INSIDERS' GUIDE®

INSIDERS' GUIDE® SERIES

INSIDERS' GUIDE® TO
KANSAS CITY

SECOND EDITION

KATIE VAN LUCHENE

INSIDERS' GUIDE®

GUILFORD, CONNECTICUT
AN IMPRINT OF THE GLOBE PEQUOT PRESS

The prices and rates in this guidebook were confirmed
at press time. We recommend, however, that you call
establishments before traveling to obtain current information.

To buy books in quantity for corporate use
or incentives, call **(800) 962–0973, ext. 4551,**
or e-mail **premiums@GlobePequot.com.**

INSIDERS' GUIDE®

Text design: LeAnna Weller Smith
Maps by XNR Productions, Inc. © The Globe Pequot
Press

ISSN 1542-7404
ISBN 0-7627-3453-1

Manufactured in the United States of America
Second Edition/First Printing

Union Station/Skyline. CVB OF GREATER KANSAS CITY

[Top] *Full moon over downtown skyline.* CVB OF GREATER KANSAS CITY
[Bottom] *Downtown at twilight.* CVB OF GREATER KANSAS CITY

Downtown skyline. CVB OF GREATER KANSAS CITY

[Top] *Truman Library.* CVB OF GREATER KANSAS CITY
[Bottom] *Nelson-Atkins Museum of Art.* CVB OF GREATER KANSAS CITY

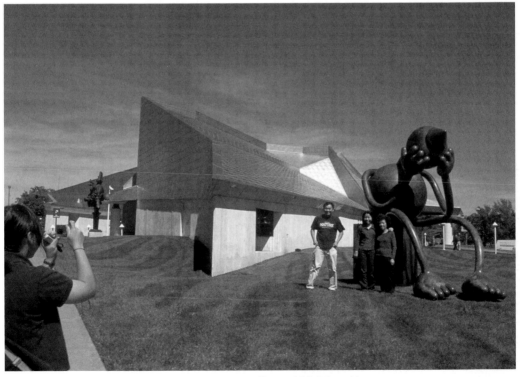

[Top] *Toy and Miniature Museum.* CVB OF GREATER KANSAS CITY
[Bottom] *Crying Giant statue at the Kemper Museum.* CVB OF GREATER KANSAS CITY

[Top] *Kansas City Chiefs football team.* CVB OF GREATER KANSAS CITY
[Bottom] *Kauffman Stadium.* CVB OF GREATER KANSAS CITY

Kansas Speedway. CVB OF GREATER KANSAS CITY

Jazz at the Phoenix. CVB OF GREATER KANSAS CITY

[Top] *Gem Theater.* CVB OF GREATER KANSAS CITY
[Bottom] *Starlight Theatre.* CVB OF GREATER KANSAS CITY

[Top] *Produce at City Market.* CVB OF GREATER KANSAS CITY
[Bottom] Arabia *Steamboat Museum at City Market.* CVB OF GREATER KANSAS CITY

City Market entrance. CVB OF GREATER KANSAS CITY

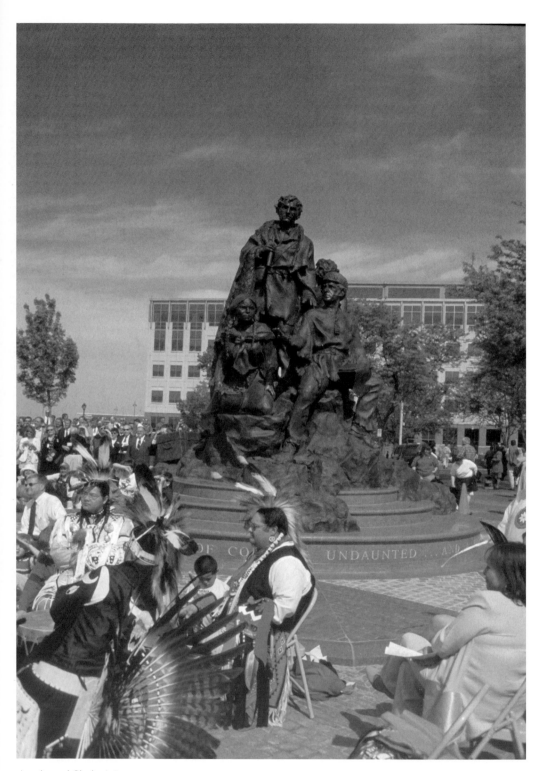

Lewis and Clark statue. CVB OF GREATER KANSAS CITY

[Top] *Diana Fountain in front of the Fairmont Hotel.* CVB OF GREATER KANSAS CITY
[Bottom] *J. C. Nichols Fountain.* CVB OF GREATER KANSAS CITY

The Scout. CVB OF GREATER KANSAS CITY

CONTENTS

Preface xxv

Acknowledgments xxvi

How to Use This Book 1

Area Overview 4

Getting Here, Getting Around 14

History 20

Accommodations 38

Restaurants 59

Nightlife 105

Shopping 120

Attractions 146

The Arts 172

Kidstuff 186

Annual Events and Festivals 201

Parks, Lakes, and Recreation 239

Sports 250

Day Trips and Weekend Getaways 264

Media 274

Worship 284

Relocation 288

Index 351

About the Author 365

Directory of Maps

Greater Kansas City xix

North of the River xx

River Market, Downtown, Crown Center xxi

CONTENTS

Country Club Plaza and Westport xxii

East Metro and South Kansas City xxiii

The Kansas Side of the River xxiv

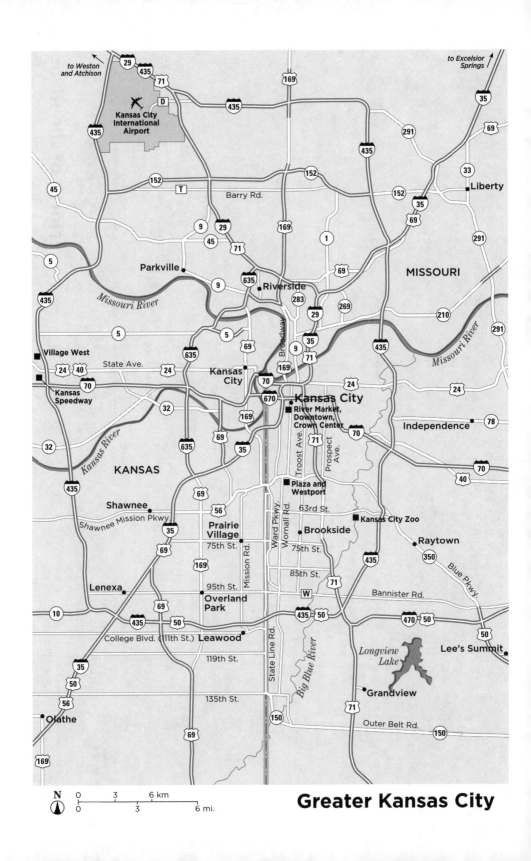

Greater Kansas City

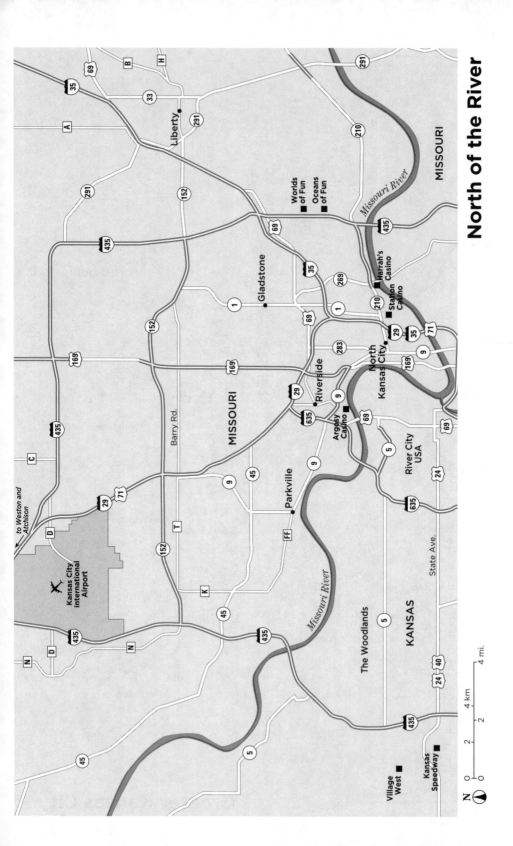

North of the River

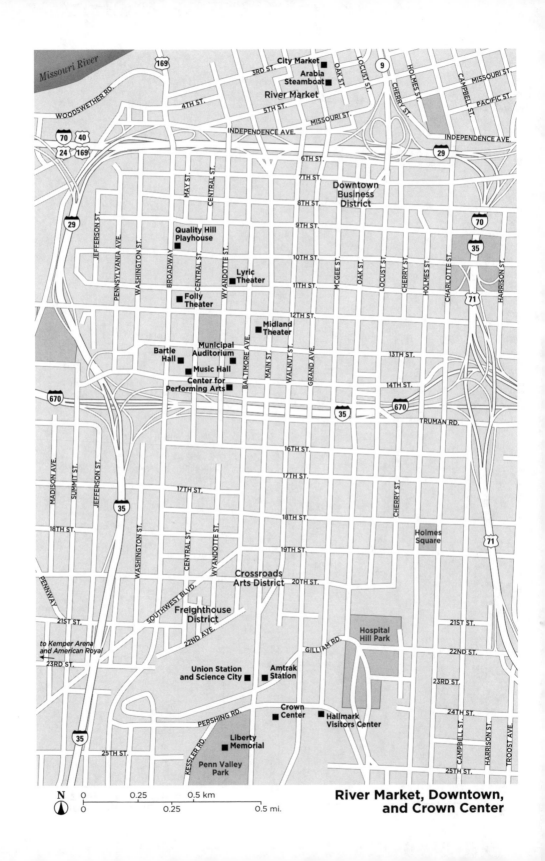

River Market, Downtown, and Crown Center

Missouri River

169

City Market
Arabia Steamboat
River Market
WOODSWETHER RD.
4TH ST.
5TH ST.
3RD ST.
OAK ST.
LOCUST ST.
CHERRY ST.
HOLMES ST.
CAMPBELL ST.
MISSOURI ST.
PACIFIC ST.
9

70 40
24 169

INDEPENDENCE AVE.
MISSOURI ST.
6TH ST.
7TH ST.
INDEPENDENCE AVE.
29

29

MAY ST.
CENTRAL ST.
Downtown Business District
8TH ST.
9TH ST.
70

35

Quality Hill Playhouse
JEFFERSON ST.
PENNSYLVANIA AVE.
WASHINGTON ST.
BROADWAY
CENTRAL ST.
WYANDOTTE ST.
10TH ST.
McGEE ST.
OAK ST.
LOCUST ST.
CHERRY ST.
HOLMES ST.
CHARLOTTE ST.
HARRISON ST.

Lyric Theater
11TH ST.
71

Folly Theater
12TH ST.

Midland Theater
Bartle Hall
Municipal Auditorium
BALTIMORE AVE.
MAIN ST.
WALNUT ST.
GRAND AVE.
13TH ST.
Music Hall
Center for Performing Arts
14TH ST.

670
35
670
TRUMAN RD.

16TH ST.
17TH ST.

MADISON AVE.
SUMMIT ST.
JEFFERSON ST.
35
17TH ST.
18TH ST.
Holmes Square
71

18TH ST.
WASHINGTON ST.
CENTRAL ST.
WYANDOTTE ST.
19TH ST.

PENNWAY
Crossroads Arts District
20TH ST.

21ST ST.
Freighthouse District
SOUTHWEST BLVD.
CHERRY ST.
21ST ST.

to Kemper Arena and American Royal
22ND AVE.
Hospital Hill Park
22ND ST.
23RD ST.
GILLIAM RD.

Union Station and Science City
Amtrak Station
23RD ST.

PERSHING RD.
Crown Center
Hallmark Visitors Center
24TH ST.

35
KESSLER RD.
Liberty Memorial
CAMPBELL ST.
HARRISON ST.
TROOST AVE.

25TH ST.
Penn Valley Park
25TH ST.

N

0   0.25   0.5 km
0   0.25   0.5 mi.

River Market, Downtown, and Crown Center

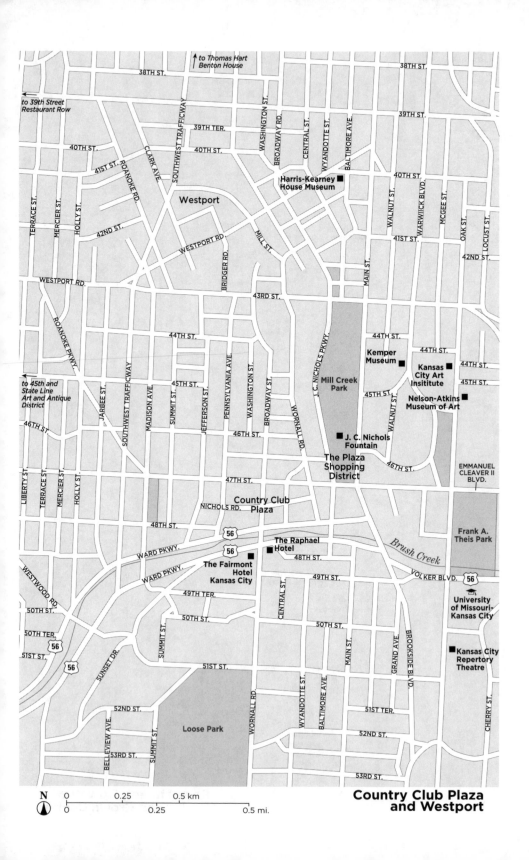

**Country Club Plaza
and Westport**

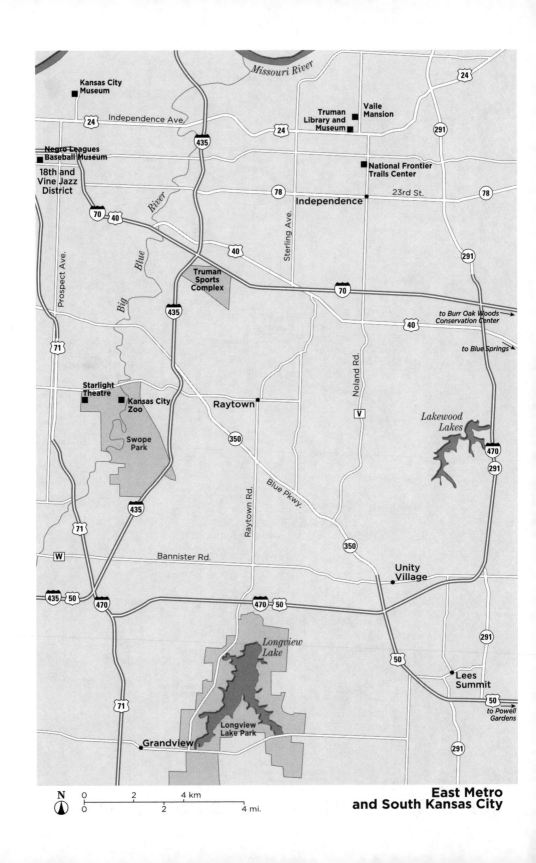

**East Metro
and South Kansas City**

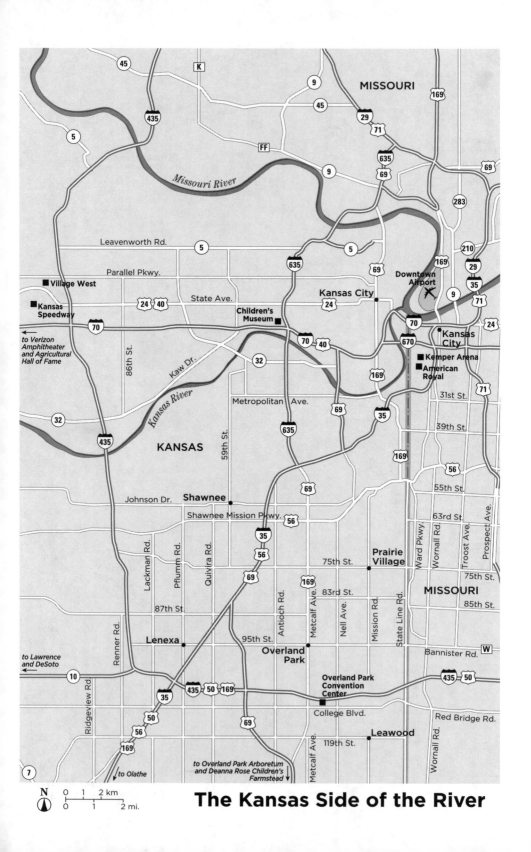

The Kansas Side of the River

N

0   1   2 km
0   1   2 mi.

PREFACE

Listen. What's that sound? It's a buzz . . . the noise created when crowds of people start talking about an exciting discovery, a hidden gem, the Next Big Thing.

In our town, the Buzz-O-Meter is off the charts as the rest of the world catches up to what we've known all along: Kansas City is a vibrant, cosmopolitan metroplex with an unmatched mix of art, architecture, and activities that simply must be experienced firsthand.

In the past few months alone, dozens of newspaper and magazine reporters have arrived to see what the buzz is all about. They've shopped in designer boutiques and bohemian lofts, covered our jazz scene, proposed girlfriends' getaways to scout for shoes and antiques, and caught the action at our new NASCAR racetrack. And when an outdoor-goods emporium in Kansas City, Kansas, became that state's number-one tourist attraction within weeks of opening, the media took notice.

They've dubbed us the official "Artland" of the Midwest thanks to our Crossroads Arts District, a mile-wide neighborhood that's home to more than 40 galleries and artist studios, eclectic shops, and unique dining choices from funky coffee shops to upscale restaurants. Recently, *Elle Travel* called this area "groovy," *National Geographic Traveler* pronounced it "trendy," and AAA *Traveler* simply asked, "What are you waiting for?"

Our lively restaurant scene hasn't gone unnoticed, either. Always a mecca for great steaks and barbecue, in recent years we've gone global with cuisine from Argentina to Thailand and everywhere in between. But of all the delicious choices, what did a writer for the *London Times* fall in love with? Our ribs!

You'll be glad to know all this attention hasn't gone to our heads. Kansas City still retains its well-known hospitality. In fact, check in with Fido at the Fairmont Hotel and he'll be treated to snacks from our own Three Dog Bakery.

So welcome. Like everyone else, you'll soon fall in love with the many facets of this remarkable city: the romance of outdoor cafes and horse-drawn carriages, the quiet beauty of lush gardens, and the spirited beat of an outdoor music festival.

View some of the country's most stellar examples of Art Deco architecture, try your luck at a riverside casino, tuck into a platter of lip-smacking barbecue, or travel back in time to President Truman's Oval Office, the James Gang's hideout, or a Civil War battlefield. Nowhere else on Earth can you find such a varied and marvelous mix of attractions, from a wild-west rodeo to a world-class art museum.

As for the steady buzz in the air? You'll get used to it. We have. So start reading—you might find yourself humming right along with us.

ACKNOWLEDGMENTS

This book is a public love note to all the musicians and artists, chefs and shop owners, historians and innkeepers whose passions and talents make this city positively vibrate with excitement. And for the thousands of mentors, teachers, caregivers, philanthropists, and volunteers: You're the reason we're known as the Heartland.

But I'm saving my personal love notes for my husband—my hero—Jerry Foulds.

HOW TO USE THIS BOOK (?)

Naturally, as a travel guide, this book is ideal for anyone planning a visit to Kansas City, whether it's a vacation, as home base for a series of day trips, or a few days before or after a business meeting. Search these chapters for the best the city has to offer in attractions, restaurants, nightlife—anything of interest to movers and shakers.

We've also put together a helpful guide just for the *movers*. If you're thinking of making Kansas City your new home, you'll find information about the local real estate market; a tour of wonderful neighborhoods; and an overview of area health care, child care, and education options in the Relocation chapter. This section also includes a listing of service providers, such as gas companies and new neighbor groups, to help you quickly feel at home in your new town. This chapter makes the *Insiders' Guide* an ideal resource for real estate companies to send to potential out-of-town buyers and for companies to give to employees who are being transferred to the City of Fountains.

Traveler or transplant: Welcome! But perhaps the optimum use for this book is the reader who lives in Kansas City but hasn't really lived it up yet. Consider this writer's story: Always a hometown booster, I really didn't fully appreciate our city until I began researching this book. You might say our friendship blossomed into a full-blown, head-over-keyboard love affair. I've toured neighborhoods otherwise unknown, tapped my foot at jam sessions, talked to natives and newcomers, met with historians and artists and gardeners and zookeepers. And, oh, the food! I've gained five pounds—all in the name of good journalism.

Using this book as a guide, start your own romance. Along the way you're guar-

anteed to discover more about the city and its surrounding small towns . . . and you might just learn more about yourself by taking part in the poetry readings, pottery painting, tango lessons, and cooking classes listed throughout these pages.

If you have children, this guide will help quiet that "There's nothing to doooo" whine. There's *plenty* to do in Kansas City for kids of all ages. Open to Kidstuff and give each child a different colored highlighter. This guide might also encourage a student to learn more about the history of the Midwest.

For pioneers headed to Santa Fe, Oregon, and California, Kansas City was the gateway to the future. But for you it might be the gateway to your past. Independence, Missouri, is home to not one but two vast genealogical libraries. Family history seekers come by the busloads to the Mid-Continent Public Library's Genealogy and Local History branch and the Jackson County Historical Society Archives and Research Library in the Independence Square Courthouse.

So whatever the reason for purchasing this book, we sincerely thank you and hope you'll enjoy it—and Kansas City—to its fullest. *NOTE*: Unless otherwise indicated all listings in this book are located in Kansas City, Missouri; other cities and

---

No wonder one of our nicknames is The City Beautiful. Kansas City maintains 36 public fountains, in addition to those on private property, as well as 55 monuments and sculptures. And you'll find 201 public parks within our borders, 19 with swimming pools, 36 with tennis courts.

---

towns will be designated MO (Missouri) or KS (Kansas).

HOW THIS BOOK IS ORGANIZED

Travelers familiar with the *Insiders' Guide* series will recognize the easy-to-use format used throughout this book. Those friendly features you appreciate are all here, including Insiders' Tips—designated with an ▇—that let you in on (shhh!) local secrets and Close-ups that provide an in-depth look at some of our top attributes.

Like all *Insiders' Guides,* this one has been organized to help make the most of your trip to the City of Surprises, from how to navigate our streets to where to find the culinary dish you crave. If that happens to be barbecue, we shudder to picture you hunched over the hotel room's yellow pages trying to choose a winner from the 100 or so barbecue restaurants listed. We'll tell you where to find a smoked brisket that will bring tears to your eyes. Want fries with that? Skip the Idahos: You won't want to miss the sweet potato fries at one popular joint.

If you're new to the *Insiders' Guide* series, here's a quick overview of what you'll find in several of the chapters and a suggestion about where to start, depending on why you're here.

You might want to spend a few minutes with Getting Here, Getting Around. It explains how to divide Greater Kansas City (which actually encompasses 18 different counties in two different states) into five manageable areas. The rest of the book refers to these districts to make finding a particular place easy.

▇ *You may have such a good time visiting Kansas City you won't want to leave. Our many charms have earned us a spot in Expansion Management's "American's 50 Hottest Cities for Expansions and Relocations." We rank way up there at No. 4.*

Because many of you will be looking for a particular type of food (is that Kansas City strip calling your name yet?), restaurants are indexed by fare. Lucky for you, no matter what food you fancy—whether it's a luscious eggplant casserole at Eden Alley (even this carnivorous city has a strong vegetarian contingency!) or the garlicky chicken spiedini at Garozzos Ristorante—it's never more than 20 or so minutes away.

If, however, your passion is dashing for a dressing room at a chichi boutique, you're in luck. In Shopping you'll discover the inside scoop on where to find fashions, antiques, decor, and discount shoes.

In The Arts you'll discover our world-class museums, symphony, ballet, live theater, and opera. You'll also see why Kansas City is gaining national recognition as an art town, thanks to the Crossroads Arts District, a cluster of artist studios and galleries between Downtown and Crown Center.

Next we suggest you head to Annual Events and Festivals. Chances are there's a music festival, street fair, tour of a historical area, or neighborhood block party going on right now. You wouldn't want to miss the revelry while you're reviewing this book.

Looking for more outdoor fun? Spend an afternoon at our Kansas City Zoo or one of our beautiful arboretums or lakes and you won't miss the mountains or beach; pack a picnic basket (find out where in the Food and Gifts section in Shopping), then open the book to Parks, Lakes, and Recreation.

Perhaps your culinary choices run more to hot dogs and roasted peanuts—fare that's best savored at the ballpark. You won't go wanting here: With Royals baseball, Chiefs football, and professional hockey and soccer teams, there's a game in town nearly every week. And our brand-new Kansas Speedway offers NASCAR fans an exciting day at the races. Start your engines in Sports.

Whew! That should get you started. Pace yourself, go easy on the incendiary salsa at Southwest Boulevard's Mexican restaurants, and you should do just fine.

Finally, the small print. We made every attempt to provide the most accurate and up-to-date information to help make your visit to Kansas City a success. But if you disagree with anything or discover a hot spot we missed, please let us know.

Send your comments or suggestions to editorial@GlobePequot.com, or write to:

The Globe Pequot Press
Reader Response/Editorial Department
P.O. Box 480
Guilford, CT 06437

AREA OVERVIEW

If Kansas City were a box of cereal, we'd have a huge starburst printed on the front reading "New! Bigger! Better!"

So much has happened to this fair city since the first edition of *Insiders' Guide to Kansas City* was published, we can't help but boast. For one thing, there's more of us to love. We've recently grown from 11 counties to 18 in both Kansas and Missouri, representing more than 9,100 square miles filled with two million happy, friendly folks.

So now more than ever, when you say "Kansas City," you're really talking about one diverse, exciting region that encompasses two states and 50 unique communities. Our unified advantage—along with our central location, well-educated and productive workforce, and low cost of running a business or buying a home—makes us a magnet for corporations to build headquarters here. And our enviable quality of life means individuals and families are thrilled to make their homes here. In fact, we have a new slogan that shows off our city's strength in numbers: "OneKC."

As for the "New" boast on the cereal box? Just witness the brand spanking new entertainment area in Wyandotte County, Kansas, that quickly became the number-one attraction in the state. Village West zoomed into being with the NASCAR Kansas Speedway, Cabela's outdoor gear emporium, Nebraska Furniture Mart, and Great Wolf Lodge. Restaurants and attractions followed, and now—just two years after opening—the area draws more than seven million visitors a year.

The "Better" promise? That's easy. Visitors and locals alike are being treated to a renaissance of our urban core. A new library—one of the most beautiful in the nation—plus a thriving art and shopping scene in the Crossroads Arts District have people talking up Kansas City. Our skyline, already a beauty, is getting a fabulous makeover with the H&R Block Headquarters, Kansas City Live Entertainment District, $250 million sports arena, Performing Arts Center, and other draws planned for the next few years.

But for right now, there's plenty to love about our town. So let's get started with a whirlwind tour.

Although the metroplex known as Kansas City encompasses just over 9,000 square miles, locals think of home as separate neighborhoods (such as Brookside), destinations (Country Club Plaza) or geographical areas (the Northland). Before your eyes glaze over, we've divided the region into five handy little areas, described below. Maps of each are found in the front of this book. We'll refer to these areas throughout the book. And remember, just about any destination in the metro is 20 minutes away or less.

METROPOLITAN AREAS

North of the River

In 1972 when the city planners approved the new Kansas City International Airport a whopping 21 miles north of downtown they expected an immediate surge in housing and services in the Northland. It took 25 years before new homes and golf courses began to dot the hillsides facing

Resources for More Information

Hungry for more? Although this book provides a portable entree into the City of Surprises, following are sources to enhance your visit.

MEDIA

Our daily newspaper, the *Kansas City Star,* publishes several photo-rich books on a variety of subjects from history to barbecue to the Flood of '51. Write to Kansas City Star Books, Attn. StarInfo, P.O. Box 410457, Kansas City, MO 64141-0457, or call (816) 234-4636.

The local NBC affiliate, KSHB, has complied fascinating, short vignettes about our city's culture, events, and people called "Kansas City Crossroads." Volumes one through four are available in VHS and DVD formats at local bookstores.

Kansas City magazine provides a well-rounded, well-written look at the town's most interesting people, places, and sometimes-quirky habits. Each monthly issue also includes a calendar of events and quick takes on local restaurants. It's a must-read for locals and welcome lifeline for expatriates. Call (913) 894-6923 for subscription information, or check out www.kcmag .com for a taste.

TOURISM SITES

Well before your trip, access these chamber of commerce and visitor center Web sites for up-to-the-minute information about festivals and events. Or call to receive brochures, maps, and special offers by mail.

CONVENTION AND VISITORS BUREAU OF GREATER KANSAS CITY

If you only have the time—or patience—to contact one visitor center, this should be it. Their quarterly magazine, *Goin' to Kansas City*, lists a calendar of events, information about dining and nightlife, kid-friendly activities, and even area day trips. The staff is adept at helping out-of-towners plan successful conventions and even family reunions. Write to the bureau at 1100 Main, Suite 2550, Kansas City, MO 64105-2195; call (816) 221-5242 or (800) 767-7700; or log on to www.gointokansascity.com or www .visitkc.com. Their satellite locations at Union Station and 4709 Central on the Country Club Plaza offer a wide variety of brochures and maps.

the Mighty Moe. But the real reason to head north isn't for new delights but old: the charming city of Parkville with its storefronts filled with art galleries and festive eateries. And if gambling floats your boat, you'll want to cross the bridge to reach our four riverboat casinos.

River Market, Downtown, Crown Center

Here's where it all began 150 years ago. And despite the mass exodus to the suburbs during the 1950s and 1960s, the cen-

Contact Information for Other Area Towns

Atchison, KS
(913) 367-2427
www.atchisonkansas.net

Blue Springs, MO
(816) 228-0209
www.bluespringsgov.com

Bonner Springs, KS
(913) 422-1020
www.bonnersprings.org

Cameron, MO
(816) 632-2177
www.cameron-mo.com

Chillicothe, MO
(660) 646-4281
www.chillicothemo.com

Clay County, MO
(816) 468-4989
www.clayedc.com

De Soto, KS
(913) 583-1585
www.desotoks.org

Excelsior Springs, MO
(816) 792-7733
www.ci.excelsior-springs.mo.us

Gladstone, MO
(816) 436-2200
www.Gladstone.mo.us

Grandview, MO
(816) 761-6505
www.grandview.org

Independence, MO
(816) 325-7111
www.visitindependence.com

Jackson County, MO
(816) 881-4440
www.co.jackson.mo.u.

Johnson County, KS
(913) 715-0748
www.jocoks.com

Kearney, MO
(816) 628-3343
www.kearneyareadevelopment.com

Lansing, KS
(913) 727-6111
www.lvarea.com

Lawrence, KS
(785) 865-4411
www.lawrencechamber.com

Leavenworth, KS
(913) 727-6111
www.lvarea.com

Leawood, KS
(913) 498-1514
www.Leawood.org

tral core remains the heart of our city. Thankfully it's coming back into its own thanks to entertainment venues such as the River Market, newly refurbished urban lofts that draw upscale professionals, and late-night attractions like the 18th and Vine Historic Jazz District.

Popular galleries throughout the Crossroads Arts District have attracted some of the area's most dynamic restaurants to the area, while just south, Crown Center offers a stay-and-play mecca for travelers with its hotels, restaurants, and shopping. This city-within-the-city is linked via skywalks to the newly refurbished Union Station that houses Science City, an interactive museum for kids, a three-story Extreme Screen, the region's only 3-D theater; and dining options that range from lobster to burgers.

Coming up are a new sports arena, an exciting entertainment district, and a performing arts center.

Lee's Summit, MO
(816) 525-6617
www.leessummit.org

Lenexa, KS
(913) 888-1414
www.Lenexa.org

Liberty, MO
(816) 792-6033
www.ci.liberty.mo.us

Miami County, KS
(913) 294-4045
www.miamicountyks.org

North Kansas City, MO
(816) 274-6040
www.nkc.org

Olathe, KS
(913) 764-1050
www.edc.olathe.org

Ottawa, KS
(785) 242-1000
www.ottawakansas.org

Overland Park, KS
(800) 262-PARK (7275)
www.opcvb.org

Parkville, MO
(816) 505-2227
www.parkvillemo.com

Platte County, MO
(816) 270-2119
www.plattecountyedc.com

Shawnee, KS
(913) 631-6545
www.shawnee-edc.com

Southwest Johnson County, KS
(913) 764-6566
www.swjocoks-edc.com

St. Joseph, MO
(816) 764-6566
www.saintjoseph.com

Topeka, KS
(785) 234-2644
www.topekachamber.org

Warrensburg, MO
(660) 747-0244
www.warrensburgecodev.com

Weston, MO
(816) 640-2909
www.ci.weston.mo.us

Wyandotte County, KS
(913) 371-3070
www.kckcvb.org

Country Club Plaza and Westport

Any trip to Kansas City must include a day of shopping on the Country Club Plaza, a 14-city-block potpourri of over 180 stores, boutiques, and dining establishments set among 40 fountains and 50 sculpted works of art. If the "Rodeo Drive" of the Midwest is a little too upscale for you, Historic Westport offers a more laid-back social scene.

Nearby is the popular 39th Street corridor that boasts more top-notch restaurants than any other real estate in town, and the 45th and State Line Art and Antiques district will thrill the collectibles hunter. The Plaza and Westport area is also home to the nationally respected Nelson-Atkins Museum of Art and the Kemper Contemporary Museum of Art. Take a short drive south past neighborhoods filled with million-dollar homes to find Brookside, an old-fashioned Main Street USA

enclave with a collection of cafes, a toy store, an ice-cream parlor, and even a five-and-dime store complete with creaking wooden floors.

East Metro and South Kansas City

Independence, Missouri, is still Harry's town, with the Truman Presidential Museum and Library all spiffed up and ready to tour along with his home. Our famed double-header sports complex also bears the 33rd president's name; tickets to a Chiefs football or Royals baseball game draw sports enthusiasts from all over. South Kansas City is also home to the Kansas City Zoo, where hundreds of animals from exotic lands gambol and roam in their natural habitats.

The Kansas Side of the River

Just a few years ago this guide would have discounted the "other" Kansas City across the state line completely. But thanks to forward-thinking mayor Carol Marinovich, Wyandotte County in Kansas has zoomed into the picture with its new Kansas Speedway that brings droves of NASCAR fans from a four-state region. Bring your earplugs. And bring your credit cards to the shopping havens sprinkled throughout Prairie Village, Overland Park, and Leawood.

OUTLYING AREAS

Earlier we mentioned that Kansas City recently added seven counties to our region. Welcome, we say: The more the merrier! You can learn more about each county's many charms by logging onto their Web sites listed in "Community Pro-

files," found elsewhere in this chapter. But for now, here are snapshots of some of our favorite new neighbors.

Atchison, Atchison County, KS

Located 50 miles northwest of downtown Kansas City and only 35 miles from Kansas City International Airport, the town of Atchison is a historic town known for its picturesque setting on the Missouri River and Victorian mansions on brick-lined streets. But its real claim to fame is Nell Hill's, a home decor emporium that draws busloads of shoppers from surrounding states. Discover details about this proud little community in Day Trips and Weekend Getaways.

Topeka, Shawnee County, KS

Topeka, Kansas's capital city, offers a quality of life that includes a terrific zoo, parks, festivals, and Washburn University. A newly remodeled Topeka and Shawnee County Public Library designed by noted architect Michael Graves is considered the most modern library in the country.

St. Joseph, Buchanan County, MO

A hop, skip, and a jump from downtown Kansas City, St. Joseph provides a wealth of attractions that celebrate both our Wild West roots (you can visit the Jesse James home and the Pony Express Museum, for example) and our cosmopolitan upbringing, evidenced by drop-dead-gorgeous Victorian homes like the Shakespeare Chateau, which is now a bed-and-breakfast. Walking tours of the Museum Hill and

Cathedral Hill neighborhoods will introduce you to glorious residences from long ago.

Excelsior Springs, Clay County, MO

You might say this town is all wet. But that's a good thing: Once dubbed "the Health Center of the Nation" thanks to its therapeutic waters, today the town's two spas have undergone extensive renovations. Once a favorite of President Harry S Truman and Al Capone (but never on the same weekend!), the Elms Resort offers a graceful style with new amenities; see details in Accommodations. And the Hall of Waters boasts the longest mineral water bar in the world, along with pampering spa services.

Lawrence, Douglas County, KS

To Kansas University alumni, Lawrence has always seemed like part of Kansas City as Kansas Highway 10 becomes bumper-to-bumper Jayhawkers going back and forth on game day.

With an exciting arts community and thriving downtown, it's no wonder Lawrence is one of the fastest growing areas in the region. Get the scoop on what we affectionately call Larry Town in Day Trips and Weekend Getaways.

THE CENTER OF IT ALL

Although it's true that Kansas City is just 250 miles from the geographical center of the United States, we like to think that the term "heartland" refers more to our lovable people than the logistics. After all, we're home to Hallmark Cards, Helzberg Diamonds, and Russell Stover Candies—so you might say Cupid is a permanent resident.

If you're coming to Kansas City in the summer, do you pack a sweater or sun-tan lotion? Maybe both. A recent July day topped out at 99 degrees, but the recorded high was a bit warmer at 103. The lowest temperature on record for that date was 55 degrees. To get current temperatures plus a five-day forecast, log on to www.kansascity.com.

We're all heart, too, when it comes to helping people in need and supporting the arts. Perhaps our generosity of spirit is a holdover from the days when homesteaders showed up with hammers and hampers of food to help a neighbor raise a barn.

Today, it's *money* we're raising to make Kansas City a better community. In fact, if you have the cash, conscience, or closet space you can attend a different black-tie fund-raiser every weekend, all year long. If you'd rather provide a little sweat equity instead, you can participate in a charity road race, bike ride, or golf tournament most weekends from spring through fall.

When we're not giving, we're taking— taking in the sights and smells of our town, that is. Some of the best aromas come from hickory smoke swirling around the barbecue restaurants that dot our city. We'll admit we didn't invent this method of slow cooking—we just perfected it.

Just ask the members of the Kansas City Barbecue Society, the largest organization devoted to the artform in the world. The group, whose motto is "Barbecue: not just for breakfast anymore," sanctions more than 120 national barbecue contests each year, including the granddaddy of 'em all, the American Royal, held next door to our celebrated stockyards each fall. See the Restaurant chapter for more information about Kansas City barbecue as well as a listing of some of our most celebrated joints.

But don't box us in as just a place to get barbecue—or world-famous steaks for that matter. We offer the hungry visitor a variety of dining experiences that rival any other cosmopolitan city.

Kansas City Vital Statistics

Mayors: Kay Barnes (Kansas City, MO) and Carol Marinovich (Kansas City, KS)

Governors: Bob Holden (Missouri) and Kathleen Sebelius (Kansas)

United States senators: Christopher Bond and James Talent (Missouri); Sam Brownback and Pat Roberts (Kansas)

Average maximum temperatures (degrees Fahrenheit): 38 (January); 65 (April); 89 (July); 69 (October)

Average minimum temperatures (degrees Fahrenheit): 21 (January); 45 (April); 70 (July); 48 (October)

Average precipitation (in inches): 1.30 (January); 3.37 (April); 4.02 (July); 2.98 (October)

Average annual snowfall (in inches): 21

Total population (as of March, 2004): 1,901,070

Kansas counties: Atchison, Leavenworth, Wyandotte, Johnson, Franklin, Miami, and Linn

Missouri counties: Caldwell, Clinton, Clay, Ray, Jackson, Lafayette, Cass, Johnson, and Bates

Total combined region: More than 9,100 square miles; 132 miles from the northwest tip of Atchison County to the southeast corner of Bates County

Median age: 35.4

Average household income: $66,700

Median price for house: $137,700 (vs. $161,400 nationally)

Major airports: Charles B. Wheeler Downtown Airport, Kansas City International Airport

Major interstates: I-435, I-35, I-70, I-29, I-635, I-670

Total consumer spending: $35.9 billion

Hotel and motel rooms in the area: More then 25,000

Nicknames: City of Surprises, City of Fountains, The City Beautiful, Number 1 "Kid-Friendly City" (Overland Park, KS)

Major colleges and universities: Avila University, Johnson County Community College, MidAmerica Nazarene University, Park University, Rockhurst University, University of Missouri–Kansas City, William Jewell College

Famous Kansas Citians: Harry S Truman, Jean Harlow, Casey Stengel, Ginger Rogers, writer Calvin Trillin, Walter Cronkite, golfer Tom Watson, handbag designer Kate Spade, actor Chris Cooper, jazz musician Pat Metheny, and Maurice Greene, the fastest man on Earth

Just passing through (important people who lived in Kansas City): Count Basie, Ernest Hemingway (journalist at the *Kansas City Star* for six months), and Walt Disney

Homegrown companies: Hallmark Cards, Sprint, H&R Block, Helzberg Diamonds, AMC Theatres, Lee Jeans, Russell Stover Candies, American Century Investments, Applebee's, Black & Veatch, Yellow Corporation, and Three Dog Bakery

Products invented here: McDonald's Happy Meal, K. C. Masterpiece Barbecue Sauce, Teflon Coating, Valomilk, Eskimo Pies, Hostess Twinkies, Rival Crock Pot, the multiscreen movie theater, the outdoor shopping center, and the swing style of jazz

Notable events in Kansas City's history:

June 26, 1804: Lewis and Clark camp here during their first expedition to the Louisiana Territory.

1821: Francois Chouteau, a Frenchman from St. Louis, establishes a fur company at the Kaw River.

1821: Missouri is admitted to the Union.

1833: John Calvin McCoy opens a supply store four miles south of the river on the Santa Fe Trail.

June 1, 1850: Town of Kansas (in Missouri) is incorporated.

1854: Kansas-Nebraska Act; many historians consider this the beginning of the Civil War.

1859: Thriving town welcomes 1,500 steamboats.

July 3, 1869: Hannibal Bridge opens, first rail bridge to span the Missouri River and provide a direct rail link to Chicago.

1871: Stockyards expand, giving us the start as prime meatpacking center. That means steaks, folks.

1889: Town becomes officially Kansas City, Missouri.

1899: City's first convention hall is built.

1900: Convention hall burns to the ground.

1900: Three months after its destruction, convention hall is rebuilt, just in time to host Democratic Convention.

1903: Missouri River floods the West Bottoms, leaving 22,000 people homeless.

1905: William Strang Jr. builds an interurban railway to encourage residential area in what is now Overland Park, Kansas.

1910: Joyce Clyde Hall sells postcards out of his suitcase at the YMCA—the start of Hallmark Cards.

1914: Union Station is built; during its heyday, 271 trains passed through daily.

1915: Parks and boulevard system is built, earning us the title "City Beautiful."

1921: The Liberty Memorial site is dedicated; completion is on November 11, 1926.

1923: The Country Club Plaza opens for business.

1931: While the rest of the country sagged under the Depression, Kansas City thrived, thanks to the Ten-Year-Plan, which created jobs and saw the construction of the City Hall, new courthouse, and miles of new roads.

1933: Nelson Gallery of Art opens.

1943: Kansas City Monarchs, the all-black baseball team, celebrates 43 straight wins.

October 15, 1949: WDAF, Kansas City's first television station, begins regular programming.

Friday the 13th, 1951: The Kansas River floods the West Bottoms again, leaving more than 20,000 homeless.

1960: The Chiefs football team plays its first season in Kansas City.

April 8, 1969: The Kansas City Royals play their first game.

January 12, 1970: Chiefs win Super Bowl IV, beating the Minnesota Vikings 23–7.

1972: River Quay, entertainment area near the River Market, takes off.

1972: Kansas City International Airport opens.

1973: Worlds of Fun opens, as does Crown Center's hotel and entertainment complex.

1974: Westport, a restaurant and entertainment district in midtown, becomes shopping and dining magnet.

1976: Kansas City hosts the Republican National Convention.

1985: Royals win the World Series.

1988: City hosts the NCAA Final Four basketball tournament.

1991: Emanuel Cleaver II becomes the first African American mayor of Kansas City. He serves until 1999, when Kay Barnes is elected the first woman mayor of the city.

1996: Voters across five counties pass the Bistate Cultural Tax, the first two-state effort of its kind in the country. Work begins to restore Union Station.

1997: 18th & Vine comes back to life with jazz venues, the Kansas City Jazz Museum, and the Negro Leagues Baseball Museum.

2000 and beyond: Kansas City, Missouri's urban areas begin a revitalization period, thanks to warehouses being converted to lofts. Neighborhoods like the Crossroads Arts District attract artists, unique shops, and restaurants.

2001: Kansas Speedway opens in Kansas City, Kansas, home to NASCAR races. It's soon joined by a 400-acre tourism district called Village West.

2004: Bill passes to build a downtown arena; also on the drawing board is a new downtown entertainment district and a Performing Arts Center.

Have a hankering for Argentine chimichurri sauce or crawfish étouffée? How about authentic pollo mole, osso buco Milanese, sauerbraten, or spanikopita? Do you savor sushi or designer pizza? Brittany-style mussels or Moroccan lamb kabobs on your mind? Dim sum sound good? Or would an ice-cold beer and chili dog hit the spot?

Answer yes to any of these culinary cues and you've come to the right place.

Jazz and Blues

Our music came to us from cities like New Orleans by way of the Mississippi and Missouri Rivers. And, like our barbecue that incorporates tomatoes for texture and molasses for sweetness, we created our own distinct recipe for jazz.

Musicians like Count Basie took aspects of gospel, ragtime, and blues and turned them into swing, an infectious rhythm that got people out of their chairs to dance at the Reno Club in 1936. Charlie "Bird" Parker's alto sax propelled the art form even further with a new manic yet compelling sound called bebop.

The 12th Street nightspots where these geniuses jammed are long gone, but you can still hear live music in clubs, restaurants, and festivals all over town. A new jazz museum and nightclub at 18th and Vine celebrates their influence and provides a forum for today's talented newcomers.

Our Climate, Both Weather-wise and Culturally

You'll find Kansas City to be a casual, friendly place where shirtsleeves—even nice shorts and sandals in summer—are appropriate for most restaurants. When in doubt call to ask, but long gone are the days when diners were handed ill-fitting jackets in order to be seated.

As for the temperature, the old saw "if you don't like the weather, just wait a few minutes and it will change" is certainly true here. Situated in the temperate zone, Kansas City's annual average temperature is a pleasant 55 degrees, with a few days in winter that drop below 20 and a few in summer that go above 90.

It's hard to pick a favorite time to visit: Nature has blessed us with a paintbox of pleasing hues throughout the year. Spring comes early in the heartland, wearing a little girl's wardrobe of pink dogwood and yellow daffodils. Summer means corn-flower blue skies, emerald lawns, ripe red tomatoes at the farmers' markets, and enough outdoor festivals to keep you from noticing the humidity.

In fall the landscape becomes a jewelry store window of crimson and gold as elms, maples, and giant oaks take on autumn's hues. In fact, many first-time visitors are amazed at the forestlike vistas throughout our city. Our forested bluffs, parks, gardens, and tree-lined boulevards are never more inspiring than when the weather turns brisk. During winter the colors—although man-made—are no less brilliant as 250,000 holiday lights outline the towers and spires of the Country Club Plaza, our spectacular Spanish-style outdoor shopping and entertainment district.

You'll be glad you brought a just-in-case umbrella any time of year. Here in the home of corn-fed beef, we rarely complain about the rain that grows that golden crop. You won't either the first time you taste a char-grilled Kansas City strip at Plaza III The Steakhouse.

GETTING HERE, GETTING AROUND

You might take a train, you might take a plane . . . but no matter how you get here, you'll enjoy it just the same!

GETTING TO KANSAS CITY

As you're driving in from the airport or on an interstate you might wonder, "Where's the city?" We assure you, it's here—and worth the trip. But before you see our skyline rising like the Emerald City out of limestone bluffs, you'll pass fields of corn and pastures of bovine. And just to prove the Midwest isn't all flat plains, on the way you'll be treated to gently rolling hills lush with trees: pink redbud in spring, garnet-hued sycamore in autumn. Relax and enjoy the view as your vehicle becomes a decompression chamber: You're in Kansas City now, where the pace is carefree and the natives are so nice that you'll want to stay longer than you'd planned.

Getting to the City from the Airport

Chances are if you're flying the friendly skies to our friendly city, you'll be coming into Kansas City International Airport, or KCI. (Read more about this award-winning airport in the Close-up.)

The KCI Shuttle provides transportation between the airport and more than 90 metro-area hotels and runs from 4:00 A.M. to 11:55 P.M. daily. Ticket counters are located near each airline baggage claim area, or dial "5000" on a white airport courtesy phone. Expect to pay around $14 from the airport to the Plaza or $23 round-trip. Call (816) 243–5000 or (800) 243–6383 for more information, or log on to www.mtsi-kc.com.

A private car service is a convenient way to go—and besides, isn't it an ego-booster to be greeted at the airport with your name printed on a sign? K-Mo Limo has courteous drivers and plush Lincoln Town Cars at your disposal. Call (913) 780–6200 or (800) 782–6201.

Other Area Airports

Although Kansas City International handles all scheduled commercial flights, several smaller fields support private pilots flying into town. Kansas City's old Municipal Airport, located just north of downtown, is now called Charles B. Wheeler Downtown Airport and serves arriving and departing corporate jets and charter flights. For more information call (816) 243–5248 or check www.flykci/downtown.com. Other airports include the New Century AirCenter in Johnson County, (913) 782–5335; Independence Memorial Airport, (816) 795–8774; and Lee's Summit Municipal Airport, (816) 251–2492.

Private Air Charter companies serving the metropolitan area are Air Charter Team, (816) 283–3280 or (800) 205–6610, and Executive Beechcraft, Inc., (816) 842–8484 or its KCI location at (816) 243–6440.

ℹ *When buying tickets online, enter KCI (for Kansas City International Airport) and you might wind up in Kono, Indonesia. (How's the weather?) You'll find us instead at MCI, a holdover from our Mid Continent International days. And because all the airport codes starting with "K" were taken, we'll remain MCI.*

GROUND TRANSPORTATION
Bus Services

We'll admit our city bus system isn't as convenient or all-encompassing as those of other cities our size. But until—make that if—Kansas City voters ever agree to a light rail system, it's the best we've got.

The Kansas City Area Transportation Authority maintains the city bus system we call the Metro, which serves primarily the central corridor of Kansas City, Missouri. Bus lines 56, 57, and 51 go from downtown through Crown Center, Westport, and the Plaza along Main Street and Broadway. For a cheap, two-hour tour of the city, catch the 51 Ward Parkway line, which passes through some pretty neighborhoods. Call (816) 221-0660 for schedules or log on to www.kcata.org.

Not that many SUV-wielding suburbanites take the bus, but those who do have access to the Johnson County Transit, affectionately called "The Jo." The buses stop at park-and-ride locations throughout the county and cover the county before heading across the state line. The blue buses take on a scarlet hue when hundreds of Kansas City Chiefs football fans don red jackets and caps to party all the way to the stadium. For schedules and fare information call (913) 362-3500 or go to www.thejo.com.

The Downtowner is a fun and cheap way to see the sights from City Market to Crown Center and anywhere in between for a quarter. The colorful buses run every ten minutes weekdays from 6:30 A.M. to 6:00 P.M. Look for the brightly marked Downtowner Shuttle Stop signs located throughout midtown or call (816) 221-0660. All vehicles are wheelchair accessible.

Taxis

You'll find taxis in Kansas City, just don't expect to find them queued up on every street corner as in Chicago. Most taxi companies have direct-connection phones at the airport, but a cab ride to the Plaza will cost around $40; better to choose the shuttle or limo service listed above. Most large hotels have taxi stands, or call Yellow Cab at (816) 471-5000 for round-the-clock service. The entire fleet is air-conditioned and drivers accept credit cards. Wheelchair-accessible vehicles are available.

Trains and Interstate Buses

On December 17, 2002, after a 17-year absence, Amtrak returned to Union Station with a new $4.6 million ticketing and boarding facility. The waiting room in the renovated train station features five of the original wooden benches and a large, historic wall clock.

Passengers enter at the northeast corner of Union Station's Grand Hall (with a capital G), adjacent to Pierpont's Restaurant. Short-term parking is available in front of the station; long-term parking is provided in the West Yards parking lot.

Three trains with four departures daily serve Kansas City: the Southwest Chief, between Chicago and Los Angeles; the Ann Rutledge, between Kansas City and Chicago; and the Missouri Mule, which makes two runs daily between Kansas City and St. Louis. For station information only call (816) 421-3622. For reservations and schedules call (800) 872-7245 or visit www.amtrak.com.

Greyhound and Jefferson Bus Lines share terminals at 1101 Troost Avenue in downtown Kansas City, Missouri, and at

Wearing your seatbelts isn't just a good idea; it's the law on both sides of the state line. In both Missouri and Kansas, children ages four and younger must be in car seats.

CLOSE-UP

Welcome to the World's Friendliest Airport

If Kansas City International is your starting point you may not care for the airport's location—20 miles northwest of downtown or about a half hour drive—but you're certain to appreciate the user-friendly design. Opened in 1972, its innovative layout connects three C-shaped terminals to a central loop. From the air it looks like Mickey Mouse's head sporting an extra set of ears. This configuration provides the shortest distance from curb to gate—75 feet—of any major U.S. airport. Check-in counters, baggage retrieval, and parking are also just steps away. One trip here and you'll see why *Travel Digest* in 2000 named KCI the world's "Most People-Friendly Airport."

How friendly, you might ask? Well, we recently spent $62 million for 15,000 economy parking spaces. While we're wondering where's the economy in that figure, you might like to know that the spaces are just part of a 10-year, $1.2 billion renovation project that includes some pretty spiffy artwork, including designs imbedded into the floors.

Facelifts are fine, but what you'll really enjoy are the expanded dining options throughout our three terminals. Now you can savor our famous Arthur Bryant's BBQ while waiting for a flight, or enjoy a cold brewsky from one of the Midwest's best microbreweries at Boulevard Brew Pub. And that reminds us: We've also added roomier lounges and more restrooms, including those that are more convenient for passengers with disabilities and persons traveling with children.

PARKING

Now, about that parking. The nearest parking lots to the terminals (A, B, and

---

730 State Street in Kansas City, Kansas. Call (800) 231-2222 for fare and schedule information. A word of caution here: These locations are not the safest in town, especially at night.

Car Travel

Depending on where you're staying during your visit, you can certainly enjoy areas of Kansas City without a car. On the Country Club Plaza, for example, some of the city's best dining, shopping, and nightspots are just a lovely stroll away from several fine hotels. Westport, too, offers the car-less crowd plenty to see and do. Stay at Crown Center and you won't even need an umbrella: overhead skywalks link the two hotels with entertainment, shopping, and the newly renovated Union Station, which houses Science City Museum.

However, if your lodging is in a suburb like Overland Park, you'll need a car to get around. There's nothing scarier than watching a group of conventioneers with name tags sprint across six busy lanes of Metcalf Avenue in search of burgers and beers.

C) provide free parking for the first half hour. After that it's $1.00 for one-half to one hour and $2.00 per hour up to a maximum of $18 per day. Circle parking is the same price, except the maximum is $10 per day. Economy parking is available at satellite lots for $5.00 per day. To reach these lots, take Paris Street off Cookingham Drive before you reach the terminal. Park in the lot (again, A, B, or C) that matches the terminal for your flight. For instance, if you're flying on Southwest Airlines, park in Lot B. The free shuttle will take you to your terminal.

AIRLINES SERVING KCI

	Phone	Terminal	Gate
Air Canada	(888) 247-2262	A	10-14
America West	(800) 235-9292	C	72, 73
American	(800) 433-7300	C	76-79
Continental	(800) 523-3273	C	67-69
Delta Connection Comair	(800) 354-9822	B	56-60
Delta	(800) 221-1212	B	56-60
Frontier	(800) 432-1359	A	16
Midwest Airlines	(800) 452-2022	A	17-19, 21
Northwest	(800) 225-2525	C	61-64
Southwest	(800) 435-9792	B	40-52
United	(800) 241-6522	A	10-14
USAirways	(800) 428-4322	A	6-8

Auto Rental Companies

Avis, (816) 243-5763, (800) 331-1212
Budget, (816) 243-5757, (800) 527-0770
Dollar, (816) 243-5600, (800) 800-4000
Enterprise, (816) 966-8188 or (913) 383-1515 in Kansas, (800) 736-8222

Freewheelin' Freeways and Roundabout Roads

Wherever you want to go in the metropolitan area, you can get there if you have directions and about 20 minutes. Since opening our first expressway, Southwest Trafficway, in 1950, we've developed a network of roadways that circle and circumvent the city. Today the Kansas City area has far more freeway miles per person than any other major U.S. city.

As you'll learn in the History chapter, Kansas City began its life at the banks of the Missouri River. Numbered streets—those running east and west—follow a grid that starts at the river and are numbered sequentially both north and south. Main Street divides the town between east and west. Kansas City, Missouri, and most of Johnson County, Kansas, follow this pattern, but there are exceptions to the rule.

Traveling through Kansas City is far more luxurious today than for the 360,000 or so pioneers setting out on the Santa Fe and Oregon Trails in the early to mid-1800s. Back then 1 in 10 died. Learn their stories at the National Frontier Trails Center in Independence by viewing films, maps, and artifacts and reading diaries kept on the trip.

Some streets meander along the land's natural contours, creating ribbonlike roads around lakes and ponds. Some of the prettiest such avenues pass through Mission Hills and Sunset Hills, where Tara-like mansions stand on acres of manicured lawns and back up to golf courses. No trip to Kansas City is complete without an eye-popping drive through these neighborhoods. Go ahead and gawk; we still do.

As in many other cities, it can be confusing to follow driving directions when streets change names at a whim. For instance, head to the airport from the Fairmont Hotel on the Plaza and you'll change streets five times within 4 miles as Ward Parkway becomes Baltimore, then J.C. Nichols Parkway. Cross Westport Road and the street sign says Broadway, then Pennway Park before becoming West Pennway—then (urrgh!)—Broadway again. Our advice? Take a limo, or the KCI Shuttle, or call a friend.

In both Missouri and Kansas you may turn right on a red light after stopping unless otherwise posted. Failing to do so—and pronto, buster—is a sure way to get a beep from the car horn behind you. We're a friendly bunch, but behind the wheel some drivers go from nice to nasty. Tailgating, changing lanes without signaling, and driving through red lights are some of the bad habits you may encounter, although some districts are putting up stoplight-mounted cameras to catch these last lawbreakers. Simply give an "I'm new here" shrug and forgive our manners. Please. Thank you.

As in all cities, you'll want to lock your car doors and place valuables like cameras

and suitcases in a locked trunk. And avoid walking alone at night. Unfortunately, that isn't just on deserted downtown streets; there have been incidents of crime, albeit rare, in nearly every area of greater Kansas City.

If you're planning to drive here in the middle of winter, check out the road conditions posted by the departments of transportation. For Kansas it's (800) 585-7623 or www.kanroad.org, and in Missouri (800) 222-6400 or www.modot.state.mo.us/roadcond/. But by the time you finish typing this last one, the flurries may have ended.

Tours

Discover Kansas City while you leave the driving to. . . well, somebody else. Kool Nites Limousine Inc., for instance, can escort you (and about 30 of your closest friends) around town in one of their three red-and-green trolleys featuring original oak-and-brass interiors. Or hop one of their "Prison Buses,"complete with a semi-functional electric chair for the guest of honor. To add to the fun, the driver sports a prison guard uniform. But the pokie was never this plush: The prison-gray bus has a 19-inch color TV, a wet bar with sink, and a CD player with surround sound. Call (816) 690-6100 or visit www.koolnites-limousine.com for details.

You won't need a get out of jail free pass, but we do recommend comfortable shoes to view our town's diverse architecture on a Historic Kansas City Foundation walking tour. These popular excursions include downtown's Art Deco buildings; our first exclusive neighborhood, Quality Hill, featuring homes dating from 1865; Union Cemetery, the final resting place for many of Kansas City's founders and Civil War casualties; 18th and Vine, with museums devoted to Kansas City jazz and the Negro Baseball Leagues; the Country Club Plaza; and more. Tours, which are led by enthusiastic volunteers, last from 45 minutes to 90 minutes and cost—what a bargain!—around $6.00 per person, with a six-person minimum. Call (816) 931–8448 to reserve a tour at least two to three weeks in advance. Some of the tours are adaptable for van or buses.

Agenda Kansas City can plan sightseeing tours of your choice, including historical sites, a day of shopping, or night on the town via vans, minicoaches, or limos. Call (913) 268–4466 or (888) AGENDAKC, or check out www.agendakansascity.com.

Some of the best views of Kansas City can be found at the Liberty Memorial tower at Penn Valley Park, the glass-enclosed elevator at the Fairmont Kansas City at the Plaza, and the City Hall Observation Deck at 414 East 12th Street.

HISTORY 🏛

There's real drama in our town's 180-plus-year history, a story filled with fascinating heroes and colorful rascals. Yet, unlike an old-fashioned Western it's not always easy to tell if the central characters are wearing white hats or black.

In our struggle to change from mudville to metropolis, we've endured heartbreak like cholera, fires, and a Civil War that left emerging towns on both sides of the state line bloodied and raw. And like every city that dared to stake its future on a river—in our case, two rivers, the Missouri and Kansas—there have been devastating floods.

Yet our history is also filled with stories of pluck and perseverance. Our up-from-your-bootstraps triumphs over natural and man-made tragedies earned us the slogan "Kansas City Spirit." We've always been a town that drew people of grit and tenacity. Our early trailblazers—men like McCoy, Swope, Nelson, Van Horn, Vanderslice, and Volker—often came here looking to make a buck or build a reputation, fell in love with the town, and became our most staunch boosters. Their names are carved into cornerstones, printed on street signs, and embellished on entry markers throughout the city they loved.

Today, a century and a half later, we honor the new pioneers who are taking us forward with vision and vitality. The last part of this chapter is devoted to the men and women whose names adorn new buildings, art centers, and organizations that were created to assist families, find cures for diseases, and train tomorrow's leaders.

Our story starts where it all began: at the river.

WHERE THE RIVERS MEET

Our landscape—fertile valleys and tallgrass prairies, limestone bluffs and wide rivers—was formed when glaciers inched across the shallow seas covering the areas now known as Kansas and Missouri. Ages later other emigrants traveled here by way of the Missouri River. Indians came—the Hopewell, Shawnee, Delaware, and the Kanza who gave us our name—in wooden canoes. French traders arrived in pirogues and keelboats. These were followed by steamboats, often magnificently appointed, before railways and roads crisscrossed our lands.

On June 26, 1804, explorers Meriwether Lewis and William Clark camped on the confluence of the Kansas and Missouri Rivers during their first expedition to the Louisiana Territory. The view they saw from the bluff that would become Quality Hill is still a commanding one today. A handsome statue commemorating the expedition stands at Case Point near Downtown. (See details in Attractions.)

It would be nearly two decades before the town really came into being. In 1821—the same year Missouri was admitted to the Union—a Frenchman from St. Louis, Francois Chouteau, established the American Fur Company at Kawsmouth to feed Europe's craving for beaver-felt hats. Five years later Chouteau's post was destroyed by flood. Would he leave this spot? Mon dieu! At the time his enterprise brought in what would now amount to $5 million a year. He moved to higher ground upriver near what is now Troost Avenue. It wouldn't be the last time the river (America's second longest after the Mississippi) would turn on the people who tried to tame her.

By 1833 the area just east of Indian Territory had captured the attention of another early entrepreneur. John Calvin McCoy, a college-educated surveyor and son of a Baptist minister, opened a supply store 4 miles south of the river on the Santa Fe Trail. He called the place West Port. Today Westport is still a thriving center of commerce, filled with restaurants, shops, and bars. One of its most popular,

Kelly's, started life as a tavern in 1836.

McCoy also founded Westport Landing on a rock ledge across the river from Chouteau's settlement. In 1838 McCoy and 13 other men formed a company and bought a 271-acre tract surrounding the river landing for $4,220. The growing town needed a name and, perhaps inspired by the passing of a jug, the group rejected Possum Trot and Rabbitville for Town of Kansas. The name stuck, and the town was incorporated on June 1, 1850. We wouldn't become Kansas City until 1889.

The township thrived, thanks in part to the romanticized depictions of the frontier by writers like Washington Irving. How many Easterners packed up possessions to travel halfway across a continent after reading *A Tour on the Prairies* in 1832? How much wanderlust was inspired by the description in *The Oregon Trail* of a land "at the height of its freshness"?

Yet travelers seeking the land of the quixotic passages in books and newspapers were disappointed by their first glimpse of our corrugated landscape. By 1840 the settlement was a square mile of land carved out of 130-foot limestone canyons so rugged its 500 residents called it Gully Town. Thick vines and dense forests of oak, hickory, elm, hackberry, and walnut awaited workers. The land was slashed with deep ravines plowed out by rushing streams. After a rain, Gully Town became Mudville.

Yet still they came.

CHOLERA STRIKES

In 1849 the burgeoning settlement met with its first serious setback when cholera killed nearly 30 percent of its residents and drove out hundreds more. There were scarcely enough people left to bury the dead.

Yet by March 1853, less than three years after the plague, the port was thriving once more, driven in part by the Mexican trade over the Santa Fe Trail and the discovery of gold in California. In a frontier version of "Last gas for 50 miles," the wagon trains fueled up on provisions at

> *Trek to Clark's Point at Eighth and Jefferson to take in the view of the river below and imagine what it was like for the area's first visitors like Lewis and Clark. The overlook didn't get its name for half the famous expedition party, however. It was named to honor former city councilman Charles H. Clark in 1933.*

the westernmost point reachable by Missouri River boats. In 1850, 600 wagons got their start at Kansas City. Just ten years later the trade amounted to 16 million pounds of merchandise each year. In 1859, 1,500 steamboats landed at the site.

Tens of thousands arrived here before heading west. Many decided to stay, and today our diverse personality comes from the immigrants who moved here and brought their colorful cultures. Over the decades Scandinavians went to work in the packinghouses. Italians grew the produce sold at the City Market. Five thousand Greeks arrived in Kansas City within a 14-year span and called their community around Fifth Street "Athens." The Irish, Germans, and Jews came, each bringing rich traditions along with suitcases and knapsacks. African Americans were brought to the area by white slaveholders. A Serbo-Croatian community sprang up on Strawberry Hill, overlooking the Kaw River in Kansas City, Kansas.

The city's first hotel—a two-story frame structure at Main Street and the levee—was established in 1846 by Thompson McDaniel to handle the travelers.

At the same time the Wyandot tribe owned and operated a ferry across the Kansas River, then known as the Kaw, which today's Lewis and Clark Viaduct now spans. The name of the tribe has presented some debate: Wyandot is the correct Indian spelling. The English added another "T," and the French tacked on an "E." But that's nothing compared to the confusion created when the township was incorporated as Kansas City, a duplicate of the larger city across the water.

Get a glimpse—actually an eyeful—of what our river town must have looked like around 1840. A mural that depicts riverboats and a tiny settlement on the bluffs has been painted on a brick build-ing just east of the Broadway Bridge in the River Market area.

THE CIVIL WAR

But soon the division between Kansas and Missouri was deeper than the river that cut through the land. By 1850 one in five Jackson County residents was African American. Of these, nearly 3,000 were slaves. Communities, even families, were divided on the issue of slavery.

Many historians trace the beginning of the Civil War to May 1854, when the Kansas-Nebraska Act opened the former Indian Territory to settlement. The conflict between abolitionists and pro-slavery groups plunged the land, known as "Bleed-ing Kansas," into political and military strife. The fighting gained intensity when William Clarke Quantrill and 450 guerrillas swooped into nearby Lawrence, Kansas, before dawn and slaughtered more than 200 men and boys. A year later a battle known as the "Gettysburg of the West" was waged across Westport and west into what is now Mission Hills.

The Civil War decimated both sides of the state line. In Kansas City, Missouri, the population dropped 25 percent to 3,000 or so. The city treasurer's statement showed municipal assets were $16,120.20 and its liabilities, $13,090.84. Cash on hand was $87 and change.

A RETURN TO PEACE AND PROSPERITY

In 1863 the government sent troops to protect the Santa Fe traders and business began to boom once more. The chamber of commerce was organized and real estate became salable again. A vacant lot on Sixth near Main brought $500; another on Walnut near Fifth sold for $305.

Yet the city, after four years of neglect, was in deplorable shape. The streets were quagmires, hub-deep with mud even weeks after a rain, and washouts and gullies made traffic almost impossible. In the spring of 1865 the city negotiated a loan of $60,000 to improve road conditions and open thor-oughfares. Once again things began to hum, and soon the hotel on Main Street was registering 27,000 arrivals a year.

In the meantime the settlement across the Kansas River was also growing, although more slowly. In 1855 a group of Kansas City, Missouri, businessmen pur-chased the core of the town from the Huron Indians. Growth escalated when its first packing plant was built in the Central Industrial District in 1868, and it soon devel-oped a solid base of railroads, stockyards, and industries. Later that year the Town of Wyandotte, along with the adjacent towns Kansas City, Kansas, and Armourdale, were incorporated into a single city.

During this time Kansas Citians began riding to work, school, and the movies on a "bunch of bananas": yellow streetcars that numbered 700 at the height of their eight-decade run beginning in 1869. For a 2-cent fare travelers could get quite a thrill tra-versing the city's hilly streets; the Ninth Street line from Quality Hill to the West Bottoms was as steep as anything San Francisco had to offer. The influx of rubber-tired buses and personal vehicles retired the last of the streetcar bells in June 1957.

BRIDGE TO THE FUTURE

In those days, despite our growth, the towns of Leavenworth, Kansas, and St. Joseph, Missouri, were leaving Kansas City, Missouri, in their dust. They had pop-ulations of 15,400 and 15,000, respec-tively, to our 4,000. But what these lusty rivals didn't have were city boosters like Robert Van Horn and Kersey Coates, who helped secure the first rail bridge to span the Mighty Mo and provide a direct rail link to Chicago. On July 3, 1869, the opening of the Hannibal Bridge was celebrated by a parade, barbecue, and fireworks. More than 20,000 people watched as the Hannibal, the pride of the Hannibal & St. Joseph Railroad, steamed across the bridge with 10 railcars in tow.

Other railroads followed from every direction until the present great aggregation of systems was built up and Kansas City's future was assured. Within five years our population had soared to 32,000, while the other cities had only grown by a few thousand each. A Main Street lot worth $400 in 1856 brought $11,000 in 1871.

SIN CITY AND ITS SAVIORS

Yet not all of our newfound prominence was positive. According to writer Charles Gleed, by 1878 the town was filled with "renegades, Indians, demoralized soldiers, unreformed bushwhackers, and border ruffians, thieves, and thugs imported from anywhere, professional train-robbers of home growth, and all kinds of wrecks from the Civil War."

Those homegrown train robbers were, of course, Frank and Jesse James. In 1866 the James Gang began its crime spree by robbing a bank on Liberty, Missouri's, town square. Along with 10 compatriots they made off with $62,500; one bystander was killed. The James farm near Kearney, Missouri, was one of several safe havens for the boys, but in truth they had plenty of willing help. Many Southern sympathizers saw the outlaws as romantic Robin Hoods who were avenging the loss of the Civil War. During the 1870s the gang was linked to nearly two dozen heists.

There was plenty of money to go around. In those days we had more gambling houses than any other city in the nation. One of these, Marble Hall, was a favorite of Wyatt Earp, Bat Masterson, Buffalo Bill Cody, and Wild Bill Hickok.

This era also marked the start of our meatpacking industry. Two plants for

Civil War history buffs will want to pick up two brochures produced by the Civil War Round Table—a 25-stop driving tour that includes important battle sites throughout the Kansas City region and a walking tour that details important locations, including Loose Park and the John Wornall House. Call (888) 397–1236, or write to the Monnett Battle of Westport Fund, P.O. Box 22528, Kansas City, MO 64113-0528.

slaughtering cattle and hogs were opened, and in 1871 the stockyards were expanded in the West Bottoms. Cowboys who moved the herds spread news about the "Queen of the Cowtowns" where saloons had French glass, gleaming mahogany bars, and no last call.

By 1878 the freewheeling town had a growth rate of 70 percent and was labeled a Modern Sodom by the local newspaper. There were 80 saloons, actually a lifesaver because the murky water supply made drinking whiskey a virtue. Annie Chambers's posh brothel at Third and Wyandotte Streets was doing brisk business as well, and if customers tired of her establishment, they had 40 other bordellos to sample.

Our prosperity also brought conveniences. In 1879 the Missouri and Kansas Telephone Company printed its first directory, listing 46 subscribers in Kansas City, Missouri, and 12 in Kansas City, Kansas. We had an opera house, Exposition Hall, a public waterworks system with 15 miles of water mains, and a two-man fire department.

Yet when William Rockhill Nelson moved to Kansas City from Indiana in 1880, he was appalled to find unpaved roads and haphazard walking boards instead of sidewalks. Soon he was using his newspaper, the *Kansas City Evening Star,* to instigate change. After he won his crusade for better fire protection and street lamps, he focused on public recreation and parks. Read more about this benevolent bear of a man in the Media chapter.

Nelson also convinced others of the importance of green spaces and planned roadways. Colonel Thomas H. Swope donated the largest gift of land in the city's history, before or since: a 1,334-acre tract of land 4 miles from downtown. It became the park that bears his name: the second largest public green space in the United States after New York's Central Park.

In 1891 landscape designer George Kessler was hired to create boulevards and parks using classical architecture while celebrating our eccentric topography. He carved roadways out of gorges and around hills to create wonderful scenic drives. By 1915 we had a feature that would forever rival cities blessed with mountains and ocean views: a parks and boulevard system that earned us the title "City Beautiful."

Buildings were springing up as fast as the roses in one of the city's loveliest green spaces, Loose Park. By the late 1880s a building spree had given the town the nickname "Athens of the West," based on architecture with high ornamentation and neo-Gothic styling. We built the third largest train station in the world, Union Depot, in the West Bottoms and constructed the luxurious Coates House Hotel and Coates Opera House. . . never mind that the latter was next to a cow pasture.

Real estate developers were following Kessler's boulevards to the south. J. C. Nichols built Crestwood, a small shopping area, at 55th and Oak to serve his residences. He sited homes on generous lots that kept the existing terrain as natural as possible, often creating curving streets to save large trees and preserve brooks and streams. His Mission Hills area, with its rolling meadows, ponds, and walkways, set examples that were repeated by developers all over the country.

By 1890 we had 25 schoolhouses, 35 miles of cable car track, and nearly 6,000 new houses. Scottish immigrants laid out the city's first golf course in the Hyde Park neighborhood in 1894. The game was a hit: These days 240,000 Kansas Citians—or 15 percent of our population—are golfers.

KANSAS CITY SPIRIT

In 1899 the city's first convention hall, designed by Frederick E. Hull, opened to the rousing music of John Philip Sousa's band. The cost was high—double the original estimates—but the structure was debt-free thanks to the donations of generous Kansas Citians. It's a legacy of philanthropic pride we follow today.

A year later, fire destroyed the building just three months before the Democratic Convention was to be held, an event boosters hoped would bring us national acclaim. But even as the fire blazed people circulated through the crowd soliciting donations for its reconstruction. A frenzied 90 days later, the convention nominated William Jennings Bryan in one of the world's largest indoor arenas—certainly its newest. The phrase "Kansas City Spirit" was coined that day. Locals strutted around town wearing badges boasting, "I Live in Kansas City—Ask Me."

Six hundred visiting journalists picked up the story and soon newcomers were jamming the streets. One person drawn to the vivacious city was 18-year-old Joyce Clyde Hall, who in 1910 sold postcards from a suitcase under his bed at the YMCA—the start of Hallmark Cards.

The city's resolve would be tested again in 1903 when spring rains turned the Missouri River into an inland sea, flooding the West Bottoms. It destroyed bridges, swept away the stockyards, filled the Union Depot, and left 22,000 people homeless. Public relief money came pouring in, and the area began to rebuild within days.

The trauma of the flooding drove William B. Strang Jr. to develop a flood-free residential area in Johnson County, Kansas. To encourage development he built an interurban railway in 1905 to take residents from downtown to home and back. It extended to the small town of Olathe farther west. The Strang Line building is still standing, now home to Traditions Furniture Store in Old Overland Park.

Another peril—this time man-made—soon took over the West Bottoms and eventually spread over the entire city. The infamous Pendergast political machine started when Jim Pendergast opened a saloon in the area. Soon his younger brother, Tom (profiled in this chapter's Close-up), was named superintendent of streets.

Those same streets continued to carry Kansas City's population southward and away from its river origins as urban sprawl settled in. J. C. Nichols began selling houses for $1,000 in Kansas City, Kansas.

By 1912 the city had 55,000 telephones, 221 churches, 72 public schools, 2,100 acres of parks, 70 miles of boulevards, and 260 miles of street railway. It also had 81 movie theaters with an average weekly attendance of nearly 450,000, almost twice the population of the city. General Hospital, an institution built to serve the city's 24,000 black residents, became the first hospital in the nation to be completely run and staffed by African Americans.

We had other reasons to be proud. Workers hung a 6-foot clock in the archway at Union Station in the fall of 1914. The Beaux Arts–style station replaced the Union Depot in the flood-worried West Bottoms. The new $60 million station at Pershing Road and Grand featured a 95-foot ceiling in the Grand Hall, three 3,500-pound chandeliers, and a North Waiting Room that held 10,000 people. During its heyday, 271 trains passed through the depot daily. Read more about Union Station's sad decline and remarkable restoration in Attractions.

By 1914 the city had another important industry, this time in the service sector. The Federal Reserve Bank opened that year and by 1921 ranked fifth in bank-clearing volume nationwide. This attracted other federal agencies to the area, and by 1939 more than 100 federal offices were located in the metropolitan area.

Money was indeed flowing during the Gilded Age. Millionaires built mansions to rival any in the country. To give his Corinthian Hall the northeast bluff view he desired, lumberman Robert A. Long moved three smaller mansions down the street. His 72-room townhome cost $1 million to build and furnish—shocking in that day. Today the majestic building houses the Kansas City Museum and Planetarium. Read more about this fascinating display in Attractions.

Ladies were decorating more than just their parlors. Charles Tivol opened his jewelry store on Petticoat Lane, where a suitor could purchase a one-carat diamond for $175. The diamonds are a bit pricier these days, but the service is still unmatched at the family-owned business now located on the Country Club Plaza. Petticoat Lane—so named for the lacy lingerie ladies would show on windy days—was also home to the Emery, Bird, Thayer general store.

THE JAZZ AGE: GOOD TIMES AND BAD

On January 16, 1920, prohibition of liquor became part of the U.S. Constitution, yet here the Pendergast political machine kept the city wide open. It was the start of the Roaring Twenties, and no town bellowed louder. Nightclubs flourished thanks to police who were paid to ignore gambling, prostitution, and liquor. Tom Pendergast's own gambling hall had two windows, marked DONATIONS and REFUNDS.

Jazz musicians knew they could always get a gig in Kansas City. Duke Ellington, Cab Calloway, and other bandleaders stopped here on tours, and our local groups kept the beat with the best of them. Pianist William "Count" Basie got his start with Bennie Moten's Kansas City

Kansas City's Colorful History

- Artist Frederic Remington sold his first painting in Kansas City. The 23-year-old arrived here in 1884 and his commercial endeavors—a hardware store and a saloon—failed miserably. His paintings, however, were popular and he sold them through an art supply dealer before moving to New York.

- In 1904 Lyda Burton Conley studied law and became the first Native American woman lawyer in the country. She used her new degree to petition Congress to pass a bill prohibiting the removal of the Huron Indian Cemetery in downtown Kansas City, Kansas. The resting place remains there today, a small plot of land surrounded by businesses between Sixth and Seventh Streets on Minnesota Avenue.

- The City Union Mission received a much-needed boost from a most

unlikely patron when, in 1934, 92-year-old bordello owner Annie Chambers was moved to tears during a funeral sermon by Reverend David Bulkley. She deeded her opulent brothel to his cause, and her residence at Third and Wyandotte Streets was converted into a women's shelter.

- One of the world's most successful companies started at the YMCA. In 1910, 18-year-old Joyce Hall arrived in Kansas City from Norfolk, Nebraska, with a shoebox of postcards, which he kept under his bed at the Y. His room became the company's first address, and today the "Shoebox" brand of cards honors that humble beginning.

- A mural in the Missouri Capitol in Jefferson City by Kansas City artist Thomas Hart Benton depicts our rambunctious town in the 1930s. The central character in the colorful painting was Boss Tom Pendergast—for which

Orchestra. Music poured out of nightclubs along 12th Street and 18th and Vine. The Reno Club, Harlem Nite Club, and big dance halls like the El Torreon kept swinging all night. One young player frequented the Reno Club to listen to his idol, saxophonist Lester Young. Eventually this young man, Charlie Parker, would create a musical style all his own.

Kansas Citians had plenty of other amusements. Fairyland Park opened on 80 acres of farmland at 75th and Prospect Avenue in 1923. That same year the first retail building on the Country Club Plaza made its first sale and the Pla-Mor Ballroom, billed as America's largest indoor

amusement center, opened in 1927. It was soon attracting 4,000 dancers nightly. When they weren't shopping, dancing, or riding the Ferris wheel, residents could listen to four local radio stations.

We stopped moving long enough to salute when five prominent Allied commanders, including General John J. Pershing and French Marshal Ferdinand Foch, joined Vice President Calvin Coolidge to dedicate the site of the Liberty Memorial in 1921. It was the country's only monument to World War I. Coolidge, by now president, returned on November 11, 1926, to formally dedicate the completed memorial with its majestic 200-foot shaft rising from

Pendergast himself posed—dealing with real estate developer J. C. Nichols and banker William T. Kemper.

- When John Calvin McCoy married Virginia Chick in 1838, he was late for the wedding. His future father-in-law sent out a search party and found him—in his wedding attire—feverishly finishing a neighbor's barn roof just minutes ahead of a thunderstorm. Six years later a tornado hit the McCoy house, blowing three-month-old Spencer—crib and all—out of the house. He was found some distance from the destroyed home, uninjured and still in bed.

- Mayor Milton McGee laid out Grand Avenue—the first road from the Missouri River to the town of Westport—just wide enough to get his horse and buggy turned around without having to back it up.

- *The Muse of the Missouri* fountain between Eighth and Ninth on Main celebrates the river's importance in Kansas City's history. Sculptor Wheeler Williams had planned to model the fish fountainheads after native Missouri River fish. But when he deemed our catfish too ugly he fashioned his own hybrid with a carp body and bluefish head.

- At one time Alexander Majors's Pony Express freight and stagecoach company employed 4,000 circuit riders, including 15-year-old wagonmaster Billy Cody. But by 1860 the telegraph and railroad spelled doom for the operation, and "The Great Bullwhacker" lost his fortune. In 1895 the entertainer, now known as Buffalo Bill Cody, made his former employer part of his Wild West show. Majors's home at 81st Street and State Line is now a museum. Read more about it in Attractions.

a hill overlooking Union Station.

We had other heroes to celebrate as well. Formed in 1919, the all-black Kansas City Monarchs baseball team traveled the Midwest in the 1920s and 1930s, when baseball was segregated. The players thrilled fans with 43 straight wins in 1943. A team member, Jackie Robinson, was the first black player to sign with a major league team, the Brooklyn Dodgers, in 1947. Pitcher Satchel Paige eventually played for the Cleveland Indians and the St. Louis Browns before returning to Kansas City to star for the A's.

Another Kansas Citian got his start during this decade. Harry S Truman,

unsuccessful as a haberdasher, was handpicked by Tom Pendergast to run for a post on the administrative court that governed Jackson County. He won, but Pendergast soon learned that Truman would not become one of his lackeys. Independence is still Harry's Town; you can visit his museum and farmhouse. Find out more in Attractions.

HIGH TIMES

Kansas City said "What Depression?" and continued to thrive during the nation's darkest days, thanks in part to Pender-

ℹ️ *Some of our city's liveliest history happened in nightspots along 18th and Vine
during the Jazz Age. You can relive
those days—to a more refined degree—
at the district's American Jazz Museum;
the Blue Room, which doubles as a
museum and nightclub; and during jazz
jams on Saturday night at the Mutual
Musicians Foundation. Get event information on the 24-hour Kansas City Jazz
Ambassadors' Hotline, (816) 753-5277.*

gast. In 1931 the Ten-Year Plan created
jobs and spawned a new City Hall, a
courthouse, and miles of new roads. The
Art Deco–style Kansas City Power & Light
building was completed at 14th and Baltimore. For years it was the tallest building
in Missouri; it remains the most stunning,
especially at night when its prismatic
glass and automated lighting system
change the tower's colors. Two years later
the Nelson Gallery of Art and Atkins
Museum opened on the property formerly
occupied by newspaper publisher William
Rockhill Nelson.

It was the end of a decade—and the
end of an era—when in 1939 Pendergast
pleaded guilty to income tax evasion and
was sentenced to 15 months in Leavenworth Prison.

WAR AND RESURGENCE

When the United States went to war,
Kansas Citians went to work. Before the
1940s our economy seemed forever
grounded in livestock, grain, and freight.
But our central location—and farmlands
full of willing workers—made the Midwest
ideal for wartime industry. Remington
Arms Company built an ammunitions
plant on 3,200 acres east of Independence, and within three years the Lake
City Ordnance Plant was churning out
200 million rounds of ammunition a
month. When the Army Air Corps picked
Kansas City for a bomber plant, it pre-

dicted it would employ 8,000 to 10,000
workers. But when the announcement was
made—one year to the day before the
bombing of Pearl Harbor—no one could
have guessed the factory would soon
have a workforce of 26,000.

Defense jobs drew 40,000 workers to
Kansas City between 1940 and 1943. Most
of them clocked in at the Pratt & Whitney
aircraft engine plant at Bannister Road and
Troost Avenue, where former homemakers
and farmhands built the 2,000-horsepower
engine used in Navy fighter planes. The
facility was the first major employer on the
suburban south side and required new
four-lane roads and trolley tracks. There
were six cafeterias to feed the riveters and
workers, 40 percent of whom were women
and 6 percent black. And they did the city
proud: Kansas City companies consistently
won prestigious "Army-Navy E" awards for
production performance. The garment district, in the meantime, outfitted America's
fighting forces.

On August 14, 1945, Missouri's favorite
son, President Harry S Truman, declared
that the war was over. The troops came
home, minus some 1,250 soldiers from
Jackson County who died in action.

The jubilant country was dancing to
Charlie Parker's bebop music. And here in
the Midwest, we stared at our Philcos as
the town's first television station, WDAF,
began regular programming on October
16, 1949. By the fall of 1950 kids were
watching Whizzo the Clown on KMBC-TV.
His audience was growing fast; during the
next decade 100,000 babies were born in
Kansas City.

As we celebrated the centennial of the
city's incorporation, things looked rosy. We
had a new outdoor theater, Starlight Theatre. Mickey Mantle played outfield for the
Kansas City Blues, a team in the American
Association. And the Katz Drug store was
selling Davy Crockett coonskin caps for 98
cents.

Then, on Friday the 13th, 1951, after 40
days of rain the Kansas River poured over
its dikes to flood the Argentine district and
the West Bottoms . . . again. By Saturday

the Kaw had engulfed the stockyards and factories in the area and forced the evacuation of 15,000 people. City crews dumped junked cars onto the embattled levees to fight the surging water and try to keep the Municipal Air Terminal dry. Five people died and 20,000 were made homeless.

Once again the city rallied. In memory of the city's mettle when it rebuilt the Convention Hall in three months in 1900, workers rebuilt the destroyed American Royal facilities in time for the livestock show weeks later. The country marveled at the collective Kansas City character. Illustrator Norman Rockwell painted *The American Spirit* showing a worker rolling up his sleeves while holding a blueprint.

In 1956 the Hannibal Bridge was replaced by the Broadway Bridge. Kansas City streetcars made their final run in 1959, and only 20 trains a day pulled into Union Station. In the following decade, news about transportation would continue to fill the front pages of the *Star.*

THE TIMES THEY ARE A-CHANGIN'

By 1962, when Interstate 70 was replacing U.S. Highway 40 as the primary entry from the east and west, city commuters were already touting the new 55-mile Interstate 35. Soon it would link folks who lived in Johnson County with their downtown jobs. Within a few years office parks and shopping malls would pop up in every direction to take workers and shoppers out of the inner city.

The exodus from Downtown began in earnest in 1947 when Sears Roebuck and Co. opened its first suburban store on the Country Club Plaza. The movement gained momentum in 1958 when Blue Ridge Mall opened in east Kansas City and Ward Parkway Center opened to the south. They were followed by Metcalf South Shopping Center and a parade of other malls in the suburbs, whose expanding populations packed the parking lots. Downtown stores became increasingly irrelevant. Emery,

Bird, Thayer closed in 1968. Dillard's, which replaced the venerable Macy's store, moved to the suburbs in 1989. Only the Jones Store Co. was left, and it turned off the lights in 1998.

The city's central core also lost its airport. The Municipal Airport just north of Downtown was too confining for growth; pilots and passengers complained that landings seemed to miss nearby skyscrapers by inches. Its replacement, Kansas City International, opened in fall 1972 on a 5,000-acre tract of land northwest of the city.

Some teenagers, in the meantime, were getting high on their own. The Midwest had its share of hippies during the 1960s. Most hung out at Volker Fountain (now called Thies Park) and neighborhood coffeehouses, where they heard local musicians like Brewer and Shipley. Some participated in protest marches.

Some historians were protesting, too— not for change but for conservation. It was a time when landmarks were destroyed to make room for expressways and parking lots. More than 125 buildings came tumbling down, including the former Lyric Theater at 622 Main Street, Kansas City's first public school at Independence Avenue and Cherry Street, and Bob Potee's glittering gambling house at No. 3 Missouri Avenue in the area now known as River Market.

But the '60s also brought plenty to cheer about. The Chiefs professional football team played its first season in Kansas City after owner Lamar Hunt transplanted the team from Dallas. Kansas City voters approved an ordinance that required tav-

Where will you find the only monument and museum in the world dedicated solely to World War I? It's not Washington, D.C., or Normandy—it's the 217-foot-tall Liberty Memorial right here in Kansas City. Major renovations, started in 2002, have returned the site to its former glory and added a fascinating museum.

CLOSE-UP

Thomas J. Pendergast

The powerful Pendergast political machine began, fittingly enough, with a horse race. Jim Pendergast used his winnings to launch a saloon below the bluffs in the West Bottoms, an area filled with warehouses, rail lines, and livestock pens. His watering hole also served as a bank for the working class. He was elected alderman in 1892 and soon extended his influence to the north end of the city. Eighteen years later his younger brother, Tom, replaced him as alderman. The Pendergast tradition of finding jobs for the unemployed and feeding the poor during holidays continued, even after Tom moved out of the West Bottoms into a mansion at 5650 Ward Parkway.

Boss Tom parlayed five years on the city council into a 30-year reign over graft, prostitution, gambling, and rigged elections. And he determined that real power and wealth was tied to business. His Riverside Racetrack pulled in plenty of dough, his Jefferson Hotel was the place to buy liquor and a little action, and his Ready-Mix Concrete Company paved Brush Creek, which fronts the Country Club Plaza.

The Pendergast power reached its zenith (many would say its nadir) between 1925 and 1939. Hundreds of nightclubs operated around the clock. Operators, gamblers, and prostitutes didn't fear police raids; they knew they'd soon go free.

The rest of the nation was noticing. NBC Radio tagged Kansas City a "hot spot" for hoodlums. In 1938 the *Christian Science Monitor* called Kansas City "wider open than any place outside Reno" and blasted residents for being "astonishingly complacent about it all." Not everyone was. Missouri Governor Lloyd C. Stark—who had once sought Pendergast's support and was denied—called for a federal probe of Boss Tom. The crime? An insurance fix he set up through the statehouse, a place referred to as "Uncle Tom's Cabin."

Crime may have been high during this period, but so, too, was the city's growth. Some say Kansas City avoided the worst of the Depression because the Pendergast connections attracted federal funds to the area. Pendergast supported a $40 million public works project, a 10-year plan that changed the city's skyline. By 1930 the city had impressive new buildings, including the Federal Reserve Bank Building, Board of Trade, Kansas City Power & Light building, the 29-story City Hall, Jackson County Courthouse, and the Municipal Auditorium, these last two constructed with concrete from Pendergast's concrete company. The 200-acre Lee's Summit Lake kept work crews busy as well. Pendergast's company also provided the materials for the Nelson-Atkins Art Gallery and the runways at the new Municipal Airport.

erns, amusement parks, and public pools to admit minorities. And on September 17, 1964, the Beatles played a half-hour concert to screaming fans at Municipal Stadium. The Fab Four would eventually record their own version of "Kansas City," the city's anthem.

Another crowd filled the stadium when the Kansas City Royals pitched its first ball on April 8, 1969. It was Ewing Marion

Pendergast handpicked politicians, including a Jackson County judge, Harry S Truman, who became a candidate for the U.S. Senate in 1934. Truman, a celebrated straight shooter himself, admired Pendergast's ability to get things done but stood up to Boss Tom when it came to shady dealings. According to Truman, he only received one request from Pendergast, to support a political ally. Truman refused, saying he was already backing another man, and that was the end of that.

Was Pendergast a friend or foe? Most historians admit he was both. To workers, particularly immigrants who came to a new city without connections, he was a godsend. The city paid 400 Pendergast captains to stop by houses during the 1930s and 1940s to make sure there was enough coal for the winter, enough food for hard times, a job if you needed one. At Christmas the captain—who would mention his allegiance to the Jackson Democratic Club—would show up with food, heating fuel, even toys for the children. The gift tags simply said "A friend," but people knew Pendergast was behind it. The grateful masses kept electing Pendergast's picks.

Ballots, in fact, would be Boss Tom's downfall. Over 60,000 of those votes were found to be cast by "ghosts" who were falsely registered. A funeral parlor listed 17 voters. Vagrants were paid 25 cents for every vote. Eventually 259 Pendergast supporters were convicted by federal juries for conspiracy involving voting fraud.

"Boss Tom" Pendergast ran Kansas City for 30 years. SPECIAL COLLECTIONS DEPARTMENT, KANSAS CITY PUBLIC LIBRARY, KANSAS CITY, MISSOURI

Pendergast's own betting addiction ended his glory days. He was arraigned in 1939 for failure to pay taxes on a bribe he took to pay off gambling debts. After serving 15 months in prison, he lived quietly at his home at 5650 Ward Parkway until his death in 1945. His stronghold on city government was over, but he left another legacy: When the books were audited the city was $22 million in debt.

With a new reform group in control, what we lost in revenue and vibrancy—slot machines were trucked away and jazz clubs lost their crowds—we made up for with a renewed civic pride.

Kauffman, the man who started Marion Labs, who brought the team to Kansas City after the A's moved to Oakland.

We crowded the streets on January 12, 1970, to welcome home the Chiefs, who had just won Super Bowl IV in New Orleans, beating the Minnesota Vikings 23–7. We continued our move to official sports town with the construction of a twin stadium. The Arrowhead Stadium opened for the Chiefs in fall 1972; Royals Stadium housed the Royals a year later. Today the baseball facility is called Kauffman Stadium—or simply "The K"—to honor the baseball team owner.

We were going after crowds of tourists as well with two shining new attractions that opened in 1973. Worlds of Fun created a loopy new skyline of roller coasters and rides on 175 acres in North Kansas City. And the Crown Center complex replaced an eyesore called Signboard Hill across the street from Union Station, offering a city-within-a-city of shopping, restaurants, and hotels linked by glass-enclosed skywalks.

When we hosted the Republican National Convention in 1976 Crown Center impressed delegates and media representatives, as did the elegant new Alameda Plaza Hotel, the first large luxury hotel to grace the Country Club Plaza. Its popular Rooftop Lounge and restaurant offered unparalleled views, food, and libations. Those looking for a more casual atmosphere could find it at the Gilbert-Robinson Plaza restaurant, Houlihan's Old Place.

If anyone visited River Quay (pronounced *key*), an entertainment district near the City Market, it would be their last chance. The area opened in spring 1972 with 13 antiques shops, restaurants, and art studios taking over refurbished buildings, some dating back to the Civil War. Within a year the streets along Delaware and Wyandotte were jammed every weekend. This was, after all, where it had all started for Kansas City, and preservationists and partygoers were pleased. Then organized crime took over and sleazy bars began to proliferate. Several buildings were leveled by suspicious explosions, and before the end of the decade River Quay was kaput.

But good things often come from disasters, and the demise of River Quay also helped signal the end of organized crime in Kansas City. Thankfully for visitors today, the area, now called River Market, is stronger than ever with dining spots and shops set around the outdoor farmers' market. On weekends festivals and music fill the streets. And it has become one of

the trendiest places to live, thanks to dozens of lofts that have transformed warehouses into sleek condos.

While River Quay was folding, Westport was growing. By fall 1974 extensive sections of the old town were being revitalized for restaurants and shops. With restaurants from casual to fancy, and bars that cater to sports crowds to cigar-smoking highbrows, Westport is our city's most happening place, especially for the younger crowd. Along these brick-lined streets, last call doesn't come until the wee hours of the morning.

Early on one of those mornings our city was once again ravaged by floodwaters. In mid-September 1977, residents in northwest Wyandotte County and Bonner Springs were driven out of their homes and a wall of water hit the Country Club Plaza. The death toll eventually reached 25 and property damage (mostly on the Plaza) was over $100 million. Within days the U.S. Army Corps of Engineers and the city began to work out plans to deepen and widen Brush Creek's channel that fronted the famed shopping district.

The 1970s was also the decade when Kansas City started to take a long look at its public persona. We were proud of our city's natural beauty and growing sophistication. Now we wanted the rest of the world to discover our many charms. We began to shirk our cowtown image while holding tight to our midwestern values. The phrase, "It's a great place to raise children," after all, had long been a selling point for real estate agents.

We began to embrace and encourage public art. We had a head start thanks to the fountains and sculptures throughout the Country Club Plaza. And thanks to the pull of students to the Kansas City Art Institute and artists to Hallmark Cards, art appreciation had a strong base in Kansas City. So the world may have been surprised—but we weren't—when world-famous artist Christo chose our Loose Park for one of his high-profile displays. For two weeks in October 1978, bright orange fabric ribboned and swirled around 3 miles of the park's walkways. It was fascinating, it was frivolous, it was fun.

HIGH INFLATION, HIGH EXPECTATIONS

Like every other American city, we were hit hard in the 1980s with skyrocketing inflation rates and high unemployment. But we momentarily forgot 17 percent mortgage rates when the Royals won the 1985 World Series. A champagne-soaked Ewing Kauffman celebrated with third baseman George Brett, pitcher Dan Quisenberry, the other players, and 41,628 screaming fans. Within days Grand Avenue was wall-to-wall with revelers as we gave the team a rousing victory parade.

At the ballpark, more and more license plates read Johnson County as that county grew by 85,000 residents during the decade. Money continued to shift from Missouri to the Kansas side as mini-mansions sprang up in Johnson County subdivisions like Hallbrook, which opened in 1989. Houses in this enclave cost on average $550,000.

Kansans had other things to celebrate: In 1986 voters did away with the past century's temperance law and approved liquor by the drink, a state lottery, and racetrack betting. The Woodlands dog- and horse-racing track opened in Wyandotte County a few years later.

Local business was racing ahead as well when a local company, US Telecom, merged with the long-distance arm of GTE in 1986. The world headquarters of the resulting company, Sprint, became one of the area's largest employers.

Kansas City continued its reputation as a sports town when we hosted 15,000 visitors for the NCAA Final Four basketball tournament in April 1988. We celebrated other sports heroes, for reasons that often went deeper than skills with a club or a bat. Golfer Tom Watson resigned from the Kansas City Country Club (where he learned to play golf) in 1990 because the club would not allow a Jewish business-

man, Henry Bloch, to join. In 1992 George Brett made the 3,000th hit of his career at Royals Stadium. Two years later he retired, perhaps because his biggest fan, Ewing Kauffman, was no longer in the stands to watch him play. The philanthropist had died the year before.

WORKING TOGETHER

As we started looking toward our 150-year anniversary, city leaders began to push for a renewed interest in our central core. At the top of the list was the dilapidated Union Station. It was clear that revitalizing the once-beautiful landmark would take cooperation—and money—from both sides of the state line. In 1996 voters across five counties passed the Bistate Cultural Tax, the first two-state effort of its kind in the country. Work began to convert the grand old depot into a science museum and entertainment venue, a project that would cost more than $200 million. Soon voters were also saying "Yes" to restoring Liberty Memorial.

Sprawl continued to move the city in all directions. By the mid-1990s the Northland was a boomtown with new, luxurious subdivisions popping up in Clay and Platte Counties. More than 100,000 residents were drawn to the area's rolling hills and lush-treed landscapes dotted with lakes and golf courses.

Everyone, it seemed, headed north of the river to try his or her luck at the new gambling casinos. Today we're home to four casinos where guests can play games of chance before sitting down to a bounteous buffet, elegant dinner, or stage show featuring national headliners. We bet you'll want to see the Attractions chapter for more information about these exciting venues.

We maintained our interest in public art. Bartle Hall got its *Sky Stations*—some call them "hair curlers"—in 1994. Giant *Shuttlecocks* dotted the lawn at Nelson-Atkins Museum of Art. We continued our love affair with fountains: Water displays define the entrances to business parks, government buildings, and neighborhoods.

We stopped razing and started restoring historic buildings from the River Market area to the downtown Garment District, Hyde Park and the Northeast area, Quality Hill and West Bottoms to the east side of town. Meanwhile places like Parkville and Weston added to their "Main Street USA" charm with new cafes, galleries, and shops.

We also began to honor our history by paying tribute to the people, places, and events that formed our city. In 1997 we opened the Negro Leagues Baseball Museum and the Kansas City Jazz Museum at 18th and Vine Streets, once the heart of the African-American neighborhood. The driving force behind these redevelopments was Emanuel Cleaver, a Methodist minister who was mayor of Kansas City from 1991 to 1999. Cleaver made history as the first African-American mayor of the city. His replacement, Kay Waldo Barnes, was the first woman to hold the office.

Other cities within the metropolis began to thrive under fresh leadership. Even the sister-city across the river awoke from more than a century of slumber. Carol Marinovich, the new mayor/chief executive of the United Government of Wyandotte County/Kansas City, Kansas, thrilled residents and surprised some neighboring cities when she announced plans for the new Kansas Speedway. The track, which opened in 2001, sponsors three NASCAR-sponsored races each year to bring an estimated $170 million boost to the city's economy, the equivalent of a Super Bowl every year. Surrounding it is Village West, a 400-acre entertainment and shopping district anchored by Cabela's outdoor emporium that—along with camouflage on every conceivable piece of apparel—includes a 55,000-gallon walk-through aquarium and a museum-quality African diorama with trophy elephants, rhinos, lions, and water buffalo. No wonder the average visitor stays three and a half hours. Village West is also home to Nebraska Furniture Mart, billed as the largest home furnishings store in the world, and the Great Wolf Lodge, a combination hotel and indoor water park (see more in the Shopping, Attractions, and Accommodations chapters).

Meanwhile, Ed Eilert, mayor of Overland Park, Kansas, for 20 of the city's 40 years, has transformed the bedroom community into the state's fastest-growing city. This suburb is continuing to go after a tourism market with a handsome new convention-and-hotel center (See Accommodations).

LOOKING FORWARD

Visitors and newcomers have always been surprised to find in Kansas City a town that's vibrant and varied, friendly yet sophisticated. The best is yet to be. There's a palpable new energy here, especially in the urban core that's been neglected for so long. Like many positive changes it started on two fronts. Corporate leaders stopped waiting for a master plan and slowly began to put their money and influence into opening offices, living spaces, and cultural venues downtown. Meanwhile young artists began to create lofts and studios out of abandoned buildings between Downtown and Crown Center, creating an exciting avenue of arts that brought in patrons and encouraged restaurants and retail shops. Even the storied West Bottoms are coming back with new art galleries, cafes, and businesses.

Looming on the horizon are a downtown entertainment district, a performing arts center to rival any in the country, and a new sports stadium. Adding to the mix will be more hotel rooms, condos and lofts, restaurants, and shopping venues. And thanks to a "Let's share" attitude among the 18 different counties that make up the region, we're busy attracting even more business to our area. It's a great time to work and live in Kansas City—and an exciting time to visit.

KANSAS CITY'S PROMINENT CITIZENS

Kansas City's leaders are continuing a tradition that began almost as soon as the town took hold: that of giving back to the community through endowments, expertise, and plenty of cash. There is, however, an important distinction between our early-day givers and those of today: The patriarchs of a century ago have been replaced, in many cases, by pairs as husbands and wives jointly decide how best to use their time and funds. In many cases the feminine half of the marriage controls a separate foundation with its own unique mission. In one case a daughter is brilliantly heading the foundation named for her late mother.

There are, of course, thousands of do-gooders whose names will never appear on a bronze plaque; these are the folks who build homes for Habitat for Humanity, spending weekends each fall to paint, clean, and fix up inner-city houses through an organization called Christmas in October. They send a $5.00 or $50.00 check when they read about a family in trouble, donate coats in winter, fans in summer, and toys for holidays. They volunteer to visit the elderly and read stories to children, line up for blood drives, and sign up for their turn in food kitchens. And their cash contributions have made Kansas City one of the top philanthropic cities in the country: The Greater Kansas City Community Foundation recently received nearly $120 million in contributions and distributed $90,145,000, making it the third largest in grants made among 582 community foundations nationwide.

So cheer these modern-day heroes—named and unnamed—who continue to make this city a great place to live and work. As you'll see in the profiles below, their reach often extends beyond our borders to help millions through education and medical research.

Henry Bloch

The cofounder, with brother Richard, of H&R Block Inc., the national tax preparation firm, has enhanced the lives of many residents. Since 1985 the Henry W. and Marion H. Bloch Foundation has provided money to expand facilities at the University of Missouri–Kansas City business school, now called the Henry W. Bloch School of Business and Public Administration. The Blochs have also financed scholarships at Avila College and capital improvements at the Kansas City Art Institute. And when Mr. Bloch retired in 2001, his company's parting gift didn't arrive in a watch box: His name is on one of the city's newest and most exciting fountains in front of Union Station.

The late Richard Bloch founded the R. A. Bloch Cancer Foundation with his wife, Annette. The foundation's cancer hotline offers support to those newly diagnosed and has established cancer survivor parks in 15 cities across the United States, including a lovely sculpture garden on the west side of the Country Club Plaza.

Donald and Adele Hall

"When you care enough to give the very best," could be the slogan for this couple's generosity as well as that of Hallmark Cards, the company founded by Donald's father.

For more than four decades Donald Hall has changed the landscape of the city for the better, with his Crown Center complex, the Henry Moore sculpture garden at the Nelson-Atkins Museum of Art, and funds for Union Hill housing and Union Station's renovation. Adele Hall has donated time and money for the Nelson-Atkins Art Gallery expansion, the United Negro College Fund, Wayside Waifs, and countless other organizations. She's had the rare honor of being named both

Kansas Citian of the Year and Johnson Countian of the Year.

The couple recently sent the city "its very best"—a $60 million check to the Nelson-Atkins Museum of Art. That brings to a total of $100 million the amount the Hall Family Foundation has contributed to the museum over the years.

Barnett and Shirley Helzberg

Open any Sunday's *Star* society page and there's Shirley Helzberg at a gala fundraiser for Starlight Theatre, the Kansas City Symphony, the Shakespeare Festival, and the new Arts Council of Metropolitan Kansas City. Yet she doesn't just show up on Saturday night—she's deeply involved in these organizations and dozens more.

As for cold cash, the couple gave one of the largest personal gifts to save Union Station, $1 million for a garden at Starlight, and seed money for a new Kansas City charter school.

Barnett, who was mentored by Ewing Kauffman, has made helping young entrepreneurs his second career after selling his jewelry business to Warren Buffet of Berkshire-Hathaway. He established the Helzberg Entrepreneurial Mentoring Program in 1995. And Rockhurst University, where he has been an adjunct professor for more than 10 years, recently renamed its business school the Helzberg School of Management to honor the couple.

Shirley also spent untold millions renovating an old schoolhouse south of Downtown into a marvelous antiques store called Webster House. See Shopping for more on this classy venue.

R. Crosby Kemper Jr.

Kemper's banking empire, UMB Financial Corporation, spans several states, yet his generosity remains chiefly in his hometown. In 1973 he donated $3.2 million to construct Kemper Arena in the West Bottoms, and a $6 million gift in 1990 resulted in the Kemper Museum of Contemporary Art. Kemper has always been one to come through for a worthy cause, such as his $1 million gift to rebuild the city's bankrupt orchestra, now the Kansas City Symphony, and a $2 million donation to the Liberty Memorial restoration fund.

James and Virginia Stowers

A decade ago few people around town had heard the name Stowers. Although his fortune from the mutual fund empire he founded, American Century Investments, put them at the top of Kansas City's elite, the reserved twosome shunned the limelight.

Yet today this couple is turning the city into a center for biomedical research. As cancer survivors, they've poured millions into the Stowers Institute for Medical Research, a handsome center built along the thriving Brush Creek Corridor. And they're proving wrong the experts who advised them to develop the institute on one of the coasts. After all, what respected international scientist would want to move to the Midwest? Since opening its doors in 2000, the Stowers Institute has attracted the world's top research talents, who, incidentally, have fallen in love with their adopted home town.

Ewing and Muriel Kauffman

Everyone in Kansas City knows the story about how Mr. K saved the Royals baseball team, and most have heard of his Project Choice program that helped students succeed on both sides of the state line (we cover Project Choice in the Higher Education section of the Relocation chapter).

But Kauffman is also credited with encouraging entrepreneurs through mentoring programs. Today the Ewing Marion Kauffman Foundation has about $2 billion in assets and includes the Kauffman Center for Entrepreneurial Leadership. His vivacious wife helped get a 911 system in the Kansas City area, and the Muriel McBrien Kauffman Foundation has assets of about $300 million.

Muriel's daughter, Julia Irene Kauffman, now oversees the foundation's works. Its most generous gift to date is $105 million for the new Metropolitan Kansas City Performing Arts Center that will turn a hilltop just south of Bartle Hall into a $300 million civic landmark when it opens in the next few years. (Read more about this exciting project in the Arts chapter.)

Kenneth and Helen Spencer

This third-generation coal mine owner built the Spencer Chemical Company and left a personal estate of more than $15 million, which his widow used to establish the Spencer Theatre in the University of Missouri-Kansas and the Spencer Museum of Art at the University of Kansas.

OTHER RESOURCES

We celebrate our rich history at dozens of museums and visitor centers throughout Kansas City. You'll find listings for interesting places like the Grinter House, the first home built in Kansas City, Kansas; Missouri Town 1855; the Jesse James Farm and Museum; President Harry S Truman's farm and museum; and the Gem Theater, which showcases our jazz heritage in the Attractions chapter under History.

TRACE YOUR OWN FAMILY HISTORY

The Kansas City area—in particular Independence, Missouri—offers genealogists and family historians a wellspring of information. A good place to start your search is the Jackson County Historical Society Archives and Research Library, located in the Jackson County Courthouse at 112 West Lexington Avenue, Room 103. It contains 20,000 photographic images and a 2,000-volume library of reference books, periodicals, letters, and more. The society's bookshop sells more than 600 titles, including maps and books relating to Jackson County, the westward expansion, and the Civil War. The society also operates two historical sites, the 1859 Jail Museum and Clinton's Old Fashioned Soda Fountain, where a young Harry Truman once worked. Call (816) 461-1897 for information.

The Mid-Continent Public Library and its adjacent 12,000-foot Genealogy and Local History Department are wonderful resources for tracing ancestors. The collection includes the U.S. population censuses for 1790 to 1920 as well as family and county histories. The branch is located at 317 West 24 Highway, Independence; call (816) 252-7228 for hours.

The Black Archives of Mid-America, Inc., at 2033 Vine, Kansas City, Missouri, is one of the largest collections of African-American memorabilia, artifacts, and research materials in the Midwest. There is an admission fee. Call (816) 483-1300 for information.

At the Johnson County Archives you'll find documents relating to the history of Kansas and the county, including marriage licenses, wills, and naturalization records from the late 1880s. The center is located in the County Administration Building, 111 South Cherry, Suite 500, Olathe, Kansas; call (913) 715-0400.

ACCOMMODATIONS

When staying in Kansas City for a night, a weekend, or a month, you can expect to be treated to the friendly service that defines our town. That means the person behind the front desk will actually look up and smile as you approach. Innkeepers—sometimes accompanied by a tail-wagging dog—may greet your arrival with a plate of fresh-baked cookies. Then there's the owner of an Overland Park motor hotel who paid a guest's bail one Saturday night. We trust you won't test our hospitality quite that far.

Good manners abound, yes, but you'll also find great accommodations. Your footsteps will echo across lobbies lined with enough marble to rebuild ancient Rome, and when one hotel boasts of running water, they're referring to the five-story waterfall to your left. Plenty of famous folks have registered at our front desks over the years, including movie stars and rock stars, glamour queens and gangsters—Al Capone used one area resort as his hideout—and more than our share of presidents. Harry S Truman, in fact, showed the world he was still commander-in-chief, despite the headlines, at one of our downtown hotels.

There are rooms to fit every taste and pocketbook, from ultraposh retreats and bed-and-breakfast inns to budget-pleasing motels and even campsites. Naturally for a city our size, every hotel, motel, and extended-stay chain is represented—just right for ratcheting up your frequent-travel points. In addition to these national names, we offer some one-of-a-kind lodging choices. To see a complete roster of available accommodations, check out the Hotel and Motel Association of Greater Kansas City's Web site at www.kansascity lodging.org.

Guests with special needs will find that most hotels offer nonsmoking or allergen-free rooms—sometimes even entire floors—and unless specified, every hotel listed is partially or wholly wheelchair-accessible. To be on the safe side, we recommend that you call ahead to check. Travelers with small children or pets should also check on services available. Speaking of pets, the Fairmont Hotel on the Country Club Plaza treats your pooch like royalty with a special dog bowl filled with goodies from Kansas City's own Three Dog Bakery. Unless otherwise noted, the accommodations in this chapter accept major credit cards and offer rooms with color TV with remote—most with cable and/or pay-per-view channels—private baths, and air-conditioning.

As for where to stay, it depends on what you desire during your visit. The downtown area is home to our financial, business, and convention services. It's also where you can see our city in stages. Or "on" stages, as it were. Our grandest theaters—many of them turn-of-the-20th-century gems—are downtown. And between Downtown and Crown Center are dozens of art galleries and artist's studios in an area called the Crossroads Arts District. During nice weather the neighborhood becomes a street party as art lovers go from gallery to gallery. And where the crowds go, great restaurants are sure to follow. The Crossroads and nearby Freighthouse District seem to sprout a fabulous new restaurant every month.

Speaking of Crown Center, we call this complex a city-within-a-city because it combines two luxury hotels and dining, shopping, and attractions all in one neat package, along with an old-fashioned town square that sports an outdoor ice-skating rink, fountains, and live entertainment. Union Station and Science City are connected to the center via an elevated, climate-controlled walkway called The Link. And it's all in the shadow of our magnificent Liberty

Memorial, the country's only museum and memorial dedicated solely to World War I.

Locations in and around Westport and our famous Country Club Plaza offer so many dining, shopping, and nighttime entertainment options you could book a room for a month and not see it all. This area also boasts two world-class art museums, lovely parks, and the reason we're called the City of Fountains. If gambling is your game, it's a sure bet you'll enjoy our riverboat casino-hotel resorts. History buffs who are wild about Harry will find hotels and bed-and-breakfasts close to his museum and home in Independence.

But don't discount accommodations in outlying areas. For instance, Overland Park offers some of the best shopping west of Fifth Avenue. And when we say take it outside, we're not being rude: Johnson County has miles of walking trails linking public parks and waterways. Dozens of private and public courses make this a golfer's paradise. Wyandotte County, Kansas, will tempt you with brand-new hotels in Village West, the 400-acre entertainment area surrounding the NASCAR race track.

As for *when* to come, spring and fall are our most glorious times of year, when gardens and trees look particularly pretty, and during summer there's a festival or event every weekend. Every winter our entire city dresses for the holidays. We open our decorated homes for tours, offer cookies and hot cider in shops, and invite the world to watch as 250,000 colored lights illuminate the Country Club Plaza on Thanksgiving night. Hotel rooms overlooking the magical ceremony—our version of Mardi Gras—are often booked a year in advance. Come anyway; the dazzling view continues through mid-January.

Reservations are always recommended. Kansas City is a popular convention town, drawing groups of 40,000 or more, because it seems folks can't get enough of our blues and barbecue. And during racing season at Kansas Speedway, rooms go as fast as the NASCAR cars. So it won't hurt to call well in advance for reservations; you'll have that much longer to dog-ear pages in this book.

So let's get you checked in. We've divided this chapter into four categories: Hotels and Motels, Extended Stays, Bed-and-Breakfasts and Inns, and RV Parks and Camping. The first two categories are listed by location. The others are listed alphabetically. All places to stay are located in Kansas City, Missouri, unless otherwise noted.

PRICE CODE

Prices reflect the average rate for high season, double-occupancy accommodations. Keep in mind that most hotels offer a price range based on size of room, amenities, and desirability. Prices listed do not include special services such as babysitting, valet laundry, parking (if charges apply), telephone calls, room service, or hotel-motel taxes. Many hotels and most bed-and-breakfasts offer packages, several places provide Internet-only discounts.

$	Less than $60
$$	$60 to $110
$$$	$111 to $160
$$$$	$161 and up

HOTELS AND MOTELS
Country Club Plaza and Westport

Embassy Suites Hotel $$
220 West 43rd Street
(816) 756-1720
www.embassysuites.com
The waterfall and mini-rainforest in this all-suite hotel's 12-story atrium is so gorgeous you might want to pitch a tent. But check out your room instead; the bedroom and separate living room make it ideal for families and business travelers. Each suite offers home-away-from-home amenities like two TVs, refrigerator and microwave, coffeemaker, and more.

CLOSE-UP

The Fairmont Kansas City at the Plaza

Step into this marble-lined lobby and you could be at a Fairmont in any great city: London, San Francisco, New Orleans. All stellar to be sure, but none of the others have what the Fairmont Kansas City has: the world-famous Country Club Plaza just a heartbeat away.

Kansas City's only Four Star, Four Diamond hotel began its life in 1969 as the Alameda Plaza with a Spanish theme to coordinate with the Country Club Plaza's architecture. It changed briefly to the Ritz-Carlton, and then became the Fairmont in 2000. A $10 million renovation has once again elevated it to the city's premier hotel.

It's only right that a grand hotel in the City of Fountains would have a liquid landmark. The waterfall that fronts the Fairmont is a backdrop for a statue of Diana, goddess of the hunt, and her three adoring cherubs. The sculpture—a copy of one made for the Moreton estate in Warwickshire, England, in 1912—was commissioned for the site in 1970 by Plaza developer J. C. Nichols.

The hotel's entrance is located at the end of a short drive around back, a con- figuration that saves all the best views for guest rooms and public areas. It's an especially pretty picture from the lobby lounge, where fresh sushi is served every evening along with more than 300 types of martinis, including the signature "Plazapolitan." Local jazz artists wow the crowds every evening. No wonder the Oak Bar was recently named one of the top hotel bars in the world by Continental Airline's *Inflight Magazine*.

The Oak Room is tucked just beyond the lounge. This elegant restaurant is open for breakfast, lunch, and dinner, when it serves fabulous steaks, fresh fish, and pasta dishes. The dining room's recessed lighting coves with silver accents give the illusion of falling oak leaves, a beautiful contrast to the twinkling Plaza scene across the bridge. The view is even more mesmerizing from the Rooftop Restaurant and Lounge, which are available for private parties and special events such as holiday dinners.

The 12-story Fairmont has 366 guest rooms, including 20 suites, 3 wheelchair-accessible rooms, and 220 nonsmoking rooms. Rooms are luxurious retreats with

More pluses include a made-to-order complimentary breakfast and an afternoon manager's reception where you'll be treated to your favorite beverage. And the location, halfway between the Plaza and Westport, means you have 60 or so restaurants to choose from within minutes. Now aren't you glad you booked another day?

Hampton Inn & Suites $$
4600 Summit
(816) 448–4600, (877) 410–4600
www.hamptoninnkc.com
Here's how to have the Country Club Plaza practically at your front door and still have enough cash left for a big-shot dinner out. This nine-story hotel has 203 oversized guest rooms, including two-

marble bathrooms, three telephones (including one in the bathroom), and an in-room safe. All the suites and the 23 rooms on the Club Floor have access to a private lounge with complimentary food presentations throughout the day and the personal services of a concierge.

Self-parking in the covered parking lot is free; valet parking is also available. The outdoor heated pools overlook the Plaza from one story above street level, and on-call massage services are available seven days a week at the fitness center. A variety of meeting rooms, banquet space, and a 12,000-square-foot ballroom makes this one of Kansas City's preferred addresses for weddings and other celebrations.

The decor and amenities, to be sure, are exquisite. But it's the special events that set this hotel apart. Christmastime is truly enchanting, when children are treated to breakfasts with Santa and storytime tea by the fireplace. When traveling with your furry friends, bark—or book—a room at the Fairmont, where Fido or Fluffy is a welcome guest.

Then there are "Dive-in" movie nights, when movies are shown on a large screen on the patio and the best seat in the house is in the pool. And the Uptown-Dine-Around package includes appetizers and dinner at two of Kansas City's top restaurants with a bottle of champagne and dessert waiting in a Plaza-view room.

If that sounds like fireworks, wait until you see the spectacular display on Thanksgiving night, just moments after the Plaza's famous lighting ceremony ends. Fireworks timed to hundreds of musical cues appear over the rooftop to leave spectators breathless, especially those with the best vantage points throughout the hotel. It's a thrilling addition to the lighting extravaganza that has defined the Plaza for more than 72 years.

No wonder Plaza-view rooms are often booked a year or more in advance. Just remember, kids, the holiday lights stay on through mid-January. And with indulgences like these, there truly isn't a bad room in the house. The Fairmont Kansas City at the Plaza is at 401 Ward Parkway; for more information call (816) 756-1500 or (800) 866-5577, or visit www.fairmont.com.

room suites with fully equipped kitchens bigger than many apartments. A continental breakfast and evening reception with appetizers and beverages are complimentary. There's also a fitness room and indoor pool to help you keep in shape for those days of nonstop shopping. The Hampton is a top pick for family reunions and other group get-togethers.

Holiday Inn Express-Westport $$
801 Westport Road
(816) 931-1000, (800) HOLIDAY

A Holiday Inn is a Holiday Inn—right? Well, that's true until you toss in a little history. A plaque above the door shows that this site was once part of the original Santa Fe Trail, while a trail map in the lobby shows the westward route.

The hotel continues the Western theme with Southwest fabrics and a Frederic Remington sculpture. Rooms—109 in all—offer workstations, dataport phones, and coffeemakers. The executive kings have separate sitting areas, and welcome baskets greet guests. A complimentary continental breakfast is included, and of course there's that terrific location next door to Kansas City's favorite entertainment center, Westport.

The Quarterage Hotel-Westport $$
560 Westport Road
(816) 931-0001, (800) 942-4233
www.quarteragehotel.com

Don't let the modern brick exterior fool you; inside, the Quarterage is a 19th-century beauty with warm oak, tin ceilings, and marble appointments. A cozy wood-burning fireplace beckons you to hunker down with a good book, and even the complimentary full breakfast and evening cocktail hour seem like an innkeeper's thoughtful touches from days gone by.

You'll also appreciate the 21st-century features such as a health club with aerobic classes, soothing hot tub and sauna, and two-line phones with high-speed data connections. It may be hard to leave, particularly if you have a prime spot near the fire, but the excitement of Westport beckons. Just steps away are some of the city's best nightspots, restaurants, and shops.

The Raphael Hotel $$$
325 Ward Parkway
(816) 756-3800, (800) 821-5343
www.raphaelkc.com

Villa Serena, a name that sounds like a Spanish lullaby, was the 1927 apartment hotel that would become the Raphael. In 1975 legendary hotelier Phil Pistilli created a treasure out of the nine-story structure by expanding rooms while keeping the Andalusian architecture borrowed from the Country Club Plaza across Brush Creek. Today this beloved boutique hotel is in the capable hands of General Manager Cynthia Savage. You might say it's still in the family; Cynthia is Mr. Pistilli's daughter.

The Raphael more than lives up to its reputation as the city's most romantic hotel. Sometimes Cynthia and her staff play cupid to set the stage for proposals. One suitor requested rose petals leading from the lobby, into the elevator, and through hallways, ending with a dozen roses and an engagement ring in the suite. "She said yes," Cynthia recalls.

The Raphael Restaurant has also served up amorous scenes like diamonds frozen in ice cubes or tucked into bouquets delivered to the table. But even without a solitaire in sight, this dining room is special. Chef Peter Hahn develops a new menu weekly by giving new continental twists to classic American fare. Dark smoky mirrors, deep recessed booths, piano music filtering in from the bar lounge—it all makes for a wonderful dinner out where—get this—you can actually hear your dinner partner. You can read more about this Kansas City favorite in the Restaurants chapter.

The Raphael has 35 rooms and 88 spacious suites filled with amenities as plush as the robes. Business travelers will enjoy extra touches like computer dataports, a state-of-the-art voice mail system, and even ergonomic work chairs in every room. If you ever want to leave your room, an entire 14-block wonderland of shopping, entertainment, and dining awaits you on the Country Club Plaza. Loose Park, with its famed rose garden, duck pond, and walking paths, is just a stroll up the hill. The Nelson-Atkins Museum and Kemper Museum are close by as well. And of course the hotel staff will be happy to arrange trips to other attractions around the city.

You didn't hear it from the hotel's staff—they would never impinge on a guest's privacy—but when performers like Sting end their gigs in town, they often end the evening with an impromptu concert at the piano in the Fairmont Hotel's lounge.

The Raphael will also woo you with special packages such as Plaza Memories, which includes two nights' stay, a keepsake silver picture frame, and a bottle of wine. The Romance Package takes a cue from that suitor from years past—or is it the other way around?—with Plaza-view accommodations, two keepsake monogrammed robes, and rose petals scattered across the pillows. Hold our calls.

Crown Center

Hyatt Regency Crown Center $$–$$$
2345 McGee Street
(816) 421–1234, (800) 233–1234
www.hyatt.com
The Hyatt's lobby lounge makes quite a first impression with a dazzling sculpture that drops from the two-story ceiling like golden raindrops. It's an elegant place to listen to piano music or the restful sounds of a fountain while you enjoy a cocktail. With Hyatt's renowned attention to detail and Kansas City's friendly charm, you may never want to leave.

You won't have to. The hotel is connected to the 85-acre Crown Center complex via an elevated walkway, so you can stroll in climate-controlled comfort to shops, restaurants, live theater, and movie houses. Crown Center Square, called Kansas City's "Rockefeller Center" by National Geographic's Traveler, is host to year-round entertainment and the city's only outdoor ice-skating rink. Another skywalk takes you to Union Station, the city's historic train station that includes an interactive science museum, great restaurants, and unique entertainment choices.

The Hyatt's 731 rooms and suites feature 24-hour room service, minibars, and movie channels. Other amenities include a complimentary health club, all-weather pool, tennis courts, and a downtown view.

And within the Hyatt are two dining choices so superb they'll forever change your concept of "hotel restaurants." You'll find detailed descriptions in the Restaurant

How many balls are suspended in the sculpture hanging in the lobby of the Hyatt Regency Crown Center? Give up? We've counted them for you: The striking artwork designed by Vermont artist Irv Harper contains 1,965 small silver globes.

chapter, but for now think about the Peppercorn Duck's rotisserie-roasted duck and buffet filled with every chocolate dessert imaginable. Or combine a little sightseeing with your grilled steak at Skies, the hotel's revolving rooftop restaurant. The lounge provides a breathtaking view as well.

The Westin Crown Center $$$$
1 Pershing Road
(816) 474–4400, (800) 228–3000
www.westin.com
Thank goodness for the Hall family, owners of Hallmark Cards, who converted an eyesore called Signboard Hill into one of the city's most exciting tourist areas. At its heart is the Westin, whose five-story lobby waterfall makes dramatic use of the original hill's natural limestone.

The 725-room hotel's location just keeps getting better and better. Its neighbor is the newly renovated Union Station, with several excellent restaurants, entertainment, and Science City, all accessible via an elevated walkway that looks like something out of Disneyland's Tomorrowland. And hotel guests are just a brisk walk from our beautifully restored Liberty Memorial and a taxi ride from the vibrant Crossroads Arts District neighborhood.

But you can enjoy plenty of action without leaving Crown Center. Enjoy a burger in a streetcar, take in a movie, or shop dozens of unique boutiques. Kids can learn new artistic skills at Kaleidoscope or simply color a placemat at Crayola Cafe. (See Restaurants, Attractions, Shopping, and Kidstuff for details.)

As a guest of the Westin, you'll have a ringside seat for the activities at Crown Center Square, including summertime concerts, hunting for the Great Pumpkin, and lighting the Mayor's Christmas tree. Even when there's nothing happening outside, the downtown skyline view from Benton's rooftop steakhouse is stunning.

Downtown

Doubletree Hotel $$-$$$
1301 Wyandotte Street
(816) 474-6664, (800) 843-6664
www.doubletree.com

This 28-story high-rise has had several names and personalities, beginning as the Americana in the 1970s. It closed its doors in 1994 and reopened to great fanfare as the Omni three years later when it helped usher in a renaissance of the downtown area. Today, as the Doubletree, it's more handsome than ever, graced with rich woods, mission-style furnishings, and a hint of the Art Deco architecture found in many of its surrounding buildings. The location puts Kansas City's cultural attractions and business services at its door.

A $26 million renovation made sure the 388 guest rooms and 99 king suites have comfort and luxury to match the company's reputation. Then, of course, there are the signature Doubletree chocolate chip cookies waiting for you after a day of exploring the City of Fountains.

The Doubletree is also a fashionable choice for grand events. Its crown jewel, a circular rooftop ballroom, offers a breathtaking view of the city's skyline. Bistro 1301 offers guests American cuisine and wood-fired pizzas, complemented by a 2,000–bottle wine cellar.

---

i *The Link—the 880-foot-long, enclosed elevated walkway between Hyatt Regency Hotel and Crown Center's shops—contains 2,000 panes of glass, which are cleaned three times a year. A second, 810-foot link was added in 2000 to connect the Westin Crown Center to Union Station.*

Historic Suites of America $$-$$$
612 Central Street
(816) 842-6544, (800) 733-0612
www.historicsuites.com

When the owners of this downtown gem combined three turn-of-the-20th-century buildings into one hotel, it was a challenge to say the least. The adjacent structures—the Builders and Traders Exchange, Burnham-Munger building, and the Barton Brothers Shoe Company—ranged in style from neo-Romanesque to Second Renaissance Revival. But the diversity is what gives this lodging choice its special flavor. You'll have 32 different floor plans to choose from, including loft styles with circular staircases in sizes up to 1,800 square feet!

Each suite includes a fully equipped kitchen—a nice way to "stay home" while you travel—and amenities include a complimentary breakfast buffet, evening reception, exercise rooms, whirlpool tub, and indoor and outdoor pools. One of its best features is the location. Historic Suites is within walking distance of Downtown's theaters, pubs, and clubs. And River Market—home to the City Market, entertainment options, unique shops, and artist studios—is just across the bridge.

Kansas City Marriott
Downtown $$$-$$$$
200 West 12th Street
(816) 421-6800, (800) 228-0290
www.marriotthotels.com

With an ideal downtown location, underground link to the convention center, and superb meeting facilities, the Marriott is convention central. It's also the place where Kansas Citians stop in for cocktails before heading across the street to a night at The Folly, Midland Theatre, Music Hall, Lyric Opera, or Kansas City Symphony. Riverboat gambling is nearby, and Crown Center, Westport, and the Country Club Plaza are just a trolley or short cab ride away.

In 1997 the 573-room Marriott nearly doubled in size by merging with the historic Muehlebach Hotel at 1213 Wyandotte. During its prime the Muehlebach was Kansas

City's favored host for celebrities, presidents, and four musicians from Liverpool who held a news conference in the ballroom on September 17, 1964. Other news was made here as well: In the wee hours of November 3, 1948, Harry S Truman hurried back to the hotel to join his campaign staff to announce that he had won reelection.

A recent renovation has reclaimed the Muehlebach's gracious past: Sparkling crystal chandeliers once again cast a warm glow on the lobby's mosaic tile floors, and deeply carved mahogany gleams. Along with a tantalizing feeling of "If these walls could talk," the Muehlebach offers guests 410 rooms and 37 suites.

The two hotel towers are now linked via a covered walkway. Together the properties offer 10,000 square feet of meeting space, including two ballrooms, 32 breakout rooms, and a 12,000-square-foot exhibit hall. The complex features a fully equipped health club and indoor pool, full-service business center including secretarial services if requested, and gift shop. Attached, covered parking is available for a fee; valet service is available.

There are also plenty of places to dine, enjoy a cocktail, or simply relax. For breakfast, lunch, or dinner head to Lilly's or the Pam Pam Room, a Kansas City tradition for generations. The Muehlebach Lobby Lounge offers a refined cocktail hour, and the 12th Street Bar on the lobby level of the Marriott adds jazz to the mix on Friday and Saturday nights.

Hotel Phillips $$
106 West 12th Street
(816) 221-7000, (800) 433-1426
www.hotelphillips.com
Even before this address was transformed into an exquisite boutique hotel, it had a place in Kansas City's heart. When completed in 1931, the 20-story, 450-room hotel was the tallest in town. It was also the most high-tech: Every room had a radio receiver—the first commercial structure in the Midwest so equipped—which gave the crews a syncopated beat during construction. Even the site's first occupant,

The 60-foot waterfall in the Westin Crown Center hotel's lobby often contributes to more waterworks—by way of happy tears. The beautiful spot has been the site of more than 100 weddings since it opened in the late 1960s.

the Glennon Hotel, which was razed to make room for the Phillips, had a story to tell. Among its first-floor shops was a haberdashery operated by Harry S Truman.

In 1979 Hotel Phillips was placed on the National Registry of Historic Places as a stunning example of Art Deco architecture. The lobby is particularly handsome, with twin staircases, intricate metalwork, and black glass on the ceiling to create the illusion of endless space. The centerpiece is a gilded 11-foot likeness of the goddess of Dawn created by Norwegian-born sculptor Jorgen Dreyer. In classical mythology Dawn was the mother of the stars. At this hotel she's the patron saint of travelers passing through Kansas City.

The new owner, Marcus Hotel group, spent $20 million to restore Phillips Hotel to its magnificence while adding to its comfort. There are now 215 spacious guest rooms and two suites, each smartly decorated with exquisite fabrics and furnishings.

Even the restaurant is something special: Phillips Chophouse offers perfectly prepared steaks, chops, and fish with impeccable service. The room itself is stunning, with ornate marble and walnut lining the walls. And the 12 Baltimore lounge is a trendy place to entertain guests or enjoy a cocktail and appetizers.

East Metro

Adam's Mark $$-$$$
9103 East 39th Street
(816) 737-0200, (800) 444-ADAM
www.adamsmark.com
At this handsome high-rise you can almost hear "Play ball!" coming from Kauffman Stadium. Its convenient location across

from the ballpark makes it a top choice for sports fans. The fact that it's also close to Worlds of Fun and Oceans of Fun, the Kansas City Zoo, and the IMAX Theatre makes it particularly family-friendly.

Amenities at this 374-unit hotel include indoor and outdoor pools and a health club with saunas. And when a hot dog at the stadium just won't do, Adam's Mark serves up American fare at Remington's Steak and Seafood Grill and casual dining at the Pantry. At Players Sports Bar a big-screen TV and a cold beer are waiting for you. Better yet, take advantage of one of the hotel's packages that include Chiefs or Royals tickets plus shuttle passes.

Drury Inn Stadium   **$**
3830 Blue Ridge Cutoff
(816) 923-3000, (800) DRURYIN
(378-7946)
www.drury-inn.com
Baseball and football fans have a winner in this budget-pleasing hotel just 2 blocks from the stadiums. There are a surprising number of amenities for the tariff, including free breakfast and evening beverages, an outdoor pool, and exercise room. And you won't have to venture far for a casual meal: Denny's restaurant is adjacent to the 133-room hotel, Old Country Buffet is within walking distance, and say! Do you smell hickory-smoked ribs? Yep, Gates Barbecue is just down the road.

Hotel Savoy   **$$-$$$**
Ninth and Central Streets
(816) 842-3575, (800) SAVOY-88
As the oldest continually operating hotel west of the Mississippi River, the Hotel Savoy provides a fascinating glimpse of our city's growth and prosperity during the late 1880s.

The hotel was built in 1888 by the owners of the Arbuckle Coffee Company, two brothers who may have coined the phrase, "Money is no object." When completed, the six-floor Italian Renaissance building boasted a magnificent ballroom and rooftop garden, Corinthian columns, Italian tile floors, marble walls, and deeply carved woodwork. The lobby's centerpiece was a domed Art Nouveau–style stained-glass skylight in the lobby designed by Frank Anderson.

As the first hotel seen by travelers coming by cable car from the old Union Depot, the Savoy's opulence gave Kansas City quite a cachet. Along with cattlemen, grain merchants, and travelers headed west, the Savoy served such famous guests as Teddy Roosevelt, William Howard Taft, and John D. Rockefeller. Performers like W. C. Fields, Will Rogers, Lillian Russell, and Sara Bernhardt returned to their rooms between curtain calls at Kansas City's grand theaters and opera houses.

In 1903 a west wing was added along with the Savoy Grill, making it the city's oldest restaurant. It, too, was an impressive sight, with high-beamed ceilings, stained-glass windows, an enormous carved oak bar, and elaborate gaslights. Artist Edward Holslag was commissioned to paint 12 murals depicting the arduous travels on the Santa Fe Trail. See details in Restaurants.

While a guest at the Hotel Savoy, Harry Houdini's skills as an escape artist were tested in an unusual way. While the magician was using a public phone booth, a traveling salesman used a broom handle to lock him in. After some jiggling and quite a bit of yelling, a humbled Houdini was released from his temporary jail.

In 1975 both the hotel and restaurant were entered into the National Register of Historic Places. And in 1985 owner Don Lee began transforming the hotel into luxurious bed-and-breakfast suites.

Lee has done a masterful job of renovating the hotel. The stained-glass skylight still graces the lobby, and the guest rooms are spacious and airy with 12-foot and 8-foot ceilings. Appointments include brass fixtures, stained-glass windows, and original antiques. Several suites have fireplaces, and some have French doors separating the sleeping and sitting rooms. Even the baths have turn-of-the-20th-century charm with claw-footed tubs with shower fixtures and pedestal sinks. Thanks to its historic appeal, the hotel has been featured in the films *Mr. and Mrs. Bridge* and *Cross of Fire*. The hotel also has 8,000 square feet of space available for meetings, parties, or receptions.

Breakfast is a gourmet affair, with a 32-item menu that includes the Savoy Grill's famous lobster bisque, smoked salmon with caviar, medallions of beef, or a light continental breakfast. Guests are encouraged to linger over another cup of Kona coffee; checkout isn't until 1:00.

Hotel Savoy offers 22 rooms from standard to deluxe suites. Breakfast is included in the room rate. Larry Green is the innkeeper.

North of the River

Ameristar Casino Hotel $$–$$$
3200 North Ameristar Drive
(816) 414-7000, (800) 499-4961

If your interpretation of "a little R & R" is "I'm ready to roll the dice," the Ameristar is for you. The 184 guest rooms and suites are quite nice, but it's the entertainment outside that keeps the reservations phone ringing.

The casino's decor—with an arched, blue-sky ceiling and dancing water fountains—makes it one of the most beautiful in the Midwest. Guests can partake of more than 160 table games, Kansas City's largest collection of slot and video poker games, 18 state-of-the-art movie theaters, or a stroll along the Victorian-era streetscape. And everyone gets lucky at the hotel's restaurants. Choose from Orlean's, a white-tablecloth seafood restaurant; Arthur Bryant's, an offshoot of the famous barbecue joint downtown; an international buffet; and an ice-cream parlor. And Ameristar makes sure children have fun while parents play; Kids Quest provides activities in a safe, supervised environment.

Ameristar's three live music venues pay off big as well. The Grand Pavilion hosts top touring talent like Chris LeDoux, Chuck Mangione, Diane Schurr, and Glen Campbell, while the Hofbrauhaus brings down the house with rock 'n' roll and blues. At the Phoenix, a twin of the popular downtown nightclub, you can enjoy jazz and blues with steaks, barbecue, or pasta.

The Elms Resort & Spa $$
401 Regent
Excelsior Springs, MO
(816) 630-5500, (800) THE-ELMS
(843-3567)
www.elmsresort.com

You never know whom you might meet at this retreat just 30 minutes from Kansas City; Presidents Harry S Truman and FDR slept here. So did Al Capone. In fact, plenty of national celebrities and much of Kansas City's society have stayed here. The Elms's history actually precedes its grand opening date of 1912: The property was originally built in 1888 as a luxury resort to take advantage of the purported healing properties of the area's mineral waters. When the building's wide wooden verandas and pine interiors were twice destroyed by fire, it was replaced by native Missouri limestone.

The hotel is still a haven of serenity and style, with 152 guest rooms and suites. A world-class spa and wellness center includes Swiss and Vichy showers and services such as mud, seaweed, and aloe wraps; massage treatments; facials; manicures and pedicures; and a blissful rose-petal-and-salt-scrub body polish. You can relax with yoga and meditation classes or rev up with water aerobics and body sculpting. The fitness center features a sauna and steam room, indoor and outdoor pool, and hiking and biking trails. There is also a challenge course—popular for corporate retreats—with climbing wall, rope course, and Burma bridge. With its 16 acres of gently rolling hills, the Elms also provides plenty of opportunity for an afternoon stroll or jog.

When you're ready for cocktails you can unwind in the lobby lounge or the second level library lounge where a scenic view accompanies your favorite libation. The Elms's upscale dining room, Adega, serves innovative American cuisine with style. A more casual option is the Dining Room, where guests can enjoy breakfast, lunch, and dinner in a graceful setting with high ceilings, a wood-burning fireplace, and a wall of windows overlooking the landscaped grounds.

If you can pull yourself away from that late-morning massage, there's plenty to do in Excelsior Springs. Along with golf courses and antiques shops, there's the fascinating Hall of Waters Spa and Mineral Baths, where you can choose your favorite bottled water from around the world or indulge in other spa treatments. And the Jesse James Farm and Museum in nearby Kearney, Missouri, provides a fascinating look at the area's favorite bandit hero. You can find more information about these in Attractions, or through links on the resort's Web site.

**Harrah's North Kansas City
Casino & Hotel $$-$$$
One Riverboat Drive
North Kansas City, MO
(816) 472-7777, (800) HARRAHS
www.harrahs.com**

Harrah's hotel and convention center is so attractive that you might come here without so much as peeking in the gaming area. The 200 rooms and suites are luxurious and amenities abound, including 24-hour room service, an indoor swimming pool, and an exercise room. There's even an arcade to keep kids and teens happy for hours.

But you'll be tempted to play once you see Harrah's 30,000-square-foot addition to its Mardi Gras Casino, highlighted by marble floors, sparkling chandeliers, and a spectacular fountain. With over 2,000 slot machines and plenty of tables, we're betting you'll find lots to keep you entertained.

When you're hungry head to one of four themed restaurants, including the Fresh Market Square Buffet with specialties from around the world, hand-carved meats, and an enormous salad bar. At Cafe Andreotti Italian food is the specialty, and The Range rustles up sizzling steaks, seafood, and prime rib in an upscale Southwestern setting. Every meal includes

a loaf of warm honey-wheat bread, a choice of Caesar or trip to the incredible salad bar, and scrumptious poblano-spiked salsa with blue corn chips. And speaking of chips, if you can't bear to be away from the games too long, the Winning Streaks Stadium Cafe serves up tasty burgers and thick milk shakes fast. Or relax and stay awhile, especially on Tuesday, when a 17-ounce grilled porterhouse steak with all the trimmings is just $12.99.

**Park Place Hotel $$
1601 North Universal Avenue
(816) 483-9900, (800) 821-8532**

A five-acre lake with meandering walking trail makes this a little bit of heaven just north of downtown. Amenities include indoor and outdoor pools, a health club, on-site restaurant and lounge, and lakeside dining in nice weather.

A convenient central location puts it across the street from the Kansas City Market Center, a popular convention and exhibition space, and close to downtown's business sectors and cultural attractions. And a shuttle takes guests to Kansas City's favorite playgrounds like Worlds of Fun, Oceans of Fun, and the Truman Sports Complex. And the casinos are so close you can almost hear the jackpots ringing.

Overland Park, Kansas

**The Doubletree $$-$$$
10100 College Boulevard
Overland Park, KS
(913) 451-6100, (800) 222-TREE
www.doubletree.com**

This hotel's name is certainly appropriate: It's surrounded by a densely forested park that includes a 4-mile hiking and biking trail, wildflower meadows, and park benches. In fact, guests have watched deer graze, herons glide silently by, and families of ducks paddle along the streams that meander through the woods.

Expect to find some creature comforts inside as well, starting with Doubletree's signature chocolate chip cookies. Each of the 356 rooms and 17 suites on 18 floors is tastefully decorated and well appointed for both business and pleasure travelers. The hotel's entertainment options include a lounge where you can relax over cocktails while watching the sun set over that magical parklike vista.

And the Rotisserie Restaurant, with its beautiful fountain and multitiered design, is a favorite with the Johnson County set. The dining room serves regional cuisine for breakfast, lunch, and dinner accompanied by piano music. Each Sunday an eye-popping champagne buffet brunch gives you a reason to head downstairs, where chefs will prepare omelets to your liking, carve juicy roast beef, or place a piping-hot Belgian waffle on your plate. Other tables are filled with cold shrimp, fresh salads and fruits, grilled vegetables, baked goods, hot egg dishes, sausage and bacon, and desserts.

The Doubletree is also tops when it comes to location. Guests soon realize there's plenty to do in the southern part of our metropolis. If you like to shop, you're just minutes away from Oak Park Mall, one of the largest shopping centers in Kansas. Anchors include Nordstrom, Dillard's, and JCPenney along with 185 specialty shops like Coach, Aveda, Ann Taylor, and Gap. Back at the hotel, take a stroll along the adjacent hiking trail or head to the bowling alley across the street. Dozens of great dining options are close by as well.

And NASCAR fans will be glad to know the Doubletree is just two minutes from the new Kansas Speedway. . . if you drive like Jeff Gordon. For the rest of us it's about a 15-minute journey.

The Marriott $$–$$$
10800 Metcalf
Overland Park, KS
(913) 451–8000, (800) 228–9290
www.marriott.com
This 390-room hotel is an island of style in the heart of bustling Overland Park. The public areas are plush and inviting, and three distinct dining choices give you plenty of reasons to make this your home-

away-from-home. At Pitcher's the bartender can toss you a highball or beer to enjoy with appetizers, burgers, or salads from midafternoon until late at night. Allie's is a popular lunch spot, serving all-American cuisine like fried catfish, burgers, and soups and salads along with a breakfast menu.

The Marriott is also home to Nikko Japanese Steakhouse, which combines an evening's entertainment with fabulous food. Skilled chefs chop and prepare tappan-style dinners in front of you on large stainless-steel grills. And if you smile just right you might get a shrimp tossed into your open mouth! Nikko is open for dinner only.

To work off your meal, do some laps in the indoor pool, head to the fitness center, or take advantage of nearby outdoor activities. Swing by a golf course or check out one of the area's beautiful public parks. Or slip on comfortable shoes and head to the shopper's paradise known as 119th Street, where a shopping center, mall, or major store is on every street corner. Big names include Ann Taylor, Talbot, Restoration Hardware, and Coldwater Canyon, and there are boutiques, spas, and more. When it's time for lunch or dinner, tuck into one of the area's great restaurant choices, from barbecue and burgers to upscale cuisine. And isn't it nice to know your fluffy pillow is waiting for you back at the Marriott?

Sheraton Overland Park Hotel
at the Convention Center $$–$$$
6100 College Boulevard
Overland Park, KS
(913) 234–2100, (888) 625–5144
www.sheraton.com
It's really the second half of this lodging's title—the Convention Center—that's its claim to fame. Opened in November 2002, this 240,000-square-foot facility is helping put sleepy suburban Overland Park on the tourism map. The space boasts the largest ballroom in Kansas and a 60,000-square-foot exhibit hall that's often filled with conventions and meetings . . . and always filled with regional art. More than 60 pieces of fine art enliven the space, including massive

metal sculptures and landscapes that capture our glowing sunsets in oil.

The Sheraton Hotel, which is connected to the convention center via landscaped courtyards and an all-weather walkway, offers 412 rooms, a fitness center, and high-speed Internet access.

Its restaurant, 1906 Bar and Grille, takes its name from the year in which William Strang developed the railroad that led to the development of Overland Park. The 148-seat restaurant has the feel of a masculine chop house, done in rich shades of hunter green, cream, and khaki. And because this is beef country, expect thick, juicy steaks to dominate the menu, along with double-cut pork chops.

White Haven Motor Lodge $
8039 Metcalf
Overland Park, KS
(913) 649-8200, (800) 752-2892
www.white-haven.com
Since 1957 the White family has been turning guests into friends at their pretty little motor lodge. And even though Metcalf has become cluttered with car dealerships and retail shops, White Haven continues to be a nifty place to stay. Its charm, after all, comes from a blast-from-the-past design with a swimming pool out front, retro sign that was once considered modern art, and furniture that leans toward French provincial. It provides the kind of comfort, value, and friendliness that make you expect to see Ward and June Cleaver and the boys pull up in a station wagon.

Brothers Bob and Eugene, along with their wives, children, and grandchildren, maintain 100 neat-as-a-pin rooms here, from singles to spacious suites. Stay as long as you like; lots of folks rent the rooms for weeks. To encourage the extended stay trade, every room has a refrigerator, and a continental breakfast is served each morning in the coffee lounge. Expecting a fax? They'll take it at the front desk and deliver it personally. Lock your keys in the car? They'll get it open. One of the sons is a mechanic who has helped many a stranded traveler get back on the road.

It's this kind of special service that keeps the flowers and candy coming from satisfied customers; one guest even sent fresh eggs from her farm. And it must have been some thank-you gift after Bob paid bail to get a guest out of jail one night.

Repeat business and word of mouth keep the NO VACANCY sign lit, particularly during summer, so reservations are in order. And say, isn't that Wally and the Beav in the swimming pool?

Wyandotte County, Kansas

Chateau Avalon $$$-$$$$
701 Village West Parkway
(Interstate 435 and State Avenue)
Kansas City, KS
(913) 596-6000, (877) KC-AVALON
(52-282566)
www.chateauavalon.net
What's Cleopatra doing on the plains of Kansas? Looking pretty pleased with herself, relaxing in a two-person jetted spa with Chroma therapy lighting, that's what.

This latest entry into the wildly successful Village West entertainment district is a cross between a bed-and-breakfast and a high-end resort. The plush amenities include custom-made mattresses and posy linens, 60-inch flat-screen TVs with DVD players and surround sound, a rose-petal turndown, and made-to-order in-room breakfast. Cleo, baby, you never had it so good.

Chateau Avalon offers 23 luxurious themed suites, including six two-story accommodations like the Castaway Isle, where being shipwrecked may not be a bad idea. The hurricane left your ship in a tree on this tropical island paradise. Coconut oil, anyone? Or perhaps the *Casablanca* is more to your tune; here you'll slumber in a replica of 1940 Morocco, complete with piles of plush pillows and a DVD of the famous movie.

The hotel is also destined to be a popular site for weddings and events, thanks to its opulent French country design and lavish landscaping, including fountains and courtyards.

Great Wolf Lodge $$$-$$$$
10401 Cabela Drive
Kansas City, KS
(913) 299-7001, (800) 608-WOLF (9653)
www.greatwolflodge.com

Dorothy, I don't think we're in Kansas anymore. That overused line suddenly had new meaning when this massive northwoods lodge opened in the Village West entertainment district in 2003. From its hand-carved totem poles to the rustic furniture throughout the lodge, it could be situated on a snowcapped mountain peak.

But the main draw is pure tropics: an indoor water park where an eye-popping assortment of fountains, pools, slides, and jets stay a pleasant 84 degrees year-round. Every few minutes a giant bucket atop the 12-story tree house tips and drenches the crowd below. Hold on to your swim trunks!

It's a vacation for the entire family, with waterslides, hot tubs, and Treehouse Island, where kids of all ages can explore 12 levels of interactive water fun with more than 60 amazing water features, cargo nets, and web crawls. At any moment, a fountain or water jet might soak you.

After dinner in the Bear Claw Cafe, a chance to win prizes in the Northern Lights Arcade, and an ice-cream treat, it's story time in the lobby as children cuddle with parents by a massive stone fireplace. Sleepy eyes snap open when a menagerie of animated woodland creatures bring a giant clock tower to life. One of the most compelling attractions of Great Wolf, however, is its six different themed suites, including the Wolf Den with a decorated enclosure for tired little cubs.

Great Wolf Lodge came just in time for those sports enthusiasts who want one more day to shop at nearby Cabela's outdoor-goods emporium or families in town to attend a NASCAR race at the Kansas Speedway. But with its year-round watery wonderland, it's become a favorite of locals looking for a fun birthday venue

or an overnight getaway. Moms can get their own version of water therapy with a trip to the Aveda Spa on the premises.

EXTENDED STAYS

With Kansas City's growing base of national and international corporations, extended-stay facilities are popping up all over to give newly hired executives a homey place to board. Individuals and families relocating to our city will find temporary residences that truly feel like home. Following are a few choices, ranging from rooms with efficiency kitchens to luxe townhomes with fireplaces. For more options, Accommodations by Apple (913-492-7252, 800-700-8160; www.kcaccommodations.com) matches fully furnished apartments, duplexes, and homes to specific needs.

Crown Center

Residence Inn by Marriott-
Union Hill $$-$$$
2975 Main Street
(816) 561-3000, (800) 331-3131

When Hallmark hires a new manager from out of town, they'll often treat the trainee to these deluxe townhomes overlooking the company's headquarters at Crown Center. The services are amazing, including complimentary grocery shopping, van transportation up to 5 miles, breakfast, and an evening hospitality hour with beverages and a light meal. During nice weather the social hour moves to the pool area, where burgers and hot dogs are on the menu.

Accommodations include studios, doubles, and a two-level penthouse that includes a queen-size bed on each floor, plus a pullout sofa bed. Some rooms have fireplaces. And of course, the location is superb, with the entertainment, restaurants, and shopping at nearby Crown Center, plus Downtown, Westport, and the Plaza just a van drive away. No wonder guests stay 30, 60, even 90 days or more; why would you ever want to leave?

The Country Club Plaza and Westport

Vanity Fair Plaza Suites $-$$
700 West 48th Street
(816) 561–2900
www.vanityfaire.com

At Vanity Fair you won't be staying *near* the Plaza, you'll be right *in* it. Want to see if there's a table available at your favorite restaurant? Just look out your window. Vanity Fair's Tudor-style architecture matches its name, but the apartments are stylishly decorated in modern black and white. And although the rooms are cozy (that's "small" in accommodation terms), they provide all the accoutrements of home, including a fully furnished kitchen, phone with answering machine, linens, and accessories. Other services such as catering, maid service, chauffeur, and use of a health club can also be arranged. If checking out the Web site, please note the spelling discrepancy.

South Kansas City

Windsong Corporate Apartments $
114 West 103rd Street
(816) 942–5997, (800) 692–2468

A convenient location, attractive units, good value—prices equate to about $40 a day—and friendly service? No wonder so many corporations book their transplanted employees and managers here. Windsong has 89 apartments ranging from one to three bedrooms, all completely furnished including all household supplies. There's also weekly maid service, a laundry room in each building, and carports. Windsong is located just south of I-435, so it's convenient to every part of the city, and the new Sprint campus is just minutes away.

BED-AND-BREAKFASTS AND INNS

Rocking chairs on wide verandas, breakfast sausages grilled on a tree-shaded patio, a grand piano in the parlor, and fresh flowers on your nightstand . . . for those who treasure the personal touches found only at a bed-and-breakfast, we have just the cozy spot for you. Several, in fact. This list includes urban settings, Plaza addresses, and a horse ranch in the tallgrass prairies of Kansas. And what, pray tell, could be more fun than sleeping in a renovated church?

Circle S Ranch Guest Ranch &
Country Inn $$
3325 Circle S Lane
Lawrence, KS
(785) 843–4124
www.circlesranch.com

If the welcoming committee seems particularly happy to see you, you've just met Tater. The friendly black Lab is one reason guests of the Circle S feel at home immediately. Another is Mary Stevenson's smiling face welcoming you to her inn nestled amid rolling hills 40 miles west of Kansas City.

It may as well be a million miles away. The inn is set in 1,200 acres of sprawling prairie and wooded glens that have been in Mary's family since the mid-1800s. Since opening in May 1998, Circle S has won enough awards to turn a cowgirl's head. It's become a popular place for everything from business meetings to marriage proposals, but rarely in the same weekend.

In fact, Mary has coordinated dozens of weddings, from sweet ceremonies in the wildflower meadow to blowout bashes at the Party Barn. This 5,000-square-foot barn, when not hosting a hoedown, is a mini-agricultural museum with farm implements, tack, and tools hanging on walls and from ceilings. Little cowpokes can even ride a 1950s-era grocery store mechanical horse for a dime.

Back at the inn, 12 spacious guest rooms feature decor ranging from pioneer quaintness to cowboy whimsy—witness the showerhead in a bucket—plus private bath and breathtaking view. An eight-person hot tub in the silo will give you something to talk about for months. It was built by Jack Cronemeyer, a fifth-generation carpenter who also crafted most of the inn's beautiful woodwork.

If you're looking for peace and quiet, you'll find it in these endless blue skies and pastures. The only sounds are soft mooing of the cattle, an occasional scream from a peacock, and—early in the morning—the timpani of tree frogs. Late at night you might hear the unmistakable arr-arr-arrooooo of a far-off coyote.

Unless you want to rise at 5:00 A.M. to bottle-feed a motherless calf like one guest did, mornings start at 8:30 with a ranch hand's breakfast of scrambled eggs, biscuits and gravy, crispy hash browns, and—if you're lucky—some golden preserves from Mary's grandmother's apricot tree. Spend the rest of the day browsing boutiques in nearby Lawrence, or stay home. Call dibs on a rocking chair on the wraparound porch, explore the tallgrass prairie on mountain bikes, or stroll the trails until a hammock calls your name. Chances are you won't be alone: White-tailed deer, quail, and wild turkey share the ranch with 200 head of cattle and quite a few bison.

If you take along a picnic basket, ask for extra apples for Pepper, Cricket, and Crazy Alice. When these horses aren't working the land, they're hoping a guest shows up with a red Delicious and a soft spot for big brown eyes. And if you have horses of your own, bring 'em; you can ride the trails with the ranch hands and help out with daily activities during summer months. For the safety of the other animals, however, Circle S cannot accept pets.

Along with personal retreats and special occasions, Circle S has found a niche with old-fashioned slumber parties—adult style. Mary greets guests with whirling blenders of margaritas while manicures, pedicures, and massages await. All-night videos and popcorn complete the theme.

And Saturday stays include a four-course dinner of grilled salmon, chicken, or filets with big fluffy baked potatoes. Non-guests are welcome with reservations.

By the way, the innkeeper's last name is now Cronemeyer. She and Jack were married on a recent spring morning in the meadow. No doubt Tater served as best dog.

The Inn on Crescent Lake $$–$$$
1261 St. Louis Avenue
Excelsior Springs, MO
(816) 630–6745
www.crescentlake.com

Motor up the long curving drive to this majestic 1915 Georgian-Colonial with stately white columns and you might expect Scarlett O'Hara to sashay down the steps. Instead a contemporary—yet just as gracious—couple welcomes you into their majestic inn. The setting is spectacular as well: 22 wooded acres including two crescent-shaped ponds that inspired the inn's name.

If the inn looks familiar, that's because it's been featured on Bob Villa's *Restore America* on HGTV and in *Travel Holiday, Midwest Living,* the *Columbus Dispatch, Kansas City* magazine, and half a dozen other publications. Soon you'll discover what the buzz is about. When Anne and Bruce Libowitz turned the home into an inn in 1997 they kept its architectural charm—like the sun-filled solarium and sweeping staircase—while providing modern conveniences. Scarlett wouldn't have been nearly as petulant after soaking in a 6-foot whirlpool tub.

Each of the six rooms and three suites has a private bath and unique personality. The black-and-white Art Deco room features a red claw-footed tub, the third-floor Treehouse Suite offers a cozy bower feeling, and the Train Room appeals to the inner child with a model train circling an overhead track. The ballroom, also known as the Honeymoon Suite, is the most requested room. Painted a buttery yellow, the airy room has a king-size iron bed draped in lace, separate sitting room, and daybed-filled dormers that create lots of places for curling up together.

Two new suites are particularly appealing. The Garden Room's private deck comes complete with a hot tub for wishing on a star. It also affords a private entrance and is wheelchair-accessible. The two-story Cottage, separate from the main house, is a little love nest that would be perfect for a weekend of bliss or a week of reconnecting with each other. It offers a living room, half bath, and kitchen on the lower level and king-size bed, sitting area, whirlpool tub for two, and walk-in shower above. A TV and stereo system are on each floor, but the real entertainment is a few steps away at the lunar lakes. . . or perhaps back in the bubbly tub.

The water does, indeed, beckon guests during nice weather. Share a paddleboat; take a dip in the pool; or aim a fishing pole at the bass, sunnies, or catfish. Or take a walk around the estate's paths. Off-site activities include golf, antiques shopping in Olde Town, or driving 30 minutes to Kansas City's attractions. During winter, retreat to the warmth of the solarium to watch snow fall gently on the expansive lawn.

Or simply while away the hours anticipating dinner. Anne and Bruce aren't merely good cooks, they're fabulous chefs. The couple met at the French Culinary Institute in New York, taking classes from the likes of Jacques Pepin, and have been treating inn guests to their skills ever since. A three-course dinner—an option for overnight guests at $35 per person—might include cauliflower soup with saffron, marinated rack of lamb, and fruit cobbler with homemade ice cream. Jackets and ties are recommended. Anne usually takes kitchen duty for breakfast, when the fare might include blueberry pancakes or herb-infused scrambled eggs.

The inn is also available for corporate events and the most glorious wedding imaginable. Packages include a one-night "Gotta Getaway" and a romance weekend that combines a suite for two nights with dinner, champagne, and massage. Draw our bath, please; we'll be there in 30.

The James Inn $$
342 North Water
Liberty, MO
(816) 781-3677
www.thejamesinn.com

This bit of heaven-on-earth was originally the St. James Catholic Church, built in 1913. By the 1980s the parishioners had outgrown the place, and a decade later David and Mary Anne Kimbrell began turning the belfry, vestibule, and bell tower into a lovely bed-and-breakfast. Mary Anne was baptized in the very space that is now the dining room.

The architecture lends itself beautifully to its new purpose. Exposed bricks and aged beams make wonderful backdrops to the couple's antiques and Oriental rugs. Sunlight floods the rooms through tall arched gothic windows, and fireplaces that once warmed churchgoers now add a glow to guests. The guest rooms are special as well, with queen-size four-poster beds, fireplaces, goose-down mattresses, comforters, and pillows. Jetted tubs overlook the bedrooms from lofts above.

A licensed therapist/aesthetician is available for a massage, body wrap, or spa treatment, and the inn's gift shop sells lotions, bath salts, and aromatherapy candles so that you can scent your room as well. The pampering continues in the hot tub located on a two-tiered deck.

Guests also delight in meals here: David's Belgian waffles and quiche are sinfully good, and on Friday night there's prime rib to enjoy by candlelight. These dinners sell out quickly, so it's best to book well in advance. David and Mary Anne also host wine-tasting events and murder mystery weekends, and non-guests can reserve room at the table for Saturday and Sunday brunches.

The inn is also popular during parents' weekends at nearby William Jewell College. And it is just 2 blocks from Liberty Square, a place to shop for antiques or visit the bank Jesse James robbed. And if you missed David's prime rib, there's the Hardware Cafe on the square, a place that once sold hammers instead of ham steaks.

LaFontaine Inn Bed & Breakfast $$$
4320 Oak Street
(816) 753–4434, (888) 832–6000
www.lafontainebb.com

Prepare to be spoiled at this stately 1910 Georgian Colonial home on a quiet street off the Plaza. Innkeeper Lionel Martin will greet you with wine and hors d'oeuvres every evening and a sumptuous breakfast to start your day. His specialties include baked German apple pancake and a recipe he calls Honeymoon Casserole: ramekins of shredded potatoes, jalapeño cheese, ham, and eggs that will make you want to get married all over again.

LaFontaine's setting is ideal for a weekend's worth of shopping, dining, art gallery hopping, and listening to the jazz and blues that made our city famous. Or you could make your own music on the baby grand in the living room. One gentleman sat down and gave a roomful of astonished guests an abbreviated version of his recent concert at Carnegie Hall.

The five guest rooms with private baths are exquisitely decorated—not a teddy bear in sight—with antiques, reproductions, and luxurious fabrics. The Spring Room is especially pretty. With two walls of windows overlooking a grove of oak trees, guests feel like they're sleeping in a tree house. The luxurious bath area features a dressing room, double-size hot tub, and separate shower. The Winter Room has a four-poster rice bed and marble-trimmed wood-burning fireplace; a large hot tub and glass shower that doubles as a steam room add to the creature comforts.

The Truitt Carriage House Suite is the ultimate in privacy. With its own kitchen, jetted tub for two, and lovely bedroom overlooking the estate's gardens, it's the ideal place to spend a honeymoon or anniversary. Actually, the romance starts the moment you call for a reservation and hear Lionel's charming French-Canadian accent.

Ophelia's $$
201 North Main
Independence, MO
(816) 461–4525
www.ophelias.net

Cocktails, dinner, a little light jazz, and you're off to dreamland. It's all part of the package at Ken and Cindy McClain's stylish inn just upstairs from the restaurant of the same name. The couple has even tossed in a little history: Ophelia's is across the street from Clinton's Soda Shop, where a young Harry Truman used to dish up ice cream.

At the inn, as well as at the restaurant below, Cindy's artistic talent is on view with beautifully decorated rooms, special touches, and a few paintings displayed here and there. There are seven rooms and one spacious suite, each with a private bath. The amenities rival those of a fine hotel, with down comforters and pillows, voice messaging, cable TV, and modem capability. A continental breakfast is brought to your door in a basket.

Ophelia's is on historic Independence Square with its centerpiece, the Jackson County Courthouse. Part of the original 1836 building remains today, and the office Harry Truman occupied as county administrative judge is largely unchanged. It's a fascinating look back in time, or you could get your nostalgia fix at one of the many antiques shops within the square. There are five restaurants as well, but if you've experienced executive chef Ryan Klover's lunch or dinner menu at Ophelia's, you won't want to stray far from the inn.

For more information about other nearby attractions, including the Truman Museum and home, the buck stops at the Attractions chapter.

Southmoreland on the Plaza $$–$$$$
116 East 46th Street
(816) 531–7979
www.southmoreland.com

Perhaps the Midwest's most celebrated inn, the Southmoreland is a magnificent 1913 Colonial Revival on a quiet residential street just 2 blocks from the Country Club Plaza. Inside you'll understand its long list of kudos, including six-time winner of the Mobil Four-Star award, one of America's Top 25 Favorite Inns, and Inn of the Month from *Travel and Leisure*.

In 1999 owners Mark Reichle and Nancy Miller Reichle didn't so much buy the inn as inherit it from its founders. The couple treats it like the precious gem it is, continuing the tradition of ambience and adding a few amenities of their own. The best of these is the new carriage house suite named for George Kessler, the landscape architect who designed the inn's namesake park. The suite is separated from the main building by a lovely brick courtyard and offers unmatched privacy and comfort. Guests can relax in front of the wood-burning stove—bright red to match the room's cheery wallpaper and bed linens—or in a jetted tub for two. There's a king-size antique iron bed, small balcony, and on the antique walnut dresser, a book describing local flora and fauna from Kessler's day.

Similar charming details appear in the inn's other 12 rooms, which are named for Kansas City celebrities. Guests in the pastel Clara and Russell Stover Room, for example, find a tiny box of chocolates on their pillows, and the Satchel Paige knotty pine sleeping porch re-creates the baseball legend's favorite fishing cabin. Pictures of the Kansas City Monarchs line the wall.

Each room has a private bath and special treats like a fireplace or jetted tub. And in one, shafts of upward-beaming light from Frank Lloyd Wright's 1940 Community Christian Church make a delightful nightlight. Other thoughtful in-room touches include cut-crystal decanters of sherry, fresh flowers, and a copy of the book *Here Lies Kansas City* opened to the section about the room's namesake.

You'll also appreciate what's happening in the kitchen. Guests are treated to wine and hot hors d'oeuvres upon arrival. For dinner you'll have your choice of dozens of restaurants on the Plaza, or request dinner in your room via a restaurant delivery service. After an afternoon of museums and shops, a fresh batch of Monster Cookies—a combination of chocolate chips, oatmeal, and peanut butter—await your arrival.

In the morning awake to an incredible breakfast that may include the inn's famous French toast stuffed with Swiss cheese and brown-sugar ham, fresh fruit, and chocolate-zucchini bread. In warmer weather Mark often treats guests to grilled sausage or ham steaks on the patio shaded by sugar maples. It's just one highlight of what makes staying in a bed-and-breakfast so special—you're treated like family.

If you're lucky (or quick) enough to book a room over Thanksgiving, you'll arrive home from the famous lighting ceremony on the Country Club Plaza to find about 30 types of homemade pies waiting in the dining room. Dibs on Mark's Key lime!

Woodstock Inn $$–$$$
1212 West Lexington
Independence, MO
(816) 833–2233, (800) 276–5202
www.independence-missouri.com
Sweet dreams are nearly guaranteed at this lovingly restored inn in the historic district of Independence. The original 1900 building was Ruby Short-McKim's studio, where the artist designed quilts and created her famous Kimport porcelain dolls until the 1980s. Charles Woodstock turned it into an 11-room bed-and-breakfast in 1987, and today it's owned and managed by Todd and Patricia Justice. The couple, who met in Korea where they taught English, brought back several things from their world travels, including a sensitivity to guests' needs and some beautiful furnishings. The Oriental Suite, for example, features a museum-quality antique wedding bed and black lacquer and mother-of-pearl armoire from the country where the innkeepers fell in love.

Love, in fact, is the overriding emotion at Woodstock Inn. Details like fresh flowers, fireplaces, silky bed linens, and lace-draped canopies help set the mood, and honeymooners will find a page of love quotes in their rooms.

All 11 guest rooms have private baths, many have jetted tubs, and some have fireplaces. In the morning, a delightful breakfast will stir you from beneath cozy bedcovers. Todd's specialty is malted Belgian waffles topped with fresh fruit sauce; other creations include apple and peach crepes, ham-and-cheese-stuffed French toast, and garden-fresh frittatas.

A short walk to the sights of Independence will help work off the calories. Historians often choose Woodstock while exploring the world of Harry S Truman, and Kansas City's other attractions are a short drive away.

The inn offers several special packages, including the Romantic Rendezvous that includes chilled champagne or sparkling grape juice, a 27-exposure one-use camera to capture those special moments, and a dinner voucher for one of the area's premier restaurants.

RV CAMPSITES AND RESORTS

Basswood Country Inn and
RV Resort $$–$$$
15880 Interurban Road
Platte City, MO
(816) 858–5556, (800) 242–2775
(reservations only)
www.basswoodresort.com
Here's a campsite and fishing resort that hits all the right notes. At least that's what Bing Crosby and Rudy Vallee thought when they were guests of millionaire A. G. Stephens's Basswood Sportsmen's Club in the 1940s. Hedy Lamar often stopped by, and Bess Truman hosted her bridge club here for many years. At one time it was on the railway line that linked Kansas City with St. Joseph between 1913 and 1933.

But like so many grand places of that era, the sporting lodge lost favor and was neglected. Don and Betty Soper saved it in 1979 and spent eight years returning it to

its former charm. Today the bed-and-breakfast inn, country store, and modern RV resort, according to *Peak Magazine,* is "perhaps the most beautiful wooded lakefront setting in the Kansas City area." It's without a doubt the fishiest: four freshwater lakes, fed by the original spring that Stephens once bottled and sold worldwide, are stocked with catfish, bass, crappies, and carp. Check the resort's Web site for a photo of one happy angler hoisting a 19½-pound catch.

Basswood packs a summer's worth of activities into the site, including a swimming pool, volleyball, shuffleboard, children's playground, and walking trails. There's a large selection of videos to rent at the store, where you'll also find basic groceries, RV and camping supplies, packaged liquor, and gifts.

Accommodations include the private Mother-in-Law Cottage with two bedrooms and full kitchen; the Celebrity House Suites where Bing Crosby, Rudy Vallee, and the Trumans often stayed; and Country French Suites. There are 119 full hookup RV sites (30 and 50 amp) plus 20 water/electric-only sites for tents and pop-ups, including 14 deluxe sites with patios. Guests can use the two picnic shelters, playground, spacious laundry facilities, and superclean bathhouses with shower stalls and vanities. A meeting hall is available for parties and family reunions.

Basswood Resort, open year-round, is just 5 miles from the Kansas City International Airport and near the attraction-packed towns of Independence, Parkville, Weston, and St. Joseph.

Jackson County Parks and
Recreation Campgrounds
(816) 229–8980
www.co.jackson.mo.us
(click on "Parks and Recreation")
Discover the reason we don't miss beaches and mountains here in the landlocked Midwest. Our breathtaking lakes, timberlands, and parks provide plenty of recreation and relaxation. Our well-maintained campsites give outdoor enthusiasts a chance to

rough it just enough. Just be sure to practice your "Kum ba yah" before it's your turn to lead the campfire sing-along.

Jackson County, Missouri, offers three public campgrounds with a total of 236 camping sites, all about 15 minutes from Kansas City proper. They are available by reservation for stays up to 14 days, and at least one camper must be 21 or over. The camping facilities include showers, restrooms, attendants, picnic tables, and ice.

Longview Lake Campground is within nearly 5,000 acres of parkland and includes a 930-acre lake with full-service marina including disabled fishing docks. Attractions include a 4-mile nature trail, horse park, launching ground where colorful hot air balloons take off and land, swimming beach, and 27-hole public golf course. The campground is open April 27 through September 30. Its 119 sites include 59 with electricity at $14 to $17 per day and 60 tent-ready at $10 to $13 per day.

Lake Jacomo Campground is within beautiful Fleming Park, at 7,800 acres, the largest parkland in Jackson County. At its heart is 970-acre Lake Jacomo, and there's a smaller Blue Springs Lake as well. More than 1,300,000 visitors a year make the best of its many pleasures, including a nature preserve, an Audubon center, a marina that hosts a sailboat regatta nearly every weekend, a swimming beach, nature trails, and more. Watch for things flying overhead, like Frisbees—this is a popular dog hangout—and model airplanes. The campground has 60 large, tree-lined sites: 10 full hookup, 38 electric, and 12 tent, for $10 to $23 per day. The site is open year-round; call for specific availabilities.

Blue Springs Lake Campground, also within Fleming Park, is open from April 13 to October 31, with 57 sites (20 full hookup, 17 electric and water, 20 electric) that range in price from $14 to $23 per day. This site is five minutes from the beach.

RESTAURANTS

Of all the things that surprise first-time visitors to Kansas City—from our cosmopolitan ambience to our far-from-flat topography—nothing seems to floor them more than our food. Not how *good* it is, mind you, but how diverse it is.

Tourists already know about the superiority of our beef thanks to Calvin Trillin's 1974 book, *American Fried,* which begins, "The best restaurants in the world are, of course, in Kansas City. Not all of them; only the top four or five." Other writers picked up the scent and have been gushing about our steaks, barbecue, and burgers ever since.

But here's the amazing thing: You don't have to be a card-carrying carnivore to eat well here. Foodies can have a world tour of authentic cuisine from Mexico to Mongolia and cooking styles from Cajun to Catalan. Vegetarians can get their five-a-day at a number of excellent eateries in town. And even the staunchest of steakhouses offers at least one meatless dish.

Enjoy fresh fish? We'll get along swimmingly. We may be landlocked, but we can still serve you a piping-hot sea bass 36 hours after it met its last fisherman. And wine aficionados will want to raise a toast to this city. *Wine Spectator* hands out awards around here like party favors. Two of our restaurants have received the magazine's Grand Award, a distinction only 100 in the world can claim. But sometimes it's what's not on the menu that makes it worth your trip. Lots of dining rooms serve a side of blues or jazz with their burgers or beef-steaks. For a complete list, see Nightlife.

Hungry yet? Following are a few tips to keep you from being disappointed in your quest for a fabulous meal. We've done our best to provide current information about the restaurants listed, but we suggest you call first before heading out the door. As for payment, major credit cards are accepted unless noted. And a word about reservations. Actually two: Make them. On weekends there's often a wave of people trying to get into the flavor of the month—which can create up to a two-hour wait at places that don't take names. Houston's comes to mind, although their roasted chicken is so divine you'll gladly accept a pager at the door.

Speaking of Houston's, you'll find this and just about every other national chain here, including Ruth's Chris Steakhouse, P.F. Chang's China Bistro, Cheesecake Factory, and Morton's Steak House. We have (at last count) 21 Applebee's, which makes perfect sense because it was born and raised here. These are all fine dining experiences, to be sure, but this book focuses on independent restaurants to introduce you to our regional cooking and original recipes.

Although we cover a lot of dishes in this chapter, you can find additional restaurants listed in the *Kansas City Star* Friday Preview, monthly issues of *Kansas City* magazine, and *Pitch Weekly,* where Charles Ferruzza's tart-as-Key-lime-pie wit makes for entertaining restaurant reviews. We'd give him the last curl of calamari on our plate any day. Another handy resource is the *Restaurant Guide* of Kansas City, a free quarterly magazine available at hundreds of restaurants, hotels, and outdoor boxes. It's published by Kathy and Laurent Denis, a couple who met in his hometown of Bordeaux, France, moved back to her home state, and now share their love of fine food with the rest of us. The guide's Web site (www.kcrestaurantguide.com) also provides restaurant links that include up-to-date menus, recipes, and maps. You can even purchase gift certificates online.

Finally, in this chapter we've listed restaurants by cuisine rather than location because in KC we'll drive across town for the ribs and onion rings at Fiorelli's Jack Stack barbecue or the pasta special—no questions asked—at YiaYia's in Overland Park. A 40-minute trek to Weston for Avalon Cafe's baked Brie? Toss it on the grill, David, we're on our way.

To help you find your way, we've added a geographic key in parenthesis beside the restaurant's name. Or you can simply follow your nose. All restaurants are in Kansas City, Missouri, unless otherwise noted.

PRICE CODE

Our price code is based on dinner for two, without appetizers, dessert, alcoholic beverages, tax, or tip. Your own bill may be higher or lower depending on what you order and normal fluctuating prices. Lunch prices are generally less. Bon appétit.

$	Less than $20
$$	$21 to $40
$$$	$41 and up

AMERICAN/CONTINENTAL

**The American Restaurant
(Crown Center)** $$$
**25th and Grand Avenue
(816) 545-8000
www.americanrestaurantkc.com**
With a glamorous movie star entrance and sparkling view of downtown, this American beauty is the place to woo a lover or wow a client. The soaring space was designed by Walter Platner two years before he did Manhattan's late, great Windows on the World, and it's stunning. Curving wooden louvers adorn the 20-foot-tall ceilings—a lacy valentine to the city from the American's owner, Hallmark Cards. Shutters on the floor-to-ceiling windows are opened just at sunset, often to applause from a room of delighted diners. During the winter holidays the view includes a twinkling 100-foot Mayor's Christmas tree in the Crown Center Square below.

The food easily matches the theatrics. The legendary James Beard was brought in as a consultant in 1974 to create refined yet soul-warming interpretations of classic American cooking.

Kansas City's only Mobil Four Star hired executive chef Celina Tio in 2001 when celebrated couple Michael Smith and Debbie Gold left after six years to open 40 Sardines in Overland Park.

Celina's menu continues to pay homage to the Midwest's bounty of meats, game, and produce. But before you think "meat, potatoes, and plenty of gravy," take a look at a recent midwinter menu: duck breast and thyme-roasted spaghetti squash with orange-juniper oil and antelope and braised chestnuts with a syrah grape reduction. And grandma never made a shepherd's pie like this; here it's studded with lobster, wild mushrooms, and roasted cipollini onions and served with truffled mashed potatoes.

Thanks to maitre d' Victor Hugo Berndt Jr., the service is stellar as well. And although the American has been trying to lighten its formal reputation—jackets at dinner are merely *suggested* now—it's still a refined restaurant where you might see black tie and ball gowns before opening night at the Lyric Opera.

The American is open for lunch Monday through Friday and dinner Monday through Saturday. Call to ask about cooking lessons. Maybe Celina will teach you how to make that Lobster potpie.

Avalon Cafe $$
**608 Main Street
Weston, MO
(816) 640-2835**
The simple charm of this 150-year-old home-turned-cafe doesn't begin to hint at the food served inside. Instead of down-home cooking, guests are treated to French-trained chef David Scott's masterpieces, like smoked duckling topped with lingonberries and Chambord, or beef filet topped with exotic mushrooms and a bourbon sauce. Can't decide? Try the Weston Trio, which usually features one of David's revered wild game dishes plus fish and steak.

But it's the Brie that's positively addictive. The rich cheese is drizzled with garlic-infused olive oil and then grilled into that perfect oozing state for slathering on French bread along with the garlic. Served alongside are spring greens in vinaigrette, seasonal fruit, and grilled vegetables. It's a terrific lunch for two, an ideal starter for four, or a feast to keep all to yourself.

During the day when tables are filled with locals, longtime fans, and tourists, the tiny rooms create a convivial atmosphere as patrons compare dishes. At night the mood is more amorous, with candlelight, fresh flowers, and the flush that comes from wonderful food. Or it may be from the desserts, which are all made in house. David's bread pudding is legendary, and his five-layer Chocolate Damnation—with mousse, cheesecake, cake, praline, and ganache— is a chocoholic's dream. And people flock to Avalon (One regular drives three hours from Omaha.) for wine dinners that feature specials like a tricolored peppercorn–crusted steak with a Burgundy glaze.

Avalon is open for lunch and dinner Tuesday through Saturday, and reservations are recommended. For more information about visiting the historic town of Weston—an antique lover's paradise—see Day Trips and Weekend Getaways.

Bluestem (Midtown) $$$
900 Westport Road
(816) 561-1101
www.kansascitymenus.com/bluestem

When husband-and-wife chefs open a restaurant, it can't help but be high on the romance meter. That's the mantra at this 43-seat bistro that Colby and Megan Garrelts opened in spring 2004—and it has been rocking the local foodie contingent ever since. What makes it romantic is the pacing—don't expect to eat and run to catch an eight o'clock movie. Dinners start with *amuse-bouche,* a complimentary sampling of tastes. This is your first glimpse of the chefs' attention to detail: Each miniature canapé is presented like a gem at a jewelry counter.

Appetizers include fois gras glazed in Sauterne jelly and served with fig jam and brioche, just as luscious as it sounds. Entrees might have you reaching for your camera before tucking into such masterpieces as wild salmon with crispy sweetbreads or a beautifully grilled strip steak next to mahogany-colored roasted onions. The chefs also offer a six-course fixed-priced dinner menu accompanied by paired wine from their impressive list. Megan's skill with pastries is evident in the dessert selection, which includes a citrus crème brûlée and silky malted-chocolate sponge pudding.

Bluestem also offers a brunch where eggs are served Benedict style, topped with smoked salmon and asparagus. Health-nuts may opt for the crunchy house-made granola.

Brunch, dinner, or a late-night sweets spree—Bluestem is the perfect date spot.

Eat up! You'll pay less to eat well in Kansas City, according to Zagat. *The rating guide says we're the number-one dining bargain of all the major cities it reviews. An average meal here costs $14.01, compared with $29.28 in New York City, which was ranked the most expensive.*

Cafe Sebastienne
(Country Club Plaza) $-$$
4420 Warwick Boulevard
(816) 561-7740

No one would blame executive chef Jennifer Maloney if she skimped on food presentation; her restaurant's location within the Kemper Museum of Contemporary Art should be visual stimulus enough. But her menu and its plating are more than up to the challenge. And now that a covered courtyard is open for year-round dining, there's more room for the hungry masses.

Her salads—like the ode to autumn, with seasonal greens, smoked Gouda, turkey, pears, honey-baked pecans, and curry-mustard dressing—are works of art. The foie gras–stuffed quail and risotto are simply dreamy, the roasted beef tenderloin with turnip-and-fig gratin divine. And for some fans, the meal isn't over until they've polished off a wedge of chocolate budino, a decadent flourless torte served with fresh fruit and whipped cream. Lunch is served Tuesday through Sunday, and dinner is available Friday and Saturday.

You may read more about the Kemper Museum in The Arts. But for now you'll be thrilled to learn that admission is free seven days a week. Spend the savings on a serving of budino.

Cafe Trocadero (Midtown) $$$–$$$$
401 East 31st Street
(816) 756-3400
www.cafetrocadero.com

With a name this campy, the food had better be good. It's better than that; this tony restaurant opened in 2003 and quickly had the biggest buzz in town. It has the whole package: an elegant blond-wood bar; servers with names like Thore (yes, really) who look like they're waiting for a call from their agents; and inspired menu items served beautifully.

The building itself got a major makeover from its days as the popular R.T.s' Deli, with exposed brick walls, a pressed-tin ceiling, and cherry-wood floors, all made more romantic with seductively low lights. And the location couldn't be trendier, thanks to owner Chris Sefreyn's two other Union Hill hangouts, the Velvet Dog martini bar and the stylish Empire Room that's part bar, part screening room, and all cool.

At the Troc, patrons park in back and enter through the smoky bar, which is the only drawback . . . unless you count the fact that the tables are too small for all the dishes you'll want to try. Starters include a tower of seared coarse-ground polenta with luscious wild mushroom compote and salmon cakes with roasted corn cilantro broth. A salad standout is the warm goat cheese with cubes of Yukon Gold potatoes and tender greens in a citrus vinaigrette.

Entrees lean toward the seafood side, including jumbo sea scallops accompanied by basmati rice studded with tart cherries

and a lovely roasted lemon sole stuffed with spinach, shrimp, and oysters. You'll quickly notice that—unlike some restaurants that automatically serve mashed potatoes with everything—here the sides and sauces are as thoughtful as the main dishes. Jalapeño cheddar polenta continues the Southwest theme of the masa-seared red scarlet snapper; porcini mushrooms and a black pepper sauce stand up to the brawny KC strip steak.

The lunch menu includes savory soups like the chilled yellow tomato and avocado—a refreshing delight on a midwestern summer day—and a roster of sandwiches, including a seared vegetable burger and sliced pork steak with Gruyère cheese served with Napa cabbage slaw. Lunch entrees will set you back $12 to $16, but the wild mushroom tart with spring vegetable risotto is worth every penny on your expense account.

The dessert menu is a nice change from the obligatory crème brûlée and tiramisu. If you can't choose between the Frozen Cashew Brittle Glacé or duo of blood orange and blackberry sorbets with spearmint syrup, order the Trocadero Taster, a chef's tour of the entire selection on one beautifully presented platter for just $12. It's about the only reason we can think of to have another birthday.

Along with specialty cocktails and coffee drinks, the restaurant serves a sophisticated wine list with about 60 selections; 15 or so are available by the glass. Call or check on the Web site for upcoming wine dinners; there's even a wine club you can join.

Californo's (Westport) $$
4124 Pennsylvania Avenue
(816) 531-7878

You can't go wrong with whatever table you're given at Californo's, a cozy bistro-type affair in the heart of our city's most energetic entertainment scene. The sidewalk seating feels like a Parisian cafe, the four-tier redwood deck out back is shaded by trees, and inside a flickering fireplace is reflected in your wine glass.

But it's the eclectic food that keeps people coming back.

It started when chef Brenda Burn and husband Terry ignored the bedlam outside and opened on St. Pat's Day 1988. By the time they received a four-star rating in the *Kansas City Star* the crowds were *in* the restaurant, not on the street. A popular salad based on one served at the Prospect, a beloved but gone Westport restaurant, combines buttery bib lettuce with hearts of palm, toasted pecans, and a lively blue cheese vinaigrette. Another salad—ideal for a quick lunch—takes an Oriental turn with snow peas, chicken, and mandarin oranges.

At night the pastas, steaks, and fresh fish dishes are tops, and frankly, whatever Brenda offers as a special is just dandy with us. There's no finer ending to an afternoon of shopping in Westport—or an evening of listening to blues down the street—than a meal at Californo's. Or have a pretend picnic on the deck, hang around until the stars come out, and make your own music.

Californo's is open for lunch and dinner Monday through Saturday.

Classic Cup Cafe
(Country Club Plaza) $$
301 West 47th Street
(816) 753-1840
www.classiccup.com

This longtime Plaza favorite offers a running fashion show as bags tagged with Sak's Fifth Avenue, Gucci, and Halls pass by its row of tables on the sidewalk. Didn't get a front-row seat? Don't worry. There's a huge deck out back, and the inside tables have wall-to-wall windows plus a fireplace for coolish weather.

The food is good from any vantage point. Half the lunch crowd seems to be sighing over the spicy Thai pizza. Other top picks are the salads and pastas. If you're ravenous after all that power shopping, go for heartier fare such as the grilled tenderloin medallions with a creamy blue cheese sauce.

Dinners might start with gnocchi, Italian potato dumplings served in a tomato-basil

or Gorgonzola-walnut sauce. Entrees continue the world tour with specialties like grilled rack of lamb and roasted chicken. To accompany your meal there are 40 wines by the glass as well as an 800-bottle wine cellar. You'll be glad you saved room for dessert once you taste Classic Cup's legendary bread pudding with hot caramel sauce. If chocolate is more to your liking, the pot de crème is made with dark Belgian chocolate and espresso from Kansas City's own Roasterie Coffee.

Classic Cup is also one of those rare restaurants that offer gourmet breakfasts. Many a business meeting has taken place over their buttermilk griddlecakes, eggs Benedict, or biscuits and gravy. The breakfast menu is available weekdays and Saturday, and on Sunday the options increase during brunch with selections like a Florentine ham frittata with layers of spinach, ham, and Jack cheese baked in a savory egg custard. The grits and grillades—grilled Italian sausage atop garlic cheese grits with red sauce—will make any Southerner feel at home. Classic Cup is open seven days a week, and reservations are a good idea.

One more note: If you're in town when the Classic Cup offers a wine or beer tasting dinner in the wine cellar, we suggest you sign up. Along with good spirits and excellent food, experts from celebrated wineries or breweries will explain their craft. It's a wonderful evening, usually at a remarkably good price. The restaurant's Web site lists upcoming events.

EBT Restaurant $$-$$$$
1310 Carondelet
(Interstate 435 and State Line,
in the atrium of UMB Bank)
(816) 942-8870

It's always fun to introduce someone new to EBT. First there's the location. The restaurant is on the ground floor of what may be the least-attractive bank in the region. But step inside its big cement edifice and you'll see why it's one of our picks for a romantic anniversary or first date.

The name comes from Emery Bird Thayer, our town's first department store, founded in 1863 at 11th and Grand. The grand store closed in the '60s, and decades later its gorgeous mezzanine tea-room was reborn as EBT Restaurant using such artifacts as the massive sandstone column capitals, exquisite chandeliers, and stained glass. But what really sets the room apart are the private dining booths in the ornate brass elevator cages.

Other special touches are the live jazz on Wednesday through Saturday, wine dinners, and tableside flamed desserts that lend an old-fashioned sophistication to an evening.

But the menu is clearly up to date and masterfully done. A recent springtime choice was sesame-encrusted ahi tuna with zippy wasabi whipped potatoes served with Tobiko caviar and pickled ginger. Meat entrees include prime beef and a rack of lamb with a cranberry–port wine demi-glace. General Manager Ed Holland is always there to make sure your dinner is superb . . . he's even been known to flambé a mean Cherries Jubilee.

At least once a night, someone orders the tableside theatrics where medallions of beef tenderloin are flamed in brandy and served with a peppercorn sauce as rich as any holdings in the bank upstairs. Too showy? Perhaps you'd enjoy the selection of small plates offered in the dining room or the bar: seared scallops with a vodka and tomato concassée, or a lamb chop on a wild mushroom–flavored polenta.

And EBT serves what may be south Kansas City's best bargain: Sunset Dinner Specials from 5:00 to 6:30 P.M. Tuesday through Friday, when a three-course dinner is less than $16. It's lovely to end the evening on an even higher note with live piano music in the lounge.

40 Sardines   **$$–$$$**
11942 Roe Avenue
Overland Park, KS
(913) 451–1040
www.40sardines.com
A world-class restaurant in back of a shopping center in Overland Park? Absolutely! The fact is that we'd follow its

owners and chefs, Michael Smith and Debbie Gold, anywhere. This celebrated couple rose to stardom as executive co-chefs of the American Restaurant, winning accolades and awards since 1994. She trained with Michelin-starred chefs in France, he trained at La Presqu'ile in the South of France, and they met in the kitchen of Charlie Trotter's in Chicago. They've hosted the Friends of James Beard Benefit at least five times—that's like taking home a quintet of Oscar statuettes—and helped put Kansas City on the culinary map. When they left the American in 2001, fans prayed the husband-and-wife team would remain in the city, and they have, only now it's a Johnson County suburb that gets the national spotlight.

At their own restaurant, on the back-side of upscale Hawthorne Plaza Shopping Center, they serve what they call "contemporary American bistro" fare, influenced by the cuisine of the countries where they have lived or traveled, including France, Italy, and Spain. The small but stylish room includes a private dining room and communal table in front of the open kitchen. This premium spot is the hottest ticket in town—and we don't mean from the gas flames. We recommend calling well in advance for reservations. It will be a memorable meal, guaranteed. Lunch served weekdays; dinner, seven days a week.

Grand Street Cafe
(Country Club Plaza)   **$$**
4740 Grand
(816) 561–8000
www.eatpbj.com.com
This is the PB&J restaurant group's flagship place, designed with an exuberant floral-pattern wallpaper, handsome rattan chairs, and food that lives up to its slogan, "Dining so amazing, so refined, so memorable, they named a thousand dollar bill after us." You'll agree with your first slurp of the potato, leek, and smoky bacon soup, a rib-sticking chowder so popular they sell a staggering 10 gallons a day. But it's the double-cut pork chop that will

cinch the deal. With executive chef Marc Valiani at the helm, it's always juicy and flavorful, and the stewed apples on the side are the perfect touch. We like to introduce guests to the dish and watch them try to finish the entire thing.

Like most other great Kansas City restaurants, the Grand does a fine filet of beef. But don't overlook the succulent seafood. The signature dessert is a chocolate ganache in phyllo pastry served with vanilla crème anglaise and raspberry puree.

During nice weather there's romantic alfresco dining on the deck overlooking the Plaza's meandering Brush Creek. The main dining room can get a bit crowded and noisy, but it's grand fun to dine at the bar and watch pasta getting saucy in the open kitchen. And the normally packed entrance and bar area overflow during happy hour when people queue up for flavored martinis and discounted appetizers. Things are more serene during Sunday brunch, a fine start to an afternoon at the Nelson-Atkins Museum of Art a few blocks away. Grand Street provides the whole package—food, service, and atmosphere—seven days a week.

Grand Street Cafe is open for lunch Monday through Saturday, dinner daily, and brunch on Sunday.

The Grille on Broadway (Midtown) $$
3605 Broadway
(816) 531-0700

There's an inside-secret feeling to this cafe in a seen-better-days part of town. For one thing it's tiny: Just 32 lucky souls can crowd in here at one time. For another, it's easy to miss among the block of bars, late-night diners, and storefronts; a striped awning with big block letters helps. Despite its size the Grille has a huge following thanks to owner and chef Sean Cummings's way with seafood, pasta, and continental fare. And although the gregarious Sean and two servers hustle, the ambience is relaxed, so you can savor every bite. Let them know if you're due to the Symphony or Lyric Opera by eight; this is a favorite preperformance venue.

Reward yourself for finding the place by ordering Sean's fabulous crab cakes or barbecued oysters, spicy little devils cooled by a blue cheese sauce on the side. The regular menu includes seared pork tenderloin with rhubarb compote and a remarkable New Zealand rack of lamb with tomato chutney. But the restaurant's strong suit is incredible fish specials. One night it might be blackened coho salmon, mild wahoo in lobster broth, or Chilean sea bass wrapped in a potato crust and pan sautéed until golden. Some diners gasp when they see the mashed potatoes; the addition of guajillo chile peppers turns the dish a deep red color and provides a robust flavor.

Desserts include a blueberry crème brûlée, Triple Chocolate Threat that will definitely threaten your willpower, and peaches marinated in port with vanilla ice cream. Have one of each.

The Grille is open for dinner only, Tuesday through Sunday.

Several Kansas City restaurants try to encourage early-evening dining by offering fixed price three- or four-course dinners before 6:30 P.M. at reduced prices. It's a great way to try a new place for little cash or as a quick bite before the theater or ballet.

Ivy's (Gladstone) $$
240 Northeast Barry Road
(816) 436-3320
www.ivyskc.com

Ignore its strip mall location, because Ivy's is the most happening thing north of the river thanks to a lively menu by executive chef Samuel E. Cross III and the live jazz on weekends. While local jazz greats Max Groove or Angela Hagenbach serenade you, enjoy a cocktail or selection from Ivy's award-winning wine list. The menu is an enormous litany of steaks, seafood, and chops. While you're ruminating there's time to enjoy an appetizer of calamari with a zippy chipotle-garlic sauce or pan-seared rare ahi tuna toasted with black and white sesame seeds.

For entrees you can't go wrong with the Kansas City strip coated with cracked pepper and topped with a brandy-mustard cream sauce. The lamb chops are also popular; here they're brushed with Dijon mustard, dusted with pistachios and breadcrumbs, and then roasted. Ivy's also lets you take a turn as chef: Order the Pasta Kitchen and you'll get to choose a pasta shape, topping, and sauce, and then watch it prepared before your eyes. It's fun to watch guests walk back to their tables with a steaming plate and big smile.

If jazz isn't your thing or you prefer a more intimate evening, request a booth in one of the other cozy rooms. You can always sit in the bar after your meal to enjoy the music. Ivy's serves lunch and dinner Monday through Saturday and is closed on Sunday. Jazz is offered Friday and Saturday from 7:00 to 11:00 P.M.

Some of our top restaurants make happy hour positively giddy by offering hors d'oeuvres and cocktails for pocket change. Pierpont's serves around 10 appetizers; Morton's, steak sandwiches; and McCormick & Schmick's, shrimp cocktails and burgers with fries for $1.95.

Jardine's Restaurant and Jazz Club
(Country Club Plaza)   **$-$$**
4536 Main Street
(816) 561-6480
www.jardines4jazz.com
Live jazz seven nights a week and on Saturday afternoon may be the biggest pull for Beena Brandsgard's cozy nightclub near the Country Club Plaza, but it serves some mighty fine food along with the tunes (see Nightlife for details). Chef Antonio Gaytan's menu is a symphony of steaks, chops, and seafood, including a luscious peppercorn-crusted filet of beef with brandy cream sauce, fried catfish,

and some inventive pasta dishes. Everything, including the salad dressings, is made in-house.

Lunch items are priced extremely well, with a nice selection of salads and sandwiches for around $7.00. But the best bargain is that there's no cover charge for evening performances. Dinner reservations are always a good idea and a must on weekends when popular stylist Angela Hagenbach or Ida McBeth is on stage.

JJ's (Country Club Plaza)   **$$**
910 West 48th Street
(816) 561-7136
www.jjs-restaurant.com
In 1996 JJ's was one of only six restaurants worldwide to be awarded the Grand Award by *Wine Spectator* magazine. Although the list has grown to 85, some say that Jimmy Frantze's intimate bistro still has no equal when it comes to ambience. Part of its charm is the location—a quiet tree-lined side street just west of the Plaza, hidden among apartment buildings and defined by its tile roof and deep-red awnings. By late afternoon the tables in the sunny bar start to fill with neighbors reading the paper over a glass of wine, catching up on gossip, or waiting until their favorite table is open.

Dinner is served through the arched doorway where white-linen topped tables and tall plants divide the open space. Exuberant paintings by local artist Mike Savage add color to the walls. There's colorful food as well, starting with Paco's Shrimp, a savory appetizer of jumbo shrimp stuffed with a horseradish sauce, deep fried, and served with a mustard sauce and red-pepper coulis.

The menu focuses on steaks, including a pan-seared filet medallion with a peppercorn and red wine cream sauce. Fish, pasta, chops, and chicken are available as well, all expertly done. The wait staff is friendly without hovering and well trained on which wines will perfectly complement your meal. JJ's is open for lunch on weekdays and for dinner seven days a week.

Joe D's Wine Bar-Cafe (Brookside) $$
6227 Brookside Plaza
(816) 333-6116
www.joeds.com

Lots of us discovered that not all wine comes in screw-top bottles at this cafe's previous incarnation, called the Monastery. The brown-robed, sandaled servers are long gone, but you might say the building stayed in the family: Good local Catholic boy and Notre Dame alumnus Joe DiGiovanni bought the place in 1986 and has kept it packed ever since. In fact, that's him at the door making even strangers feel like long-lost friends. He swears that's the only place he's welcome, since the chef won't let him cook and the wait staff won't let him near the tables.

The Joe-free kitchen is in the talented hands of chef Todd Schulte, who prepares an amazingly diverse list of soups and salads, pastas, and entrees defined by fresh seafood, steaks, and chops. Peruse the menu by all means, but don't miss the long list of daily specials printed on a chalkboard. Recent entries included shrimp and artichoke hearts in a lemon basil cream sauce over pasta, duck enchiladas, and mixed grill of Denver elk and veal tenderloin served with a gin and raspberry demiglace. Todd, you are a genius.

The place to be from mid-May until late fall is the patio, where Brookside neighbors congregate and others stop by with cones of Foo's frozen treats from down the street. Get there early for a ringside seat, as these tables are first-come, first-served. Reservations, however, are taken for the inside rooms. And instead of coveting that ice-cream cone, order Joe's famous bread pudding with chocolate and caramel sauces and see who's jealous now.

Joe D's is open for lunch Monday through Friday and dinner Monday through Saturday.

Joe D's on 39th (Midtown) $$-$$$
1815 West 39th Street
(816) 561-3663
www.joeds.com

True Kansas City foodies were heartbroken when local celebrity chef Steve Cole closed Cafe Allegro, his swanky eatery that turned this neighborhood into Restaurant Row. But now Joe DiGiovanni, owner of the wildly popular Joe D's in Brookside, has taken over the space, and the result is a fun place to get good food and great drinks and enjoy a spring evening on the newly opened upstairs deck. They don't let Joe up there on sunny days lest he burn that gorgeous bald pate.

He's brought over some favorites from his Brookside place, including a black mussel appetizer in a creamy white wine and garlic sauce and an osso buco that rivals any in town. Make that the country. We're also partial to the boneless pork loin chop that's plump with a bread-sausage-apple stuffing and then finished with a cider Dijon glaze.

As a public service, Joe serves a "Morning After" Sunday brunch. You might just forget that hangover when you see your server, dressed in pajamas, coming your way with a crabmeat-draped eggs Benedict and a San Marino Mary (that's a Bloody Mary made with Absolut Peppar and a few secret ingredients served in a pint glass).

Check Joe D's Web site for upcoming wine dinners and special events. There's live piano music every evening during dinner, but you'll have to handle Monday night on your own: the restaurant is closed.

MelBee's Bar & Restaurant $$-$$$
6120 Johnson Drive
Mission, KS
(913) 262-6121

This little gem looks like it was plucked from a trendy Chicago neighborhood and plopped into a block of retail shops on busy (and frankly, boring) Johnson Drive. Inside is one of Kansas City's sexiest spaces with low lights, a curvy bar where the martinis are top drawer, live piano music nightly, white linen–draped tables, and an ever-changing art display. The food presentation is just as sexy: Instead of huge portions, entrees are served like

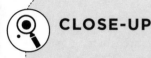

Kansas City Originals

Like all *Insiders' Guides,* we try to focus on local flavor, whether in shopping destinations, coffee shops, bookstores, or restaurants. It's not that there aren't some fine national chains in town; it's just that we like to celebrate the independent owners and chefs who are driven by a desire to offer something unique and homegrown.

In Kansas City we're lucky to have Kansas City Originals, an organization that supports the cause of restaurants with one or at most two locations. At this writing, 31 individual dining spots make up the roster, with more coming on board every year.

You'll find a terrific online directory on the organization's Web site (www.kc originals.com) with links to individual restaurant sites that include menus, directions, and hours. Watch for special events, too, such as food-laden fund-raisers and parties, and discount certificates that encourage you to give a local chef's fare a try.

So here you go: a different restaurant for every day of the month. And then, of course, you'll have to start over because menus will have changed. You'll find many of these restaurants elsewhere in this chapter, but the entire Kansas City Originals roster is worth repeating. All addresses are in Kansas City, Missouri, unless otherwise stated.

Aixois
2501 East 55th Street
(816) 333-3305
www.kansascitymenus.com/aixois

American Restaurant
2450 Grand Avenue
(816) 426-1133
www.americanrestaurantkc.com

Bluebird Bistro
1700 Summit
(816) 221-7559
www.kansascitymenus.com/
bluebirdbistro

Cafe des Amis
112½ Main Street
Parkville, MO
(816) 587-6767
www.cafedesamikc.com

Cafe Maison
408 East 63rd Street
(816) 523-3400
www.cafemaisonkc.com

Cafe Sebastienne
Kemper Museum of Contemporary Art
4420 Warwick Boulevard
(816) 561-7740
www.kemperart.org/café

Cafe Trocadero
401 East 31st Street
(816) 756-3400
www.cafetrocadero.com

City Tavern
101 West 22nd Street
(816) 421-3696
www.citytavern.net

40 Sardines
11942 Roe Avenue
Overland Park, KS
(913) 451-1040
www.kansascitymens.com/40sardines

Frankie's on the Plaza
100 Ward Parkway
(816) 931-2525
www.frankiesontheplaza.com

Frondizi's
4558 Main Street
(816) 931-3322
www.frondizis.com

Gia's Italian Cucina
2905 Southwest Boulevard
(816) 531-7770
www.giaskc.com

Governor's Meeting House
Restaurant & Catering
10910 West 60th Street
Shawnee, KS
(913) 631-2661
www.governorsmeetinghouse.com

Hereford House (four locations)
20th and Main Streets
(816) 842-1080
www.herefordhouse.com

Jardine's
4536 Main Street
(816) 561-6480
www.jardines4jazz.com

JJ's
910 West 48th Street
(816) 561-7136
www.jjs-restaurant.com

Joe D's
6227 Brookside Plaza
(816) 333-6116
www.joeds.com

Joe D's on 39th
1815 West 39th Street
(816) 561-3663
www.joeds.com

La Bodega
703 Southwest Boulevard
(816) 472-8272
www.labodegakc.com

Le Fou Frog
400 East Fifth Street
(816) 474-6060
www.lefoufrog.com

Macaluso's
1403 West 39th Street
(816) 561-0100
www.macalusoson39th.com

The Majestic Steak House
931 Broadway
(816) 471-8484
www.majesticsteakhouse.com

Marina Grog and Galley
Gate 1 at Water Edge
Lake Lotawana, MO
(816) 578-5511
www.kansascitymenus.com/marina
grogandgalley

MelBee's
6120 Johnson Drive
Mission, KS
(913) 262-6121

Pierponts
30 West Pershing Road (Union Station)
(816) 221-5111
www.kansascitymenus.com/pierponts

Piropos
1 West First Street
Parkville, MO
(816) 741-3600
www.kansascitymenus.com/piropos

PotPie
904 Westport Road
(816) 561-2702

The Raphael (inside the Raphael Hotel)
325 Ward Parkway
(816) 756-3800
www.raphaelkc.com/restaurant

re:Verse
618 Ward Parkway
(816) 931-7811
www.reservekc.com

Shields Manor Bistro
121 Main Street
Platte City, MO
(816) 858-5557
www.shieldsmanorbistro.com

Suzi's
408 East Bannister Road
(816) 444-5650
www.suzis.net

Tatsu's
4603 West 90th Street
Prairie Village, KS
(913) 383-9801
www.tatsus.com

V's
10819 East 40 Highway
Independence, MO
(816) 353-1241
www.vsrestaurant.com

Webster House
1644 Wyandotte
(816) 221-4713
www.websterhousekc.com

Zin
1900 Main Street
(816) 527-0120
www.zinkc.com

jewelry on small plates with glistening sauces done in dots and swirls. It's an elegant, quality versus quantity way to dine.

We suggest each diner choose one or two entrees from the list of 30 or so cold and warm selections and then share. The Artisan Cheese Plate is a smart way to start or end the meal; four or five premium cheeses from around the world are presented along with rough crackers and a smattering of fruit. Favorite entrees include the sumptuous wild mushroom potpie (just the cognac-kissed aroma under that puffed pastry will make you swoon) and the sautéed halibut with mango Thai chilies, a lovely composition in red and gold. Or opt for the prix fixe dinner and choose from four or five selections to enjoy with a cocktail or glass of wine. Service is poised and friendly at MelBee's, and the clientele is a sophisticated mix of straight couples and gays.

Lunch is also special here, with a variety of soups, salads, and sandwiches. The MelBee Club, made with chicken breast, prosciutto, Havarti, and smoked tomato aioli, is terrific, especially when crisp, bronze sweet potato fries share the plate.

Ophelia's $$
201 North Main
Independence, MO
(816) 461-4525
www.ophelias.net
When Ken and Cindy McClain turned this boarded-up space into a hip, urban restaurant and inn, they gave after-hours

life to historic Independence Square. The American regional cooking with European flair is as artfully done as Cindy's paintings on the walls. Favorites include his brandy-laced crab soup and roasted rack of lamb. And at just under $18 the salmon and jumbo sea scallops in a saffron white wine beurre blanc isn't just a culinary standout, it's a bargain.

Lunch is casual with a kick, such as chicken salad with port wine apples and candied walnuts and a smoked pork sandwich with pickled red cabbage. A low-fat spa menu is also available for lunch and dinner, a thoughtful touch for guests staying at the inn upstairs. Lunch and dinner are served every day but Monday, and brunch is available on Sunday. On Friday and Saturday evenings there's live jazz in the bar; the large open space makes it easy to listen and still enjoy a conversation.

To turn a delightful evening into a good night, reserve a room at the inn, where Cindy has worked her creative magic with seven rooms and one luxurious suite. See Accommodations for more information.

Pachamama's $$–$$$
161 Quail Creek Drive
Lawrence, KS
(785) 841-0990
www.pachamamas.com
When this handsome restaurant opened a few years ago, it gave us a reason besides KU basketball to drive 30 minutes to this college town. Despite a location behind a

Hy-Vee grocery store, Pachamama's food is distinctive and the atmosphere is romantic. In fact, the two-story windows, bleached-wood rafters, and lush greenery create a rainforest effect, a visual reference to the restaurant's Incan name, which means Mother Earth.

That's where the maternal theme ends: Mom never cooked like this. Chef/owner Ken Baker's menu takes us around the world with stops in Asia, India, Mexico, and Italy. A roasted portobello and carrot tower, for example, is enhanced with a ginger-soy-mirin essence; spaghetti verde brings together roasted poblano chiles, tomatillo, and cilantro crema; and a rolled pork loin is cured in a maple-red chile rub and served with wild rice pilaf and balsamic wild cherry sauce. If the Tahitian vanilla bean crème brûlée is on the dessert list, order two. It's too good to share.

Dinner here is always exciting but even more so during a wine-tasting dinner or cooking class events. Call or check the Web site for details and dates. Pachamama's is open for dinner only, seven days a week.

Peppercorn Duck Club
(Crown Center) $$–$$$
2345 McGee
(816) 435–4199

The folks at Hyatt Regency somehow missed the memo that said hotel restaurants must be mediocre. Even after two decades the Peppercorn is *still* one of the best places to seal a business deal or pop the question. Any celebration is more special with a trip to the over-the-top Ultra Chocolatta dessert bar. Before you say "no thanks," just remember this chocolate-lover's paradise is complimentary. And didn't your mother tell you it's impolite to refuse a gift?

As befitting its name, duck in all its crisp and succulent glory reigns supreme on the menu, fresh from one of the rotisseries on view. The duck strudel—prepared with portobello mushrooms, Boursin cheese, and a truffle demi-glace—is particularly delicious. Other popular choices

include barbecued shrimp in a spicy sauce that calls for extra napkins, and game including pheasant, venison, and bison. You can indulge for lunch on weekdays, dinner every night, and brunch on Sunday. Service is as smooth as you would expect in a venue this plush. There's more royal treatment: a matchbox printed with your name and a rose presented to each lady. And be sure to leave something on your plate: Leftovers arrive in duck-shaped aluminum foil packages.

Phillips Chophouse
Hotel Phillips $$$–$$$$
106 West 12th Street
(816) 221–9292
www.hotelphillips.com

A gorgeous space with rich carved oak and marble appointments, impeccable service including tableside flambéed desserts, and a sophisticated menu . . . what more could you want? Perhaps a luxurious hotel room upstairs? You've got it! In fact, the Chophouse is one of those rare finds—a hotel restaurant you'll want to visit even if you're not staying the night.

True foodies will appreciate the presentation as much as the well-executed food, such as the mashed potatoes that are molded into a standing pear shape, dusted with paprika for a faux rosy color, and topped with a twig and leaf. It's the sort of culinary surprise that keeps you talking for days. Other sides are scrumptious as well: Balsamic-marinated cipollini risotto accompanies the cedar-planked salmon, and seafood cassoulet—starring house-made seafood sausage—complements a meltingly tender pan-roasted monkfish. The steak choices are always top notch, too.

If the gourmets are satisfied, wine aficionados will be beside themselves here; the glasses are Riedel, a fitting tribute to a fine wine selection and a wait staff knowledgeable enough to suggest stellar vintages. Just save room for the bananas Foster, flamed at your table. You could also ignite your own flame upstairs (see Accommodations).

Lunch service is smooth as well, if you can get past the fact that the attractive lady at the next table is the mayor. Here's where Kansas City's movers and shakers seal deals, pitch ideas, and celebrates new business. Or sometimes they just come to enjoy good food, like the duck spring rolls or BLT with seared diver scallops nestled among the smoked bacon and tarragon aioli on sourdough.

Pierpont's (Crown Center) $$
Union Station, Pershing and Grand
(816) 221-5111
www.herefordhouse.com

When Union Station opened in 1914, even the women's and children's lounges were grand affairs, with marble stonework and ornate oak leaf plaster. In 1999 Rod Anderson, owner of the Hereford House, turned these rooms into one of the city's most glamorous restaurants. The bar is particularly stunning with its dark woods, richly detailed high plaster ceilings, and mirrored liquor shelves that bartenders reach by climbing a 14-step rolling ladder. It gives a whole new meaning to "I'll take that straight up."

Named "best place to entertain out-of-town guests" by the local press, Pierpont's is also a top choice for small groups thanks to its swanky private Wine Cellar dining rooms. Close the French doors and you'll have the space to yourselves. Larger banquet rooms overlook the grand dining space below. Although the restaurant has a sophisticated feeling, it also attracts casually dressed clientele during happy hour when a variety of appetizers—including hamburgers, calamari, and skewered chicken—are available for less than two bucks. It's a terrific light meal before heading to one of the theater venues within Union Station.

But we suggest you reserve a dark, cozy booth and stay for dinner. This is part of the Hereford House group, remember, so the steaks are superb. Pierpont's is also known for its fresh seafood, and the duck is fabulous, spit roasted and served with a raspberry-hoisin sauce that suits the rich duck meat. But for rich, you can't get more decadent than the macaroni and lobster casserole made with shiitake mushrooms, fresh asparagus, and smoked Gouda cheese sauce.

Rod has made a commitment to his wine cellar, with more than 300 labels on the menu and 3,000 more stored below. It makes for a terrific wine tasting dinner. Reservations are necessary for these monthly events and highly recommended for lunch and dinner, served seven days a week.

Raoul's Velvet Room $$
119th and Metcalf
(Rosana Square Shopping Center)
Overland Park, KS
(913) 469-0466
www.raoulsvelvetroom.com

Truth be told, Raoul's is better known for its cocktail-party atmosphere and entertainment like acoustic jam sessions, dance raves with a DJ, and costume parties where the beautiful people get a chance to expose even more of their toned bods. (Read more about this popular place in Nightlife.) But Raoul's is also a fine restaurant with an impressive wine list. And despite its swanky looks, the prices are remarkably low. The Brie-and-mushroom-stuffed chicken breast with herb risotto and baby veggies in a port wine demi-glace is just $14.00, and the pan-seared crab cakes are served with sautéed leeks, roasted tomatoes, and spinach with a lemon butter sauce for a mere $9.00. The most expensive regular-menu item, the filet mignon, is a very reasonable $24.00, especially when it comes with the perfect sides: grilled portobello mushrooms, garlic mashed potatoes, sautéed asparagus, crispy onions, and an herbed Madeira veal glacé. Oh, yeah.

Even the bartenders like to get into the culinary act with martini concoctions like the Chocolate Chip Cookie (made with vanilla vodka and chocolate chip cookie liqueur) or the Black & Bleu, where the olive is stuffed with blue cheese. No, thanks, we'll stay with our pimiento, please.

The bar is also where to find reasonably priced wines by the bottle and glass, as well as a very respectable list of fine Scotches and cigars.

Join the online mailing list to keep up with such events as Wine Raves, featuring some stellar pours for around $10 per person, and popular Midwest musical acts. It can get pretty hot and crowded on the dance floor, but nobody minds. There's an icy mango martini waiting at the bar.

Hipsters will be happy to know that Raoul's is open until 2:00 A.M. seven nights a week. Doors open at precisely 4:44 P.M. You'll have to ask why yourself.

Raphael Restaurant
(Country Club Plaza) $$
325 Ward Parkway
(816) 756–3800
www.raphaelkc.com

For decades, patrons have referred to the Raphael as the most romantic restaurant in town. It could be the piano music coming from the lounge, the dark paneling with smoked glass and mirrors, the private booths, or the food that can make even the toughest customer starry-eyed. Or it could be that, unlike so many other bistros in town, you can actually hear your partner's sweet nothings whispered from across the table.

Adding to its lovey-dovey ambience is the fact that the Raphael Hotel's lobby is just a few steps away. In fact the restaurant has served as preamble to many an amorous evening, and general manager Cynthia Savage and her staff have contributed to marriage proposals by hiding ring boxes under dinner domes or inside bouquets of roses.

Although the restaurant's atmosphere and service say Old World, chef Peter Hahn keeps the menu fresh with items borrowed from Asian, French, Italian, and even Southwest cuisines. Appetizers, for example, include grilled sea scallops with papaya and an orange-cilantro sauce and prosciutto-grilled pears with a Gorgonzola-walnut relish and port wine glaze. Even the spinach salad is special here, enlivened

with smoked salmon bacon and a lemon-horseradish dressing.

The entrees change weekly to take advantage of the season's bounty. Past menus have included bison rib-eye steak rubbed with chili oil then grilled to medium rare and served with roasted corn-poblano mashed potatoes. A delightful veal scaloppini is stacked with pancetta, fried tomatoes, and Stilton cheese; and vegetarians can be very happy with the eggplant Parmesan. Entree descriptions include wine suggestions from the Raphael's extensive list. Desserts include a macaroon nut tart that would be lovely with a cream sherry. . . or there's always that chocolate waiting on your pillow upstairs.

Lunch and dinner are served Monday through Saturday. Breakfast is served daily.

Rozzelle Court (Country Club Plaza) $
4525 Oak Street
(816) 751–1279

Perhaps it's the setting that compels us to place this cafeteria-style eatery in the same category as the most lauded, and often luxurious, restaurants in town. The space is a trip to Tuscany with carved stone, a ring of arched openings in the balcony above, a gurgling fountain, and the golden glow from skylights three stories above. And where else can you fold your napkin, stand up, and say, "Now where do you suppose they keep the Rembrandt?"

Frankly, once you've tasted the food you won't mind pushing a brown plastic tray through the line. You might think artists have arranged the salads here, especially the grilled salmon on spring greens dressed with balsamic vinaigrette. The soup of the day never fails to impress, whether it's curried chicken or rich seafood bisque. Desserts are always delectable as well, ranging from Key lime pie to almond cheesecake.

Lunch is served Tuesday through Sunday (the museum is closed Monday), and the live music that accompanies Friday dinners turns this enchanting room into one of the most popular in town. Admis-

An On The Town Passport Unlimited card (888-273-6392; www.passportunlimited .com) gets you a free entree when you pay for one of equal or higher value. The roster includes around 36 places ranging from brewpubs to fine dining, and you could easily recoup the $87 annual membership fee over a long weekend in town.

sion to the museum is free, and the food is reasonably priced. Now *that's* art. Read more about the Nelson-Atkins Museum of Art in the Close-up in the Arts chapter.

Savoy Grill (Downtown) $$$
219 West Ninth Street
(816) 842-3890

As the city's oldest restaurant, there simply isn't another place in town so imbued with history, romance, and gentility. If those accolades sound dated, so be it. The deeply carved wood paneling, stained glass, and cushy dark booths certainly worked for Harry S Truman, who was such a regular customer they named Booth No. 4 in his honor.

While you're contemplating your order, take a note of the surroundings, which haven't changed much since 1903. The lanterns were once gaslights, and the 12 murals were painted by Edward Holslag to depict the pioneers' arduous trek on the Santa Fe Trail. The first mural near the entrance shows steamboats arriving at the Missouri River levee with limestone bluffs in the background—what would become downtown Kansas City.

But the Savoy didn't make or keep its reputation with artwork alone. Perfectly grilled steaks and steamed lobsters are the mainstays here, and dinner might start brilliantly with steamed mussels brought to the table in a big tin bucket. Owner Don Lee and white-jacketed waiters with impeccable service will make sure your meal is perfection. Take your time; after all, it took a scene in *Mr. and Mrs. Bridge* 14 hours to film here.

Reservations are a must for both lunch and dinner. Lunch is available Monday through Saturday, dinner seven days a week. And here's good news for theatergoers and night owls: Dinner is available until midnight on Friday and Saturday. And if you're celebrating a birthday or anniversary, why not splurge by reserving a room at the bed-and-breakfast inn upstairs? Your key is waiting in the Accommodations chapter.

Skies (Crown Center) $$-$$$
2345 McGee
(816) 435-4199

Breathtaking panoramic views of the skyline are on the menu at this revolving restaurant on the 42nd floor of the Hyatt Regency. In fact, with 72 windows and 23 color murals gracing the walls, you're surrounded by the sights of Kansas City wherever you look. There's no chance of getting dizzy, however; the rotation is so smooth you may not notice it until the red neon Western Auto sign is out of sight.

Although the menu offers nothing revolutionary (sorry, we couldn't resist) the mesquite-grilled steaks are expertly prepared. Other choices include tender steamed crab legs and a mixed grill of fish, chicken, and beef. For dessert, bid farewell to your diet and go for the Sky High Pie, three layers of homemade ice cream on a graham cracker crust. Or head to the lounge for an after-dinner drink and tell the bartender, "One more trip around the city, please." Skies is open for lunch on weekdays, cocktails and dinner seven days a week, and brunch on Sunday.

Starker's Reserve
(Country Club Plaza) $$$
201 West 47th Street
(816) 753-3565
www.starkersreserve.com

This Kansas City gem provides everything fine dining should be: beautifully prepared food served with Old World style in a gorgeous setting. Owner Cliff Bath also founded Harry's Starker's around the corner, a much-loved restaurant named for a gregarious 15th-century British gourmand. Harry, it was said, often indulged in whiskey and wine before engaging in naked public jaunts, hence the phrase "stark naked." Starker's, alas, served its last meal in 1996. But by then the elegant Mr. Bath had opened the current space as a private restaurant.

Today Starker's Reserve is open to public dining as well, making it one of the most coveted reservations in town. The surroundings are exquisite, with country French furnishings, lovely second-story views of the Plaza, and chandeliers crafted of wine bottles that reflect color and light around the room. Dinners here are long, leisurely affairs featuring contemporary cuisine and the freshest ingredients. A winter menu could start with butternut squash–leek soup with bacon and chives or pan seared shrimp dumplings with lobster broth and crème fraîche. Maroon-colored roasted baby beets enliven a watercress and goat cheese salad with spiced pecans and Pommerey mustard vinaigrette.

Entree specialties include rack of lamb served with sundried tomato and porcini risotto sauced with a mint demi-glace, and a potato-wrapped salmon so moist its dill-flavored buerre blanc sauce might go untouched. Are you sighing yet? Perhaps the chocolate truffle mousse will send you over the edge. And it gets better: Starker's wine cellar is stunning. It was the first Missouri restaurant to earn a Grand Award from *Wine Spectator*. It remains on the esteemed list today. Reservations are a must here, and although casual attire is welcome, Starker's is worth dressing for. Hear that, Harry?

Starker's Reserve serves dinner Tuesday through Saturday.

Yahooz $$
4701 Town Center Drive
Leawood, KS
(913) 451-8888
www.eatpbj.com
We wouldn't steer you wrong; don't let the cowboy-like decor (think spurs, lots of

tooled leather, and rawhide 'round the lamps) keep you away from this place. It is, after all, part of the PB&J group that owns Grand Street Cafe and YiaYia's, so you couldn't get a bad meal here if you tried.

Hefty steaks, naturally, are on the menu, but other items might tempt you as well. Yahooz makes the most of locally raised products, including pork from Alma Farms and free-range chickens from regional farms. The dishes are always expertly prepared and served with great sides like cheddar scalloped potatoes. You'll want to eat every bite, so make sure you don't fill up on the cast-iron skillet of warm corn bread with honey butter before dinner.

Kids will love the place thanks to its giddy-up look, comic books, and special menu with corn dogs, cheeseburgers, and peanut butter and jelly sandwiches. And the wait staff seems to be selected for their aptitude in making children feel special. One server offered to whip up some applesauce from scratch when a young diner requested the nonmenu item.

Yahooz is open for lunch Monday through Saturday and dinner every night and rustles up a Sunday brunch fit for a hardworking cowboy. Along with carved ham and roast beef, the buffet offers made-to-order omelets, smoked salmon, an egg-cheese-and-sausage casserole, fresh fruits, breakfast pastries, and desserts. Reservations are recommended, especially on weekends. Watch for their famous wine dinners.

YiaYia's Eurobistro $$
4701 West 119th Street
Overland Park, KS
(913) 345-1111
www.eatpbj.com
The PB&J group went all out in designing this striking decor with limestone walls, slate floors, and a lodgelike ambience. The menu is heartwarming too, with appetizers like wild mushroom ragout over creamy polenta. We've noticed people trying hard not to pick up the shallow bowl to slurp every last bit; thank goodness the

servers provide crusty sourdough bread for that task.

The menu offers flavorful choices for lunch and dinner including a grilled salmon salad and tasty oak-fired gourmet pizzas. The linguini with shrimp, spinach, and oven-dried tomatoes in a rich brown butter sage broth is one of the best pasta dishes in the city, and the sautéed sea bass with rock shrimp and fennel risotto is a work of art. No wonder the servers seem proud to bring the custom-designed charcoal-and-white plates to your table.

The nightly specials—typically grilled fish, pasta, and pizza—are always winners. As a nice touch they offer the pasta servings in two sizes; order a half portion and you'll still be amazed at the number of noodles placed in front of you. Half of Johnson County must have Styrofoam boxes in their fridges marked with "YY" and the date. But the double-cut pork chop is so savory you'll want to eat every morsel in one sitting. Ditto for the grilled beef tenderloin with a black pepper and Gorgonzola-Chianti sauce served with marinated vegetable kabobs and mashed potatoes.

The desserts are fine as well. Order the crème brûlée and you'll get a trio of tiny pots: chocolate, raspberry, and a classic version. It's the perfect way to share a dessert with the rest of the table. You'll see plenty of families and large groups dining here, but you can still find a romantic booth in a corner. On a balmy evening, a table on the plant-lined patio is worth requesting. Lunch is served Monday through Saturday, and dinner is available every night. A brunch menu is offered on Sundays.

Webster House Restaurant (Downtown/ Crossroads) $-$$$
1644 Wyandotte
(816) 221-4713
www.websterhousekc.com

In this beautifully renovated schoolhouse-turned-antiques shop, it's the dining rooms that go to the head of the class. Whether you're seated in the red room,

sunny market, or New York–style library, this is a popular place for the ladies who lunch, folks who work downtown, and shoppers who have discovered the nearby stores in the Crossroads Arts District.

Chef Tim Johnson keeps the mix fresh with a menu that changes daily, but with any luck the list will offer the goat cheese soufflé—a tender mound of baked cheese served with greens and sliced fruits of the season. Add one of the desserts, like the just-tart-enough lemon bar, and it's a lovely way to spend an afternoon before searching the rooms for stunning 18th- and 19th-century European and American antiques and unique giftware (see write-up in Shopping).

This is also one of high society's favorite spots for special events such as wedding receptions and parties. The galleries filled with antiques make a stunning background for brunch, luncheons, and after-hours soirees. Chef Johnson can create an elegant repast specifically for your needs, or you may choose from one of Webster House's private dining menus. For special occasions the antique school bell may be rung in honor of the celebration. For us, the Webster's roast rack of lamb with walnut crust and pear-bourbon sauce is a bell-ringer!

Zin (Downtown/Crossroads) $$-$$$
1900 Main Street
(816) 527-0120
www.zinkc.com

Alex Pryor's trendy restaurant in the Crossroads Arts District is the place to see and be seen, particularly at night when wall-to-wall windows turn it into a glowing jewel box beckoning from the street. Reviews have been glowing as well for the chef's upscale version of Midwest's meat-and-potato fare. His potatoes are the fingerling variety, which combined with haricot vert, nicoise olives, and greens make a lovely salad. Another culinary twist is the house-made rabbit sausage-potato hash topped with a poached quail egg.

Entrees include a pistachio-crusted red snapper served with roasted spaghetti squash and a swirl of red-pepper coulis. The rich flavor of Australian lamb enhances a cassoulet of flageolet beans, mushrooms, rosemary, and tomatoes.

Can't decide? Let the chef choose for you: Zin offers a three-course prix fixe menu for lunch and a degustation—a five-course tasting—every night.

ASIAN

Saigon 39 (Midtown)   **$**
1806 ½ West 39th Street
(816) 531-4447
This family-owned Vietnamese cafe is often voted the best in Kansas City thanks to its award-winning dishes. Stir-fried dishes are very popular, and the spicy pineapple soup is a unique taste sensation you could easily learn to love. Think you can take the heat of the kitchen? Better watch how you order your dishes—mild, medium, or hot—because the cooks will comply. An extra-spicy version of the crabmeat-and-squid soup has become an ad hoc prescription during cold and flu season; it's guaranteed to knock the germs right out of you.

Other soups, as well as stir-fries, can be customized with combinations of meat and fish or served vegetarian style. Order a side of their ethereal spring rolls and you have a fine meal. Bring cash—nothing else is accepted—and call ahead because Saigon 39 is open on a limited and ever-changing schedule. But their curry dishes alone are definitely worth a phone call.

Thai Place   **$-$$**
9359 Santa Fe Drive
Overland Park, KS
(913) 649-5420

11838 Quivira
Overland Park, KS
(913) 451-THAI

732 North Seventh Highway
Blue Springs, MO
(816) 229-3292

4130 Pennsylvania (Westport)
(816) 753-THAI

100 East Seventh Street
(Arun Thai Place Grill)
(816) 472-THAI
www.kcthaiplace.com
There may be no other cuisine as marvelously diverse and intricate as Thai, and Ann Liberda does it to a "T." Since opening her first Thai Place in Overland Park, she and her son, Ted, have introduced Kansas Citians to unusual sauces that include everything from slightly sweet coconut milk, refreshing basil and lemongrass, to a head-exploding concoction flecked with slivers of bright red peppers we've nicknamed "hurt me." It's all delicious, as long as you understand that hot and spicy means just that.

Although it's fun to experiment with new dishes (huge servings make it easy to share), you can't go wrong with the popular seafood *phad Thai*, a delightful marriage of sweet, salty, and spicy flavors made with rice noodles, shrimp, mussels, squid, and crabmeat in a fermented fish sauce called *nam pla*. We've decided that most of the menu sounds like a teenager who just came home with a pierced tongue. Just point and smile, and let your friendly server do the rest.

Large groups might want to try a variety of appetizers such as the fried mussels, four huge garlic tempura-battered fritters served over stir-fried bean sprouts; cordovan-colored pork ribs; and delicate, translucent spring rolls fat with grilled chicken, cilantro, and carrot shreds. Entrees include Chilean sea bass, and a ginger-laced Duck Paradise in a rich brown sauce alongside fried rice studded with roasted cashews and pineapple instead of peas and carrots. The curry dishes are particularly lush blends of sweet and savory flavors.

The newest location at Seventh and Walnut is a boon to city workers hungry for more than a burger at lunch. Service is quick, the food superb, and free parking across the street a real bonus. Expect crowds at lunch, but for now you'll have the place almost to yourself for dinner while our Downtown reinvents itself.

BAKERIES, DELIS, AND DESSERTS

Andre's Confiserie Suisse (Midtown) $
5018 Main Street
(816) 561-3440
www.andreschocolates.com

This combination European-style tea shop, bakery, and candy store is wildly popular with ladies who lunch, midtown office workers, and even men who do eat quiche. In fact, the only way to sample the elegant food is to get here before 11:15 A.M. or after 1:30 P.M. because Andre's doesn't take reservations and there's always a crowd. No matter. People will gladly wait in line for the prix fixe lunch, which includes a choice of two specials such as goulash or vol-au-vent, plus a fresh-baked roll, choice of confection from the dessert tray, and beverage for less than $11. A quiche or two always appears on the menu as well. All the desserts are incredible, but the Linzer torte is simply to die for.

Marcel Bollier, son of the late founder, Andre Bollier, runs the tiny place, and his mother, Elsbeth, oversees the ever-changing menu. Together they make sure Andre's famous quality continues. Before you leave the shop—and you can bet someone in line hopes you will—stop by the cases of exquisite handmade chocolates and desserts. The artistry of the truffles and chocolate boxes filled with confections is superb. Out of town fans can order from the Web site.

Andre's is open for lunch Tuesday through Saturday.

Angie's Italian Ice and Frozen Custard (Midtown) $
1710 West 39th Street
(816) 931-2423

Look for the bright red awning for a little bit of heaven within the 5 blocks known as Restaurant Row. Here's where to indulge in traditional frozen treats like malts, shakes, cones, and frozen custard, a thick concoction worth every second of a brain freeze. Angie's also makes indescribably good Italian ices (called gelato back East) in flavors like mango, black raspberry, strawberry, and lemon. Can't decide? Get a cone that combines frozen custard and gelato.

Angie's is also one of the few places in town to get an authentic Chicago-style dog; for the poor souls who have never had one, it's a Vienna beef wiener with celery salt, chopped tomatoes, and peppers on a bun. There are a few benches nearby where you can sit to enjoy your treat, or take it on a walk along the eclectic 39th Street neighborhood.

Angie's is open seven days a week at this location and has a stand at the City Market. You'll also find their concession at a few annual events like the Spirit Festival.

d'Bronx Deli $
3904 Bell
(816) 531-0550

This cheerful, bustling New York–style deli serves massive sandwiches but perhaps is most beloved for its thin-crust pizza piled nearly 2 inches high with toppings. Its 30-inch version is a party in a box whether you're taking it home for a night in front of the tube, back to the office for lunch, or sneaking it past the hotel's front desk. But the best part is eating in because of the never-ending stream of people. You'll see suited business execs, construction crews, moms with hungry kids, and starving artists. This place is the great equalizer because no matter what your background, everyone faces the same dilemma: What sandwich should I order today? There are 50 on the menu, but here's a hint: The Italian meatball is hard to beat. Or try a house specialty like the Wild Bill, which is salami, provolone, coleslaw, and spicy mustard and horseradish on rye. Let's rodeo!

And while you're waiting for your food, don't be surprised if a television crew shows up. d'Bronx has been featured on

Food TV's *The Best Of,* a program that spans the nation looking for top eateries. And just in case you doubt the name's authenticity, d'Bronx owners Janet and Robert Bloom are originally from that famous neighborhood. More important, they beat out plenty of famous New York addresses to be named one of the six top delis in the country.

The deli is open from 10:00 A.M. to 10:00 P.M. Monday through Saturday, so folks often stop by for pastrami on rye after a night of barhopping, or pie and coffee after a late dinner. And the soothing homemade chicken soup might be just the thing to send you off to dreamland.

**Foo's Fabulous Frozen Custard
(Brookside)** $
**6235 Brookside Plaza
(816) 523–2520**
What could be better on a sultry night than sharing a Sticky Hickey? Especially when the treat is actually a concrete—a richer, denser version of ice cream—mixed with marshmallow, caramel, and chocolate chips. Foo's is fun anytime of year but especially when you slurp your cup, cone, or sundae as you window-shop the beautiful Brookside neighborhood. You can choose from dozens of ingredients to mix with your frozen custard, including fruits, nuts, chunks of Snickers and Heath Bar, and flavorings like maple, rum, and coffee. Make your own recipe or go for a Foo's favorite like Mint Oreo Twist or a Blue Devil that incorporates raspberries, crème de menthe, and chocolate chips. Divine.

**Murray's Ice Creams & Cookies
(Westport)** $
**4120 Pennsylvania Avenue
(816) 931–5646**
Murray's may be the reason we don't mind the heat and humidity in mid-July—it gives us one more reason to head to Murray's. This tiny spot at the end of a horseshoe-shaped loop in Westport lists 16 or so flavors on the wall with around 200 other recipes waiting their turn. With any luck Chocolate Flake Fromage will be

on the list when you visit. This cream cheese-flavored ice cream with semisweet chocolate flakes has its own fan club. Other specialties are smooshies, which merge ice cream with toppings like chunks of candy bars, and lumpies, which are malts made chunkier than normal. Try to control yourself.

Murray's has a few tables indoors and out, but most people prefer to walk around Westport to window-shop and people-watch. During December and January, when Murray's is closed, you'll just have to dream about Fudge Raspberry Rhapsody or One Drunk Monk. But they do a very nice send-off: On the last Sunday in November all ice-cream tubs are half price. See? Now you have plenty of time to buy a bigger freezer.

Plan to visit? Here's the scoop: Murray's opens at noon Tuesday through Sunday and closes between 9:00 and 10:30 P.M. depending on the day. Closed Monday.

BARBECUE

Arthur Bryant's Barbeque (East Side) $
**1727 Brooklyn
(816) 231–1123**
Celebrities and presidents have made the pilgrimage to this landmark since 1930, and today, despite the spot's location in a neglected neighborhood, the lunch line still forms by 11:30. Even then you'll wait as much as half an hour to yell "Beef and fries" to the man standing in front of that smoking pit, but it's worth it to get your hands around 4 inches of brisket.

In fact, it's worth the wait just to witness the decades-old ritual as the counterman slaps two pieces of Wonderbread on a plate and—using his catcher's mitt–size hand—grabs a fistful of just-sliced beef brisket to completely cover the bread. No tongs, no gloves, and no complaints from us. He then slathers on a thick layer of sauce using a paintbrush. The sauce is an alarmingly orange mixture that's a bit more vinegary—and a lot grainier—than anything else in town. You'll no doubt notice big vats of the stuff curing in the front windows. Although they introduced a sweeter, tomato-based version a few years back, go for the original; after all, it's one reason *New Yorker* columnist Calvin Trillin named Bryant's "the single best restaurant in the world." The sandwich is accompanied by an enormous portion of unpeeled fries hot from a lard bath. Don't forget to fish a good number of pickle slices from the jar on your way to the cash register.

The beer is served in a frozen mug that turns the brew into a slushee for adults. You can eat in the restaurant or have your meal to go, whereupon it will be wrapped in two layers of butcher paper that will only partially protect your car's upholstery. Eat in or take out, take the time to savor every morsel. After all, it's been cooking for 13 hours or so.

Bryant's serves lunch and dinner seven days a week, and because it's just a block from the historic 18th and Vine district, it's a tasty way to make a day of killer 'cue, cold beer, and hot jazz.

Burnt ends might sound like a restaurant reject, but around here it's a delicacy. The dish is cut from the ends of a barbecued brisket and served alone with sauce or as a sandwich. The high-flavor, slightly chewy treat is on the menu at just about every barbecue joint in town.

**BB's Lawnside Bar-B-Q
(South Kansas City)** $
**1205 East 85th Street
(816) 822-7427**

For a full shot of what Kansas City does best—blues and barbecue—you can't beat Lindsay Shannon's roadhouse. The Louisiana-style gumbo is mighty good, but BB's excels at hickory-smoked ribs. The aroma alone will practically pull you from the front seat of your car and into the front door. Grab your barbecue and a locally brewed Boulevard Beer and pull up a chair at one of the long tables filled with tempo-rary strangers. Once the ragtime, boogie-woogie, or blues starts up you'll be sitting next to your new best friends. A seat at the bar will give you a vantage point to plenty of people-watching. BB's is open for lunch and dinner Wednesday through Sunday, and there's live music every night. Check out the listing in Nightlife for more information about this popular joint.

Boardroom Bar-B-Que $
**9600 Antioch
Overland Park, KS
(913) 642-6273**

Who says they can't serve good barbecue in the 'burbs? By the time pitmaster Scott O'Meara opened this place near a busy shopping center, he already had a loyal following from years of winning barbecue contests. Although the restaurant is comfortable and the servers friendly, this place does a phenomenal take-out business, especially on Sunday, when a meaty slab of ribs costs just $12.99. The smoky brisket is also a standout, and you might want to prime your appetite with some buffalo chicken wings, called "nuclear" because of the incendiary sauce. And speaking of sauce, the restaurant displays more than 1,000 different brands. Join their Sauce of the Month Club and you can eventually try them all. The Boardroom is open seven days a week for lunch and dinner.

**Danny Edwards Famous
Kansas City Barbecue
(Downtown)** $
**1227 Grand Boulevard
(816) 283-0880**

Dan's not kidding; this is the kind of 'cue that made Kansas City famous. But eat fast; there's seating for only 18 people in this 600-square-foot smoky emporium. Owner Danny Edwards learned well from his pop, legendary smokemaster Jake Edwards. He dry-rubs his ribs in a secret spice mixture before smoking them out back for about eight hours. The result is a deep-down flavored slab that's tender but with just enough chewy texture to make you work at falling in love.

The brisket sandwich—arguably the most tender in town—is the top seller, with ribs and burnt ends running close behind. Danny also does a mean barbecued chicken. Don't look for fries or onion rings at the joint; there's simply no room for a fryer. But perhaps a fudgy brownie from McLain's Bakery will provide the missing calories. The place is packed for lunch Monday through Friday; it is, alas, closed on weekends.

Fiorella's Jack Stack Barbecue $-$$
1344 Holmes (South Kansas City)
(816) 942-9141

9520 Metcalf
Overland Park, KS
(913) 385-7427

22nd and Wyandotte
(Freight House District)
(816) 472-7427
www.jackstackbbq.com
Around here, we tend to steer clear of barbecue chains. A famous rib place tried to infiltrate our town a few years ago and soon went back to North Miami wondering, "What happened? They loved us in Dallas!" But Jack Stack's growing empire is just fine with us, because they started right here in the 1950s.

The latest location, next to Lidia's in the bustling Freight House area near Union Station, is a fancy-pants version with a gorgeous bar, soaring ceilings, and cushy booths. One diner walked in, whistled, and said, "This is where gluttony gets an etiquette lesson." If purists refuse to eat 'cue at any restaurant with a wine rack it's their loss; Zagat reviewers say this is the best barbecue in the nation. And it's casual enough to show up in jeans.

The original restaurant in Martin City is definitely laid back. It looks like a house that's been expanded a few times to make room for relatives. The second location, on Metcalf, is an attractive space with a huge parking lot that is still overflowing on weekends. The menus at all three locations are big enough to blanket the table, filled with a mind-boggling selection of barbecued meats, hickory-grilled poultry and

fish, and certified Angus steaks. Kiss your low-fat diet goodbye and start with a rack of thick-cut, battered onion rings big enough to wear as bracelets. They come to the table stacked like a kid's toy on a copper skewer. Other side dishes include a rich cheesy corn casserole, slightly sweet coleslaw, and fabulous hickory pit beans thickened with chunks of burnt ends, ham, and meat drippings.

Jack Stack serves five types of ribs, including pork and beef spare ribs, baby back, and lamb ribs that got rave reviews in the London Times and New York Times. Along with steaks, sausage, pork chops, and crown prime rib, there are fire-grilled chicken, fish, and shrimp. Sandwiches include the Martin City Mayor—named for the restaurant's original home—made with chopped burnt ends topped with coleslaw on a French bun.

All three locations are open for lunch and dinner seven days a week. And here's good news for you unfortunate souls who can't get to Kansas City often enough: Jack Stack's ships their award-winning ribs and other smoked meats anywhere. Check the Web site or call for information.

Gates Bar-B-Q $
1325 East Emanuel Cleaver II Boulevard
(816) 531-7522

2001 West 103rd Street
Leawood, KS
(913) 383-1752

3205 Main Street (Downtown)
(816) 753-0828

1221 Brooklyn (East Side)
(816) 483-3880

10440 East 40 Highway
Independence, MO
(816) 353-5880

1026 State Avenue
Kansas City, KS
(913) 621-1134
www.gatesbbq.com
It's always fun to watch a tenderfoot walk through the door and take a step back-

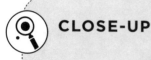

Kansas City Barbecue

Welcome to the Barbecue Capital of the world. Oh, we know: The Carolinas claim to be the cradle of American barbecue, and Texas has the brisket circuit sewn up. But here in the Midwest we've perfected the technique so well it's often referred to by the generic term "Kansas City barbecue," as if the city and the food are forever intertwined.

To really appreciate barbecue you've got to talk the talk. First off, true aficionados consider "barbecue" a noun, not a verb, although the rest of us tend to use it both ways. It refers to beef or pork that's been slow-cooked over wood—often hickory, cherry, or apple wood to add a subtle flavor—for hours. And we do mean hours. It's a commitment of time and constant attention, turning it into a recreational sport that calls for cold beer and good friends. A brisket or slab of ribs can take eight hours or more of monitoring the fire to make sure the temperature doesn't vary more than a dozen degrees. This patient technique makes barbecue distinctly different from Kansas City's preferred method of cooking steak, grilling quickly over a flame stoked as high as 1,400 degrees F.

The result is a succulent morsel of meat. But saying ribs are so tender they fall off the bone is not necessarily a compliment; it may mean they've been parboiled—a real no-no that local experts call *faux que*. Say it fast and you'll get the message.

And don't expect your barbecue to show up slathered with sauce. Although meat is often dry-rubbed with a spice mixture before going into the smoker, the sauce—if applied at all—is mopped on right before serving or during the final minutes of cooking so the sugars in the sauce don't burn. That's another thing: Although there are exceptions like the vinegary version at Arthur Bryant's, for the most part Kansas City sauce is on the sweet side thanks to its molasses-spiked tomato base. If you want more sauce with your brisket sandwich, you'll usually find a bottle or two of the thick, mahogany-colored liquid on the table, often sporting the restaurant's label. Don't even think about asking for the recipe. Around here ingredients are guarded as carefully as Zsa Zsa Gabor's birthdate.

If you're getting the idea that barbecue isn't merely a food group but our city's true identity, you're halfway there. Or as members of the Kansas City Barbecue Society like to say, "Barbeque. It's not just for breakfast anymore." Membership in KCBS—the world's largest, with 2,500 members in 50 states and 11 countries—is $30 a year. Contact them at 11514 Hickman Mills Drive, Kansas City, MO 64121. Or call (816) 765-5891 or (800) 963-KCBS, or visit www.rbjb.com.

KCBS members—and the rest of us—are eternally grateful to Henry Perry. He introduced the food group to Kansas City in the late 1920s when he started selling ribs out of a trolley barn at 19th and Highland. A slab back then—wrapped in pages of newsprint—cost 25 cents. Henry's barn became 'Cue University for local legends like George Gates and Charlie Bryant. Charlie eventually bought the place and expanded it with help from his brother Arthur. After Charlie died Arthur tinkered with the sauce—the original was so hot it nearly caused blisters—and moved the business to 1727 Brooklyn. The lunch lines have never stopped.

As for its preparation, while the main ingredients and basic techniques passed down from Henry are universal, the sauce recipe and even the hardwoods used for smoking are often closely guarded secrets. In Kansas City, saying one barbecue restaurant is the best in town can start a heated debate. Heck, we can't even agree on one single spelling of the name: barbecue, barbeque, BBQ, or bar-b-que. When it comes time for locals to pick their favorites, the criteria are usually split into categories like best fries, best ribs, best brisket, or best sauce.

We'll let you decide. But pace yourself; there are 80 or so barbecue outlets in town. We've listed some of the top achievers in this chapter. But before you go, here's a quick primer, courtesy of the Kansas City Barbecue Society, to help you place your order.

- **Baby back ribs:** Also known as loin back ribs, these are cut from the pork loin and usually weigh about two pounds per slab.

- **Barbecue:** To slow cook meats over hardwood (some folks use charcoal or a mix of the two) at a temperature of 200 to 375 degrees F.

- **Burnt Ends:** Blackened, somewhat charred pieces of brisket that are too charred to slice. These are served with plenty of sauce and highly prized at restaurants. Sometimes they're called "brownies."

- **Glaze:** A finishing sauce applied to meat—what's called mopping—during the final minutes of barbecuing.

- **Long end spare ribs:** The first six ribs from the breastbone on back.

- **Pit:** The cooking unit used to barbecue. You'll see everything around here, from black barrels on legs to cement or brick open structures. A good smokemaster can produce great barbecue from a hole in the ground.

- **Rib tips:** The breastbone at the top of a slab of spare ribs.

- **Rub:** A dry marinade—usually a closely guarded mixture of dry spices and herbs—that's liberally massaged into meats to impart flavor.

- **Short end spare ribs:** The last seven or eight ribs in a slab of spare ribs. We're calling dibs right now.

- **Wood chips:** Small chips of wood used to impart smoky flavor to barbecued meats. Hickory is perhaps the most popular, but plenty of experts use fruitwood like apple or cherry because it's slightly sweeter. Some people cut the bitterness of hickory by mixing in fruitwood.

If preparing barbecue sounds like a huge commitment in time and trouble, we have a solution: Skip the wood, get on the road, and let a master smoker prepare it for you. You'll find some of the city's most popular barbecue restaurants elsewhere in this chapter. Happy eating.

ward when assailed by a loud "May I help you?" from behind the counter. Answer quickly because with these crowds, they don't ask twice. The menu is printed on the wall above the open kitchen, but if you get flustered just remember you can't go wrong with the ribs and fries.

Or go for the mixed plate to try the ribs, beef brisket, and beef sausage. Once you're handed your plate of smoky 'cue, head to the side table to load up on one or all four flavors of sauce. The mild version makes a fine catsup substitute for dipping fries. And don't be surprised if you find yourself heading back to the line, this time yelling back at the order taker, "Yeah, you can help me. Give me a slab to go."

Lunch and dinner hours vary by location. Call ahead.

Hayward's Pit Bar-B-Que $
11051 Antioch Road
Overland Park, KS
(913) 451-8080
www.haywardsbbq.com

Hayward Spears and his family have been adding a smoky haze to Johnson County since the mid-1970s. Far too classy to be considered a barbecue joint, Hayward's offers a chance to relax and enjoy succulent ribs and sandwiches piled high with beef, pork, ham, or combinations. For lots of flavor condensed into a bite-size package, try the burnt ends as a sandwich or part of a combo meal. The onion rings are big, fat crunchy affairs, and the beans have plenty of meaty chunks.

This place does a huge take-out business, and Hayward was smart enough to build a separate order-taking alcove so that things don't get quite so crowded on Friday and Saturday nights. If you're eating in, check out the collection of Angus and Hereford horns on the walls, 3-foot testaments to our cowtown heritage. Hayward's is open for lunch and dinner seven days a week and does a brisk catering business.

L.C.'s Bar-B-Q (East Side) $
5800 Blue Parkway
(816) 923-4484

This is the place to find true Kansas City lip-smacking barbecue: smoky ribs, brisket that will make you weep, and perhaps the best fries in the world. Although not as famous as Arthur Bryant's, it's usually on the top-five list of people who really know their smoked meat. The sauce is sweet and tangy. You'll want to eat until you hurt.

Table space is generally gone by a quarter to noon, and when there's a Saturday game at Kauffman Stadium, cars line up early. Be forewarned, though: This is far from a fancy location. Perhaps there's a good reason for the bars on the windows, and even the smoker in the parking lot is chained to a utility pole. Lunch and dinner are served Monday through Saturday.

Oklahoma Joe's BBQ $
47th and Mission Road
Kansas City, KS
(913) 722-3366

No doubt Jeff and Joy Stehney heard every imaginable joke using "gas" and "restaurant" in the same sentence when they started serving barbecue in a space shared by a Total filling station, convenience store, and liquor store. Now they're laughing all the way to the bank as people line up noon and night for award-winning fare. The walls are lined with just a few of the 300 or so trophies Joe and his team have won at contests around the country, including a coveted Grand Champion statue the size of a three-year old.

This is simply outrageously good barbecue. And while competitors often excel at one or two items, at Oklahoma's everything is superb. Favorites include lip-smacking ribs, burnt ends, and Carolina-style sandwiches, that Southern treat of pulled pork topped with spicy slaw. The gumbo, a rather unusual menu entry, is thick with chunks of smoked chicken, ham, and okra. It's as good as anything served in New Orleans. By 11:30 the lunch line to Joe's snakes around the corner, with folks sharing stories of their first time here or eager to get their mitts on a Hog Heaven (pulled pork and sliced sausage on a bun) or a Lean-n-Mean (smoked turkey on Texas toast topped with spicy slaw).

They'll slap smoked meats on anything here, including salads. You can have your greens topped with shredded pork, cold sliced brisket, or hot boneless chicken. Have a salad if you must, but don't skip the fries. In supersize-me portions, they're some of the best in the city. So are the rest of the sides, which are—along with that mighty fine gumbo—available in pint and quart containers to go. The sauce is also for sale, a garnet-colored, slightly sweet concoction called Cowtown Bar-B-Q that ranked first at the 2001 American Royal Barbecue Contest. Jeff also sells four seasonings to rub into meats before smoking or grilling. And of course you'll want an "I got smoked to the bone" T-shirt designed by local cartoonist Charlie Podrebarac.

The line starts to form again for the dinner specials. Prices can't be beat: on Monday and Tuesday half a smoked chicken with two sides and Texas toast is just $5.95. Thursday is rib night, when a full slab goes for just shy of 13 bucks. The menu suggests a slab will serve two to three people; they obviously haven't watched some of us eat.

Oklahoma Joe's has a great atmosphere where families, couples, and singles pack into three booths, 16 tables, and a long counter facing a view of regular and premium pumps. The beer is flowing, the barbecue is smoking, and the stereo is blaring, "Got My Mojo Workin'." Can it get any better than this? Well, yes. They could be open on Sunday. And if they would just do something about that name.

Rosedale Barbecue $
600 Southwest Boulevard
Kansas City, KS
(913) 262–0343
Naturally this joint knows how to smoke meaty ribs and flavorful brisket. They've been doing it since 1934, longer than anyone else in Kansas City. For years this no-frills place was called a "bucket shop"

because it sold beer in metal cans. Although a little more sterile since remodeling a few years back, it still retains a slightly funky atmosphere. And Rosedale certainly passes the litmus test for good 'cue: Lines extend out both side doors by noon. It can be a madhouse, but you can always show up when the crowds are gone; it's open until 10:00 P.M. Monday through Saturday and until 8:00 P.M. on Sunday.

Fans go for the hearty beef, pork, and ham sandwiches, or "half bird and fries," tasty barbecued chicken and crispy zigzag-cut fries served hot in a waxed paper bag. The baby back ribs are tender and lean but are only available on Sunday. And Wednesday brings another rare treat: all-you-can-eat riblet dinners. If you don't care for barbecue—say it isn't so!—there's also homemade chili and a kielbasa sandwich.

CAJUN/CREOLE

Jazz—A Louisiana Kitchen $–$$
1823 West 39th Street
(816) 531–5556
Kick the fun up another notch at this rowdy Kansas City mainstay where the walls are covered with Mardi Gras posters and graffiti from past visitors. You'll want to add your own comment or signature after digging into traditional Cajun dishes like blackened seafood, gumbo, oysters on the half shell, and po'boy sandwiches. Or just order the all-you-can-eat hushpuppies for $139; the order includes a free bottle of Dom Perignon.

At night this becomes party central as live jazz, Dixieland, and blues play five nights a week. During the day it's often a hangout for interns from the KU Medical Center up the street looking for a little relaxation and roux between rounds. They can replace their stethoscopes with Mardi Gras beads. Make sure to get your own colorful necklace before you leave.

Jazz is open from 11:00 A.M. to midnight daily.

CASUAL DINING FAMILY STYLE

**Stephenson's Old Apple Farm
(East Side)** $-$$
16401 East 40 Highway
(816) 373-5400

Stephenson's opened more than 50 years ago as a tiny diner next to the family's orchard, simply a way to extend the market for the bountiful fruit. Today it's where generations have spent countless Sunday dinners and celebrated untold birthdays. You'll understand its popularity as soon as you walk through the vine-covered courtyard or taste a sample of apple cider while waiting for your table. For something with a little more punch, order a delectable apple daiquiri.

There's more down-home goodness waiting at the table, whether you choose to dine in the Parlor, the Cupboard, the Yard, the Backporch, or the Larder. Your meal includes samples of savory corn relish and hot apple fritters with homemade apple butter. Many a diner has filled up on these, but try to pace yourself. There's fork-tender barbecued brisket waiting, along with baked chicken in cream and hickory-smoked ribs. Some folks show up just for the green rice, a custardlike concoction flecked with parsley, a dish that has single-handedly sold thousands of the restaurant's cookbook.

It should come as no surprise that apple dumplings top the dessert list. Or you could always take your dessert with you; during harvest time apples are lined up along the windowsill for you to take

your pick. The cookbook, cider, and other farm-made goodies are available in the original country store.

Stephenson's serves lunch Monday through Saturday and dinner daily.

Stroud's (South Kansas City) $
1015 East 85th Street
(816) 333-2132

There's just one reason to wait an hour or two inside this rickety 1920s roadhouse on Friday and Saturday nights: to get your mitts on the best pan-fried chicken you've ever tasted. Reservations are not taken; you simply give your name to the guy with the clipboard the moment you walk in. During summer some folks avoid the line by ordering dinners to go, and then setting up tailgate parties in nearby parking lots.

But most people don't mind the wait—except perhaps for parents with small children—because the crowd is festive, there's a full bar, and the aroma of fried chicken serves as a constant reminder of the final reward. Once seated, remember that everything is served family style, so whatever chicken dinner you order will arrive at the table on large platters and in bowls to pass around. Don't worry, we've never seen a table run out of fluffy mashed potatoes, slow-cooked green beans, peppery cream gravy, cottage fries, or french fries. Skip the catsup and dunk the fries in gravy like most guests do.

To start you'll have your choice of chicken noodle soup or salad, and every dinner ends with a basket of warm cinnamon rolls. Like magic your server will show up with doggie bags and packets of hand wipes. But back to that chicken. Stroud's serves it steaming hot from the 14-inch cast-iron skillets. The crispy golden brown crust falls away to reveal tender, juicy chicken that was deemed "the best chicken on the planet" by the *New York Times*.

If chicken isn't your thing, there are tasty pork chops served pan-fried or broiled in garlic butter sauce, chicken-fried steaks, pan-fried catfish, and deep-fried shrimp. The waitresses are friendly, efficient, and polite enough to laugh at what-

---

i *Dining out with little ones? Lots of our restaurants cater to kids, with special menus, coloring books, or toys to keep them happy and occupied. Some of the best are Yahooz! in Leawood, the Crayola Cafe in Crown Center, and Winstead's, where children can share a Skyscraper ice-cream soda and listen to the jukebox.*

ever chicken joke you care to share, and the piano player knows everyone's favorite song. And if you're looking for a reminder of your visit beyond that doggie bag, buy a "We Choke Our Own Chickens" T-shirt.

Stroud's is open for lunch Friday through Sunday and dinner daily.

Winstead's (Country Club Plaza and other locations) $
101 Brush Creek Boulevard
(816) 753-2244
Since 1940 this has been the place to come for burgers and shakes, and other than a few menu updates not much has changed since then. The waitresses still wear jaunty uniforms, the jukebox still plays great tunes—no quarters required, just punch in your favorite rock 'n' roll tunes—and most important, they continue to live up to their 60-year motto, "We grind U.S. choice steak daily for the sandwich."

For newcomers, it's only fair to describe the famous Winstead's steakburger—available as singles, doubles, or triples. But don't expect quarter-pound patties. These are flat, thin circles of beef that are broiled on a greaseless grill. In fact the onion slice is thicker than the burger, so you won't be remiss if you order a double. But it's the combination of flavors—the grilled beef with slightly crispy edges, fat slice of sweet onion, tangy mustard-and-ketchup sauce, pickle sliced the long way, and unadorned bun—that beats all other burgers hands down. It's even wrapped in paper and presented on your plate like a gift.

To complete your experience get the Special Chocolate Frosty, "the exclusive Winstead drink you eat with a spoon." They mean it, try to suck this creamy concoction through a straw and we know for a fact your head will cave in. Only after the drink has partially melted, on the off chance there's any left, should you even consider unwrapping the straw. During hot summer days the limeade is a refreshing substitute, made with plenty of shaved ice and a perky hat of lime sherbet. For families or a table of teens it's great fun to order a Skyscraper Soda; this monster of

an ice-cream treat is served in a glass about a foot tall and is meant to be shared by two to four people.

Winstead's is open daily for breakfast, lunch, and dinner.

CHINESE

Blue Koi (Midtown) $-$$
1803 West 39th Street
(816) 561-5003
The sponged aqua walls of this relative newcomer to Restaurant Row isn't the only cool thing about this dumpling and noodle shop. The menu lists unexpected dishes that appeal to both vegetarians and carnivores alike. And for the kid in all of us there are 11 flavors of bubble tea, which is all the rage in San Francisco's China Town. This iced milk and tea drink is made with tapioca balls that float to the bottom of the glass, waiting for you to slurp them up through a straw. Like your tea straight? You'll find an extensive list of aromatic brews, including a slightly floral scented jasmine, to go with your meal. If you have the time or interest, invest in the Gong Fu tea ceremony, available from 2:00 to 5:00 P.M., which includes an array of small cups and fragrant tea that's been scented seven times.

But it's the Chang family's comfort food that has people filling the long, narrow space for lunch and dinner. The Chinese pot roast, a slab of slow-roasted, fork-tender beef ladled over wide strips of noodles, is addictive. Or follow the menu's lead and order Ants on a Tree, a Taiwanese dish of sautéed minced pork and shredded cabbage served with amber-colored cellophane noodles.

Seven types of dumplings are available to order either boiled or pan-fried as a meal or an appetizer to share. The duck wrap is another excellent starter; shredded roasted duck is mixed with cucumber, cilantro, and a tangy and slightly sweet hoisin sauce and served in a soft breaded wrap.

Vegans will be happy to find several tempting dishes, including a vegetarian dumpling, lettuce wrap, and braised tofu with shiitake mushroom entree.

Bo Lings $
9055 Metcalf Avenue
Overland Park, KS
(913) 341-1718

4800 Main Street (Country Club Plaza)
(816) 753-1718

9574 Quivira Road
Lenexa, KS
(913) 888-6618

7105 West 135th Street
Overland Park, KS
(913) 239-8188
www.bolings.com

When Kansas Citians are hungry for Chinese food, those in the know head for one of Richard and Theresa Ng's restaurants. Their original place, a beautiful showroom in pale teal and dark wood in the Plaza's Board of Trade Building, gained them a loyal following. Johnson County fans were thrilled when they opened three more locations closer to home.

Richard's food is fresh, flavorful, and authentic; in fact he often visits Hong Kong's best restaurants for ideas to bring back home. The extensive menu includes Cantonese lettuce wraps, General Tso's Chicken, shrimp, and scallops in garlic sauce, sizzling black pepper beef, and fried noodles. Even the rice is special: a blend of aromatic jasmine and fluffy American long grain. A house specialty is succulent Beijing roasted duck. These plump, rice-fed ducks are cooked in custom-designed hanging ovens that let the fat drip away as the skin becomes crisp and russet colored. The duck is then carved and tucked into soft steamed buns along with slivers of cucumber, green onion, and sweet plum sauce. It may become your new favorite dish.

On Saturday and Sunday a dim sum brunch is served at the Plaza and Metcalf locations. This wildly popular event offers over 50 appetizers, including steamed barbecue pork buns, shrimp dumplings, and stuffed eggplant. All four locations are open seven days a week.

Genghis Khan Mongolian Grill (Midtown) $
3901 Bell
(816) 753-3600
www.genghiskhankc.com

This large corner restaurant with exposed brick walls and wooden floors is always packed thanks to the variety of food, a fun atmosphere, and incredible value. Although the menu offers tempting dishes, most regulars ignore the printed list and head for the all-you-can-eat buffet.

For lunch grab a plate and start piling on your choice of 20 different fresh vegetables and sliced beef, chicken, pork, crab, catfish, and squid. At night the selections expand to include shrimp, scallops, lamb, Chinese sausage, and mahimahi. Then add a splash of sauce. You can create your own flavor from 20 ingredients like soy sauce, ginger, and garlic, or use the handy recipes provided. Finally, hand your overflowing plate to the barbecue cook, who will grill it before your eyes. Prices include appetizers like crab rangoon and spicy chicken wings and dessert.

Expect a crowd by noon, when this becomes a hangout for interns and staffers from nearby KU Med Center, vegetarians, and anyone else looking for fresh flavorful food at a bargain price. Lunch starts at just $7.50, and dinner is around $13.00 depending on whether your creation includes meat. Genghis Khan is open for lunch and dinner Monday through Saturday, and offers unique cocktails that add to the fun.

FRENCH

Even though our first official settler was French, it would be some 150 years before we acquired more than one restaurant serving Gallic food. Today we have some of the finest French bistros this side of the Atlantic, attended to by chefs who, more often than not, came here for love and ended up falling in love with the city as well.

Aixois (Midtown) $$
251 East 55th
(816) 333-3305

Pronounced *Ex-WAH*, this chic bistro came to be when Megan and Emmanuel Langlade met at another French restaurant in Parkville, fell madly in love, married, and left to open their own place. And what a charming rendezvous it is, snuggled in the back corner of a block of antiques and design shops in the gentile Crestwood neighborhood. In fact, to reach the restaurant you can enter through the delightful Bloomsday Books or its own door, where you'll pass by a tiny coffee bar. The coffee service alone hints of what's ahead; stirrers are mismatched silver spoons rather than white plastic sticks.

Inside the bistro, mustard-yellow walls and exposed bricks and ceiling beams set the mood. And while the menu is small, there are enough daily specials to warrant a weekly reservation. Many devotees would be quite happy to order Emmanuel's truite saumon meunière every single day; this ruby trout sautéed in lemon butter and topped with slivered almonds is so popular it's served for both lunch and dinner. For sheer presentation, it doesn't get much better than coppery salmon peeking out from beneath a golden brown parchment paper package.

But if a restaurant can make its name simply for potatoes, this one can. We hate to use the term french fries when describing pommes frites because no fast-food joint ever offered such crisp-tender slivers of spuds. They're served with a number of items, including the peppered flank steak, Kansas City strip, and Prince Edward Island mussels in a luscious cream sauce. Starters are also delicious, especially a classic salade niçoise, a lovely composed salad of tuna, tomatoes, tiny black olives, and hard-boiled egg on a bed of greens with a tangy vinaigrette, and the peppery arugula and strawberries with warm goat cheese. The luxurious pâtés are all made in-house.

If you can't decide which dessert to have, have them all with the assiettes Aixoise, a decadent display that includes crème brûlée, chocolate mousse, fresh fruit with puree, and profiterole with chocolate. Aixois serves lunch and dinner Tuesday through Saturday. The coffee bar is open seven days a week.

Cafe des Amis $$
112½ Main Street
Parkville, MO
(816) 587-6767
www.cafedesamiskc.com

It's easy to pretend you're in a village in France while sitting on this sun-dappled deck with the fragrance of roast duck swirling around you. The clincher is handsome owner Didier Combe's accent as he asks if the escargot is to your liking.

Didier's recipes, from his mother's kitchen in Aix-en-Provence, are brought brilliantly to life by chef Frank Marciniak. The menu includes classics such as coquilles Saint Jacques and new masterpieces such as a casserole of organic vegetables, aromatic herbs, and tangy goat cheese. For lunch there are lovely crepes, and at night the filet in a sauce of cognac, peppercorns, and Roquefort will have you swooning.

Desserts include crepes filled with a dark chocolate sauce and a shimmering tart served with caramel sauce. While the deck seating is divine, the bistro also has small—and we do mean small—rooms inside. But no one's complaining; the close quarters give you one more reason to sit knee-to-knee with your sweetheart.

Cafe des Amis serves lunch Wednesday through Saturday, dinner Wednesday through Sunday, and Sunday brunch from noon to 3:00 P.M.

Cafe Provence $$
3936 West 69th Terrace
Prairie Village, KS
(913) 384-5998
www.cafeprovence.net

Hannah Bistro Cafe owner Patrick Quillec opened his second location to the delight of his legions of Johnson County fans.

And if the windows look out over a parking lot rather than the Seine, who cares? It's the food that counts, and the chef does not disappoint. As for atmosphere, the television at the bar is always tuned to a French station, where even a traffic report sounds romantic.

And the food—especially the sunny, saffrony bouillabaisse—looks like you've traveled to Provence. But if you really want to savor your seafood, opt for the mussels in a white wine, garlic, and shallot sauce so decadent you'll beg for more bread. Other classic French dishes include steak tartar and pan-seared frog legs served with a rosy tomato coulis. And, ah, for dessert, there's crème caramel, lemon tart, and profiteroles, which are pastry puffs topped with ribbons of chocolate ganache and served with homemade ice cream. Lunch is available weekdays; dinner is served Monday through Saturday.

Hannah Bistro Cafe   **$$**
7070 West 105th Street
Overland Park, KS
(913) 383-1000
www.hannahbistro.com

This fashionable place is so special it requires two qualifiers: bistro and cafe. Fans have no such confusion about chef Patrick Quillec's food, however. The French-inspired American cuisine, with just a dash of Asian flavors, is considered some of the finest in town. The menu is divided into small and large plates, so it's easy to put together a meal to match your appetite or share bites with tablemates. Can't decide between the soups? Have the sampler and taste all three flavors of the day. Patrick likes to create combinations that balance each other in taste and texture, so one day the trio might include roasted yellow bell pepper bisque, apple and Brie, and cheddar and ale. Add the marvelous crab cakes layered between paper-thin leaves of potato and pesto aioli and you have the perfect lunch. A lighter choice might be the best-selling salad that features fried goat cheese on a bed of butter lettuce with cumin vinaigrette.

If you go a little weak at the knees over the Brittany-style mussels, you won't be alone. Patrick prepares 150 pounds a week of the fresh shellfish in a white wine, garlic, and cream sauce. The most popular entree is the grilled filet mignon crowned with a pesto and shallot confit and served with potato gratin. And fans begged Patrick to bring back Shrimp Philip, a pasta dish he named for his son. And just who is Hannah? Why, she's the chef's pretty daughter.

Save room for the apple tart, warm caramelized Granny Smith apples in puff pastry served with homemade cinnamon ice cream. Hannah's is also one of our favorite piano bars, a very romantic place for cocktails before dinner or cognac after. Lunch is available weekdays; dinner is served Monday through Saturday.

Le Fou Frog (River Market)   **$$–$$$**
400 East Fifth Street
(816) 474-6060
www.lefoufrog.com

It only makes sense that this cozy French bistro would land in the historic River Market district not far from where our famous first Frenchman made his home. The rest of us are just glad chef Mano Rafael followed his heart—and his bride, Barbara, a Kansas City native—to our river town as well. The move was easier for him than you might think, because the area reminds him of the port city of Marseille.

Since opening in 1997 Mano has thrilled guests with classic French dishes such as escargot with garlic butter and seared rack of lamb coated with Dijon mustard and herbs. Order the steak au proivre with pommes frites, those thin and crispy fried potatoes, and pretend you're sitting in a small cafe on the rue de la whatever.

After more than eight years, there's still a steady buzz about Mano's moules marinieres, which are Prince Edward Island mussels steamed in a broth of white wine, shallots, mustard, and heavy cream. But don't overlook the osso buco Corsican, slow-braised veal shanks in a red wine veal broth topped with thin slices of prosciutto and shaved mozzarella. His cassoulet of duck breast is a savory mixture of sausages from Toulouse, lamb, flageolet beans, rosemary, and garlic. If there's room left for dessert, the warm apple tart is a fitting ending to the evening.

Le Fou Frog, which means the crazy Frenchman, serves lunch Wednesday, Thursday, and Friday and dinner Tuesday through Sunday. It also hosts events like a Bastille Day celebration, wine tastings, and a Valentine's Day feast that features food declared to be aphrodisiacs. To turn even a winter's evening into a party, a heated tent is available year-round. One bit of warning: This place is very noisy and boisterous, and that's just how the owner and most of the patrons like it. But if you're looking for a quiet, intimate evening, this may not be your best choice.

Tatsu's $$
4603 West 90th Street
Prairie Village, KS
(913) 383-9801
www.tatsus.com

Don't let the location in an unassuming strip mall dissuade you from coming here. Just pop in a French CD and pretend you're driving your Renault past the Eiffel Tower rather than a firehouse in Johnson County. Inside, the space is lovely with candlelight, fresh flowers, and even fresher food. Japanese-born owner and chef Tatsu Arai has been adding a delicate touch to classic French cuisine to the delight of his longtime fans since 1980. Specialties include braised oxtails cooked in a red wine sauce and Jacques a la Moutarde, which is poached shrimp, scallops, and mushrooms in mustard sauce served in a puff pastry shell. Entrees come with salad, fresh vegetables, and home-baked bread. And after you've fallen in love with the house-made salad dressing, you'll be glad to know it's available by the bottle.

By now we hope you've ordered the Grand Marnier soufflé. It's a lovely sight on a pool of crème anglaise and stripes of dark chocolate sauce. And notice, please, the two dollar signs in Tatsu's heading. It is

truly amazing to find food and service this splendid for so few francs.

Lunch is served Monday through Friday; dinner is served Monday through Saturday.

INTERNATIONAL

La Bodega (Midtown) $$
703 Southwest Boulevard
(816) 472-8272
www.labodegakc.com

This boisterous cafe is where you'll find out which of your friends learned to share in kindergarten. For at La Bodega, most of the menu is composed of hot and cold tapas—little savory appetizers—that are meant to be passed around the table. We've come to love the Basque way of socializing so much we often graze this way for hours, with a different dish arriving every few minutes to a round of applause. Complete the Spanish tradition with a glass of sherry. La Bodega also serves lovely old ports, wines, and a fabulous sangria.

Top-selling cold tapas include marinated olives, roasted red peppers stuffed with tuna and rice, and asparagus spears wrapped in smoked salmon. Hot versions to try are skewered chicken and chorizo with garlic-cumin mayo, squid sautéed in olive oil and garlic, and Pimento Del Piquillo Relleno, meatballs in a spicy garlic cream sauce. This last dish is so savory you'll want to make a boat with your bread—*hacer una barco* in Spanish—and sail it around the plate to pick up every bit of sauce.

If you still have room for entrees, two of the most popular are grilled steak with blue cheese and the Spanish paellas. The seafood version is loaded with shrimp, chunks of whitefish, scallops, mussels, and littleneck clams and served with lots of saffrony-yellow rice. Skip the dessert and spend your last pesos on the special coffee made with several types of liqueurs. As you're sipping you'll have time to study the colorful decor, especially the mosaic bar and fabulous mural by local artist Peregrine Honig.

Lunch is available Monday through Saturday. Dinner is served daily.

Piropos   **$$-$$$**
1 West First Street
Parkville, MO
(816) 741-3600
www.piroposkc.com

In Buenos Aires the women are so beautiful that admirers have created an art form—loosely translated into piropos—for paying them compliments. The lovely Cristina Worden received a particularly fine piropo from husband Gary; he built a restaurant to showcase her country's cuisine.

The view alone will have you whistling in admiration. The restaurant's walls of windows and deck make the most of a hilltop setting overlooking downtown Parkville, the Park University spire, and the lights of Kansas City's skyline in the distance. And if you miss out on an outside view a mural provides additional charm. Can you spot Cristina and Gary among the painted figures?

At Piropos the food is the star, especially since it's based on ingredients we appreciate in the Midwest: excellent steaks and fresh salads. It's the trio of sauces that sets this cuisine apart: creamy garlic aioli; criolla made with peppers, tomato, celery, and vinegar; and chimichurri, that Argentinean staple made with parsley, garlic, vinegar, and olive oil. The sauces are served in tiny pots along with empanadas—the spiced beef version is especially flavorful—so you can pick your favorite.

There are some surprises on the menu. The fact that nearly half of Argentina is made up of Italians is evident in pasta dishes like ricotta and spinach stuffed ravioli with a walnut-studded butter sauce. A pan-seared halibut brushed with a roasted red pepper puree leads the fish choices. But it's the grilled meats that stand out at Piropos, including succulent steaks, lamb, and pork chops. You'll find yourself asking for more sauces for dipping.

The desserts provide another nod to the Argentinian way of life. Dulce de leche—a caramel known in South America

as milk candy—is drizzled over creamy flan, chocolate cake, and apple-filled crepes. Piropos serves dinner only, Tuesday through Sunday.

re:Verse (Country Club Plaza)   **$$**
618 Ward Parkway
(816) 931-7811
www.reversekc.com

La Bodega owner James Taylor had an instant hit when he opened this hip place on one of the Plaza's most visible corners. The Beat Generation theme doesn't matter to the mostly twenty-somethings at the bar, but the retro cocktails certainly do. The list includes grasshoppers, stingers, and martinis and a refreshing mojito made by adding white rum to a muddled mix of mint, sugar, and lime. The cocktails keep coming until 1:30 A.M., making it one of the late-night lounges of choice.

The decor is just as stylish as the crowd, with lipstick-red walls and ceiling, stainless steel panels, and viewing screens that let you peek into the kitchen. It can be quite a show on busy nights. The menu stars tapas, like its sister restaurant on the Boulevard: spicy tidbits to share with dining partners. The trio of ahi tuna slices is a nice choice; they're seared, tied with scallions like little packages, and served with a peanut-chili sauce. The sautéed calamari and spicy chorizo is a sensual delight on a stark white plate.

Pasta dishes are just as artfully dressed, and the grape-leaf wrapped sea bass is roasted then placed on a bed of sautéed chard and creamy Israeli couscous. It's a dish that's big enough to share, especially if you've spent the first half of the evening trying several tapas. Re:Verse is open for lunch Monday through Saturday and dinner seven nights a week. For early birds, it serves espresso starting at 6:45 A.M. and breakfast from 7:00 to 10:30 A.M. Monday through Friday.

Shiraz (Crossroads Arts District)   **$$**
320 Southwest Boulevard
(816) 472-0015

Stephanie and Ali Shirazi's first eatery was

the West Side Cafe, a phone booth-sized place in a reconditioned gas station. When they moved to a bigger and prettier space a few blocks down the street loyal fans followed, hungry for Ali's black beans and rice, tandoori chicken, and anything he decided to curry that day.

With its exposed brick walls, artwork from local artists, and metal cutouts at the windows casting intricate shadows at noon and night, Shiraz has a welcoming bohemian atmosphere. Low lights, flickering candles, and the heady fragrance of exotic spices make for a very sexy evening. If you notice that half the patrons have ordered the roasted red pepper appetizer, there's a reason. This terra-cotta colored dip of peppers, walnuts, pomegranate syrup, and tahini is addictive. It's served with warm toasted pita bread, and for another dollar a tasty black olive hummus will share the plate. Split the appetizer with a friend, add two fresh Greek-style salads, and you have a marvelous lunch.

Standouts on the dinner menu include pork chops served with a piquant pomegranate glaze, and Ali's signature dish, gormeh sabzi: lamb shank braised with aromatic Persian herbs and sun-dried lemons until tender and flavorful. His eggplant Marrakesh stuffed with rice, tomatoes, and feta cheese is one of the most coveted vegetarian meals in town. Listen carefully to the dinner specials as well; if the server mentions sea bass, raise your hand immediately. It's always meltingly tender, a dish you'll dream about for weeks. With food this flavorful and plates filled to brimming, it's hard to save room for dessert. But it would be a shame to miss the flourless chocolate cake, hazelnut praline crunch, and chocolate mousse served with hazelnut ice cream. It's divine.

During nice weather ask for a table in the courtyard where, especially on balmy Saturday nights when a guitarist is playing lush flamenco music, there simply isn't a more romantic urban setting. Shiraz is open Monday through Friday for lunch and Tuesday through Saturday for dinner.

ITALIAN

Carmen's Cafe (Brookside) $-$$
6307 Brookside Boulevard
(816) 333-4048
This tiny place truly is a family affair, with the three Bautista brothers, Juan, Gabrielle, and Francisco, serving Mama Carmen's recipes. Regulars feel like family as well, particularly those seated at the counter where they can watch the kitchen staff working in a space roughly the size of a Buick's backseat.

Despite the kitchen's dimensions the menu is huge and displays a Spanish influence with tapas and flaky empanadas. Most people, however, show up for Italian food like linguini with white clam sauce and chicken spiedini.

Garozzo's Ristorante $-$$
526 Harrison (East Side)
(816) 221-2455

Garozzo's Ristorante Due
12801 East 40 Highway
Independence, MO
(816) 737-2400

Cafe Garozzo
9950 College Boulevard
Overland Park, KS
(913) 491-8300
Some people have a standing reservation at the original Garozzo's on Harrison every Friday night, rebuilt after a fire destroyed it in 2003. Is it the 5-inch high lasagna, Frank Sinatra tunes in the background, or owner Mike Garozzo singing along in his gravelly voice? Sorry, Mike. It's the food.

We love to eat. On average, every man, woman, and child in Kansas City spends $938 dining out each year, according to the National Restaurant Association. That puts us third in U.S. metropolitan areas; just $30 less than first-ranking New York City and $17 less than Washington, D.C. We spent $29 more per person than San Francisco!

This multiroom restaurant is where many of us tasted our first chicken spiedini, that flavorful rolled breast of chicken smothered in a piquant garlic-lemon sauce. It's a recipe Mike brought from the Italian section of St. Louis known as the Hill in 1989, and every year more of us fall in love with the tangy taste, especially since he seems to add another restaurant every five years or so and all locations are open for lunch and dinner seven days a week.

Spiedini fans may find it hard to branch out, but the menu offers other wonderful items, particularly specialties named for Garozzo family and friends like the Gambretti Angelina, charbroiled, jumbo shrimp in a white wine butter sauce with mushrooms and fresh broccoli. The Bistecca Salvatore Alla Siciliano is a 16-ounce porterhouse that's breaded, charbroiled, and basted in amogio sauce, that garlicky lemon concoction that defines so many dishes here. Thanks, Sal, wherever you are.

All entrees are served with a house salad, pasta or vegetable on the side, and bread and butter. Skip the yellow spread and dip your bread in what's known as Italian butter, a small plate of olive oil, freshly ground black pepper, grated Parmesan cheese, and a sprinkling of red pepper flakes. The appetizers are hard to pass up. Pray that cream of artichoke is the soup of the day; it's worth every bit of butter and cream. The Heaven and Hell is a pesto-stuffed ravioli and lawn prawn charbroiled in fiery diablo sauce.

Pastas are, naturally, excellent here, and a variety of tubular and ribbon noodles are available with tomato sauce, Alfredo, or simple crushed tomatoes and garlic. If you're lucky somebody will order the Three Way Pasta, a platter overflowing with ravioli, spaghetti, and mostaccioli and topped with a softball-sized meatball. We've been waiting to see it polished off in one sitting. And on Thursday the lunch specials often include short ribs that are so delicious they often sell out early.

You'll be happy to know Garozzo's also sells house-made sauces, salad dressings, and its own line of pasta at each restaurant and several grocery stores throughout the Kansas City area.

Jasper's (South Kansas City) $$–$$$
1201 West 103rd Street
(816) 941–6600
www.jasperskc.com

For nearly five decades the Mirabile (pronounced *Mir-AH-bill-ee*) family, led by Jasper Sr., collected culinary rating stars, diamonds, and a multistate fan club for serving classic Italian food at its formal dining room on Wornall Road. When it moved south patrons followed the aroma of grilled sausages, roasted lamb shanks, and garlic to its new home. And now thanks to a more casual atmosphere—it's not unusual to see shorts in summer—a younger crowd has discovered this Kansas City treasure. Loyal customers were happy to see favorites like baked lasagna and veal scaloppini on the menu even after the patriarch passed away.

Jasper Mirabile Jr.—friends call him JJ—has been running the kitchen for many years. His respect for traditional Italian cuisine and genius for creating new dishes have earned him accolades around the world. He's been a guest chef at the James Beard House—the first Kansas City chef so honored—and featured in the *New York Times, Midwest Living,* and *Italy's Cucina.* And he's always improvising: A tour of Venice inspired entrees like grilled sea bass with truffle sauce and fire-roasted duck with blood orange and dried cherry balsamic demi-glace. Did we mention his lobster and ricotta ravioli? Bellisimo!

JJ also finds time to share his passion with others. He teaches cooking classes at the Culinary Center of Kansas City (see www.kcculinary.com for schedules) and at the organic farmers' market at Barstow School each summer.

Finding the door to the restaurant can be a bit confusing. You enter through the family-owned Marco Polo's Italian Market, a tiny shop filled with cheeses, meats, condiments, and homemade take-out dishes like savory Italian meatloaf. Make a mental note to stop by during lunch for a grilled sausage and pepper sandwich.

On pleasant evenings ask for a table on Jasper's patio, where the quiet gurgle of Indian Creek and canopy of trees can make you forget you're near a busy intersection. The restaurant is open for lunch and dinner seven days a week, and reservations are accepted for parties of six or more. For smaller groups, you may call an hour or so before you plan to arrive and ask to be placed on a wait list.

Lidia's (Freighthouse District) $$
101 East 22nd Street
(816) 221-3722

It was quite a coup when famed restaurateur and public TV cooking show host Lidia Bastianich chose Kansas City for her first restaurant outside New York. Locals who'd been dazzled by her northern Italian cuisine at Becco and Felidia helped create a buzz that hasn't abated even after several years.

Lidia and her team decided to open in the Freighthouse District near Union Station, an area that had been neglected for decades. It's now the hottest area in town thanks to the nearby art galleries and shops in the Crossroads Arts District. The three-story room is dominated by spectacular blown-glass balloons fashioned into chandeliers, which are reminiscent of Dale Chihuly's famous work. Oversized wine bottles in silhouette create another dramatic decoration.

For those who thought Lidia's would raise the bar on restaurant prices, the opposite is true. Servings are generous and prices are surprisingly low. It may be hard to select just one entree from the expansive, evocative menu, so no one will blame you for simply ordering the pasta trio. It takes "all you can eat" to an entirely new level as servers circle the rooms to refill plates with pastas fresh from the kitchen. The selection changes daily but usually includes a ravioli, sauced ribbon shape, and aromatic risotto. For around $14 it is without a doubt the most delicious bargain in town.

The regular menu includes roasted veal shank with saffron-scented barley risotto and grilled salmon over braised lentils with a zesty chive-mustard sauce. Even the rib-eye steak gets an Italian lesson with a rosemary, sea salt, and anchovy rub before it's grilled.

Lidia has left her namesake restaurant in the capable hands of executive chef Dan Sweeny and pastry chef Cody Hogan, whose contributions include bonet al caffe, a molded custard flavored with chocolate, amaretto, and espresso, and a tiramisu some consider the best in town. No room for dessert after your fifth helping of pasta? Then end the evening as the Italians do, with a caffe corretto, "corrected coffee," that's braced with shots of grappa and liqueur.

Lidia's is open for lunch Monday through Saturday, dinner daily, and brunch on Sunday.

Macaluso's (Midtown) $$
1403 West 39th Street
(816) 561-0100

This slice of heaven on Restaurant Row is a fine example of what makes independently owned restaurants so special. It starts with the owner, Tom Macaluso, who's there to take your reservation, greet you at the door, and stop by to make sure you're having a wonderful time. Don't, however, expect Tom to break into "O Solo Mio" during dinner. This transplanted Easterner can seem a bit standoffish to newcomers, but he warms up quickly, even to the point of personally preparing special dishes for longtime patrons.

And where else would you find wind-up toys at the bar? That's one way to make waiting for a table fun. It gets even better once seated and your order of crab cakes arrives. Chef Warren's versions are pan seared and served with a spicy pancetta sauce. His gnocchi appetizer is also a hit: tender puffs in roasted red pepper sauce dappled with garlic beurre blanc. Caesar salad fans will be thrilled to see the classic version here: crisp romaine dressed with a mash of anchovies, garlic, lemon, and good olive oil and topped with freshly toasted croutons and shaved Parmigiano-Reggiano.

The entree list includes several pastas, expertly prepared seafood and steaks (the tenderloin topped with foie gras and sauce béarnaise is decadent) and a cioppino that tosses salmon, shrimp, clams, mussels, and calamari over pasta with a tomato-fennel-rosemary couli. Expect to take a good portion of your meal home; most entrees are served with two vegetables, including red cabbage simmered in red wine. By all means, ask for a box so you'll have room for dessert. No one else does a white chocolate cheesecake quite this good. And chocolate lovers will go for the dark chocolate mousse served with Kahlua whipped cream.

Service is friendly without being fussy, and the noise level—with friends yelling hello across the room—can get rather loud at times. For most people it simply adds to the convivial atmosphere. On Monday expect an even bigger crowd when local jazz singers show up. We'll be the ones sitting at the bar fighting over the wind-up dinosaur egg.

Macaluso's is open for dinner only, Monday through Saturday.

MEXICAN/SOUTHWESTERN

Canyon Cafe
(Country Club Plaza)   **$-$$**
4626 Broadway
(816) 561-6111
Although you won't find authentic Mexican fare here (go to one of the family-owned eateries on Southwest Boulevard for that) Canyon Cafe's location and gorgeous interior deserve mentioning. The entrance is up the hill from the Pottery Barn and marked by a burning caldron. Inside is more drama, with an open staircase dividing the two-story space. The upstairs bar provides a pretty view of the Plaza, and some killer margaritas.

The appetizers include a chili-spiked blend of Southwestern specialties such as poblano chicken chowder and upscale versions of classics. The quesadillas incorporate goat cheese with Monterey Jack, and tacos are available with fried whitefish or shrimp in a zesty chipotle sauce. Entrees range from beef like the tenderloin brushed with garlic smoked jalapeño marinade, flame grilled and served with caramelized red onion-jalapeño marmalade, to fish and pastas.

All in all, it's a recipe for a delightful lunch or evening: icy-cold margaritas, zesty food, and a beautiful view. Canyon Cafe is open for lunch and dinner seven days a week; Sunday's lunch offers a special brunch menu. There's live music on Wednesday and Sunday nights.

La Fonda El Taquito (Midtown)   **$**
800 Southwest Boulevard
(816) 471-1675
Drive up and down Southwest Boulevard and you'll find the real deals: Mexican restaurants where the owner's grandmother stirs the pork chili while a younger sister presses tortillas one at a time. El Taquito is just such a place. It got its start in 1978 when Augustin Medina opened a tortilla factory in a tiny storefront. When he began serving lunch to help with the cash flow, the food was so tantalizing it became his chief business.

Twelve years ago La Fonda moved to its current location at the corner of Summit and Southwest Boulevard, where those fresh tortillas scoop up succulent pork chili. Like true family-style Mexican food, the flavors are not hot, but you can crank up the heat by adding freshly made salsas in temperatures ranging from mild to wild.

Flavorful pork is also used for the taquito carnitas, soft-shell tacos that satisfy right down to your soul. The taquitos can also be ordered with chicken or chorizo. Burritos are popular as well, but leave room for the sopapillas, fried bread dusted with cinnamon sugar, or the smooth flan.

On Friday and Saturday nights live Latino music turns the front area into a salsa and merengue dance floor. Things cool down a bit a few hours later, just in time for a Sunday brunch when huevos rancheros and other classic dishes liven up the menu. La Fonda is open seven days a week.

SEAFOOD

Fresh seafood lovers, your ship has come in. Thanks to overnight shipping, several restaurants receive fresh fish and shellfish shipments six days a week. Then they fry, grill, roast, blacken, or pan sauté them with finesse. Following are some of the seafood restaurants that really float our boat.

Bristol Bar and Grill $$–$$$
5400 West 119th Street
Overland Park, KS
(913) 663-5777
Fans of this Kansas City classic were crushed when it left its longtime spot on the Country Club Plaza (where Capitol Grill now resides), but they didn't have long to pine. It reopened, gorgeous stained-glass dome and all, near our *other* open air shopping center, Town Center Plaza. The Bristol also kept their slightly sweet drop biscuits that servers bring around throughout your meal as well as the beloved Sunday brunch. This button-popping buffet features dozens of dishes including seafood pasta, cheese grits, crab soufflé, peel-and-eat spiced shrimp, carved prime rib, scrambled eggs and egg casseroles, fresh fruit, a Belgian waffle bar, and decadent desserts like Key lime tarts, bread pudding, and chocolate-dipped strawberries.

At lunch and dinner, however, it's the seafood that rules. Several types of fish are available seared, grilled, baked, or blackened, including yellowfin tuna, salmon, and mahimahi. The Bristol is open seven days a week for lunch or brunch and dinner, and the huge parking lot is always filled on weekends, when reservations are a must.

McCormick & Schmick's
(Country Club Plaza) $$–$$$
448 West 47th Street
(816) 531-6800
Is it our imagination, or does this place look like a casting call for *Friends?* Perhaps it's the cosmopolitan martini that casts a rosy glow. Whatever the reason, here's where the beautiful people show up to see and be seen and partake of happy hour appetizers. The rest of us get happy by heading to a dinner table. And if you want to get positively silly, reserve one of the booths (called a "snug") with curtains that can be drawn discreetly shut.

Good luck choosing from this eye-popping menu of no less than 30 fresh seafood entrees. And they do mean fresh: Fish is shipped in six days a week. You might start with oysters on the half shell from Washington, Long Island, Prince Edward Island, and British Columbia; a sampler plate will get you a few from each location. During cold weather the traditional oyster stew is the perfect comfort food.

The menu changes daily based on the latest coastal catch, but usually includes specialties such as salmon roasted on a cedar plank and served with a pinot noir sauce or stuffed with crab, shrimp, and Brie; and cashew-crusted talapia with a Jamaican rum butter sauce. Grilled steaks and imaginative pasta dishes are also available.

For dessert, there's a delightful white chocolate mousse encased in a dark chocolate bag served with fresh berries and whipped cream. Now don't you wish you'd requested one of those secluded snugs?

Lunch and dinner are served Monday through Sunday. Reservations are highly recommended for the main dining rooms and the outdoor patio overlooking the Plaza.

SOUL FOOD

Madry's Dash of Flavor (East Side) $
26 East 39th Street
(816) 753-3274
This family-owned restaurant on the corner of Walnut Street features an all-you-can-eat buffet overflowing with down-home goodness. Most of the

patrons have been coming in for years, but they're always happy to see a new face. As you enter the restaurant, head for the right-hand corner to pay before you sit down to eat. This is one tab you'll be happy to cover: It's just under $8.00 for everything, including your choice of beverage and a dessert. Carryout is an additional dollar.

It has everything you'd expect a soul food haven to have, including crispy fried chicken, fried catfish, barbecued ribs, sausage, pork chops, green beans that have been stewing in onions and ham chunks all day, sweet potatoes, grits, macaroni and cheese, and corn bread that proves that from-scratch baking is the only way to go. It's enough to make you want to hug the person at the next table. And after 10 meals, your next visit is on the house. Now that's soul. Hours are 11:00 A.M. until 7:00 P.M. Tuesday through Saturday and until 4:00 P.M. on Sunday. Come hungry.

Three Friends' Restaurant & BBQ
(East Side) $
2461 Prospect
(816) 231-9753
Show up for the Sunday buffet, by all means, but just make sure you're dressed for it. People come here straight from church, so they're looking good: ladies in fancy hats, gentlemen in suits and ties, even little kids fidgeting in their finery. There's nothing fancy about Mattie and Cornelius Jewell's place—unless it's that feathered hat on the lady across the room—but the food is delicious, especially the barbecue, catfish, fried chicken, and pork chops.

Side dishes are just like mama used to make (or you wished she had): macaroni and cheese, greens, grits, applesauce, and just-baked corn muffins and biscuits. For dessert—tell us you saved room!—there's hot peach cobber. And that's just the buffet. Downstairs is a full-service dining room where you can order more of the same from the menu. Three Friends' is only open on Friday and Saturday from noon to 1:30 A.M. and Sunday from noon to 8:00 P.M.

STEAKHOUSES

As the city that gave the world the Kansas City strip—please don't ask for a New York strip around here—we're known for our steaks. This particular cut came to be in 1946 when Eddie Williams bid $35.05 per pound—10 times the going rate—for a champion Hereford at the American Royal livestock auction. It made T. O. Pride's 16-year-old owner $44,375 richer and created national attention for Kansas City steaks. Following is a cowtown primer on cuts of beef, along with a few suggestions about where they do them up royally.

- **Filet:** Selected from the finest beef tenderloin, this cut is the tenderest, melt-in-your-mouth of all red meats. Usually available in 6-, 8-, and 10-ounce cuts.

- **Kansas City strip:** A beautifully marbled, boneless cut loaded with flavor. Typically available in 10- and 12-ounce sizes.

- **T-bone:** A very thick, very juicy cut that's fit for a king or queen. Better save room for this one; it's often served in 22-ounce cuts.

- **Rib-eye:** Very juicy and flavorful, this steak is hand-cut from the naturally aged prime rib.

The Capital Grille
(Country Club Plaza) $$$
4740 Jefferson Street
(816) 531-8345
When *Pitch Weekly* named this the best steakhouse in town, they raised a few eyebrows. Frankly, it's rare that a transplant—and a 15-location national chain at that—can win the hearts of such a loyal crowd. But this ultraplush restaurant earns its accolades. It provides just the right clubby atmosphere, starting at the handsome granite-and-mahogany entrance. There's even a signature martini, the Stoli Doli, made with slices of pineapple marinating in glass crocks of Stolichnaya vodka on the bar.

The seating is sumptuous whether you're in a plush booth, at a white linen–draped table, or in one of the private dining rooms that are usually taken by the bigwigs from our football organization. As you're escorted to your table, you'll pass the glass case where beef is dry aging for 14 to 21 days. When it's at the peak of flavor steaks are hand-cut, well seasoned, and seared at 1,100 degrees Fahrenheit to seal in the juices and provide that distinctive caramelized crust. And that, according to executive chef Ray Comiski, is the key to the Capital's extraordinarily good steaks.

Purists will simply order a 14- or 20-ounce Kansas City strip or filet sans topping, but the steak au poivre with Courvoisier cognac cream sauce is pretty remarkable, too. So are the signature veal chops with Roquefort butter sauce.

But first things first. Dinners can start with cold baby lobster with confetti mayonnaise, a sinfully rich lobster bisque, or the "Wedge," an enormous portion of iceberg lettuce with blue cheese and crumbled bacon. As for lunch, the steak salad is large enough for two, or one diner with dreams of a second meal.

Service is refined yet friendly, with servers who say "My pleasure" to any request—and mean it. Don't be surprised if you receive a handwritten note a day or two after your visit. An impressive wine list includes more than 300 bottles ranging from $27 to well over $500. A few large and half bottles are available as well. And true wine connoisseurs will appreciate the fine crystal glassware without a rolled rim. At about $12 a stem, it's an investment in quality that sets the right tone. Wine lockers are available to store your personal collection; the brass plaques lining the wall read like a "Who's Who" of Kansas City elite.

If you need one more reason to make a reservation, consider the deep-dish Key lime pie with toasted pistachio crust. The restaurant is open for lunch on weekdays and dinner seven days a week, including a 10:00 P.M. last call on Sunday.

Hereford House   **$$–$$$**
20th and Main Street (Downtown)
(816) 842-1080

5001 Town Center Drive
Leawood, KS
(913) 327-0800

19721 East Jackson Street
Independence, MO
(816) 795-9200

6th and Wakarusa
Lawrence, KS
(785) 842-2333
www.herefordhouse.com

Since 1957 the Hereford House's downtown restaurant has been serving perfectly aged, trimmed, and grilled steaks seven days a week to willing carnivores. It's even rumored that the phrase "juicy and tender" was coined in this very spot.

So naturally longtime fans were relieved when new owner Rod Anderson kept the restaurant's ambience and most of its tenured staff when he remodeled the downtown landmark in 1987. A year later he opened a location in Leawood, then Independence, and now he's planted his brand in Lawrence, Kansas.

For real beef lovers, the thrill begins with a charred carpaccio sliced paper thin and served chilled with a peppy chipotle mayonnaise. Or try plump mushroom caps stuffed with shrimp and crab in a creamy cheese sauce. The steaks, of course, are delicious, either simply grilled or topped with a cracked pepper and blue cheese sauce or Dijon mustard and brown sugar glaze. Fish is done right here as well, particularly the cedar-planked salmon that's oven roasted and served with a garlic herb butter. Side dishes include the signature cowboy baked beans and twice-baked potato. As for the signature creamy Italian and cheddar cheese salad dressings, regulars refer to them as "pink" and "yellow" and usually order a little of both.

Hereford House is also a business lunch mecca, usually packed with nearby office staff and conventioneers who've heard about the daily specials like twin beef medallions, French dip, or meat loaf with mashed potatoes and gravy. Leave room somehow for the heavenly white chocolate bread pudding or peach cobbler served with vanilla ice cream.

All four restaurants are open seven days a week. The Leawood location offers kosher dinners with advance notice. The dress is casual, and reservations are recommended. For a beef-eater's bargain, try the Sunset Dinner special.

J. Gilbert's $$-$$$
8901 Metcalf
Overland Park, KS
(913) 632-8070

This restaurant has the high honor of being named for Joe Gilbert, the beloved restaurateur who helped build the Gilbert-Robinson empire. It's a fitting tribute. The interior is a handsome mix of stone and dark woods with an enormous bar area and some of the friendliest bartenders in town. While you're enjoying a cocktail you'll have time to sample the addictive house-made potato chips with blue cheese sauce.

The dining areas are beautiful as well, with a cozy fireplace, big cushy booths, and a golden glow from the low lighting. Take your time with the menu; although J. Gilbert's fashions itself a steakhouse, they offer some excellent seafood, chicken, and pasta dishes like a five-spice chicken penne with a smoked Gouda sauce.

But this place definitely knows how to put the sizzle into a steak. They select only cornfed Black Angus beef, then sear the steaks on a wood-fire grill hot enough to seal in the flavorful juices within seconds. Purists will go for the tender filet mignon, and those who hanker for something fancy might like the bourbon-based sauce. The side dishes really shine here as well, especially the poblano potatoes au gratin.

J. Gilbert's provides the right atmosphere for a romantic anniversary dinner, yet is casual enough for families. It's open for dinner only, Monday through Sunday.

Jess & Jim's Steak House (South Kansas City) $$
517 East 135th Street
(816) 941-9499
www.jessandjims.com

A tornado took this place off the map in the 1950s, but it landed forever on the culinary map in 1972 when Calvin Trillin announced in *Playboy* that it served the best steak in the universe. The notoriety resulted in expansion—twice—and a new menu that included a 25-ounce Playboy Strip.

The restaurant's namesakes are gone; Jim for good in 1981 and Jess on the West Coast, where he no doubt misses Midwest beef. But the tradition lives on with Jim's kin, the VanNoy family. And just to prove that lightning *can* strike twice, Jess & Jim's was recently mentioned again in *Playboy*, when the magazine called it "the quintessential midwestern steakhouse." The article got it right; the place is next to railroad tracks, meat hangs in the window, and the waitresses are stunned if someone asks to see a dessert menu.

There are 12 steaks available, including filets ranging in size from 5 to 14 ounces, and an eye-popping, button-flying 30-ounce porterhouse. Steaks are served sizzling on big hot silver platters. You can order them anyway you like, but please note that steaks cooked beyond medium well are not guaranteed.

Other entrees include lobster—available either steamed or battered and fried—frog legs, chicken gizzards, and shrimp. And most come with your choice of a football-sized baked potato, fabulous cottage fries, plus soup or salad and homemade garlic toast. There's even a surprisingly varied wine list including 23 cabernets.

Jess & Jim's steaks are also available for carryout, as are gallon jars of their famous pickled beets. And here's a secret: Sometimes you'll find a money-saving coupon on their Web site. The promotion changes based on the time of year, but you can bet it has nothing to do with dessert.

The restaurant is open for lunch and dinner Monday through Saturday.

The Majestic Steakhouse (Downtown) $$$
931 Broadway
(816) 471-8484
www.majesticgroup.com

This slim three-story building once housed Fitzpatrick's saloon and a bordellomaking it a popular place for gangsters and political bigshots during the 1930s. Pressed tin ceilings, tile floors, and stained-glass lights reveal its turn-of-the-20th-century age and helped put it on the National Register of Historic Places.

Since 1993 the landmark has gone from making history to serving historically good steaks. The Majestic is justly proud of its 21-day dry-aged prime beef. True carnivores will simply point to the 12-ounce Kansas City strip, a marbled steak so flavorful you may not notice the flaky baked potato and sautéed vegetables on the side.

And that brings up a good point regarding prices. Unlike a lot of steakhouses that offer salads and side dishes a la carte, the Majestic's entrees come fully loaded, including a salad with a tasty house-made basil-walnut dressing. Owner Doug Barnard a wine buff himself—has peppered the 800-label wine list with bottles starting at just $12. All in all it makes for a rather reasonable evening out, especially when you add in the free entertainment. You can hear some of Kansas City's finest jazz musicians seven nights a week in the lower level, and there's never a cover charge. Lunch is served weekdays and dinner every night.

And don't hesitate to order a before- or after-dinner drink here; Prohibition has been over for years. Not that it mattered when Tom Pendergast ran the city from this address. You'll find out more about him in the History chapter, but in the meantime you can visit his cigar club on the third floor, complete with walk-in humidor, stained glass, and leather chairs. Although it's a private club you can be a temporary guest of the restaurant as long as there's no special event going on.

Plaza III The Steakhouse (Country Club Plaza) $$$
4749 Pennsylvania
(816) 753-0000

The fact that this place still packs them in, even after big-name national steakhouses moved into the neighborhood, is affirmation of its excellent food and great service. The Spanish-style decor hasn't changed much since duo Joe Gilbert and Paul Robinson, along with Joe's son Bill, opened it in 1963.

Dinners start with complimentary chilled vegetables and ranch-style dip, but our advice is to save yourself for what's on the menu. Standout appetizers include the famous Plaza III Steak Soup, a thick broth of ground beef and vegetables, and a spinach salad with spiced roasted walnuts and hot bacon dressing. Side dishes include a one-pound baked Idaho potato and delectable creamed spinach, and crispy latkelike hash browns with onions.

But let's get down to why Plaza III is consistently rated one of the country's top steakhouses. It's the beef. They hand-select only cornfed, center-cut USDA-graded prime beef and then age it from three to four weeks in their own beef locker. Optional diable, béarnaise, and pan-gravy sauces are available but totally unnecessary with steaks of this caliber. If you're not in the mood for steak, lobster and salmon are also on the menu.

The extensive wine list has won acclaim from *Wine Spectator.* And before or after dinner you can head to the cozy bar through the side door or downstairs to the jazz lounge for live music.

Beyond barbecue and steaks, we have a few other hometown recipes to sample. The Plaza III steaksoup is a perennial favorite, as is the baked potato soup at the Grand Cafe. You'll also want to try a brew from Boulevard Beer, and finish your meal with java from the Roasterie Coffee. Several top restaurants also serve their own blends.

Lunch and dinner are served Monday through Saturday. Dinner only is available Sunday.

VEGETARIAN

Vegans and the diet conscious can usually find at least one or two meatless meals on the menus of most of the restaurants listed above. But the following places cater to those who love veggies and grains.

Blue Bird Bistro (West Side) $
1700 Summit
(816) 221-7559
At this storefront cafe located above the downtown bluffs, you'll see a diverse crowd enjoying inventive dishes and a cozy atmosphere. Although dishes with free-range chicken and chemical-free beef have been added, many still consider this their favorite vegetarian menu.

Salads include a quinoa with peppers, red onion, dried apricots, and currants with a lemon and olive oil dressing. Add a cup of curried red-lentil and tomato soup and it's a dandy lunch. The whole-wheat thin-crust pizzas topped with an assortment of vegetables and homemade tomato sauce are popular any time, as is the veggie lasagna.

There's also a full bar, where you can try a chilled Japanese sake. Lunch and dinner are served Monday through Saturday, with a Sunday brunch.

Eden Alley (Country Club Plaza) $
707 West 47th Street
(816) 561-5415
Hidden in the basement of the Unity Temple on the Plaza, this fun and funky place evokes the feeling of a hippie hangout from the 1960s. The patrons, however, are a mixed bag. At any given table you can see business types from surrounding offices, book club participants, and, yes, vegetarians looking for delicious dishes starring whole grains, beans, and greens.

The day's menu appears on a blackboard above the tiny kitchen, and always includes tasty salads and a veggie burger that could change your mind about meatless fare. Other frequent offerings include pizza and cheesy quesadillas. With what you've saved in animal fat, you can splurge on a yummy cake or brownie. But be sure to bring cash, because Eden Alley doesn't take credit cards or checks. It's open for lunch and dinner Monday through Friday and is closed Saturday, Sunday, and the first Tuesday of each month.

SUNDAY BRUNCH

Some folks save all their calories for Sunday, when several restaurants offer items from an a la carte menu or a brunch buffet. Show up and you'll be rewarded with made-to-order omelets, boiled spiced shrimp, carved prime rib of beef, fresh pastries, and everything in between. And on special occasions like Easter, Mother's Day, and Thanksgiving, lots of other places fire up the chafing dishes, so call ahead and ask. If a restaurant listed below does not appear elsewhere in this chapter, we include the address in its description.

Readers of the *Bristol*, a local newspaper, rate the brunch at **Rotisserie** in Overland Park, Kansas's Doubletree Hotel "The Best in Kansas City." One look at the six-station feast and you'll understand why. Chefs will prepare omelets to your liking, carve prime rib as thick as you'd like, and pop out hot, crispy Belgian waffles. There are also peel-and-eat shrimp, fresh fruits and salads, grilled asparagus and red peppers, a medley of fresh breakfast pastries, fluffy scrambled eggs, ham, crisp bacon, and desserts including brownies, chocolate cake, lemon tarts, and the chocolate chip cookies this hotel is known for.

Ophelia's on Independence Square serves brunch items from its inventive menu and is a great place to begin a trip to nearby Truman's Library and Museum. Brookside is the location of **Cafe Maison** (408 East 63rd Street, 816-523-3400), where the brunch menu includes a superb smoked salmon hash and French toast stuffed with walnuts and Granny Smith apples. Items on the limited cold buffet line include croissants, cheeses, sliced ham, bagels, pasta salad, and a few desserts. It's worth waiting in line for a table.

At **YiaYia's Eurobistro,** where the service is like a big comfortable hug, a diverse brunch menu greets you every Sunday. Two standouts are Corey's crab omelet and the Big Guy, an eye-popper that includes eggs Benedict, lox and bagel, a blueberry pancake, strawberry French toast, oven-roasted potatoes, and bacon or sausage. Add a cup of YiaYia's private coffee blend and you're set for the day. At **Yahooz,** its cousin across the street, you can enjoy a brunch buffet that includes egg-based casseroles, roasted meats, fruit parfaits, and more.

Brunch may be the best—certainly the quietest—time to try **Tomfooleries Restaurant & Bar** (612 West 47th Street, 816-753-0555) because all the twenty-somethings are still in bed. You'll be treated to an amazing number of pastries, hot dishes, cold shrimp, made-to-order omelets with 50 choices of ingredients, and unusual buffet items like cold pizza and hot corned-beef hash.

ALFRESCO DINING

During nice weather it's grand to dine outdoors on a deck or patio where you can hold hands with your date or hold court with a group of friends. Following are some suggestions, many of which you'll find detailed elsewhere in this chapter.

Piropos in Parkville provides one of the most romantic views anywhere with a bird's-eye view of the river town and Park University's towers in the distance. While you can't have dinner outside, it's a lovely place to enjoy appetizers and cocktails before being seated indoors. At **Lidia's** umbrella-dotted patio you can enjoy dinner or simply dessert and Italian coffee while listening to the gurgle of a water fountain or the roar of a freight train rushing by. The scent from the restaurant's herb garden adds more appeal. The skinny brick-lined patio at **Shiraz** is popular on pleasant evenings. With soul-stirring guitar music

and Ali's fabulous menu, this is an urban paradise. The **Classic Cup** on the Plaza is the place to see and be seen, particularly if you get a coveted spot on the front sidewalk, where the people-watching is as lively as the food. There's also a large deck in back. During a sunset or on a starry night, there's perhaps no better place to be than the tiny European-style balcony at **Figlio** on the Plaza overlooking beautiful Mill Creek Park and the J. C. Nichols fountain. A few blocks away **Frondizi's** (4558 Main Street, 816-931-3322) offers the same view through an expanse of trees. The awning-covered deck in back is a terrific place to share wine and fried calamari with friends.

For a lovely waterfall view and fabulous Italian food, head to **Jasper's** patio. Here, surrounded by shady trees and the quiet splashing of Indian Creek, you'd swear you were at a private retreat instead of in suburban Johnson County. And at **Joe D's** in Brookside, any table will guarantee you a wonderful meal, but during nice weather patrons fight over the last seat on the patio. His newer place, **Joe D's on 39th,** offers a fun upstairs deck.

HIDDEN GEMS

Following are some favorite dine-in or take-out restaurants that get votes for serving consistently great food at reasonable prices. What's *not* remarkable is their locations: You'll have to hunt for them amid drab shopping centers or boring strip malls. But we promise once you taste the food you won't care if you're parked in front of a dry cleaner or dentist's office.

Cafe Casbah $
8609 College Boulevard
Overland Park, KS
(913) 469-9999
Around here the road to Morocco begins just west of the corner of College Boulevard and Antioch. There's where you'll discover Cafe Casbah, a pretty little restaurant serving exquisite Mediterranean classics like dolmas, baba ghannouj, and

stuffed mushrooms. More adventurous types might try the stuffed squid, and the luscious seafood bisque and cream of almond soup are worth every calorie.

The list of entrees is surprisingly large for this tiny place and includes chicken and shrimp curry, duck with honey-date-walnut sauce, salmon with champagne sauce, stuffed lobster tail, and rack of lamb with garlic. The veal Oscar is worthy of applause as it's brought to the table: Two large tender medallions of veal are dappled in a creamy sauce and then topped with two whole crab legs and fat shrimp. Low-fat and low-salt entrees are available by request, an example of the personalized service found here. Cafe Casbah has a full bar and a limited wine list. Lunch is served Tuesday through Friday; dinner is available Tuesday through Saturday. But here's fair warning: Word of mouth about the food and prices have made this a Johnson County favorite. We suggest you make reservations, especially on weekends.

Greek Cuisine $
11811 College Boulevard
Overland Park, KS
(913) 338-0657

Dozens of customers have standing orders at least one night a week; they show up at this family-owned restaurant at the usual time and their take-out orders appear as if by magic. The food—all prepared in-house by owners Balban and Paramjit Gill—is fresh and flavorful, particularly the grape leaves stuffed with ground beef and rice and flaky phyllo-wrapped tiropita and spanakopita. These three appetizers, along with plenty of roasted lamb and pita bread, make up the small combination plate. Add a large Greek salad and it's plenty for two to three people to share—and a bargain at less than $14 for the entire meal.

The dinner combination plate is even heartier, with mousaka, a classic Greek dish of layered eggplant, meat sauce, and cheese in béchamel sauce; pastitsio, a casserole with sauce and macaroni; slices of lamb; and two appetizers.

The gyro sandwich is the biggest seller by far. Entrees, which come with a small salad and pita bread, include chicken and beef shish kabob and roasted leg of lamb. Children enjoy the chicken and fish tenders, parents like the prices, and everyone loves Paramjit's baklava, that heavenly creation made with honey and ground nuts in layers of phyllo dough. The restaurant has about 10 tables and is a little tricky to find: It's behind Par Exsalonce Day Spa in the College Village shopping center at the southeast corner of College Boulevard and Quivira Road. Lunch and dinner are available Monday through Saturday.

Iliki Cafe $-$$
6431 North Crosby Avenue
North Kansas City, MO
(816) 587-0009
www.iliki.com

Christian and Cristal Fuller have created a culinary oasis in the Picture Hills Shopping Center, where the tantalizing aromas of smoked eggplant, lamb, and garlic often turn a stop at the wine bar into dinner for two. The food is as complex and colorful as the beautiful rugs hanging on the walls: red pepper dip sweetened by pomegranate syrup, grilled marinated shrimp with Thai chili paste, spicy Armenian beef sausage served with a cool yogurt and cucumber sauce.

The menu lists cold and hot mezze (appetizers) along with entrees that provide their lyrical Middle Eastern names as well as English descriptions. Halloum, for example, is pan-seared sheep cheese from Cyprus on a bed of lemony cucumbers and tomatoes; gambari translates to plump shrimp sautéed in garlic and white wine served on a bed of basmati rice. Sound tempting? Wait until you savor them in person. Prices here are very reasonable; service is friendly and efficient. And about that wine bar: It features one of the largest wine lists in the city, including 70 wines by the glass and beers from such far-flung spots as Poland, Greece, Belgium, and St. Louis. No wonder it's a favorite place for Northlanders to congregate on Friday and Saturday nights. Lunch is available weekdays, dinners every night but Sunday.

NIGHTLIFE

To taste the *true* essence of our town, you simply must spend an evening listening to jazz. It was that syncopated, soulful, savory stew of many different musical styles, after all, that put Kansas City on the musical map.

That, and the atmosphere that surrounded it. During the Jazz Age, Kansas City earned the name "Paris of the Plains," not so much for our wide boulevards but for the variety of vice available 24 hours a day. At one time this wide-open town was home to hundreds of nightclubs, speakeasies, cabarets, dance halls, and honky-tonks, chiefly clustered around 12th Street and Vine on the east side of town.

Along with jazz, Kansas City had another thriving entertainment option in the 1920s and 1930s: female impersonators. The city's most popular drag club was Dante's Inferno on Independence Avenue. The club is long gone, but its sign lives on in the front window of Retro Inferno, an ultracool vintage furniture store in Downtown (see more details in Shopping).

Those honky-tonk days are long gone, but on any given night and even some afternoons you can still hear jazz pouring out of clubs and restaurants, on street corners on the Country Club Plaza, and at annual festivals such as the Juneteenth Celebration, Parkville's River Jam, and the Jazz Lover's Pub Crawl (see Annual Events and Festivals for information). But today "Satin Doll" shares air space with other musical styles, including rock, R&B, zydeco, Irish folk songs, country, and reggae.

When you get enough people together to listen to music, it's a sure bet many of them will want to get up and dance. Whether you want to scoot your boots, learn the tango, or practice your West Coast Swing, you'll find an open dance floor somewhere in town.

Night owls can also find plenty of other entertainment around here. We have our share of comedy clubs and bars and taverns, including some that serve up their own microbrewed beer. Before you head out, however, a bit of housekeeping: In both Kansas and Missouri, the legal drinking age is 21. Most of our nightlife is clustered in the Downtown, Westport/Midtown, and Plaza districts, and a few are within walking distance of one another; club hoppers will most likely need a car.

Enough of the rules, already, let's go! To make it easier to locate your personal predilection, we've divided this chapter into entertainment categories.

COCKTAIL LOUNGES, BARS, AND TAVERNS

When it's cocktail time, you can order a cold one at bars found within some of the city's finest restaurants such as Plaza III–The Steakhouse and McCormick & Schmicks on the Plaza and Pierpont's in Union Station, where the bartenders will climb a ladder to fetch the mixings. But if you *really* want to get high, head to Skies, the revolving restaurant and lounge atop the Westin Regency Crown Center Hotel. When you've seen the red neon Western Auto sign go by for the fourth time, it's your cue to call it a night.

Here's a list of other places ready to serve up your drink order. For a real taste of Kansas City, order a pint of our hometown brew, Boulevard Beer.

Empire Room
334 East 31st Street
(816) 561-2640
This place is so hip its ad in the alternative newspaper *Pitch Weekly* doesn't even list the address. But here it is, the little sister to the Velvet Dog, serving up martinis until the wee hours seven days a week. Food is served until midnight. Order your

---

If you've had too much nightlife around the holidays, get a ride or call a cab when it's time to hit the road. Each year Holiday Cab offers free rides home (the first $25 worth of fare, or about 20 miles) between Christmas and New Year's from 7:00 P.M. to 3:00 A.M. Call (816) 276-7899, or ask the bartender for the free cab.

gourmet pizza, then head for a cozy booth to watch second-run movies—the original *Ocean's Eleven*, perhaps?—and sports events on the big screen TVs.

Kelly's Westport Inn
500 Westport Road
(816) 561-0635
www.kellyswestportinn.com
History buffs might like to know that Kelly's is the oldest building in Kansas City. Well, at least they have a bronze plaque saying it is. Even the owners aren't sure. What they do know is that this corner establishment was once a grocery store run by Daniel Boone's grandson and became a saloon by 1933. Since then it's been where a cross section of the city—lawyers, salespeople, real estate agents, and artists—meets for lunch on Friday and never seems to make it back to the office. Perhaps it's the bright-red Jell-O shots that get to them: at $1.00 a pop; they do seem to slide down easy. By evening the crowd is younger and rowdier and, in summer, barely dressed. Kelly's is such a tradition on St. Paddy's Day that in 1989 they closed the doors for fear that the floors would cave in. Get a glimpse of the mob scene on the Web site. On weekends those wooden floors are wall-to-wall with returning college kids and boomers who make regular pilgrimages to their favorite hangout.

Mike's Tavern
5424 Troost Avenue
(816) 444-3399
www.mikestavernonline.com
Mike's is just what a neighborhood bar

should be, with friendly bartenders, a casual atmosphere, and cheap drinks. Students and alumni from nearby University of Kansas City–Missouri and Rockhurst University congregate in the afternoons to play pool, hang out at the bar, and watch sporting events on one of 15 or so screens. The jukebox plays mostly fifties rock, there's karaoke every Wednesday night, and local bands often show up on weekends. If that's not enough, there's always a game of darts, Golden Tee, or the half-pound burgers and crispy Tater Tots to keep you happy.

The Velvet Dog
400 East 31st Street
(816) 753-9990
www.velvetdog.com
Located a few blocks from Crown Center (the KCMO TV tower is an excellent landmark) the Dog is where the hip crowd goes for flavored martinis and a game of boccie ball (that's Italian lawn bowling) on the back patio. If you don't know how to play, have no fear: There's usually a martini-toting expert ready to demonstrate. Create your own cocktail party with savory tidbits like artichoke fritters and tomato bruschetta, or try the Spicy Thai Pizza. As for those martinis, you'll have 17 to choose from, including a chocolate version, each for $7.00.

Even the Dog's Web site is cool, with a slot machine game that announces your winnings with a barking pooch. Back in reality, when it's time to move on you won't even have to repark the car; just head for the owner's other bar, The Empire Room.

For fabulous dining, try the new Cafe Trocadero, owned by the same groovy group, in the same neighborhood (see Restaurants).

COMEDY CLUBS

Since the days of burlesque, Kansas City has always been a circuit for top-name comedians, a tradition that continues today thanks to more than our share of comedy clubs. Over the past decades we've welcomed up-and-comers like Rosie O'Donnell, Ellen Degeneres, and a guy named Jerry Seinfeld. At one time our first official comedy club, Stanford & Sons, located above the Westport restaurant by the same name, was ranked first in the Midwest and third in the nation by *Rolling Stone* and *Variety.*

If the comedy scene seems a little heavy on the "Stanford" names, it's because patriarch Stanford Glazer started the whole shebang in 1975 and later was joined by his sons. Legal matters and egos broke the family up; although it was no laughing matter, Kansas City now has more clubs than most cities our size.

ComedyCity
300 Charlotte
(816) 842-2744
www.comedycity.cc
Home of Kansas City's original Comedy Sports, where tag teams improvise to suggestions from the audience. You won't hear the "blue" language used in other clubs; this is good, clean family fun that's appropriate for groups of all types and sizes. And when the audience participates and the players are on, this can be a hilarious night out, Wednesday through Sunday.

Stanford & Sons Comedy Club
106th and Metcalf
Overland Park, KS
(913) 385-3866
This popular nightspot is located behind Hooter's—now *that's* funny—in a strip mall on busy Metcalf Avenue.

DANCE

Nearly every night in our fair metropolis, couples are putting on their dancing shoes and twirling, dipping, or boogying to music somewhere in town. Perhaps surprisingly, the fastest-growing age group at dancing events is twenty-somethings, who are taking to the Lindy Hop and West Coast Swing with wild abandon. For a complete list of venues, classes, and dance organizations to join, complete with pictures, check out Mike Strong's well-organized Web site (www.kcdance.com). Following are a few of the most popular locations.

Barumba in Mi Cocina
620 West 48th Street
(816) 960-6426
Getting an invitation to this Latin lounge in the downstairs of a popular Mexican restaurant on the Country Club Plaza harkens back to the "are you cool enough?" days of Studio 54 in New York. If you're not a regular, you have to have dinner upstairs first and then meet the approval of the manager. Once in, though, the music is hot, the dancing is hotter, and the patrons are friendly. It's the cocktails that will get you: Specialty drinks like the Mambo Limousine will run you over fast. You'll have plenty of time to nurse that highball, though. The nightclub, which opens at 10:00 P.M., stays open until 2:30 A.M. No food is served.

El Caribe Cafe & Lounge
12112 West 87th Street Parkway
Lenexa, KS
(913) 599-2270
At this restaurant located 1 block west of Quivira, it's time to put down your Caribbean Jerk Chicken when the Latin dance lessons start at 8:30 P.M. or you might be wearing the spicy brown sauce. By the time the DJ arrives at 10:00, the place is generally packed, and the sensuous salsa and tango moves continue until 2:00 A.M.

XO
3954 Central
(816) 753-0112
www.xonightclub.com
The name is short for oxygen, and you might find yourself searching for a mask if you're not in prime condition when the action starts around midnight. The mostly under-25 crowd doesn't show up until 11:00 P.M. (when the cover charge jumps from $5.00 to $10.00), but once they're there the

throbbing music and laser light show keeps them in a lather until 3:00 A.M. Wednesday through Sunday. If you could actually *see* through the moody piped-in smoke you'd be able to check out what the cool kids are wearing these days. XO is where locals take visitors to prove that Kansas City can still move with the best of 'em.

If you're taking a cab, be aware that— unlike some other major cities—taxis here don't cruise, so allow time for the doorman to call one, and make sure you keep the cab phone number handy.

GAY AND LESBIAN CLUBS

Bar Natasha
1911 Main Street
(816) 472-5300

Since opening on New Year's Eve 2003, this bon vivant of a bar and nightclub has attracted the city's most sophisticated gays along with mostly urbane straight couples. When it first opened there was a sense of secrecy to the place—almost as though you needed a special knock for admittance. There was no sign over the door as there is now, and from the sidewalk the cabaret seemed like another office building on the block.

The secret-club atmosphere may be gone, but the cavernous space still has several things going for it: a piano smack dab in the center of the room where a variety of artists perform (if you know the lyrics to popular show tunes, you're in) and lead sing-a-longs; a tasty menu that raises the bar for typical bar food; and a statuesque co-owner, Missy Koonce, who can be seen mixing a cocktail, greeting her immense network of friends, or belting out a tune on stage. This popular Kansas City actress named her club for Natasha Fatale, the cartoon character she played in a production of *Rocky & Bullwinkle* at the Coterie Theatre.

The menu is short—about 12 savory items and six sweets—with prices that range from five bucks for a chutney cream cheese spread with crackers to $70 for blini with caviar. The most popular dish is the sliced steak with blue-cheese butter; at $10 it's a terrific meal paired with the cheese platter and a chocolate flourless cake chaser. The singing may drown out your party's conversation, but no matter. Sing right along and enjoy the fun.

Bar Natasha is open from 4:00 P.M. to 1:00 A.M. Wednesday through Saturday, and is a popular venue for events like private birthday parties and fund-raisers, particularly those that benefit AIDS research.

LIVE MUSIC

Some of the venues below offer a true nightclub atmosphere with cocktail tables surrounding a stage and an appreciative audience that's there to actually *listen* rather than gab with tablemates. Answer a cell phone here and you might find yourself stared down or even out on the street.

There are also dozens of places— restaurants and hotel lobbies all over town—where trios or piano players provide background music to clinking glasses and conversation. But whether you take your jazz with a side of sirloin or like it a la carte, you'll discover talent that can soar above the din.

Some locations charge covers ranging from $3.00 to $5.00 depending on the night and the talent; many invite you to sit and enjoy the music gratis as long as you order an occasional cocktail or two.

Blues and Rock 'n' Roll

Rhythm and blues was the father of jazz, and papa never really left the Kansas City music scene. These days there are as many blues venues in town—and at least as many fans—as there are jazz emporiums. You can catch a case of the blues nearly anywhere, any night in Kansas City.

For times and locations, check out the schedule on the Kansas City Blues Society's site at www.kcbluessociety.com.

A word about tickets: For the venues that bring in major bands (like Grand Emporium and the Uptown), advance tickets, which are highly encouraged, are available at the nightclub's box office or on its Web site. Tickets can also be purchased through Ticketmaster (816-931-3330, www.ticketmaster.com), or at ticket centers including Hen House grocery stores and other outlets detailed on the Web site. Be aware that Ticketmaster charges a substantial additional fee.

BB's Lawnside Bar-B-Q
1205 East 85th Terrace
(816) 822-7427

Owner Lindsey Shannon combines his passions for blues, beer, and barbecue in this homey roadhouse, which plays live music Thursday through Sunday. The food's pretty hot, too; try the spicy jambalaya, Smoky Jo's Gumbo, or ribs and burnt ends. And to wash it all down order a "Bucket of Blues," which will get you five Pabst Blue Ribbons in a galvanized tin. Nothing fancy here, but when the joint is jumping with blues, jazz, or Terence O'Malley's ragtime piano, it's a guaranteed good time. See if you can identify the lineup of blues greats on the mural behind the stage.

Blayney's
415 Westport Road
(816) 561-3747
www.blayneys.com

You might miss this quintessential blues spot unless you know where to look. Take the stairs underneath Rose's Express in Old Westport, pay at the door, and get ready for good rockin' tonight. Blayney's is the sort of hangout where bartenders have your usual draft ready before you sit down, where the entire space—and many of the patrons—are in desperate need of daylight, and the dance floor is so crowded you may find yourself dancing with several people at once. In short, it's a blast. Folks from all age groups and walks of life show up to hear longtime favorites like the smoky-voiced leader of the Bob Harvey Band, the Nace Brothers, and Four Fried Chickens and A Coke (that's a band, not a menu special) six nights a week. It's easy to figure out the owner's given name: bartenders wear T-shirts saying, "I work for Dick. . . but I prefer cash." It's our pick for best Kansas City souvenir.

During the warm weather the deck out back is the place to be.

Grand Emporium
3832 Main
(816) 531-1504
www.grandemporium.com

It's obvious the moment you enter—once your eyes adjust to the inky interior, that is—that this place has soul. Built in 1912, the building once served bathtub gin in the speakeasy downstairs and other vices in the bordello above. But since 1985 owner Roger Naber has made it famous for the blues, reggae, rock and rockabilly, jazz, and swing it serves up seven nights a week; in fact it's the only establishment to be twice voted "Best Blues Club in America" by the Blues Foundation.

As of spring 2004 it has a new owner, proving that old rockers never die—they just get married and have children. Naber may be gone, but the music continues in a slightly tidier space.

Headliners usually gear up at 8:30 or so, and the box office opens at 11:00 A.M. daily; 1:00 P.M. on Sunday.

The place seats 175, but often it's too crowded to even see the chairs, let alone find one, as 300 folks move en masse to the music. And since all that foot shuffling will make you hungry, Amazing Grace dishes up her award-winning barbecue for weekday lunches and before and after the shows, Tuesday through Saturday. Even during lunch there's music, thanks to the jukebox that's loaded with 100 rare 45s from Howlin' Wolf to James Brown. The Emporium also hosts the monthly Kansas City Blues Society Jam and is available for private parties. Even the for-sale merchandise is cool here; along with the standard

T-shirts and caps they offer authentic (and used!) mechanic's shirts with the Grand Emporium flaming insignia on the back. If there's a downside to the place it's that parking is limited and on the street.

The Hurricane
4048 Broadway
(816) 753-0884
www.hurricanekc.com
By Wednesday of every week, there's usually at least one personal ad in the city's alternative newspaper along the lines of, "Met you at the Hurricane Friday night but didn't get your name." Perhaps it was too noisy to hear it. This 16-time winner of "Kansas City's Best Nightclub" is *the* place for loud music, crowded spaces, and rowdy Gen-Xers who show up for drink specials seven nights a week. It's certainly one of the reasons Westport is Kansas City's liveliest entertainment district. During warm weather the deck is the place to see and be seen. Cover charge.

Jilly's on Broadway
1744 Broadway
(816) 221-4977
One by one, small bars like Jilly's are turning the lights on again Downtown. This cozy place offers live music on Thursday and Saturday, a DJ who spins what he calls "the future sound of retro" on Friday, and a very cool open-mic singer/songwriter showcase every Wednesday. When the weather's fair, the deck is a great place to party and pick out your next condo . . . because with neighborhood spots like this, you're going to want to move to the city. No cover.

John's Food and Drink
928 Wyandotte Street
(816) 474-5668
There's no better view of the city than from this three-story rooftop known to regulars as simply "the deck," where downtown workers head after punching out to hear rock 'n' roll and rendezvous with friends. But don't miss out on the other two floors. DJ John packs the second-level dance floor every weeknight while nondancers head straight for the pool tables.

The second floor is also where you can find one of the best bargains downtown: a lunch buffet for under $6.00. The first floor's diner has served lunch and dinner to downtown workers for more than 20 years. The huge menu features mostly sandwiches (the fajita steak version is especially tasty), pastas, salads, and burgers. On Friday, two pounds of crab legs will cost you just under $12, ready to be washed down with discounted shots of liquor. What a way to start the weekend. John's is also one of the only downtown joints that's open seven days a week and until 3:00 A.M. on weekends.

The Levee
16 West 43rd Street
(816) 561-2821
www.thelevee.net
Truth be told, about half of Kansas City tipped back their first tequila shooter right here in this neighborhood bar just north of the Plaza. Long popular with folks from 21 to the well-over-50 crowd, the Levee is the place for dancing on the tables (go ahead, we've all done it at least once) and listening to flat out blues and rock 'n' roll Monday through Saturday. The fun continues until 3:00 A.M. and often spills out onto the deck or patio.

Regulars were thankful when Pyramid Pizza took over the food service. Along with pies they offer salads, sandwiches, and something they call B'onz, an appetizer made from pizza dough stuffed with three cheeses, dipped in garlic butter, and baked. And pssst! Look for printable food coupons on Levee's Web site. There's plenty of parking in a lot across the street, but on warm summer weekend nights, there's often a line to get in. Expect a cover charge.

The Madrid
3810 Main
(816) 753–4909
www.madridtheatre.com
Opened in 1926 as a 1,500-seat silent movie house, this distinctive Spanish revival–style palace was plush inside and out with ornate plaster and terra-cotta trim. Back then you could hear house organist Carl W. Stalling introduce the movies. Later, after a stint with Walt Disney, he moved to Warner Brothers, where he contributed the quirky compositions to Bugs Bunny cartoons. Howard Hughes bought the Madrid in the '30s, but by 1944 it fell silent. Current owner Kerry Duffin rescued it in 1995 and began the slow restoration process. Today it's home to local groups or national acts, typically in the rock (Leo Kottke was a recent show), heavy metal, and hip-hop genres. During those nights the crowd generally runs to the young and the pierced. But on Friday night when there's salsa and ballroom dancing, the dress code calls for nice casual to dressy. The same is true for the Sunday brunch that includes foot-stomping, body-swaying gospel.

And here's a tip: Don't get paranoid if you think someone is videotaping you walking from your car; the Old Westport neighborhood is up in arms about the noise and parking problems the Madrid has created. Please be respectful of nearby homeowners.

Raoul's Velvet Room
119th and Metcalf (Rosana Square Shopping Center)
Overland Park, KS
(913) 469–0466
www.raoulsvelvetroom.com
Who says there's no place to party in sleepy suburban Overland Park? You'd never know it from the outside of this club

smack dab in the center of a shopping mall off busy 119th Street, but inside it's a throwback to the ritzy supper clubs of the 1930s, with a smoke-filled bar and a separate, dark and moody dining area. Cocktail tables and a dance floor surround the stage area, where you can hear a variety of music from acoustic guitar to jazz to Disco Dick and the Mirror Balls. Raoul's is open seven days a week from 4:44 P.M. (and not a minute too soon) until 2:00 A.M. But don't worry, it's easy to find your car in that big parking lot. Also see the write-up in the Restaurants chapter.

A few years ago Kansas City caught martini mania in a big way. Several of our bars and restaurants have entire martini menus, with everything from the classic to a chocolate version. Some of the longest lists are found at the Fairmont's Lobby Bar, Raoul's Velvet Room, and the Velvet Dog.

The Uptown
3700 Broadway
(816) 753–8665
www.uptowntheater.com
God bless Larry Sells, the man behind the restoration of this magnificent movie palace. When it opened in 1928, the Uptown thrilled patrons with its elaborate Mediterranean courtyard design complete with balconies, twinkling stars, and mechanical flying birds. Ten years later the theater copyrighted the "Fragratone" system, which piped fragrances through the ventilation ducts.

Through the years all the greats played here, from Bob Hope to Bob Dylan, and it continued to serve as a live concert venue until it closed in 1989. After a $15 million restoration, it has reopened in all its glory. And although the opulent decor and red velvet curtain might contrast with the occasional heavy metal acts that appear on stage, it provides the appropriately upscale atmosphere for performers like

Ben Vereen or Nancy Wilson. Even when there's nothing happening on stage, the new Nowhere Club is a fun place to enjoy a cocktail and happy hour buffet four nights a week.

Along with an event calendar, the Web site offers photos and 3-D views of this breathtaking place with the curved marquee. And if you're looking for a delightful preconcert dinner, there's the Grille on Broadway (816–531–0700); we provide more information in Restaurants. Tickets may be purchased at the Uptown or through Ticketmaster.

The Wild West Border Deli and Bar
1717 West Ninth Street
(816) 472–1355

You can yippee-tie-one-on in the historic West Bottoms now that this fun, young bar has opened amid small art galleries and studio spaces. The antique pressed-tin ceilings and Art Deco floor tiles hint of the former Pabst-Milwaukee building's 100-year history as a ballroom and speakeasy. There's even a secret trapdoor to the basement, the better to hide the hooch during Prohibition. These days the booze is legal and when a bluegrass, funk, or rock band is playing on weekends, the mood is festive. When it's time to sit one out you can grab a sandwich at the deli.

You'll see a range of patrons here, from suburbanites seeking the inner-city experience to black-clad Art Institute students. No surprise that the latter crowd shows up: The landlord is Peregrine Honig, a talented local painter who provided the club's logo and 3-D mountainscape above the entrance. Her artwork also graces the back wall at La Bodega, a tapas restaurant on Southwest Boulevard.

Casino Entertainment

Although Kansas City's four casinos provide plenty of gaming action, you can exchange the blackjack tables for a cocktail table to hear live music in a variety of pavilions and piano bars. In Attractions we provide additional details about each casino.

Ameristar Casino
8201 Northeast Birmingham
(816) 414–7000, (800) 499–4961

Consistently voted "Best Casino" by readers of Kansas City magazine, Ameristar could also win prizes for the entertainment lineup in its Grand Pavilion. Since 1997 it has brought in such acts as David Lee Roth, Spyro Gyra, Chuck Mangione, and Chris Ledoux to its elegantly appointed stage. Tickets range from $12 to $65. Or head to the more intimate piano bar, the Phoenix, a smaller version of the popular Downtown jazz bar of the same name.

Argosy Casino
777 Northwest Argosy Parkway
Riverside, MO
(800) 270–7711
www.argosycasinos.com

The stars may be overhead at the four-star Constellation restaurant, but they're on stage at the 600-seat nightclub when entertainers like country crooner Pam Tillis show up on weekends. For a more casual dining option, order a bucket of shrimp for just $7.50 while you listen to the vibes. There's jazz, along with one of the city's best brunches, on Sunday.

Harrah's
One Riverboat Drive
(816) 472–7777
www.harrahs.com

Although Harrah's bills itself as the place for serious slots, when it comes to music the emphasis is on fun. Your first hint is the Mardi Gras jazz fountain in the lobby; your second is the sound of sassy horns coming out of the handsome entertainment pavilion. Here, bands like Nigel Mack and the Blues Attack can easily drown out the ding-ding-ding of slot machines several rooms away. Located on the northern bank of the Missouri River 3 miles from downtown, Harrah's offers a classy play-and-stay option with an attached hotel, as well as four dining options to keep you happy for an evening or a weekend. There's even a car wash so you can get your automobile cleaned and detailed while you enjoy yourself.

Isle of Capri Casino
1800 East Front Street
(816) 855-7777, (800) THE ISLE
www.islandcapricasino.com
You can't miss this casino with lights outlining the paddleboat so bright it rivals the nearby downtown skyline. Inside, the music is lively as well, with steel drums beating out a Caribbean beat to continue the island theme, or jazz trios on weekends that link Kansas City's heritage with calypso.

Country

Although we sometimes try to ignore our cowtown heritage like a pesky younger brother who follows us around, there's no disputing our Western roots. Throughout much of 1980, in fact, the most popular radio station and most of the jukeboxes in town played nothing but country hits. Most of us have hung up our spurs these days, but you can still join in a line dance at these two nightspots when the mood strikes.

The Beaumont
4050 Pennsylvania
(816) 561-BOOT (2668)
The first thing you notice upon entering this popular club in Westport is the mechanical bull. How convenient that it's right in front of one of three bars in the joint, all the better to wrestle up some nerve. If that action is a little too much for you, perhaps taking a free line dance lesson is more your style.

Thanks to its size and open design, the Beaumont can bring in some top-name acts that are too big for other clubs. Don't

be surprised, however, to hear decidedly noncountry bands here; there wasn't a single Stetson in sight when rock band They Might Be Giants appeared. And then there are the Friday salsa nights when professional dancers practice sensuous moves on the giant dance floor while crowds gather to watch.

But the Beaumont's "Urban Cowboy" appeal is its best draw. You've just gotta love a band called Insane Clown Posse. It's closed Sunday, which is why, we suppose, even cowboys get the blues.

Denim and Diamonds
1725 Swift
North Kansas City, MO
(816) 221-7300
www.denimdiamonds.com
Although there's no live music here, the place is plenty lively without it thanks to a great staff and an enthusiastic crowd. Loosen up those new Levi's with free dance lessons Wednesday through Sunday from 7:30 to 8:30 P.M., then be ready to two-step all night. The crowd often breaks into a line dance, and even if you don't know the steps you'll have fun. Double D is known for some of the prettiest cowgirls in the Midwest, especially on Thursday, which is Ladies Night.

Irish Pubs

The success of our stockyard industry in the West Bottoms was built, for the most part, on the broad backs of Irish workers who moved here in the late 1800s. They brought their music, dance, and a passion for a pint to their new home, and the rest of us become at least a little Irish when we partake of it. No wonder ours is the third largest St. Patrick's Day parade in the country. But you won't have to wait until March: There's an Irish festival or sing-along nearly every weekend somewhere in Kansas City.

We even lay claim to one of the finest Irish soloists, Connie Dover, who resides in

Weston (a charming town just north of Kansas City; see Day Trips and Weekend Getaways) and appears at local festivals when she's not touring the world or appearing on National Public Radio's *Prairie Home Companion*. With the voice and face of an angel, she can bring a crowd to tears—or its feet—with a simple ballad. See her schedule at www.conniedover.com. Other local talent includes Eddie Delahunt, Bob Reeder, and groups like the Shenanigans. Hear them at the following locations, or purchase their CDs at Browne's Market (3300 Pennsylvania; 816-561-0030; www.brownesmarket.com), Kansas City's oldest retail establishment and the oldest Irish business in the country.

Donovan's Grille & Pub
6825 North Oak Trafficway
Gladstone, MO
(816) 420-9099

Sample some authentic fish-and-chips or Irish stew between turns playing darts at this friendly pub. And every Friday night at a pint past eight there's live Irish music. Audience participation is nearly mandatory.

Harling's Upstairs
3941-A Main Street
(816) 531-0303

Harling's is just outside the craziness of Westport, but you won't miss it once the music starts. In fact, you might not even find it unless you're looking; its largely unmarked entrance is a single door that leads to a staircase that opens to huge rooms with an eagle's-eye view of the busy street down below. Its Irish heritage comes out when crooner Eddie Delahunt gets the crowd going with Gaelic songs Wednesday and Thursday. Blues is served on Sunday from 2:00 to 6:00 P.M. to help bid a soulful farewell to the weekend.

O'Dowd's Little Dublin
4742 Pennsylvania Street
(816) 561-2700
www.odowds.com

On summer nights the upstairs deck of this Plaza establishment is packed with young, attractive people whose motto seems to be the more the merrier. Many a date has been made on the slender staircase that joins the two floors. You can enjoy live Irish music, often erupting into sing-alongs, with your ale and traditional Irish fare. With its busy Plaza corner location, it's a fine place to meet up with friends or make new ones.

O'Malley's Pub
500 Welt Street
Weston, MO
(816) 640-5235
www.westonirish.com

When a German immigrant named John Georgeans started a brewery (the oldest brewery west of the Hudson River) in the early 1840s, he dug three rooms 55 feet underground and lined them with limestone blocks to create an even temperature for the fermenting process. At one time the brewery produced up to 20,000 barrels of beer a year before it was closed during Prohibition. Today the trilevel space is home to Sean O'Malley's Pub, which is the perfect escape on a hot summer evening. Just upstairs, Sean's parents operate the American Bowman Restaurant and the Inn at Weston Landing, so you can literally dine, drink, and deposit your weary body into a downy bed without leaving the premises.

When entertainers take the stage, the atmosphere is unlike anything else in town. Every October, Sean hosts an Irish Festival with three additional stages outside (see more in Annual Events and Festivals). There's authentic Irish food, imported libations, and great entertainment, including balladeer Bob Reeder, who sings and tells bawdy limericks. Watch for appearances by Connie Dover.

W. J. McBride's Irish Pub
12030 Blue Valley Parkway
Overland Park, KS
(913) 451-3100
www.wjmcbrides.com

Close the blinds to block out the view of the Super Target store and you'll think you're in Ireland. In fact, most of this pub's rich wood interior was constructed in Ireland and then shipped to the Midwest, and you're likely to hear a true Irish brogue from the management and staff. Certainly the music is legit; here's where to hear Bob Reeder (yes, he does seem to get around), Eddy Delahunt, and the popular Irish rock band, the Elders. Just for good measure, other contemporary artists and groups grace the stage now and then. We cover the dining options in the Restaurants chapter, but until then you haven't lived until you've had McBride's grilled pork chops marinated in garlic and rosemary.

Jazz

The Blue Room
1600 East 18th Street
(816) 474-2929
www.americanjazzmuseum.com

Back in the 1930s and 1940s, the Blue Room, located in the swank Street Hotel, was one of the hottest nightspots in the country. Six decades later it serves as a museum by day, with a wall of images of local musicians who made Kansas City swing. The glass-topped cocktail tables are display cases filled with rare artifacts like Count Basie's 1936 Musician's Union card, while the jukebox serves up tunes and videos from performers like Louis Armstrong, Charlie Parker, Billie Holiday, Fats Waller, and John Coltrane. Don't miss seeing Charlie Parker's saxophone or Ella Fitzgerald's rhinestone eyeglasses among the displays.

At night the Blue Room comes to life as a jazz club where four nights a week it welcomes local and national jazz greats. Since opening in September 1997, the club has built a loyal and ever-growing following. Although food and smoking are prohibited to preserve the artifacts, alcoholic beverages are available at the bar. The crowd tends to be older and well dressed. The Blue Room is part of the American Jazz Museum but has its own entrance. No cover charge.

The Kansas City Jazz Ambassadors can provide a pub crawl for you any time of year. The all-night party includes visits to at least three hot jazz spots, plenty of local music history, and authentic barbecue. They'll even provide live music on the bus. Tariffs start at $40 per person for groups of 40 or more. Call (913) 967-6767 or (816) 478-8378.

The Club at Plaza III
4749 Pennsylvania Street
(816) 753-0000

It could be the perfect date: Share a chateaubriand at Plaza III—The Steakhouse on the Country Club Plaza before heading downstairs to its elegant nightclub for great jazz and a nightcap. Once home to Kansas City's trendiest disco, the space now treats performers royally with a great sound system and a sophisticated crowd generally there to hear music. The place attracts national acts as well as local talent like the bossa-nova beat of Boko Maru Wednesday through Sunday. Expect a cover charge of around $5.00. Check out the dining room's write-up in the Restaurants chapter.

The Gem Theater
1615 East 18th Street
(816) 474-6262
www.americanjazzmuseum.com

Opened as a movie theater in 1912, the facade of the Gem, with its stained-glass and distinctive neon marquee, is still beautiful. But inside it's been updated to a 500-seat theater with the latest in lighting, sound, and acoustical design. The theater has hosted concerts, workshops and symposiums, and an annual Jammin' at the Gem Concert Series featuring outstanding national performers such as Lionel Hampton and James Moody. Call for event information, or check the Web site.

Kansas City—and All That Jazz

During the 1920s and 1930s, Kansas City was at the heart of the music scene. As a railroad hub, some of America's best musicians would stop here on their way to or from New Orleans, Chicago, or New York, and many, like Bill "Count" Basie, liked what they saw and heard and soon made the city their home.

Kansas City was a prosperous place during these decades and patrons had their pick of grand palaces like the Pla-Mor, which opened Thanksgiving Day 1927 at the northwest corner of Linwood and Main. The "million-dollar ballroom" featured an enormous dance hall along with a bowling alley, swimming pool, and ice-skating rink that doubled as the home ice for the town's minor league hockey team. Local stars shared marquee space with top-name touring acts such as Louis Armstrong. And Hoagy Carmichael pre-miered a new tune called "Stardust" on the Pla-Mor's stage.

The city's seedier side was repre-sented by joints like the Chesterfield Club, where waitresses were clad in noth-ing more than Cellophane.

But no matter whether the nightclub was ritzy or raunchy, it was packed with talent. Local musicians like Count Basie, Charlie Parker, and Joe Turner eventually influenced jazz across the nation. Basie practically invented the infectious, synco-pated style called swing at his piano at the Reno Club, bringing in soaring solos to drive the crowds wild.

Parker is generally considered most responsible for the creation of bebop, taking the music known as jazz into its modern incarnation. Certainly, others like Dizzy Gillespie and Thelonious Monk contributed mightily. But even among his peers, Parker was recognized as a leader, one of the rare musicians who actually earned the tag "genius." Had he not died in his thirties he might have gained even more of a mainstream following.

The legendary "cutting session" between tenor sax greats Lester "Pres" Young and Coleman "Bean" Hawkins depicted in Robert Altman's film *Kansas City* really happened. It went down on December 18, 1933, and continued until the wee hours at a joint called the Cherry Blossom. Pianist and bandleader Bill "Count" Basie kept time.

Some say famed saxophonist Charlie Parker came by his nickname "Yardbird," later shortened to just "Bird," because of his fondness for fried chicken. But others say his handle came from his "free as a bird" lifestyle that would cause his untimely death.

As musicians like Basie and Parker became better known, they often left for the East Coast and bigger gigs. But it was the fall of political boss Tom Pender-gast (read more about his reign in the History chapter) that marked the end of the Jazz Age in Kansas City. Once reformers closed the nightspots, the remaining bands took the A Train to places like New York and Chicago.

So the term Kansas City jazz is a handy handle for a musical mix that owes its life to gospel, ragtime, blues, swing, and bebop. No wonder it's so hard to define. Our advice? Don't overanalyze it. Just listen.

The sound that put Kansas City on the musical map—jazz—can still be heard at night-clubs, restaurants, and courtyards all over town. RICK MCKIBBEN

You'll have plenty of chances. Kansas City has given birth to some remarkable jazz talents over the decades, and it continues today. A few, like singer Kevin Mahogany and Grammy-winning guitarist Pat Metheny, have moved away. But others are happy to call the heartland home between tours to Chicago, New York, and Europe. While they're touring there are others to keep your fingers snapping: A two-page list of local musicians printed in *JAM,* the Kansas City Jazz Ambassadors' bimonthly magazine, includes 85 bands, 55 vocalists, and one tuba player. You'll find them performing almost every night at some nightclub or restaurant or head-lining at music festivals all over town. Look for listings in the *Kansas City Star*'s Friday Preview or *Pitch Weekly,* or call the 24-hour Kansas City Jazz Ambassadors' Hotline at (816) 753–5277.

By the way, when Charlie Parker's plastic horn came up for auction at Christie's in New York, forward-thinking Kansas Citians, led by then-mayor Emanuel Cleaver II, outbid a Japanese investor to bring it back home for $145,000. The instrument is now displayed at the Kansas City Jazz Museum at 18th and Vine.

Ivy's Restaurant & Jazz Club
240 Northeast Barry Road
(816) 436-3320
www.ivyskc.com
Owners Sam and Carol Cross took a real chance when they upgraded their strip-mall diner into a swanky restaurant and jazz club in the 1980s, but the gamble has paid off handsomely. Part of the draw is the talent they book—including Angela Hagenbach, Soul Solution, Max Groove, and Stan Kessler—but plenty of people show up just for the food and award-winning wine list. The luscious roasted lamb chops coated with Dijon mustard and crushed pistachios is a not-to-be-missed specialty. As one of the few jazz outlets north of the river, the place tends to pack them in every Friday and Saturday, so reservations are highly recommended. And if you really want to hear the jazz, request a table near the stage. If you prefer a more romantic dinner, there are private nooks and crannies to be found throughout the restaurant. Check out Ivy's Web site for a handy map and directions. No cover.

Jardine's Restaurant & Jazz Club
4536 Main Street
(816) 561-6480
www.jardines4jazz.com
Beena Brandsgard's cozy club has become one of Kansas City's hottest night spots to hear some of the city's top performers, including Angela Hagenbach, Mike Metheny, and Lisa Henry, every Tuesday through Saturday. And when blues stylist Ida McBeth has a birthday, she cele-

brates in this hideaway with several dozen of her closest friends and fans. The late-night jam session is also popular every Saturday after midnight when musicians show up after ending gigs elsewhere; anyone with a voice or a horn is encouraged to get up on stage.

The restaurant serves better food than you might expect, too (see listing in Restaurants). Everything—from the skillet-fried chicken and crunchy-crusted fried catfish—is made from scratch. Want to really live? Reserve a cozy, dark booth and order the peppercorn-crusted filet mignon in brandy cream sauce. And here's good news for night owls: Jardine's is one of the rare places that serves dinner until midnight on weekends. Just a stroll from the Country Club Plaza with plenty of well-lighted parking in back. No cover.

The Majestic Steakhouse
931 Broadway
(816) 471-8484
www.majesticgroup.com
If walls could talk they'd drown out the music played seven days a week at this historic nightspot. Originally built in 1911 as the Fitzgerald Saloon, the handsome brick building served as bordello, speakeasy, and office where politicians met with lobbyists and thugs, businessmen, and favor seekers. The downstairs space now provides a cozy nightclub featuring some of the city's favorite vocalists like Julie Turner. No cover charge.

This is another example of great food nearly upstaging the entertainment; the dry-aged steaks here are renowned (see more details in Restaurants). In fact, locals remember the Majestic from its 40-year span at East 31st Street and Holmes. Although you won't be able to hear the jazz in the dining room, a solo acoustic guitarist provides music to dine by.

The night isn't complete without at least a peek at the members-only, third-floor Pendergast Cigar Club with its brick walls, leather chairs, and walk-in humidor. Memberships cost from $500 to $3,000 a year, but here's a real Insiders' tip: For the

---

Although you'll see plenty of jeans and even shorts during summer, lots of jazz club patrons tend to dress up a bit on Saturday night. So pull out that cocktail dress and black suit when you paint the town red. Didn't pack the fancy duds? Don't worry: You'll be welcome no matter what you're wearing.

---

cost of dinner—no sacrifice there—you can be escorted up the stairs as a guest of the restaurant as long as there isn't a private party in session.

The Mutual Musician's Foundation
1823 Highland Avenue
(816) 471-5212

This living shrine to jazz is where Charlie Parker, Jay McShann, Bennie Moten, Lester Young, Mary Lou Williams, and other greats got their start and where today, musicians jam from around midnight until dawn—or as long as the audience is there. There's no cover charge, but donations are gladly accepted at the door, and you'll want to pony up a few bucks after a particularly soulful solo.

Located in the 18th and Vine District, the building was designated a National Historic Landmark in 1982 after undergoing major reconstruction. The district is also home to the Negro Leagues Baseball Museum and the American Jazz Museum, both well worth a visit (information is available in Attractions), along with the Gem Theater and the Blue Room, described earlier. If you hurry you might still see some of the movie sets from Robert Altman's 1995 film, *Kansas City*.

Phoenix Piano Bar & Grill
302 West Eighth Street
(816) 472-0001

You can't miss this cozy neighborhood club; just drive around downtown until you hear music or spot the giant smiling face mural painted on its brick wall. Folks inside are grinning as well, thanks to the friendly atmosphere and co-owner Tim Whitmer, one of Kansas City's most popular piano players. He and his band, KC Express, hold court here along with regular visits from top performers like internationally respected jazz stylist Karrin Allyson (who lived in town for a while), Max Groove, and the Dave Stephens

Swing Band. The menu features steaks, pasta, and fresh seafood for lunch and dinner, but the main pull is the live music and casual vibe. Originally the Phoenix Hotel built in the 1880s, today it's where to get your weekend started right. No cover.

SPORTS BARS

Kansas City is officially a sports town, so nearly every bar in town—even the more sophisticated versions with highly polished wood and real ferns—has a big screen or two tuned to a game, tournament, or race. And when a professional sports team or college game is on the tube, one of these bars is the place to go to commiserate or celebrate with friends.

Harpo's
4109 Pennsylvania
(816) 753-3434

With nightly happy hour specials from 4:00 to 7:00, a menu loaded with appetizers and burgers, and plenty of strategically placed TVs, it's no wonder Harpo's was named best sports bar by *USA Today*. There's even a nifty courtyard when you want to escape the nonstop cheering or grousing during a Chiefs game. The fun continues until 3:00 A.M.

River Market Brewing Company
500 Walnut Street
(816) 471-6300

During the day and most evenings this attractive brewpub does a brisk lunch business serving beer, salads, burgers, and pretty good barbecue. But woe is the couple expecting a quiet evening out when a KU or MU football game is being televised on what seems like an endless number of screens. That's when noisy alumni take over the wooden booths and barstools to cheer on the teams.

SHOPPING

In the mid-1800s, as the last civilized stop on the way out West, we welcomed wagon trains and riverboats with provisions, pickaxes, and camaraderie. Shoppers still come here in droves, although today they show up for style rather than mere sustenance.

In fact, several times a year entire busloads of ladies debark at the shopper's paradise known as Kansas City. Shoppers from hundreds of miles away make annual, sometimes quarterly, pilgrimages to our city-sized antiques centers, enormous outlet malls, and one-of-a-kind emporiums like Nell Hill's in nearby Atchison, Kansas.

Of course, the high-winter holidays wouldn't be the same without a visit to the Country Club Plaza, our 14-block extravaganza of retail stores and entertainment with 250,000 glowing Christmas lights outlining every building, spire, and arch. And for those who enjoy one-of-a-kind shops rather than big-name stores that could be in any city in North America, there's the Crossroads Arts District, a vibrant neighborhood with more than 70 art galleries, boutiques, and showrooms, all within a mile walking radius. We'll give you the full tour in this chapter's Shopping Districts section, but we've also singled out a few shops in cross-referenced categories, such as antiques.

Our shopping opportunities are so stupendous that when people call us a sports town, they're often referring to the action in the *aisles,* not the stadiums. Our renowned buying power and sophisticated lifestyle have naturally attracted giant retailers, often for their first forays into the Midwest. Examples include Nordstrom, Ralph Lauren, and Saks Fifth Avenue. And where these giants go, smaller exclusive boutiques and stores such as Armani, St. John Knits, Dean & Deluca, MAC Cosmetics, and Mark Shale follow, giving us

enough cachet to be considered the heartland's Rodeo Drive.

Other retail adventures await you just outside our city limits. Drive just 40 miles or so to Weston, Missouri, or Lawrence, Kansas, and you'll find charming, old-fashioned downtowns filled with antiques shops and flea markets, art galleries, unique fashion emporiums, and more. We take you there in the Day Trips and Weekend Getaways chapter.

And don't overlook the dozens of one-of-a-kind shops you'll find only in Kansas City. Asiatica fashions exquisite garments from antique kimonos, and Retro Inferno sells designer furniture from the 1930s to 1970s in prime condition, just right for that so-in loft look. Both shops were "discovered" by collectors in New York and Los Angeles before their own hometown. Ditto for local artists Markus Pierson, whose famous Coyote series is owned by the rich and famous; his wife Sheryl Pierson, whose collages grace the homes of Whoopi Goldberg and Sir Elton John; and Tom Corbin, who counts Jack Nicholson, Tom Hanks, and Alec Baldwin as fans. Their studios are a few blocks apart in the River Market area. It must be the water.

Don't be shy about calling or dropping by any of the places mentioned. One thing you'll learn about shopping in Kansas City is that, unlike some other cities, you'll be greeted by a friendly hello whether you're in a major department store or a tiny shop with a tinkling bell above the door. Go ahead and touch the goods, sit down to test the cushions, and ask where to get a good meal nearby. And don't be surprised if they place your purchase in a gift bag complete with tufts of tissue paper and a jaunty bow.

Expect most of the shops to be open Monday through Saturday, unless listed otherwise. But because many of the stores are owner- or artist-operated, it's always best to call ahead.

The shops in this chapter are grouped by category of goods and then listed alphabetically. All the shops are in Kansas City, Missouri, unless otherwise noted.

Many of these special places are unadvertised, and several are off the beaten path. When the shopkeepers ask how in the world you discovered them, just say an Insider gave you the scoop. So put on those comfortable shoes, grab that credit card, and let's go shopping!

ANTIQUES AND COLLECTIBLES

It's true: We're one of the country's best-kept secrets when it comes to the quality and value of the antiques available here. And often, just to make the hunting even more delightful, we've grouped dozens of shops together in a huge antiques mall or neighborhood. You can literally shop all day at one location, returning to your vehicle just long enough to store another treasure in the trunk. When it's time for a break, a cafe or coffee shop is usually just a shopping bag's throw away.

Antiquities & Oddities
Architectural Salvage
2045 Broadway
(816) 283-3740
If the name doesn't get you, just driving by the beautiful two-story Broadway Bank-turned-antiques-shop with intriguing treasures peeking through the windows will. For decades, long before slightly chipped architectural remnants, bronze urns blackened with age, and enormous marble sculptures became the look for upscale gardens and homes, Architectural Salvage has been collecting interesting and priceless pieces from razed buildings, churches, and movie palaces and selling them to interior decorators, set designers, and savvy shoppers.

Here's where to find massive carved wooden doors, rusted gates, salvaged church pews, stained-glass windows, Tara-sized porch columns, discarded fireplace

mantels, and red velvet fold-down seats. You can spend hours just digging through boxes of doorknobs and cases of rescued hardware. Pace yourself, and leave the nice clothes at home; it can get pretty grungy here. But to find that perfect gargoyle for your garden, what's a little 80-year-old dust? Be warned, though. This isn't a spur-of-the-moment shopping spree. The store is only open Thursday through Saturday or by appointment. Owner Rick Bettinger may have just the baluster or newel post you need.

Asiatica Ltd.
4824 Rainbow Boulevard
Westwood, KS
(913) 831-0831
Fans of this shop report Asiatica sightings all over the world—in a posh hotel lobby in New York City, in the shadow of the Sistine Chapel—because their fashions made from old Japanese kimonos are so distinctive. Each year Elizabeth Wilson and Fifi White travel to the Far East to hand select silk kimonos from the 1920s to the 1950s, then bring them back home to get glorious new lives as vests, flowing jackets, blouses, and wraps.

These gorgeous garments are available only through Asiatica's showroom near the Country Club Plaza and a handful of trunk shows in major markets around the country. Each piece of clothing is a work of art, a one-of-a-kind artifact created from a nonrenewable resource.

The shop also offers an ever-changing selection of antiques, Japanese chests, ceramics, scarves, and jewelry picked up from around the world. And you never know when you'll be tapped on the shoulder somewhere in Rome with a question, "Say, aren't you wearing Asiatica?"

Brookside Antiques
6219 Oak Street
(816) 444-4774
www.brooksideantiques.com
Some shop owners willingly share their expertise with customers who stop by. Ron Zoglin put his advice on paper in

Antiquing for Dummies, a nifty guide he cowrote with Deborah Shouse. His enormous store a few blocks south of the Brookside shopping district gives readers a great place to ply their newfound knowledge. Known nationwide for his extensive Chinese collection, including altar tables, carved benches, and tea stands, Ron also offers rare Venetian glass, silverware, 18th-century American and European furniture, and objects of adornment like exquisite shell cameos and pocket watches. His Web site shows just a sample of a 300-piece collection of jade figurines and jewelry worn smooth by years of rubbing for luck. Your luck can change with one visit.

You'll find a number of charming, old-fashioned "Main Street" shopping districts throughout Kansas City, each filled with unique stores and antiques shops. Some of the best are in Parkville, Brookside, Independence Square, 45th and State Line, Crestwood, and the eclectic Crossroads Arts District.

Cheep Antiques
500 West Fifth Street
(816) 471-0092
The name sounds like "bargain," but the quality and variety of antiques found inside this three-story shop in the River Market is about as rich as it gets. There are so many hall stands, armoires, buffets, bedroom sets, dining tables, and washstands in this 30,000-square-foot space that you'll have to squeeze between them sideways to get to the next room.

The bounty also includes rugs, clocks, upholstered furniture, and an odd assortment of baskets, boxes, and even humidors. The Porter family (one is always in residence, ready to share the history of each piece) can convert nearly any armoire into an entertainment or computer center. Layaway and delivery are available. Look for the big sign on the building 1 block west of the Broadway Bridge.

Churchill at Crestwood
309 East 55th Street
(816) 363-3938
www.churchillincrestwood.com
This gem of a find is in the delightful, blocklong shopping-and-dining destination known as the Crestwood Shops. And while Churchill is known for its incredible selection of antique furniture, it's also the place to spy accessories and jewelry favored by Hollywood's young A-list stars like Kate Hudson and Gwyneth Paltrow. Chances are the booty in the coveted Oscar gift basket is on Churchill's shelves before the telecast is over. Just how does a tiny shop in the heart of Missouri get such a scoop? Leave it to Churchill's vivacious owner, Sally Hilkene.

Frankly, we'd follow this trendsetter anywhere. Sally's unerring eye for taste (she was a much-sought-after interior designer for more than 20 years) serves her well, as she fills her shop with an eclectic collection of treasures for the home and personal adornments. Fancy the handbag on Sharon Stone's arm in a celebrity magazine? Check with Sally first. Those fabulous scented stones Elton John likes to give as gifts? Churchill's, again. And this warm and energetic merchant is becoming known for her exquisite one-of-a-kind jewelry, culled from estates all over the world—like the glorious pair of chandelier earrings one famous actress wore on a fashion magazine cover.

While Sally follows the trends, her inventory consists of pieces that will stand the test of time. And speaking of that, did you see her selection of divine watches?

The Curious Sofa
329 Southwest Boulevard
(816) 221-6600
www.curioussofa.com
Stopping by Debbie Dusenberry's antiques and home furnishings shop is like a minivacation as your senses are assailed by scented candles, offbeat treasures longing to be touched, and "Moon River" on the stereo. On any given day you might find a peeling-paint medicine cabi-

net, funky mirror covered in shells, or beaded Barbie-size chandelier. Her selection of new and antique jewelry is divine.

Here, vintage is cleverly mixed with made-to-look-old new items like the Shabby Chic line of furniture.

Give this delightful proprietress a call before heading her way; she's a willing resource to help plan your own Kansas City scavenger hunt. Or check her Web site, which is pretty ooh-and-ahh worthy itself, for links to other independent businesses in the vibrant Crossroads Arts District.

45th & State Line Antique, Art & Design Center
45th and State Line Road
(816) 531-4414

If you have a penchant for the old, the unique, or the collectible, then snoop to your heart's content in this quaint historic district that features over 20 antiques shops and galleries, all within charming row houses. Despite the number of shops in one place, they rarely repeat each other, so it's a sure bet you'll be here for hours. The prices bring back buyers again and again.

One not to miss is Christopher Filley (816–561–1124), where unique antiques and decorative arts are stacked to the rafters. Although it specializes in garden art including architectural remnants, statues, bird fountains, and pitted stone balls, you'll also spy hand-carved santos, a nice selection of mercury glass, mirrors set inside enormous industrial gears, and other delightfully quirky finds. Prices are not marked, but don't be afraid to ask Christopher or his associate, Rich Hoffman. You'll get a price and perhaps a fascinating story about the item's history.

European Express (816–753–0443) may sound like a fast-food cafe, but it's actually three floors filled with antiques, including enormous armoires and marble washstands. And make sure to stop by Morning Glory Antiques, Earl's Court, and. . . oh, what the heck. Visit them all; each is totally different, all are wonderful. And the proprietors are truly happy to greet you and answer questions. During the holiday open house they'll even set out cookies and hot spiced cider.

When it's break time, the 45th Street Coffee Shop's comfy sofas and light-filled window seat will feel just like home. They serve breakfast pastries, light sandwiches, and salads along with coffees and fruit smoothies.

GR Interiors
1450 West Lexington
Independence, MO
(816) 254-0964
www.frontofthehousedecor.com

If you've ever been to a restaurant whose walls are filled with interesting antiques, vintage posters, and eclectic doodads like canoe paddles and wondered, "Where do they find these things?," well, this is the place. Originally part of the famed Kansas City Gilbert-Robinson restaurant group, this storeroom has outfitted dining rooms like Houlihan's around the country.

Since husband-and-wife team Ernie and Leigh Laber took over the enterprise, they've shifted their energies to creating customized mirrors, lighting fixtures, and artwork incorporating stained and leaded glass. Most of the work is done for restaurants, such as an $80,000 stained-glass dome for a bistro in California and a marvelous mirror for J. Gilbert's here in Overland Park, but they also create art for residential clients. A pub mirror, for example, complete with family name and year established, would cost around $500 depending on the design and size.

The four artists who fashion these pieces are masters at their craft, turning out Tiffany-quality work. And according to artist Rick Hanks, they can handle any project using your concept or theirs. He's particularly proud of a recent installment in a Kansas City lake home: a 7-foot window with an etched nature scene. The price? Don't ask.

GR Interiors still has an amazing display of treasures accumulated from estate sales, barns, attics, and curio shops from all over the world; anything, Ernie says, that you can hang on a wall or stand on a

shelf. The booty, naturally, changes constantly. Open weekdays from 9:00 A.M. to 5:00 P.M. and weekends by appointment. Rumor has it they may be moving soon, so please call first.

Joey O'Connor Antiques and Oriental Rugs
4740 Rainbow Boulevard
Westwood, KS
(913) 384-2424

For more than 25 years this ball of energy has managed to find some of the best antiques and accessories in town. But don't drop in expecting $10 coffee tables. Here, the consigned goods include prized antiques, fine artwork, and sought-after Oriental rugs that go as high as $65,000. A handsome mahogany dining table is set with $18,000 worth of Imari dinnerware in pristine condition. Joey's price is about half of retail.

Other choices might include Staffordshire porcelain cats, an American Federal desk, massive carved armoires, and an antique wooden hat mold. Notice the "might" in that sentence, the goods always go fast thanks to regular customers and interior designers who stop in several times a month, often just for a dose of Joey's irreverent sense of humor. Looking for something specific? Give her a call. She may have it now, expect to get it soon, or can find it on one of her many buying trips. The shop is open Tuesday through Friday.

Locust Grove Antiques & Interiors
25180 Missouri Highway JJ
Weston, MO
(816) 640-3203

Locust Grove isn't an antiques *mall*, but with its barnlike size it may as well be. It's amazing that two partners own the entire inventory, which is part antique, part new, all sensational. Kate Parsons, a talented interior designer, teamed up with daughter Christy Shafer to create small vignettes of themed treasures to make browsing fun and collecting a breeze.

A recent walk-through spied a dining room area with pierced silver servers, topiaries, and a tapestry throw; a bar service with silver cocktail picks in a vintage shot glass and an old seltzer bottle; and a glorious bedchamber with antique bedroom set, vintage linens, and needlepoint pillows. They also have some of the most incredible faux florals and botanicals available, including dried wreaths. Locust Grove is definitely worth the 40-mile drive out of town, especially if you're heading to Weston (see Day Trips and Weekend Getaways) for the afternoon or weekend. The shop is open every day but Monday.

Mission Road Antiques
4101 West 83rd Street
Prairie Village, KS
(913) 341-7577
www.missionroad.antiquelandusa.com

Better get plenty of rest the night before you plan to attack this 50,000-square-foot mall, considered to be one of the finest in the Midwest. The building is as historical as some of its contents; 60 years ago it was a stable for Thoroughbred horses, including the 1938 Kentucky Derby winner, Lawrin. Today the "stalls" have been taken over by 350 dealers displaying their wares, which include European antiques, primitives, stained glass, vintage housewares, Oriental porcelain, estate jewelry, military collectibles, and more.

Some vendors specialize in one category, such as original oil paintings or Christmas decorations, but most offer an engaging array of goods. Expect to spend at least half a day to see it all. And just as you've reached sensory overload, there's a cozy cafe in the mall to offer a place to sit down to some tasty food. The Bloomsbury Bistro's menu changes every Friday, but expect to find items like veggie lasagna and chicken salad along with soups and wraps. The chef knows her way around a cake pan, too. Homemade desserts include pies and German chocolate cake.

River Market Antique Mall
115 West Fifth Street
(816) 221-0220
No wonder this mall has been voted "Best Antique Shop in Kansas City" by readers of *Pitch Weekly*. First, there's the size. With more than 30,000 square feet of booths and showcases spread out over four floors, it's enough to make you just plain giddy with anticipation of what you'll find. Here's just a teaser: American, European, and primitive furniture including mission and Wakefield; pottery and glassware featuring plenty of Roseville; vintage clothing and jewelry; quilts and lamps; antique toys; and old advertising art. The vendors are friendly enough to answer questions and point you to another booth if you're seeking something specific. And the location creates the perfect environment for finding treasures as old as our city: The mall is a few blocks from the very spot where our town began.

Webster House Antiques and Restaurant
1644 Wyandotte
(816) 221-4713
If you're from the old school of thought, you'll love shopping for antiques in what's considered to be Kansas City's oldest surviving schools. While renovating the Romanesque Revival building, built in the late 19th century, workers removed plasterboard to find blackboards with homework assignments written in chalk.

Now the rooms hold the marvelous antique and decorative accessories that used to grace Crestwood Galleries Antiques & Cafe, which spent 30 years at the Crestwood Shops at 55th and Oak. Thanks to owner Shirley Bush Helzberg's vision, the new location has more than double the retail space, plus room for a charming restaurant and additional galleries on the second floor. Loyal fans of Crestwood Galleries will be thrilled to see the same friendly faces at Webster House, including general manager Keitha Kaminski and talented designer Joe Haas. And, yes, that aroma wafting around the Chinoiserie and Chippendales is executive

chef Timothy Johnson's chipotle shrimp with sautéed corn cakes.

Woodson Place Antiques & Interiors
318 West Walnut
Raymore, MO
(816) 331-2701
Sleepy little Raymore's population nearly doubles when Roy and Jane Park announce they're back from Europe with the latest container of antiques. Caravans of buses, cars, and vans show up at this turn-of-the-20th-century home turned shop set back from a busy commercial street. Thank goodness there's plenty of parking—and a separate warehouse to hold the overflow.

It's Jane's unerring eye for quality that draws customers from 12 states—she has an instinct for what people want—but it's the jaw-dropping prices that keep them coming back. Recently a magnificent tiger mahogany armoire, circa 1860, sold for a mere $1,789. Bring measurements and be ready to buy as soon as you fall in love; at these prices nothing lasts long enough to tarry. Raymore, Missouri, is located about 40 miles south of Kansas City. Be sure to call for dates of the next open house.

BED AND BATH GIFTS

Indigo Wild
3189 Mercier
(816) 221-3480, (800) 361-5686
www.indigowild.com
This tiny company produces delightfully scented bath and beauty products made of good-for-you ingredients. The Zum bars, for example, include goat's milk, pure essential oils, and herbal extracts and come in lots of yummy scents like lavender-mint and sandalwood-citrus. The bars, which look like tie-died artwork with swirls and chunks of colors, come in fun, corrugated shapes. The company also makes paraffin-free candles, baby care products, body lotions, and all-natural lip balms in flavors like tangerine. That's Zum kiss! Products are

available by phone, online, or through a clever catalog.

**Perfect Scents
608 West 48th Street
(816) 753-8117, (800) 223-9819**

**5037 West 119th Street
Overland Park, KS
(913) 469-1737
www.perfectscentsinc.com**
"Come inside and play," Nancy McAnany beckons to those who enter her shop of earthly and ethereal delights. Since 1989 she's been turning customers into alchemists as they create unique body lotions, massage oils, and home products using dozens of aromatic essential oils. Nancy figures there are at least 3,424 different custom-scented products you can conjure up. Or choose one of her designer oils that smell like expensive versions without the hefty price tags.

The shelves and counters reveal other treats, like spearmint-flavored lip balm, gentle baby care products, lamp rings that send a subtle fragrance throughout the room, and car diffusers that do the same for that long drive home. And who could resist the red mineral facial treatment she calls the "Hoover Vacuum Cleaner" of masks? The stores are located on the Country Club Plaza and Hawthorne Plaza.

**Scandia Down—Kansas City
501 Nichols Road (Country Club Plaza)
(816) 753-4144
www.scandiadownkc.com**
Welcome to Ursula Terrasi's little corner of the world. Literally. This merchant—with the grace of Italian royalty and the warmth of a Midwesterner—searches the globe for luxurious bedding (can you count to 800 threads per inch?), hand-finished furniture, heavenly scented bath potions, and beautiful tableware for her shop on the Country Club Plaza. But it's the meringue-high, down-filled comforters that have shoppers wanting to jump in bed. Each cozy store vignette has been dressed to the nines in sumptuous fabrics and masses of pillows.

No wonder Scandia Down is favored for its bridal registry service: Climb into one of these sumptuous confections every night and the honeymoon may never end. And following Mother Nature's course, the shop has a new line of beds and accessories for babies.

The shop is located on the corner of Pennsylvania and Nichols Road, at the delightful Penguin Courtyard, where live musical concerts are held from spring through fall. If Ursula has her way, they'll play a medley of Dean Martin hits.

BOOKSTORES

Here in Kansas City, reading ranks right up there as a favorite hobby. Perhaps it's our way of getting through cold winter nights or a tough day in the sun at poolside. We encourage early readers, too, through readings at bookstores and libraries. And two of our best corporate citizens, AMC Theatres and the *Kansas City Star,* do their part by sponsoring ongoing reading programs for students.

Adult readers have plenty of opportunities to turn the page, too, thanks to bookstores that seem to be on every street corner and twice as many in most malls. Naturally we have our share of national book dealers like Waldenbooks, Borders, and Barnes & Noble. But we also have an amazing number of independent booksellers who succeed because of their special services. Rainy Day Books, for instance, consistently brings well-known writers to town for speaking engagements. At Bloomsday Books and Reading Reptile, the owners have found a market and nurture it so well customers wouldn't think of being disloyal. So here, dear readers, are some of our best and brightest booksellers.

**Bloomsday Books
301 East 55th Street
(816) 523-6712
www.bloomsdaybooks.com**
Lawyer-turned-bookseller Tom Shawver is thrilled to take your gently used books in

for trade; it's his confirmation that one more person has the reading bug. The bookstore's location is ideal: a large sunny space in the quaint Crestwood Shops, where his neighbors include antiques stores and bustling bistros. The shelves are well organized with varied categories, and the staff is made up of avid readers who can talk about nearly any book or author.

Relax with an espresso and croissant, scone, or slab of peanut butter fudge from the Aixois Coffee Bar on the other side of the door, part of the bistro (see Restaurants) by the same name. Then take your beverage back to Bloomsday, choose a chair in the sun-filled window, and relax while you make your literary selection. Tom certainly won't rush you: There's no doubt this guy holds literature—and especially the works of Irish author James Joyce—in high esteem. He named his shop for Leopold Bloom, the central character in Joyce's *Ulysses,* and every June 16 holds a nonstop reading of the novel. Hold the latte; could you make that an Irish coffee, please?

The Complete Traveler
7321 West 80th Street
Overland Park, KS
(913) 648-1560
If you're planning a trip, make Bill Abrams's well-stocked travel store your first stop. Beyond a staggering collection of travel guides, globes, and personal travel accessories like money belts, he can dispense valuable advice. Tell him your vacation goals—insights into the culture, romantic getaway, or family fun—and Bill can point you to the right book. He might also include some personal tips on what to do once you're there. Chances are if Bill hasn't been there one of his globetrotting customers has.

The Complete Traveler is an authorized representative for Eurail and BritRail passes and is one of a few retailers to carry the Thomas Cook European Rail Timetable, which Bill calls the Bible of European rail travel. And because you have

to put your new travel guide in something, the store stocks a nice supply of luggage.

The Last Chapter Bookshoppe
11128 Antioch
Overland Park, KS
(913) 339-6616
Twenty-five years in the book-selling business? Now that's a story! Jane Schaumburg has kept her independent shop thriving thanks to personal service, an enviable inventory, and loyal customers who have followed her to her latest location in a busy shopping center at the corner of Antioch and College Boulevard.

Jane hosts authors for book signings several times a year—hugely popular events that have fans lining up for hours—and maintains long calling list for new publications. Love a good mystery, romance, western, or cookbook? You'll learn about it here first. Jane and her employees are also helping encourage young readers: The shop provides books for the Blue Valley school system's summer reading lists.

Rainy Day Books
2706 West 53rd Street
Fairway, KS
(913) 384-3126
www.rainydaybooks.com
Vivien Jennings and Roger Doeren somehow manage to convince top authors that they can't sell a single book unless they appear in Kansas City. Since 1975 Rainy Day has hosted thousands of book signings—several a month—for authors including Ray Bradbury, Anne Rice, Jack Welsh, Martha Stewart, Garrison Keillor, and Erin Brockovich.

This corner store in Fairway near the Country Club Plaza is all that a bookseller can hope to be: a friendly place where there's someone on the staff who can recommend a book whether the subject is murder, cooking, home repair, romance, or coping with a baby sister. Rainy Day also sponsors writers' seminars throughout the year to encourage local authors to keep those bookshelves filled. And Vivien writes a regular column, "Book Ends," in a weekly society magazine, the *Independent*. Heavens, if *she* can find time to read, anyone can.

Reading Reptile
328 West 63rd Street
(816) 753-0441
www.readingreptile.com
Is this someone's living room or a book-store? Actually, it's both. Since 1988 own-ers Pete and Debbie have made this cheery shop their home-away-from-home, where they've brought up their four adorable kids, made lasting friendships, and introduced hundreds of children to the joys of the written and spoken word. They hold free story hours for preschool-ers and school-aged children every week and host book clubs for young readers.

Once a year Reading Reptile sponsors a two-day event (a literary love-in, they call it) so that children, adults, teachers, and librarians can meet some of the top authors and illustrators. The store is fun, the Web site is a hoot, and the T-shirts, in which a fellow implores his dog to "Read, Dammit!" would make a fine gift for the serious booklover.

CLOTHING AND ACCESSORIES

Act II
1507 West 47th Street
(816) 531-7572
Yes, it's true that Act II is a consignment shop, but owner Gloria Everhart is so picky about quality that the goods might as well be right off the retail rack. Savvy women shop here first for eveningwear

Local folklore credits Olathe bootmaker Charles H. Hyer with the innovation of making boots shaped differently for right and left feet in the late 1800s. Before that, shoes were identical, and—one would imagine—a little tough to break in.

with labels from Bill Blass, Calvin Klein, Adolfo, and other designers. The after-five and ball gown selection is amazing thanks to the number of black tie affairs held each year in Kansas City; some social denizens attend four or more a season and wouldn't dare wear the same sequined number twice.

Gloria also sells tailored suits, casual clothes, outerwear—yes, even furs—and like-new handbags and shoes. The store is just up the hill from the Plaza, and her men's consignment shop is a few blocks away.

Bob Jones Shoes
1914 Grand
(816) 474-4212
www.bobjonesshoes.com
You're bound to find your soul-mate at Bob Jones. At any given time more than 100,000 pairs of designer shoes line the racks at up to 70 percent off retail. Sure, a few in the back room are a little dated, unless you want bright blue pumps with six-inch heels, but 98 percent of the inventory consists of top names found at the finest department stores. For women that includes Enrico Gori, Via Spiga, Stuart Weitzman, Joan & David, and Calvin Klein. Men can choose from Johnston Murphy, Kenneth Cole, Bostonian, Rockport, and more. Bob Jones also carries a limited number of athletic shoes and unique women's handbags. Just look for the wooden Indian in front.

DISCOUNT MALLS AND STORES

Bushnell Factory Outlet
8500 Marshall Drive
Lenexa, KS
(913) 752-6166
www.bushnell.com
Take a look at the pair of binoculars in your hall closet or backpack; if they're good, chances are Bushnell is printed on the case. This Kansas City–based com-pany has been manufacturing high-

performance optics for more than 50 years, but until they opened this outlet you'd have to pay retail prices at sporting goods stores. You'll still pay retail for some merchandise, including first-run binoculars, telescopes, night-vision scopes, and laser rangefinders. But you'll find significant discounts, from 25 to 50 percent off retail, on discontinued items, and up to 75 percent off retail on factory demonstration goods that are still in great shape.

The outlet holds plenty of attraction for any birder, astronomer, or sports enthusiast, even if that means someone who pulls a beer tab at a football game instead of a trigger. Plus Bushnell carries Bolle and Serengeti, some of the most stylish sunglasses in the world.

The Great Mall of the Great Plains
I-35 and 151st Street
Olathe, KS
(913) 829-6277, (888) FUN MALL
www.greatmallgreatplains.com

This enormous mall, the largest in Kansas, has more than 100 factory outlet, discount, and specialty stores under one roof. Anchors are Marshall's and Burlington Coat Factory plus Linens 'n Things, Eddie Bauer, Old Navy, Nautica, Black & Decker tools, Carter's, and Levis. Specialty stores include Noble House jewelers and Ritz cameras. And if shopping isn't your bag, there's a 16-screen movie theater.

You won't have to look hard for convenience, either. The fully carpeted space is all on one level, stroller and wheelchair rental is complimentary, and there's a Jeepers! children's play area in the center of the 800-seat food court that offers everything from Cajun food to cinnamon rolls.

Prime Outlets
1452 West Old Missouri Highway 40
Odessa, MO
(816) 230-5697
www.primeoutlets.com

Drive 30 minutes for a bargain? You bet. And plenty of folks have done just that since this attractive open-air mall opened

in 1995. There are 50 shops in all, including biggies like Eddie Bauer, Reebok, Levi's, Gap, Casual Corner, and OshKosh B'Gosh, and housewares favorites like Mikasa, Farberware, and Corning Revere. The food court offers deli sandwiches and pizza, and for a sugar fix there's a fudge shop.

Cargo Largo
(formerly Recovery Sales Outlet)
1390 East 35th Street South
Independence, MO
(816) 350-6100
www.cargolargo.com

This may be the only place on earth to find a limited-edition Italian fountain pen worth $3,000, an antique Japanese tansu chest, a 10-pound bag of kitty litter, and a Big Bird costume all in the same place. But don't bother rushing over for the yellow feathered suit: it's long gone by now. In its place is something else just as bizarre. Cargo Largo handles about 15,000 shipments of lost, unwanted, or otherwise undeliverable cargo every week, all discounted up to 80 percent off the retail price.

In fact, its parent company, Kansas City-based Recovery Management Corp., is the biggest single buyer of all misdirected freight in the country. And although it does a big Internet business, most of the goods end up on shelves in this airplane hangar-size warehouse. Here's a recent haul for one shopper: a Winston fly-fishing rod at half its $700 price, an Oriental rug for $60, a fax machine, a floor lamp, Doc Marten boots, and massive quantities of caulking supplies. He passed on the framed Red Sox shirt signed by Ted Williams and Budweiser neon sign in the shape of a football helmet.

Cargo Largo also holds a Thursday-afternoon bid sale, which is more fun than a barrel of monkeys; a container of live simians is perhaps the only thing you won't see. Items include retail, commercial, industrial, and hard-to-classify categories. The sale is held in Unit 800 of Carefree Industrial Park (call Cargo Largo for directions) every Thursday from 2:00 to 8:00 P.M.

The Country Club Plaza

What do you get when you combine an art and sculpture gallery, shopping center, flower garden, and jazz club? You get the Country Club Plaza, and admission to this outdoor extravaganza is free of charge.

Nestled against the banks of Brush Creek, this architecturally stunning, 14-block plaza offers everything you could want—shopping, dining, hotels, services, and entertainment—all within walking distance. Or if you're so inclined, you may view the elegant surroundings from a horse-drawn carriage.

The Plaza was the brainchild of Jesse Clyde (J. C.) Nichols, a real estate developer who changed a swampy tract of land into the country's first shopping center in 1922. He envisioned a shopping area that was automobile-friendly at a time when many thought the auto was a passing fad. And he wanted his little village filled with the romantic courtyards, ornate towers, red-tiled roofs, ornate ironwork, art, and sparkling fountains he had admired in Spain. Today the artwork alone is worth far more than the $1 million he originally paid for the 55-acre site.

In the early 1920s new shops opened and thrived on the Plaza, and soon long-standing downtown stores opened second locations here. It became the center of style and fashion. The permanent wave was introduced in a Plaza beauty salon, and top Hollywood movies debuted at the ornate Plaza Theater. J. C. continually looked for ways to attract shoppers.

In 1925 a single strand of lights heralded the start of the holiday shopping season. It's a celebration that has grown into a world-famous event as 250,000 jewel-colored bulbs outline every spire, swag, and tower beginning Thanksgiving evening. And it doesn't matter if the weather is frigid; with more than 300,000 people packing the streets it's always warm. The lights continue to shine until mid-January.

During the Depression the Plaza Art Fair began in 1932 as a promotional tool to encourage visitors. More than 70 years later, the event is the Midwest's premiere art fair, drawing an annual crowd of more than 275,000 during the three-day event. This celebration of the arts transforms 9 blocks into a giant art gallery representing more than 250 artists from nearly every state. Entertainment includes a free children's workshop, culinary specialties from 25 Plaza restaurants, and live music on three stages. The event is held each fall near the end of September.

Before J. C. Nichols died in 1950 he had seen his idea influence other developers around the country. Miller Nichols built on his father's dream, adding hotels and apartments to the Plaza's landscape and buying outstanding artwork and fountains from around the world to adorn his museum without walls. Some of the most spectacular pieces include the J. C. Nichols Memorial Fountain by Henri Gerbert, the Pool of the Four Fauns, the 130-foot-tall reproduction of the famous Giralda Tower of Seville, and the endearing *Sleeping Child* sculpture that slumbers in the median of a busy street. An illustrated Walking Art Tour is available from the Plaza Customer Service center (816-753-0100) at 4745 Central on the southwest corner of Hall's, or find photos and maps at www.countryclubplaza.com.

For some, shopping is an art form, and the Plaza provides plenty of opportunity to practice it. Among more than 150 unique stores you'll recognize retailers like Saks Fifth Avenue, Polo Ralph Lauren, Brooks Brothers, Coach, Eddie Bauer, Laura Ashley, Z Gallerie, Betsey Johnson, Gap and Gap Kids, J. Jill, St. John, Tiffany and Co., AIX Armani Exchange, Banana Republic, MAC Cosmetics, Anthropologie, The Sharper Image, Barnes & Noble Booksellers, and Tommy Bahama.

But we're perhaps even more proud of the hometown retailers presented here. They include Halls, an elegant emporium with fashions for men and women, fine jewelry, giftware, and accessories for the home; five jewelry stores including Tivol, Swirk, and Helzberg Diamonds; Diebels Sportsman Gallery; Three Dog Bakery with treats for pets; Superlatives, a world-class antiques and home decorating shop; and Scandia Down, where the service matches the exquisite display of European linens and gifts.

The culinary arts are well represented as well. Nearly 40 restaurants, bistros, and pubs will tempt you. Frequent travelers will be happy to know their favorites are here, including Ruth's Chris Steakhouse, McCormick & Schmick's Seafood Restaurant, The Capital Grille, Houston's Restaurant, P. F. Chang's China Bistro, Pizzeria Uno, and the Cheesecake Factory. But don't miss some of our hometown dining experiences; one taste of Bo Ling's Chinese Restaurant, Baja 600, re:Verse, Starker's Reserve, The Raphael Restaurant, or Plaza III The Steakhouse and you may find a new favorite. Look for details about some of the best in the Restaurants chapter.

The Plaza is also home to 14 or so specialty food options, including The Better Cheddar, a purveyor of gourmet food and wine; Panache Chocolatier, where you'll find decadent fudge, truffles, and

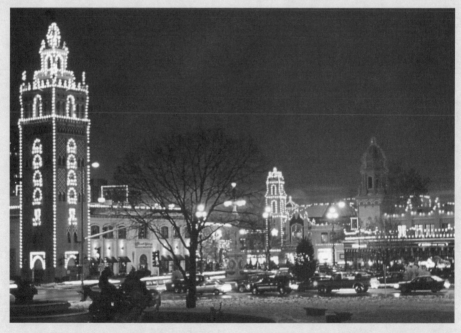

The holiday shopping season officially begins Thanksgiving night when the Plaza lights are turned on. CVB OF GREATER KANSAS CITY

addictive chocolate-dipped popcorn; and Topsy's Popcorn Shop, the place to get freshly popped treats and perhaps the world's best limeade. And because you shouldn't have to go too far without an espresso, LatteLand has two separate locations on opposite ends of the Plaza.

Just as J. C. Nichols intended, the Plaza is a self-contained city with personal services galore. Get your shoes shined or repaired, suits tailored, and boxes shipped, handy for all those purchases you plan to take home. Looking for a new hairdo or personal pampering? The Plaza boasts five salons or spas, including Mario Tricoci Salon & Day Spa and the Elizabeth Arden Salon in Saks Fifth Avenue. To pay for it all, you'll find four ATM machines within the area.

Kansas City's musical heritage is well represented on the Plaza. Beginning each May, free "Plaza Live" concerts bring some of the area's best jazz, blues, and folk musicians to the outdoor courtyards. The entertainment goes from 5:00 to 8:00 P.M. every Thursday, then again each Saturday and Sunday from noon to 5:00 P.M. It's the perfect way to enjoy a latte or lap some ice cream, sit on the side of a fountain or find a bench, and listen to stylists like Ida McBeth confessing the blues. Music lovers can also hear tunes at several venues throughout the Plaza, including the ritzy jazz bar below Plaza III The Steakhouse and at The Fairmont and Raphael hotels.

It's true, there is a lot to see and do on the Plaza. May we give you a lift? One of the most exciting ways to experience the magic is in a carriage. Two companies, Pride of Kansas City and Surreys Ltd., will escort you around the open-air marketplace in a festive old-fashioned carriage pulled by horses. For a truly enchanting evening choose Cinderella's Coach, a pumpkin-shaped carriage outlined in sparkling white lights.

If all this shopping, dining, and sailing has you exhausted, sweet dreams are just a stroll away at four hotels—The Fairmont, Raphael, Four Points by Sheraton, and Hampton Inn & Suites—and The Southmoreland Inn, an award-winning bed-and-breakfast. You'll get officially tucked in the Accommodations chapter. Or simply rejuvenate after a busy day at Kansas City's newest spa, Lenora Ellen (816–753–2820), across from the Fairmont.

The Country Club Plaza was a gift to Kansas City from J. C. and Miller Nichols. And this visually stunning, wildly exciting fantasyland of shopping, dining, music, and entertainment is our gift to the rest of the world.

FARMERS' MARKETS

We're blessed to be surrounded by dozens of small farms and orchards, many of them certified organic. Farmers drive to town in the wee hours every Saturday and Sunday to bring us fresh sweet corn, snap beans, juicy peaches, and tomatoes so good you can eat 'em like apples. Following are some of the most popular markets where the rows of nature's best are laid end-to-end like colorful quilts.

Barstow Organic Farmers' Market
11511 State Line Road
Leawood, KS
(816) 942-3255
This market doesn't draw nearly the

crowds of others in town. But that's just fine with the picky consumers who show up at the Barstow School grounds every Saturday from May through mid-October. Shorter lines mean you can actually talk to the farmers about their green beans, fingerling potatoes, apples, peaches, and exotic-looking Japanese eggplant. But don't expect picture-perfect specimens. A few bug-ravaged tomatoes prove that everything is certified pesticide and chemical free.

Many of the growers also bring prepared foods like jellies, jams, salsas, and even hand-milled soap.

City Market
Fifth and Walnut
(816) 842-1271
www.kc-citymarket.com

This is the big kahuna, the biggest open-air market in six states, where nearly 200 vendors hawk fresh produce on Wednesday, Saturday, and Sunday year-round. For the pick of the crop, it's best to get here early, around 7:00 on Saturday, 9:00 otherwise. That's when all the chefs arrive to sniff cantaloupe, inspect zucchini, and plan for that evening's special. That pale yellow ear of corn might end up in a chipotle-laced chowder tonight.

Restaurants aren't the only ones buying in bulk; you'll see couples lugging flats of strawberries to cars parked down the street. And beyond ripe produce, expect to see a hodgepodge of arts and crafts like twig furniture, jewelry, and paintings from local artists. It's always a party atmosphere, especially on weekends when crowds can swell to 30,000 or more a day. If the fruits and vegetables make you hungry, get lunch on the go from one of the street vendors. At Frank's you can get a two-pound turkey drumstick and ear of corn; Great Scott Santa Maria serves a terrific grilled beef tri-tip sandwich. Or treat yourself to Angie's frozen custard or Italian ice. If you have time, tour the steamboat *Arabia,* a riverboat that sank during the early days of our town. It's a fascinating museum that we cover in Attractions.

Marche du Jour
3848 West 75th Street
Prairie Village, KS
(573) 584-3385

Every Saturday from May through October, Mother Nature shows up in the guise of Sally at Widgeonwood Farms (even the name sounds like something organic) with just-picked heirloom tomatoes, wild plums, slender asparagus stalks, and other organic delights. And for Sally, a dusty pickup truck wouldn't do: She displays her colorful fare in the courtyard of Delaware Interiors (913–384–0330), a delightful home furnishings shop whose goods are almost as glorious as the glossy eggplant on display outside. The store is also a working studio where proprietor Paula Leigh and her staff of interior designers help clients create the same warm, inviting surroundings displayed within the rooms. Walking past the lovely antiques, rich fabrics, and artwork on your way to flavorful produce. . . well, it's a sensual treat that can set the tone for the entire weekend.

But some regulars come to Marche du Jour to stock pantries rather than vegetable bins. Each week brings new jars of treats like dilled green beans, Italian parsley pesto, port wine cranberry relish, tomato-basil-Vidalia dressing, and wild plum butter. There is rarely enough to go around; get there by 9:00 or you may be disappointed. Sally also makes decadent sweets, including biscotti dipped in white chocolate, chocolate English toffee, and chocolate raspberry truffle sauce. Here's our recipe for heaven: a couple of truffles and a warm bath fragranced with her rosemary-and-lavender French bath salts.

Stores on the Country Club Plaza stay open until 9:00 P.M on Thursday nights year-round to give you an opportunity to hit your favorites while in town. And beginning Thanksgiving night, the stores stay open every night except Sunday during the holiday season to help make the seasons bright.

Thank goodness you needn't go the entire year without a jar of Sally's gazpacho. She hosts a holiday market in early December at Delaware Interiors. Call for details; they also ship.

Overland Park Farmers' Market
**Marty Street between 79th
and 80th Streets
(913) 642-2222**
It can get pretty crowded on a summer Saturday as people stand in line for just-picked watermelons, fat blueberries, Big Boy tomatoes, and peaches-and-cream corn, a variety so sweet and tender you can practically eat it raw. There's always a display or two of cutting flowers in bouquets, locally produced honey, and more. To keep things lively, several times a month a live band will entertain the crowds at the Clock Tower, an old-fashioned public square a few stairs up from the market area. Get there early for a seat outside, or duck into Mildred's Coffee Shop for a cappuccino and a muffin and grab a chair on the patio.

FINE ART

We have more than our share of talented artists in Kansas City, thanks in part to the influence of the Kansas City Art Institute and Hallmark Cards. We cover the galleries that show their work in the Arts chapter. But in the meantime, here's your chance to visit the studios, showrooms,

---

You can buy one of Rhett Johnson's found-art sculptures at his studio in Dearborn, Missouri, or simply admire them at a Hen House grocery store. The store commissioned Rhett to create 6-foot-long chickens out of tractor seats, painted steel, gelatin molds, and various gizmos. The Hen House at Quivira and College Boulevard in Overland Park , Kansas, has the fanciful fowl hanging above the produce display.

---

and even classrooms where they create their craft.

Corbin Bronze Ltd.
**201 Wyandotte Street
(816) 842-0496
www.corbinbronze.com**
You can see Kansas City sculptor Tom Corbin's work at the Firefighter's Memorial Fountain at Penn Valley Park, the Kauffman Memorial Garden near the Plaza, and in galleries and designer's showrooms across the country. Or simply rent the movies *Ransom* and *A Perfect Murder,* where his stunning furniture and statuettes set the tone for the characters' privileged lifestyles.

Better yet, view the work in person at his showroom in the River Market area. Tom has sold more than $1 million worth of sculptures, furniture, and lighting, forever knocking him out of the starving artist category. His trademark is slim, ethereal female figures that seem light enough to float despite their bronze heft. Prices range from $200 to more than $100,000 each.

The Kansas City Art Institute
**Annual Ceramics Sale
4415 Warwick
(816) 474-5224, (800) 522-5224
www.kcai.edu**
Discover emerging artists and incredible bargains at this student sale at one of the country's most respected art institutes. The event is always held a few weeks before the Christmas buying season, usually the first weekend in December. Doors open promptly at 10:00 A.M. on Saturday and noon on Sunday, but shoppers start showing up hours before to secure a place in line. Once the doors open it's every art lover for himself or herself. During years when the snow is higher than a lined rubber boot, students bring out hot cider to keep things lively. Here's the drill to keep from being trampled by the crowds behind you: As soon as the doors open, grab one of the empty cardboard boxes off to the left and start moving

around the stations. When you see something you like, grab it or it will be gone.

The artwork, which demonstrates varying degrees of proficiency, includes glazed platters, vases, and teapots that would fetch hundreds or thousands of dollars at galleries or high-end shops as well as quirky little bowls only an artist's mother could love. You'll also find sculptures and three-dimensional pieces that could fill a wall. As for prices, although the students are getting savvier on market value, you can still grab a gorgeous casserole dish with lid for around $30, a stunning vase for $25. And the proceeds help keep the artists in clay and supplies, so that's a good thing.

Rhett and Kelly Johnson
Dearborn, MO
(816) 450-3616

Rhett is a monumentally talented sculptor who works with found objects like old cobalt-blue bottles, engine parts, and iron he shapes and leaves outside to rust. His garden art features graceful birds landing on arches and stakes. Kelly creates exquisite beaded art and witty painted papier-mâché masks, which she also sells at Missouri Bluffs, a women's clothing store in Weston, Missouri (see Day Trips and Weekend Getaways). Their studios in Dearborn, Missouri, just north of Kansas City, are open by appointment only and definitely worth the 35-mile trip.

Markus and Sheryl Pierson
River Market area
(816) 421-1979
www.markuspierson.com

Oh, if only we could all have as much fun as the globe-trotting, tango-dancing coyote in Markus Pierson's paintings. And if you see the word coyote and think howling-at-the-moon Southwestern art, think again. Markus's alter ego is an erudite chap in dapper suits and fedoras, casually leaning against a palm tree or despondent in jailhouse stripes as a prisoner of love. The artist's story is as fascinating as his art. He began the Coyote

series in 1986, two years after picking up a brush, and a year later his canvases were in more than 100 galleries worldwide. His first original sold for $100; now they go for up to $100,000 or so to fans like Oliver Stone, Kevin Costner, John Cleese, Sylvester Stallone, captains of industry, heads of state—and Ozzy Osbourne. Markus shares studio space with his wife, Sheryl, a talented artist in her own right. Her collages have famous fans as well: Elton John and Bernie Taupin gave each other one for Christmas. Their work is shown at Blue Gallery, 7 West 19th Street (816-527-0823, www.bluegallery online.com) in the Crossroads Arts District.

When Barnett Helzberg brought the Hope diamond to town to promote his new store on the Country Club Plaza, security was tight as the public took turns viewing the priceless gem. But when it came time to transport the legendary rock to the store's Topeka location, Barnett simply dropped it in his coat pocket and drove away.

Robyn Nichols, The Pearl Gallery
1818 McGee
(816) 474-1731
www.robynnichols.com

This raven-haired enchantress turns calla lilies, nasturtium blossoms, and gingko leaves into gleaming sterling silver jewelry so their delicate beauty lasts forever. Robyn's exquisite work is admired at high-end stores and galleries around the country. And she always draws a crowd at the Plaza Art Fair each fall as people cluster around the booth to see her jewelry and elegant serving pieces: spoons shaped like seedpods, ladles like lily pads.

The artist also creates commissioned work for individuals and companies. Her work can be viewed at her gallery, The Pearl, which also exhibits other artists' three-dimensional work throughout the year. Call for specific dates and times. And if you live in or near Kansas City, get on Robyn's mailing list; her annual holiday parties are renowned.

FOOD AND GIFTS

Andre's Confiserie Suisse
5018 Main Street
(816) 561-3440

4929 West 119th Street
Overland Park, KS
(913) 498-3440
www.andreschocolates.com
When Master Confiseur Andre Bollier and his wife, Elsbeth, came here from Switzerland in 1955 to set up a candy shop, few residents had ever tasted premium chocolates; it would be decades before "Godiva" meant anything but a lady with a horse. So the Bolliers served lunches at their tearoom while they began educating the Midwest palate. We tell you about the lunch specials in Restaurants, but for now let's rhapsodize about the confections within the glass cases.

All the chocolates, from truffles to cream- and caramel-filled assortments, are handmade and meltingly delicious. The shop's specialties are treats tied to the seasons like handpainted, edible chocolate Easter eggs; Valentine hearts filled with truffles; and chocolate wine bottles packed with chocolate-covered almonds that are perfect for any celebration. Replace the Andre's label with your own and the glossy brown bottles make extraordinary wedding and anniversary gifts. Chocoholic Johnson Countians were thrilled when the Bollier family opened a second location, in Hawthorne Plaza.

The Better Cheddar
604 West 48th Street
(816) 561-8204

71st and Mission
Prairie Village, KS
(913) 362-7575
What sets a specialty gourmet shop apart from a grocery store are unique products

and personal service. That's certainly the case at The Better Cheddar, where owner Ron Shalinsky and his gracious staff welcome you like family and encourage you to sample the wares. In fact there are so many chunks of cheeses, crackers with savory toppings, and decadent chocolate truffles to try, it's easy to have dinner while you shop.

Among the hundreds of gourmet selections are jars of The Better Cheddar's own proprietary brand; a dab of cranberry chutney on a gingersnap cracker is like getting a mouthful of Thanksgiving. There's food for thought as well: Handprinted cards describe each cheese and offer suggestions for use. The Dutch aged cheddar with black pepper, you discover, is terrific with strawberries and makes a very grownup macaroni and cheese dish.

The Better Cheddar's Plaza store also sells a nice variety of wines, a perfect accompaniment to the gourmet picnic the staff can prepare with a little prior notice. And their gift baskets are so legendary that regular customers order them delivered sight unseen.

Browne's Market
3300 Pennsylvania
(816) 561-0030
www.brownesmarket.com
When Ed and Mary Flavin opened this grocery store in 1887, it was to offer a taste of County Kerry to the thousands of Irish immigrants finding new homes here. The tradition continued when daughter Margaret married Jim Browne, and today the shelves are still stocked with treats from the homeland: sweets like Hob Nobs and Cadbury Flakes, tweed caps, Aran knit sweaters, teas, and Claddagh windchimes. The deli case features bangers and mash, soda bread, and Irish stew. And everyone, no matter what their heritage, enjoys the chocolate chip, chocolate oatmeal, and white chunk macadamia cookies, rated best by readers of *Pitch Weekly*. Show up on Cookie Tuesday and they're on sale. You might even see an impromptu Irish dance by the family's fifth generation.

Browne's is the unofficial starting point for the city's huge St. Patrick's Day parade; the party starts as early as 7:00 A.M. with an authentic Irish breakfast.

Christopher Elbow Artisanal Chocolates
320 Southwest Boulevard
(above Shiraz Restaurant)
(816) 842-1300

It's quickly become one of our favorite gifts for an open house or a birthday: a box of Christopher Elbow's chocolates. Each morsel is a work of art: glossy orbs that look like glass marbles, rainbow-colored pyramids, fat squares handpainted with swaths of color or dusted with cocoa. He infuses the truffles with unusual flavors like Brazilian coffee, French lavender, Chinese five-spice, caramel banana, and delicate Earl Grey tea.

Christopher learned his trade as pastry chef for Shiraz and The American Restaurant before becoming a full-time chocolatier. His luscious creations are available in three sizes—2, 4, or 21 melt-in-your-mouth wonders—each in an elegant, embossed white box tied with (what else?) a chocolate-brown bow.

Fervere Bread
1702 Summit
(816) 582-7323

Fred Spompinato makes breads with a tender texture and chewy crust that can only be achieved by hand kneading, lots of patience, and a special Old World oven. He named his tiny, take-out bakery for the Latin word (pronounced fur-VAIR-ay) meaning passion. That may explain why Fred sold his first successful bread company years ago when it became more of a business and less of a craft.

Now he's up to his elbows in dough again and loving every sticky minute. Using organic flours and natural ingredients, he turns out dense, crusty loaves in six or so varieties, including an aromatic olive rosemary, a country French, and an oval wonder filled with walnuts, apples, and plump apricots. During winter his holiday gift to us is a cranberry pecan loaf

enlivened with orange rind. No need to wrap it, Fred, we'll eat it here.

Fervere, which is in the bohemian neighborhood along with Blue Bird Bistro (see Restaurants) and a few artist studios, is open 11:00 A.M. to 7:00 P.M. Thursday through Saturday. There are always generous chunks of each bread, along with dishes of good olive oil for dunking, ready to sample before you buy.

Original Juan Specialty Foods, Inc.
111 Southwest Boulevard
Kansas City, KS
(913) 432-5228, (800) 568-8468
www.originaljuan.com

Forget complaining about the heat and humidity of a summer day in Kansas—it's always hot at Original Juan's where they cook up 80-gallon vats of incendiary salsas and sauces, even fruit jellies, using chili peppers and little else. Even Wilber Scoville, the guy who devised the rating system for chilis, would whimper with one drop of Da' Bomb's The Final Answer. This deep red sauce tops out at 1.5 million Scoville units and is available in a box that includes a lock and key. They're not kidding; you must be 21 or over to buy the stuff.

It's just one of about 100 products that are available through the company's Web site and catalog and at the retail counter on Southwest Boulevard. Not everything will cause your brow to sweat, though. They also carry Cheesecake in a Jar, a rich sauce to pour over ice cream or cake, and an award-winning artichoke and spinach cheese dip mix.

Planters Seed & Spice Company
513 Walnut
(816) 842-3651

At Planters the atmosphere is always festive, even without 35,000 people milling around the farmers' market down the street, as regulars show up for a monthly fix of coffee, bird seed, and half-ton bags of dog food. Not much has changed since it opened in 1924; the wooden floors may creak a little more now, but you can still get more than 200 varieties of herbs and spices in giant bins. They also offer items like chili seasoning and a wide variety of coffee beans. They also have a nice selection of loose teas in flavors like mango, black currant, and vanilla, along with pretty teapots. The sales staff can help you create gifts using complementary items, like packets of chili seasoning and dried beans in a ceramic casserole dish or bags of flavored coffee beans and a grinder in a laminated box. A handy catalog provides additional inspiration.

A large portion of the store is devoted to gardening tools, flower bulbs, and decorative items like wind chimes.

The Roasterie
2601 Madison
(816) 931-4000, (800) 376-0245
www.theroasterie.com

As a foreign exchange student in Costa Rica, Danny O'Neill fell in love with the rich, robust coffee served there. Fifteen years later his passion for the brew had him roasting beans in the basement of his Brookside home, and when he mastered the art of air roasting he knew he'd found his calling. He and buddy Norman Killman would roast in the basement, pack in the living room, and deliver the fragrant bags of beans to customers in Norm's '81 El Camino.

That was 1993. And although Norm swears he still has the car he can certainly afford to drive something a little more exotic; the brand is sold in grocery stores and gourmet shops and served in Kansas City's top restaurants. In fact, several local chefs have commissioned their own special blends, so if you dig the java at The American Restaurant or the Classic Cup, you have Danny to thank. The company makes about 40 blends and flavors in all, including a Kansas City Blend, a combination of Indonesian and Central and South American beans that's hearty yet smooth. But to be sleepless in Kansas City go for the Nitro Express, a darker roast with a pungent, smoky aroma and flavor. You can find the flavor-sealed bags at most area grocery stores.

Three Dog Bakery
612 West 48th Street
(816) 753-3647, (800) 4TREATS
www.threedogbakery.com

Yes, we know the food here is for pooches, but it's so artfully done we couldn't resist. Besides, what better gift to take home to your best buddy than a Scotty Biscotti or Puppy Petit Four? Locals Dan Dye and Mark Beckloff started the company when they couldn't find healthy snacks for their three dogs, Dottie, Gracie, and Sarah Jean. Using dough made from whole wheat flour, unsweetened carob, and low-fat yogurt powder and a $2.00 bone-shaped cookie cutter, the duo concocted treats their girls loved.

Now Dan and Mark are rolling *in* dough. Their products are available at Three Dog Bakery stores across the country (with one in Japan) and through selected Target stores. If you stop by the Plaza store you'll see several four-footed fans sampling the wares. You can also order through the dog-alog (a catalog simply wouldn't do) or the company's fun Web site.

GIFTS AND OTHER GOODIES

Animania
4818 Rainbow Boulevard
Westwood, KS
(913) 362-6889

Discover Kansas City's wild side at a store filled with animal-themed art, gifts, and interiors—in fact, everything for your home including the doghouse. Jan Kyle's clever shop is next to Dr. Wayne Hunthausen's busy Westwood Animal Hospital (www.westwoodanimalhospital.com), so there's usually a pet or two going back and forth through the shared door.

And because Jan and Wayne are married, you can bet the good doctor approves all the collars, books, and pet training items. You can even pick up one of his pet behavioral books and award-winning videos about teaching children to be safe around animals.

Collector's Choice Trains
15105 Metcalf
Overland Park, KS
(913) 681-6830

Hobbyists and collectors, your train has come in. Norman Hussey's shop offers the largest selection of O- and G-Gauge model trains in Missouri and Kansas, including a limited-edition diesel locomotive, the Kansas City Southern's *Southern Belle*. She's a beauty with roof fans that spin, cab doors that open, and nifty digital sound effects so you won't have to do that annoying "Woo-woo!" noise. Collector's Choice also stocks Lionel and MTH starter sets with hundreds of engines, cars, and accessories. The shop is closed Sunday and Monday.

Gallup Map Company
1733 Main
(816) 842-1994

The maps, charts, and atlases displayed in this shop are so intriguing even men wouldn't mind asking for directions. They carry maps from all over the world, but the real reason to visit is the chance to study the plots and diagrams of our town's far-flung city limits. Hey look! I can see my house from here!

Gallup also has globes of all kinds, including nifty inflatable versions, the better for packing as take-home gifts. You'll also find sports team banners and national park hiking guides. And just try to get your companion away from the showroom wall covered in maps of the world, the United States, and our little corner of the universe.

Moon Marble Company
600 East Front Street
Bonner Springs, KS
(913) 441-1432
www.moonmarble.com

You say you've lost your marbles? Bruce Breslow can make you a new set—while you wait! This big kid doesn't run a store, he owns a giant toy box filled with yo-yos,

When rocker Neil Young is in town for a concert, his first stop isn't backstage but out south to Collector's Choice, a model railroad store. The musician has a vested interest: Not only is he an avid collector but he's also part owner of the Lionel Company that manufacturers model trains.

colorful tin rocket ships and robots, magic tricks and silly pranks, jump ropes, jacks, game boards, and more. And while you're browsing, he'll be busy creating marvelous marbles out of glass. Moon Marble is a favorite field trip for groups of all ages; in fact there's usually a WELCOME SCOUTS message on the chalkboard sign in front. Individuals are welcome as well, but you must promise to have fun.

Marble collectors will recognize the names of the artists represented here, including Bruce, Jim Hart, Drew Fritz, and Jody Fine. The rest of us will simply admire the colors, patterns, and swirls that make these treasures look like 1-inch planets. Some of the most prized ones cost around $40, or you can get a bucket of shooters—a full eight pounds—for a mere $45.

Nate's Swap Shop
8200 East 63rd Street
(at U.S. Highway 350 and Interstate 435)
(816) 353-1627

This drive-in movie theater becomes a rollicking swap meet on Saturday and Sunday, when spilled popcorn and hot dog wrappers are replaced by weird and wonderful loot. Dozens of vendors sell just about anything you could ever need—and tons you didn't know you needed until now—like car parts, endless rows of tools, pots and pans, Army fatigues, dilapidated furniture, decapitated dolls, videos, CDs, and all those 8-track hits you've been missing. Admission is $1.00, cheap enough for an entire morning of fun.

HOME FURNISHINGS AND ACCESSORIES

Aesthetica
1817 Wyandotte
(816) 421–5455
www.aesthetica-kc.com

James Carver's creativity (he was a designer for Disney for years) is on parade in this shop filled with fascinating home decor, giftware, and gourmet food. The range of inventory may be wild—from precious gifts for baby to sophisticated martini glasses—but it's all so expertly selected and stylishly displayed, you'll want it all. Every purchase leaves the store with a gift bag and tissue, but pay a little extra and watch James do his magic. He'll create a gift package or clever container tied to a theme like a home spa or gourmet chocolates. In fact, James has an entire corner of his shop devoted to exquisite papers and ribbons, so the gift you take to a birthday bash might never get opened because it's just too pretty.

For personal gifts such as jewelry, handbags, and books, there's nothing like Aesthetica. And James even makes buying business gifts a breeze: Simply call him with a price range and he'll e-mail photos of options along with ideas for wrapping. Choose one and he'll do the rest, including shipping to the lucky recipient.

Black Bamboo
1815 Wyandotte
(816) 283–3000
www.black-bamboo.com

As an interior designer for an international architectural firm, Tim Butt envisioned beautiful and functional spaces for clients. Through his business travels, he was drawn to the simple, elegant lines of Asian and modern furnishings, so when he opened his new shop he filled it with a mix of each. He personally selected pieces from Burma, China, Thailand, Bali, Vietnam, and elsewhere.

In his handsome new space, which formerly housed a vintage Corvette restoration shop, Tim gives each piece of furniture its due with room to breathe and great lighting. The inventory includes an ever-changing collection of antiques, such as a lovely blue-painted secretary from the mid-1800s, to sterling-and-jade jewelry and artwork.

The look of the place says expensive, but you might call it Asian minor: Prices range from $3.50 for a silk-screened greeting card that could easily be framed to a large cabinet handcrafted of Asian Yuma for around $3,000. In between are a wonderful array of sofas, chairs, side tables, and accessories—all reflecting Tim's keen sense of style.

The Home Gallery
7517 West 119th Street
Overland Park, KS
(913) 451–6262
www.thehomegallery.net

You can buy a low-mileage luxury car for a fraction of its original sticker price and gently worn clothes at consignment shops. Wouldn't it be great if you could get the same deals on furniture? That's the concept behind Dan DeLeon's business. He takes advantage of our fickle furniture tastes—what were you thinking with that Southwest look, anyway?—by acquiring nearly new furniture on consignment.

The quality is so good many first-time shoppers think it's a new furniture store, albeit more eclectic than most. Expect to see a bit of everything: a sleek enameled entertainment unit, antique German headboard, tooled-leather side chairs, Oriental screen inlaid with mother-of-pearl. The best items go fast, so if you see something you like, grab it. On busy Saturdays you're likely to hear "I saw it first!" and the sounds of running from across the floor. The Home Gallery also stocks new accessories including lamps, clocks, pottery, scented candles, and more.

Nell Hill's
501 Commercial
Atchison, KS
(913) 367–1086
www.nellhills.com

In the birthplace of Amelia Earhart, merchandise is flying out of the home furnishings store that's become one of the hottest retailers in the nation. Or perhaps the draft is *incoming* as vans and busloads of buyers from Omaha and Des Moines storm the place several times a year. During the holidays, when the store is aglitter with $300,000 worth of Christmas decorations, there's often a line snaking around the corner.

You might think, *What's the big deal?* at first sight of Mary Carol Garrity's modest two-story building on the corner, but, oh, what wonders await inside. Room after room is filled with European antiques next to all-American red-plaid sofas mingled with Indonesian tables topped with baskets, vases, and dishware. Everything is so artfully arranged you'll want to say, "I'll take the whole room, please." No problem; delivery is free. But the affable Ms. G would rather help you develop your own look, a service she does every day for customers who bring in photos of rooms and a plaintive "Help me, please."

Personal service and inventory aside, some people come to Nell Hill's just for the price tags. The petite owner is a powerhouse when it comes to negotiating discounts, often importing tons of goods to get the best deals. She confides that she buys her wicker from the same village in the Philippines as Ralph Lauren but pays Pier 1 prices. Gifts such as silverplate bowls, sets of crisp white linen cocktail napkins, and wire baskets are so well priced it pays to just grab several and figure out who will get them later.

For more treasures, walk just a few paces to *the* G. Diebolt's (608 Commercial, 913-367-2395; www.gdiebolts.com), which features fanciful bedding, oodles of candles, mirrors, cashmere throws, and inspiration to create your own luxurious sanctuary, or her new antiques emporium, Garrity's, at 121 North Fifth Street (913-367-1523). Be sure to pick up a copy of Mary Carol Garrity's decorating books *Nell Hill's Style at Home* and *Nell Hill's Christmas at Home.*

Pryde's Old Westport
115 Westport Road
(816) 531-5588
It's a three-decade Kansas City tradition: When a young woman gets engaged, she heads to Pryde's to register *before* picking out her dress. Owner Louise Meyers has helped newlyweds, as well as college-bound seniors, singles, and empty nesters, outfit kitchens for more than 20 years. She's the pretty blonde in a dark green Pryde's apron greeting customers by name, making sure displays look inviting, and offering coffee to visitors. Say yes: Pryde's signature blend is so terrific you'll want to buy a pound or two to take home.

Or you might try using a trail of coffee beans to help you find your way back to the front door. The array of cutlery, cookware, dinnerware, linens, and serving pieces is so staggering you can get lost within the multifloored, many-roomed space. Turn a corner and there's a wall of kitchen utensils you didn't know existed, barbecue tools of every design, candles, glassware, and more. Pryde's has a splendid collection of dinnerware to set an elegant or casual table, including England's finest stoneware, Portmeirion, and Emile Henry from France. But one of the store's best commodities is advice. Louise and her staff are more than happy to help you choose the proper tool for the task, demonstrate a pasta machine, or put together a gift basket for a bridal shower. Gift-wrapping is always free, and Pryde's can ship anywhere.

Retro Inferno
1500 Grand Boulevard
(816) 842-4004
www.retroinferno.com

Some of the city's best gift shops are found in art museums. The Nelson-Atkins Museum of Art and the Kemper Museum of Contemporary Art both feature shops that offer books, posters, note cards, wearable art (such as jewelry and painted silk scarves), and handcrafted pieces like vases and teapots.

Truth be told, collectors and interior designers on both coasts are more familiar with Rod Parks's collection of mid-20th-century furniture than many Kansas Citians are. With wall-to-wall primo modern designs in his groovy location, it's a sure thing you'll find the Herman Miller, Knoll, Dunbar, McCob, Russell Wright, or Heywood Wakefield piece you seek. Don't recognize the names? It doesn't matter; you'll identify the clean lines from any stylish Katharine Hepburn movie you've ever seen. These tables, credenzas, low-slung sofas, and stylish bars are shown next to white chairs sculpted like an open palm, boomerang-shaped cocktail tables, and Sputnik light fixtures from the fifties: just the stuff you could kick yourself for passing up at garage sales years ago. Or selling at your own!

Retro Inferno also sells accessories such as vintage cocktail shakers, Murano glassware, pink ice crushers, and even some vintage cocktail dresses that may have spent the evening at the Inferno Lounge, the disco that gave the shop its name. The nightclub is long gone, but the neon light lives on in Rod's front window. And you might even leave with a pocketful of cash; he buys quality vintage furniture and accessories, so that Electrolux gathering dust in the closet could pay for your trip. Here's an Insiders' tip: Park in back rather than the street; You may avoid a parking ticket.

JEWELRY

Helzberg Diamonds
Various locations at shopping malls and the Country Club Plaza
www.helzbergdiamonds.com
From one tiny storefront in Kansas City, Kansas, this enterprise has become the personal jeweler to customers at more than 75 stores across the country. Morris Helzberg began the dream in 1915, but it was his son, Barnett, then Barnett Jr., who grew it into one of the most successful retailers in the country. These marketing geniuses added an element of fun to the sometimes all-too-serious task of buying jewelry. In the 1930s the company offered free "aeroplane" rides with the purchase of a $49 Benrus Pilot watch, and to launch the new Country Club Plaza store Barnett Jr. brought in the Hope diamond, which the public could view for free if they made a contribution to the United Way.

This benevolent tradition continues today: Although retired from the gem business, Barnett Jr. and Shirley Helzberg are two of the most generous Kansas City citizens of all time. But it was their engagement in 1967 that sparked one of the store's most successful promotions, the "I Am Loved" pin. Barnett originally thought of the idea as a pre-engagement stall tactic. Since then the red-and-white pins have been used in schools to teach children self-esteem, sent to American troops in Vietnam, translated into eight languages, and featured in the "Charlie Brown" comic strip. To date the store has handed out more than 35 million of the red-and-white tokens of love.

Swirk Jewelry
310 West 47th Street
(816) 753-1949, (800) MR SWIRK
www.swirkjewelry.com

Seems like 1910 was a good year to open a jewelry store in the Midwest. Swirk's has built a loyal following buoyed by personal service, a small but lovely selection of diamond and gemstone jewelry, many estate pieces, and the fix-anything skill of its repair team. Here's where Kansas City brings its tired timepieces and broken bracelets. Visit the small shop above Buca de Bepo restaurant on the Country Club Plaza. You'll get a handshake whether you buy something or not, most likely from somebody named Swirk.

Tivol
220 Nichols Road
(816) 531-5800

4721 West 119th Street
Overland Park, KS
(913) 345-0200
www.tivol.com
In 1910 when jeweler Charles Tivol opened a store in downtown Kansas City his ledger registered $105,000 the first year. Today the store often does that in one sale. It's come a long way from $95 diamond rings, but it's never wavered from a commitment to customer service. It doesn't hurt that Charles's son, Harold, has a knack for marketing; in fact the 70-something still shows up in the company's clever ads.

The store moved to its current location on the Country Club Plaza in 1951, where it remains the area's crown jewel with breathtaking window displays and even more stunning creations inside. Top designer names are represented here, and in Kansas City the only proper engagement ring comes in a Tivol's black-and-gold box.

Harold swore he'd never move from the Plaza, and he hasn't, but when son and daughter Tom and Cathy accepted the reins they opened a second location in Hawthorne Plaza to cater to their customers out south. But don't let the luxurious surroundings keep you from entering. The friendly salespeople are happy to let you try on a dozen diamond line bracelets, whether your wrist is clad in denim or mink.

SHOPPING DISTRICTS

Crossroads Arts District
(1-mile-wide area between Downtown
Kansas City and Crown Center)
www.kccrossroads.org
Every big city has one—a neighborhood where unique boutiques, antiques stores, showrooms, art galleries, and restaurants have popped up to become the trendiest place in town to shop. In Kansas City that destination is the Crossroads Arts District.

Part of its charm is that the studios and storefronts have emerged out of brick warehouses, abandoned office buildings, and lofts, many still sporting handsome concrete moldings and wooden beams. This is shopping the way it used to be, where the person behind the counter is the owner, friends gather over wine in the evening, and there's not a Starbuck's in sight.

When a handful of the art gallery owners banded together to stay open late on Friday, First Friday was born. In past years it's become Kansas City's official street party, with crowds walking to the 40 or so galleries and artist studios, catching trolleys to visit ones that are a bit farther away, and shopping in stores that aren't in the typical shopping mall. Restaurants offer anything from a quick bowl of spicy noodles to a white-tablecloth, four-course meal.

And where art starts, lofts are sure to follow. The Crossroads and surrounding areas are the hottest addresses for loft-living, with new spaces being converted every month.

We've profiled several shops like Aesthetica, Curious Sofa, Black Bamboo, Retro Inferno and Webster House Antiques within this chapter; art venues like Blue Gallery; and restaurants including Shiraz and Zin.

Other must-see stops include High Cotton Home Furnishings (118 Southwest Boulevard, 816–471-3561) and Hudson Home, a showroom filled with fabulous modern furniture and lighting (1619 Walnut, 816–421–3649). You'll find information about and links to dozens more on the Web site, which includes a map. Or pick up a brochure when visiting any location within the neighborhood. The general boundaries are Truman Road to the north, Interstate 35 to the west, the KC Terminal railroad tracks to the south, and Troost Avenue to the east. Nearby hotels include the Westin and Hyatt at Crown Center and the Phillips House (see separate listings in Accommodations).

Downtown Parkville, MO
(816) 505-2227
www.parkvillemo.com

This riverfront village is a charming little getaway for a day of shopping, yet is close enough to drop in for lunch. The real pull is its mix of two dozen one-of-a-kind shops and galleries filled with gifts, decor, and fine art. Home Embellishments (816–505–1022) is like an always-open art fair representing work from more than 60 artists. Look for wacky metal masks, steel garden sculptures of frogs and flowers, folk art frames, funky jewelry, and a collection of knobs and pulls owner Jan Gunn rightfully calls "gutsy." Across the street, at 201 Main Street, is River's Bend Gallery (816–587–8070), where owners Rick and Kristy McKibben share their love of fine arts and crafts with the rest of us. This is gift central, for you or someone special, with gorgeous etched-glass vases, whimsical ceramic and glass martini glasses, wearable art including painted vests and flowing tunics, vivid pastel landscapes you'll want to get lost in, and silver and pewter jewelry at terrific prices. Rick's own award-winning photography is also shown.

A short walk up Main Street, Dixie Dunnaway turned a charming home into an even more charming shop called Rivendell (816–746–9506). It's the place to find gorgeous lamps and picture frames and throw pillows. You'll wish your home could smell as good as La-De-Da, and it can (816–741–6711). This delightful shop sells pretty sachets, glycerin soaps in flower

designs, unusual candles, and potpourri, all wonderfully displayed among stylish upholstered chairs, rattan and metal tables, and lamps. One brick wall is filled with room-making clocks inspired by antiques from Paris, London, and Portobello.

Ready to drop? You'll have your choice of restaurants ready to recharge your energy level. Cafe des Amis (816–587–6767) serves country French fare on a lovely treetop deck. The pizzas at Stone Canyon (816–746–8686), especially the roasted potato and chicken version, are legendary. If you have more time, the view from Piropo's (816–741–3600) is breathtaking and gives you a chance to admire the spires of Park University, the river, and downtown Kansas City's skyline while you dine on Argentine-inspired steaks, empanadas, and pastas. And because you'll be overlooking Parkville's Main Street, you can make a list of the other shops you'll want to visit. Or work off your meal with a stroll along the groomed trails that meander through 115 acres of river valley woods and wetlands, complete with a romantic waterfall. Read more about this nature sanctuary in the Parks, Lakes, and Recreation chapter.

Westport
Westport Road and Pennsylvania
(816) 756-2789
www.westporttoday.com

At night this neighborhood becomes party central, but during the day you'll find unique shops and specialty stores worthy of an entire day of browsing. Go online (www.westporthistorical.org) or stop by the Westport Merchants Association (4123 Mill Street, 816–756–2789) for a map showing the historic places within this neighborhood, including the Nathan Scarritt Home built in 1850 and the Chouteau Society Plaque, which commemorates the town's first white inhabitants.

When the history lesson is over, it's time to shop. Natural Wear (816–531–9082) is a longtime favorite women's store featuring casual clothes made from natural fibers, along with accessories, hats, jewelry, and sandals. The fragranced candles alone will pull you into the eclectic galleries lining the streets that showcase work from several area artists and crafters. Display cases and shelves are filled with picture frames, candles, leatherbound journals, and interesting handcrafted boxes.

If you notice a line forming midafternoon, it's the fan club for Chocolate Fromage ice cream at Murray's Ice Creams & Cookies (816-931-5646). They scoop 16 different flavors at a time—with 200 waiting in the wings—along with lumpies, which are malts made with chunks of ice cream. Yum! Westport is also known for its nightlife and restaurants; see those chapters for details.

SOUVENIRS AND GIFTS

The Best of Kansas City
314 Ward Parkway (Country Club Plaza)
Crown Center Shops
(816) 842-0200, (800) 366-8780
www.thebestofkc.com
One taste of our food and you'll want to take it all back with you. Now you can, with a gift basket from the Best of Kansas City. For years they've been putting together big, gorgeous gift baskets bursting with hometown products like Laura

Little's Fudge, Andre's Chocolates, Strawberry Hill nut loaves, Fritz's smoked meats, Hereford House Steak Sauce, and Wolferman's muffins. Nonfood items include CDs and books from local talent, coffee mugs, and caps. The two locations offer about 25 packages from sweet to savory.

Kansas Sampler
9540 Antioch Road
Overland Park, KS
(913) 383-2920

Town Center Plaza
(913) 491-3004

Mission Mall
(913) 432-3355
www.kansassampler.com
When you realize, Dorothy, that you're not in Kansas anymore, you'll wish you had some fun souvenir to remember your trip. Here's just the place to find it. Peg and Tim Liebert have put together a wonderful collection of Sunflower State–themed goodies like T-shirts, sampler boxes filled with locally made gourmet food and goodies, books about the region, CDs from local artists, and Kansas magnets to add to your refrigerator collection. A favorite is the Pet Tornado and delicious sunflower-seed cookies.

ATTRACTIONS

ooking for a fabulous family vacation? Romantic weekend for two? A new place to call home? Congratulations! You've come to the right place. With so much to see and do, Kansas City is the perfect choice no matter how you define fun.

In fact, here's where our unique mix of citified culture (la-de-da) and Wild West rowdiness (yee-haw!) really pays off. You can spend your day contemplating a Rembrandt or attending a rodeo, and then dine by candlelight or campfire. . . all within our city's boundaries.

History buffs will be taken aback; although another city is rightly called the gateway to the West, we were the *gate* that outfitted more than half a million travelers on the Oregon, California, and Santa Fe Trails during the mid-1800s. You can relive their stories at dozens of museums, historic sites, and restored antebellum homes. And if your taste runs to more modern architecture, things are looking up . . . way up. Our downtown skyline has nearly 60 Art Deco buildings from the 1920s and 1930s.

Naturally in this chapter you'll also see attractions that have wowed tourists for decades, like our renowned Nelson-Atkins Museum of Art and the 14-block shopping mecca known as the Country Club Plaza. But for those frequent KC visitors who are thinking, *been there, done that,* get ready for a few surprises. A citywide cultural renaissance is taking place just in time for your visit. We're busy updating and renovating some of our most treasured landmarks and historical districts while adding new destinations on both sides of the state line. That means there's bound to be a snappy little bonus for the art lover, sporting nut, and shopaholic in your entourage. We're proud to show it all to you.

The attractions are grouped by category and listed alphabetically. Because hours frequently change, it's best to call for updated information. All attractions listed are in Kansas City, Missouri, unless otherwise noted.

You may wish to start at the Observation Points where you can see our city from on high.

ART MUSEUMS

Kemper Museum of Contemporary Art
4420 Warwick Boulevard
(816) 753-5784
www.kemperart.org
When locals describe Kansas City's *other* art museum, they simply say, "It's the one with the spider." This one could be the model for a sci-fi thriller. The sculpture by Louise Bourgeois weighs 1,600 pounds and is roughly the size of a New York apartment. A much smaller crawler can be seen on the building's exterior wall.

Opened in 1994, the museum is a gift from R. Crosby Kemper, chairman and CEO of UMB Financial Corporation. At its core is the stunning collection of Kemper and his wife, Bebe, that includes works by Jasper Johns, David Hockney, Robert Motherwell, Georgia O'Keeffe, Willem de Kooning, and Frank Stella. A Dale Chihuly blown-glass chandelier is one of the most stunning displays.

If Wayne Thiebaud's *Cakes and Pies* painting makes you hungry, you'll find relief in Cafe Sebastienne. Consider this delightful restaurant part of the art tour because the walls are filled floor to ceiling with 110 canvases by Frederick James Brown. The works, commissioned by the Kempers, tell "The History of Art," and it's fun to pick out references to masters like Picasso, Matisse, and Van Gogh. If you're stumped about a particular piece, the cafe has a printed guide.

Along with permanent displays, the museum hosts exhibits throughout the year, usually by cutting-edge artists. Want one more reason to thank the Kempers? Admission is free. The museum is open every day except Monday, and the cafe serves lunch Tuesday through Sunday and dinner Friday and Saturday. When you visit, take time to walk around the grounds of the Kansas City Art Institute next door; several of the students' sculptures are good enough to be in the museum.

Nelson-Atkins Museum of Art
See Close-up on page 148.

CASINOS

In Kansas City you'll have a chance to go rollin' on the river. Sort of. Our riverboat casinos are, shall we say, permanently docked. But that doesn't mean you won't have a boatload of a good time as long as you're 21 or older. And here's an easy way to cruise over to the boats: Catch a ride on the Casino Cruiser, the No. 173 Metro Bus, which makes the loop from Crown Center and Downtown hotels to the casinos. For information call the Metro at (816) 221–0660 or ask your hotel's front desk for more information.

Ameristar Casino Hotel
3200 Ameristar Drive
(816) 414–7000, (800) 499–4961
You'll find two casinos for the price of one here, with more than 3,200 slot and video poker machines (the most in the city) plus more than 140 table games, including craps, roulette, and mini-baccarat. In fact, Ameristar boasts the largest poker room in the Midwest. Go fish.

This pleasure palace also holds the cards to lots of other entertainment. The Grand Pavilion hosts top comedians, headline entertainers, and live professional boxing, and Depot #9 offers live music. You'll also find an 18-screen movie theater, an authentic Bavarian brewpub, an international buffet, a fine Italian restaurant, and nine cafes serving everything from Arthur Bryant's famous barbecue to fried rat-

tlesnake to custom-made ice-cream cones. There's also an attached luxury hotel.

Argosy Casino
777 Argosy Drive
Riverside, MO
(816) 746–3100, (800) 900–3423
www.argosycasinos.com
Casino decor can range from over-the-top to elegant, and Argosy is definitely the latter. The public areas and restaurants follow a romantic theme with midnight-blue skies and twinkling stars. It's particularly appealing in Journey Wood Fired Steaks, where chefs grill steaks to perfection over mesquite—a nice dining choice even if you don't plan to play. At Crazy Olives, order your favorite martinis, appetizers, and sandwiches to go with a side: live entertainment. Terrace Buffet's cozy environment will tempt you with breakfast, lunch, and dinner selections seven days a week.

For real action go from the dining table to a gaming table. There are 42 in all, plus what *Casino Player* magazine calls "Missouri's Loosest Slots." You can try your luck at 1,750 of them for a nickel to $10 a pull. The Casino Stage Bar is where to find live entertainment Thursday through Saturday.

Harrah's North Kansas City
Casino & Hotel
One Riverboat Drive, North Kansas City
(816) 472–7777, (800) HARRAHS
www.harrahs.com
Harrah's offers the whole package: an exciting casino, a luxury hotel, five restaurants, and exciting live music in the Pavilion. You may never want to leave, especially when you see the gorgeous two-story Mardi Gras casino. Take your winnings, or at least your hunger, to a buffet bonanza, Italian restaurant, or sizzling filet at The Range Steak House. Or count your coins back in your suite and order room service, available 24 hours a day. More good news? Harrah's is putting their money where their guests are. In 2004 they doubled the number of rooms and

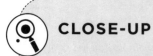

The Nelson-Atkins Museum of Art

At the heart of Kansas City's vibrant art scene is the Nelson-Atkins Museum of Art, ranked among the top 15 art museums in America. The city owes this treasure to two people: one larger-than-life benefactor whose name is symbolic to the city, the other virtually unknown. The two never even met. William Rockhill Nelson was a huge man with a big heart for his adopted hometown. He used his enormous power and prestige as owner of the *Kansas City Star* to turn a rough and rowdy town into a cultured city by pushing for sidewalks, streetlights, boulevards, and parks. He was also a passionate patron of the arts and bequeathed $11 million to the city for art acquisitions. His daughter and son-in-law donated the family's 20-acre estate, Oak Hall, for the site.

The museum's other benefactor was Mary Atkins, a reclusive former schoolteacher who married late but well. She was introduced to great art during travels to Europe and determined that her hometown should have a world-class museum. By the time she died, her late husband's estate was worth $1 million.

With the funding in place, groundbreaking began in 1930. By 1933 the building was complete: an imposing rectangle six stories high and larger than a city block. Its classic design boasts 32 gigantic columns on four sides and 12 30-foot-tall black Pyrenees marble columns define the vestibule. The tab was just shy of $3 million. The museum's name honored both benefactors. The William Rockhill Nelson Gallery of Art and the Mary Atkins Museum of Fine Art was later abbreviated to the Nelson-Atkins Museum of Art. Today we simply call it the Nelson.

Most museums start with an impressive collection, but the Nelson didn't have so much as an etching to its name. Trustees had to start from scratch, and the timing couldn't have been better. Their buying spree began during the Great Depression, when excellent works were available for a song. In another stroke of luck, the committee hired Laurence Sickman, a 23-year-old graduate student in China, who had impeccable taste. Soon unimaginable artifacts began arriving in wooden crates: an earthenware Wei orchestra (the only one of its kind to survive from the sixth century), T'ang dynasty bowls, and rosewood Ming furniture. If the collection had only resulted in the Chinese Temple Room, it would have been enough to make the city proud. The vast Asian collection brought the museum immediate respect, and it is still considered one of the finest in the Western world.

Other treasures await. More than 28,000 items dating from 3,000 B.C. to the present are thoughtfully arranged in 58 galleries and period rooms. Each gallery contains no more than 10 to 12 items to allow ample viewing space while providing a sense of intimacy. You'll need an entire day, comfortable shoes, and help from the information desk to see just a portion. And if you're visiting with little art lovers, a *Looking Together* brochure may be as important as the "don't touch anything" talk you had in the car. Youngsters usually make a beeline for the "Armor for Man and Horse" from 1565 located just beyond the entrance. Think you're carrying around a little extra weight? This poor chap's metal garb tops out at 60 pounds.

Other highlights include rooms decorated with European and American furniture and art from 1200 to 1960, including furniture by Frank Lloyd Wright, Gustav Stickley, and Ludwig Mies van der Rohe. The modern and contemporary art includes canvases by Willem de Kooning, Jackson Pollock, and Franz Kline, along with an icon of the minimalism movement, sculptor Robert Rauschenberg's *Tracer.* And don't miss the chance to fool someone with Duane Hanson's lifelike *Museum Guard,* complete with blotchy skin, rumpled uniform, and thinning hair.

Local pride abounds in the American art wing, where George Caleb Bingham and Thomas Hart Benton are represented. Benton's lush masterpiece *Persephone* once hung in Billy Rose's Diamond Horseshoe Bar in New York. The collection also includes works by Winslow Homer, Edward Hopper, Georgia O'Keeffe, John Singer Sargent, and Andrew Wyeth. European masters include Rubens, Rembrandt, Van Gogh, and Gauguin. An entire wall is filled with the poetry of Claude Monet's *Water Lilies.* The ancient art collection contains exquisite Egyptian, Greek, and Roman artifacts from 3,000 B.C. to A.D. 300. Highlights include a 4,000-year-old wooden statue of a nobleman with still-vivid colors and Greek vases from the sixth and fifth centuries B.C. that celebrate the human form as much as the artists' skill.

Along with permanent displays, the Nelson hosts traveling exhibits, classes for all ages, lecture series, and tours of private collections and museums in other cities. The best way to keep up-to-date is by joining Friends of Art (816–751–1363), which gains you free admission, invitations to previews, and discounts at the bookstore and cafe.

Some of the museum's most stellar displays are outside in the Sculpture Garden. This 17-acre park is dotted with seated figures and reclining women, and

The exquisite Temple Room within the Nelson-Atkins Museum of Art is part of a world-class collection. RICK MCKIBBEN

we don't mean visitors lounging on a lunch break. The gardens contain 13 massive Henry Moore bronzes, the largest collection in the country. But their rounded whimsy is nothing compared to four 18-foot shuttlecocks placed at angles on the lawn as if the museum were a badminton net. The fiberglass-and-aluminum sculptures, by internationally known pop artists Claes Oldenburg and Coosje van Bruggen, were installed in 1994. Love them or hate them—there's rarely a gray area—you'll have to admit they add lighthearted fun to the austere granite building. Feel free to bring a picnic lunch and relax under the shade of a birdie or bronze sheep, or choose a leafy gingko tree. Audio tours are available. Be aware that during the Nelson's multimillion-dollar renovations, parts of the museum, and nearly all the grounds, are off-limits (unless you consider cranes and bulldozers high art).

Don't miss lunch at what *Travel Holiday* magazine calls "the prettiest cafe in the Midwest." The open-air Rozzelle Court restaurant is a one-way ticket to Tuscany, with stone columns and arches with golden light coming from skylights above. A fountain provides musical accompaniment. The cafeteria-style line might pull you back from your mental vacation, but the food won't disappoint. The selection includes artistically arranged salads, delicious soups and sandwiches, and yummy desserts; wine is available by the glass. Rozzelle Court is open from 11:00 A.M. to 3:00 P.M. Tuesday through Sunday, when it serves a buffet brunch. Dinner is served most Fridays, when you can dine to the sounds of live jazz or classical music.

It's all waiting for you, if you can pull yourself away from the new underground garage. It's been called one of the most beautiful parking structures in the world thanks to its undulating ceiling and shimmering light coming from windows in the reflecting pool above. It's just one element of the 140,000-square-foot expansion, the museum's first since opening in 1933. The five-year, $134 million project will also include a new Ford Learning Center and Noguchi Sculpture Court. As before, the trustees have chosen well; the project architect, Steven Holl, was recently named "America's best architect" by *Time* magazine. Holl's most elegant contributions are his five irregularly shaped glass lenses, described as "great quartz crystals spilling neatly on the side lawn" by the museum's director, that will provide light and space to underground spaces. The largest of these will be the Bloch Building, which will contain a main lobby, museum shop, reference library, dining room, and exhibition space. A new grand staircase will connect the old and new areas.

The Nelson is at 45th and Oak Streets, 3 blocks northeast of the Plaza shopping district, and is open daily except Monday and major holidays. Admission is free, and free guided tours are offered Saturday at 11:00 A.M. and 1:00 P.M. and Sunday at 1:30 and 2:30 P.M. We suggest you call or check online (816–561–4000, www.nelson-atkins.org) for updated information, especially during the expansion, which will continue through 2006.

suites, upgrading gambling and dining choices to the tune of $100 million. That's a lot of chips!

Isle of Capri Casino
1800 East Front Street
(816) 855-7777, (800) THE ISLE
(843-4753)
www.isleofcapricasino.com
Welcome to the islands, Mon, and have a nice day. The Isle of Capri is like visiting a tropical resort with bright colors, a two-story waterfall, lush landscaping, and the sound of island drums. If your button-down shirt gets in the way, simply replace it with a festive print at the Banana Cabana kiosk. The casino floor offers more than 1,000 slots and 30 table games and a chance to win $100,000 at Missouri's only Free Pull Machine. If you've worked up an appetite, Farradday's is ready to comply with New Orleans crawfish bisque or a steak. There's also Calypso's all-you-can-eat buffet, quick bites at Tradewinds Marketplace, or homemade chili and ice cream at Island O'Aces.

The Woodlands
99th Street and Leavenworth Road
Kansas City, KS
(913) 299-9797
www.woodlandskc.com
Until the Kansas Speedway showed up, this was the biggest thing to hit Wyan-

dotte County in years. It's still an impressive racetrack, sitting off to the east of northbound Interstate 435 with an electronic sign announcing race days. Greyhound races are held six times a day Wednesday through Sunday year-round. Horse racing season is October through November, Wednesday through Saturday. If you miss the ponies in the off-season, don't despair; the Woodlands offers simulcast betting on out-of-state horse races. All race schedules are subject to change, and bettors must be 18 or over.

The Woodlands also offers a fabulous Sunday brunch and other daily specials. And here's a real Insiders' tip: It's an ideal spot to park your RV when visiting the Kansas Speedway 2 miles away.

ENTERTAINMENT DISTRICTS

Oh sure, you'll want to spend at least one day on our famous Country Club Plaza. But don't miss our other areas that offer festivals and fairs along with enough nightclubs, unique shops, and restaurants to keep you entertained for an afternoon or a weekend.

The Country Club Plaza
Plaza Customer Service, 4745 Central
(816) 753-0100
www.countryclubplaza.com
No matter what you've read or heard about the Plaza, you're bound to be amazed by its beauty. Picture 14 blocks of Spanish-style buildings filled with retailers and restaurants, nightclubs and coffeehouses, antiques shops, and tiny boutiques. And in every corner and alleyway, courtyard and median you'll discover a sculpture in bronze or marble, a lacy wrought-iron gate, a painted tile mural, a fountain, or flower bed. Entire books have been devoted to the Plaza, and you'll need three brochures just to try to see it all: a walking tour of artwork and fountains, a dining and entertaining guide, and a retail map. You'll find all of these and more at

the customer service office at 4745 Central (at the southwest corner of Hall's) and reproduced on the Web site above.

Better yet, tuck the map in your pocket and simply walk around. Show up in spring and you'll share sidewalks with the 6-foot-tall Easter bunnies that have delighted generations of children and adults; this is also the season when flowering bulbs fill the gardens and people fill the sidewalk cafes. During summer you'll enjoy the free weekend music series, as well as the ice cream, iced cappuccinos, and icy martinis waiting at dozens of cafes and shops. In September the Plaza Art Fair turns the place into a giant neighborhood block party with 250 artists, live music, and food vendors. And starting on Thanksgiving night, miles of colored lights outline every spire and arch and swag—the Plaza's holiday gift to the world.

Plan to leave plenty of room in your suitcase; the Plaza puts Rodeo Drive to shame with more than 180 stores and boutiques. You'll find fashion's aristocracy like Armani, Brooks Brothers, BCBG, Ann Taylor, Betsey Johnson, St. John, and Laura Ashley and floor after floor of choices at such department stores as Halls Plaza, Mark Shale, and Saks Fifth Avenue. Make yourself over at MAC Cosmetics or Aveda, or make over your home with something from Pottery Barn, Restoration Hardware, or Scandia Down. Younger kids will go for places like Discovery Channel; bigger kids will like the toys at Sharper Image.

Whew! Ready for a break? Then you'll love the fact that the Plaza is home to 40 restaurants, bistros, and pubs, from one-of-a-kind eateries like re:Verse, Starker's

When planning a day at an area attraction, don't forget that Kansas City's weather can change at the drop of a rain hat. Check the weather to see if you need to bring a warm wrap, umbrella, or sunscreen—or all three. Updated weather can be found online at www.kansascity.com.

Reserve, and Bo Ling's Chinese Restaurant, to national favorites like McCormick & Schmick's, The Capital Grille, and Cheesecake Factory.

If you're ready to have someone else do the walking for a change, take a carriage ride with Pride of Kansas City Carriage (816–531–1999) or Surrey's Carriage (816–531–2673). These tours-on-the-hoof are fun during the day but really turn on the romance at night with white lights and glowing lanterns. There's even a pumpkin-shaped Cinderella's carriage! And there's still time left to drop into Tommy Bahama's for that tropical print shirt you saw in the window.

Crown Center
2450 Grand Boulevard
(816) 274–8444
www.crowncenter.com

In 1968 Joyce C. Hall, founder of Hallmark Cards, and his son, Don J. Hall, turned an eyesore called "Signboard Hill" into one of the city's most vibrant entertainment centers. Crown Center became one of the nation's earliest mixed-use developments and a model for how to do urban redevelopment right. You'll need a guidebook just to see it all, and thank goodness Crown Center offers a terrific one at the information booth on the lower level just past the main entrance. A separate map takes you past marvelous outdoor sculptures, including an Alexander Calder, plus fountains and landmarks throughout the 85-acre complex and surrounding neighborhood.

You can get to nearly everything via a glass-enclosed elevated walkway called The Link that connects Crown Center with Union Station and the Hyatt Regency. But what makes this complex the "Rockefeller Plaza" of the Midwest is the Crown Center Square, with fountains and terraced lawns where events take place all year. The Entertainment Pavilion with its free-form tent is home to free family activities throughout summer, and from November to March it's transformed into the city's only outdoor ice-skating rink. Each winter

the 100-foot Mayor's Christmas Tree becomes the square's glowing focal point.

Within Crown Center are more than 50 unique shops and restaurants, a movie complex, and two live stage venues: the American Heartland Theatre and the Coterie Family Theatre. The Hallmark Visitor Center provides a look at the greeting card company's history (you'll learn why the wackiest line is called Shoebox), and at Kaleidoscope kids can exercise their creative muscles. Parking is free for the first three hours; just remember to get your ticket validated at any retail shop or restaurant. Van-accessible handicapped parking is available on Grand Boulevard near the main entrance, and the parking garage includes handicapped parking with ramps to allow easy access. You can also rent strollers or check out wheelchairs at Customer Service.

River Market
North of Fifth Street from Broadway
Bridge to Heart of America Bridge
(816) 842–1271
www.kc-citymarket.com

When it comes to attractions, this one really produces, literally. Since 1857 it's been home to the biggest farmers' market in the Midwest. But there's plenty happening here besides ripe tomatoes. The River Market is a laid back neighborhood that's fun to explore on foot. You might even find a treasure to ship back home at the Kansas City Artists Coalition (816–421–5222) at 201 Wyandotte, where a variety of artists show work from cutting edge to classic.

Then follow your nose to Planters Seed and Spice Company at 513 Walnut, where you'll find bins overflowing with every fragrant herb, seed, and coffee bean imaginable. Antiques hunters will go nuts in the 30,000-square-foot Cheep Antiques (816–471–0092) at 500 West Fifth Street. Other antiques are on view—this time reclaimed treasures from a boat that sank in 1856—at Arabia Steamboat Museum, 400 Grand Street (see listing in Museums).

When you need a break head for River Market Brewery (500 Walnut), the first place to open (officially, anyway) when Prohibition ended. River Market also hosts wild and wonderful street parties with music and dancing nearly every weekend from spring through fall. Check the Web site or call for dates.

Westport
Westport Road between Main Street and Southwest Trafficway

Westport got its start in 1833 when John Calvin McCoy built a trading post on the northeast corner of Westport Road and Pennsylvania. By 1836 the area's colorful population of 50 or so included scouts Kit Carson and Jim Bridger as well as John Sutter, a guy who skipped town to escape creditors and look for gold. The area also played a bloody role in the Civil War when the Battle of Westport became known as the Gettysburg of the West.

Today Westport is still a stopping point for thirsty and hungry travelers. Lucky for you, prairie dog is no longer on the menu; instead you'll find dining choices from gourmet to casual, plus bars and live music venues. And instead of spurs and cattle prods, shops offer candles, hand-crafted jewelry, and garden art.

Most of us agree that a trip to Kansas City isn't complete without visiting Kelly's Westport Inn (500 Westport Road, 816-561-5800, www.kellyswestportinn.com), the city's oldest standing building. Built in 1837, it was once a grocery store operated by Albert Boone, grandson of Daniel. It was designated a national historic landmark in 1959, which means hands off on changing the creaky-floored structure. Frankly, current owners Pat and Kyle Kelly and their legions of loyal customers wouldn't have it any other way. This is the place to be on St. Pat's Day when the streets outside become a sea of green and a river of spilled beer.

Pick up a walking map of historic buildings and sites at Westport Merchants Association (816-756-2789) at 4123 Mill Street,

or check out their Web site at www.westporttoday.com. An informative and entertaining online tour is available on Dr. Ronald Miriani's site (www.kcculture.com), which also offers walking tours of Parkville and the West Side.

HISTORICAL CHURCHES

Cathedral of the Immaculate Conception
416 West 12th Street
(816) 842-0416

In 1882 the dome of this neoclassic-style church was the highest point in the city. Today it's dwarfed by its steel-and-glass neighbors, but the gleam from the 23-karat gold leaf outshines everything in sight. The dome was gilded in 1960, and the church was recently renovated. Masses are held at 12:15 P.M. Monday through Friday; at 2:30 and 4:30 P.M. on Saturday; and at 9:00 and 11:00 A.M., and 6:00 and 8:00 P.M. Sunday.

Community Christian Church
47th and Main
(816) 561-6531

When Frank Lloyd Wright designed this church in the 1930s, technology couldn't produce the shaft of light he envisioned coming from the top of the dome. The beam would have to wait another 60 years for artist Dale Eldred to make it work, but even he wouldn't be around to see it. A year after his death, in December 1994, the Steeple of Light, which includes four xenon lights at 300 million candle-power each, was switched on. The lights shine heavenward every weekend and nightly through the holiday season.

The church itself is pretty amazing as well. Curved walls are covered with a textured white surface and, typical of Wright's style, the overall design is stark. But the brilliant architect knew what he was doing. Because he created a sanctuary without needless adornment, we can focus our attention on the things that matter most.

Community of Christ Temple and Auditorium
1001 West Walnut
Independence, MO
(816) 521–3045
www.cofchrist.org

With its silver spiral reaching skyward, the Community of Christ Temple is one of the country's most visually stunning structures. From the inside, looking up toward the ceiling as it rises 195 feet, the design becomes organic—a giant seashell glowing bright white.

In 1831 Joseph Smith designated Independence as the new site for the city of Zion, and today this international Mormon headquarters serves a denomination of 250,000 members. Visitors are welcome to experience the Worshiper's Path, a reflective walkway filled with symbolic artwork leading to the 1,600-seat sanctuary. The room is large, but when the 102-rank pipe organ is played, the very walls seem to vibrate with the powerful sound. Time your visit for one of the free recitals, which are held daily from 3:00 to 3:30 P.M. June to August and every Sunday from 3:00 to 3:30 P.M. September to May. Tours of the Temple are on Monday through Sunday, but not from noon to 1:00 P.M., when the Daily Prayer for Peace is taking place. You are invited to take part; the service begins at 12:30 P.M.

The auditorium was designed in the 1920s and features a 5,800-seat chamber with seating in the round beneath a domed ceiling. President Truman made history here when he signed an executive order to desegregate the armed forces in 1948. Within the auditorium is the Children's Peace Pavilion, an interactive museum dedicated to promoting peace through example. The Pavilion is open Tuesday through Saturday free of charge.

Mormon Visitors Center
937 West Walnut
Independence, MO
(816) 836–3466

Learn about the key role the Church of Jesus Christ of Latter-Day Saints (the Mormons) played in the early and often tempestuous history of Independence. The visitor center houses rare artifacts and artwork documenting the history and beliefs of the Mormons. Exhibits include a re-creation of a log cabin; the two-story mural entitled *The Second Coming of Jesus Christ* is splendid. The center is 1 mile south of the Truman Library on the corner of River Road and West Walnut and is open from 9:00 A.M. to 9:00 P.M. daily for free guided tours.

Unity World Headquarters
1901 Northwest Blue Parkway
(816) 524–3550
www.unityworldhq.org

Unity Village's beautiful, 165-foot-tall bell tower can be seen for miles throughout the southwest part of the city; its teachings touch lives around the world. Unity has been offering nondenominational ministry, prayer, and education since 1889, and its monthly spiritual publication, *Daily Word,* is translated into nine languages with an annual circulation of 1.3 million. Its Silent Prayer ministry receives more than two million requests for prayer assistance annually.

Unity Village's Mediterranean-style buildings, two of which are on the National Register of Historic Places, are situated among 1,400 acres of beautifully landscaped grounds, with meditation chapels, fountains, and reflecting pools. The showplace rose garden, with more than 800 rose bushes and 50 varieties, is at its prettiest June through October.

Free tours start at the visitor center at 9:00 A.M., noon, and 1:00 and 5:00 P.M. Monday through Friday. Saturday tours are held at 9:00 A.M., noon, and 1:00 and 4:00 P.M. May through October. The guided walking tour, which includes a 12-minute video presentation about Unity's history, takes about an hour and is equal to 2 city blocks; there are two flights of stairs. The tour can be modified to be wheelchair-accessible with advance notice.

HISTORICAL HOMES

If you like looking at homes—really old homes—we've got 'em. Several of these mid-1800s era houses are on the National Register of Historic Places. Although you'll see a wide variety of styles, from simple cabin to opulent Victorian, there is a recurring theme. Most of these homes were directly on or near the famous trails heading west; in one case the backyard was turned into corduroy by thousands of wagon wheels. The homes are open for individual tours, or let Ann Malita-Smith of Kansas City Adventures (816–920–5513, www.kansascityadventures.com) plan a terrific itinerary of historic homes, churches, or other sites to match your interests. Ann lives in a 1909 shirtwaist in a lovely northeast neighborhood, so she respects old bricks, wood floors, and cranky furnaces.

Alexander Majors Historic House and Museum
8201 State Line Road
(816) 333–5556

Today this nine-room house is surrounded by office buildings and banks, but in 1856 it served as an outfitting base for the growing Santa Fe Trail trade. Its owner, Alexander Majors, cofounded the Pony Express, which quickly became the largest overland freighting operation in the country, at one time employing 4,000 men and 3,500 wagons. But within 18 months the telegraph displaced the need for wagons and riders and Majors lost his fortune. He would eventually get a job touring with a former employee, Buffalo Bill Cody, and his Wild West show. The house is filled with period furnishings, and the adjacent barn houses a working blacksmith shop and restored wagons. The site is open on weekends; closed during winter. Admission is $3.00 for adults, $1.50 for children.

Bingham-Waggoner Estate
313 West Pacific
Independence, MO
(816) 461–3491
www.bwestate.org

If there was ever a superhighway in the mid-1800s, it was the Santa Fe Trail, and this estate had a front row seat. In fact, in 1999 wagon "swales" were discovered on the southern 19 acres, which suggests this was a shortcut to the trails. You can see these paths by going behind the house, crossing the footbridge, and looking along a line of trees.

History was made inside the 1827 house as well. Of its many colorful residents, the most famous was George Caleb Bingham, an artist and early-day political activist who used brushstrokes to demonstrate his feelings about the Civil War. When a Union general issued the infamous command that left countless residents of Jackson County homeless, Bingham painted *Order No. 11* here. Other works are in the American Paintings section of the Nelson-Atkins Museum of Art. In 1870 he sold the home and moved to Kansas City.

The Waggoner family purchased the house in 1879 and produced their "Queen of the Pantry Flour" in the mill across the street. Three generations of this family occupied the home over the next 100 years. Today the house and its acreage are recognized as one of the more significant historical sites in western Missouri. Inside are many furnishings of the time, including a massive dining room table and a walk-in icebox. The home is open for tours from April to October and during the Christmas season. Admission is $4.00 for adults, $2.50 for seniors, and $1.00 for ages 6 to 16.

1859 Jail, Marshal's Home, and Museum
217 Main
(816) 252–1892
www.jchs.org

Just think: In the mid-1800s prisoners didn't have TVs or phones. Okay, no one did. But you'll still be amazed at these dungeonlike cells that held Frank James, William Clark Quantrill of Quantrill's Raiders, and others crossways with the law. Actually, the cell that held Frank James was opulently outfitted by his many adoring fans, and he took his meals with the jailer's family. But in other "guest" quarters, barred windows, double iron doors, and leg chains provide a chilling look at frontier justice. The jail and the marshal's home have been restored to period and contain an outstanding historical collection. Tours are given seven days a week March through December. Closed Thanksgiving, Christmas, January, and February. Admission is $4.00 for adults, $3.50 for seniors, $1.00 for ages 6 to 16, and free for under 6.

Harry S Truman Home
219 North Delaware Street
Independence, MO
(816) 254-9929

The simple charm of the Summer White House speaks volumes about the man who chose to be buried in his hometown rather than beside a towering monument in Washington, D.C.

Bess Truman's grandparents built the Victorian home in 1885; she grew up here, and she and Harry lived here when they weren't in Washington, D.C. The furnishings are just as they were when she died in 1982, right down to the dishcloth by the sink and Harry's hat by the door. The house is open year-round and tours are conducted every 15 minutes. We suggest you arrive early because tickets are issued starting at 8:30 A.M. on a first-come, first-served basis. Tickets are available at the Truman Home Ticket and Information Center at Truman Road and Main Street, where you can watch a short slide show about the Trumans. Admission is $2.00, free for those under 17. Guided walking tours of the neighborhood leave from the center daily at 10:00 A.M. and 2:00 P.M. Memorial Day through Labor Day.

Harry S Truman Office and Courtroom
112 West Lexington
(816) 795-8200

The office where the 33rd U.S. president began his political career as a county judge is chiefly unchanged since the day he left for a higher calling. An audiovisual show traces Truman's life before his presidency. Tours are available Tuesday

through Thursday and Saturday; the courthouse is closed on federal holidays.

Independence Square
(816) 252-0608
www.jchs.org

Independence has it all: infamous outlaws and hometown hero, bloody border battles of the Civil War, and opulent homes. At its heart is Independence Square, which marked the beginnings of Harry S Truman's political career and the journey for thousands heading west. Within the old-fashioned town square you'll find the 1859 Jail and Truman Office and Courtroom (described below) as well as antiques shops, unique stores, and restaurants. And there's a phosphate or banana split waiting for you at Clinton's Soda Fountain (100 West Maple) where a young Harry once scooped ice cream and mopped the floor. He'd later say his weekly salary of three silver dollars looked like three million.

Jesse James Bank Museum
Court House Square
Liberty, MO
(816) 781-4458

Did the James Gang really steal $60,000 from this bank in February 1866? We'll never know for sure, but it makes a great story. Regardless of who done it, this is the site of the first daylight peacetime bank robbery in the United States. You can tour the bank with its stone vault, iron safe, and Civil War–era teller's window. The bank museum is open year-round. Admission is $4.00 for adults, $3.50 for seniors, $1.50 for ages 8 to 15, and free for those under 8.

Jesse James Farm and Museum
21216 Jesse James Farm Road
Kearney, MO
(816) 628-6065, (800) FUN-CLAY

Where else but in the Wild West would people idolize a man who robbed trains and banks? But Jesse James wasn't just a typical hoodlum. His boldness and flamboyance—helped along by sensationalized newspaper articles and dime novels—

turned him into a modern-day Robin Hood. Jesse was born in this house in 1847, the son of a Baptist minister. The young man's religious upbringing apparently didn't take; after a stint in the Civil War he joined with other former Confederate guerrillas to lead the James Gang.

A tour of the home begins with a short film recapping the exploits of James and his older brother, Frank. Artifacts include Jesse's boots and spurs and Frank's letter of surrender. You can also stroll along the stream where the boys played as youngsters and pass Jesse's original burial site, where his mother once sold souvenir stones from his grave. The woman figured since visitors were taking them anyway, she might as well make a profit. Although there are no stones left unturned, the on-site gift shop offers books and souvenirs.

The famous bandit was shot in the back in 1882 and is now buried in Mount Olivet Cemetery in Kearney, about 20 miles northeast of downtown Kansas City. But there's always been talk that the bandit faked his death and lived out the rest of his life in the East. When his heirs agreed to have the body exhumed in 1995, the rumors were laid to rest (so to speak) when DNA and forensic evidence determined that the man in the grave really was Jesse. The home is open year-round and often hosts dramatic reenactments. Admission is $5.50 for adults, $4.25 for seniors, $2.50 for children 8 to 15, and free for those under 8.

John Wornall House Museum
146 West 61st Terrace
(816) 444-1858
Today this stately 1858 Greek Revival structure sits peacefully amid other lovely homes near Loose Park. But during three days in October 1864, the antebellum home's wide front porch was stained with blood when it served as an army hospital. The home's 500-acre farm was at the vortex of the Civil War's largest battle west of the Mississippi.

As a museum, the Wornall House provides an intriguing look at the lives of early settlers. Well-informed docents and staff take visitors through rooms filled with period furnishings, including a foursquare grand piano in the parlor and Lincoln rocker in the master bedroom. From October through May actors re-create a typical day in the mid-1800s. Several programs are mounted throughout the year, such as holiday candlelight tours and Civil War reenactments on the grounds. The museum is part of a 25-stop driving tour of the Battle of Westport; other sites include Loose Park and a rise near the Big Blue River that was known as "Bloody Hill." Brochures are available from the Parks and Recreation Department (816-513-7500, 4600 East 63rd Street, Kansas City, Missouri). The museum is open Tuesday through Sunday; closed in January. Admission is $3.00 for adults, $2.50 for seniors, $2.00 for ages 5 to 12, and free for ages 4 and under. Call for hours, which change with the seasons.

Rice-Tremonti Home
66th and Blue Ridge Boulevard
(816) 358-7423
In 1844, Archibald Rice's 160 acres was a popular place to camp while waiting for spring before heading west on the trails. The homestead wasn't as fancy as some others still with us today, but that's the key to its fascination; its furnishings provide a glimpse into the way families lived in what was once wilderness. The home is now on the National Register of Historic Places.

One of the most interesting attractions is a replica of Aunt Sophia's cabin, where the family's slave lived. Sophia would cook the meals here and then carry them to the main house. Tours are available Saturday and Sunday from May through September.

Thomas Hart Benton Home and Studio
3616 Belleview
(816) 931-5722
If you're a fan of this famous Kansas City artist, this tour is a must. If you're not familiar with his work, there's ample opportunity to discover it in the Benton

section of the Nelson-Atkins Museum of Art and from a mural that fills a wall at the Truman Library.

His painting style was bigger than life, a colorful montage of voluptuous women, powerful men, and landscapes that seemed to rise and swirl as if in a tornado. The Benton home remains exactly as it was when the artist went outside to sign a painting and dropped dead in 1975. His brushes and paints, pipe, and harmonica are casually placed as if waiting for his big rough hands to take them up. His wife, Rita, died a few months later, but her famous spaghetti sauce lives on. Make sure to pick up a copy of her recipe in the kitchen. The tour is open seven days a week; admission is $2.00 for adults, $1.25 ages 6 to 12. If you have time, stroll around the lovely Belleview homes district; minimansions line the streets, and the landscaping is exquisite, particularly in spring when the pink and white azaleas are in bloom.

Union Station
30 West Pershing Road
(816) 460–2222
www.sciencecity.com
After a second flood devastated the Union Depot in the West Bottoms, the city knew it needed to build a rail station on higher ground. Several years and $5.8 million later, the result was the City Beautiful movement's most spectacular testament to date. When Union Station opened on October 30, 1914, it was the third largest train facility in the world after New York's Grand Central and Pennsylvania Stations. More than 100,000 people jammed the 400- by 800-foot Grand Hall for the

When you go to Union Station, remember that there really was a Union Station Massacre. It happened on June 17, 1933, when four people were killed during an attempt to free a notorious federal prisoner. You can still see the stray machine-gun bullet lodged in a wall near Union Station's east entrance.

grand opening ceremony, with thousands more pushing into the football field–size North Waiting Room.

This magnificent Beaux Art structure was more than a train terminal; it was the city's town hall, where people came to dine at Fred Harvey's restaurant and dance on New Year's Eve. "Meet me under the clock" was a common phrase as friends looked for familiar faces under the 6½-foot-wide dial. Army boots echoed through the marble halls as more than half of all World War II soldiers boarded trains here.

But by 1950s travel by rail was a thing of the past, and the station's depot was relegated to a walk-up window on one side. The last Amtrak train pulled out in 1985. The once-beloved station was forgotten, its now-empty halls echoing only with breaking glass, falling plaster, or the steady drip, drip of water leaking through a stained roof. Over the following decades several groups promised to rebuild it, but the projects failed one by one. Finally, city leaders had two choices: Restore it or tear it down.

They decided to bring it back to life, financed with a bistate cultural tax in 1996, the first such two-state, five-county program in the country. After more than $250 million and years of work, Union Station and its new Science City museum opened in November 1999. As you walk through the Grand Hall and North Waiting Room, be sure to look at the ornate ceilings 95 feet above you. These plaster swirls and ribbons, oak leaves, and rosette medallions—sky-blue, gold, and terra-cotta—were meticulously restored by artisans, including a team from Liverpool, England, that helped restore the fire-ravaged Windsor Castle. Crystal chandeliers, all 3,000-pounds of them, sparkle like new.

Union Station is once again a place to celebrate and meet friends under the clock before enjoying an elegant meal at Pierpont's, where the gorgeous bar alone is enough to make a conductor whistle. Within the massive station is Science City, an interactive museum for children with activities that prove science is everywhere in our lives. Adults and kids alike will enjoy the live theater and giant-screen Extreme Screen within the complex. For details, including ticket prices and times, see the Kidstuff chapter.

Vaile Victorian Mansion
1500 North Liberty
Independence, MO
(816) 325–7430
www.ci.independence.mo.us
As pretty as a wedding cake, this 31-room mansion features gables and towers, lacy trim, and Gothic windows. Its highest peak is adorned with grillwork that looks like a crown, a fitting reference for a town called "Queen City of the Trails."

The house was built in 1881 for Harvey Merrick Vaile, a prosperous lawyer, rancher, and, as you'll see, a rather wicked fellow. At one time the estate included a lake, boathouse, and lushly landscaped gardens. The home was just as elaborate within, filled with unheard-of conveniences like flushing toilets and a 48,000-bottle wine cellar. In the master bedroom a reclining woman (minus more than just her high-button shoes) was painted on the ceiling. Other interesting but less scandalous art-work appears elsewhere: As was the norm, the builder used inexpensive pine in the upper floors and then had it painted to look like more costly mahogany or cherry wood. If you look closely at the faux grain-ing in the second-floor smoking room, you'll notice faces and animals incorpo-rated into the swirls and dips.

After the owner's death in 1894, the home became a sanatorium and then a nursing home. It was nearly demolished before the DeWitt family bought it in the 1960s. The family, along with members of the Vaile Victorian Society, restored this home to a fare-thee-well and are pleased to invite you in. The group hosts a Mad Hatter's Tea Party in March, a strawberry festival in June, and holiday tours in December, when the home is beautifully decorated. The home is open seven days a week from April through October and cer-tain days in December; please call for a current schedule. Admission is $4.00 for adults, $3.50 for seniors, and $1.00 for ages 6 through 16.

HISTORICAL MUSEUMS AND SITES

American Jazz Museum
18th and Vine
(816) 474–8463
www.americanjazzmuseum.com
Jazz. It was America's music, and in the 1920s and 1930s no place played it with more passion than Kansas City. Some of the greats, like Count Basie, Bennie Moten, and Charlie "Yardbird" Parker, got their start, made their name, or honed their craft here. Many stayed; some headed to the even brighter lights of New York. The American Jazz Museum is the first in the country devoted exclusively to this art form.

Dozens of interactive displays provide a glimpse of this historical, hysterical time when music poured out of dozens of nightclubs 24 hours a day. You can become part of it, if only for an hour or so, by listening to hundreds of the greatest jazz recordings ever made, including Ella Fitzgerald scatting through "A Tisket, A Tasket," and Big Joe Turner singing—what else?—"Goin' to Kansas City." Catch more than two dozen jazz performances on a video jukebox, and watch *Jazz*, an original film starring Jay McShann, Max Roach, and Shirley Horn. Special displays, including the world's most expensive saxophone, honor talents like Charlie Parker, Louis Arm-strong, and Duke Ellington.

Little hipsters aren't left out. In the Wee-Bop Room, children can play audio engineer at the mixing station; experiment with harmony, melody, and rhythm; and learn the range and sounds of different instruments. The museum is open Tuesday through Saturday, noon to 6:00 P.M. Admission is $6.00 for adults, $2.50 for children. A combination ticket to the American Jazz Museum and the Negro Leagues Baseball Museum costs $8.00 and $4.00, respectively.

Arabia Steamboat Museum
400 Grand Avenue
(816) 471–4030 (information),
(816) 471–1856 (group reservations)
www.1856.com

Who hasn't dreamed of finding buried treasure? Bob Hawley and sons Dave and Greg, along with Jerry Mackey and their families, put their dreams to work by uncovering the steamboat *Arabia* 132 years after it sank on its way from Westport to Parkville, Missouri. When the 171-foot boat went down, a quick-thinking crew got all 130 passengers off safely, with the exception of one lone mule. But 222 tons of goods drifted to a watery grave, including frontier-bound tools and dishware, shoes, and buttons . . . and 400 barrels of Kentucky bourbon. A few ladies were devastated to learn they wouldn't get the perfume they'd ordered from France.

Using an old river map, the Hawley and Mackey team located the boat in a cornfield one-half mile from the river's edge and began excavation in 1988. It would be three torturous weeks before they uncovered the splintered remains of the left paddle wheel. Soon the men were bringing up box after box of treasure. The museum is a fascinating look at these remarkably preserved supplies, which National Geographic *Traveler* calls "A King Tut's tomb. . . a time capsule of another age!" It's believed to be the largest single collection of pre–Civil War frontier artifacts in the country. Once inside, visitors will see a replica of the *Arabia*'s side-wheel paddle slicing through the water; there's even part of the walnut tree that was its downfall. After a short movie about the steamboat's history and its excavation you can ask questions, and often the person with the colorful answers is named Hawley.

You can then walk through the display areas by yourself or attend one of the tours—worth waiting for—that begin every half hour. Children eight years old and up will enjoy the museum, and it is wheelchair-accessible. A gift shop sells books about the *Arabia* written by Greg and Don Haw-ley, including a cute children's book, and an 1856 perfume based on bottles found within the dig. Allow at least 90 minutes to see it all. Admission is $9.75 for adults, $9.25 for seniors, and $4.75 for ages 4 to 12.

The museum is open seven days a week, closed on major holidays. Call for hours. Food is not allowed in the museum, but an ice-cream parlor is just outside the entrance, and several casual-style restaurants are within walking distance. And here in Kansas City, we're eagerly waiting the excavation of a steamboat the Hawley family says was even grander than the *Arabia*. Stay tuned!

18th and Vine Historic District
1616 East 18th Street
(816) 474–VINE (8463)

From the 1920s through the early 1940s, the 18th and Vine neighborhood was the center of Kansas City's African-American culture, commerce, and entertainment. It's where jazz musicians like Charlie Parker, Count Basie, and hundreds of others played, and it's home base for the Negro Baseball Leagues. We pay tribute to their heart and soul in this $24 million, 50,000-square-foot complex that opened in 1997. Within its walls are separate museums devoted to jazz and the Negro Leagues (both described later in this chapter) as well as the Horace M. Peterson III Visitor Center, which tells of the contributions black citizens made to the city's social and economic development. The center also contains the Blue Room, a nightclub that re-creates the music's heyday. During the day this club is a minimuseum filled with artifacts; four nights a week it becomes a stage for some of KC's best jazz musicians. The Blue Room has its own entrance at 1600 East 18th Street. Call (816) 474–2929 for event schedules.

Two other attractions are close by. The Gem Theater Cultural and Performing Arts Center, a 500-seat facility that hosts dance and musical events, is across the street at 1615 East 18th Street, and the Charlie Parker Memorial is 1 block north between

Vine Street and The Paseo. (You can read more about this tribute in Landmarks above.) The 18th and Vine District is five minutes from downtown and Crown Center, 2 blocks south of Interstate 70 at The Paseo exit. Free on-street parking is available; the area is also served by Kansas City's Metro No. 108 Indiana bus and the trolley. For more details about the two main museums within the complex, see the American Jazz Museum and the Negro Leagues Baseball Museum listings.

Elmwood Cemetery
4900 Truman Road
(816) 231-0373, (877) 231-0373
www.historickcelmwood.org
Many of Kansas City's most important civic leaders were laid to rest in this European-style cemetery, their wealth and social status evident in enormous monuments and mausoleums. Even the grounds are historic, created by the city's most respected landscape architect, George Kessler. The 43 acres served as an early drawing board for the parks and green spaces he would design during his career. Stop by the cemetery's office or go online for biographies of famous people buried here; guided tours are available for groups of 10 or more with advance reservation. There may be a fee; certainly donations are always welcome at this not-for-profit historic treasure.

In a sea of massive monuments, the most impressive by far is the Armour Chapel, a stone Gothic sanctuary dedicated to the memory of meat packing magnate Kirkland Armour (1854–1901). Other elaborate resting places belong to Jacob Loose, founder of Sunshine Biscuits, whose estate donated the land for Loose Park, and Kersey Coates, an influential leader who helped develop downtown's Quality Hill. His Coates House Hotel was one of the finest in the Midwest.

A much smaller tombstone was laid for a very large woman, 6' 10" Leannah Loveall Kearnes, also known as Annie Chambers. Kansas City's most notorious madam, Annie changed her ways late in life and left her City Market property to the City Union Mission. Along with famous people, more than 700 Civil War veterans are buried here, as well as many who died in border wars. There are also a large number of Jewish burials from Congregation B'nai Jehudah Temple in two southwest acres, all facing east.

Detailed biographies of several of these famous citizens can be found in Wilda Sandy's fascinating book, *Here Lies Kansas City.* Self-guided tours of Elmwood are welcome until dusk Monday through Friday. Please check with the office before attempting to take any monument rubbings. At this time there is no fee.

Call ahead to find out if attractions offer tours, as these can greatly enhance your visit. One example is the Arabia Steamboat Museum *in the River Market area where the tour guide is usually one of the people who discovered the buried treasure. Often you can reserve space in the tour to guarantee your seat—not a bad idea during the busy summer or on weekends.*

Harry S Truman Library and Museum
500 West U.S. Highway 24
Independence, MO
(816) 833-1400
www.trumanlibrary.org
Independence is still wild about its native son, the 33rd president, who grew up in this town. When the library opened in 1957 it became only the second such archive in the country.

Fresh from a $22.5 million renovation completed in 2001, the museum and library does more than just tell Truman's story. As he wished, it challenges visitors to explore the decision-making process of that era and how it affects our lives today. Two new permanent exhibits include "The White House Decision Center," a behind-the-scenes look that lets visitors take on the roles of the president and his aides in a re-creation of the West Wing. A multimedia exhibit contains dozens of original artifacts and documents from before, during, and after Truman's presidency. Other features include the gravesites of Harry and his wife, Bess, the documentary film *Harry S Truman: 1884–1972,* and a replica of Truman's Oval Office where you can listen to a tape of his voice and see the original THE BUCK STOPS HERE desk plaque.

This is a fascinating look at a leader who may be better regarded today than when he was in office as we find a new appreciation for his honesty and frank-talking ways. And visitors are often surprised to discover the many ways Truman changed history: He proposed the first national health care plan, announced the end of the war in Europe, and signed peace treaties with other countries. He was also the president who dropped the first atomic bomb. And although his Whistlestop Campaign has been copied in recent years, no one has done it as successfully. Children might enjoy looking at 10,000 or so documents, photographs, and political cartoons about this train ride across America at www.whistlestop.org.

Museum admission is $7.00 for adults, $5.00 for over 61, and $3.00 for ages 6 to 18. It's open seven days a week. Plan on spending at least one hour to view the permanent displays and any special touring exhibit. Or consider making a day of it touring the other "Man from Missouri" attractions in Independence, including Independence Square and the Truman Home, both detailed in this chapter.

Huron Indian Cemetery
Seventh and Ann Street
Wyandotte County, KS

This two-acre tract tucked between office buildings and banks provides a story both heartbreaking and triumphant. The cemetery was established in 1843 for members of the Wyandot Indian Nation (the name became Wyandotte later) who died of typhoid, cholera, and the elements after being forced from their homeland in Ohio. The fallen were brought to this sacred ground at a high point overlooking the meeting of two rivers. It's estimated that 400 to 500 members of the tribe are buried here, many in unmarked graves.

Through the years as the town grew up around it (Kansas City, Kansas, was incorporated in 1886) there were attempts to buy the land or simply take it over despite the tribe's wishes. After one near-sale in 1906, three sisters—Lyda, Helene, and Ida Conley—built a small lean-to over their parents' graves and took turns defending the area with a shotgun. A more lawful fight occurred when Lyda, a lawyer, became the first Native American woman to present a case before the U.S. Supreme Court. The land was placed on the National Register of Historic Sites in 1971, and today you can tour the cemetery and see Helene Conley's tombstone, which reads, CURSED BE THE VILLIANTHAT MOLEST THEIR GRAVES. Read more about the Huron Cemetery and those feisty sisters, including references to a possible curse, at www.kckansas.com/2001huron. There is a spirit here that is palpable.

Johnson County Museum of History
6305 Lackman Road
Shawnee, KS
(913) 631-6709
www.digitalhistory.com

Although baby boomers might take issue with things from their childhoods ending up in a museum, the truth is that everyone will enjoy the 1950s All-Electric House. The ranch-style house, built in 1954 to showcase all the modern electric conveniences, was actually a model home in Prairie Village, a tidy Johnson County suburb. Now *this* was the life: a painting that slides back to reveal a black-and-white television, a remote control near Dad's recliner that closes the drapes and turns on the stereo, and a bedside dial that controls the lights throughout the house. Guess they hadn't discovered "clap on, clap off' technology yet. Other displays include actual home movies, toys from the '50s, and a snazzy 1955 two-tone Chevy Bel Air.

The main museum chronicles the county's growth from its beginnings as

Indian Territory in 1820, its change to farmland then suburbs, and now its role as
edge city and one of the fastest growing
areas in the two-state region. Exhibits
show—through more than 500 artifacts,
documents, photos, and maps—various
and often competing versions of "the
good life." The first inhabitants, the
Shawnee, are represented by items such as
ceremonial clothing and an 1859 edition of
Hymns in the Shawnee Language. There
are also interactive displays and profiles of
33 individuals who helped shape the area
over the past 175 years. The museum is
open from 10:00 A.M. to 4:30 P.M. Tuesday
through Saturday and 1:00 to 4:00 P.M.
Sunday. The All-Electric House is open
Tuesday through Saturday from 1:00 to
4:00 P.M. Admittance to the museum is
free; the house tour costs $2.00 for adults
and $1.00 for children 12 and under. Poodle
skirts not required.

Kansas City Museum of History and Science
3218 Gladstone Boulevard
(816) 483-8300
www.kcmuseum.com

Believe it or not, at one time this majestic
building was a private residence. Well,
they certainly don't make 'em like they
used to. When lumber baron Robert A.
Long built his 70-room villa called
Corinthian Hall in 1911, it cost a whopping
$750,000, unheard of in those days. He
was content with everything except the
view. To improve it he moved three 4,000-
square-foot mansions down the street.
Perhaps that's where the phrase, "Not in
my backyard" originated. The palatial
space is now the Kansas City Museum,
which houses interactive displays about
the pioneering spirit of our early settlers.

Kids in particular will enjoy exploring
the culture of the Osage Indians, visiting
Chouteau's trading post, and climbing
aboard a covered wagon heading west.
Everybody will go for the 1910 soda fountain, where they still scoop a pretty good
ice-cream cone. A tour of the mansion
gives you a taste of how fortune's favored

lived . . . but who needs a bowling alley
anyway? The planetarium hosts seasonal
star shows and educational programs
throughout the year.

Take a self-directed tour Tuesday
through Sunday; student and group tours
are also available with reservations. Admission is free, but suggested donation is
$2.50 for adults and $2.00 for seniors and
those 17 and under.

Negro Leagues Baseball Museum
1616 East 18th Street
(816) 221-1920, (888) 221-6526
www.nlbm.com

Before the multimillion-dollar contracts,
before the megabuck endorsement deals,
there were men who played baseball just
because they loved the game. And they
continued to suit up and take the field
even when major league teams shut them
out because of their color. This museum,
the only one of its kind in the country, follows the history of the Negro National
League, beginning with its formation at
nearby Paseo YMCA in 1920. Out of that
came the Monarchs, one of the league's
most exciting teams thanks to players like
Satchel Paige, Cool Papa Bell, Connie
Johnson, and John Jordan "Buck" O'Neil.
Oh, man, could these guys play ball.

Two short videos tell the stories of
games played here and on the road, and
an impressive display of memorabilia
brings them to life. You'll see documents
and photos that demonstrate the highs
from wins and fans' adulation as well as
the lows caused by segregation and
racism. In this regard the exhibits tran-
scend sports and hit at the very heart of
our country at the time. Eventually the
Negro Leagues ended for the same reason
they started: sheer talent. The Brooklyn
Dodgers recruited Monarchs player Jackie
Robinson in 1945, and others soon followed. The leagues played their last game
in 1960.

One of the museum's most striking displays is the Field of Legends, where life-
size bronze players are positioned on a ball
diamond. The 10 statues represent the first

Negro League players inducted into the Hall of Fame in Cooperstown, New York. Trivia games test your knowledge about these heroes.

With any luck, during your visit Buck O'Neil will be there; just look for the snappy dresser with the million-dollar smile. A former Kansas City Monarchs player who became its manager and then successful baseball scout, today Buck serves as chairman of the museum board and living legend. Does he have a bronze statue here? Yes, indeedy. The museum is open Tuesday through Sunday; admission is $6.00 for adults, $2.50 for 12 and under. Combination tickets to the Negro Leagues Baseball Museum and the American Jazz Museum are $8.00 and $4.00, respectively.

Union Cemetery Walking Tour
28th and Walnut
(816) 472-4990
When 49-acre Union Cemetery was deeded in 1857, its planners thought it would provide enough burial space for the towns of Kansas and Westport for all time. Shortsighted? Not for two communities (we didn't become Kansas City until 1889) that only had 3,000 residents between them. It's estimated that 55,000 are buried here, including veterans from every American war and cholera victims by the score. Some of our city's most famous citizens lie here as well, individuals whose granite-etched names are repeated on city street signs, schools, and historic home sites. Alexander Majors, whose company founded the Pony Express, is here, as is artist George Caleb Bingham. Lesser known (except to those he assisted) is Tillman Crabtree, Kansas City's first policeman. One of his duties was to carry women across the city's muddy streets.

The cemetery is open for self-guided tours seven days a week from 8:30 A.M. to 3:30 P.M. Maps with biographies of the most famous are available in a small box near the entrance gate or at the sexton's cottage. Or contact the Union Cemetery Historical Society (816–472–4990), 227

East 28th Street Terrace, Kansas City, MO 64108. Be sure to bring large sheets of paper and charcoal pencils to create rubbings of interesting stones.

LANDMARKS

The Kansas City Power & Light Building
14th and Baltimore
www.skyscrapers.com
(click on Kansas City)
The same year that New Yorkers were admiring their tallest skyscraper so far, the Empire State Building, we were agog at ours. In 1931 the Power & Light Building became the tallest building in Missouri. Architectural team Hoit, Price & Barnes knew this 31-story Art Deco beauty would eventually lose its tallest-structure status, so they added a bonus: a 97-foot pillar of lights at top that cycle among white, amber, red, and green. The building's setbacks, which give it a telescoping look, are also dramatized at night with hidden floodlights. The Art Deco theme is repeated inside with a sunburst motif in the brass elevator doors, radiator grills, and even the water fountain.

Charlie Parker Memorial
The name of sculptor Robert Graham's 17-foot bronze head of Charlie "Bird" Parker is *Bird Lives*. He certainly does through his music. The Kansas City, Kansas, native, who changed the sound of jazz, is memorialized on a plaza behind the American Jazz Museum in the 18th and Vine Historic District.

Pioneer Mother
The inscription on this large bronze tells the story of thousands of women who gave up homes and families back east to start new lives. The passage from the Book of Ruth reads, "Whither thou goest, I will go and wither thou lodgest, I will lodge. Thy people will be my people, and thy God, my God." The sculpture is in Penn Valley Park, south of the entrance to the Liberty Memorial.

Rosedale Memorial Arch
35th Street and Booth
Kansas City, KS
Based on the Arc de Triomphe in Paris, this monument pays tribute to soldiers who fought in World War I. It was designed by Rosedale resident John LeRoy Marshall and dedicated in 1923. The "War to End All Wars" wasn't, and 70 years later a monument was added to honor the soldiers of World War II, Korea, and the Vietnam conflict. High on a hill, the Arch can be seen from miles away.

The Scout
This impressive statue of an Indian on horseback wasn't even meant to be ours; it rested here temporarily on route to its intended home at San Francisco's 1915 Panama-Pacific Expo. But Kansas Citians loved the sculpture so much they raised $15,000 to buy it. Now *The Scout* forever watches over our skyline from a hill in Penn Valley Park between Southwest Trafficway and Broadway, just off 31st Street.

Sky Stations/Pylon Caps
atop H. Roe Bartle Hall
13th and Central
When these metal sculptures were mounted on tall, slender pylons 200 feet above Bartle Hall in 1994, they became one of our most dramatic landmarks—and one of the most hotly debated. Some pundits refer to them as "three whirligigs and a curling iron." George Jetson may disagree, but R. M. Fisher's designs were influenced not by the space age but by the Art Deco designs found throughout our downtown skyline.

NEIGHBORHOOD DRIVES

Take a rubbernecking drive through some of our most beloved neighborhoods filled with charming Tudors or jaw-dropping mansions. Most of the stunners were built between 1900 and 1940, but there are some up-and-comers, particularly on the Kansas side. And take note of the number of trikes and basketballs in the driveways of homes costing $1 million or more. Where do these whippersnappers get all that cash? We know for sure it's not from writing travel guides. Following are some of our favorites drives.

Hallbrook
West of State Line, north of College Boulevard in Leawood, Kansas
What Hallbrook lacks in maturity—the area was developed just two decades or so ago—it more than makes up for in sheer glamour. Its villas and minimansions lean toward Spanish and country French in design. Look for one jaw-dropper that's based on Tara from *Gone with the Wind*.

Mission Hills
Southwest on State Line Road and 53rd Street, west of the Carriage Club
This lovely drive is another blessing from landscape architects and builders who let the lay of the land determine where streets and houses should be placed. Roads dip here and there, jogging gracefully around streams and skirting ancient trees. And the homes caught up in all this natural glory are simply magnificent. As you drive southwest you'll pass Mission Hills Country Club and Kansas City Country Club golf courses on the west.

Rich & Famous Tour
(913) 338-0129, (816) 763-9401
It's common knowledge that Jean Harlow, Walt Disney, and Ernest Hemingway lived in Kansas City at one time, but did you know Mickey Rooney, Red Skelton, Burt Bacharach, and stripper Sally Rand hung their hats—or fans, as the case may be—here as well? Local writer Don Davidson offers a fascinating drive-by tour of these homes as well as other celebrity abodes, including those of Casey Stengel, actor Craig Stevens, Walter Cronkite, Ginger Rogers, and sports greats Marcus Allen and Joe Montana.

Former and current politicians, business owners, and media personalities are included, and you'll learn how Daniel

Boone, Harriet Nelson, and other famous folks are connected to our town. There are more than 100 homes in all, and Don describes them all in detail. A fun 20-minute trivia quiz will see who's been paying attention. This is an ideal tour for groups from 20 to 40 and lasts from 9:00 A.M. to 4:00 P.M. with a stop for lunch. The fee depends on the total number in the group but is typically around $25 per person. Tours are by appointment only.

Ward Parkway
Beginning at West 53rd Street, southwest of the Country Club Plaza
No one will ask for your ticket to this attraction: It's a 4-mile drive on one of the country's most beautiful boulevards. We adore it, HGTV–TV devoted an entire hour to it, and if you're visiting friends in Kansas City you're bound to get the grand tour at least once.

Ward Parkway has some of the priciest real estate in town. But even some locals don't know that it didn't cost a dime when J. C. Nichols began developing homes on these 500 acres near the turn of the 20th century. Businessman Hugh Ward, donated the land to the city, but died before the papers were signed. His wife, Vassie James Ward, followed through on the plan and requested that it be named for her late husband.

The new boulevard became a magnet for money, and during the early 1900s some of the most prominent families chose to build their homes, villas, and mansions here. The Tom Pendergast house at 5650 Ward Parkway is one of the most famous, while certainly the most striking is the Corrigan-Sutherland House on the corner of 55th and Ward Parkway. In 1912 Barney Corrigan commissioned flamboyant Kansas City architect Louis Curtiss to design the splendid 25-room home (a room for each of his 18 children with space for more, it would seem). The modern Art Nouveau style was constructed of concrete with a Carthage cut-stone facing and magnificent tree-motif stained glass. The estate cost around $200,000, but, alas, the

66-year-old Corrigan didn't live to see it finished. He died on January 6, 1914, on his way to inspect the home's progress. The property was then purchased by the Sutherland lumber family, who remained here for several decades.

While the homes' opulence turned this into a street of dreams, the green spaces made it a paradise. Today people jog, walk dogs, and bike along its tree-shaded sidewalks, and kids play tag football on wide medians that form miniparks. The boulevard was designed by renowned landscape architect George Kessler along with father-and-son team Hare & Hare. As for the remarkable fountains, sculptures, and urns that grace Ward Parkway, those were gifts from J. C. Nichols.

Westwood Hills
West of State Line Road on 50th Street
Although this is one of the smaller cities in both size (less than one square mile) and number of residents (around 390), it's earned the right to its nickname, "the Prettiest Little City in Kansas." Darling cottages and elegant estates are sprinkled along roads that dip and twist, and massive trees cross the streets to create overhead umbrellas. Be sure to stop in for a mango-flavored Jet Tea at the Hi Hat Coffee Shop (5012 State Line, 913–831–0341); there's enough ginseng in this golden-yellow smoothie to power your trip back home.

OBSERVATION POINTS

City Hall Observation Deck
414 East 12th Street
(816) 274-1444
www.kcmo.org
The only place to get a better look at the city is from an airplane. Our stunning Art Deco–style City Hall provides a breathtaking view from its 30th floor open-air deck 425 feet above downtown. And while you're waiting for the elevator, check out the friezes and celestial-themed lighting fixtures in the lobby. The art continues outside with 16 panels just above the sixth

floor that depict major events in our city's history. This steel and limestone stunner, designed by architect firm Wight & Wight, was completed in 1937 at a cost of $5 million. The deck is open Monday through Friday from 8:00 A.M. to 4:15 P.M. To reach it take the lobby elevator to the 28th floor, and then take the stairs. There's no charge.

Cliff Drive
Gladstone Boulevard and Elmwood
You're just in time to enjoy this 6-mile roadway that was recently restored to its turn-of-the-20th-century splendor. Although today the view from Cliff Drive isn't so hot—a jumble of train tracks and industrial buildings—it's a pleasant diversion with places to pull over and consider what it must have been like to negotiate the curves in a horse and carriage.

You can thank landscape architect George Kessler for retaining its natural beauty back in 1893 along with the surrounding 282-acre North Terrace Park. In fact you might see rappellers risking knees and elbows on the rugged limestone cliff that gives the road its name. For a more civilized look, stay in the car; that way you can also tool around the historic Northeast area, including the Scarritt Renaissance neighborhood bound by Independence Boulevard and the park. More than 120 homes and churches are listed as local historic landmarks. A good place to start is the Kansas City Museum on Gladstone Boulevard (see details in Museums), a 71-room mansion-turned-museum that hints of the area's opulence at one time.

Lewis and Clark Point
Eighth Street and Jefferson
Stand at the bluffs overlooking where the Kansas and Missouri Rivers meet and try to imagine what Meriwether Lewis and William Clark were thinking on September 15, 1806. The expedition team was returning from an arduous trip to Oregon. They were exhausted and no doubt thirsty, but they wouldn't find refreshment here. Clark had deemed the Kaw "disagreeably

Looking for a bird's-eye view of our beautiful city? Take the elevator to the top of the Liberty Memorial's 217-foot column in the sky. You'll overlook our skyline and, just below the monument, our grand Union Station.

tasted" on their first stopover two years earlier. No doubt.

The three-day 1806 encampment is now memorialized by Eugene Daub's sculpture *Corps of Discovery* at Jefferson and Eighth Streets on the bluffs of what is now Quality Hill. Dedicated in 2001, the 18-foot-high bronze depicts Lewis, Clark, their Shoshone Indian interpreter Sacagawea, Clark's black slave York, and Lewis's dog, Seaman. It's the nation's largest monument to honor the expedition. Check the back of Seaman's tail for a surprise: the artist's face!

Liberty Memorial Observation Tower
100 West 26th Street
(816) 221-1918
At this monument's groundbreaking ceremony in 1921, the crowd watched as General John J. Pershing and the four other principal Allied commanders took the stage. It was the first and only time these men ever appeared in one place. Five years later, before a crowd of 100,000, President Calvin Coolidge dedicated the country's only memorial honoring the men and women who died during World War I. The city had a reason to be proud; it had only taken 10 days to raise the $2.5 million needed to build the monument. In today's dollars the contributions would be more than $20 million.

New York architect H. Van Buren Magonigle envisioned his 217-foot column as "an altar high raised in the sky with its flame of inspiration ever burning." That flame went out when the monument, crumbling and deemed unsafe, was closed in 1994. After a $30 million restoration project, the Liberty Memorial reopened with great fanfare on Memorial Day weekend 2002.

The project was financed by benefactors, private citizens, and the sale of granite bricks inscribed with names of brave loved ones long gone. Work continues on the 30,000-square-foot underground museum that will display a portion of the 400,000 artifacts, the world's largest collection from the Great War. And once again the view from the observation tower is inspiring.

OUT AND ABOUT

Deanna Rose Children's Farmstead
138th Street and Switzer Road
Overland Park, KS
(913) 897-2360
www.opkansas.org

Let's see: Old McDonald had a pig, and a cow, and a goat. . . and a *bison*? You'll find them all, along with chickens, sheep, and owls, at this fun-for-all 12-acre farm in south Johnson County. It opened in 1976 and in 1985 was named to honor Deanna Rose, an Overland Park police officer killed in the line of duty.

It's always a fun excursion but especially so in spring, when newborn animals are popping up like daffodils. Although it's fun to watch them be bottle-fed, it's a positive giggle fest to feed the goats from your hands. Bring plenty of quarters to buy pellets from the vending machines; these animals eat nearly $70,000 worth of snacks a year! Other activities include fishing (pole rental is $2.00) and pony rides and hayrides for $2.00 per person. A concession stand and picnic area are on site.

New to the area are a log fort, a country schoolhouse circa 1900, and a Kanza Indian encampment, complete with earthern lodge and tepees. No wonder the site has attracted more than 300,000 visitors annually in recent years, 75 percent from outside its Overland Park home. The farmstead is open daily from 9:00 A.M. to 8:00 P.M. April through September and closes at 5:00 P.M. in October. It's closed November through March. Admittance is free, but donations are gladly accepted.

The Kansas City Zoo
6800 Zoo Drive
(816) 513-5800
www.kansascityzoo.org

Take a wild animal safari without leaving the country at this natural habitat zoo set in 200 rolling acres. The areas are divided into different "countries," which you can visit by walking, riding the train, or taking a safari boat ride. In Africa you'll see elephants giving each other mud baths to cool off on a summer afternoon, herds of sable antelope and impala running free, and giraffes necking. Watch for the youngest animals, like our baby hippo or three playful lion cubs. The newborns and toddlers are always some of the zoo's most popular sights. The Australian exhibit includes an aviary with 20 species of birds and mammals, and acres where kangaroo, emus, and dingoes roam. Here's where you can catch a ride on a camel or pony. Some of the older exhibits remain favorites, especially with kids who love to watch the sea lions splash in the pool. Farmland USA has a petting zoo and pot-bellied pigs, miniature horses, and goats.

The zoo also hosts several events throughout the year, including a Halloween party and Earth Day celebration. And Nocturnal Safaris give children a chance to play zookeeper for one night at a campout under the stars. This exciting, educational program is ideal for families, scouts, and church groups for ages six and up. Reservations are on a first-come, first-served basis starting March 1. The safaris are held Friday and Saturday from late May through September, and the cost is $30 per person.

You can also catch a flick (a really big one) at the Sprint IMAX Theatre, which boasts a 6½-story-tall screen and 12,000 watts of digital sound. Call (816) 871-IMAX for day and evening show times and ticket information. You can attend IMAX without visiting the zoo (tickets range from $4.00 to $10.00), but the best value is a combination ticket.

The zoo is open daily from 9:00 A.M. to 5:00 P.M. April 1 through October 14 and 9:00 A.M. to 4:00 P.M. the rest of the season. From June through August the zoo stays open later to take advantage of cooler temperatures. It's closed Christmas Day and January 1. Admission is $7.50 for adults, $6.50 for seniors, $4.50 for ages 3 to 11, and free for 2 and under. On Tuesday everyone gets in for $3.00. Parking costs $2.00 from April 1 through October 14; otherwise it's free.

Kansas Speedway
1333 Meadowlark Lane
Kansas City, KS
(913) 328–RACE (7223)
www.kansasspeedway.com
"It's purrrty," drawled NASCAR legend Richard Petty when he first saw this $260 million ICS-owned facility that opened in June 2001. It's also biiiig. In fact you could fit both Kauffman and Arrowhead stadiums and their parking lots in the racetrack's infield. And while size does matter, this 75,000-seat (with plans to increase the number soon), 1½-mile tri-oval track was designed for the comfort and convenience of the fans and racing. One example is the infield Fan Walk that gives racing fans an up-close look at the garages, inspection stations, and Victory Lane. And there's not a bad seat in the grandstand, thanks to a low infield and elevated backstretch that creates an unimpeded sight line. An even better view, along with a wet bar and private restrooms is available in one of 68 luxury suites. Turn around between laps and you can see the Kansas City, Missouri, skyline from this vantage point.

Season tickets go as fast as a modified Monte Carlo, with Kansas residents taking the lead at 40 percent of total tickets sold. Fans from 46 states and four Canadian provinces purchase tickets; apparently people in Hawaii, Maine, Rhode Island, West Virginia, and Washington, D.C., didn't get the memo. Individual seat prices range from $170 to $330. Varrooom. You can lap up more information in the Sports chapter.

If you plan to visit such attractions as the Kansas City Zoo or the Nelson-Atkins Museum of Art more than once, you might save money by purchasing a membership card. Benefits often include free or discounted admittance, discounts on food or gifts, and invitations to special events. And a season's pass at Worlds of Fun can quickly pay for itself.

Powell Gardens
1609 Northwest U.S. Highway 50
Kingville, MO
(816) 697–2600
www.powellgardens.org
This roadtrip for the soul begins with a 30-mile drive out of town, just enough time to listen to Vivaldi's Four Seasons while you anticipate what's coming up. . . literally. With 915 acres of perennial gardens, a shady rock and waterfall trail, wildflower meadow, and a lovely island garden set in the 12-acre lake, there's enough variety to thrill any nature lover. Even the buildings, designed by Arkansas architect Fay Jones, are breathtaking. The Marjorie Powell Allen Chapel's soaring ceiling, cedar-and-stone structure, and open crossed beams may remind visitors of the architect's famous Thorncrown Chapel in Eureka Springs, Arkansas. The visitor center hosts several events each year, including classes on making topiaries and birdhouses, and a Festival of Butterflies each August, when thousands of colorful wings fill the conservatory, landing on trees and the heads of delighted toddlers. Cafe Thyme, also in the center, has surprisingly good salads and sandwiches and serves Sunday brunch.

Admission to the gardens from April through October is $5.50 for adults, $4.50 for seniors, and $2.50 for children ages 5 to 12; those under 5 are free. The price is a dollar less from November through March, when the gardens are still enchanting. Guided tours are available for a fee. You can read more about this magical place in Parks, Lakes, and Recreation.

Worlds of Fun and Oceans of Fun
4545 Worlds of Fun Avenue
(816) 454-4545
www.worldsoffun.com
This 175-acre side-by-side theme park will earn an A+ with kids. Worlds of Fun opened in 1973 and has been adding new rides every year. One of the most popular is the Mamba, ranked as one of the world's top-10 roller coasters, which sky-rockets 205 feet up before dropping at 75 miles an hour, the equivalent of 3½ Gs of fun. The 12-story-tall Boomerang lives up to its name by twisting backward and forward through corkscrew turns, upside-down loops, and 125-foot lifts at—gulp!—50 miles per hour. There are plenty of other rides, including a less hair-raising choice: a 60-foot-high Ferris wheel. And smaller kids will enjoy Camp Snoopy, where huggable versions of the beloved cartoon characters come to life.

Worlds of Fun is generally open from late May to early September at 10:00 A.M.; closing times are as late as 10:00 P.M. A single day pass for adults and children 48 inches or taller is $36.95 plus tax; for children 4 years old and shorter than 48 inches it's $14.95 plus tax. After 4:00 P.M. the admission price is reduced, and season passports and group events are available. Prices usually increase every year, so call or check the Web site for specifics.

Oceans of Fun is the sister attraction right next door, a 60-acre playground with a giant pool complete with 4-foot-high waves, a sandy beach, and 43-foot water slides. After one afternoon your kids will never be content with the thumb-over-the-garden-hose again. Parents will find other liquid pleasures in Castaway Cove, an adults-only pool with swim-up refresh-ments. Oceans of Fun is generally open from late May to early September at 10:00 A.M.; closing time varies. A single day pass for adults and children taller than 48 inches is $24.00; for children 4 years old and shorter than 48 inches it's $12.95. Prices are subject to change; call for specifics.

TOURS

Boulevard Brewing
2501 Southwest Boulevard
(816) 474-7095
www.blvdbeer.com
Since 1989 John McDonald has been single-handedly (well, actually he has 40 helpers now) resurrecting Kansas City's 150-year-old tradition as a brewery town. That's when he rolled out his first barrel of Pale Ale, and he has since added brews like Unfiltered Wheat, Dry Stout, and Bully! Port, which won a gold medal at Chicago's Real Ale Festival.

Boulevard's production is up to 40,000 barrels a year now, which means they're no longer a microbrewery but a regional spe-cialty brewer. The category doesn't matter; this is beautifully crafted beer universally respected for its distinctive hop character-istics. Alas, it's only available in eight states, but that's how John keeps on top of the quality.

You can get a minilesson on brewing on the Web site. Better yet, hop to it and attend a tour. They're given every Saturday at 1:30 P.M. by reservation only. You can also purchase some great merchandise with the company's cool logo at the brew-ery, online, and by phone.

Federal Reserve Bank of Kansas City
925 Grand Boulevard
(816) 881-2000, (800) 333-1010
www.kcfrb.org
If you promise not to walk in and chirp, "Show me the money," we'll let you in on this interesting tour. The guided walk-through includes an overview of the Fed's responsibilities in monetary policy and reg-ulation and a look at the bank's operating areas. The real fun comes, though, when you see the high-speed sorter that can count, sort, and destroy cash faster than a 16-year-old daughter: up to 100,000 bills an hour. The Money Museum tells the story of U.S. currency from its start during George Washington's administration to the current electronic processes. Coin collec-tors, in particular, will find the museum

interesting. Tours, which last about 90 minutes, are given at 9:30 A.M. and 1:30 P.M.
Monday through Friday. Call for groups of
six or larger. And leave your money at
home; the tour is free.

Harley-Davidson Final Assembly Plant
11401 North Congress
(816) 270-8488, (888) 875-2883

Get your motor running at this facility
where you can watch the assembly line
action and drool over some shiny new
rides. Tours are free, but there are a few
rules. Children must be at least 12 years
old and accompanied by an adult. No
open-toed shoes are allowed. Anyone
over 18 will need a photo ID. Cameras are
prohibited in the factory area, and all visitors will pass through a metal detector.
But don't worry. Lockers are available to
store your camera and the four pounds of
keys that held up the security line.

Tours last approximately one hour. We
suggest you call ahead, because tours are
not available on holidays, during summer
and Christmas shutdown, and when the
plant is off-limits during special production
work. The museum and tour center are
open from 8:00 A.M. to 3:00 P.M., and logo
merchandise is available in the gift shop.
Some enthusiasts barely make it past the
parking lot, which looks like one gigantic
Harley dealership.

Historic Kansas City Foundation
201 Westport Road
(816) 931-8448

Some of us consider this passionate group
our city's best friend. The foundation
began in 1974 when concerned citizens,
led by the irrepressible Jane Fifield Flynn,
began trying to save historic structures
from demolition. Since then they've rescued beauties like the Coates House, the
President Hotel, and a group of apartment
buildings on the Plaza known as the
Poet's Row. The group gives several public
walking tours a year to showcase a different neighborhood or area such as Hyde
Park, Union Station, and the Garment District. During these time-machine travels,
volunteers describe architecture and tell
interesting tidbits about famous residents.
Most tours simply require showing up at
an appointed time and paying $3.00 or
so; others require preregistration and
$10.00 to $15.00 each.

The foundation also hosts private walking tours for groups of 10 or more with a
two- to three-week advance notice. The
donation is $5.00 per person. Tours last
from one to two hours and some are
adaptable for vans or buses. Potential
areas include downtown's Art Deco buildings, River Market, 18th and Vine, and
Northeast neighborhoods. Volunteers are
also available for speaking engagements.

THE ARTS

Kansas City: the art capital of the world. Well, darn close anyway. When you factor in our museums, art spaces and galleries, orchestras, musical groups and soloists, and millions of dollars of public artwork like fountains, sculptures, and murals—well, it's enough to make any city seem downright highbrow. And the phrase "All the world's a stage" may well have been coined for Kansas City; we have more professional theaters than any other city our size in the United States. With more than 300 cultural organizations, our town is an exciting destination and, more important, a great place to live, work, and raise a family.

You can attribute our amazing cache of culture to early philanthropists like William Rockhill Nelson, who decided his adopted hometown deserved boulevards and a world-class art museum; J. C. Nichols who gave us enough fountains to make even Rome seem second-rate; that city may boast more fountains, but we have more that actually work.

Current-day angels with names like Hall, Helzberg, Bloch, Kemper, and Kauffman keep the "home is where the art is" tradition going. And now they, along with thousands of musicians and singers, artists, writers, poets, and dancers who call Kansas City home, would like to share the wealth with you.

The listings in this chapter are presented in alphabetical order by category. All organizations are located in Kansas City, Missouri, unless otherwise noted.

ART GALLERIES AND SHOWROOMS

Art lovers and collectors, get out your wallets. Kansas City has a wealth of places where you can find artwork from cutting edge to traditional. . . and yes, something to go over that sofa. In the last few years, dozens of galleries, from tiny lofts to glamorous showrooms, have sprung up, especially around the Crossroads Arts District.

Many of these, along with art spaces in the emerging West Bottoms area, are open on weekends, by appointment, and during the First Friday Gallery Walks held the first Friday of each month. The *Kansas City Star* Friday Preview does a great job listing gallery events, and the Artist's Coalition has a handy map that pinpoints many of the most exciting studios and galleries. Or contact one of the galleries listed below; often they'll place you on a mailing list.

For now, following are a few galleries that consistently carry artwork worth coveting. What's more, the gallery owners are down-to-earth folks who will gladly answer questions about a style or particular artist—or disappear if you want to be left alone.

Blue Gallery
7 West 19th Street
(816) 527-0823
www.bluegalleryonline.com
This gallery in the Crossroads Arts District caters to both novice buyer and serious collector with a thoughtful mix of styles and prices. The large, bright space is divided into areas where you can take your time and study a piece, step back from a large sculpture, or sit and contemplate an oil. Owners David and Kelly Kuhn (she's beautiful enough to be an artist's model) have a knack for attracting artists with a salable look. Nothing here is so out-there that you instantly feel like the only person in the world without a tattoo or pierced appendage.

Like many gallery owners, they will bend over backwards to help you own the art you fall in love with. They'll let you take it home to live with for a few days; they'll even come out to take a picture of your intended wall, then digitally drop in the artwork to see how it would look. Out-of-town buyers can peruse art on the Web site and have it shipped.

Leedy-Voulkos Art Center
2012 Baltimore
(816) 474-1919
www.leedy-voulkos.com
Owned by Jim Leedy, whom many consider the father of the Crossroads Arts District, and in many ways Kansas City's evolution into an art center, this gallery is an enormous, light-drenched space that mixes paintings and sculpture with crafts like ceramics and fiber. Along with regional and national artists, Jim's diverse talents are showcased here. Known for his expressionist ceramics, he has had a major exhibition nearly every year somewhere in America since 1962. His Opie Gallery provides exhibition space for emerging local artists as well. This is usually the starting point for First Fridays, art tours that take place throughout the area the first Friday of every month during decent weather.

River's Bend Gallery
201 Main Street
Parkville, MO
(816) 587-8070
www.riversbendgallery.com
What happens when your personal art collection overruns your home? You either donate it to a museum or open a gallery. Lucky for us, Rick and Kristy McKibben did the latter, so we have a chance to buy instead of just browse. River's Bend, in a sunny shop on Parkville's quaint Main Street, has a diverse grouping of art, both oils and pastels, including mesmerizing landscapes that seem to glow with their own sun; unique and extremely well-priced jewelry, photography, and martini glasses from whimsical to downright sexy. There's always something new to catch your eye and imagination.

The focus, however, is on art glass—gorgeous vases in a kaleidoscope of colors, iridescent jellyfish caught in elongated globes—that makes you wonder how they could have ever been in a molten state. In fact, everything in the gallery warrants a second look or an answer from a willing shop owner. And that's the beauty of buying from a gallery where the person at the desk is often the buyer: He or she can tell you enough about the artist that you'll feel you're buying from a friend.

ART MUSEUMS

The Kemper Museum of Contemporary Art
4420 Warwick Boulevard
(816) 561-3737
www.kemperart.org
This dynamic art space features a dazzling core collection that includes work by Georgia O'Keeffe, Jasper Johns, Robert Motherwell, and Frank Stella. The museum also presents exhibits taken from its permanent collection as well as several shows a year starring internationally known artists such as Dale Chihuly, Herb Ritts, and an amazing bead art display by Liza Lou. It's easy to find the place; just look for a gigantic spider sculpture on the front lawn. Yikes! The museum is open Tuesday through Sunday. Call for the times. Admission is free. The Kemper is described in detail in Attractions.

The Nelson-Atkins Museum of Art
4525 Oak Street
(816) 561-4000
www.nelson-atkins.org
This magnificent neoclassic building put Kansas City on the art map, not just in the country but also in the world. Along with pieces by Rembrandt, Renoir, and Caravaggio, the Nelson boasts one of the world's finest Oriental collections and more Henry Moore sculptures than anywhere outside the artist's hometown. Thanks to a monumental expansion program that will continue through 2006, expect to see perhaps the most impressive parking garage in the universe. We've included a close-up on the Nelson in the Attractions chapter. The museum is open Tuesday through Sunday. Call for opening and closing times.

Find out about 150 other arts organizations, from individual graphic artists to puppeteers to orchestras, at the Arts Council of Metropolitan Kansas City Web site, www.artslinks.org. You'll also see a listing of current events happening in and around Kansas City.

DANCE

Kansas City Ballet
1601 Broadway Boulevard
(816) 931-2232
www.kcballet.org
This 47-year-old company of two dozen dancers is thriving under new artistic director William Whitener, who has also contributed some of the troupe's newest ballets. Classical, modern, dramatic, and even comedic work makes up the rich and varied dance tapestry, and each year Whitener expands the repertoire. He enjoys shaking up the audience, and challenging the dancers, by bringing in new choreography and giving vibrant new life to pieces that haven't been performed in decades. One look at the evocative *Frankie and Johnny* set to 1930s swing music and you'll realize this ain't your grandmother's ballet.

The tutus come back on, however, for other productions. Four are presented each season, including an annual *Nutcracker*, which is performed at the Midland Theatre during the holidays. The other programs are held at the Lyric Theatre. In addition, the dancers take their toe shoes on the road to grace stages at other venues. In the Wings is a unique choreographic workshop performance where the artists create and perform new dance pieces, then turn up the lights to allow audience members to ask about the process of dance and choreography. Ballet in the Park is a delightful series of free outdoor performances held each fall at different green spaces throughout Kansas City, including Powell Gardens, the Loose Park Rose Garden, and the Crown Center Pavilion.

FINE ART SPACES

Pick up a copy of *Review* (816-471-2343), a free publication devoted to visual arts in Kansas City, at midtown galleries and coffee shops and you'll see a list of at least 150 places where artwork is shown and sold on any given day. Although the majority is in galleries and studios, you can also find paintings just hanging around coffee shops, libraries, restaurants, and bank lobbies. Next stop: car washes. Before making your art discovery trek, call for information about hours and days open; a few are by appointment only, and many are closed one or two days a week.

Gallery of Art
Carlsen Center, Johnson County
Community College
12345 College Boulevard
Overland Park, KS
(913) 469-2344
Under the direction of Bruce Hartman, this small gallery located off the lobby of the Carlsen Center has established a national and international reputation for presenting emerging and established artists. The 3,000-square-foot gallery exhibits five major shows annually with more than 50,000 people attending. Each opening features a public lecture by the artist, curator, or a critic. The gallery is free to the public and open seven days a week, except for summer, when it's closed on Sunday.

This talented—and very busy—curator also supervises a much larger gallery, one that's spread over the community college's 234-acre campus and courtyards. The Oppenheimer-Stein Sculpture Gallery has been valued at more than $1 million and includes stunning contemporary pieces in bronze, marble, and metal. A playful bronze hare is perched on a bell in the campus courtyard, and *Walking Man* is forever striding along the roof of the Commons Building. More than 200,000 people visit this oasis of art in the suburbs annually. In addition to the Oppenheimer-Stein collection, the campus is home to dozens of other works, both indoors and out, including sculptures, large canvases, and ceramics. Look for a free 24-page guide that describes all the displays. And thanks to gifts from the Oppenheimers and Jerry Nerman and his family, the college will be home to a new $2.5 million Gallery of Art.

H&R Block Artspace
16 East 43rd Street
(816) 561-5563

When the Kansas City Art Institute got a grant from a Missouri cultural trust program, it was able to renovate a small warehouse near its campus into a gallery and arts education space. That cash infusion begot more, this time from benefactor Henry Bloch, and voilà: a home-away-from-school for art students. Open since 1999, the gallery hosts several exhibits a year that bring this concrete shell to life with ideas and vitality. Granted, a few exhibits have guests whispering, "Am I missing something, Edna?" but most are insightful works by very talented and as yet undiscovered artists.

Kansas City Artists Coalition
201 Wyandotte
(816) 421-5222
www.kansascityartistscoalition.org

Since 1975 the Kansas City Artists Coalition has provided support, exhibition space, and a voice for established and emerging artists both local and regional. More than 400 artists use its white walls as an ever-changing art gallery, and dozens of artists have nervously watched the public pick apart or praise their first exhibition here. Art lovers show up in droves (and SUVs) every February for the KCAC Benefit Art Auction when some of the region's best artists donate work to be auctioned to the highest bidder. This is a chance for the artists to give back to an organization that played an important part in their early careers.

The coalition also produces the wildly popular Open Studios Tour every other year, with plans to make it an annual event. The first tour, which took place on two weekends in October 2000, exceeded all expectations. More than 213 artists in 14 counties participated, gaining a new audience for their work and giving art lovers a chance to meet the artists and their environment. More than 19,000 art pieces were purchased, with total sales of almost $100,000. Not bad for four days!

LITERARY ARTS

Prospero's Books
1717 West 39th Street
(816) 960-7202
www.prosperosbookstore.com

Described as an artistic community masquerading as a used book store, this is the home of The Pit, Kansas City's largest open-mic poetry reading. And if you're picturing a handful of hopefuls waiting their turn, you'll be surprised to see the crowd. Each month between 40 and 100 writers show up to read original works to a sensitive and encouraging audience; after all, most of them have faced that microphone.

Readings begin at 5:30 P.M. on the fourth Sunday of each month. The bookshop also publishes some of the best work in *Prospero's Pocket Poets*. And if music is more to your liking, Prospero's turns into an intimate space for original music by some of the area's best songwriters on most Fridays and Saturdays. You'll hear a broad range of folk, Celtic, punk, jazz, and country.

The Writer's Place
3607 Pennsylvania
(816) 753-1090
www.writersplace.org

Entire books could be written *about,* not just in, this literary community center. The large stone structure with a turret was built as a private residence in 1909, then spent time as an apartment house, brothel, and church until becoming a homey place for writers to take classes, get advice, and share their work in 1992. You might call it a ghostwriter's place because several workers and guests have seen, felt, or heard a

Welcome to the 'artland

You won't need a ticket to see some of Kansas City's most exciting odes to culture. Art is all around us, gracing parks and shopping areas, defining neighborhoods, fronting office buildings and libraries, providing beauty on brick walls. It's our public art, and many newcomers to our town are simply blown away at the amazing array.

In Attractions we listed two areas, Crown Center and the Country Club Plaza, that are really outdoor art galleries filled with sculpture, mosaics, and fountains. Tim Janicke, esteemed photo editor of the *Kansas City Star* Sunday magazine, collected a stunning array of our public art in a new book, *City of Art*. It's available in local bookstores or through the *Star* (816-234-4436). While you're waiting for your copy, we'll take you on a brief tour of some of our favorite outdoor art, our fountains.

Our city's most beautiful landmarks were originally established to fill the needs of people and provide water for horses. There were plenty of takers; in 1910 the equestrian population of Kansas City was 70,000. Later they fed our desire for beauty and celebration. The City of Fountains Foundation (816-842-2299, www.kcfountains.com), established in 1973, partners with the Parks and Recreation Department of Kansas City to maintain existing fountains and help establish new ones. The foundation has a beautifully illustrated brochure to help you locate our liquid art around town.

Fairmont Kansas City at the Plaza
Corner of Wornall Road and Ward Parkway

The hotel's front is defined by one of the tallest man-made fountains, a concave curtain of water 56 feet wide and 17 feet high. The waterfall provides a backdrop for a sculpture of the goddess of the hunt and her entourage of cherubs. Diana has an arm raised as if taking in the magnificent scene before her. But we think she's actually saying, "Hand me one of those fluffy Fairmont robes, will ya?"

J. C. Nichols Memorial Fountain
47th Street and Nichols Parkway

Kansas City's signature fountain was dedicated in 1960 to the memory of J. C. Nichols, the developer of the Country Club Plaza, and Mr. Fountain as far as we're concerned. He was instrumental in turning our town into a water wonderland by acquiring fantastic fountains from Europe and shipping them home. This particular beauty depicts four equestrian figures that each represent a famous river of the world. The multiple water jets spray 30 feet from the center. Even in winter, when part of the fountain has become a blue ice sculpture, it is magnificent.

Crown Center Fountain on the Square

Known as one of the most spectacular and playful of our water displays, this fountain serves as a centerpiece to the "city within a city." Occupying a full 200 square feet, the fountain area consists of a cobblestone-paved surface with no visible sign of nozzles or hoses. Water soars magically from the fool-the-eye fountain as far as 30 feet into the air. At night it is illuminated by colored lights and is particularly pretty from restaurants, shops, and hotels overlooking the square. During summer days it's not unusual to see a few kids of all ages run through the fountain. But you didn't hear it from us.

Local artist Tom Corbin sculpted these frolicking children at this sparkling fountain in North Kansas City. CVB OF GREATER KANSAS CITY

Boy and Frog Fountain
Nichols Road and Central
One of the Plaza's most endearing and amusing fountains, this charmer was purchased in 1929 in Florence, Italy. It shows a toddler who's surprised by a shower from a friendly bronze frog.

The Children's Fountain
North Oak Trafficway and Missouri 9
Local sculptor Tom Corbin truly has captured the fountain of youth in this delightful display of six children frolicking in jets of water. The entire fountain itself is massive; the basin measures 60 feet by 100 feet.

Heritage Fountain
23rd and Topping
This spectacular tower of water in Blue Valley Park can be seen for miles around. Dedicated in 1977, this fountain stands on a site some 400 feet above the base of the park and consists of an 85-foot steel pylon with 16 water jets at its summit.

Kauffman Stadium Fountain
Truman Sports Complex
One of the things that makes Kauffman Stadium one of the premier sports venues in the world has nothing to do with sports. The water fountains that operate during Royals home games are simply thrilling every time one of our hometown boys hits a home run. The skyrocketing fountains also entertain the crowd between innings and serve as a spectacular foreground for the fireworks display at the end of every game.

The Town of Kansas 1850 Mural
204 West Third Street
Although this isn't a fountain, it does have a watery theme. Close to where our city began is a wonderful monument to the thousands of people who came here by way of the Missouri River. A mural on the side of a brick River Market building depicts a steamboat chugging along next to a raft in the muddy Missouri. Cows and a settlement are seen on the bluffs above,

all under a cloudy midwestern sky. The artwork, based on a well-known 1853 lithograph, was painted by Jesus Ortiz, Alisha Gambino, and Joseph Faus. River Market loft developer Mel Mallin came up with the idea, raised the money, got the building owner's blessing, and hired the artists. A few years later, this spunky octogenarian commissioned the same team to paint a mural depicting the Lewis and Clark Expedition's stop at our river area. It's located in the River Market area. Bravo, Mel!

presence they call Clara. Apparitions aside, the center houses a gracious lounge on the first floor, which is used for public events or smaller meetings, plus a gallery displaying art and texts. Classrooms, an extensive library, and offices take up the second and third floors.

The Writer's Place is a wonderful resource for local authors to share ideas, get tips from published writers, or commiserate over rejection letters. Several programs are held throughout the year, including book and poetry readings, a monthly book club, student writing competitions, and art exhibits. The public is invited to attend or participate for a small fee, and membership to the organization costs around $30 a year. And you may get to meet Clara.

MUSIC

Ah, the city where the blues and jazz officially met. Naturally we offer plenty of opportunity to explore the music scene of harmonicas, electric guitars, and drums. If you need a nudge, check out the dozens of nightclubs and restaurants offering live music seven days a week in the Nightlife chapter. But you'll also find classical music throughout our fair city. Hear that? Someone is tuning up right now. Please take your seat.

The Friends of Chamber Music
(816) 561-9999
www.chambermusic.org

In the late 1970s, Cynthia Siebert took a chance that Kansas Citians would sit through an evening of chamber music, let alone pay for the privilege. She was delighted by the enthusiastic response, and today as executive director she continues to bring in the world's finest chamber music, pianists, and early music ensembles. To her credit, and to the audience's delight, she seeks out performers who bring passion and a freshness to their craft, not just a famous name. The 18-concert series takes place at four remarkable venues: the Folly Theatre, Grace and Holy Trinity Cathedral, Carlsen Center, and Redemptorist Church in midtown. Ticket prices are around $25.

Kansas City Symphony
1020 Central, Suite 300
(816) 471-1100 (office),
(816) 471-0400 (tickets)
www.kcsymphony.org
A night at the symphony is whatever you make it: black tie or jeans, romance or revelry. Fond memories of the last time you heard "Pictures in an Exhibition" or an exciting new venture into the music of Phillip Glass. You'll hear it here first, thanks to a full season that includes a dozen or so classical concerts at the Lyric Theatre, the Music Hall, and other venues such as Yardley Hall at the Johnson County Community College.

The symphony also presents a Pops series of crowd pleasers like the Count Basie Orchestra. Its Family Series introduces youngsters to the joy of classical music, pain free. Just try to keep a four-year-old from dancing in the aisle to "Snoopy Does the Samba." Tickets vary by performance, with prices ranging from $15 to $40. Check online; the symphony sometimes has nonadvertised deals such as $13 tickets that are upgraded to the best available seats in the house—free. Now that's what we call a musical score!

Lyric Opera of Kansas City
Lyric Theatre, 11th and Central
(816) 471-7344
ww.kcopera.org
Not crazy about opera? The Lyric may change your mind. Since 1958 it has been presenting glowing productions that have turned blasé audiences into opera lovers. What's the secret? For one thing, although the performances are in the original languages, supertitles shown above the stage let you know what that large man is bellowing about. Four productions are offered each season, including a blockbuster like *Tosca* or *Madame Butterfly* and an American opera (for which supertitles may still be necessary). Long-term subscribers may have noticed an upgrade in singers and production values since 1998, when artistic director Ward Holmquist took the helm.

The Lyric Theatre's history reads like a tale by Puccini. Originally built in 1926 as the Ararat Temple for $1 million, the building went into foreclosure in 1939 and by 1942 had been stripped of its seats and sold to the American Red Cross as a blood donation center during the war. When the war ended the building was once again home to legitimate theater, then a movie house before the opera company purchased it in 1970. (One would assume for a song.) It is stunning, with a Greek Corinthian facade that echoes the American Beaux Arts architecture used in neighboring structures. And although the auditorium is dressed in finery, you needn't be. As at most Kansas City performance art venues, you'll see everything from ballgowns to chinos in the audience. Come as you are, they like to say, but just come.

Quality Hill Playhouse
303 West 10th Street
(816) 421-1700
www.qualityhillplayhouse.com
When you're hungry for a sophisticated evening filled with the singable tunes of Cole Porter, George Gershwin, and Henry Mancini, this intimate theater has your seat ready. J. Kent Barnhart serves as emcee and musical director—and brilliant pianist—for cabaret reviews that have covered themes such as great duets, musical divas, and Sinatra songs. Ken's other talent (along with a quick wit and perfect timing) is choosing the right singers for the selections. In Kansas City he's blessed with some standout performers who can give us goosebumps with showstoppers like "My Man" from *Funny Girl* and "Try to Remember" from *The Fantasticks*.

The two-hour shows are slick and professional, and the small, seven-row arrangement ensures a great seat. The audience laps it up seven nights a week. To be sure, more than a few get in with a senior discount, but you'll also see plenty of young music lovers in the audience, especially those who appreciate haunting lyrics and music to hum all the way home. Quality Hill Playhouse produces four shows a year, with performances every night and matinees on Sunday and some weekdays. Single tickets are $23, with discounts for groups and seniors. Covered parking is adjacent to the playhouse, and Sienna Bistro (816–527–0220), serving lovely pastas, fish, and steaks, is right next door.

THEATER COMPANIES

American Heartland Theatre
Crown Center, Third Level Shops
(816) 842-9999
www.ahtkc.com
The actors must have been chanting "Break a leg!" nonstop when this theater opened on April 1 more than 20 years ago. Luck was obviously on its side, however, because the American Heartland contin-

ues to thrive. What keeps it so fresh is the variety of productions that include musical comedies, mysteries, and drama. Past seasons have offered *You're a Good Man, Charlie Brown, Rainmaker,* and its signature holiday presentation, *Nunsense.* If you don't laugh at the antics of this order of nuns (which includes the hapless Sister Amnesia) you may get your knuckles rapped with a wooden ruler.

The 420 seats rise sharply from the stage, ensuring that everyone has an unobstructed view. Unique features include a full-service bar (patrons can take beverages to their seats), a private suite for 36 guests, and free covered parking. Single ticket prices range from $19.00 to $27.50, with the holiday shows costing a few dollars more.

Not sure about what to wear to the ballet, symphony, or opera? Although opening night is usually business dress or evening wear, other performances are typically anything goes. To learn more, including program guides, terms, and even when to applaud (when everyone else does!), check out the major performing arts' groups Web sites. They'll also give you age restrictions for children.

Barn Players
Little Theatre at Shawnee Mission
Northwest High School
12701 West 67th Street
Shawnee, KS
(913) 381-4004

"Hey kids! I've got a barn, and my sister can sing and dance. Let's do a musical!" That's probably close to what happened in 1955 when this group held its first production, making it the longest continuously operating community theater in Kansas City. The group presents three productions a year, ranging from *California Suite* to *Little Shop of Horrors.* The group also has a scholarship fund for college-bound high school students interested in the performing arts.

The Coterie Theatre
Crown Center
(816) 474-6552
www.thecoterie.com

This professional theater for young adults has been a Kansas City favorite for more than 20 years, thanks to artistic director Jeff Church's mission to create an experience that all age groups can enjoy—with or without the kids in tow. The Coterie focuses on imaginative adaptations of beloved stories and fairy tales but isn't afraid to tackle deep subjects like the Holocaust. The artistic integrity is so high that *Travel and Leisure* rated it one of the country's top-10 children's theaters. A new grant is allowing the Coterie to expand its classroom space and construct a lobby. See Kidstuff for information about auditions and tickets.

Gorilla Theatre
31st and Broadway
(816) 471-2737
www.gorillatheatre.org

For more than 13 years this just-off-Broadway theater has presented a unique combination of entertaining and enlightening programs unlike anything else in town, ranging from classic drama, to new playwrights, to avant-garde theater, to alternative musicals. The work, whether from George Bernard Shaw or Sam Shepard, is always thought-provoking.

But the Gorilla is best known for giving local writers a chance to be heard. Each year the winners of its Annual Playwriting Competition see their work performed on stage, and the company also hosts several poetry readings through its Million Monkeys Poetry Series. One of the company's most popular productions is the Annual Sunrise Show, held outside at 7:30 in the morning. Begun as a grassroots effort in 1991, its audience has grown to more than 1,000 and the effort has received extensive media coverage, including in the *Wall Street Journal.* Venues have included the steps of the Nelson-Atkins Museum and nearby Theis Park at 49th and Oak. The early-bird event is free, with donations encouraged. Tickets for the regular series range from $8.00 to $12.00.

Kansas City Repertory Theatre
UMKC Campus, 50th and Oak
(816) 235-2700
www.kcrep.org

From its humble beginnings in a wooden playhouse on the University of Missouri-Kansas City campus in 1964, this company has grown into a nationally respected theater that attracts actors and directors of national and international acclaim. For our money, though, it's the local actors we come to see. Before the curtain rises patrons are usually busy checking the program to see if favorites like Gary Neal Johnson, Merle Moores, and Mark Robbins will be appearing that night.

The Kansas City Rep produces six main productions during its September through June season, each running a minimum of 24 times. The repertoire includes classical and contemporary dramas and comedies, each beautifully staged, with costumes and lighting that are always top-notch. The Rep also gives the city a wonderful holiday gift, *A Christmas Carol*, when artisans and stylists create sets that are more fantastic every year. The not-for-profit organization's success is due in great part to a sense of continuity; in more than 40 years it has only had three artistic directors, beginning with Dr. Patricia McIlrath, then George Keathley, who retired after 15 years. Peter Altman assumed leadership in 2001.

The New Theatre Restaurant
9229 Foster
Overland Park, KS
(913) 649-7469
www.new-theatre.com

This dinner theater puts the emphasis on dinner, with a tempting buffet of entrees and side dishes that might have you wondering why they bother with a show. But you'll be glad you waited for the production; chances are the person on stage is a beloved TV star like Don Knotts, Marion Ross, or Loretta Swit. With all that, plus

nearly 700 seats in a beautiful stepped arrangement that gives everyone a great view, it's no wonder the *Wall Street Journal* calls this "The best dinner theatre in the country."

Founders and co-artistic directors Dennis Hennessey and Richard Carrothers put on five shows per season, four of which star characters like Ritchie's Mom or Hot Lips. But audiences also enjoy seeing local actors on stage, like Lori Blalock, Jim Korinke, and Debra Bluford. Apparently it's a recipe that works. The New Theatre enjoys an average 94 percent attendance 52 weeks a year. And 40,000 to 50,000 of those people are out-of-towners, including several hundred who fly in from California and catch a show before heading to Branson or back home. Yes, indeed, it does cater to the mature audience. But you'll also see plenty of young adults laughing at the jokes. It's hard not to when Barney Fife is staring right at you. Ticket prices range from around $19 to $38, but better hurry. The majority of seats belong to season ticket holders.

Starlight Theatre
4600 Starlight Road in Swope Park
(816) 363-7827
kcstarlight.com

Starlight opened its theater under the stars on June 25, 1951, with *Desert Song*. At the time about 40 professional, self-produced outdoor theaters existed in the country; today only two remain, both in Missouri. During its early days, seasons consisted of 10 shows that included operettas and new Broadway musical comedies. One of its unique features came from a disgruntled star. In 1958 Jerry Lewis was unhappy with the distance between the stage and the audience. An extension, paid for by the comedian, was built to cover the orchestra pit and remained in place until a new stage was built in 2000.

One "star" was a hard act to follow. Former President Harry Truman was happy to appear as himself in a play, until an appendicitis attack forced an early curtain call—into a waiting ambulance. By the

1970s, facing the exorbitant costs of mounting lavish Broadway musicals, Starlight turned to variety shows, and attendance dropped every year. Now the big shows are back, with five Broadway-style shows each May through September season, including classics like *My Fair Lady* and *The Music Man*.

A new $10 million, 12,000-square-foot, fully enclosed stage allows for huge, complex sets, such as a helicopter landing in *Miss Saigon*. The design incorporates two new towers to complement the existing ones that are the theater's trademark.

Tickets cost from $9.00 to $70.00— quite a range, but with 8,000 seats the cheap ones seem an acre away from the stage. You can tell the season ticket holders; they come armed with a chair cushion, binoculars, and an umbrella. You should, too. Starlight is also host to several top-name entertainers every year, from James Taylor to the Four Tops.

The audience has ample opportunity to dine under the stars, too. The Applause Club is a catered dining area open to season ticket holders only. The rest of us are happy to make do with concession food like tasty hot dogs and lemonade.

Theatre in the Park
Shawnee Mission Park
79th and Renner Road
Shawnee, KS
(816) 464–9420 (info line),
(913) 631–7050
www.theatreinthepark.org
A summer night, a star-filled sky, and Curly singing something about a beautiful morning. There are few better ways to spend an evening than watching talented local actors and singers bring new life to classic Broadway shows, especially if you've packed a wedge of cold watermelon in your picnic basket.

The season consists of four musicals, and more than 3,000 people show up each night, far more than just parents of lead actors. The crowd attests to the fact that the talent is top-notch. Ticket windows open at 7:00 P.M., and our advice is

to get there early because the line can get long. The programs begin at 8:30 P.M. A concession stand and public restrooms are available. Admission is $5.00 for adults, $3.00 for children ages 4 to 12, and free for those under 4.

Theater League
301 West 13th Street
(816) 421–7500
www.theaterleague.org
Here's where Kansas City gets to see those thrilling Broadway productions like *A Chorus Line* and *Rent* not long after they win Tony statuettes in New York. Sets are breathtaking displays, such as a miniature lake lit with thousands of candles for *Phantom of the Opera*.

The venue is pretty spectacular, too: the gorgeous 1930s Art Deco music hall at 13th and Wyandotte, with romantic private balconies overlooking the stage and sumptuous decor. Theater League mounts four major shows a year as well as special engagements such as concerts. And although individual tickets are available, it's the season ticket holders who get the best deals. With prices ranging from $140 to $200 per season, the package includes first dibs on special engagements and everything from free desserts to 50 percent discounts at several restaurants on the night of the performance.

Unicorn Theatre
3828 Main Street
(816) 531–PLAY (7529)
www.unicorntheatre.org
"Edgy," even "risky," are words often used to describe the topics portrayed on Unicorn's stage. In fact artistic director Cynthia Levin likes to describe it as contemporary, controversial, and consistent. Naturally, it appeals to a dedicated audience of free thinkers who want something more to discuss post-performance than what the protagonist was wearing . . . or not.

The professional theater has produced more than 200 plays, with more than 45 world premieres, since it began in 1974 as an acting workshop in what is now the

River Market area. In the late 1990s Unicorn moved to its current location in the midtown business district, transforming an old garage into a modern, intimate arrangement utilizing a thrust stage and a seating capacity of 150. Regular performances are shown Tuesday through Sunday, with ticket prices ranging from $12.50 to $25.00.

THEATER VENUES

The play's the thing—and so is the musical, comedy act, and concert. Kansas City is home to some stellar theaters, including three historic buildings that are nearly as interesting as what's on stage. And you can share in the buzz about our new Metropolitan Kansas City Performing Arts Center, due in 2007.

Carlsen Center and Yardley Hall
Johnson County Community College
12345 College Boulevard
Overland Park, KS
(913) 469–4445
www.jccc.net

Part of the behemoth community college campus on a windswept hill, Carlsen Center is a 165,000-square-foot complex that houses four theaters, an art gallery, and an espresso bar along with classrooms and offices. Its size allows for a sweeping lobby with an 85-foot glass ceiling above a granite entry floor.

The exterior is brick, with a graceful arched doorway providing the only adornment, but it's the interior bricks that will catch your eye. Kansas artist Donna Dobberfuhl has created a series of figures that portray the history of theater, dance, and music. The carved-brick sculptures appear on the walls facing the entrance to Yardley Hall, an auditorium known for its superb acoustics and comfortable seating. Since its opening in 1991, the space has hosted such productions as Broadway plays and the Moscow State Symphony Orchestra, as well as current popular singers. More than 200 performances are held here every

year, making the extensive, free parking a real perk.

Folly Theatre
12th and Central
(816) 474–4444

Our only surviving theater palace from the 19th century, the Folly has gone through many names, including the Standard, the Century, Schubert's Missouri, and (unofficially) the Grand Old Lady of 12th Street. Despite a few face-lifts on the inside, the south facade given her by local architect Louis Curtiss is still intact. It's a stately face with simple lines embellished only with an elegant three-story Palladian window.

The theater originally cost $250,000 to build and opened September 23, 1900, with a series of touring vaudeville and burlesque comedies. It continued serving rather blue and rowdy fare until the Schubert family made the 22-year-old legit at last. The Marx Brothers, Shirley Booth, and Humphrey Bogart performed here until once again the feathers were flying. In 1929 an unknown 16-year-old named Rose Louise Havoc made her debut here before she adopted her stage name, Gypsy Rose Lee.

The hall limped through the Depression and finally closed in 1974. Two local philanthropists, Joan Kent Dillon and William Deramus III, saved her from the wrecking ball and mounted a community effort to restore her beauty. The Folly reopened in November 1981 and has remained a vital part of our entertainment scene. She hosts the Friends of Chamber Music, the Harriman Arts Program of William Jewell College, and the Civic Opera Theater of Kansas City, as well as an international jazz series. When you visit the Folly, take a moment to realize that her bricks were laid by Civil War veterans.

Metropolitan Kansas City
Performing Arts Center
16th and Baltimore

A new crown jewel for the city is on the horizon—literally—on a hillside setting overlooking Downtown to the north and Crown Center and our visual arts districts to the south. The Metropolitan Kansas City Performing Arts Center will be a world-class attraction consisting of 400,000 square feet of space. More than just audiences and civic leaders are thrilled about the news; the $305 million center will be home to the Kansas City Ballet, the Kansas City Symphony, and the Lyric Opera, companies in desperate need of growing room. In addition, the 1,800-seat concert hall and 2,200-seat proscenium theater will attract Broadway shows and other large productions.

The new addition to our cultural landscape comes by way of Julia Irene Kauffman, who heads up the Muriel McBrien Kauffman Foundation named for her colorful mom. It was her late mother's dream to leave something so vital and lasting that this city would never forget her. Ms. Kauffman has committed $105 million to make that dream come true, one of the largest single gifts to a cultural project in the country. Another $200 million will come from private donors, foundations, and taxpayers.

The architect, Moshe Safdie, who has transformed urban areas from Canada to Jerusalem, is known for dramatic curves, intriguing textures, and a generous use of windows and open space. You can expect to see as many gardens as buildings in the 6-block setting that is scheduled to open in 2008.

The Midland Theatre
1228 Main Street
(816) 471–8600 (event line),
(816) 471–9703 (administrative offices)
Listed on the National Registry of Historic Places, the Midland is the grandest historic theater within a 250-mile radius of Kansas City. It was built by Marcus Loew in 1927 for an extravagant cost of $4 million.

One of only 300 theaters designed by celebrated architect Thomas Lamb, it's often been called Lamb's "favorite theater" and was certainly the most elegant of its day with over 6 million inches of gold leaf. Its five massive Czechoslovakian hand-cut

crystal chandeliers, precious antique furniture, and spectacular wood and plasterwork are irreplaceable in today's market. The enormous auditorium seats 2,800 and is five stories high, with balconies and stylish opera boxes. It was the first theater in the country to have air-conditioning and is now among only 25 of its kind still standing.

The Midland presented silent pictures and stage shows during its early years. It was purchased by Kansas City's American Multi-Cinema (AMC Theatres) in 1966. The theater showed motion pictures until 1981, when once again it became the venue for Broadway plays, concerts, ballets, and special events. Stars such as Tony Bennett, Dolly Parton, and Harry Connick Jr. have performed on this stage during the past several years.

The Municipal Auditorium,
Music Hall, and the Little Theater
301 West 13th Street
(816) 513–5000
The Municipal Auditorium, an Art Deco wonder that was built in 1935 for $6.5 million ($2 million over budget), fills a city block with its hulking mass of limestone. Linear geometric designs and bas-relief medallions are its only external adornments, a severity that makes entering the grand foyer even more of a thrill.

The auditorium houses three large spaces—a multipurpose arena, the Music Hall, and an elegant little ballroom known as the Little Theatre—each with its own lobby, to accommodate any size or type of event including conventions, sporting events, exhibitions, concerts, plays, and lectures. It has been the scene of everything from political conventions to philharmonic performances to circuses.

The arena has seating for 10,500 people, and its unique roof-support system, which eliminated the need for pillars or posts, provides an unobstructed view from every seat. The 92-foot ceiling is high enough for a trapeze, and its 24,000-square-foot floor, built of oak two-by-fours, is strong enough to support an elephant—

which it has. More college basketball Final Four games have been played here than in any other building in the nation. Now that's good hang time.

The Music Hall, built in 1936 as a home for the Philharmonic Orchestra, is entered through a splendid Art Deco lobby on 14th Street. It features pale gray Italian marble floors and walls, which create a nice echo until the room fills with theatergoers, chan-deliers, and beautiful floor-to-ceiling murals. It seats 2,500 patrons in elegant splendor amid tones of burgundy, deep green, and gold and has an antique pipe organ that once accompanied silent movies. The Little Theatre is accessed through a door on 13th Street and boasts a sweeping, doublewide stairway. The space seats 3,000.

KIDSTUFF

As you'll see, Kansas City is a great place to be a kid, raise a kid, or act like a kid again yourself. You can even *pet* a kid at a children's farmstead in southern Johnson County. From hands-on creative workshops to captivating historic sites, there's something for every tot and teen in your entourage. In fact, we're so kid happy here we don't have just one action-packed theme park, we have two.

And just to prove you can bring a kid to culture and still make him think, Kansas City offers lots of fascinating museums, including the interactive Science Museum at Union Station. There are plenty of indoor and outdoor activities so that youngsters can burn off all that energy, as well as kid-approved restaurants where they can gain it back.

Although we adore children, we're also partial to parents. That's why we tell you about several attractions that are cheap or absolutely free. You'll find other family activities and events to help fill the photo album in the Festivals and Annual Events chapter and the Attractions chapter. But the following ideas should keep the youngest members of your party busy for days. Soon you'll be hearing, "Mom? Dad? Can we move to Kansas City?"

The attractions in this chapter are listed alphabetically by kid-friendly category. All are located in Kansas City, Missouri, unless otherwise noted.

CREATIVE KIDS

All Fired Up
7659 Northwest Prairie View Road
(816) 584-0060

7915 Santa Fe Drive, Overland Park, KS
(913) 385-5456
www.justglazeit.com
What's that sound? Oh, it's silence, broken only by an occasional, "Look, Mom, I

painted a butterfly!" You'll be amazed how much quiet fun your children can have creating their own masterpieces at this paint-your-own-pottery workshop in downtown Overland Park and in the Northland. The owner, Teddy Wright, has a soft spot for kids, so she makes sure they, and you, have a great time. Little artists can choose from dozens of ceramic items to paint, including stepping-stones, mugs, picture frames, holiday ornaments, and plates. Adults may choose more elaborate pieces, including pretty urns with curvy handles, large platters, and birdhouses.

Then it's time to get creative. You can help your little artist choose a theme such as "I love Grandpa," bones on Fido's feeding bowl, or simply go with doodles and dots. For inspiration Teddy has finished projects and pictures to look through. Lightly pencil in the image, then add paint using brushes, stamps, sponges, and stencils. It's impossible to make a mistake; until the piece is fired the paint will wipe right off to start again. Once your child is finished with the artwork, it's left for Teddy to glaze and fire in the kiln. It will be available to pick up a day or two later, so you may want to schedule your trip here near the beginning of your vacation.

Both locations are grand for birthday parties and scout outings, as well as adult-type fun like margarita parties, when groups make their own glassware using special paints. Call to find out when the shop is open. Prices for the pottery pieces range from $3.00 to $48.00 each. Studio fees for adults are $7.00 per hour or $10.00 unlimited time; for ages 12 and under studio fees are $6.00 per hour or $8.00 unlimited.

Build-A-Bear Workshop
95th Street and Quivira
Overland Park, KS
(813) 307-0328
www.buildabear.com

Now here's a souvenir from Kansas City that won't land in the closet the moment you get home. At this colorful workshop in Oak Park Mall, your child gets to help construct his or her very own best buddy from 25 different animal styles. The fun comes when they make it their exclusive toy by selecting a sound to place inside or even recording their own voiced message to replay any time they want. "You're the coolest!" comes to mind.

Your child can help create a birth certificate with name and "date of birth" or choose from seven different storybooks starring the new pet. After a quick stuff and fluff, it's time to choose an outfit and accessories from a wardrobe of over 200 items. And to take the new furry friend home in style, there's even a Cub Condo carrying case. The basic plush animals are priced from $10 to $30; outfits are an additional charge.

Kaleidoscope
25th Street and Grand Boulevard
(816) 274-8301
www.hallmarkkaleidoscope.com
Every child is an artist at this workshop run by Hallmark Cards. In fact, the entire place looks like a giant greeting card, with themed areas where children ages 5 through 12 can spend an hour creating masks and other crafts with leftover materials from the card maker. Rather than being given a set project, children are encouraged to explore their own sense of color and design. Your child can come away from this visit with a new sense of expression and self-confidence.

Admission is free, limited to one 55-minute session per child, and open to walk-in visitors on Saturday throughout the year and Monday through Saturday in summer. Reservations are required on weekdays during the school year and for groups of six or more at any time. Tickets are available starting at 10:00 A.M. for walk-in sessions. Children must be accompanied by an adult. Call to check on what hours it's open.

Kaleidoscope also offers wonderful workshops taught by staff and volunteers

where children can build or decorate a take-home project like a birdhouse or tie. There's a small fee for these programs, and reservations are required. And don't miss the free worksheets that detail additional activities families can do together at home; they're available at the receptionist's desk on the way out.

And here's another bonus: The Hallmark Visitor Center, also in the Crown Center complex, gives children in third grade and above a chance to learn how the Hallmark artists make their magic. Adults will adore the displays as well.

The center includes an interesting film on the creative process as well and an exhibit about Hallmark's history. Did you know it started right here in Kansas City? Kids get to make a bow to take home, and artists are around to demonstrate their skills and answer questions. This is free as well, but reservations are required for groups of 10 or more or if you would like a guided tour. The visitor center is open Monday through Saturday. For more information call (816) 274–5672 or point your paintbrush to www.hallmark.com.

HAVE A BALL

Cool Crest Family Fun Center
10735 East Missouri Highway 40
Independence, MO
(816) 358-0088
www.coolcrest.com
The Patterson family has been entertaining everyone from tiny tots to tottering grandparents since 1950 at this 4½-acre playground. There's something to keep everyone happy, including four 18-hole miniature golf courses (watch the Green Dragon hazard; it's a doozie), go-karts, batting cages, and a 7,000-square-foot game room with video and pinball machines galore. The nifty fifties-style pizzeria serves up cheesy pies plus hot dogs, ice cream, and slushees. Cool Crest is lovingly maintained and seems to have another new attraction every year. Event planners can help make sure your birthday

party or group outing is a success. Cool Crest is open year-round, and golf is available when weather permits. Prices vary based on activities. Because the hours vary depending on the day, call ahead for details.

Family Golf Park
1501 Northeast MO 40
Blue Springs, MO
(816) 228-1550
www.familygolfpark.com
If your kids can't find something exciting to do at this huge play area, it's time to ship them home. This beautifully landscaped park features 36 holes of miniature golf that wind through a lake setting, a par-3 golf course, putting green, game arcade, and bumper boats. Ker-splash! The golf practice facility is open year-round, and golf lessons are available. Hours are 8:30 A.M. until 10:30 P.M. weekdays and until 11:30 P.M. on Friday and Saturday. Rates vary depending on the activities.

Incred-A-Bowl
8500 West 151st Street
Overland Park, KS
(913) 851-1700
www.incredabowl.com
When former Royals pitcher Danny Jackson and his, wife, Jody, couldn't find an entertainment center the entire family could enjoy, they built one themselves, and it's a beauty. This 65,000-square-foot, state-of-the-art center includes a 40-lane computerized bowling alley, an arcade filled with more than 100 of the latest interactive and virtual reality games, a three-story set of play tubes for the tikes, a new laser tag center, and a miniature golf course. Whew!

The complex's claim to fame, however, is Cosmic Bowling every Friday and Saturday night until 1:30 A.M., with groovy black lights, fog, glow-in-the-dark balls and pins, and upbeat music. Incred-A-Bowl also has a pro shop, gift store, and snack bar. Now if only those shoes weren't so dorky.

Call Incred-A-Bowl for opening and closing hours.

Jaegers Subsurface Paintball
9300 Northeast Underground Drive
(816) 452-6600
www.jaegers.com
What a brilliant use of our subterranean limestone caves! With 180,000 square feet in this paintball arcade, there's plenty of places to hide and go . . . splat! Players can choose from 6 to 10 different games for any number of participants. The center is open daily at various hours. Call for details. A three-hour session, including gun and paintballs, costs around $25 per player. Jaegers is located east of Interstate 435 and just north of the Missouri River.

HOT DOG! TIME TO EAT!

The Crayola Cafe $
2450 Grand Avenue
(816) 426-1165
www.crowncenter.com
This colorful restaurant in the Crown Center Shops caters to kids with a tin of crayons and ready-to-color placemats at each seat. And you'd swear a five-year old—and a picky eater at that—dreamed up the menu. It features grilled-cheese sandwiches (crustless, of course), a double-decker peanut butter club, chicken drumsticks, and mac and cheese. Over 20 specialty fountain drinks and fruit smoothies keep the blenders buzzing. Parents can order theirs with alcohol (the piña coladas are great) along with grown-up menu items including sandwiches, salads, and pastas.

After lunch or dinner you can extend the color-me-happy experience at the adjacent Crayola Store. Along with oodles of crayons and logo-emblazoned clothes and accessories, you'll find interactive computerized displays and games.

Fritz's Railroad Cafe $
2450 Grand Avenue
(816) 474-4004
www.crowncenter.com
Get your vacation on track at this train-inspired restaurant in the Crown Center

Shops. It's quite a trip to call in your order on the telephone at your booth, and then watch it chuga-chug-chug to your table on an overhead electric train. The outrageous fun will delight your kids, and so will the menu of made-to-order burgers, hot dogs, sandwiches, and shakes. Parents will get on board as well, with tasty items like bowls of Fritz's famous chili.

Rainforest Cafe   **$-$$**
11327 West 95th Street
Overland Park, KS
(913) 438-7676
www.rainforestcafe.com
Your kids will be wide-eyed and wonderstruck even before they sit down at this restaurant in Oak Park Mall. In this lushly vegetated place, thunder cracks, animals seem to come to life, and tropical fish mesmerize onlookers. It's almost too stimulating to eat, but when kids are handed their very own menu they usually change their minds. While they're having a blast, your children will be learning about ecology from talking trees and jabbering birds.

Birthday packages include invitations, treasure maps with crayons, and safari pith helmets (say that fast three times!). As for the food, prices are a bit high but portions are huge—and for a trip to the Amazon without boarding a plane, it might be worth it. There's even a full bar. Reservations are a must, particularly on weekends; walk-ins can expect at least an hour's wait.

ICE IS NICE

AMF Ice Chateau
8788 Metcalf
Overland Park, KS
(913) 648-0129
Perhaps your child will aspire to an Olympic gold medal at this regulation-sized indoor rink. Even without a triple-anything, it's a guaranteed good time. Open skating is available from noon until 4:30 P.M. or so most days, and lessons are available for all ages and levels. On weekends, kids and teens have a blast during

Ice Xtreme, when the lights come down and the music cranks up. The fun starts at 8:00 P.M. on Friday and 7:00 P.M. on Saturday and lasts until 11:00 P.M.

Hockey leagues practice their moves here as well, and there's drop-in hockey every Sunday starting at 8:30 P.M. Non-skaters can head to the bowling alley, pool tables, and game arcade. A concession stand provides the fuel for all this fun. Admission is $4.50 for 7 and under, $6.50 for 8 and older, plus $2.50 for skate rental.

Crown Center Ice Terrace
2450 Grand Boulevard
(816) 274-8411
www.crowncenter.com
Kansas City's only outdoor ice rink is a scene worthy of Currier and Ives: couples, arm-in-arm, gliding across the ice to music, children in snowsuits making frantic arm circles to keep from falling. . . oops, too late. The setting for this living Christmas card is Crown Center, which appropriately enough is the Hallmark Cards headquarters. A free-form tent provides shelter so even during inclement weather the ice is perfect.

The terrace is open seven days a week, 10:00 A.M. to 9:00 P.M. from November through March. Fees are $5.00 per person; skate rental is $2.00. Groups of 20 or more save the rental fee, and the rink is available for private parties before or after regular hours; reservations are necessary for these activities. Bring plenty of quarters for the vending machines that dispense hot cocoa and cappuccino.

Pepsi Ice Midwest Skating Rink and Fitness Center
12140 West 135th Street
Overland Park, KS
(913) 851-1600
www.pepsiicemidwest.com
This sparkling new, sprawling center features three ice rinks used for hockey and ice-skating competitions and practice. In fact this facility recently became the new home of one of the country's oldest ice-skating groups, the Silver Blades.

The ice is available for free skating at various times during the week, usually from 10:00 A.M. to early afternoon on weekdays, and two sessions on Saturday. Check the Web site or call for specific hours. Fees are $6.50 for adults, $5.00 for children under 7 years of age, and $2.00 for skate rental. Lessons are also available, and the rink can be rented for birthday parties. The center also has a fitness center, game room, and deli.

Snow Creek Ski Lodge
Missouri Highway 45,
5 miles north of Weston
(816) 640-2200
www.skipeaks.com
We'll admit Missouri is a few peaks short of Colorado, but that doesn't mean kids can't have fun on skis here. This ski lodge is on a natural hill with a 300-foot vertical drop and enough varied terrain to give beginners and experts a (ski) run for their money. Trails are accessed via two triple chairlifts, one double chairlift, and a rope tow. Thanks to 40 snowmaking machines, the snow base ranges from 24 to 60 inches, enough to provide powdery fun for the crowds that pack this place on evenings and weekends. There are plenty of gentle slopes and flat areas for beginners to practice their wedges without getting blasted by the big kids.

A 10,000-square-foot lodge features a cafeteria, bar, and lounge and also houses the ski school and gift shop. The rental shop offers shaped skis with plenty of junior sizes, plus snowboards and ski boards—just the ticket for Jason's Run, an area with enough jumps, bumps, mounds, pipes, and tabletops to keep expert boarders counting the days until Snow Creek opens in mid-December. Weather permitting, the lodge stays open seven days a week through mid-March.

The park is always popular, but never more so than during the midnight sessions when lights turn the ice a pale gold and music adds to the party atmosphere. Midnight sessions start the last weekend in December, and on special nights the lodge is open until 3:00 A.M. Check the Web site or call for specific hours.

Prices range from $16 to $33 for a one-day pass, equipment rental another $16 to $20. Group rates and season passes are available. Lessons cost around $12 an hour for beginner or refresher; private lessons are also available. The Web site shows plenty of photos, including some pretty cool boarding competition. See you on the slopes, you snow bunny, you.

LIONS AND TIGERS AND GOATS, OH MY!

Deanna Rose Children's Farmstead
138th Street and Switzer Road
Overland Park, KS
(913) 897-2360
www.opkansas.org
If your children have never been up close and personal with a cow—or even if they have—they'll love this miniature 12-acre farm. The farmstead opened in 1976 and in 1985 was dedicated in memory of Deanna Rose, an Overland Park police officer killed in the line of duty. This attraction is so wonderful it was the "extra credit" that earned Overland Park its rating as "Most kid-friendly suburb in the US" by Zero Population Growth.

Within the barnyard are Bluefeather the bison, plus rabbits, pigs, chickens, sheep, and goats that like to play king on the mountain in their rocky playing field. In spring the place is filled with fuzzy little newborns; it's quite a treat to feed the babies from a bottle. Older animals, particularly the goats, are tame enough to eat from the palm of a two-year-old. Make sure you have enough film for your camera. You'll also want to bring plenty of quarters to buy feed from the vending machines.

There are other activities to keep your child, and you, entertained for hours. At Grandpa Bob's Fishing Pond, you can rent a pole for $2.00 on a strictly catch-and-release system. Pony rides and hayrides are available for $2.00 per person from

10:00 A.M. to 2:00 P.M. Monday through Saturday and noon to 4:00 P.M. on Sunday. Brick pathways wind through the park past flowers, vegetables, and shrubbery maintained by the Johnson County Extension Master Gardeners, and there's usually an expert or two on hand to tell you exactly how they get those begonias so perky. New attractions include an Indian encampment, a prairie playground, including a log fort, and a country schoolhouse.

A concession stand and picnic area are handy for when your little farmhand gets hungry. The farmstead is open daily from 9:00 A.M. to 8:00 P.M. April through September and closes at 5:00 P.M. in October. It's closed November through March. Admission is free, but you'll gladly give a generous donation; this kind of good old-fashioned fun is priceless.

The Kansas City Zoo
6800 Zoo Drive
(816) 513–5800
www.kansascityzoo.org

The Kansas City Zoo had humble but heartwarming beginnings when it opened in December 1909 as a shelter for abandoned circus animals. Since then it's gone through as many skins as a python. Two decades ago, as at many other zoos around the country, visitors could only stare at bored animals held behind cages. Today it's entirely different, with 200 acres of natural habitats that let the animals roam freely. And while there's no guarantee you'll see a lion—he may be snoozing in the brush out back—you'll appreciate the realistic environment almost as much as these beautiful beasts.

The zoo is continuing to grow and improve, and its endangered species breeding programs are getting positive results and accolades from across the country. It's already the tenth largest zoo in the United States and, with 200 more acres available, could become one of the top zoological parks anywhere.

It's already one of the most exciting. One of the newest additions is the African exhibit, 95 acres of land that's home to more than 400 animals. Take a tour through Botswana, where the elephants roam, keeping cool by taking mud baths during summer's heat. Sometimes these pachyderms become Picassos as they paint on canvas, holding brushes in their flexible trunks. Crossing into Kenya, animal lovers can gaze over 17 acres of plains filled with sable antelope, beisa oryx, impala, and greater kudu . . . as in "kudu hand me the camera, please? I think I just saw a cheetah!"

Hop on a safari boat ride to tour Lake Nakuru, where you might see one of the zoo's newest stars, our adorable baby hippos, or Kifaru Malika, the East African rhino born in fall 2000. She's one of only 660 black rhinos in existence today. Want to see eye-to-eye with a giraffe? Then perhaps you'd like to picnic in the treetops while they forage for food nearby. Our zoo has been blessed with two giraffe births in recent years, and it's always a delight to watch these graceful animals grow up. And up. Three lion cubs provide plenty of feline antics as well.

In the Congolese Forest you'll see leopard, bongo, and lowland gorillas, and in Tanzania the chimpanzees will keep you entertained. In the final stop, Uganda, you'll view baboons, lemurs, jackals, and an enormous Aldabra tortoise.

The Australia tour begins at Gundagai Station with a free short movie highlighting the colorful wildlife from the world's smallest continent. An aviary with 20 species of birds and mammals marks the start of this area, followed by more than 30 kangaroo and emus that roam free to allow for up-close viewing. Dingo, wallaby, cassowary, and tree kangaroo can also be spied. If you want a bird's-eye view, take a camel ride at the station; kids can also get pony rides here. Or hop a train for a tour of the park, browse the gift store, or gaze at the 40-foot-long aboriginal mural, the largest installation of aboriginal art in the United States.

But don't focus just on the new exhibits. Children love traditional areas like the sea lion pool, where the sleek enter-

The best time to see animals in their natural habitats at the zoo is summer, of course, but don't discount a wintertime visit. Many of the animals prefer colder temperatures (the polar bears become positively giddy), and Wildlights, huge lighted animal sculptures, are on view from mid-November through the end of the year. They can be viewed from the train that circles the zoo.

tainers dive and splash and bark in unison during feedings. At Farmland USA, potbellied pigs, miniature horses, and goats are favorites. This area also includes pony rides and a terrific playground.

The zoo hosts several events throughout the year, including a Halloween party called Boo at the Zoo, and Party for the Planet, which celebrates Earth Day. From June through August, Sunset Safaris take advantage of cooler evening temperatures when the animals are more active. During these days the zoo stays open until 8:30 P.M. and offers activities like train rides, live music, and cool beverages.

Parents will also be glad to know there are several snack bars throughout the zoo as well as two sit-down restaurants. Selections at the new "Beastro" are quite tasty. But, especially during the hot days of summer, it's a good idea to bring plenty of water along with sunscreen and hats.

The zoo also features the Sprint IMAX Theatre, which puts you right in the center of the action with a 6½-story-tall screen and 12,000 watts of digital sound. Recent shows included cave explorations and journeys into outer space. Call (816) 871–IMAX for day and evening show times and ticket information. You can attend IMAX without visiting the zoo (tickets range from $4.00 to $6.00), but the best value is a combination ticket.

But for our money, the biggest thrill for kids is a Nocturnal Safari, where they spend the night at a campsite after a day of playing junior zookeeper. Next morning, is that a tummy growling or a big cat wak-

ing up nearby? Never fear, the campers are safe and breakfast is waiting. This exciting, educational program is ideal for families, scouts, and church groups for ages 6 and up. Reservations, which go as fast as a cheetah, start March 1, and the safaris run Friday and Saturday from late May through September. It's one more reason to become a member of Friends of the Zoo; FOTZ members pay only $30, nonmembers pay $35, and nonmembers who live out of town pay $40. Call (816) 513–5700, ext. 24673, for membership information.

The zoo is open daily year-round from 9:00 A.M. to 5:00 P.M. April 1 through October 14 and 9:00 A.M. to 4:00 P.M. the rest of the season, except for Sunset Safaris described above. It's closed Christmas Day and January 1. Admission is $7.50 for adults, $6.50 for seniors, $4.50 for ages 3 to 11, and free for 2 and under. On Tuesday everyone gets in for $2.00. Parking costs $2.00 from April 1 through October 14; otherwise it's free.

LOOP-THE-LOOPS AND LOTS OF WATER

Jeepers!
The Great Mall of the Great Plains
Olathe, KS
(913) 393–3535, (800) 533–7377
www.jeepers.com
Although Jeepers! is located in a huge discount shopping mall, you'll have no trouble finding the entrance: Just look for the 15-foot-tall grinning ape. Inside is a day's worth of giggles, with bumper cars, laser tag, rides, and sports challenges that pay off in super prizes for ages 2 to 12. Toddlers will find tubes, chutes, slides, and soft games that encourage hand-eye coordination. You can test yours by getting a buffalo chicken wing in your mouth without hitting your chin. In fact the Rino Diner offers something for everyone in your group, including pizza, hot dogs, chicken fingers, milk, and soft drinks. Snacks like popcorn and cotton candy are also available.

Adults are encouraged to enjoy games and rides right along with the youngsters. If you're planning a birthday party for your little one, however, you can leave the entertainment to the friendly staff while you sneak out to shop at a few of the mall's stores. Jeepers! is all indoors, which makes it ideal during rainy or cold weather. It's open seven days a week as late as 10:00 P.M. Call ahead to check on opening and closing times for the day of your visit.

Admission is free, but rides require tokens. An all-day pass is $7.99, $5.99 for kids under 36 inches. Single ride tickets are available for $1.00. The Web site often has discount coupons ready to print.

**Worlds of Fun and Oceans of Fun
4545 Worlds of Fun Avenue
(816) 454–4545
www.worldsoffun.com**

Kansas City sent the fun-o-meter off the charts when Worlds of Fun opened in 1973 with 175 acres of roller coasters, rides, and musical shows. The park is based on Jules Verne's Around the World in Eighty Days, with distinct areas representing Europe, Africa, Asia, and the Americas. Frankly, kids might not even make the connection with the continents. All they want to know is how fast the rides go.

The answer is very fast indeed. The Mamba, ranked as one of the world's top-10 roller coasters, blasts riders 205 feet up then drops 'em 184 feet at 75 miles per hour. Your kids aren't making faces, Mom, they're just getting 3.5 Gs of fun. The Detonator lifts riders 200 feet in the sky, pausing just long enough to catch a breath before plummeting back to Earth. And the Boomerang is a 12-story-tall scream machine that rockets forward and backward through corkscrew turns, upside-down loops, and 125-foot lifts at up to 50 miles per hour. You might want to rethink those breakfast plans. Another popular ride is the Timber Wolf, a 4,320-foot roller coaster with hairpin turns and a unique 560-degree helix. A more sedate choice might be the Skyliner Ferris wheel, which provides a panoramic view from 60 feet up.

Worlds of Fun also keeps the smaller kids in mind with their very own Camp Snoopy. In this one-acre playland, the beloved Charles Schultz characters come to life and a small-scale tower ride can make your children feel like the big kids without getting scared. A kiddy train and Red Baron airplane ride round out the activities.

To make your stay more enjoyable there are food concessions and stroller rentals available. Worlds of Fun is generally open daily from late May to early September at 10:00 A.M.; closing times are as late as 10:00 P.M. Get out the ruler folks, here are the pricing policies: A single day pass for adults and children 48 inches or taller is $36.95 plus tax; for children 4 years old and shorter than 48 inches it's $14.95 plus tax. After 4:00 P.M. the admission price is reduced, and season passports and group events are available. Prices usually increase every year, so call or check the Web site for specifics.

Next door is Oceans of Fun, a 60-acre wet and wild adventure that includes a million-gallon pool with 4-foot-high waves, sandy beach, children's "sprayground," 43-foot water slides, and Castaway Cove, an adults-only pool with swim-up refreshments. Oceans of Fun is generally open daily from late May to early September at 10:00 A.M.; closing time varies. A single day pass for adults and children over 48 inches tall is $24.00; for children 4 years old and under 48 inches tall it's $12.95. Prices may change; call for specifics.

MUSEUMS FOR YOUNG MINDS

Mention a museum to kids and watch how fast they run from the room. We understand. But if you can get them in the door of one of these exhibitions, you may have a hard time getting them to leave. Pick something your child is passionate about, like dinosaurs, or give him or her something new to learn about such as astronomy. Suddenly that next science project is in the can.

When available we've listed the museum's Web site so that you can pre-plan your visit to get the most out of your valuable time. Here's another plus: The wide variety of choices means there's something to interest every age group from toddlers to 'tweens and above. And don't miss our premier children's interactive museum, Science City.

Children's Museum of Kansas City
4601 State Avenue
Kansas City, KS
(913) 287–8888
www.kidmuzm.org
Imagine a museum where instead of warning your children to keep their hands to themselves, you get to say, "Go ahead and touch everything." At this wildly popular museum in the Indian Springs Marketplace, hands-on activities are designed to stimulate creativity, jump-start imagination, and teach motor skills and problem solving. There are role-playing sections where kids shop for groceries and ring them up using scanners. Backstage at the theater participants learn about lighting and sound effects and get to try on costumes and face paints. If they have a short poem, song, or speech, they can test it out on stage. And like they say, if you can make it in Kansas City, Kansas, you can make it anywhere. The wellness center has actual medical equipment including a stretcher, hospital bed, and crutches, a good way to help ease a child's fears before a scheduled hospital stay or doctor's visit.

The recycle center gives children, parents, and teachers an opportunity to pick up arts and crafts supplies on the cheap. And usually a new exhibit is making the rounds, such as a giant toothbrush that turns dental health into playtime or a puppet show.

The birthday parties are at the top of our list, however. You can choose a theme such as space travel or go all out with a Victorian Tea Party, where 8 to 10 little girls dress in fancy hats and clothes, dine on dainty food, and even get a Victorian etiquette lesson from the party hostess. At

the Monster Morph, partygoers are transformed into monsters with costumes and face paint. Gruesome cupcakes and mysterious potions are served, a party we guarantee they'll remember for years.

The museum is open year-round, Monday through Saturday, from 9:30 A.M. to 5:00 P.M., Sunday 1:00 to 5:00 P.M. During the school year (September through May) it is closed on Monday. Admission is $3.50, free for under age 2. Please be aware that the Children's Museum may be moving within the next few years, so please call or check the Web site before making your plans.

The Toy and Miniature Museum
of Kansas City
5235 Oak Street
(816) 333–2055
www.umkc.edu.tmm
Tell your children to "think small," and then take them to this fascinating museum filled with one of the world's most extensive collections of miniatures, antique toys, and folk art. Although girls of all ages are drawn to the exquisitely furnished dollhouses, boys will find plenty of interesting exhibits as well. They seem to love the transportation room with trains chugging overhead, and cast-iron scooters, stagecoaches, and cars are featured below. In the 15 Decades of Toys display, children see simple tin toys from the 1850s, cast-iron banks, an early teddy bear, Barbie and GI Joe, Cabbage Patch dolls, and toys named for TV celebrities. Kids may get the biggest kick from parents pointing and saying, "I had one just like that!" And nearly everybody giggles at the sight of a naked doll, "Frozen Charlotte," named for a girl so vain she refused to wear her frock and froze to death. Kids, don't try this at home.

One of the museum's most enduring exhibits is the display of miniatures such as an American Indian bowl with 1/8-inch-long frog handles and an 8-inch-high English Georgian secretary desk with working locks and 19 secret compartments. Wow! These objects are built to scale and often crafted from precious materials such as bone and sterling silver. Others were made of every-

CLOSE-UP

Science City at Union Station

For children (or adults for that matter) who consider science their least-liked subject, the Science City interactive museum will change their minds. Here, visitors learn that science is all around us in our everyday lives. And rather than viewing artifacts displayed behind glass, children are encouraged to play, interact, and learn.

Science City offers plenty of places for pooped-out scientists and their parents to refuel without leaving Union Station. Get a quick bite at Union Cafe in the heart of the station. Or head across The Link, the enclosed elevated walkway kids consider a fun event all by itself, to Crown Center's food court and restaurants. Be sure to get your ticket or hand stamped at Science City if you plan to return.

Science City is open 10:00 A.M. to 5:00 P.M. Monday through Saturday and noon to 5:00 P.M. on Sunday. General admission is $9.00 for adults, $8.00 for seniors, $7.00 for children 4 through 12, and free for under 3 years of age. Parking is free for up to five hours; if you're staying longer, get your parking ticket validated at the event you're attending.

The Theater District, which is separate from Union Station, comes alive in the evening with four exciting stages. The City Extreme Screen's five-story-tall screen and two- and three-dimensional projection brings films to life. City Dome combines video, lasers, special effects, and multichannel sound to create a planetarium show that's out of this world. City Stage is a 200-seat live theater venue offering a variety of shows from musical revues to hilarious science demonstrations. And TurboRide is a moving experience—literally. You'll strap in for a fast-paced, four-minute adventure flying with the Blue Angels, racing around Indy 500, or coming face-to-face with the dinosaurs. Single theater admissions start at $4.00 for children and $6.00 for adults or can be purchased in combination with Science City. The Theatre District is open until 10:00 P.M. and is located in the lower level on the west side of Union Station.

Union Station is located at 30 West Pershing Square near Crown Center. The main phone number is (816) 460–2000, or log on to www.sciencecity.com.

day items like wishbones, feathers, and pine cones. And don't miss the maze, a zigzag hallway lined with tiny room settings ranging from a turn-of-the-20th-century classroom to a study in the Palace of Versailles. Along with the regular exhibits there is often a special event scheduled, so plan on spending hours here.

Because there's so much to see within the 24 rooms on two floors, it's best to request a treasure hunt guide at the welcome center. Along with overviews of the

rooms, the guide suggests questions to ask children, providing thought-provoking history lessons along the way. The museum, located on the beautiful tree-lined campus of the University of Missouri–Kansas City, is open 10:00 A.M. to 4:00 P.M. Wednesday through Saturday, and 1:00 to 4:00 P.M Sunday. It is closed Monday and Tuesday, on major holidays, and on the two weeks following Labor Day. Admission is $4.00 for adults and $2.00 for children ages 3 through 12.

When visiting Union Station's Science City, don't miss the watery display out front. The Henry W. Bloch Fountain, named for the H&R Block cofounder, is an ever-changing liquid ballet that pumps 9,225 gallons of water per minute through 232 computer-controlled jets shooting as high as 120 feet. If only your tax refund had that kind of altitude!

Wonderscope Children's Museum
5705 Flint Street
Shawnee, KS
(913) 268-4176, (913) 268-8130
(recorded message)
www.wonderscope.org
Although it's true that some other museums are fancier than Wonderscope, parents tell us that children beg to return here again and again. Located in the Flint Elementary building, Wonderscope is specifically set up for children from 6 months to 10 years, one of the few places where toddlers will find plenty to do. A favorite section is the grocery store, where children get to shop for pretend groceries and scan the purchases. In the TV area your little Katie Couric or Dan Rather can direct, film, and read the evening news. In the Raceways room, children can learn about gravity, speed, and acceleration using golf balls . . . are you sure Galileo started this way? And in the Hands of Mercy area, stories of current and former patients at Children's Mercy Hospital help teach children about medical care while they get a gentle lesson about compassion.

Special programs and events range from storytelling to the Gee Whiz science demonstrations. Budding preschool artists will enjoy the art workshops, while some kids head right for the indoor sandbox. Although food isn't allowed in the exhibit areas, you can enjoy lunch and snacks from home in the indoor picnic area; a soft drink machine is available. Wonderscope is also a favorite place for birthday parties; call for information about cost and availability.

The museum is open 10:00 A.M. to 5:00 P.M. Monday through Saturday and noon to 5:00 P.M. on Sunday. Admission is $5.00 for ages 3 and up, $2.50 for ages 1 and 2, and free for under 1 year.

RIDE 'EM COWBOY (AND COWGIRL)

American Royal Museum
and Visitor Center
1701 American Royal Court
(816) 221-9800
www.americanroyal.com
Okay, so your young 'uns don't get to ride a horse or rope a steer at this museum. But they can pretend they're riding Blaze as they try out a variety of saddle styles in the Traditions area. Lots of activities and displays keep little cowpokes entertained, and for students and 4-H members interested in agribusiness, this place is a must. The center opened in 1992 as a tribute to the 100-year-old American Royal, Kansas City's annual horse and livestock shows, rodeo, and parade.

Kids get a kick out of stepping on a livestock scale to compare their weight to that of pigs, chickens, and feeder steer. They can try their hand at an interactive livestock judging game and check out memorabilia from past rodeos and horse shows. And little girls can dream while gazing at a dazzling crown from the American Royal Queen contest.

The museum is open year-round, and trained docents are available for tours. Activities are scheduled throughout the year, including spring field trips when kids can take pony rides, make butter, grind wheat, plant a soybean, and learn how to line dance. Call extension 125 for specific dates and costs and to make reservations for specific events.

SEE WHAT'S IN STORE

Following are shops where your kids can spend their allowances, or the entire family can play, poke, and peruse without spending a dime.

Brookside Toy & Science
330 West 63rd Street
(816) 523-4501
You don't need a child to enjoy this store; in fact there are plenty of solo adults walking around with big silly grins in place, reliving a childhood for an hour or so. Every conceivable toy, game, and model car kit is here, along with a very nice display of telescopes and microscopes. As the name implies, this is science project headquarters, with science kits and educational toys to pique the imagination. Jim and Mary Jo Ward, who have owned this wooden-floored wonderland since 1964, take pride in the fact that they don't sell toy weapons of any kind.

Even for an independent store (rare these days) prices are competitive with the big chains. And here's another reason to shop here first: Kids are encouraged to bring in old toys in good condition to donate to less fortunate children.

For even more nostalgia, stroll down to the Dimestore, where you'll think you've stumbled into a time warp. This old-fashioned emporium is chock-a-block with sundries, toys, household goods, art supplies, and plenty of what used to be called penny candy.

Both stores are open daily and are within the delightful Brookside shopping district, an old-fashioned main street filled with unique shops, restaurants, and an ice-cream parlor. See the Shopping chapter for more.

Crayola Store
2450 Grand Boulevard
(816) 274-7500
www.crowncenter.com
Color this store fun! This visual and sensory experience captures the universal appeal of Crayola products in 60,000 square feet of color and creativity. Naturally you'll find all sorts of art supplies, backpacks, and toys starring the crayon colors, but there are also interactive games and a crayon-making demonstration to delight most ages.

Moon Marble Company
600 East Front Street
Bonner Springs, KS
(913) 441-1432
www.moonmarble.com
The owner of this store is a big kid himself, so children always have a blast here. Along with keeping aisles filled with yo-yos, magic tricks, game boards, and old-fashioned tin toys, Bruce Breslow makes marvelous marbles while you watch. And of course there are plenty of the round wonders to buy—whole buckets of them—as well as collectible marbles from all over. Call or check the Web site for details about when Bruce will be demonstrating his skills.

Reading Reptile
328 West 63rd Street
(816) 753-0441
www.readingreptile.com
Walk into this cheery store once and you'll feel like one of the family. Since 1988 owners Pete and Debbie have been encouraging little readers with story hours, book clubs, and an annual two-day literary love-in when they bring together little readers, parents, and authors. Even when nothing special is happening, the Reptile is a cool place for kids.

TAKE IT OUTSIDE, KIDS

Kansas City is dotted with dozens of parks and lakes where kids can find enough beaches, nature trails, and campsites to fill a summer or a lifetime. You'll find descriptions of some of our favorite parklands in the Parks, Lakes, and Recreation chapter. In the meantime we'll introduce you to the following places created with kids in mind, including a park that's friendly to wheelchairs. Most parks are open from daylight to dusk daily. Call ahead for opening and closing times.

Ernie Miller Park and Nature Center
909 North Kansas
Olathe, KS
(913) 764-7759
Introduce your nature boy or girl to this 113-acre park that's been preserved in all its glorious natural state. Three trails wind through ecological habitats like grassland, meadow, and forest. It's a terrific place for birding—look for woodpeckers, sparrows, owls, and woodland songbirds—as well as sighting other wildlife like white-tailed deer. Pick up a pocket-sized guide at the Nature Center, where you can spend time with a terrific wildlife diorama and inter-pretive displays.

Roller Hockey Rink
116th and Knox
Overland Park, KS
This 120-foot by 65-foot rink at Indian Val-ley Park features a playing surface of color-coated asphalt with regulation height and width goal areas. A 5-foot-tall sideboard surrounds the playing area, and there are player benches located on both sides. Rules and safety suggestions are posted, but there are no supervisors on site. The rink, which is maintained by the top-notch Johnson County Parks and Recreation Department, is on a first-come, first-served basis. There are no fees for use.

Sheila Kemper Dietrich Park
27th Street and Gillham Road
The first things you'll notice about this mid-town park, named for a big-hearted parks commissioner, are the vivid colors and high contrasts that are especially appealing to visually impaired children. This delightful play area, a concept that has become a national model, is designed to delight chil-dren of different ages with a variety of physical and development abilities.

Another thoughtful feature is the bright animal figures signing letters, a thrill for a hearing-impaired child who can read WELCOME. The park's surface is padded Astroturf instead of sand, so it's suitable for wheelchairs and safer for little ones just beginning to walk. Children will also enjoy playing on the giant pirate ship and bouncing on springy chairs.

Skateboard Park
138th and Switzer
Overland Park, KS
(913) 893-6354
You've gotta love a community that spends $240,000 to build a facility devoted entirely to skateboarding. An Overland Park re-source officer got the balls rolling in Novem-ber 1997, organized students and parents at a local school to help, and convinced the city it was a keen idea. A committee mem-ber coordinated the landscaping as one of his Eagle Scout projects.

The area, complete with ramps, jumps, and rails for all skill levels, is popular with skateboarders and in-line skaters. On nice summer days there's usually a small crowd of people amazed at what these kids can do with a few inches of wood on wheels.

THEATERS FOR YOUNG THESPIANS

How many movie stars can pinpoint the moment they decided to become an actor? Plenty, and often that moment came while watching a play or musical as a child. Perhaps your youngster will catch the acting bug as well, or at least be entertained for an hour or so at one of these made-for-kid theaters. Some of them even offer acting classes (read more in the Education and Child Care section of the Relocation chapter), and one provides a forum for young playwrights.

The Coterie
2450 Grand Boulevard
(816) 474-6552
www.thecoterie.com
Since 1987 this professional acting com-pany has been introducing young people to the joys of live performances. The sub-ject matter is often thought-provoking, with such titles as *Free to Be. . . You and Me* and a look at the horrors of the Holo-caust. But there's light-hearted fare as

well, including a musical starring that silly Pooh Bear. The schedule, available on the Web site, lists the appropriate ages for each performance and often includes ideas for additional study on the subject, a useful feature for parents and teachers.

Regular performances are ongoing throughout the year but vary as to dates and times, so please call. You'll want to pick up the phone anyway; these productions are often sold out weeks in advance. Admission is $10.00 for adults; $8.00 for students, youths 18 and under, and seniors. It's easy to add to the experience by attending after-performance workshops or by taking acting classes that are available for preschool through 12th grade.

Each May the Coterie mounts a Young Playwright's Festival to showcase local talent. It also holds auditions for children and adults every spring; details can be found on the Web site or by calling. The Coterie is located within the Crown Center Shops.

Paul Mesner Puppets
707 West 47th Street
(816) 756-3500
www.paulmesnerpuppets.org
For more than two decades this talented puppeteer has been bringing children's books and classic fables to life using rod puppets (think Kermit and Miss Piggy) and beautifully crafted marionettes. Although the stories often have important messages, it's Paul's wisecracking humor that steals the show. Give him three minutes and you'll forget the variety of silly voices is coming from just one person behind the stage.

Programs, which are held at Unity Temple on the Plaza, usually run four times a year, typically in October, January, March, and July. Call or check the Web site for specific times and dates. Tickets are $6.00. During the rest of the season Paul and his troupe are touring the United States or giving shows at local festivals, events, and children's museums like Wonderscope. Some performances are available on videotape through Paul's

company, Reading Reptile (816-753-0441), a children's bookstore, and Rainy Day Books (913-384-3126).

Theatre for Young America
4881 Johnson Drive
Mission, KS
(913) 831-2131
www.tya.org
For more than 25 years this company's mission has been to foster educational and emotional growth of children through drama. The good news is that children don't even realize they're learning; they're too busy laughing or getting immersed in the actions on stage. TYA, as it's called, mounts eight or nine shows a year in a range of subject matters from ancient to contemporary. The plays are appropriate for preschool ages and up. The staff and volunteers also offer classes in voice, body movement, and conflict management. Individual classes as well as four-day and one-week residencies are available.

The theater is located on the second level of Mission Center Mall at the corner of Roe Boulevard and Shawnee Mission Parkway. Performances last around an hour and are generally held Tuesday through Sunday throughout the year. Single admission prices are $6.00 per person, and group rates and season tickets are available. Call for times and dates of performances.

TWINKLE, TWINKLE, LITTLE STAR

You promised your child the moon and the stars; well, here's your chance to deliver. Kansas City is blessed with a number of observatories in both urban and suburban settings. Pick a cloudless night to introduce your little star to the wonders of the universe. And for the biggest Big Bang for your buck, head out to the giant telescope at Powell Observatory just north of Louisburg, Kansas.

Johnson County Community College
College Boulevard and Quivira Road
Overland Park, KS
(913) 469–8500
www.jccc.org
The astronomy department faculty and students host an "Evening with the Stars" twice a year, usually the first weekend in April and October. After a presentation in the college's small theater, you and your children can file onto the observation deck atop one of the buildings to view the galaxies through a permanently mounted 12-inch reflecting telescope. Smaller telescopes are usually available for the events as well. If skies are cloudy the outdoor program may be canceled.

The event is free, but because of limited space reservations are necessary. Children under 16 must be accompanied by an adult.

Kansas City Museum
3218 Gladstone Boulevard
(816) 483–8300
www.kcmuseum.com
This museum, housed in a fabulous 50-room mansion, includes a planetarium with cool programs for school groups as well as seasonal shows just right for families. Winter Skies, for instance, is held December 11 through March 5. The program lets kids ages 8 and up explore some of the most widely recognized constellations, including Orion the Hunter, Taurus the Bull, and Gemini the Twins. Showtimes are 1:30 P.M. on Friday and 1:00, 1:45, 2:30, and 3:15 P.M. on Saturday and Sunday. The cost is $3.50 per person. Call or check the Web site for other event information.

Powell Observatory
Louis-Young Park
Louisburg, KS
(913) 438–3825
www.askconline.org
This, to use a purely scientific term, is the big Kahuna. Located far from the lights of the city, Powell Observatory has a reflecting telescope with a 30-inch mirror. It's the largest telescope in a five-state area and among the largest in the country that

is available for public viewing.

Members of the Astronomical Society of Kansas City built and maintain the facility and host programs here such as "Starbright Saturday Night." Held every Saturday night from May through October beginning at dusk, the program includes a discussion about a current astronomical event and a short video. A tour of the observatory concludes with taking turns viewing the stars, galaxies, nebulae, moon, and planets through the 30-inch and new 16-inch telescopes. The suggested donation is $3.00 per person. Bring lawn chairs or blankets, and don't forget the bug spray!

In addition to the huge display, society members are usually outside with their own telescopes and are happy to let visitors take a peak. The observatory is also open during major astronomical events; upcoming ones are detailed on the Web site. A map to the site, which is 20 miles south of Kansas City in Lewis Young Park, is also included. You can also book the observatory for special groups such as scout troupes and birthday parties; reservations are required.

Warkoczewski Observatory
800 East 52nd Street
(816) 235–1606
Locate Orion faster than you can say . . . "Warkoczewski," through this 16-inch telescope mounted on the roof of Royall Hall on the University of Missouri–Kansas City campus. The observatory is named for the late Stanley Warkoczewski, a retired sound engineer who, along with his wife, Helen, spent 10 years constructing the telescope in his basement before donating it to the school. A member of the university's physics department, he often gave lectures on astronomy and taught many students how to build their own telescopes. Stan died in 1997 at the age of 91, but we think he's up there, just to the east of Pegasus.

The observatory is open one hour after sunset on clear Fridays from April through November. It's best to call the number above to confirm that it will be available.

ANNUAL EVENTS AND FESTIVALS

A while back a gentleman wrote to the editor of the *Kansas City Star* complaining about what he considered a tragic lack of things to do in our town. Where, he implored, could he take his family when they came to visit in early July? For the next week or so, letters to the newspaper answered him with long lists of fascinating attractions . . . and more than a few offers to help him move out of town.

Perhaps he had missed the previous week's edition listing (for one Saturday alone) festivals celebrating Slavic, Greek, Scottish, African-American, and Hispanic cultures; three garden tours; a rock fest; a folk dance; three free jazz concerts; a fishing derby; the Monkees at the Midland; real monkeys at the zoo; a sailboat regatta; and Elvis Presley's cousin singing "Blue Suede Shoes." And that doesn't even include standbys such as Worlds of Fun, Oceans of Fun, the Truman Library, theaters, art exhibits, or lazy afternoons at a park or lake. Mister, if you can't find something to do in that group, you're not trying hard enough.

So here's our calendar for the rest of you. As you'll see, around here we'll throw a party or start a parade based on little more than that it's Tuesday. Perhaps our love of celebrating comes from our days as a pioneer town; make it through the winter with a few pigs left and one of those porkers will be the guest of honor at a community pig roast. Our Wild West roots also show up in rodeos and barbecues, including the granddaddy of 'em all, the American Royal, but those of you with more refined tastes won't be disappointed. Cultural activities are plentiful whether you're into dance, music, or fine arts. Flamenco guitar in a rose garden, check. *Nutcracker*

Suite from a balcony, check. A 10-city-block outdoor art show, double check.

One of our finest treasures, our diversity, is evident in the number of ethnic festivals held throughout the year. You'll have a chance to taste spanikopita, kimchee, bangers and mash, or alligator on a stick (tastes just like chicken) while listening to a bagpipe, electric guitar, bouzouki, fiddle, steel drum. . . or accordion if you must.

Take a holiday—take two!—and few cities celebrate it better than KC. Our St. Pat's Day parade is third in the country after New York and Philadelphia. Fourth of July takes off with a bang and a boom with no fewer than 24 separate fireworks displays. Even our Halloween is spooktacular, with a dozen haunted houses and pumpkin patches. Winter brings holiday tours of historic homes and the world's most thrilling display of Christmas lights. So come soon, and come often. No matter when you arrive we'll have something wonderful waiting for you.

The events are in Kansas City, Missouri, unless otherwise noted.

JANUARY

Country Club Plaza Holiday Lights
Just in case you haven't seen the Plaza illuminated with 75 miles of jewel-colored lights, you still have until mid-January before they're put away for another year. Then it becomes just your run-of-the-mill, 14-block Spanish-style outdoor shopping center with big-name shops, 40 or so restaurants, and about a million dollars of artwork and fountains. Our favorite view can be seen coming down from the hill on Wornall that runs between the Fairmont and Raphael hotels. It's a breathtaking

moment as the entire postcard picture opens up.

Crown Center Ice Terrace
2450 Grand
(816) 274-8411
www.crowncenter.com
Put on your woolies and catch some frozen action at the city's only outdoor skating rink. You'll be warmed by the hot cocoa and the entire storybook scene. The hours are 10:00 A.M. to 9:00 P.M. daily, and skating lessons are available for little Winter Olympic wannabes. Admission is $5.00 and skate rental is $2.00. And when you're ready to duck inside, the entire Crown Center Complex is at your frozen feet.

Martin Luther King Jr. Celebration
William Jewell College
Liberty, MO
(816) 781-7700
Several communities and churches throughout the Kansas City area honor Dr. King's memory with music, dance, and educational programs so that children and teens can learn about his teachings. The City of Liberty has hosted one of the largest, "Building a Community: Shaping a New Generation," since 1985. Past years have showcased local groups including the Wylliams/Henry Danse Theatre and the William Jewell Concert Choir. The event is free to the public.

Snow Creek Ski Lodge
Weston, MO
(816) 640-2200
www.skipeaks.com
You can hit the ski slopes and still be home in time for dinner at Weston, Missouri, just 40 minutes away. The mini-ski resort offers enough variety to give beginners and expert skiers an afternoon or evening of fun. The 24- to 60-inch base is courtesy of Mother Nature, helped along by 40 snowmaking machines, and trails are accessed via two triple chair lifts, one double chair lift, and rope tows. Après-ski activities take place in the lodge that sports a cafeteria, bar, and lounge along

with a rental shop where the hottest things going—literally—are the snowboards thanks to the 2002 Winter Olympics. There's plenty of time to practice your loops and jumps; weather permitting, the lodge stays open seven days a week through mid-March. Check out more of the cool news in Kidstuff.

FEBRUARY

Art Auction
Kansas City Artists Coalition,
210 Wyandotte
(816) 421-5222
www.kansascityartistscoalition.org
Hope you have some dough left after the holidays, because you'll want to buy something here. The Artists Coalition was formed in the early 1970s as a place where emerging artists could exhibit their work and learn a bit about the other side of creating: publicity and marketing. In 1984 they started this annual event to showcase about 200 artists in categories from ceramics and glass to pastels, found-art sculpture, and oils. For two weeks the work is displayed in the gallery, leading up to the night of the event, which includes a silent auction and live bidding. It's definitely an eclectic crowd, with art patrons in suits and cocktail dresses mingling with artists in blue jeans; sometimes it's the other way around. Actually, no one cares what you're wearing; it's just a wonderful opportunity to see a wide variety of artwork and meet the creators in one place. Appetizers and refreshments are included in the ticket price.

Groundhog Run
Hunt Midwest Underground Facility
Subtropolis
(816) 746-1414
There may be 4 inches of snow on the ground, but it's a relatively toasty 58 degrees in this underground cave. Nearly 3,000 runners vie for prizes in this 5K and 10K race. More than the balmy temperatures, the participants love the flat running

surface. Entrants pay around $15, which gets them a T-shirt and the knowledge that they helped raise funds for a local charity.

Have a Heart for Hope House
B.B.'s Lawnside Bar-B-Q,
1205 East 85th Street
(816) 461–4188, (816) 822–7427

Since 1995 this event has married the four things Kansas Citians love best: jazz, blues, barbecue, and benevolence. The music comes in the form of some top entertainers like Mama Ray, the Rich VanSant Band, and Big John and 39th Street Blues Band. The barbecue doesn't get much better than the ribs at B.B.'s. And it's a fine cause: Hope House is a shelter for women and children who are victims of domestic violence. The joint rocks from noon until seven or so on a Sunday in late February. Advance tickets cost $8.00, $10.00 at the door.

Metropolitan Lawn & Garden Show
Bartle Hall, 13th and Central
(816) 931–4686, (816) 513–5000
www.kcconvention.com

What perfect timing! Just when Midwest-erners can't take another day of gray skies and brown lawns, it's time for the Mid-west's premier lawn and garden show. Landscape designers try to outdo one another with fabulous displays of flower-ing bulbs, trees, and the latest in water gardens. One year's display included 6,000 square feet of waterfalls, fountains, ponds, and even a jumping water demon-stration. Garden ornaments, outdoor furni-ture, and fountains are well represented, and garden experts present programs on lawn care; planting flowers, herbs, and vegetables; and tree maintenance. And if you're still on the fence about fencing, patio materials, and decking, this is the place to ask questions of the dozens of vendors on hand. The three-day event typically takes place in early February. Admission is $7.00 for adults; children under 12 get in free. See the description below for a two-for-one show price.

Remodeling & Decorating Show
Bartle Hall, 13th and Central
(816) 931–4686, (816) 513–5000

This may be the best deal of the year; you can attend this show and the Metropolitan Lawn and Garden Show for the same admission fee. Just wear comfortable shoes because you'll be pounding the concrete for hours. Homeowners who are tackling a major remodeling job will find great products and ideas here, or at least someone to commiserate with. Even folks living in sparkling new houses will want to watch demonstrations on faux painting, wallpapering, and turning bedsheets into fancy curtain swags. More than 250 com-panies, covering almost 200,000 square feet of exhibit space, show the latest home decorating trends as well as prod-ucts and services for roofing, skylights, kitchens and baths, spas, pools, and win-dows and doors. Demonstrations continue throughout the weekend. One year the Duct Tape Guys stuck around to show audience members the many uses of the do-it-yourselfer's best friend. See the lawn and garden show for ticket information.

When attending an event at Bartle Hall, allow an extra 20 minutes for parking. The adjacent garage and lots charge $5.00 and fill up fast. It's often quicker to park a few blocks away (bring change for street meters) and walk back. With 40,000 spaces you're sure to find something. Sometimes a shuttle service is available.

Harlem Globetrotters
Kemper Arena, 1800 Gennessee
(602) 258-0000
www.harlemglobetrotters.com

These court jesters have been entertaining Kansas City for decades, but their antics—and shooting arms—never seem to get tired. Audience participation is a big part of the fun, and there's always a lucky little kid or pretty teen called out on the court. The history is as remarkable as that one-finger basketball trick; since 1927 the team has performed before over 120 million people in 115 countries. That's a lot of dribbling. Logo merchandise including balls, caps, and jerseys is available. Tickets start at $12.

Annual Kansas City Boat Show
Bartle Hall, 13th and Central
(816) 513–5000, (816) 931–4686
www.kcconvention.com
We may be landlocked, but Kansas City has more than its share of recreational lakes dotting our landscape, and the fabulous Lake of the Ozarks is just a few hours away. For more than 25 years this show, the Midwest's biggest, has put thousands of boating and fishing enthusiasts, as well as party-cove sun worshippers, in the mood. It's a pretty awesome sight as Bartle Hall is transformed into a water wonderland complete with an indoor lake just to tempt you to finally buy that first boat, upgrade an existing one, or at least check out the latest fishing gear. All manner of luxury cruisers, fishing boats, ski boats, personal watercraft, and apparel are seeworthy. And if that's not enough, there's usually a celebrity guest appearance. (One year it happened to be a live alligator show.) You'll have plenty of opportunity to see more than 100 boats on view; the show typically lasts Wednesday through Sunday. Adult tickets are $7.00; tadpoles under 12 get in free.

World of Wheels at Bartle Hall
13th and Central
(248) 650–5560
www.worldofwheels.com
You'll see plenty of flash, add-ons, and paint here . . . and that's just the bikini contest participants. Every year about this time, Bartle Hall practically vibrates with testosterone as they roll in every kind of hot rod, rebuilt classic cars, and fancy-detailed motorcycle imaginable. Some of the most popular displays are customized vehicles and bikes that feature incredible paint jobs and pounds of extra chrome. Proud owners vie for top prizes, others just show up to drool. The ticket price of

$12.50 will also let you stand in line to ogle celebrities, women wrestlers, and scantily clad beauties . . . just don't ask to look under the hood. The show usually runs Friday through Sunday.

The RV Show
Bartle Hall, 13th and Central
(816) 513–5000
www.kcconvention.com
Once a year Bartle Hall becomes a super-highway with hundreds of motor homes, trailers, fifth-wheels, custom vans, campers, and minihomes that prove you actually *can* take it with you. And of course dozens of recreational vehicles are on display, ranging from a few thousand dollars to palaces-on-wheels that top out at more than $1 million. Vendors are also on hand with the latest in camping gear and every type of accessory, appliance, and aftermarket product available to make your home-away-from-home more comfortable. Admission to this three-day show is $7.00; children under 12 get in free.

Annual Jazz Ambassador's Fund-Raiser
(816) 753–5277 (recorded message)
www.jazzkc.org
Although the venue and performers change from year to year, this evening always brings out some of the area's most exciting jazz musicians. One year, "Ladies Sing the Blues" provided hours of pretty ballads to get-down-with-it-sister torch songs by Myra Taylor, Lisa Henry, and Sharon Thompson backed by talented trios. The night's proceeds help raise money for musicians in need, everything from paying a gas bill to picking up medical costs. The 400-member Kansas City Jazz Ambassadors started the fund in 1992. Check the Web site or call the information line to find out other jazz performances around town.

Mardi Gras Blues Pub Crawl
Various locations
(816) 531–7557, (913) 649–0383
Count 'em: 21 clubs, 21 bands, and several hundred of your best friends. It all adds

up to the Kansas City Blues Society's annual portable party, when vans take you from club to club all over town. It's a great way to discover a new little joint in Westport or a happening place at 18th and Vine while you leave the driving to someone else. Tickets for the gig—always on Fat Tuesday—cost $10 in advance or $12 at the door of any participating club. The roster includes popular places like Grand Emporium, Blayney's, the Phoenix, and Winslow's City Market BBQ. The highest concentration is midtown, but you can start anywhere and hit as many clubs as you'd like. Just remember that eventually you'll have to navigate your own vehicle safely, so pick a designated driver.

Annual "Little House" Birthday Celebration
Cave Spring, 8701 East Gregory Boulevard
(816) 358-2283
www.cavespring.org
For anyone who loves Laura Ingalls Wilder's books, or the television show they spawned, this charming afternoon party is a must. Activities for young and old include storytelling and a chance for youngsters to experience the daily burdens of pioneer life by grinding wheat and churning butter. Old-fashioned games like sack races and egg tosses keep everyone entertained, plus there are arts and crafts and birthday treats. And here's an interesting twist: Adults get in free while children pay $5.00 in advance or $8.00 at the door. You can learn more about Cave Spring, a marvelous 36-acre nature park and historic site, in the Parks, Lakes, and Recreation chapter.

Polar Bear Plunge
Shawnee Mission Park, 7900 Renner Road
Overland Park, KS
(913) 236-9290
www.kansastorchrun.org
Brrrrr! Since 1998 hundreds of folks have braved icy waters and potential head colds to jump into Shawnee Mission Park Lake. There'd better be a good reason, you say?

There is: Money raised goes to benefit Special Olympics Kansas. Once participants stop shivering (tents are provided for changing into dry clothes), it's time to head to the post-plunge party at Barley's Brewhaus, 16649 Midland. Say, barkeep, can you warm that beer for me please? Prizes are awarded for wimpiest plunge and most outrageous plunge wear, among others. Same-day registration is available for a $50 fee, and participants are encouraged to obtain sponsors to bring in more cold cash. The annual event is hosted by Kansas police officers. Special Olympics is an international program of sports training, education, and athletic competition for individuals with mental retardation. In Kansas, more than 6,000 Special Olympians participate in 21 official sports.

MARCH

First Fridays in the Crossroads Arts District
(816) 472-4546
www.crossroadscommunityassociation.org
Although this street-party-cum-gallery opening happens the first Friday of every month, the crowds really start showing up around March when the weather's better. This near-mile-wide Downtown neighborhood, bounded by 15th Street and Interstate 35, is chock-full of artist studios, galleries, unique shops, and trendy restaurants. In most months, a colorful trolley will take you around the area for free. Most galleries are open until 9:00 P.M.

Annual Easter Egg Hunt
Lake Jacomo
Blue Springs, MO
(816) 795-8200
A tisket, a tasket, grab your Easter basket and join this fun-filled morning when children from three years to third grade scamper for candy-filled eggs. Special guests, like Lulu Bell the Clown and the Easter Bunny, are usually on hand to cheer the little hunters on. A few "magic" eggs with special prizes are hidden

among the others. Registration costs $5.00 and is limited to the first 600 participants, so early reservations are recommended. Make a day of it and enjoy the rest of Fleming Park, which includes the 970-acre Lake Jacomo.

Breakfast with the Easter Bunny
Powell Gardens
Kingsville, MO
(816) 697-2600
www.powellgardens.org
Could anything be sweeter than a three-year-old girl in an Easter bonnet or a toddler in his first tie? You'll see hundreds of them in all their pastel and plaid glory as they anxiously await the arrival of the Easter Bunny. While they're waiting they can dig into pancakes in flavors like blueberry, banana, and chocolate chip. Eggs, however, are not on the menu; they're saved for the Easter Egg hunt when kids up to age 10 scatter throughout the gardens looking for plastic eggs filled with toys and candy. Seeing Powell Garden's display of thousands of spring bulbs is reward enough for most adults. Breakfast with the big guy is typically held the two Saturdays before Easter; the hunt follows the second date only. Breakfast is $6.00 for adults and children over 3, $4.00 for under 3, and it costs $5.00 to participate in the egg hunt, which includes garden admission. Reservations are required for both events.

Annual Home Show
Bartle Hall, 13th and Central
(816) 513-5000
www.kchba.org
Keeping up with the Joneses is a national obsession, and for over 50 years this show has been showing area residents how to do it right. At more than 600 displays in space equivalent to eight football fields you'll see the latest techniques, products, and services available to remodel, decorate, secure, or beautify your home. There must be a dozen bubbling hot tubs alone. If you're in the market for a new home, you'll have a chance to meet with area builders and look through sample house plans.

And because this event is combined with the Kansas City Flower, Lawn, and Garden Show, you'll get expert advice on landscaping, or simply a chance to tiptoe through the tulips in the waterways and floral displays. Demonstrations showing everything from tree pruning to floral arranging are staged throughout the weekend; past shows have brought in nationally known experts like Mr. Fix-It. Concession stands offer hot dogs, snacks, and beverages. You can even take home more than just a bag full of product brochures; Wayside Waifs will be on-site with adorable, adoptable cats and dogs. In past years more than 100 pets have found new homes at the show. The Home Builders Association of Greater Kansas City sponsors the four-day showcase. Admission is $7.00 for adults, $6.00 for seniors and students. Children 12 and under are admitted free.

Snake Saturday Parade and Festival
Downtown North Kansas City, MO
(816) 274-6000
www.nkc.org
Yes, Bridget, there is a St. Paddy's Day parade north of the river, and it's a doozy. This pretty little community practically doubles in size—or at least in shades of green—as 100,000 people show up the Saturday before St. Patrick's Day for an all-day party. A parade winds its way downtown with more than 150 cars, bands, and floats, and the post-parade activities offer something for the entire family. Enjoy carnival rides, arts and crafts booths, and enough green beer to forever change the course of the Missouri River. Irish dance troupes and musical groups perform as well. The fun starts at 9:00 A.M. and is free.

Brookside St. Pat's Warm-Up Parade
Meyer Boulevard and Wornall
(816) 523-5553
www.brooksidekc.org
You might call this our St. Patrick's Day parade on training wheels, but it's still an impressive sight as floats, bands, clowns, community groups, antique cars, and

dogs dressed in green wind their way through this pretty neighborhood. Come to think of it, with thousands of spectators, this parade is bigger than most cities put on all weekend, and we're just getting started. The parade starts around 2:00, but get here earlier because there are always fun goings-on like musical entertainment, dancing, food, and ale. But pace yourself: The big parade is less than 24 hours away.

St. Patrick's Day Parade
Downtown
(816) 931-7373
www.kcirish.org
Although our official St. Patrick's Day parade got a late start compared with some other cities, we soon showed them how to transform green crepe paper into a world-class float. Outrageous radio host Mike Murphy got the ball rolling on March 17, 1972, while having lunch (and perhaps a beer or two) with three friends at a downtown restaurant. They decided what Kansas City needed was a St. Pat's parade, by golly, so they whipped up a sign, put a green bow on somebody's dog, and began a tradition that's become the third largest parade in the country. These days about 350,000 people crowd the streets to cheer on more than 200 colorful floats, politicians in convertibles, high school marching bands, pretty girls dancing jigs, pipe and drum corps, an Elvis look-alike or two, and a contingency of kazoo players. It hasn't been without its problems; one year we watched in horror as a radio station mascot, a 40-foot inflatable fox with sunglasses and a guitar, got caught in overhead wires. They had to shoot him.

For those really in the spirit, the day starts at Browne's Market (3300 Pennsylvania Avenue), where an authentic Irish breakfast is served along with music and dancing as early as 6:00 A.M. After the parade it's traditional to join the masses on the streets of Westport. Once the crowds were so large they actually had to close the doors to Kelly's Westport Inn.

APRIL

Art at the Center
(formerly Art in the Woods)
Overland Park Convention Center
6000 College Boulevard
Overland Park, KS
(913) 895-6357
www.artkc.com
The Overland Park Arts Commission has been setting up this temporary art gallery since 1982. In 2003 it moved to a new home in the lower level of the new convention center. More than 120 artists are represented each year in the juried show, with work that includes photography, oils, watercolors, and abstracts. The art is for sale; prices range from $200 to more than $9,000. The free show is usually open for two or three weeks beginning in late April.

Civil War on the Border
Mahaffie Stagecoach Stop,
1100 Kansas City Road
Olathe, KS
(913) 782-6972
www.olatheks.org
As the first overnight stagecoach stop on the Santa Fe Trail outside Westport Landing, this place saw its share of wranglers, riders, and families heading west. It also got caught in the border skirmishes between Missouri and the Free State. In fact, these battles predated the Civil War by four years. Reenactors dressed as infantry, cavalry, and artillery soldiers will relive Civil War days as Yanks and Rebs mix it up during this two-day event. The cannon booms will be enough to knock you out of your seat! More cordial activities are on tap as well: an 1860 fashion show, a wedding, and a Missouri Town Dance. Demonstrations throughout the weekend will shed light on the frontier town lifestyle, and the vittles and sarsaparilla will tide you over until the next stagecoach pulls up bound for Dodge.

Earth Day at the Zoo
Kansas City Zoo
(816) 513-4630
www.kansascityzoo.org
This annual Party for the Planet offers a
chance to commune with nature and talk
to the animals. Tree-huggers can participate in a 3-mile walkathon for a $10 con-
tribution, and interactive games for every
age are found throughout the park. And
here's your chance to pick up some Zoo
Manoo at the compost sale. A small container goes for $6.00, a truckload is
$70.00. So *that's* Harry's secret to his two-
pound tomatoes! Admission to the day's
activities is $6.00 for adults and $3.00 for
kids. If you ask us, it's a dung deal.

Kansas City Indian Market and
Southwest Show
Overland Park International Trade
Center, 6800 West 115th Street
Overland Park, KS
(913) 451-7691
www.indianmarket.net
America's top-rated festival for Indian,
Southwest, Western, and wildlife art has
set up shop on the Kansas plains (actually
a very nice exhibition hall) for more than
12 years, attracting more than 300 artists
from 40 states and five countries. This is a
rare opportunity to talk to and buy
directly from the artists who are present
throughout the three-day show. The jewelry displays alone are staggering and
include everything from delicate earrings
for a few dollars to extravagant turquoise
necklaces worth thousands. Other art
includes pottery, paintings, woven items,
and feathered headdresses. But there's
more to do than just buy treasures; stage
acts include native Indian dances, music,
and storytelling, and an authentic tepee
shows the Plains Indian lifestyle during the
1800s. Kids will enjoy the balloon art, face
painting, and a chance to practice dance
steps set to drumbeats. The festival is well
known for its variety and exceptional pricing and typically draws as many as
20,000 visitors from as far away as Japan,
Germany, and Australia. Check the Web

site for special discounts at nearby hotels.
Adults pay $10.00 at the door, and a sin-
gle admission is good for all three days.
Children under 13 get in free. Parking is
plentiful and free.

Festival of Wines
American Heart Association Benefit
(913) 648-6727
www.standardbeverage.com/KCFW
This is one party your cardiologist might
actually prescribe. You'll get to consume
some heart-healthy wine and raise money
for the American Heart Association at the
same time. Each year more than 1,500 big-
hearted guests show up to sample 300 or
so wines from some of the world's top
vineyards. In just six years it has become,
according to *USA Today,* one of "the most
popular wine festivals in the USA." The gala
kicks off Friday night with a five-course
wine dinner (at $200 a pop) starring a
celebrity vintner such as Bob Mondavi. On
Sunday the main event includes a grand
wine and food tasting, live jazz music and
dancing, and a live auction. Festivalgoers
get a chance to schmooze with the wine-
makers while chefs from local restaurants
demonstrate tips for cooking with wine. A
live auction caps the evening as bidders vie
for rare and fine wine lots, a trip to the California wine country, giftware, and restaurant certificates. Tickets to Sunday's event
are $50 per person in advance and $60 at
the door and include a commemorative
wineglass and corkscrew. So far, thirsty
donors have helped raise more than
$500,000 for the cause. The gala is held at
a different location each year. Call for current information.

Pembroke Hill School Clothesline Sale
State Line Road & Ward Parkway
(816) 936-1200
This is without a doubt the most incredible garage sale in the Midwest. It takes
volunteers weeks just to sort, tag, and display the wares, including everything from
baby clothes to furniture, shoes to golf
clubs, and antiques to jars of marbles. For
those who don't know, Pembroke is a

school for mostly privileged students, so their families' cast-offs often sport designer labels. Oh, you'll still find the occasional lamp you wouldn't wish on your brother-in-law, but for the most part it's all primo stuff. Call the school for dates, or watch for the big banners displayed on the school grounds a week or two in advance. It costs $2.00 to shop from 9:00 to 11:00 A.M. on opening day (worth it!); otherwise it's free.

Kansas City Royals Opening Day
Kauffman Stadium
(800) 6ROYALS
www.kcroyals.com

The boys are back, the wait is over, and baseball season is officially open at "The K." Opening weekend usually falls within the first week in April, and people dress in blue and challenge their vocal cords. Sunday's game includes a special Kids Opening Day celebration including a post-game fun run and gifts. Learn more about this beautiful ballpark and the Royals in Sports.

Spring Homes Tour
(816) 942–8800
www.kchba.org

Find your new home or just see how the other half lives at the second largest scattered home show in the country. For more than 40 years members of the Kansas City Home Builders Association have been giving us their best and most beautiful every spring with abodes ranging from $120,000 to close to $2 million. The last group usually boasts closets big enough to have their own zip codes. Many are fully furnished, giving lookers a chance to check out the latest in decorating trends. The tour spans eight counties and includes close to 500 homes. Free admission, but there is a price: You may not want to go home again.

Symphony Designer's Showhouse
Different location each year
(816) 968–9711
www.showhouse.org

Some of the area's most beautiful homes and talented interior designers come together once a year to create this benefit for the Kansas City Symphony. Each year a different home is selected, but it's always a magnificent specimen, often a minimansion along Ward Parkway. The empty house is open for a week or so in February for public previews before a single can of paint is opened and then closed while more than 40 interior designers, landscape professionals, builders, architects, and artists work their magic. The finished showhouse is dressed to the nines, and it's interesting to see how each team of designers or individual interprets the room he or she has chosen to decorate. An on-site boutique sells a variety of goods such as jewelry, herb topiaries, and garden art. Preview tickets cost $5.00, and admission for the completed showhouse, which is usually open for three weeks, costs $12.00 at the door or $10.00 when purchased in advance at various outlets. No infants or children under 8 years of age are admitted.

MAY

Americana Weekend
Agricultural Hall of Fame
Bonner Springs, KS
(913) 722–9300
www.santafetrails.org

Head west—all the way to Kansas City, Kansas—to celebrate our city's importance as gatekeeper to the California, Oregon, and Santa Fe Trails. Even if you don't get something out of the history lesson, you'll find other reasons to celebrate, like good food and fun family activities. The weekend includes three different events in one, including one of the season's first official barbecue contests, the Blue Devil Cook-Off, where smokers vie for top prizes. The Prairie Winds Kite Festival, sponsored by local company Windwizards (913–856–0145, www.windwizards.com), fills the periwinkle-blue Kansas sky with colorful kites in various shapes like dragons and gigantic, two-handled dual-line fliers that require more than a little dexterity. More grounded fun comes with the yo-yo contest. Or put your feet to work by two-stepping and toe tapping to cowboy, Celtic, and acoustic music at the Santa Fe Trails Bluegrass Festival. The weekend also offers a juried craft show featuring more than 40 exhibitors and lots of food and drink. This always brings in a crowd of locals as well as out-of-town campers. Admission ranges from $5.00 to $20.00, a weekend ticket costs $45.00, and camping is available for $5.00 and up.

Annual Bachathon
Grace and Holy Trinity Cathedral, 13th and Broadway
(816) 474–8260
www.ghtc-kc.org

All Bach, all the time. Some 22 years ago someone at this downtown cathedral got the bright idea that folks might like to hear six nonstop hours of the master's most famous concerti and cantatas. They were right, and today standing-room-only crowds fill the chapel to hear a 28-voice choral ensemble and masters playing the 33,000-pipe house organ. In years past selections have included the *Brandenburg Concerto V* and *Goldberg Variations*. Although most guests choose to listen to a few selections and quietly leave (wait here, I'll be bach), it's not unusual for true music lovers to stay put for the entire program. If that's you, bring a cushion for the pew. Cookies and beverages are available, and the surroundings are divine. Mostly Norman French in architecture, the cathedral has a classic Gothic arch and two magnificent Tiffany stained-glass windows. The event is typically held the first

---

For up-to-the-minute listings of events, check the Star *Friday Preview (www.kansascity.com),* Pitch Weekly *(pitch.com), www.gointokansascity.com, and the current issue of* Kansas City *magazine.*

Sunday in May and begins at 2:00 P.M., but you'll want to be there long before then to get a seat.

Antiques on the Common
Greenwood, MO (approximately 25 miles southeast of Kansas City)
(816) 537–7822

If only magazines like *Country Living* would stop showing up, we could keep this one-day antiques extravaganza our little secret. But nooooo, they have to tell the world about the goods brought in from dealers in 15 states, the jaw-dropping prices—and the blueberry cream pie. It takes Claire Fellows about two months to set up all the tents and picnic areas, one day to sell out, and about two weeks to recuperate before she starts it all again for the September sale. Expect to find an enormous variety in every price range. If the $5,000 cabinet is too rich for your blood, check down the way; there's a less-rare version for $180. Other goodies include highly collectible tramp art, baskets, penny rugs, and tons of folk art. Ask Claire, who also owns Country Heritage and Friends antiques shop, for a flyer with directions and a list of places to stay while you're in town. And plan to get there early; about 1,500 or so shoppers with fire in their eyes and "I saw it first!" on their lips show up for this one.

Brookside Art Fair
63rd Street between Wornall and Main
(816) 523–5553
www.brooksidekc.org

The art fair season officially opens at this outdoor exhibit held in the charming village known as Brookside. It seems more tents are added each year, but still the sidewalks and streets overflow as 40,000 people wiggle their way in for a better look at silver earrings, a photo of the Plaza lights, an azure glass vase, or a pastel landscape.

About 195 artists are represented, grateful for a chance to talk to art lovers and sell work without paying commission. And because it is the first major show of the season, most of the artists do quite well, averaging $6,700 for the weekend. Children get a chance to create, too; at the Baptist Hospital tent they can create cards for patients. The art of eating well is also on display in food booths operated by local restaurants. A terrific addition for the past 10 years or so has been the Share-A-Chair Silent Auction, where area artists decorate chairs, frames, and birdhouses that are then auctioned off. Proceeds benefit two local chapters of Habitat for Humanity. The fair, usually held the first weekend in May, also corresponds nicely with the opening of Joe D's wine bar patio, a terrific place to sit and admire your new prize.

Cinco de Mayo Fiesta
Guadalupe Center,
1015 Avenida Cesar E. Chavez
(816) 471-2582
www.guadalupecenter.org
In 2001 Kansas City's Latino community had another reason to celebrate the anniversary of Mexico's victory over the French army: It broke ground for a $5.1 million cultural and culinary arts center that quadrupled the Guadalupe Center's size. It's a fitting tribute, and needed space, for a population that has doubled in Kansas and Missouri in the last decade and tripled in Johnson County. During that time the May celebration has been growing, too, with mariachi and local bands, folkloric dance, games, pony rides, and lots of tasty food. Just down the street, a Mexican breakfast and Mariachi Mass is held at Our Lady of Guadalupe Shrine. Admission is free.

Fiesta in the Heartland
City Market
(816) 472-6767
www.hispanicchamberofcommercekc.com
Just as not everyone wearing a "Kiss me, I'm Irish" button on St. Pat's Day has ties to Ireland, not everyone dancing salsa at this celebration is Latino. About 10,000 festivalgoers crowd City Market each May 1 to hear nationally known Tejano singers and Latino bands, practice salsa and cha-

cha slide dances, and sweat off about three pounds in the jalapeño-eating contest. Hola! Less incendiary foods are available as well, including grilled tenderloin, tamales, and ice cream. Children will be treated to face painting, piñatas, and visits with sports teams' mascots.

Azteca Fiesta
Rosedale Park, 35th and Booth
Kansas City, KS
(816) 931-6468
The first Azteca event in 1991 drew an impressive crowd of a few thousand; today more than 15,000 people attend the multiday festival. The fun begins on May 1 with a parade down Southwest Trafficway and then, depending on how the dates fall, continues the next weekend with a children's parade and three-day carnival with clowns and karate demonstrations. Everyone has a chance to learn more about the varied and colorful Latino culture with folkloric dance and music. Food vendors are on hand to sell delicious authentic cuisine, and fireworks illuminate the sky behind the park's majestic Rosedale Memorial Arch on Sunday night.

Kids Fishing Derby
Old Lake Jacomo on Beach Road
Blue Springs, MO
(816) 229-8980, ext. 16
Hey, kids, grab your fishing pole and head out to this fishing contest made just for little tadpoles. Since 1988 this one-day event, open to kids ages 2 through 15, reels 'em in with fun-filled activities and a casting contest. The first 100 kids to show up get a free cane pole; registration begins at 8:00 A.M. Children should bring an adult (aw, shucks), fishing pole, bait, and bucket to hold all that catch. Even if the line is a loser, every kid will take home a prize like fishing tackle and sporting goods.

Festival of Creativity
Crown Center Square
(816) 274-8444
www.crowncenter.com
Kids, parents, and teachers earn bragging

rights at this annual celebration to show-case the artistic and musical talents of high school students throughout the metropolitan area. More than 75 schools are represented by bands, dancers, and individual singers, as well as visual arts. Some of the most impressive elements are the all-metro orchestra, band, and choir that bring students from different schools together in perfect harmony—after just one day of rehearsal. The event is free.

Heritage Hikes
Various locations
(816) 235-1448 (Communiversity),
(816) 931-8448 (Historic Kansas City
Foundation)
Each spring the Historic Kansas City Foundation and Communiversity join up for educational and entertaining strolls through the city's varied and vibrant neighborhoods and historic sites. Past hikes, which usually lasted three hours or so, have included the Northeast, Downtown, and Hyde Park Districts, giving walkers an up-close look at everything from Victorian homes to turn-of-the-20th-century warehouses-turned-condos. Reservations are necessary, and fees range from $10 for one hike to $25 for three. Other walking tours are hosted throughout the year for around $3.00 each; contact the Foundation for dates and details.

Party at Barney
12th Street between Central and
Wyandotte
www.kcmo.org
This party includes plenty of music, food, and a chance to mingle with others who live and/or work downtown, along with a few folks trekking in from the suburbs. A highlight is the latest five or six public art installations along Central Street, called the Avenue of the Arts. Admission and parking are free.

Plaza Live! Courtyard Concerts
Locations around the Country Club Plaza
(816) 753-0100
www.countryclubplaza.com

You may not hear the tune, "The Best Things in Life Are Free," but you'll experience it firsthand during this free music concert series that lasts from May through the fall. Some of the area's top musicians plug it in and lay it down at courtyards throughout the Plaza, including the Penguin located by Scandia Down, Mermaid near Eddie Bauer, and Neptune outside Houston's. The music ranges from jazz and pop to blues and Dixieland, with performers like Skip Hawkins Trio, Boulevard Band, Krazy Kats, Max Groove, Ida McBeth, and Angela Hagenbach. Listen up from 5:00 to 8:00 P.M. Thursday and Friday and 2:00 to 5:00 P.M. Saturday and Sunday.

Truman Days
Independence Square
Independence, MO
(816) 325-7111
www.visitindependence.com
We prove we're still wild about Harry every year as we celebrate his birthday. It's a fine excuse to visit the museum, home, and courthouse that bear the name of the beloved 33rd American president.

Westport Irish Festival
Westport
(816) 756-2789
www.kcirishfest.org
This annual festival should tide you over during those lean months between March 17 and the Labor Day Irish fest in Brookside. And because the St. Paddy's Day party always ends up in Westport, this is a chance to reclaim any lost cars, keys, or shamrock earrings. It's also simply a fine way to enjoy the spring weather and celebrate the area's Celtic origins.

A highlight of the two-day event is always the traditional and contemporary Irish music. In the past, local beauty and internationally acclaimed Connie Dover has thrilled the crowds along with favorites The Elders, Shenanigans, and Eddie Delahunt. The children's area offers games and arts and crafts like Celtic rubbings, along with Irish dancing, pipers and exhibits for the whole family. Stout and ale flow, and authentic cuisine from across the pond is available. Tickets are $5.00 for adults; there is no charge for children under 12.

JUNE

Corporate Woods Jazz Festival
Antioch and College Boulevard
Overland Park, KS
(913) 661-5459

An opportunity to hear three days of non-stop music from Kansas City headliners—free? Count us in, along with about 40,000 other jazz lovers who've been showing up for the fresh air, great music, and Cajun sausages for more than 14 years now. Lineups have included artists like Ken Navarro, the Greg Meise Quartet, Ida McBeth, Angela Hagenbach, and the New Red Onion Jazz Babies.

The venue couldn't be better. The rolling hills of Corporate Woods, a 294-acre office park blessed with 30 varieties of trees, picnic tables, jogging trails, and a winding woodland stream, provide opportunities to get some private time with your own Sophisticated Lady. As for the Cajun 'dogs, they're just one of dozens of festival foods to tempt you, including barbecue, onion blossoms, frozen margaritas, beer, and sweet treats. Several of the artists will have CDs for sale. Festival T-shirts and raffle tickets raise money for local charities. Bring lawn chairs, picnic baskets, kids, and dogs. Parking is plentiful around the corporate park.

Croatian Day Picnic
Fourth and Barnett
Kansas City, KS
(913) 788-9758

You'll find your thrill on Strawberry Hill at this annual celebration that's more than 75 years old. It's a chance to discover the all-too-often overlooked *other* Kansas City, a town with a rich heritage and vibrant neighborhoods of Slavic families. Lively polkas will get you dancing, but it's the

food that will make you swoon: tender cabbage leaves stuffed with meat, onions, and rice; grilled sausages; and a flavorful sweet bread with layer after layer of ground walnuts and spices called povatica. Plus you'll have a chance to tour the Strawberry Hill Museum with parishioners of St. John's Catholic Church.

Dog-N-Jog Run-Fur-Fun
Mill Creek Park
(913) 596-1000
www.hsgkc.org

Each year from 800 to 1,000 dogs and their owners come out to enjoy this pretty park on the Country Club Plaza while they help contribute to the Humane Society of Greater Kansas City. Amazingly, the fur rarely flies, as most doggies enjoy the company. Plus they get massages and treats for rewards. Vendors are also on hand with pet-related products, and pure-bred rescue groups have terrific dogs available for adoption; in fact purebreds account for 25 percent of shelter animals. Participation in the fun run costs $15.

Downtown Overland Park Days
Metcalf Avenue between
78th and 83rd Streets
Overland Park, KS
(913) 642-2222

This ain't your daddy's Old Overland Park; during this two-day event, the quiet Downtown district rocks with R&B music, roving entertainers, a beer garden, and an old-fashioned street dance. An Avenue of the Arts features more than 70 local and regional artists and crafters, and the kid's carnival keeps little ones entertained with a petting zoo, clowns, and games. The farmers' market will stay open until all the luscious fresh produce has sold out, and even then you won't go hungry; more than 50 food vendors will tempt you with grilled chicken, barbecue, snacks, and frozen treats. Downtown's unique shops and restaurants will also be open to serve you. Donation is $2.00 at the gate.

Great Lenexa Barbecue Battle
Sar-Ko-Par Trails Park
Lenexa, KS
(913) 541-8592
www.lenexa-kansas.com
Ummm, smell that hickory smoke? Just follow it to find one of the country's biggest barbecue battles. The word "battle" is right: Each year about 160 teams compete for the chance to take home the coveted trophy. A panel of 300 judges rates seven categories of meat, including brisket, pork, chicken, ribs, and sausage, and although that might sound like a cushy job, it's actually hard work. The fun begins on Friday evening as the smoke masters prepare giant cookers and closely guarded sauce recipes and then stay close through the night to regulate the heat. On Saturday morning while they're sweating out the judging, the rest of us can enjoy live music and kiddie games. The best part comes after the grand champion is crowned and the crowd is invited to taste the best barbecue in the state of Kansas.

Halfway to Hollywood Film Festival
Area movie theaters
www.halfway2hollywood.com
This is a movie purist's dream, featuring 60 independent films, more than 100 screenings, and live appearances by filmmakers. The multiday, multivenue festival began in 2001 as a cultural and educational event dedicated to the exhibition and preservation of independent and classic cinema. It offers several themed series, including foreign and American independent films, most of which are premiering in Kansas City; a sci-fi fest of films made or released in the 1950s, with primitive special effects that are often hilarious; and a tribute to a producer or director. All screenings take place in KC's cool little art-film palaces like the Rio, the Fine Arts, and the Englewood. Admission is $30 for passes to all movies or all events; $50 will get you in to the whole shebang.

Heart of America Shakespeare Festival
Southmoreland Park,
47th Street and Oak
(816) 531-7728
www.kcshakes.org
The play's the thing, and since 1992 this lively event has been our opportunity to brush up on the Bard. For four weeks from late June through July, professional actors, many of whom also appear at Missouri Repertory Theatre, perform one or two of Shakespeare's plays on a rotating basis each Tuesday through Sunday. There is no performance on July 4. The plays are different each season, but you can expect a sword fight or two, love lost then found, and at least one episode of mistaken identity. And the setting is straight out of Romeo and Juliet: a lovely little park near the Nelson-Atkins Museum of Art.

Don't miss the preshow at 6:15 P.M., when actors do hilarious send-ups of the Bard's plays. Audience participation is heartily encouraged; nay, it's often mandatory as "volunteers" are plucked from the crowd of onlookers. The play begins at 8:00 P.M. Admission is free, but donations are welcome. A limited number of reserved seats are available for $10 and may be purchased through Central Ticket Office (888-286-4849) at least 24 hours in advance. Most folks simply bring a lawn chair, a blanket, and a picnic basket. Or you may reserve a boxed dinner that includes a sandwich, side dish, and dessert. Orders must be placed at least 48 hours in advance. Refreshments are also available at the site.

Jazz, Blues & Fine Arts Riverjam
English Landing Park
Parkville, MO
(816) 880-9026
www.parkvilleevents.com
What an enchanting evening this makes, sitting under the stars listening to jazz with the fairy-tale spire of Park University glowing in the distance. Parkville has always had a getaway kind of feel to it thanks to an old-fashioned Main Street filled with antiques shops and galleries.

The annual jazz fest turns the attention from shopping to its lovely park along the banks of the Missouri River.

There's always an impressive lineup of local musicians. And although it's highly unlikely you'll get bored with the music or tents of arts and crafts, you can always stroll along the groomed trails or visit the nearby nature sanctuary. See the Parks, Lakes, and Recreation chapter for more information about this 115-acre reserve. There's no charge for the jazz fest, and you may bring a cooler for snacks but no alcohol. Food, beer, wine, and other beverages are available at the festival.

Jazz Lover's Pub Crawl
Multiple locations
(816) 753–JASS (5277)
www.jazzkc.org
You'll want to get plenty of sleep the night before this annual bash, because it offers 20 or so nightclubs, dozens of top-name musicians and singers, and enough fun to last until the last bus departs. The music starts wailing at 8:00 P.M. at locations that range from River Market and Downtown, to the 18th and Vine District, to Westport and the Plaza. You'll find everything from crowded little joints to fancy-schmancy restaurants in the mix, all packed with jazz lovers getting their grooves on. Find a favorite chair and stay there all night if you like, or do what most folks do: Hit as many nightspots as you can. You're sure to discover a favorite new place or artist who takes your breath away. Tickets, available at the clubs, are $10 in advance and $15 at the door. Your hosts are the Kansas City Jazz Ambassadors, a high-class organization that's been teaching us to crawl for more than 20 years.

Jazzoo
Kansas City Zoo
(816) 513–5800
www.kansascityzoo.org
Things can get pretty wild at this black-tie gala, and we're not just talking about exotic animals pacing a few hundred feet

away. Jazzoo has Kansas City's social elite doing the jungle-boogie all night long, spurred on by music, dancing, and fine wines. And with the aroma of gourmet food prepared by 80 top chefs, it's amazing there aren't a few uninvited guests, like a hungry lion or two. At least the penguins know to dress appropriately. Tickets (at $150 a pop) usually sell out within days. Profits benefit the Zoo Learning Fund.

Juneteenth Celebration
Various locations
(816) 483–1300
www.blackarchives.org
With something for everyone—young and old, all races and backgrounds—this event has grown into a celebration of life. Black Archives of Mid-America Inc. has played host for more than 23 years, and each year the group outdoes itself with activities like a golf tournament at Swope Park, crowning of Mr. and Mrs. Juneteenth, a block party at the Historic 18th and Vine District, and a motorcycle and car show. Kids have their own activities area with games, a chance to climb on a fire engine, and a share in the African-American culture. Local musicians keep the crowds entertained, while food vendors keep everyone happy with barbecue, grilled corn on the cob, and refreshments. The grand finale always showcases a top national musical group. The public is invited to attend the main celebration for free; other events like the golf tourney include a registration fee.

Lake Fest
Missouri Town 1855
Fleming Park, Blue Springs, MO
(816) 795–8200
This is an incredible evening for the entire family, with boat and personal watercraft rides, water games, arts and crafts, and foods of the summer. Live entertainment and a fireworks display continue the fun into the night. The fun begins at 5:00 P.M. Admission is $7.00 per vehicle, $3.00 per walk-in.

Lee's Summit Festival of the Arts
Downtown Lee's Summit, MO
(816) 246–6598
www.leesummitmainstreet.org
Invite some folks over to your block party and watch your population double overnight. That's what happens as soon as music—including rock, country, acoustic, blue grass, and jazz—starts playing in every corner, alley, and parking lot within the 6-block Downtown area. Add more than 400 crafts, food, and commercial booths and, buddy, you've got yourself a festival. Plenty of people agree; the three-day fair, usually held the first week in June, can bring in as many as 80,000 guests. And just to prove they're good neighbors, admission is free.

Old Shawnee Days
57th and Cody
Shawnee, KS
(913) 248–2360
www.cityofshawnee.org
On any given day, Old Shawnee Town offers an interesting look at frontier living in the late 1800s. Its 17 original and repli- cated structures include the 1843 territo- rial jail, a general store, a bank, and a funeral parlor. But during the annual Old Shawnee Days festival, the place really comes alive (even the funeral parlor) with a parade, carnival, battle of the bands, and big musical guests. Headliners have been '70s bands like Ozark Mountain Daredev- ils, Starship, Firefall, and Liverpool, a Beat- les' cover band. Other activities have included historical reenactors, a live alliga- tor wrestling show, and a cutest baby con- test. No doubt these last two events were held on opposite sides of the fairground. All the usual festival food is available, and admission is free.

Rose Day in the Park
Loose Park
(816) 784–5300
We can't think of a more lovely way to spend the first Saturday in June than sur- rounded by thousands of rose bushes in Kansas City's prettiest urban park. This event is hosted by the Rose Society of Greater Kansas City, a club founded in 1931 to prove that roses could indeed grow here despite our zone-five rating and rather stubborn clay. And grow they do. The Laura Conyers Smith Municipal Rose Garden started with 120 bushes, and now the 2½-acre park has more than 4,000 plants in 125 varieties. This fragrant sea of pink and salmon, red and flame, lavender and deepest lipstick, also includes a fountain and reflecting pool, benches, and pretty limestone and timber pergolas. The organization hosts other events throughout the year, including classes on caring for roses.

Scottish Highlands Games
Wyandotte County Fairgrounds
Kansas City, KS
(913) 432–6823
www.kcscottishgames.org,
www.kcscot.com
It's amazing, Grace, what fun you can have at this annual festival filled with Celtic music and mirth. The traditional jigs, bal- lads, and reels go back to the 16th cen- tury, and favorites like "Scotland the Brave," "Caledonia," and of course "Amaz- ing Grace" are easily recognized. You'll hear them all performed by bagpipes, drums, fiddles, bouzoukis, and voice. The Celtic harp, in fact, provides one of the most popular hands-on events, "Cuddle a Clarsach." Traditional costumes and danc- ing are also on tap, including the thrilling Scottish National style made popular by River Dance. Children will enjoy story- telling, face painting, and a chance to pose with Nessie, the Loch Ness Monster. And of course you'll have a chance to cheer on 50 or so big, burly men in kilts as they hurl 16-pound stones and Scottish war hammers for prizes (hopefully not at the audience). Tickets to the two-day event are $8.00, $3.00 for ages 7 to 12, and free for 6 and under. Bring two cans to donate to Harvester's Food Pantry to save $1.00 on each ticket.

**St. Dionysios Greek Orthodox
Church Festival
8100 West 95th Street
Overland Park, KS
(913) 341-7373**
Why anyone would miss this festival is Greek to us. Every year the church grounds are transformed into an agora (marketplace) with a boutique filled with embroidered blouses, "worry beads," and sailor hats and a taverna set with succulent food. Fill your plate with leg of lamb, chicken baked in lemon sauce, a gyro sandwich, and traditional side dishes and pastries. While dining you'll be entertained by dancers clapping and twirling to the distinctive sounds of bouzouki. Eat fast—they need your table for dancing!

Parish members are proud of their heritage and their church, and tours are given throughout the two-day festival. The icons, Bishop's throne, and the Pantokrator painted on the ceiling are beautiful . . . but isn't the music starting up again? Opa! Admission and parking are free, and proceeds from sales of food and goods go to benefit church community services.

**Sugar Creek Slavic Festival
11520 East Putnam
Sugar Creek, MO
(816) 833-0192
www.slavicfest.com**
Here's your chance to overcome your polkaphobia with a healthy dose of Slavic food, dance, and the happy sounds of accordion music. The festival started in 1986 to celebrate customs brought over from Slovenia, Croatia, Hungary, Romania, and Poland in the mid-1800s. The savory food alone will make you want to add a few consonants to your surname, including sarma (stuffed cabbage rolls), kielbasa (Polish sausage), and povitica (rolled walnut bread). Traditional Slavic music and dancing are the mainstays of the two-day event, and guests have a chance to join in the kolo circle dances. This phrase may come in handy as you're finishing that second sausage: "Zedan Sam," which means I am thirsty. No problem; cold beer

and beverages are just a dance step away. It's all happening at the Mike Onka Memorial Building, with proceeds benefiting North American Croatian Relief and local civic improvement projects.

**Sunset Safaris
Kansas City Zoo
(816) 513-5800
www.kansascityzoo.org**
During the dog days of summer, the zoo stays open every Thursday until 8:30 P.M. to take advantage of cooler temperatures. You'll be welcomed by train rides, music and games, and animals that are usually more active in the evening. Sunset Safaris run from early June through mid-August. Check the Web site or see Kidstuff for more information about the zoo.

JULY

**Kansas City Spirit Festival
Penn Valley Park
(816) 221-4444
www.spiritfest.org**
We're a little dizzy from following this event around, but it's definitely worth nailing down. The first Spirit Fest took off on the Fourth of July 1984, and people are still talking about the lineup of '60s hitmakers like Herman's Hermits and Paul Revere and the Raiders along with stages packed with current bands.

For several years the event dominated the Labor Day roster. Its sponsors moved it to July in 2003. Check the Web site to be sure, or simply listen for the crowds; no matter when or where it lands it's always Kansas City's biggest chance to hear headliners like baby boomer favs Eddie Money, Huey Lewis and The News, and the B-52s. Other musical styles, including gospel, Tejano, country, rock, reggae, R&B, and acoustic, appear on the international and showcase stages. The electronic music showcase features forward-thinking genres like house, trance, and techno.

You can take a break from the tunes (or mindless noise from the techno groups) and catch a carnival ride, visit arts and crafts tents, or take the kids to see storytellers, clowns, and jugglers in the Children's Pavilion. More than 20 food vendors will make sure you don't go hungry or thirsty; festivalgoers aren't allowed to bring coolers, cans, and bottles. But do bring a blanket or lawn chairs and join 250,000 other partiers whenever or wherever the Spirit moves you. Advance tickets cost $8.00; they're $12.00 at the gate.

Overland Park Civic Band Concerts
Santa Fe Commons Park,
81st and Santa Fe
Overland Park, KS
(913) 642-2222

Who says we've lost that small-town flavor? It's right here at this old-fashioned town-square park in sweet little old Overland Park. They strike up the band—usually ragtime, blues, or country—each Sunday evening beginning the first week in July and continuing through August. For more old-time fun, stroll the downtown area, window-shop, or stop in for a huge chocolate chip cookie at Mildred's Coffee Shop. The concerts are free; bring lawn chairs.

Summerfest
St. Mary's Episcopal Church,
13th and Holmes
(816) 235-6222

This four-program series is incredibly popular thanks to the talents of its 10-member chamber ensemble and a repertoire that appeals to a wide audience. Each program also includes a guest artist, such as a soprano soloist, who adds depth to the selections. After you've fed your soul, take care of the rest of you with a post-concert artist schmooze that includes a lavish spread of minisandwiches, hors d'oeuvres, sweets, and beverages. And as if all that weren't enough, the concerts are presented in a stunning Gothic church that was built in 1888. Be sure to notice the high altar with deeply carved wood and the stained-glass windows. Summerfest has become quite the seasonal ticket, so

early reservations are recommended. A subscription to all four concerts costs $50 until May 25, then it's $60. The programs are offered at 7:00 P.M. each Saturday and 5:00 P.M. each Sunday in July.

Theatre in the Park
Shawnee Mission Park,
79th and Renner Road
Shawnee, KS
(816) 464-9420 (info line),
(913) 631-7050
www.theatreinthepark.org

Thirty years ago this organization opened with a few boards laid on bricks and dressing rooms in nearby bushes. Today it's one of the hottest tickets in town as 3,000 patrons show up to watch Broadway productions like *Annie, Evita,* and *The Music Man* performed by nonprofessional actors, many of whom could one day be holding a Tony of their owny. The summertime experience gives hundreds of actors, dancers, and singers of every age group a chance to perform. Four different musicals are presented each season, and each runs for two weeks on weekends. The ticket gates open at 7:00 P.M., and because there are no prior sales, the line often starts an hour earlier; the programs begin at 8:30 P.M. A concession stand is on-site, as are public restrooms. Admission is $5.00 for adults, $3.00 for children ages 4 to 12, and under 4 free. Bring a picnic basket and lawn chairs and be ready to cheer for somebody's kid.

Water Garden Tour
(816) 525-7664
kcwatergardens.com

Just when a cool splash of water would feel really good, the Water Garden Society of Greater Kansas City complies with an invitation to tour more than 60 area gardens. The offerings range from tiny koi ponds created by the homeowners to monstrous minilakes with waterfalls installed by professional landscape companies. Several have appeared in local and national garden magazines. Tickets, at $10 each, include a map and descriptive brochure and are available at several garden centers throughout the metro area. Check online for more information.

Wyandotte County Fair
1405 North 98th Street
Kansas City, KS
(913) 788-7898
www.wycofair.com

This is the real deal, where 4-H kids show off their best calves (as in little cows, not leg muscles), pies, and dresses to win blue ribbons. For everyone else, just showing up is reward enough. The grandstand (tickets cost $3.00 to $12.00 extra) has acts like Little River Band, a demolition derby, a youth rodeo, and a messy attraction called Mud Madness. The free stage offers country bands, gospel music, and folk dancing. The fairgrounds are wall to wall with tents filled with arts and crafts, carnival rides and games of chance, exhibits like chainsaw artists, clowns, a petting zoo, and a live shark show. In Kansas? Yep, plus enough cotton candy and funnel cakes to make the Whirly Bird off-limits.

You don't have to be in the 4-H club or even a Dot (our affectionate term for a Wyandotte County resident) to enter the competitions; anyone can bring a biggest tomato, best scrapbook, prettiest wreath, most impressive Lego construction, or chocolate chip cookies to vie for cash prizes. This author still treasures a State Blue Ribbon for banana nut bread won eons ago. But that's recent history; the fair has been around since 1863 and at its current 40-acre site since 1955. It's now the largest county fair in Kansas and Missouri.

Daily gate admission is $4.00 for adults, $2.00 for kids 6 to 12, and free for 5 and under. Parking is $2.00. Or get a five-day pass for $25; check online for details and a coupon for additional savings.

Fourth of July Fireworks Displays and Festivals

Ever since private fireworks became verboten in KC, we've had to get our thrills at giant community displays. Let's see: a few Black Cats and sparklers or 20 minutes of dazzling jewels and diamonds exploding in the night sky overhead. We'll take the public fireworks, thank you very much. And you won't have to go far to see some spectacular shows; in fact, in some parts of the city you can watch several going off at once. Following are some of our favorites; a two-page spread of more listings can be found in the *Kansas City Star*. We've also included other family-friendly choices around the holiday.

Booms and Blooms
Powell Gardens
Kingsville, MO
(816) 697-2600

The sounds of the Missouri Symphony Pops will thrill you as fireworks light up the sky like giant multicolored chrysanthemums. Light jazz starts at 3:00 P.M., the conductor takes up the baton at 7:00, and the pyrotechnics start as soon as it's dark. Besides the booms, there are blooms like the eye-popping display of daylilies and other lush floral gardens. You can even stay cool with a stroll in a shady glen along a waterfall stream. Cafe Thyme offers a selection of crisp salads, tasty sandwiches, and desserts. Admission to the park is $6.50 for adults, $2.50 for children.

Fire in the Sky Fourth of July Celebration
City Market
(816) 842-1271
www.citymarket-kc.com

City Market and the House of Blues put together one of the best July 4 affairs in town, with hot rhythm and blues, ice-cold drinks, and plenty of barbecue and other festival food. Tables and folding chairs are provided, and there are shady areas to escape the sun if you want to come out early to enjoy the always-festive atmosphere of River Market. The gates open at 5:00 P.M. and the fireworks, one of the city's most elaborate displays, begin just after 10:00. Advance tickets go for $10 to $15 and are highly recommended; this is often a sellout.

Independence Day at Ft. Osage
Sibley, MO

We're gonna party like it's 1812, when they were celebrating our country's 36th anniversary of independence. You're invited to join the civilians and military personnel who lived in this fort. Highlights include the firing of the cannons, muskets, and military drills in full dress uniform, which must be murder in the hot sun. Lucky for you there are cold refreshments to enjoy. Admission is $3.00 for adults, seniors, and kids from 5 to 13 and free for children under 5. The celebration starts at 9:00 A.M. and continues to midafternoon.

Independence Day at
Missouri Town 1855
Lake Jacomo in Fleming Park
Blue Springs, MO
(816) 795–8200, ext. 1-260

You say you want an old-fashioned Fourth of July? How about the way they did it back in 1855? This re-created village from our city's early days really lives it up with patriotic speeches, a town parade, period costumes and music, and children's games that don't require batteries. And it all takes place at one of the prettiest parks in the city. Admission for the 9:00 A.M. to 4:30 P.M. event goes for $3.00 for adults, $2.00 for youth ages 5 to 13, and free for under 5. Now you'll have just enough time to catch a nap before heading out to watch fireworks.

Kansas City Jaycees Pro Rodeo and
Wild West Extravaganza
Benjamin Ranch, 6401 East 87th Street
(816) 761-5055, (800) 437-2624
www.benjaminranch.com

A cowtown? You bet we are—and proud

of it, at least during the four-day Kansas City Jaycees Pro Rodeo, when 350 of the country's best professional cowboys and cowgirls try to win cash prizes. The competition has been held at the 229-acre Benjamin Ranch since 1958, and, buster, they do it up right. Thousands of folks crowd the 6,000-seat arena to watch over 150 untamed horses and Brahma bulls roped, ridden, and wrestled.

Clowns and specialty acts entertain the crowd between competitions, and little cowpokes can ride ponies and visit the petting zoo. Concession stands offer everything from hot dogs and burgers (maybe that's what makes the bovines so testy) to ice cream. Every night ends with a thrilling fireworks display that lights up the starry midwestern sky. Gates open at 6:00 P.M., and rodeo performances start at around 8:00 and last until 10:30. Tickets range from $12 to $18 each day, with proceeds benefiting the Greater Kansas City area Jaycees, Dream Factory, and Kansas City Care Team. It's a weekend your kids will never forget.

Lenexa Community Days
Old Town Lenexa, Santa Fe Trail Drive
and Pflumm
(913) 541-8592

Rise and shine early so that you can participate in the annual Freedom Run beginning at 7:00 A.M., and then catch your breath while enjoying a good old-fashioned community parade at 10:00 A.M. The rest of the day belongs to family games and activities, food vendors, and live music. For those of you still awake, the cities of Shawnee and Lenexa put on an awesome fireworks display at Shawnee Mission Park (5900 Renner Road) in the Theatre in the Park area. Bring lawn chairs and blankets. The admission is free to all events.

Overland Park Fireworks Spectacular
Corporate Woods Office Park
Overland Park, KS
(913) 451-7110

You'll be watching the skies throughout this Fourth of July celebration, first when the National Guard of Kansas flies overhead and then during a fireworks display that seems to go on forever. Musical entertainment, food and drinks galore, and an activity area for kids complete the deal. Even better, it's free.

Parkville Concert and Fireworks Display
Parkville University grounds
(816) 741-7676
The Parkville Community Band performs a concert of show tunes and favorite oom-pah marching numbers. The fireworks are especially beautiful when reflected in the still mirror of the Missouri River.

"Still More Things People Collect"
Exhibit
Crown Center Shops, Level One
Showplace, 2450 Grand
(816) 274-8444
www.crowncenter.com
What started as a lark in 1996 has become one of the coolest little happenings in town. It's certainly one of the kookiest as people from far and wide display unique and unusual things they collect. Pez dispensers? Nope, that would be far too normal. Try the largest cat whisker collection in the world, an impressive set of square-bottom ties, or a drawer full of floaty pens. You can peruse these and 75 other oddball groupings from late July through early September. Just promise not to laugh; remember one man's junk is another man's trendy art collection. The exhibit is open daily during its run. Free admission. Here, kitty, kitty, kitty . . .

AUGUST

Abdallah Shrine Rodeo
Kemper Arena
(913) 362-1293
Yippee ti yi yo! It's the biggest Shrine rodeo in North America, and we've got it. It's quite a thrill to watch 150 professional cowboys and cowgirls compete for big prizes in Brahma bull riding, steer wrestling, and calf roping. The one-handed bronc bucking event is done with

and without a saddle (ouch), and cowboy wannabes get to catch and saddle a wild horse (double ouch). The clowns jumping in and out of barrels keep the competition light, and kids can get involved in a shoe race where they have to sprint across the arena, try on shoes from a barrel, and flip-flop back. The preshow is always a kick, with Shriners dressed in costume riding outrageously decked-out go-karts. Tickets are $8.00 to $12.00 for the two-day event.

Aviation Expo
Downtown Airport
(816) 471-4946
www.kcairshow.org
If things are looking up, it must be because the Blue Angels are in town. The U.S. Navy precision flight team is just one exciting element of the Aviation Expo. Other high-flying action includes the midair acrobatics of the U.S. Army Golden Knights Parachute Team, a demonstration team from Air Force A-10s, F-117s breaking the speed limit, and stunt pilots and wing walkers. Live music throughout the two-day show, a hot air balloon show at night, and free airplane rides for kids add to the list of activities, and 40 food vendors serve up nachos, smoked brats, and snow cones.

Staged by the Mid-America Youth Aviation Association, the two-day expo helps educate young people about careers in aviation and related fields. Crowds have grown to more than 150,000 at the downtown airport, so parking elsewhere (such as the Crown Center) and catching a shuttle is a must. You'll find shuttle information on the Web site along with important safety tips like wearing ear protection and plenty of sunscreen. It gets mighty hot on that tarp, but that doesn't keep runners from participating in an early-morning race. Admission is free; round-trip shuttle fare is $2.00.

Ballet in the Park
Various locations
(816) 931-2232, ext. 375
www.kcballet.org
With leafy trees serving as stage curtains,

this series of free outdoor shows lets you get a bit of culture while wearing flip-flops and sipping lemonade. Since its start in the early 1980s, this has been one of the ballet troupe's favorite programs, both for the dancers and the audience. The diverse program ranges from ballroom dancing to neoclassic ballet, from dramatic work to modern pieces where bodies are twisted into "sculpture." The entire 25-member company is featured in some capacity, giving some of the lesser known dancers a chance to star. Venues have included the Loose Park rose garden, Crown Center Pavilion, and Powell Garden, so the surroundings are as lyrical as the artists. Performances are free and open to the public; bring lawn chairs or blankets. Dates change from year to year. Call for current information.

Blues and Bar-Be-Q Benefit
B.B.'s Lawn Side Bar-B-Q
1205 East 85th Street
(816) 822-7427
How tough is this decision? Show up to hear 13 bands, get some great barbecue, and drink cold beer while you contribute to a good cause. Past performers have included crowd-pleasers Four Fried Chickens and a Coke and Kelley Hunt. All proceeds go to the Sherwood Center, a United Way Agency that provides services for people with autism and related disabilities. Admission is $4.00 for adults; kids 11 and younger get in free. The event doesn't have a standard date; call for details.

Ethnic Enrichment Festival
Swope Park, Swope Parkway and Meyer Boulevard
(816) 333-1124
Twirling costumes, lively music, and an array of international cuisine; here's a chance to celebrate more than 40 cultures that make our city so vibrant and appealing. For two days, usually the third weekend in August, you can enjoy a different performance on stage every half hour, including steel bands from Jamaica, Samoan dance groups, Scottish pipe

bands, Mexican folkloric ballet, Japanese martial arts, and a parade of flags. Craft booths, food vendors, and educational activities are also on tap. Admission is free, but donations are cheerfully accepted.

Elvis Parade
Barney Allis Plaza, 12th and Wyandotte
(913) 677-8013
www.kyys.com
Put on your blue suede shoes, grab your teddy bear, and practice crooning, 'cause it's "now or never" to see more than 100 parade entries, Elvis impersonators, and so much more. This hilarious, often embarrassingly bad festival has been sponsored by radio station KYYS for more than 16 years. Thankyouthankyouverymuch.

Festival of Butterflies
Powell Gardens
Kingsville, MO
(816) 697-2600
www.powellgardens.org
While 150,000 people watch for Blue Angels at the Air Expo, several hundred will be enchanted by other winged creatures closer to earth. More than 6,000 guests take turns watching the multicolored miracles in the garden's conservatory during the country's largest butterfly exhibit. As cameras click, an orange-and-black Viceroy sips nectar from a purple ironweed flower, a blue Atala becomes a temporary hair bow on a three-year-old, and a rare orange-barred Sulphur flits by in iridescent splendor. More than 23 varieties emerge during this event, plus there are outdoor butterfly and hummingbird gardens, face painting for the children, and a catch-and-release party. It's a magical weekend that adds to the everyday wonder of Powell Garden; you can read more about it in the Parks, Lakes, and Recreation chapter. General admission prices are in effect for the festival: $6.00 for adults, $5.00 for seniors, $2.50 for 12 and under.

Race for the Cure
Union Station
(816) 842-4444
www.kansascityraceforthecure.com
In August the streets around Union Station become a moving sea of pink as 20,000 T-shirted runners and walkers move toward the finish line and a cure. The Kansas City affiliate of the Susan G. Komen Breast Cancer Foundation has been going strong since 1993, moving its course several times to accommodate the larger crowds. The 5K run/walk and 1-mile fun run appeal to a wide array of athletes, including those who wear photos of loved ones who have died from breast cancer or have survived it and those who are themselves fighting the disease. Water stations and cheering crowds keep the runners motivated, and music, festivities, and lots of food wait at the finish line. Registration fees range from $25 to $35. Call for this year's date.

Summer Skies
Kansas City Museum
3218 Gladstone Boulevard
(816) 483-8300
Learn to locate the constellations and stars just in time for that camping trip. You'll be able to find Scorpio, Sagittarius, Orion the Hunter, and the Summer Triangle from the museum's planetarium. Make a day of it and tour other exhibits, including photos and memorabilia from the Long family, who owned the original Corinthian Hall. Museum entry is $3.50 per person, and the star-filled event continues through early September.

SEPTEMBER

Antiques on the Common
Greenwood, MO
(816) 537-7822
Although antiques buffs try to keep this one-day sale a secret, word has gotten out and the crowds grow bigger every year. By now 1,500 or so fevered shoppers show up to dig through tent after tent of primo antiques and collectibles. Dealers from 15 states bring in the goods, including early Americana, folk art, hooked rugs, redware (highly prized in New England), baskets, quilts, and country furniture with just the right amount of peeling paint. No matter what your budget ($5,000 or $10) you'll walk away with some treasure. And a full tummy: The blueberry cream pie, bratwurst, and chicken salad in a pita are all delicious. The brain behind it all is Claire Fellows of Country Heritage and Friends, a terrific antiques store in Greenwood. Give her a call for directions and a list of motels and RV campsites; she might even send her recipe for Pig Pickin' Cake.

Art Westport
Westport Square
(816) 756-2789
Westport's motto is if you can't beat the Plaza Art Fair in size, at least have yours a few weeks earlier. And it works. But this weekend-long street party succeeds for another reason: All the work is created by local artists, so there's a sense of community and continuity that gives shoppers a chance to buy from favorites year after year. Expect to see a great variety of styles and genres, including ceramics, oils, pastels, watercolors, metal sculpture, garden art, carved wooden boxes, and handcrafted jewelry. Food vendors line the streets, live music adds to the festival atmosphere, and the people watching (as always) is as good as it gets. Admission is free, so you'll have extra cash for a new treasure.

Belton, Grandview & Kansas City
Railroad Company Train Rides
502 Walnut
Belton, MO
(816) 331-0630
www.orgsites.com/mo/beltonrailroad
It's all aboard for fun as this community relives its past as a railroad town in the 1920s. An authentically re-created open window train takes passengers on a 45-minute round-trip on Saturday, Sunday, and holidays from Labor Day through the end of October. Tickets cost $6.50 for

ages 3 and older; $15.00 to ride with the engineer (no extra charge for blowing the whistle), and $10.00 to see the world in reverse from the caboose. Special seating is limited and on a first-come, first-served basis. Other activities are planned throughout the season, including ice-cream socials and educational field trips, and photos and documents from the rail-way's heyday are displayed in the gift shop.

Brookside Irish Festival
63rd and Wornall Road
(913) 338-1962
www.brooksideirishfest.com
'Tis a long way from St. Paddy's Day, but apparently 15,000 folks who crowd the streets of Brookside don't mind—or don't notice after downing a few Irish stouts. They show up in a sea of green to hear traditional music from local talent like the Elders, Eddie Delahunt, and Bob Reeder and to watch the flashing feet of O' Riada Academy of Irish Dance. Past years have also brought in national acts like Black 47, a group that mixes hip-hop and hard rock with traditional Irish music. Kids will keep busy with games and face painting, and parents may head right for the corned beef, scones, meat pies, and Irish whiskey. You might walk away with more than a hangover; raffle tickets are sold for trips to Ireland and big-screen TVs. Admission is $5.00; children 12 and under get in free. Money raised goes to a local Irish Culture Center.

Fiesta Hispanic
Bartle Hall
13th and Central
(816) 765-1992, (913) 706-7881
There's more entertainment than toys in a piñata at this festival honoring our city's vibrant Latino community. For two days puppeteers, Tejano singers, music and dance troupes, and exhibits keep the crowds entertained while an exhibit hall showcases the culture's proud heritage. It's a fitting tribute to national Hispanic Heritage Month. Admission is free.

Greek Festival
Greek Orthodox Church of the Annunciation, 120th and Wornall Road
(816) 942-9100, (816) 491-1990
It's hard to imagine what our lives would be like without the influence of ancient Greece. Logic, geometry, medicine, and architecture (even words like *sophistication* and *philanthropy*) come from their world. Then there's the food. Here's a chance to experience it all (well, maybe just the food) at a celebration this parish has been hosting for more than 40 years. You'll find enough gyros to feed an army, enough paper-thin phyllo dough to cover the world, and enough dancing to make Zorba proud. The crowds are so huge they need three food lines to serve hungry festivalgoers. But don't worry. We've saved some baklava for you. Admission and parking are free.

Jewish Arts Festival
Jewish Community Center,
6801 West 115th Street
Overland Park, KS
(913) 327-8000
www.jewishartskc.org
This relatively new addition to the fall festival roster offers a wonderful opportunity to celebrate ancient Jewish traditions and culture. They've packed a lot of activities into one day, including several bands and soloists, an art exhibit, and interactive games for children that are so fun they won't realize they're learning about their heritage And of course you'll want to eat a little something, so there's hummus with pita, pizza, barbecue, desserts, and more (all kosher). Tickets are $5.00 in advance and $7.00 at the door; children under 12 are admitted free.

Lenexa Spinach Festival
Sar-Ko-Par Trails Park,
87th Street and Lackman Road
Lenexa, KS
(913) 541-8592
Kids may shudder at the thought of a day devoted to spinach, but there's more to this festival than simply greens. It starts

with a Kiwanis pancake breakfast and includes a polka dance, Popeye and Olive Oyl characters, and a tossing of the world's largest spinach salad, which is sold by the plateful to those who enjoy the leafy vegetable. The two-day event costs $2.00 for ages 13 and older.

March of Dimes Annual Bikers for Babies
The Kansas Speedway
(816) 561-0175
www.marchofdimeskc.org/biker
This annual charity event brings a new meaning to the phrase, "Biker Babe," as hundreds of motorcycle riders raise money to help save infants at risk. Participants are well rewarded with a free lunch, music and entertainment, great prizes, and a chance to ride through some of the Midwest's prettiest countryside. Past years have brought together 1,500 or so riders with total contributions of more than $140,000, and the crowd gets bigger every year. The fee is $25 per ride, but most participants spend months raising money for the cause. It's hard to say no to a guy in leather chaps.

Old Settlers Celebration
Downtown Olathe, KS
(913) 764-1050
www.olathe.org
No wonder this annual event is a blast; Olathe's had more than 100 years to get it right. They certainly pack enough excitement into three days, including free concerts on Friday and Saturday nights starring big-time names of the '60s and '70s like Mitch Ryder, Gary Lewis and the Playboys, and Mark Lindsay from the Raiders. But the fun starts much earlier with carnival rides on Thursday and the state's biggest parade Saturday morning. More than 150 arts and crafts booths show off local talent, and ice cream keeps everybody cool.

One of the liveliest attractions is the gabfest that allows older residents to tell young whippersnappers about the good old days, like walking to school through 3 feet of snow. Barefoot. This celebration is a

chance to discover a vibrant city with an interesting history, famous sons (including several governors, actor Buddy Rodgers, and J. C. Nichols, who developed the Country Club Plaza), and a name that means "beautiful" in the Shawnee Indian language.

Overland Park Fall Festival
Santa Fe Commons Park
Overland Park, KS
(913) 895-6357
www.opkansas.org
Get your Christmas shopping out of the way early at this outdoor arts and crafts show that's been steadily growing in size since 1980. Pace yourself; there are nearly 180 artists and crafters displaying handmade treasures like jewelry, candles, ceramic dolls, stained glass, pottery, dried-floral wreaths, oil paintings, and personalized children's puzzles. Or save all your money for the food booths with the usual summertime treats like Cajun sausages, kettle corn, snow cones, and beer. The farmers' market is also open, offering the freshest produce from nearby farms and orchards. Tables are set under big white tents, so even if it rains you can sit a spell while listening to local bands play crowd-pleasing blue grass, blues, jazz, and classic rock 'n' roll. Speaking of crowds, this event pulls 'em in, with attendance of about 18,000 over three days.

Party 'Arty
Various art galleries
(816) 751-1305
The see-and-be-seen atmosphere at this annual event has as much to do with the fashionable crowd as it does the art. Sponsored by the Nelson-Atkins Museum of Art's lively Friends of Art group, it's a great opportunity to discover a cool, little-known gallery, talk to the artists, and sip a glass of Chardonnay along the way. Most of the art galleries are clustered in the Crossroads Arts District, so it's easy to leave your car and walk, but you'll also want to check out newer galleries in the emerging West Bottoms area. In past

years this neighborhood has hosted the after-party party, so to speak, with beer, wine, appetizers, and very loud music. Tickets are $25, payable at the door. A map of the participating galleries is available by contacting Brenda Barton at yfa@nelson-atkins.org. Party hearty, art lovers.

Pig-Pickin' Chicken-Lickin' Feast
Bingham-Waggoner Estate,
313 West Pacific
Independence, MO
(816) 461-3491
At the very least this annual festival wins the prize for the best hunger-inducing name. And you can bet you'll be licking your fingers after a dinner of roasted pig, Stroud's famous fried chicken, and lots of savory side dishes. Other down-home fun includes a quilt show, silent auction, banjo music, and clogging (that's folk dancing, folks). You can also tour the home that was a popular stop along the westward trails (read more about this site under Historic Homes in the History chapter). Advance reservations are required; tickets cost $10.

Plaza Art Fair
Country Club Plaza
(816) 753-0100
www.countryclubplaza.com
Some people save up all year to buy a fabulous treasure or two at this three-day event. They'll have plenty to choose from; more than 230 of the nation's top artists turn nine Plaza streets into one big outdoor art gallery. The quality of work is incredible. In a highly competitive jury process, more than 1,200 artists from some 35 states vie for the right to have their work seen by more than 275,000 art enthusiasts. Expect to see ceramics, fiber, glass, graphics and printmaking, metal, painting, pastels, photography, wood, and some of the most exquisite jewelry around.

While browsing you'll be treated to the aroma of Thai chicken pizza, Italian sausages, and black bean chili from more

than two dozen Plaza restaurants. Desserts, icy margaritas, beer, and other beverages are also on the menu. Music fills the air as well, thanks to three stages offering everything from R&B to classical. Children can create their own masterpiece to take home in the Kid's Art Workshop or view other students' work at the Young Artist Exhibition tent. And of course it all takes place at the Country Club Plaza, which is a work of art all by itself. The Plaza Art Fair is a tradition that began in 1932 and just gets better with time.

Plaza Pzazz
Country Club Plaza
(816) 421-1753
As if the Plaza didn't have enough pizzazz, they throw a block party with music, dancing, and delectable food from the trendiest restaurants in town. The location couldn't be more chichi, either; the streets nestled along lovely Brush Creek on the Plaza are lined with booths and tents that are lit up with tiny white lights as the sun sets. The $75 ticket price goes to a very good cause: three local Ronald McDonald Houses that give shelter and support to families with seriously ill children. The charity serves more than 3,000 families a year. Tickets go as fast as an order of McDonald's fries.

The Kansas City Renaissance Festival
Bonner Springs, KS
(816) 561-8005, (800) 373-0357
www.kcrenfest.com
Buxomy wenches and men in tights? These fetching fantasies have been drawing crowds to this 16th-century shire every fall for more than 25 years. Well, that and continuous entertainment, mouthwatering foods, and a wide array of handcrafted wares. Where else can you witness a sword fight, cheer a jouster on horseback, and flirt with a king, all in one afternoon? With 16 acres and 13 stages of music, plays, and zany comedies, there's almost too much to see in one day, so you'll be thankful the festival runs for seven weekends beginning Labor Day.

Each week sports a special theme; Lovers and Fooles, for instance, hosts the wedding of the century, and Pipes and Plaids brings out the bagpipes and kilt competition. Gypsies, bandits, beggars, the royal entourage, and dozens of other costumed characters stroll the 16-acre village, engaging visitors in skits and revelry. Music is around every bend: Celtic harmonies, bawdy pub songs and sea shanties, lilting tunes on harps and hammered dulcimers. The village's shaded lanes are lined with shops showcasing goods from more than 160 artisans, including puppets, beribboned hair wreaths, tooled-leather purses, and toy swords.

Kids are in their own little realm with elephant and camel rides, a petting zoo, and dozens of games such as Slay the Dragon and Drench a Wench. Some people show up just for the food, particularly roasted turkey legs big enough for two, pork chops on a stick, root beer floats, and 80 other delights including a rather modern invention, barbecue ribs. Cider Jack, wine, and ales are also available. The festival is open rain or shine and parking is free. Before you go, practice saying the standard greeting around Canterbury: "Huzzah!" Tickets are $13.95 for adults, $12.50 for students and seniors, $6.95 for children ages 5 to 12, and free for children under 5. Check the Web site or call for discounted advance tickets.

Riverside Riverfest
Riverfront Park
Riverside, MO
(816) 741-3993
What this city lacks in history (it's only 50 years old) it more than makes up for in fun. Witness the number of activities it packs into one September weekend alone: a pancake breakfast, a vintage car show, a grand parade featuring the world-famous Anheuser Busch Budweiser Clydesdales, a carnival, a blues and jazz jam, a battle of the bands, a beauty contest, and two fireworks displays. Whew! There's plenty of entertainment for the kiddies, too, including a petting zoo. The older crowd can sit

it out at the bingo tents. The central event is free; a $12 armband will get you onto the carnival rides.

Santa-Cali-Gon Days
Independence Square
Independence, MO
(816) 252-4745
www.santacaligon.com
In the mid-1800s three routes—the Santa Fe, California, and Oregon Trails—led the pioneers to new adventures out West, and they all began in or near Independence. This festival has grown in popularity in its 30-plus years, topping out at some 250,000 visitors over the four-day span.

There's certainly enough to keep everyone of them entertained. The Main Stage is always a big draw, with past performers like the Dixie Chicks, Clint Black, Eddie Rabbit, and Asleep at the Wheel. The Community Stage hosts local talent, including Native American dancing, square dancing, and must-see events like watermelon seed–spitting contests. No contest about who's got the best food roundup for the weekend; here you can choose from barbecue, jambalaya, hamburgers, corn dogs, ice cream, lemonade, and dozens more. In fact, more than 300 commercial food and game booths are here, along with a large carnival midway. And the juried craft show has been ranked among the top in the nation by the crafters themselves.

For those interested in the historical significance of the trails, the Missouri Free Trappers exhibit portrays the life of the pioneers. Four days of fun, free admittance and parking. . . what more could you want? How about discount tickets for the carnival rides on the Web site? You'll also find information about free shuttles—a must, especially on Saturday afternoon.

Strut with Your Mutt
(816) 761-8151
www.waysidewaifs.org
Put on the dog while you help raise funds for the Wayside Waifs animal shelter. This walkathon is held every fall at a different park, and part of the fun is entering differ-

ent contests like cutest pooch, best costume, or the owner and pet who most resemble each other (scary judging when the entrant is a wrinkled sharpei). Plus there are vendor booths and doggie treats galore. $30 gets you a T-shirt and possibly a slobbery thank-you from a schnauzer.

Kansas City Symphony
Labor Day Concert
Shawnee Mission Park
(816) 471–0400
www.kcsymphony.org
You haven't lived until you've heard the Kansas City Symphony begin the first notes of the "William Tell Overture" just as the sun is setting behind a canopy of trees. This popular Labor Day tradition always includes selections the audience instantly recognizes, even if they can't recall the name, such as Copland's "Rodeo" or "The 1812 Overture." It's a fine way to introduce youngsters to classical music. The program begins at 7:00 P.M., which gives you plenty of time to enjoy the park's lake, rolling hills, and leash-free dog area. Read more about this popular green space in Parks, Lakes, and Recreation.

OCTOBER

Antiques Garden & Home Design Show
Overland Park International Trade
Center 115th and Metcalf
Overland Park, KS
(816) 756–3580
This weekend shoparama certainly lives up to its reputation as the premier event for fine lifestyles. The city's top interior designers try to outdo one another with fabulous decorated rooms while antiques dealers set up shop with exquisite furniture, estate jewelry, and fine collectibles. The "garden" in the name comes from indoor miniparks created by landscape designers; past shows have had restful Japanese gardens and bulb-happy springtime displays. The hosts are Gamma Phi Beta and KCPT-TV19, our public television station, and money raised goes to help support the station.

Admission is $7.00 in advance (tickets are usually available at Hen House supermarkets) and $9.00 at the door.

CANstruction
Crown Center Square
(816) 329–5000
www.crowncenter.com
This annual event builds its own excitement as 11 teams of architects, engineers, and contractors compete to design and build giant structures made entirely out of canned goods. Has anyone entered the leaning tower of pizza sauce yet? At the close of the monthlong exhibition, the canned goods are donated to the Harvesters Food Pantry. Admission is free, but you're encouraged to bring at least one can of food or a nonperishable item to view the display.

Christmas in October
(816) 531–5259
www.christmas-in-october.org
You've gotta love a community that comes together for two weekends each October to clean up, fix up, and rehabilitate homes belonging to low-income homeowners who are often elderly or disabled. This nonprofit group was started in 1984 by Richard W. Miller and John P. McMeel (of Andrews McMeel Publishing) with a couple of hammers and a few willing friends. These days about 6,000 skilled laborers and hardworking volunteers tackle the jobs.

Over the years this group has improved more than 5,500 homes in neighborhoods throughout the metro area, often enabling residents to remain in their homes with dignity and pride. Union craftspeople like electricians, plumbers, carpenters, and roofers handle the major repairs during the first weekend. A week later a horde of energetic workers with paintbrushes, rakes, and wheelbarrows show up to finish the job. There's a mighty big payoff for a few days of sore muscles and Eggshell Gloss in your hair: joyful tears from an 85-year-old lady who will have a warmer house this winter.

Fall Parade of Homes
(816) 942–8800
www.kcparadesofhomes.com
At this annual show you'll find about 500 reasons to buy a new home as more than 200 builders from eight counties tempt you with their finest houses. You can tour as many as you'd like in every lifestyle and price range, from less than $95,000 to more than $1.6 million. Just why does any one family need seven bathrooms, anyway? Many of the most exclusive homes are dressed to the nines by area interior designers, so you'll come away with lots of decorating ideas. To add to your choices, Downtown lofts and condos have been added to the tour. Books with floor plans are available at most of the homes, and a tour map is available online.

FilmFest Kansas City
Various locations
(816) 474–7100
What's the difference between FilmFest Kansas City and those big-deal festivals like Cannes or Sundance? Well, although we can't offer you a glimpse of Robert Redford, at least in Kansas City you'll see films. That's right, even if you're not an industry mover and shaker or member of the media, you can buy a ticket and see 50 or so movies from around the world. Aspiring filmmakers will also be interested in workshops and a chance to schmooze with producers, screenwriters, and directors. The movie lineup offers something for every taste, including sci-fi thrillers, musicals, foreign films, shorts, cinematic masterpieces, and potential blockbusters from established names. The weeklong event includes the KAN-ED filmmaking program, the precursor to the KAN Film Festival, a competitive event held every June in Lawrence, Kansas.

Hidden Glen Arts Festival
Kansas 10 and Cedar Creek Parkway
Olathe, KS
(913) 780–3540
You might say this art fair has a much larger canvas, the gorgeous, upscale homes and emerald-green golf course of Cedar Creek. But it's the 100 or so booths filled with fine art that will attract your immediate attention. Past favorites have included garden art crafted of recycled metal, delicate ceramic teapots, and gem-studded silver jewelry. Artists from 10 states are available to discuss inspirations and techniques. Little squirts have story-tellers, puppets, and a color wheel game to keep them busy while you shop. Admission and parking are free.

Historic Kansas City Homes Tour
(816) 931–8448
Ever drive by a beautiful home and wish you could peek inside? Now you can, with the owner's blessings. Each fall the Historic Kansas City Foundation chooses one neighborhood to feature, always an area filled with turn-of-the-20th-century jewels that have been carefully preserved or lovingly restored. Past tours have included the fabulous Scarritt-Renaissance and Hyde Park neighborhoods. Tickets are $10 and can be purchased at the site. Proceeds help continue the foundation's mission of restoring, renewing, and rediscovering historic buildings, homes, and areas of our city.

Hyde Park Historic Homes Tour and Festival
Hyde Park Neighborhood
(816) 561–HPNA (4762)
www.hydeparkkc.com
Get close and personal with some of the loveliest homes in Kansas City at this annual tour. You'll see everything from charming shirtwaist bungalows to stately stone mansions, brought back to glorious turn-of-the-20th-century grandeur by hardworking homeowners. Tour guides (often the residents themselves) discuss the home's history, interesting details about the restoration, and sometimes-spooky tales about ghostly visits. Typically five homes are on the list, all within a pleasant stroll, or you can hop a ride on a trolley. Refreshments and barbecue are available in the beer garden, and an art

fair and children's activity center add to the weekend fun.

Junior League of Kansas City
Holiday Mart
Overland Park International Trade
Center, 115th and Metcalf
Overland Park, KS
(816) 997-8525
Get on your mark, get set, shop! Lots of ladies finish their entire holiday shopping list in one fast-paced afternoon at this annual buyer's paradise. More than 100 gift boutiques are side by side, offering jewelry (silver, gemstone, and estate pieces), home decor, gourmet foods, apparel, pewterware, and collectibles. Many of the area's most popular shops are represented as well, including Nell Hill's from Atchison, Kansas, and Locust Grove of Weston, Missouri. Clothing booths tend to carry unique fashions like fringed leather jackets, elaborately decorated vests and hats, and fun accessories not available anywhere else in town. And of course you'll find Christmas decorations galore, including tree-trimmers, ornaments, dried floral wreaths, and exquisite Santas with price tags of $300 or more. For the most part, though, prices are so reasonable you'll be glad you grabbed a shopping basket at the door. Single-day tickets are $6.00 in advance and $8.00 at the door; multiday tickets, good for all four days, are $15.00. Call the number above for ticket outlet information.

La Strada dell' Arte
Union Station
(816) 941-3600
Each fall a corner of Kansas City becomes extra colorful with an art form borrowed from the boulevards of Rome and Paris: street painting! The fun is watching the process as more than 200 artists—professionals, students, and talented amateurs—create their 4-by-6-foot asphalt canvases in colored chalk. It's almost heartbreaking to realize that they're only temporary. Although preregistration is required, there are a few spaces left for last-minute artists who pay $20; supplies are furnished. And

for a $2.00 fee, young artists can decorate a 2-by-2-foot square. The two-day festival is free to the public; the money raised comes from sponsors and benefits a local charity.

Lee National Denim Day
(800) 521-5533
www.denimday.com
How cool is this? Wear jeans to work and instead of getting reprimanded you're considered a good citizen. Local business Lee Jeans sponsors this now-national event, with money going to the Susan G. Komen Breast Cancer Foundation. So take that $5.00 bill out of your jeans pocket and send it in.

Weston Irish Festival
O'Malley's Pub, Short and Welt Streets
Weston, MO
(866) N2 IRISH (624-7474) (toll-free)
www.westonirish.com
In Weston they turn Octoberfest into O'Toberfest with three days of fun. What else can you do when your name is Sean O'Malley and you own an Irish pub? How nice that he invites all his friends and guests to join in as dozens of top-notch Celtic singers, dancers, and musicians entertain. Headliners have included internationally known Connie Dover, who happens to be a Weston resident when not touring, the Elders, and the Shenanigans. Of course there's also plenty of Irish food and drink, authentic jewelry and clothing to buy, and CDs to have the artists autograph. Gate passes range from $5.00 to $8.00 a day. Children under 12 are free, but you may want to plug the little ones' ears when Bob Reeder starts in with his naughty limericks.

Halloween Events

We turn into the City Boo-tiful near the end of October, when you can find about 40 different Halloween activities all over town (look for current lists in the *Star*), including haunted houses, acres of pumpkins, and nonscary festivals for little trick-

or-treaters. As they say at the pumpkin patch, you can take your pick.

Blue Valley Recreation Pumpkin Patch
Blue Valley Recreation Complex
Overland Park, KS
(913) 685-6000
www.bluevalleyrec.org
For children 7 and under, this is better than a bag full of Snickers bars. They'll be having so much fun, and get so tuckered out, they may not miss the door-to-door candy collecting. Activities include hayrides, clowns, face painting, and a moonwalk, and everybody gets a pumpkin to take home. A small fee and preregistration are required.

Boo at the Zoo
Kansas City Zoo
(816) 513-5800
www.kansascityzoo.org
Looking for a ghoulishly good time for your young trick-or-treaters? This is a not-so-scary place where they can trick-or-treat from 20 candy stops, watch puppet and sea lion shows, and participate in zookeeper chats and animal feedings. And of course they'll get to see the real live versions of their little kitty-cat costumes. This all-day party is usually held the weekend before Halloween, and usual admission prices ($3.00 to $6.00) are in effect.

Halloween Family Concert Fest
Johnson County Community College
Overland Park, KS
(913) 895-6357
www.opkansas.org
How about a safe alternative to trick-or-treating that's certainly easier on the dental bills? And instead of getting a bag of sugar your kids get a dose of classical music. Don't worry about their getting bored; they may not recognize "Peter and the Wolf," but "Star Wars" will definitely ring a bell. Other activities include costume contests and prizes. There's no charge.

Powell Pumpkin Patch
25695 Spring Valley Road
Louisburg, KS
(913) 837-2212
Drive 30 minutes just to get lost? That's part of the fun at this pumpkin patch with a 20-acre maze, the largest in the Midwest. Walking through the mile of trails will take at least 30 minutes, and your reward is a chance to pick out the prettiest or at least most carve-worthy pumpkin from 30 acres of the orange globes. Admission is free, pumpkin prices vary by size.

Spooktacular at Powell Gardens
Powell Gardens
Kingsville, MO
(816) 697-2600
www.powellgardens.org
This two-day fall festival includes storybook characters, games, costume contests, and lots of treats in a friendly setting. And—mums the word—the gardens are simply beautiful this time of year. Bring your own trick-or-treat bag. Prepaid registration of $5.00 to $7.00 is required.

The Beast
1401 West 13th Street
(816) 842-4280
www.kcbeast.com
Can you tell we've gotten to the haunted house section of our list? This one is billed as "America's largest haunted house," and while we can't vouch for that, it is guaranteed to scare your socks off. Instead of having visitors walk in a line, the Beast has an open design so that guests can wander at will through several themed areas. This may not be appropriate for young children or even older kids who are easily traumatized.

It's open weekends in September and October and then nightly from mid-October until early November. The haunting starts at 7:00 P.M. and lasts until the fog lifts. Yikes. Admission is $17 Sunday through Thursday and $30 Friday and Saturday. Combo tickets to The Beast and the Edge of Hell are the best deal at $26; check online for coupons.

The Edge of Hell
1300 West 12th Street
(816) 842–4279
www.edgeofhell.com
They call this theater the granddaddy of all haunted houses, and you'll wish gramps were here to hold your hand. It's Kansas City's biggest and oldest fright fest, with a huge advantage over the others: a five-story slide. See The Beast for ticket information.

NOVEMBER

American Royal Livestock
Horse Show & Rodeo
See the Close-up in this chapter and get ready to rodeo, pardner.

A Christmas Carol
Missouri Repertory Theatre
4949 Cherry Street
(816) 235–2700, (888) 502–2700
www.missourirepertorytheatre.org
Even after more than 20 years, we never grow tired of seeing this Christmastime treat featuring outstanding costumes, staging, and acting. The chain-rattling ghosts floating in air are hair-raisingly believable, the ending is always happy, and by the time Tiny Tim makes his final memorable statement, you truly will feel blessed. Tickets for 39 performances (late November through the end of December) go on sale as early as October, and early reservations are a must for the best seats. It's the perfect way to wrap the entire family in the holiday spirit. Parking is free and plentiful around the UMKC campus. Adult tickets range from $27 to $33 depending on seats; youth tickets (18 and under) are $18. The Rep always offers three or four signed performances per season.

Crown Center Ice Terrace
2450 Grand
(816) 274–8411
www.crowncenter.com
Something to look forward to all year long: outdoor ice-skating in Crown Center Square. Opening day for the season is usually the first week in November, with a free early-morning skate from 6:00 to 9:00 A.M. including complimentary hot chocolate and doughnuts. Free morning skates continue while the terrace stays open, through late March. Regular admission is $5.00 per person plus $2.00 skate rental. The hours are 10:00 A.M. to 9:00 P.M. Sunday through Thursday and 10:00 A.M. to 11:00 P.M. Friday and Saturday. It's lovely to skate when you can see stars, as long as that doesn't mean you've just taken a fall. How many cups of cocoa am I holding up?

The Fairy Princess
Kansas City Museum
3218 Gladstone Boulevard
(816) 483–8300
Create a delightful memory as children whisper their wishes to the Fairy Princess, and with a wave of her wand, a gift magically appears! Her highness is always a vision in layers of netting and a glittering crown, and children of all ages are instantly enchanted. Wishes come true every Saturday from late November until just before Christmas. Each visit costs $5.00 per child, which includes the gift and a photo. It's an experience they'll never forget; this author certainly never has.

Handel's Messiah
Community of Christ Auditorium,
Walnut and River
Independence , MO
(816) 235–6222
When King George II heard George Friederic Handel's *Messiah* for the first time, he gave it a standing ovation. You'll do the same after hearing the 350-voice Independence Messiah Choir and the Messiah Festival Orchestra perform the stirring oratorio. The two groups practice for months for this one performance, a nine-decade gift to the community. The staging adds to the evening: a beautiful church, a monstrous 113-rank organ, and a chorus dressed in tuxedoes and evening gowns rising before you on stepped platforms. By the time the "Halleluiah Chorus" begins

you can't help but join in. The perfor- mance is held every year on the Saturday before Thanksgiving. Tickets range from $12 to $28 and are available starting in early September. Don't miss it.

Home for the Holidays Tour
Various locations
(913) 685-2802

We'll bet your home would look spectacu- lar if you had a professional interior designer and dozens of elves decorating it for the holidays. That's what happens dur- ing this popular tour when the Johnson County Young Matrons choose five gor- geous homes in an upscale area, lavish them with about a ton of ornaments and fresh greenery, and then invite the rest of us in to drool. The tour is typically held on a weekday, so hundreds of workers call in sick and hope their bosses don't show up until after dinner. Advance tickets cost $12 and are available at area grocery stores. The price increases to $15 at the door— worth every penny for the decorating ideas you'll take back to your own home.

Spirit of Christmas Past Progressive Gala
Independence, MO
(816) 461-3491

It's an old-fashioned Christmas—and we do mean old—as music, elaborate decorations, and historical reenactments transport you to the holidays of 1800. You'll visit the 1859 Marshal's Home and Jail (looking quite pretty despite its original purpose) along with the Bingham-Waggoner Estate and Vaile Mansion. You may read detailed infor- mation about each site in Attractions. The tour includes hors d'oeuvres and is usually held Thanksgiving week. Tickets are $35 each, and reservations are required.

Holiday Lighting Ceremonies and Displays

Santa doesn't need Rudolph to locate Kansas City. By the first of December

we're lit up like a . . . well, like a Christmas tree, as every community adds its own special holiday display. Following are some of the best and brightest.

Christmas in the Park
Longview Lake Campground
Lee's Summit, MO
(816) 795-8200

Children will have their little faces plas- tered to the car window when you drive slowly through this display of 175 ani- mated figures illuminated by nearly 300,000 lights. To join them, take Inter- state 470 to View High Drive, south to Third Street, and follow the signs, or just listen for the oohs and ahhs coming from vans full of kids. Free, but donations of $1.00 per vehicle or $1.00 per person for buses go to help nearly 40 local charities. The lights turn on in late November and continue through December 31.

Mayor's Christmas Tree Lighting Ceremony
Crown Center Square
(816) 274-8444
www.crowncenter.com

The holiday season is officially here when this 100-foot tree arrives in Crown Center Square the first week in November. Then it's dressed in thousands of lights and ornaments in time for the lighting cere- mony the evening after Thanksgiving. The mayor of Kansas City and a celebrity guest flip the switch for more than 7,000 white lights on the tree and an additional 50,000 illuminating Crown Center Square. This glowing tree stands as a symbol of the Mayor's Christmas Tree Fund, which has helped more than 33,000 less fortu- nate families over the past nine decades. Even after the holidays the tree has a spe- cial purpose: Its wood is used to make commemorative ornaments sold the fol- lowing year to benefit the charity.

The tree lighting is a magical finale to a day that begins when Santa appears in his horse-drawn carriage before settling into his temporary home in Crayola® Christmas Land. He'll be available for photos and to listen to secret wishes.

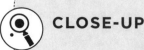

Ropin', Ridin', and Ribs

In Kansas City, when you mention the *party,* chances are you're talking about the American Royal. We've been celebrating this combination grand parade, rodeo, and livestock competition since 1899, so it's definitely here to stay. But for most of us, the American Royal doesn't mean ropin' and ridin', it means ribs. As in barbecue.

Carolyn Wells, the smoky-voiced executive director of the Kansas City Barbeque Society (the group that sanctions nearly 100 competitions across the country), calls it the Super Bowl of barbecue. Local cartoonist Charlie Podrebarac refers to it as "the Woodstock of barbecue." Even the *New York Times Magazine* has gotten in the act, dubbing it "the Academy Awards of barbecue."

All we know is that if you're new in town and looking for the competition, you won't need a map. Just look for the blue smoke rising from hundreds of cookers taking their own sweet time transforming briskets, ribs, pork butts, and sausages into tender morsels to be offered up to about 600 judges the next day. Have mercy, it smells divine as forests of hickory, oak, apple wood, and cherry give off a sweet and pungent perfume. Adding to the aromatherapy are whiffs of onion, peppers, and molasses as teams mix up carefully guarded sauce recipes or stir big pots of barbecue beans to make the most of meat drippings and chunks of brisket.

Each year teams from around the country show up at the West Bottoms, smokers in tow, to vie for more than

$60,000 in prizes and trophies as big as a side of beef. About 65 elite teams, champions all, compete in the International Invitational contest, with about another 350 or so entering the open cook-off.

The annual bash provides plenty of entertainment even for noncookers. It seems more than barbecue is being judged as teams try to outdo one another by personalizing their roped-off areas with outlandish decorations, inflatable palm trees, and live bands. Even the teams' names are a hoot, like Bite My Butt, Pig Newton, Drinkers with a Bar-B-Que Problem, and Any Pork in a Storm. The winners get more than bragging rights and some cash; a title from the American Royal can mean a real boost to business if you own a barbecue restaurant, sell your own sauce brand, or market a smoker.

There is, of course, another side to the American Royal, and without it we probably wouldn't be as well known for our barbecue. The livestock show speaks to Kansas City's century-old importance in the food chain. Here, too, some of the country's best ranchers and 4-H members come to compete for big prizes in categories like Angus bulls, heifers, lamb, and swine.

The American Royal Rodeo is one of the top 10 in the country sanctioned by the Professional Rodeo Cowboys Association and offers such events as barrel racing, saddle bronco riding, calf roping, and that ever-popular mutton bustin'. A Mexi-

Ropin' and ridin' at the American Royal Rodeo, an annual event that showcases our Wild West heritage. RICK MCKIBBEN

can Rodeo Extravaganza salutes the Mexican cowboy heritage with folkloric dancing, mariachi bands, and charro bronco riders. Even folks who don't care about the fine art of lassos show up for the big-name entertainment after the events. Country crooners like Willie Nelson, Sawyer Brown, Clint Black, and others have appeared. A huge parade down Main Street begins the whole shebang with more than 7,000 participants, including 16 saddle clubs, 25 floats, and 23 bands. A children's rodeo, horse show, and agricultural exhibitions round out the weeklong extravaganza. So now you know the answer to "Where's the beef?" It's right here in Kansas City, especially in October.

All the staged events take place at the American Royal Complex, west of Downtown in the West Bottoms. For more information, mosey on down to the Web site at www.americanroyal.com or call (816) 221-9800. And if you plan to come, remember: Cowboy boots are more than just a fashion statement.

Overland Park Mayor's Lighting Ceremony
Between 78th and 83rd Streets
west of Metcalf
Overland Park, KS
(913) 642-2222

Santa arrives a little early at downtown Overland Park, but that's just fine with the kids waiting to take a picture with the jolly old elf. Parents will get in the spirit too, with carolers, holiday crafts for sale, gay music, free cider and cookies, and an electric light parade. The mayor lights the Christmas tree at dusk, and the party continues with free carriage rides for those who bring two canned goods to donate to Harvester's.

Festival of Trees
Longview Farms
Lee's Summit, MO
I-470 at View High Drive exit
(816) 508-3300
www.marillac.org

When you first see this show arena filled with hundreds of twinkling and bejeweled Christmas trees decorated by local interior designers, florists, and artisans, it can take your breath away. More merriment comes from jugglers, choirs, bands and vocal performers, puppets and stilt-walkers, and a silent auction of seasonal gifts made by local and regional artists. The festival begins just before Thanksgiving and continues for a week. Admission is $5.00 for adults, and the money raised benefits the Marillac Center for Children, a psychiatric treatment facility for children ages 4 through 17.

Christmas Card Lane
Mission Ridge III
Olathe, KS
(913) 764-2913

This neighborhood of more than 200 homes all join together to create giant holiday card displays, lines of luminaries, and twinkling front-yard trees. The display usually runs from Thanksgiving until December 31 and is located north of 151st and west of Ridgeview at Ridgeview and Frontier. No charge, but we'd gladly pay.

Country Club Plaza

This legendary scene is perhaps our city's most treasured tradition when, starting each Thanksgiving night, more than 75-miles of jewel-toned lights illuminate every spire and swag of the Spanish-style architecture. Even when the temperature is 10 degrees below zero, a crowd shows up to help with the countdown as a celebrity guest pulls the switch. For the past few years the drama has escalated, with a spectacular fireworks display at the Fairmont hotel.

Mission Hills, KS
63rd and Ensley and Eisenhower Lake

We're not sure how this started—as a lark or a mistake—but a few years ago a homeowner tossed a string of white lights into a tree and let it fall naturally. The result was an illuminated modern art sculpture. The look caught on and now dozens of neighbors join in to create a sea of sailboat shapes along the streets of this pretty neighborhood.

Ward Parkway and Romany Road
between 69th and 71st Streets

Make this your second stop after viewing the Plaza lights. It's a fantastic sight, with hundreds of tree trunks wrapped in tiny white lights. The glowing circles are amazing when viewed in perspective from Ward Parkway.

Wild Lights at the Kansas City Zoo
(816) 513-5800
www.kansascityzoo.org

Whose bright idea was this? We're not sure, but it certainly is a magical experience. This walk-through festival features more than 45 larger-than-life animal light sculptures as well as more hands-on activities. Kids can pet live reindeer, ride the train, visit with Santa, and make holiday crafts from pine cones and such. The family fun continues every evening through December 30.

DECEMBER

Christmas in Weston
Downtown Weston, MO
(816) 640-2909

For more than 20 years this charming town has been getting all dolled up for the holidays and inviting us to visit. There's plenty to make the 40-minute drive worth your time: a walking tour of five historic homes, wandering street carolers, carriage rides through town, and visits with Father Christmas. Many of the antiques shops, stores, and boutiques offer hot cider and cookies, too. A donation of $8.00 for adults and $2.00 for children is welcome. And if you're so enchanted you want to visit Weston again, you'll find information in Day Trips and Weekend Getaways.

Drive-Through Living Nativity
Rockwood Baptist Church, 10035 Westport
Independence , MO
(816) 252-6155

More than 50 characters and live animals depict 13 scenes in the life of Jesus, creating a moving experience that reminds us of the true meaning of the holiday. Although there is no charge, donations are accepted. The drive is usually open for a week beginning the first of December.

Jazz Community Carol Fest
Community Christian Church, 4601 Main Street
(816) 561-6531

Ever hear "Silent Night" performed with a syncopated beat? You will at this happening, happy event that pairs classic holiday tunes with two dozen of Kansas City's finest musicians. Enough gospel and classic renditions are tossed in to keep everyone in the mood; it's simply not Christmas until you've heard Ida McBeth sing "O Holy Night." The $20 tickets go fast for this joyful treat that always falls on the first Sunday afternoon in December.

The Gardener's Railway
Powell Gardens
Kingsville, MO
(816) 697-2600
www.powellgardens.org

Model train enthusiasts will love watching G-gauge trains wind their way through a dwarf forest and lush greenery. Everyone else will just be thrilled to shrug off jackets in the toasty confines of a glass-encased conservatory. And there's still plenty to see throughout the rest of the gardens even in the sepia tones of winter. Regular admittance fees apply: $5.50 for adults, $2.50 for children ages 5 to 12.

The Nutcracker
Midland Theatre
(816) 931-3330
www.kcballet.com

This holiday classic continues to astound audiences, both young and old, with its magnificent sets, costumes, and special effects. (The Mouse King is truly sinister!) The performance features the beloved music of Peter I. Tchaikovsky, choreography by Todd Bolender, three casts of professional artists from Kansas City Ballet, and more than 100 youngsters ages 7 to 17 selected from Kansas City Ballet School. Children love the fantastical characters and perk up when they hear music they recognize. And the setting, historic Midland Theatre with its gilt trimming and rich velvets, adds to the magic. Tickets range from $15 to $60.

Winter Skies
Kansas City Museum
3218 Gladstone Boulevard
(816) 483-8300

Here's a wonderful way to introduce children to the heavenly world of astronomy or reacquaint yourself with favorite stars and constellations like Orion, Gemini, Taurus, and Sirius, the brightest star in our winter sky. The museum's planetarium presents two or three programs each Friday and Saturday through mid-March. Tickets cost $3.50 per person.

New Year's Eve Celebrations

Prove you can par-*tay* with the best of them with bubbles, balloons, and booga-looing at your choice of big galas or more intimate affairs. In addition to those listed below, dozens of hotels, nightclubs, casinos, and restaurants offer packages from $40 per person to more than $1,000. In one recent year, the *Kansas City Star* listed more than 50 different party events. Pop!

Hyatt Regency Crown Center
2345 McGee Street
(816) 421-1234, (816) 435-4152
www.hyattnye.com

Just you, your sweetheart, and 4,000 of your closest friends. Sound romantic? It certainly is *exciting,* especially at the stroke of midnight when they release 20,000 balloons. The evening also includes spacious entertainment areas, an indoor laser light show, and a pyrotechnic display. Packages include champagne, buffets, and open bars starting at $180 for singles hoping for a last-minute match and $275 for couples.

Union Station's New Year's Celebration
(816) 460-2020

It's been a tradition since 1933 to ring in the New Year at Union Station. At this grand palace there's plenty of room to find a cozy spot for a midnight kiss (dibs on under the clock) or link up with friends to toast the New Year. The evening includes more than just champagne; you can also visit Science City and see live stage shows in the Theater District. Prices start at $60.

Velvet Dog
400 East 31st Street
(816) 753-9990

This disco explosion has been the grooviest New Year's bash around since 1996. The crowd becomes one big groove-machine while dancing to a jukebox full of funky '70s disco hits, and next door the Empire Room's DJ takes requests for Bee Gees favorites. Better practice spelling out "YMCA" before you call for reservations. A $30 advance ticket ($40 at the door) will get you into both clubs and includes a limited open bar. This is a definite twenties crowd.

PARKS, LAKES, AND RECREATION

Kansas City and Mother Nature? We're like *that*. She blessed us with a landscape of shimmering lakes, lush green spaces, golden prairie grass, and acres of woodlands. Everywhere you look we're surrounded by the great outdoors, which might account for the dozens of sports activities and organizations you'll read about in the Sports chapter.

But for now let's see just how easy being green can be. Kansas City, Missouri, alone has 188 parks, including the third largest metropolitan park in the country, and more than 130 miles of boulevards and parkways covering some 10,000 acres. Downtown parks, sometimes shaded more by skyscrapers than sycamores, give city workers a respite from phones, faxes, and meetings long enough to enjoy lunch alfresco, listen to a jazz concert, or ogle the annual Elvis Parade. More about that later.

In addition, the city is ringed by hundreds of lakes, woods, and parks, places where you can commune with nature, possibly feed apples to bison, and most definitely feed your soul. With an abundance of rolling acres, fragrant floral displays, lakes overflowing with sporting amenities, and cool, sandy beaches, it's easy to say, "You bet!" when someone tells you to take it outside.

And how we do love our gardens. Kansas City gardeners have fought clay, rocks, and a pernicious Zone 5 to create some of the country's most stunning groupings of flowers and plantings. Drive down any street and you'll notice the fruits of their.labor as front doors are defined by masses of flowers. Each season brings another reason to celebrate. spring's iris, tulips, and daffodils give way to mounds of impatiens, splashy azaleas, and daylilies and then mums the word each fall. Where

the sun won't reach we plant hundreds of hostas. Backyards are filled with koi ponds, Japanese gardens, shady decks, and New Orleans–style courtyards. And while you may not want to stop the car to peer over a stranger's gate, you can get inspiration and fresh air at one of our public gardens described here. We highly recommend our 915-acre Powell Botanical Garden for starters.

There's far more to describe than one chapter will allow, so in the Close-up we've listed area parks and recreation departments and garden clubs where you can learn about other green spaces, special events, and classes. You may also want to peruse the Annual Events and Festivals chapter for special events regarding flora and fauna throughout the year. Perhaps there's a water garden tour or butterfly festival near you.

Chances are by the time you have that picnic basket ready, you'll have discovered a pastoral spot on which to spread a blanket. To help you find it, we've divided this chapter by activity type. Listings are in Kansas City, Missouri, unless otherwise noted.

LAKES

Fleming Park
Missouri Highway 40 on
Woods Chapel Road
Blue Springs, MO
(816) 795–8200
You bet they're happy campers in Jackson County; they're also happy boaters, fishing enthusiasts, swimmers, and hikers. Fleming Park, a 7,800-acre paradise just 15 minutes east of Kansas City, offers all these activities and more with two lakes, a

No man is an island . . . but we have one in the area. Twelve-acre Nelson Island is the only publicly accessible island in the Kansas River. It's located at the northern terminus of Mill Creek Streamway Park.

swimming beach, picnic shelters, archery range, hiking, and camping facilities. We provide camping information in the Accommodations chapter, or call (816) 229–8980 for a free campground guide.

Winding through the grounds are six trails that offer blufftop and lakefront vistas, as well as your choice of a quiet stroll to a challenging hike. The park is also where you'll find Missouri Town 1855, an antebellum farming community of more than 25 buildings dating from 1820 to 1860. This living-history museum uses original furnishings and equipment, interpreters in period attire, and rare livestock breeds to depict the lifestyles of the mid-19th century. Take a self-guided tour or watch for annual events like Children's Day in June when kids can take out the earphones and participate in a gunnysack race or pie-eating contest.

Take a safari ride through the 100-acre Animal Enclosure and you can stare a bison in the eyes and watch a family of elk play in a pasture. And, yes, please do feed the animals; be sure to bring apples and pears. Tours are given Saturdays throughout the summer, and tickets ($4.00 for adults, $3.00 for seniors and kids from 2 to 13) are available the day of the tour at Missouri Town; preregistration is not available. Call (816) 229–8980 for more information about this wild ride.

The Kemper Outdoor Education Center is a haven for nature lovers nestled on the east side of Lake Jacomo in the Fleming Park Nature Preserve. The center features aquariums, live displays of reptiles (go ahead, you touch it), a bird viewing area, and a display of rocks and minerals. The 40-acre site boasts butterfly gardens, ponds, beehives, wildlife-feeding stations, and a 1-mile nature trail through wetlands,

tallgrass prairie, and woodlands. Kemper Gardens is a popular spot for summer weddings where the bridge over the garden pool waterfall makes a lovely altar. Okay, we've fed the bison, said "I do," and filled up on blueberry pie. Now, get set to get wet at one of Fleming's two lakes.

Blue Springs Lake

Powerboats, water skis, tubes, and personal watercraft are all familiar sights on this 720-acre lake. Anglers try their hands at striped bass, bluegill, largemouth bass, and catfish. Bring your own boat or rent one at the marina, where you'll also find lakeside gasoline pumps, concession stands, and (let's think positive here) a fish-cleaning station. You can also pick up your state fishing license at the marina.

Or you can beach it at Blue Springs' sandy shoreline. Get energetic with a swim, volleyball game (volleyballs are available for rent), paddleboat, kayak, or canoe, or simply work on that tan. Certified lifeguards are on duty, and showers, restrooms, and full concessions are available, so you can simply show up with your bathing suit and a towel. Oh, and you'll need $3.00 for adults or $2.25 for kids 15 and younger. The fun starts Memorial Day.

Lake Jacomo

Set sail on this breathtaking 970-acre lake located in the heart of Fleming Park. Enjoy colorful sailboat regattas, or jump aboard a pontoon boat where the livin' is easy. The marina provides everything you'll need for a day at the lake: boat rental, concession stands, state fishing license, and tackle shop. And get that frying pan ready for some crappie, bluegill, largemouth bass, and walleye: Jacomo is an angler's dream come true.

Lake Jacomo is the place to be on any balmy day, but it's particularly appealing during special events like July's Lake Fest, when thousands of folks line the shores and take lake cruises, watch a regatta, and enjoy a spectacular fireworks display. The annual Easter Egg Hunt brings out hundreds of kids to look for goodies.

Wyandotte County Lake Park
91st Street and Leavenworth Road
Kansas City, KS
(913) 596-7077
You could easily imagine you're in the Lake of the Ozarks while driving through this 1,500-acre parkland with bluffs, heavily timbered woods, and gently rolling hills. Its 400-acre lake is where about half of Wyandotte County first placed a worm on a hook, and many of them return every spring to continue the drill. Some get an earlier start; boating and fishing are allowed from the last Saturday in February through November 30. Call about hours and permits. A horse trail and children's playground are other possibilities, and be sure to show up for free model railroad rides each second Saturday of the month from April through November.

WyCo Lake, as we call it, has 16 shelter houses, each with water, electricity, restrooms, and playground equipment; there's a reservation fee for each. Other picnic areas are free to the first group there with the potato salad. The handsome new James P. Davis Hall provides air-conditioned comfort for up to 150 guests. The lake is also home to the Korea-Vietnam Memorial, the only monument in the United States to honor soldiers from both wars. Dedicated in 1988, the structure includes a wall of marble fronted by two life-size bronze statues representing 111 who died from Wyandotte County. Kansas City sculptor Tom Corbin donated his time to create the bronzes, and a dozen labor unions donated thousands of hours to the project.

PARKS AND GARDENS

Antioch Park
6501 Antioch Road
Merriam, KS
(913) 831-3355
The Johnson County parks district purchased this park in 1956 (its first acquisition) and has turned it into one of the most popular community parks in the metropolitan area. Although at 44 acres it's not the largest, they've packed it with lots of activities like tennis and basketball courts, two small catch-and-release fishing lakes, and an accessible playground called Dodge Town where kids can climb in and out of the hotel and general store. Four picnic shelters offer tables, grills, drinking fountains, and restrooms and can be rented for around $30 for a half day from the parks department.

The park is also home to the Helen Cuddy Rose Garden and Memorial Arboretum, a picturesque wedding site found on the northwest corner of the park. More than 650 rose bushes grace the grounds, reflecting late centenarian Helen Cuddy's favorite flower. The peaceful garden, which has held many weddings over the years, also encloses a cascading fountain, a sundial, and a perennial bed containing iris, lamb's ear, hibiscus, crocus, and other old-fashioned favorites. A walkway will take you through the small arboretum, and picnic tables, a small lake with stepping-stones, and a children's play area will beckon you to stop for a while. You can remember loved ones by contributing a planting; for more information call (913) 831-3355.

Barney Allis Plaza
12th Street and Wyandotte
(816) 513-5000
Tucked between the Bartle Hall Convention Center and downtown hotels sits a city park that serves as an unofficial town square. It's a popular place to get a quick bite from a street vendor, link up with friends after work, and attend Party at the Barney block parties. Trees provide shade, and a large sloping fountain sits on the north end. To the east is the Kansas City Sports Walk of Stars, a monument to local greats that hasn't yet, if you'll forgive the pun, quite gotten off the ground. During summer months, the lunchtime crowd is treated to free noon concerts that could be jazz, blues, ragtime, or classical guitar. And every August, Barney meets the King as a dozen or so Elvis impersonators don

outlandish white jumpsuits, oversize sunglasses with attached sideburns, and sparkly belt buckles to hold a parade. Hundreds turn out to watch the quirky tribute and vote for the best outfit. Thankyouthankyouverymuch.

Although there's no charge to enjoy most of the green spaces we've described, you will need a little green to rent a shelter or a boat or spend a day at a beach. Call the numbers shown for fee information or to reserve your space. And call early; many of the most popular shelters are reserved far in advance.

Bonner Springs Park
Interstate 70 North
Bonner Springs, KS
(913) 596-7077

This 540-acre park is kept busy year-round with more than just picnics and volleyball. Located adjacent to the Agricultural Hall of Fame, the park houses the Sandstone Amphitheatre, where top-selling musical groups perform outdoor concerts. Each fall the area becomes an Old English village during the Renaissance Festival (read about this in Annual Events and Festivals). When the electric guitars and jousting stop, the park offers outdoor activities like tennis courts, ball fields, and shady picnic areas.

Deanna Rose Children's Farmstead
13800 Switzer Road
Overland Park, KS
(913) 897-2360

A favorite destination for families thanks to its petting zoo, wagon train rides, and other activities, the farmstead also contains a delightful garden maintained by the Johnson County Extension Master Gardeners. Surrounded by a white picket fence, the old-fashioned garden contains a butterfly garden; herbs; shade garden planted with hostas, lilies, and columbine; and a vegetable garden, all along a winding brick walkway. Usually a garden expert

is there, measuring the marigolds or tending to tulips, so you might get some advice during your visit.

English Landing Park
Parkville, MO
(816) 505-2227
www.parkvillemo.com

This long and narrow 64-acre greenway stretches along the natural bends and limestone bluffs of the Missouri River, providing wonderful views from its hiking trails, picnic shelters, and playgrounds. Most of the amenities are just across a turn-of-the-20th-century truss bridge. You'll find lots of folks enjoying ripe peaches and other fresh produce from the farmers' market alongside the trail. The park hosts several festivals throughout the year, including the Parkville Jazzfest and Christmas on the River.

For even more adventure, head to the Parkville Nature Sanctuary, which offers 115 acres of woods and wetlands, a waterfall, a beaver colony, and a glimpse of the area's storied past as a river town. You'll find a trailhead just north of the soccer field parking lot. And if you've had enough of the great outdoors, head back to Parkville's Main Street, where shops, galleries, and a wide array of restaurants await.

Ewing and Muriel Kauffman
Memorial Garden
4800 Rockhill Road
(816) 932-1200

This exquisite walled sanctuary is one more lasting legacy from Ewing and Muriel Kauffman. And although not large, there is much to see as you walk through each display. Brick pathways lead you past elegant ironwork, sculptures, and stained-glass windows providing a delightful mix of vistas and textures. A teak bench provides a place to pause and murmur a quiet thank-you to the Kauffmans, whose gifts are ever blooming. Garden pavilions provide shade, and pergolas brace bright blossoms nodding on vines. A lush mix of flowers and plants is changed three times each year, so the

The Men Who Turned Kansas City Green

When people visit Kansas City and swoon over our vast parks and boulevards, they're paying tribute to landscape architects George Kessler and the father-and-son team of Sid and Herbert Hare.

When a 21-year-old George Kessler came to town in 1890, he saw little more than scattered homes on little hills, occasionally separated by junglelike foliage. He soon partnered with William Rockhill Nelson, who owned and edited the *Star* and who was desperate to turn the little town into a picturesque and pleasant city. Together they, along with other concerned citizens like August Meyer, created the City Beautiful project. By 1895 Kessler was replacing shacks, dumps, and rickety signboards with verdant hillsides, tree-shaded lakes and walks, and smooth, spacious boulevards.

For 30 years he worked with the Kansas City Park Board to create Gladstone Boulevard and Cliff Drive, the Paseo, and Liberty Memorial and to turn a depressing Vinegar Hill into the majestic Penn Valley Park. George Kessler did more than just green-up Kansas City. During his 40-year career he designed 26 communities, 26 park and boulevard systems, nearly 50 parks, and 46 estates and residences in 23 states, Mexico, and China. You can learn more about his work through the George Kessler Society (P.O. Box 6685, Kansas City, MO 64123–0658, www.georgekessler.org).

Sid Hare started his career as superintendent at Forest Hill Cemetery, where he became a national authority on expanding the roles of cemeteries as botanical gardens, bird sanctuaries, and arboretums. In 1910 he started a landscaping consulting firm with his son, Herbert, who had studied with the famous Frederick Law Olmsted. During their 28-year partnership, father and son continued George Kessler's tradition of wide, beautiful boulevards and parks throughout Kansas City's landscape.

Their trademark was winding roads contoured to natural topography, preserving trees and valleys, and retaining (or creating) scenic vistas. In 1913 J. C. Nichols hired the Hares to work on the Country Club District area. In addition to laying out approximately 2,500 acres, the firm designed the grounds for many homes, including some of the 50-acre estates that made up the original Mission Hills. Herbert was responsible for designing settings for many of the imported sculptures and fountains that Nichols placed throughout his developments.

Hare & Hare also collaborated with architect Edward Buehler Delk in planning Nichols's Country Club Plaza. Other memorable works include the Rose Garden in Loose Park, which Sid completed in 1937, a year before his death, and the setting for the Nelson-Atkins Museum of Art. Herbert went on to contribute projects throughout the country, including Kansas City's masterful Linda Hall Library arboretum. He passed away in 1960, soon after completing plans for Lake Jacomo.

The legacy of Kessler and Hare & Hare continues today through programs like MetroGreen, a large-scale system of interconnected corridors that will span more than 1,000 miles to link city to countryside, suburb to urban area. More than a system of trails and bike paths, MetroGreen will conserve the unique native landscape—bluffs and woodlands and prairies, parks and boulevards—to ensure that future generations will enjoy them as well.

garden looks completely different from month to month.

A reflecting pool runs the length of the Parterre Garden, where slender female sculptures by local artist Tom Corbin are captured in midpirouette. The octagonal pool in the Green Garden offers an ever-moving water display, and shhh . . . there's one more area to be discovered. The secluded Secret Garden really does have a secret: three hidden fountains that shoot arcs of water above your head at random moments. At least once a day someone feels a drop from above and asks, "Is it raining?" The garden is open every day except some holidays, and there is no admission fee. No pets are allowed except assistant dogs. There is one animal allowed in, but he's on duty. The squirrel-chaser is Thomas, who was adopted from a shelter.

Although perhaps you'll never have a park named for you like Mr. Swope, Powell, or Loose, you could leave a legacy with a park bench, tree planting, or rose bush. Several of our public parks and gardens can arrange for a lasting memorial in your honor.

Heritage Park
159th Street and Pflumm Road
Olathe, KS
(913) 831-3355

This 1,160-acre park was dedicated on Independence Day 1981 and includes enough amenities to warrant a parade. Facilities include 10 picnic shelters; a 45-acre lake; a marina with pedal boat and sailboard rentals; concession stands; play areas; fields for softball, soccer, and football; and an 18-hole championship golf course and driving range. We're tuckered out just thinking about it.

One of its most unique features is the Black Bob Shelter House, which is on an island and also accessible by foot from the marina area. It can handle up to 300 and is available by reservation only. The shelter includes 30 tables, a large barbecue grill,

electricity, and restrooms—a good thing, because it's the only district shelter that allows 3.2 beer. Extremely popular, it is often rented months (even years) in advance.

Linda Hall Library
5109 Cherry Street
(816) 926-8747
www.lindahall.org

Most people come to the Linda Hall Library seeking knowledge and information. With more than one million volumes, it is the largest privately supported library of science, engineering, and technology in the United States. But those seeking tranquility will find it in the 14-acre urban arboretum with 450 or so trees representing 160 varieties. In late April the tree peonies, saucer-size beauties in vibrant colors, begin to bloom; they constitute one of the largest collections in the Midwest. By May the antique shrub roses scent the air as you stroll by. A butterfly garden is planted with happy marigolds, color-box zinnias, Mexican sunflowers, and nectar-rich fennel. A new area contains 50 species of indigenous perennials. Tours of the gardens can be arranged, or you may pick up a printed guide at the library's front desk for $5.00.

Loose Park
51st and Wornall Road
(816) 561-9710

Loose Park wasn't always so serene. At one time this was the site of the bloody Civil War Battle of Westport, but today the only reminders are historical markers placed throughout the 74 acres. An 8-foot-high bronze statue of Jacob Loose watches over the garden named in his honor. And early-morning joggers, Plaza workers breaking for lunch, late-afternoon lovers, and children tossing bread crusts to the ducks are all drawn to this space up the hill from the Plaza.

Within Loose Park is the Laura Conyers Smith Municipal Rose Garden, with a reflecting pool, a fragrant display of hundreds of colorful blooms, and a small lake

Welcome to Paradise

Set among gently rolling hills, Powell Gardens is one of the Midwest's most treasured places, offering 915 acres of vivid plants bursting with color, winding pathways along brooks and waterfalls, windswept meadows, and some of the region's most striking architecture. Luckily, this scene of serenity is a mere 40 miles away.

Your tour begins at the visitor center, a handsome stacked-limestone building that houses a conservatory, classrooms, a delightful gift shop, and Cafe Thyme, where upscale buffet food is served for lunch, Sunday brunch, and dinner during special events.

When you're ready to explore the grounds, you can take a free trolley ride to the different areas or cross the bridge on foot to the Island Garden set in a 12-acre lake. This is a showplace for native and exotic water plants, rock gardens, and ornamental trees—nearly 800 varieties of plants in all. A three-pooled cascading water garden acts as the focal point. The island's north side allows for an uninterrupted view of the stunning Marjorie Powell Allen Chapel, a wood, glass, and stone triangle in the sky designed by famed Arkansas architect Fay Jones.

After leaving the water garden, head to your right past the Wildflower Meadow. There you'll enter the cool and serene Rock and Waterfall Garden, dressed in every shade of green imaginable in delicate ferns and nearly 50 varieties of hostas. Sweet pinks and white appear in flowering trees in spring, and in summer raspberry-colored azaleas pro-

vide a burst of color. Hidden among these enchanted woods are picturesque decks and secluded benches for cuddling or taking time to reflect.

Just over a bridge is the 3½-acre Perennial Garden, the largest in the Midwest, with more than 5,000 plantings, including many chosen specifically as come-hithers to butterflies. In summer the place nearly pops with orange, deep reds, and brilliant yellows as 250 varieties of daylilies lift their trumpets to the skies. The curving walkways take you through twists and turns to a peaceful pavilion overlooking the lake.

Back at the visitor center you can enjoy a crisp salad or tasty sandwich or buy a book or garden tool in the gift shop. Here's also where you may take part in a class like growing orchids, constructing a birdhouse, or making holiday wreaths from natural elements. Outdoor festivals and events include the popular Booms and Blooms over Fourth of July weekend, with live music and an impressive fireworks display, and Ballet in the Park with the Kansas City Ballet. Several times a year members of the Astronomical Society of Kansas City present stargazing demonstrations.

More than 100,000 visitors enjoy the gardens (816–697–2600, www.powellgardens.org) each year. General admission April through October is $5.50 for adults, $4.50 for seniors, and $2.50 for children ages 5 to 12. From November to March the price is $1.00 less. Just one hint before you head out: Bring plenty of film.

Parks and Recreation Departments

Most cities within our metroplex have their own parks and recreation departments, staffed and managed by those wonderful men and women who plan outings; clean away debris; and keep our lakes, parks, trails, and public gardens so idyllic. Here's how to reach them. And when you do, you might say thanks!

MISSOURI

Kansas City
Kansas City Missouri Parks & Recreation, (816) 513-7500

Cass County
Belton Parks & Recreation, (816) 331-0336

Clay County
Clay-Platt Baseball League, (816) 734-3733

Clay County Parks & Recreation, (816) 532-0803

North Kansas City Parks & Recreation, (816) 274-6008

Liberty Parks & Recreation, (816) 792-6009

Grandview Parks & Recreation, (816) 763-3900

Jackson County
Jackson County Parks & Recreation, (816) 795-8200

Raytown Parks & Recreation, (816) 358-4100

Platte County
Platte County Parks & Recreation, (816) 858-3338

KANSAS

Johnson County
Blue Valley Parks & Recreation, (913) 685-6000

Johnson County Parks & Recreation, (913) 831-3355

with a tranquil lily pond. Although Jacob Loose's widow, Ella, who commissioned the park in 1927, had requested athletic fields, we're secretly glad someone dropped the ball, so to speak. Without shouts of fouls and scores, Loose Park provides a restful, peaceful retreat.

Overland Park Arboretum & Botanical Gardens
179th and Antioch
Overland Park, KS
(913) 685-3604
This hidden, 300-acre gem in south Overland Park is most definitely growing, with new ecosystems and a handsome new learning center. Five miles of wood chip–covered hiking trails meander through the area and across two 75-foot bridges spanning Wolf Creek. The trails become slightly more challenging along limestone bluffs rising above the southern banks of the creek. Views from here are marvelous, and if you linger long enough you might see a crane or other waterfowl silently land.

Eight natural ecosystems, from prairie grassland and dense woods to a wildflower meadow, provide a surprise at every turn. The highlight is the Erickson Water Garden, with four waterfalls and a bog

Lenexa Parks & Recreation,
(913) 541-8592

Mission Community Center,
(913) 722-8200

Olathe Parks & Recreation,
(913) 764-6163

Overland Park Parks & Recreation,
(913) 895-6350

Wyandotte County
Kansas City, Kansas Parks &
Recreation, (913) 596-7077

Bonner Springs Parks & Recreation,
(913) 422-7010

GARDENING ORGANIZATIONS AND RESOURCES

The Loose Park Garden Center
5200 Pennsylvania Avenue
(816) 784-5399

This is the headquarters for several garden clubs, where meetings, shows, and workshops take place. The horticultural reference library has about 1,500 books on every bloomin' thing. It's open 8:00 A.M. to 4:00 P.M. weekdays. The Garden

Center Association of Greater Kansas City, an umbrella group with about 1,000 members, meets here. Its newsletter, *Garden Bulletin,* is published bimonthly and includes a calendar of events. Membership costs $15 a year. For information call the number above.

Master Gardeners' Hotlines
These are the experts to call when your dahlia's drooping or your tomatoes are toast. Armed with state horticultural training courses and scads of experience, the volunteers can answer your questions or direct you to other resources. The Johnson County Master Gardeners work at the Deanna Rose Farmstead, 137th and Switzer in Overland Park. The hotline (913-764-6306) is staffed 9:00 A.M. to 4:00 P.M. weekdays. The Missouri Extension hotline (816-833-8733) is open 9:00 A.M. to 3:00 P.M. weekdays. Or contact the Master Gardeners' automated Infoline, (913) 393-1913 or www.outreach.missouri .edu/extensioninfoline.

with more than 100 natural plantings that attract birds, butterflies (more than 500 varieties have been identified here!), and two-footed nature lovers. Benches scattered around the area invite you to rest and listen to the restful sounds of cascading water and laughing children.

The Marder Woodland Garden is a relatively new addition with massive stone pillars supporting wooden arbors at its entrance and overlook. It's a romantic spot with the sound of falling water resonating through towering trees. And your little nature boy or girl will have fun following a spiraling walkway or watching frogs frolic

in a pond in the Children's Discovery Garden. Plants and trees are identified here, as they are throughout the garden. An easy, half-mile asphalt trail provides a nice stroll.

A visitor center hosts programs and social events and contains a small gift shop and concession stand. Enjoy your refreshment on the sunny patio. When visiting, please note that you cannot reach the arboretum by going south on Antioch. Take U.S. Highway 69 south to 179th Street, turn right, and go west about 0.5 mile. Large signs will indicate the entrance on your left. Admission is free, but donations are accepted.

Shawnee Mission Park
7900 Renner Road
Shawnee, MO

More than three million visitors enjoy this 1,250-acre park every year, more than any other park in the state of Kansas, making the district wonder why it doesn't open a tollbooth. Lucky for us, it's a public park and anyone can enjoy its many natural wonders along with a few treasures where Mother Nature got some human help.

Facilities include a 150-acre lake for boating, fishing, and sailboarding, 12 shelters and numerous picnic areas, horseback and nature trails, an archery range, and a marina. A sandy beach with a concession and bathhouse appeals to sun-lovers; a $2.00 fee gets you in. Shelters range in size from Shelter No. 3 with a lake view and seating for 32 to No. 10 in the Walnut Grove area with three grills, 20 tables, and seating for 160. Please invite us to *that* party. In fall this park has a splashy show of colorful foliage that rivals New England. Colorful trees line the main road that circles the park; take one and head to the south side of the park where a 5⅛-story observation tower provides a breathtaking view of the jewel-tone leaves.

Shawnee Mission Park is also home to Theatre in the Park, a popular summer theater venue (see The Arts for more information), and the John Barkley Visitor Center, which has an exhibit on the history of parks in Johnson County. Pet owners, however, make a mad dash to the dog park, a 70-acre fenced area that is leash-free. With access to the lake, it's a favorite with labs, who gleefully swim out to retrieve sticks. Leashes are required everywhere else.

Swope Park
Swope Parkway and Meyer Boulevard
(816) 871-5600

Topping out at 1,769 acres, Swope Park is the largest city park in Kansas City and one of the most expansive in the country. The land was donated by millionaire Thomas H. Swope and dedicated on June 25, 1898. It contains two golf courses; areas for softball, soccer, rugby, and Fris-

bee; horseback trails; and a day camp for kids. And, yes, you can rough it in the middle of a city: Hiking enthusiasts can take a guided scenic tour along the hill south of the Lake of the Woods.

The Lakeside Nature Center (4701 East Gregory Boulevard, 816–513–8960) within Swope Park is Missouri's largest wildlife rehabilitation center, caring for more than 3,300 native animals and birds. The center also has a 1,000-gallon aquarium and offers educational programs for all ages, including bird-watching, animal tracking, streamside hikes, and nature photography. The nature center is open 9:00 A.M. to 5:00 P.M. Tuesday through Saturday and noon to 4:00 P.M. Sunday. Admission is free, and the center is open year-round, closed Monday. Swope Park is also home to the 8,000-seat Starlight Theatre as well as the Kansas City Zoo and Sprint IMAX Theatre.

TRAILS

Drive around this suburban area and you might dismiss it as row after row of housing developments, shopping centers, and office buildings. But thanks to city fathers with vision, Johnson County, Kansas, is a place of green spaces, meandering streams, and pocket parks, with about 140 miles of trails for walking, hiking, and biking. You just need to know where to look. The following will give you a good head start, but to really get a lay of the land, the Johnson County Park and Recreation District (913–438–7275, www.jcprd.com) offers maps and descriptions. And if you plan to take a phone, park rangers are available through the dispatcher by calling (913) 782-0720.

The Indian Creek Trail and Tomahawk Creek Trail system in Overland Park provides more than 30 miles of hiking and biking leisure. The Indian Creek portion joins Quivira Park at 119th and Quivira and extends to Leawood City Park, where it dips in and under Interstate 435 and through commercial, residential, and office areas. The areas are shaded, a few park benches are scattered around, and you'll see a charming little waterfall along the way. You can also access the trail at several points, including Corporate Woods office park, where a drinking fountain and picnic shelter mark the entrance to a partially hidden bridge.

Tomahawk Creek Trail runs behind Blue Valley Recreation Fields near 138th Street and Antioch Road, and from Nieman Road and 135th Street around St. Andrew's Golf Course to the Deanna Rose Farmstead, which makes a great stop along your way (see Kidstuff for information about this delightful place). The trail connects with a trail at Miller's Woods.

Mill Creek Streamway Park crosses four counties as it travels along Mill Creek from Woodland Road north to Kansas Highway 10 in Olathe and then continues north

When exploring our many walking and biking trails, remember it's "Yield to the right and pass on the left." When approaching walkers from behind on a bike or in-line skates, it's courteous, not to mention safer, to announce "To your left" to allow them time to move over.

through Lenexa, Shawnee (where it dips into Shawnee Mission Park), and Merriam to the Kansas River. If you made it all the way, celebrate with a little dance on 12-acre Nelson Island, the only public-accessible island in the Kansas River, where the trail ends. Mill Creek includes wheelchair-accessible parking, drinking fountains, and shaded picnic areas.

SPORTS

Ballgames! Getcher red-hot ball-games here! In Kansas City we love our sports. Always have, always will, whether our teams are winning or not. And our sports town status began long before the Royals and Chiefs suited up. It started in 1884 when the Kansas City Unions baseball team first took the field.

But it was the Kansas City Monarchs, those champs of the Negro Leagues, that really put us on the map. Satchel Paige, Jackie Robinson, and Buck O'Neil, who's still a ball of fire well into his nineties, were so important to the sport and this city that we built the country's only Negro Leagues Baseball Museum (www.nlbm.com). You can read more about this terrific memorial in the Attractions chapter.

And no other city in America can rival our history of college tournament basketball. A tournament—Big Six, Big Seven, Big Eight, Big 12—has been played in Kansas City every year, sometimes twice a year, since 1946. But it started long before that. In 1937 what is now known as the NAIA tournament, the nation's oldest, began at downtown Municipal Auditorium. By the time the NCAA Tournament final came here in 1940, 10,000 fans packed the stands and March Madness became an official affliction. The NCAA will return in 2005 after a short stint in Texas. And after an eight-year absence, the NAIA returned to Kansas City in 2002. We remain the undisputed Tournament Town.

We're not always watching sports. . . sometimes we're participating in them. You'll find plenty of athletic activities to keep you in liniment, including golf, cycling, hiking, and running. We're also big on joining clubs so that we can talk about our sports when we're not watching or playing; for instance, for a city without a single snowcapped mountain, we have one of the country's largest ski clubs. You'll get

contact information in this chapter. But first, let's hit one out of the ballpark.

The listings in this chapter are grouped by spectator, participation, family, and kids' sports. The facilities are located in Kansas City, Missouri, unless otherwise noted.

SPECTATOR SPORTS

Kansas City Royals
Kauffman Stadium,
Truman Sports Complex
(816) 921–8000, (800) 676–9257
www.kcroyals.com
Here's a trivia question for you, sports buffs: What local team name in the late 1880s sounded a lot like the Red Sox? Give up? It was the Kansas City Blue Stockings. Honest. More than a century later we're still on that side of the color wheel, but you can bet there are more people cheering at Kauffman than at the old Muehlbach or Municipal Stadiums. For one thing, The K, as we affectionately call it, seats 40,625 fans.

The stadium was named for Ewing Kauffman, who purchased the Kansas City Royals in 1968 and turned the team into one of the most successful franchises in baseball. They won six division championships and two American League pennants. We showed our appreciation by building a fancy new Royals Stadium in 1973 and they proceeded to fill it with two million fans a year more than 11 times. Now *that's* a lot of beer and peanuts. The stadium is one of the fan-friendliest arenas in pro sports. Behind the fence in right field is a 322-foot-wide fountain, the largest privately owned water display in the world, that puts on a dazzling show between innings and when one of our boys hits a home run. In left field is a 30-by-40-foot Sony JumboTron video display board that was the largest in the country when installed in 1990. Water jets and fireworks filled the sky on October 27, 1985, when Kansas City won the World Series title with an 11-0 victory over the St. Louis Cardinals.

We said thanks to Mr. K on July 2, 1993, when the 21-year-old Royals Stadium was renamed in his honor, and there wasn't a dry eye in the dugout or stands. A month later tears came again as the only owner the team had ever had died at the age of 76. But George Brett gave us something to cheer about in 1999 when he became the first member of the Royals to be inducted into the Major League Baseball Hall of Fame.

Kansas City ushered in a new era when David Glass took over ownership in 2000. And although we haven't returned to the glory days of 1985—yet—there's always this season. Tickets range from $7.00 to $19.00.

Kansas City Chiefs
Arrowhead Stadium
(816) 920-9300
www.kcchiefs.com

Other teams hate to play at Arrowhead Stadium, and it has less to do with the opposition than the fans. Kansas City boosters are known as the loudest and most enthusiastic in the National Football League. Crowd noises have been known to challenge even the most seasoned veteran's concentration; even squinting up at that sea of blood-red jackets, hats, and sweatshirts can be intimidating.

Fans have had plenty of practice chanting in unison; of the nearly 80,000 seats, most are occupied by season ticket holders. The rest are usually snapped up when single-game tickets, at about $40 a pop, go on sale in late July.

Around here, pro football isn't a game, it's a lifestyle. Entire sections of department stores are devoted to Chiefs apparel. Every fall Chiefs flags fly from cars and front porches. Then there are the tailgate parties, when the parking lot takes on a blue haze from row after row of grills sizzling up hot dogs and burgers. The competition is nearly as fierce as what's to

come, with groups trying to outdo one another and TV cameras recording the action. You'll see everything from barbecue ribs, baked beans, and cold beer to chilled baby lobster with fine wine. We'll stick with brats, please, with plenty of mustard and kraut.

Kansas City football, too, has had a long history. It started in 1924 with the Blues (that color again!), an NFL team that changed its name to the Cowboys a year later. In 1963 Lamar Hunt moved his Dallas Texans to Kansas City and named them for the city's mayor, H. Roe Bartle, whose nickname was "Chief." The team won the American Football League championship in 1967 and 1970. On January 11, 1970, the Chiefs won the Super Bowl, and in 1972 they moved into their new stadium in the Harry S Truman Sports Complex.

Kansas City Wizards
(816) 920-9300
www.kcwizards.com

When it was announced that the new major league soccer team in Kansas City would be known as The Whiz, the management got what they wanted: plenty of attention. When the jokes threatened to overcome the players' potential, the name was changed to the Wizards in 1996. Ahhhh, that's better. The new name and jerseys must have worked; the team won the MLS Cup in 2000. If that's like winning the Super Bowl of soccer, it's appropriate because the Wizards' owner is Lamar Hunt, who also bankrolls the Chiefs.

The Wizards play their home games at Arrowhead Stadium; the season runs from April through September. Tickets cost $12.00 to $19.00 for adults and $8.00 to $13.00 for youths.

By the time you read this, Kansas City may be breaking ground for a downtown arena that will draw additional sports franchises and big-name concerts to our revitalized Downtown area.

PARTICIPATION SPORTS

Bike or run along our many trails, swing a golf club, bowl a few strings, or take to the ice. We figure you've got to stay active just to burn off all that barbecue. No matter what your pleasure or passion, you'll have an opportunity to play it here. And if you're into fishing or sailing, check out our extraordinary array of lakes in the Parks, Lakes, and Recreation chapter.

Golf

Kansas City has been in love with golf since 1894, when two Scottish duffers created the town's first course in what is now the Hyde Park neighborhood. Did we say "course?" It was actually nothing more than a deserted cow pasture near 36th and Gillham Road. Two years later a group of the original players started Kansas City Country Club, an elite organization that celebrated its golden anniversary in 1996.

By the early 1900s courses began to dot the landscape, and the increased interest attracted some of the finest golf course designers of the day, including A. W. Tillinghast and James Dalgleish. Kansas City was becoming known as a golfing town. More courses, both private and public, sprang up, and the city played host to a PGA event for more than a decade. All that practicing paid off. Kansas City native Tom Watson has won the PGA Tour Player of the Year six times and eight Majors and is considered one of the top all-time players since turning pro in 1971. Another native, Matt Gogel, is also making a name for himself.

Of the nearly two million people living in the KC metro area, it's estimated that 270,000 are golfers. No wonder, then, that we've raised some winners. Pros from our town include Tom Watson, Matt Gogel, Bruce Lietzke, and Tom Pernice Jr. (PGA Tour) and Amy Alcott (LPGA Tour).

As interest in golf grew, spurred by Tom Watson's success, Kansas City began to see a need for more public courses, and dozens of city and county greens were developed during the 1980s and 1990s. Today more than one million rounds of golf are played annually on 72 courses (46 public and 26 private) in the Greater Kansas City area. And new courses are added every year to keep up with the demand. Of the 1.6 million people who live in the metropolitan area, 240,000 are golfers, or about 15 percent. You can bet that prime home lots next to new golf courses go fast. Our private courses are superb, and we hope you'll have a chance to play on at least one during your visit; many of them have reciprocal privileges for members of other clubs. In this chapter we'll concentrate on our beautiful public courses.

And as for Tom, our hometown hero? You can usually catch him at Kansas City's annual TD Waterhouse Championship as the top Senior PGA Tour player. He also hosts the annual Children's Mercy Golf Classic, an event he's been involved with since 1979.

Please note that this list is not inclusive. The Convention and Visitors Bureau of Greater Kansas City (816–221–5242, 800–767–7700, www.kansascitygolfguide .com) publishes a handy list of all the courses. We've listed courses with a wide range of fees.

Deer Creek Golf Club
7000 West 133rd Street
Overland Park, KS
(913) 681–3100
www.deercreekgc.com
With its 162 acres of rolling terrain and plenty of mature trees, sand, and water, well-traveled golfers may immediately identify this as a Robert Trent Jones Jr. course. It's certainly one of his most beautiful. Jones has crafted not just one but two signature holes into this masterpiece. The No. 3 hole is a 422-yard hole that plays between a creek on the left and a bunker on the right. To make it you'll have to drive it dead-on. And if you didn't care

for that water hazard the first time around, you won't care for the second signature shot. It comes at No. 15, a 22-yard par 3. Monday through Friday fees are $70, $10 more on weekends.

Heritage Park Golf Course
16455 Lackman Road
Olathe, KS
(813) 829–GOLF (4653)
This popular course isn't a walk in the park, although it is in one. The course has proven its level of difficulty by being used for U.S. Open qualifying rounds. The 16th hole is the one that can trip you up on this Don Sechrest–designed course. The 215-yard, par-3 hole requires 190 yards of carry over a body of water. We'd like to have a take in that used golf-ball concession. Fees range from $14 to $20 weekdays and $16 to $26 Friday through Sunday and holidays.

Ironhorse Golf Club
15400 Mission Road
Leawood, KS
(913) 685–GOLF
www.ironhorsegolf.com
Although only open since 1995, this 189-acre course has quickly become an area favorite, winning top honors from readers of *Ingram's* magazine and accolades from *Golf Digest*. It was designed by Dr. Michael Hurdzan, and every effort was made to maintain the natural landscape, which gives the course a mature look that will only improve with time. The par-72 championship 18-hole layout offers a distinct challenge on every hole, and the creek that meanders through the course affects play on no fewer than 15 holes. Ironhorse features bent grass greens, zoysia fairways, and bluegrass and fescue roughs. Golfers can choose from five tee complexes per hole. Total yardage varies from 6,900 yards from the back tees to 4,783 from the forward tees.

The upscale homes that surround the course are as magnificent as the grounds. Fees are $46 on weekdays and $54 on weekends. Cart fees are $16.

Longview Lake Golf Course
11100 View High Drive
(816) 761–9445
Near one of the area's most picturesque lakes, this course features varying elevations, elevated tee boxes, and a little longer play. The Scottish-style links offer something for every skill level. Signature holes both include water. No. 8 is particularly challenging because of the pond running along the left side. And one of the prettiest views on the course provides its biggest trouble spot on No. 12, which is played next to Longview Lake. Weekday greens fees are $23, $26 Friday through Sunday. A cart will cost you $6.00. And consider showing up four hours before twilight, when the all-you-can-play buffet is open and costs just $24 including the cart.

If you're looking for a new set of golf clubs, you might want to check out Kenneth Smith Golf Club Company (913–631–5100), which helped win the first Masters Golf Tournament. Horton Smith from Springfield, Missouri, won the tourney with custom-made clubs from the 82-year-old firm that counts Bob Hope, Bing Crosby, Pres. Dwight D. Eisenhower, Ty Cobb, Mickey Mantle, and Sylvester Stallone among its clients, past and present. A set of irons will run $1,200 to $2,000, a driver around $280 to $400.

Overland Park Golf Club
125th and Quivira
Overland Park, KS
(913) 897–3809
The biggest hazard here is finding a place to park at 5:00 P.M. Keep driving, though, because playing here is a pleasure. Around 125,000 rounds of golf are played on OPGC per year, a tribute to its beauty, location, and value. On weekdays you'll pay $20 to walk and $34 to ride; $23 to walk and $34 to ride on weekends.

With 42 sand bunkers on 13 holes and two lakes affecting five holes, you might as

well say each hole is a challenge. The course is sited high on a hill in Overland Park with extraordinary views. As you can imagine, tee times go fast, so it's best to call several days in advance. This course also offers a popular par-3, nine-hole ladies league, and for a community course has a decent pro shop, instructors, and snack bar.

Swope Park Memorial Golf Course
Interstate 435 and Gregory
in Swope Park
(816) 513-8910
www.swopememorialgolfcourse.com

This course is carved out of Swope Park, at 1,769 acres one of the country's largest metropolitan parks. The area is also home to Starlight Theatre, the Kansas City Zoo, a hiking trail, and a nature conservatory. But with land this vast you'll feel completely insulated from the world in this natural beauty.

A. W. Tillinghast built the course in 1913, and although it's a shorter course than many more contemporary ones in Kansas City, it has many excellent features. That is, if you're ready for a challenging game. Two of Kansas City's toughest holes are here. No. 17 is slightly uphill, and adding to the tension is a bunker in the middle of the fairway. And on the 14th hole, bunkers to the left of a right turn 250 yards out can make you wonder why you ever took up the sport. Perhaps the reasonable fees will cool you off: Nine holes will cost you $12.00, with a $6.00 cart fee; 18 holes cost $20.00.

Tennis

Head out with your tennis racket to any park in the city and you're bound to find a net with your name on it. Many are free or available for a dollar or two; a few have lights that are often coin operated. During nice weather we recommend calling ahead to reserve court time.

Happy Rock Park
7600 Northeast Antioch Road
Gladstone, MO
(816) 436-2200

Four lighted courses are located in this Clay County park that gets its name from a twist on the city's name. There's no charge for court time, which can mean some wait time, but you'll have other activities to keep you entertained. The 80-acre park offers playgrounds, fitness trails, soccer fields, and beautiful open land that's just right for sailing Frisbees or flying kites.

Indian Creek Recreation Center
7401 West 103rd Street
Overland Park, KS
(913) 895-6385

Although these eight courts have no lighting, they're popular until dusk when players seem to be enjoying the great outdoors as much as a good backhand. A tennis pro is on hand during summer, and a playground, picnic shelter, and paved fitness trail are nearby. Overland Park offers 30 tennis courts in all within their park system; this one is the largest.

Plaza Tennis Center
4747 J.C. Nichols Parkway
(816) 784-5100
www.kcmo.org/parks

These are quite possibly the most glamorous tennis courts in the country, with architecture that echoes the Country Club Plaza, and the landscaped Brush Creek walkway within view. Recently expanded to add lockers, showers, and a pro shop, these 14 lighted courts include a stadium with seating.

The gorgeous new digs have attracted professional, college, and regional championships. Lessons and racquet stringing are available. Court fees range from $4.00 to $8.00 per hour with an additional $1.00 for lights, and reservations are taken up to 24 hours in advance. Annual cards are available from $50 for juniors to $225 for families; benefits include three-day prior reservations, waived court fees, and other discounts.

Fencing

Kansas City Fencing Center
9900 Antioch
Overland Park, KS
(913) 579-9535
www.kcfencing.org
Fencing helps develop agility, strength, speed, and discipline. If not, what's the point? This program is taught by some of the country's finest, including head coach Kelly Williams, the top-ranked female saber fencer in the United States. Now she's training others to succeed: Her students have placed in the top eight in United States Fencing Association competition in every age group. Classes are available for beginning, intermediate, advanced, and expert level fencers in three categories: saber, foil, and épée. Intro classes, which include two one-hour classes per week, range from $50 to $70 per month and provide equipment. Open sessions using your own equipment are also available.

Sailboat Racing

Jacomo Sailing Club
Lake Jacomo
Blue Springs, MO
(913) 707-8818
www.jacomosailingclub@usa.net
This club has been promoting the sport of sailboat racing since 1958, before the lake was even completed. And you've got to love any organization that calls a meeting in the middle of a crystal-blue lake on a Sunday afternoon. Although the majority of its members like nothing better than a good competitive regatta, some members just come out to watch, cheer, and enjoy the day on the club's nicely equipped pontoon boat. The club offers training sessions for new members, and each June

they hold an Open Sail, sort of like an open house but with boats. It's a great opportunity to learn more about the sport, see the different types of fleet boats, and get wet. If you decide to join, an associate membership costs $40 a year and includes all privileges except competing for trophies. A $95 per year membership entitles sailors to skipper their own boat and compete for trophies.

Biking

Kansas City has its share of biking enthusiasts, who enjoy our wide streets and miles of trails. The only thing missing is designated bicycle lanes throughout the metro. This may change in the next few years; the MetroGreen plan aims to encourage more two-wheeled transportation with hundreds of miles of trails linking urban to suburban areas. Until that happens, if you do venture out on your Schwinn, do so with caution. Wearing a helmet goes without saying, but also follow all motor traffic rules, be alert, and, above all, make yourself known to drivers. For companionship on the open road, plus information about scenic bike rides and annual charity rides, contact one of the clubs below.

Favored paved trails include the Blue River Parkway, which starts in Minor Park at Red Bridge Road in Kansas City; the Mill Creek Streamway Park, which extends more than 17 miles from the Kansas River to downtown Olathe; and the Indian Creek and Tomahawk Biking and Hiking Trails in Overland Park, which run about 10 miles along the northern edge of I-435. Access points include Corporate Woods and Leawood Park.

Johnson County Bicycle Club
www.jcbikeclub.org
This group started in the late 1960s as part of the local parks and rec department and went solo in 1973 with about 30 members. Today nearly 300 riders are involved, which means you can usually

Kansas City, Start Your Engines

To visualize just how big the new Kansas Speedway is, consider that both Kauffman and Arrowhead Stadiums, plus their humongous parking lots, would fit into its infield, with room left over for one particular race driver's ego.

The $260 million International Speedway Corporation–owned facility opened in June 2001 and gave Wyandotte County a sound that drowns out even the rumble of racing motors: ka-ching! Season tickets went flying out the door, with 40 percent of total ticket sales going to Kansas residents. Fans from 46 states and four Canadian provinces grabbed up the rest. Individual seat prices range from $170 to $330.

Those lucky enough to get seats are not disappointed. The 75,000-seat, 1.5-mile tri-oval NASCAR track was designed for the comfort and convenience of the racing teams and the fans. Thanks to a beautifully planned low infield and elevated backstretch, every seat from rows 1 to 65 has an unim-

peded view of all four turns and the backstretch. And although the seats are great (especially those personalized with the owners' names), the Fan Walk is even better. Guests access the infield via a tunnel located south of the grandstand. Within the infield fans get an intimate look at the garages, inspection stations, and Victory Lane. An opening in the fence provides a chance to obtain autographs.

Fans might have to wait to get a driver's scribbled name, but they won't have to wait for much else. ICS and its designers did their homework and found out that racing fans hate to stand in line, so the Kansas Speedway has 16 ticket windows, 18 concession stands (including those selling barbecue), 50 portable food kiosks, and 12 restrooms. Hallelujah!

An even better view, along with a wet bar and private bathrooms, is available in one of 68 luxury suites. The privilege costs plenty; after a one-time

find a buddy or group strapping on a helmet to hit the road nearly every day. It sponsors three annual rides of up to 100 miles and holds monthly meetings to demonstrate new equipment and discuss how gel-padded bike shorts are the best garments ever invented. Throughout the year, volunteers host free rides that vary in speed, distance, and starting location but frequently begin or end at a restaurant to further the club's unofficial motto, "Ride to eat, eat to ride!" Membership dues are $20 a year, and many of the events are open to nonmembers for a fee. Find more information on the Web site, or write to

P.O. Box 2203, Shawnee Mission, KS 66201–2203.

The Kansas City Bicycle Club
(816) 436–5641
www.toto.net/kcbc
This club, established in 1963, sponsors everything from beginner rides to all-day marathons for those who have to see what's over the next hill. The KCBC also has a United States Cycling Federation–sanctioned racing team and hosts the annual Tour of Kansas City race every fall. Quarterly meetings are held at a different location each time and always

Vrroom! Treat yourself to one of the country's most fan-friendly NASCAR racetracks, the new Kansas Speedway in Wyandotte County. CVB OF GREATER KANSAS CITY

administrative fee of $7,000, the rooms go from $29,000 to $70,000 a year with a four-year minimum commitment. Ka-ching indeed. Each one sold out immediately; now there are plans to build 100 more.

Drivers appreciate the design as well. Veteran driver Bill Elliott said it may be the best ever built. Creature comforts include garages that measure 5 to 10 feet larger than those at most tracks, increased amperage for trailer hookups, and a terrific family center and playground for their children.

Sound good? That's what everyone else thought, too. Tickets to the 2001 inaugural season were sold out, and the 2002 season did likewise. Most of the season ticket holders renewed, which they can do for 30 years, and those on the waiting list snagged any that were left. But it's not too late to get on the next list. Or simply wait until ICS decides to add a few thousand more seats. And you can still see this gorgeous new track; several nonracing events are held here each year, including a barbecue cookout and races to raise money for charities. To find out more about tickets and events, contact Kansas Speedway (913–328–RACE, www.kansasspeedway.com) 1333 Meadowlark Lane, Kansas City, KS.

include an interesting ride and a picnic. A monthly newsletter keeps members current on upcoming events, newly discovered tours, and training techniques. Annual dues are $20 for individuals, $25 for families, and $35 for sustaining members.

Running and Walking

By the time spring shows her pretty head, plenty of us are hitting the streets to gear up for road races. You'll have lots of chances to get your race-day T-shirts here; there seems to be a fund-raising run or walk every weekend. Following are three of the largest. If you'd like a few pointers before you sign up, we've included information about a local running club.

AIDS Walk
(816) 931–0959

The region's largest AIDS fund-raising event brings together around 5,500 people to raise money and awareness for the men, women, and children living with HIV/AIDS in the Kansas City area. Since 1989 it has contributed more than $1 million to research and programs. The run is usually in April, and past sites have included Mill Creek Park on the Country Club Plaza.

Groundhog Run
(816) 746-1414

This race takes place in the Hunt Midwest Underground Facility Subtropolis, a huge, underground labyrinth big enough to handle an 18-wheeler. The runners aren't too hep on the course's twists and turns, but they dig the 58 degrees in the middle of winter. The race is held every February. Get there early; this one attracts 3,000 or so runners, and the space, naturally, is limited.

Kansas City Track Club
(816) 333-RACE (7223)
www.kctrack.org

Run a few miles, get a free beer. Sounds like a plan. This track club devotes its time to teaching people how to run, keeping them motivated and safe and then rewarding them with some of the best parties around. A long-standing tradition is the 4- to 12-mile Wednesday night fun run that ends at some member's house for potluck dinner. It usually draws from 40 to 70 members, and visiting runners are always welcome. Other outings include Sunday-morning long runs and Thursday-night speed sessions.

The club also puts on 17 or so races a year, including the St. Pat's Run; the Dog and Jog Run Fur Fun, featuring 980 dogs and their masters; and the Brew to Brew, a 42-mile killer that starts at the Boulevard Brewery in Kansas City and ends at the Free State Brewing Company in Lawrence. Certainly the most scenic course is the annual Cliffhanger 5K walk/run held at the historic Cliff Drive in the Gladstone Boulevard area. Although the limestone cliffs provide some challenge, seeing the waterfall fountain is worth it.

Trolley Run
(888) 543-7223, ext. 4
www.trolleyrun.org

Following along Kansas City's long-gone urban trolley track, this is Kansas City's largest run and the fourth largest 4-mile run in the United States. It's actually just a festive street party, because the course is so flat and scenic you won't feel like you've worked at all. Starting in the Waldo area at 75th and Wornall, the run takes you through some of our loveliest old neighborhoods, where dogs and kids line the streets to cheer you on. Keep going: The final reward is a view of the lushly landscaped Brush Creek, a below-street level, 0.75-mile concrete ribbon that has a tiered waterfall at the west end.

The race ends on the Country Club Plaza with music, lots of food, and high-fives all around. On top of that the race is held in April, one of our best months weatherwise. If all that doesn't convince you, perhaps this will: Money raised goes to help the Children's Center for the Visually Impaired, an organization that provides training and help to blind and visually impaired infants and children.

FAMILY SPORTS
Camping

Basswood Country Inn and RV Resort
15880 Interurban Road
Platte City, MO
(816) 858-5556, (800) 242-2775
(reservations only)
www.basswoodresort.com

At this resort, which *Peak Magazine* calls "perhaps the most beautiful wooded lakefront setting in the Kansas City area," you can stay at a cabin or set up camp overlooking the lake. Stay where Bing Crosby and Harry Truman stayed at one of this resort's cabins, or camp out at a spot overlooking the lake. There are 119 full-hookup RV sites (30 and 50 amp) plus 20 water/electric-only sites for tents and pop-ups, including 14 deluxe sites with patios. Guests can use the two picnic shelters, playground, spacious laundry facilities, and superclean bathhouses with shower stalls and vanities. A meeting hall is available for parties and family reunions.

You'll have plenty to do with four freshwater lakes stocked with catfish, bass, crappies, and carp, plus a swimming pool, volleyball court, and walking trails through the wooded acreage. A convenience store offers videos (perhaps *White Christmas?*) and basic groceries. Basswood Resort, open year-round, is just 5 miles from the Kansas City International Airport.

Jackson County Parks and Recreation Campgrounds
(816) 229–8980
www.co.jackson.mo.us
The county offers three public campgrounds with a total of 236 camping sites, all about 15 minutes from Kansas City proper. They are available by reservation for stays up to 14 days, and at least one camper must be 21 or over. The camping facilities include showers, restrooms, attendants, picnic tables, and ice.

Longview Lake Campground is part of a 5,000-acre park that includes a 4-mile nature trail, horse park, swimming beach, and 27-hole public golf course. The 930-acre lake has a full marina with wheelchair-accessible fishing docks. The campground is open April 27 through September 30. Its 119 sites include 59 with electricity at $14 to $17 per day and 60 tent-ready at $10 to $13 per day.

Lake Jacomo Campground is within beautiful Fleming Park, at 7,800 acres, the largest parkland in Jackson County. At its heart is 970-acre Lake Jacomo, and there's a smaller Blue Springs Lake as well. Attractions include a nature preserve, Audubon center, marina, swimming beach, hiking trails, and more. The campground has 60 large, tree-lined sites, 10 full hookups, 38 electric, and 12 tent, which cost from $10 to $23 per day. The site is open year-round; call for specific availabilities.

Blue Springs Lake Campground, also within Fleming Park, is open April 13 to October 31 with 57 sites (20 full hookup, 17 electric and water, 20 electric) that range from $14 to $23 per day.

Fishing

With all our lakes and parks, you're sure to reel in the largest walleye, crappie, channel catfish, or largemouth bass you've ever seen. Since the region covers two states and nearly a dozen counties, fishing permits vary. But for the most part, Missouri requires a $3.00 per day nonresident permit, and Kansas charges $3.50 per day. You'll find information about our major lakes, including Jacomo, Blue Springs, and Wyandotte County, in the Lakes, Parks, and Recreation chapter. Following are some additional fishing spots.

Lake Olathe
625 Lakeshore Drive
Olathe, KS
(913) 764–6163
You're sure to find a place to capture a competition-size catfish, bass, or even trout somewhere in these 170 acres. There's even an assist from Old Saint Nick; each year the parks and recreation division tosses retired Christmas trees into the area around the fishing piers to create nesting places for fish.

Shawnee Mission Park
7900 Renner Road
Shawnee Mission, KS
(913) 831–3355
Anglers seeking bluegill, carp, and bass show up at this 150-acre lake, one of the most popular in the region. Boat rentals are available, but you'd better reserve yours early; each spring and fall the lake is stocked with rainbow trout. Now that's good eating.

Smithville Lake
DD Highway
Smithville , MO
(816) 532–4217
When people around here say they're "gone fishin'," chances are this is their destination. Just 20 miles north of downtown Kansas City, Smithville's 7,200 acres provide plenty of reeling action. The lake is

stocked with tiger musky, walleye, bass, crappie, and several species of catfish for an afternoon of fishing and a fine fillet that night. Boats are available for rent at the two full-service marinas, and five mul-tilane boat launch ramps ensure easy accessibility to the water. And you're in luck: Smithville has 777 campsites, one-third with electrical hookups. Call (816) 532–0803 for reservations.

Miniature Golf

Cool Crest Family Fun Center
10735 East Missouri Highway 40
Independence, MO
(816) 358–0088
www.coolcrest.com
This 4½-acre playground has been getting families together for fun since 1950. You'll have plenty of opportunity to practice your short game (and patience) because Cool Crest offers a total of four 18-hole miniature golf courses. Other activities include go-karts, batting cages, and a 7,000-square-foot game room with video and pinball machines galore. And to continue with the blast-from-the-past theme, a '50s-style pizzeria serves up pies with all the top-pings. After an afternoon here you'll find yourself singing along to their decades-old jingle, "It's a fun, family kind of place!"

Family Golf Park
1501 Northeast MO Highway 40
Blue Springs, MO
(816) 228–1550
So you're not ready to spend thousands of dollars on golf lessons, clubs, and shoes? You can still have fun knocking a ball around at this course. This beautifully landscaped park features 36 holes of miniature golf winding through a lake set-ting. The center also includes a par-3 golf course, putting green, game arcade, and bumper boats. Ker-splash! The golf prac-tice facility is open year-round; golf les-sons are available. Hours are from 8:30 A.M. until 10:30 P.M. weekdays and until

11:30 P.M. on Friday and Saturday. Rates vary depending on the activities. It's great fun for the entire family.

Bowling

Interest in this sport seems to ebb and flow depending on how people feel about the shoes. It's popular once again, not only with long-term leagues and little kids but also with teens seeking a fun Friday out with friends. Several bowling alleys in Kansas City cater to the young crowd with laser light shows and booming music.

AMF College Lanes
10201 College Boulevard
Overland Park, KS
(913) 451–6400
www.amf.com
A real plus for people staying at the Dou-bletree Hotel across the street, this center offers 32 lanes, seven billiards tables, and a lounge along with a small arcade. They crank up the music for X-treme Bowling, when black lights make the pins and balls glow, dude. And for groups of four, a Fun Pack is the way to go: $10 each will get you shoe rentals, two hours of bowling, a pitcher of soda, popcorn, and a one-topping pizza.

Incred-A-Bowl
8500 West 151st Street
Overland Park, KS
(913) 851–1700
www.incredabowl.com
This 65,000-square-foot, state-of-the-art center includes a 40-lane computerized bowling alley, an arcade filled with 100 of the latest interactive and virtual reality games, and a three-story set of play tubes for the tykes. Teens in particular really go for the Cosmic Bowling every Friday and Saturday night, when black lights, fog, glow-in-the-dark balls and pins, and upbeat music take the pain out of a gutter ball. The fun continues until long past midnight. Incred-A-Bowl also has a pro shop, gift store, and snack bar.

Ice Skating

AMF Ice Chateau
8788 Metcalf
Overland Park, KS
(913) 648-0129
This regulation-size indoor rink offers open skating from noon until 4:30 P.M. most days, with lessons available for all ages and levels. On weekends, kids and teens have a blast during Ice X-treme, when the lights go down and the music cranks up. The fun starts at 8:00 P.M. on Friday and 7:00 P.M. on Saturday and lasts until 11:00 P.M. And if you're into hockey, a drop-in game is available every Sunday starting at 8:30 P.M. Nonskaters can chose among a bowling alley, pool tables, and a game arcade, and there is a concession stand for ready fuel. Admission is $4.50 for 7 and under, $6.50 for all others, plus $2.50 for skate rental.

Crown Center Ice Terrace
2450 Grand Boulevard
(816) 274-8411
www.crowncenter.com
Kansas City's only outdoor ice rink opens to great fanfare each November and continues until March—and by that time skaters are often dressed in T-shirts and shorts! The terrace is open seven days a week, 10:00 A.M. to 9:00 P.M. Fees are $5.00 per person, and skate rental is $2.00. Groups of 20 or more save the rental fee, and the rink is available for private parties before or after regular hours. A vending machine dispenses hot cocoa and cappuccino and soft drinks for those balmy early spring days.

Pepsi Ice Midwest Skating Rink and
Fitness Center
12140 West 135th Street
Overland Park, KS
(913) 851-1600
www.pepsiicemidwest.com
You're apt to see Olympic-quality skaters practicing spins and jumps at the home of the Silver Blades, one of the country's oldest ice-skating groups. Competitions and practice take up quite a bit of ice time, but free skating is available during the week from 10:00 A.M. to early afternoon on weekdays and two sessions on Saturday. With three ice rinks, this center also hosts hockey practice and games. Fees are $6.50 for adults, $5.00 for children under 7 years of age, and $2.00 for skate rental. Lessons are also available, and the rink can be rented for birthday parties. This giant new center also has a fitness center, game room, and deli.

Snow Skiing

Kansas City Ski Club
(913) 383-9006
www.kcskiclub.org
Go figure. Here we are, miles away from a mountain, and we have one of the largest ski clubs in the country. And it's active without a flake in sight. With 3,000 members, there's always a group getting together to play volleyball or golf, socialize at an area bar, or take canoe trips in the summer. Oh, yes, and ski. The club sponsors about 31 ski trips each year with destinations as diverse as Colorado, New Mexico, Canada, and Spain. The membership more than pays for itself in what you'll save on each trip. Besides that, it's one of the best ways to meet singles in the area.

Snow Creek Ski Lodge
Missouri Highway 45,
5 miles north of Weston
(816) 640-2200
www.skipeaks.com
When ski buffs aren't in a car or van heading to Breckinridge or Vail, you might find them at this ski lodge that opened in 1985. People who expect the Midwest to be flat as a flapjack will be surprised to see a 300-foot vertical drop and enough varied terrain to give beginners and experts plenty of action. Nine intermediate trails are served by two triple chairlifts and one double chairlift, and a rope tow gets you to the beginner area. The snow base usu-

ally ranges from 24 to 60 inches thanks to 40 snowmaking machines.

A lodge features a cafeteria, bar, and lounge and also houses the ski school and gift shop. The rental shop offers shaped skis with plenty of junior sizes, plus snowboards and ski boards. Jason's Run has enough jumps, bumps, mounds, pipes, and tabletops to keep expert boarders happy. The park opens in mid-December and stays open through mid-March if the weather cooperates. It's open seven days a week, offers night skiing beginning in late December, and stays open until 3:00 A.M. for special events.

KIDS' SPORTS
Baseball

Old Ballgame Training Academy
13705 Holmes
(816) 942-9992
www.oldballgame.com
When two parents became dissatisfied with the baseball training their sons were receiving, they started this top-rated academy in Martin City. Housed in a brand-new facility complete with indoor and outdoor practice fields, batting cages, bullpens, and a fitness center that rivals any in the metropolitan area, here youngsters can get the training they need to succeed in the sport while having fun. Along with coaches' clinics, the center offers membership programs that include group and private lessons, filming and video analysis, and training camps. A standard membership is $115 per month, with a limited number of openings left.

Skateboarding and Roller Hockey

Roller Hockey Rink
116th and Knox
Overland Park, KS
No phone
Kids love this regulation, 120-by-65-foot rink at Indian Valley Park. The surface is coated for safety (well, at least it's safer), and a 5-foot-tall sideboard surrounds the playing area. Player benches are on each side. Rules and safety suggestions are posted, but there are no supervisors on-site. The rink is maintained by the Johnson County Parks and Recreation Division, and there are no fees for use.

Skateboard Park
138th and Switzer
Overland Park, KS
(913) 893-6354
After the popularity of iceboarding competitions in the 2002 Winter Olympics, this sport is sure to skyrocket. This small park was created thanks to a grassroots effort that began with an Overland Park resource officer. $240,000 later, the community got its center in 1997, complete with ramps, jumps, and rails for all skill levels. It's popular with skateboarders and in-line skaters.

FITNESS CENTERS/ HEALTH CLUBS

With three pages of health clubs listed in the Yellow Pages, it's a wonder we're still ranked as one of the country's fattest cities. Here's where those who are fit stay that way, or at least check out the cutie on the next treadmill.

The Athletic Club of Overland Park
10440 Marty
Overland Park, KS
(913) 383-9060
www.athleticclubop.com
You'll have no excuse not to get in shape at this premium fitness center. Its cardio theater includes banks of treadmills, elliptical machines, and rowing machines, and a cycle studio puts you through the paces during a spinning class. A full-size basketball gym, nine racquetball and handball courts, and even a sand volleyball court are here. The complex also includes an

indoor pool; separate area for free weights; and studios for yoga, Pilates, and aerobics. You'll also find locker rooms and lounges that are downright plush, plus a cafe that serves a variety of healthy meals, snacks, and fruit smoothies. Or you can blow that workout on a beer. Massage and spa therapies, nutrition services, a pro shop, and a day care center round out the mix.

Bally Total Fitness
6700 West 110th Street
Overland Park, KS
(913) 491-0200
www.ballytotalfitness
Is this a social club or a gym? Actually it's both, but if you're going to meet other singles you might as well see how they look in spandex. This club has it all: enough treadmills to eliminate lines, a Life Fitness lineup that makes weight training seem fun; plenty of class times throughout the day for step, yoga, and spinning; and indoor and outdoor pools. Bally's also keeps up with the latest fitness trends like

Pilates, tai chi, pre- and post-natal classes, and even salsa dancing. Membership costs vary depending on services you desire, but average costs are $50 to $65 per month after a one-time fee of $100. Bally has 350 locations across the country, including three others in the Kansas City area.

YMCA
Various locations
(816) 561-9622
The YMCA of Greater Kansas City includes 12 branches throughout the metropolitan area. Although the equipment and services vary, most have weight rooms, indoor and/or outdoor tracks, locker room facilities, and cardio equipment. Some have pools, and several offer child care. The YMCA also holds true to the "Christian" part of its name by catering to families and children. Kids are encouraged to cultivate healthy bodies and minds through sports activities, craft classes, and other programs. The YMCA of Kansas City, Kansas (913-371-4400) has two locations.

DAY TRIPS AND WEEKEND GETAWAYS

W hy anyone would want to leave the pleasant confines of Kansas City is beyond us. But the three small towns in this chapter have enough appeal to pull anyone away from a plate of our famous ribs. Each one has a unique personality and enough attractions to make it well worth the short drive.

But instead of jumping on the highway after dinner, why not slide under a down-filled duvet at a bed-and-breakfast? Each town offers irresistible options, from an antiques-filled estate to a rustic but romantic working ranch. Besides a sumptuous breakfast the next morning, staying overnight gives you one more day to explore a museum, scout out another art gallery, or stop by that pretty park you passed on the way.

There you have it: three destinations that feel like a century away. Best of all, you'll hardly need to top off your gas tank. You can be checking out that cute little antiques shop or sinking your teeth into a square of homemade fudge in less than an hour.

And now, let's get started by doing what so many travelers did in the late 1800s: heading west.

LAWRENCE, KANSAS

Lawrence is a marvelous mix of quirkiness and cosmopolitan flare that can only be found in a college town. Toss in a couple of four-star restaurants, great music venues, and . . . well, we won't expect you back tonight. In fact, for some tourists a weekend became a week that turned into forever. The town is booming thanks to graduates who stay on and visitors who fall in love with the laid-back pace, vibrant arts scene, and parks and lakes just a short walk or bike ride away. Its historical buildings also rate points: In 2000 the National Trust for Historic Preservation named Lawrence one of the dozen most distinctive and unique destinations in the country.

The varied collection of downtown shops is also a draw. At the heart of the 5-block district is Massachusetts Street, which you'll soon call "Mass" like everyone else. The tree-lined avenue is an outdoor art gallery thanks to a successive series of one-year exhibitions of sculptures by national artists. Another 30 outdoor artworks and murals serve as a nice introduction to the galleries and museums around town. On select Fridays throughout the year, most galleries join in the Gallery Walk, where artists mingle with guests. Check the Web site (www.visitlawrence.com) for dates. A sampling of art showrooms includes Phoenix Gallery, specializing in custom stained glass, ceramics, textiles, and prints; Borderline Gallery (6 blocks east of Mass on Ninth), with unique artwork like copper clocks and raku ceramics; and Silver Works, a gallery of exquisite handcrafted jewelry and crafts.

The apex of arts activities is the Lawrence Arts Center (785–843–ARTS [2787]), in the 900 block of New Hampshire. The center features exhibitions by area and nationally known artists and is home to the professional Prairie Wind Dancers and Seems-to-Be Players Children's Theatre Company.

You'll also find enough home furnishing stores to turn every KU dorm room into a palace. Many of these rival Kansas City shops for style and variety. Popular ones include Interiors, where partners Di and Dru Fritzel have combined antiques and reproductions with an amazing array of accessories, including quilts, baskets, ceramics, and garden art; and the Casbah, an exciting marketplace of furniture, lamps, and frames from several countries, all brought together in a colorful hodge-podge of treasures. The colorful star-shaped paper lamps with pierced cutouts can dress up any decor.

Plan to spend at least an hour at the Blue Heron, where they take an artful approach to life with contemporary and traditional furnishings and accessories from quirky to refined. The lipstick-red chair shaped like a lady's high-heeled pump is just an indication of what you're in for. If your footgear isn't made for walking, head into Footprints, where they stock 10,000 Birkenstock sandals. While you're slipping on a pair, take time to admire the mural of agricultural landscapes created by local artist Missy McCoy. Stop in au Marche, a European-style grocer that stocks a nice selection of gourmet cheeses, pâtés, and sausages. They can create a picnic lunch to go, perhaps to serve on a dish from Hobbs, a fun shop that specializes in reproduction dinnerware from famous restaurants around the world.

Spending the day surrounded by college students might make you yearn for a makeover. Rejuvene Day Spa (785–865–4372) can comply with a facial, massage, and body wrap, and a new 'do can be yours at the Blue Dot Salon (785–840–0407). And lots of Kansas Citians make a monthly pilgrimage to Babette's (785–749–7227), a chic shop where all the latest makeup and beauty products await. Retail shops offer everything from lingerie to vintage resale clothes.

Treat yourself to a double dipper in a homemade cone at Sylas & Maddy's ice cream, or save your appetite for one of Lawrence's world-class restaurants. In the past 10 years or so, new chefs have made this a dining destination for people throughout the region. Teller's was one of the first and is still one of the best; here's where to order salads, pasta specials, and more—and then check out the restrooms, just past the converted bank's safe.

Pachamama's (785–841–0990, www.pachamama.com) is well worth the short drive. The soaring ceilings, stone columns, and wall-to-ceiling windows, could make it difficult to concentrate on the food . . . until you're served. Chef Ken Baker turns fresh, local ingredients into memorable meals. Witness his peppered smoked pork tenderloin with souffléd garlic-cheese grits, or wood-fired breast of duckling on smoky greens. And his vanilla bean crème brûlée? Oh, mama. The restaurant serves dinner seven nights a week and also hosts Patio Grills on Tuesday, as well as Friday wine tastings. Reservations are a must.

More casual fare like soups and sandwiches is found at the Free State Brewing Company (636 Massachusetts, 785–843–4555, www.freestatebrewing.com), the first legal brewery in Kansas since pioneer days.

Before or after dinner, consider catching a performance at the Lied Center of Kansas (15th and Iowa, 785–864–ARTS [2787]), a dazzling $14.3 million multipurpose facility that's home to Kansas University's concert series, Swarthout Chamber Music, and Broadway and Beyond. Past seasons have included *Chicago,* the Girls Choir of Harlem, and the Baryshnikov Dance Project. The University Theatre (15th and Naismith Drive on the KU Campus, 785–864–3982, www.kutheatre.com) presents a wide array of plays and musical performances, including the popular Kansas Summer Theatre. Perhaps other nightlife is calling you. Lawrence offers some of the Midwest's most exciting live music venues, like the Bottleneck at 737 New Hampshire and the Granada on Mass, offering heart-thumpingly loud music from rock to alternative. Liberty Hall on Mass is a restored opera house that provides a beautiful setting for live entertainment as well as cinematic releases.

When you're ready to turn in, Lawrence has several dreamy options. The Eldridge Hotel (Seventh and Massachusetts, 785–749–5011, 800–527–0909) is the only Lawrence business in the same spot it occupied during Kansas Territorial Days and throughout the Civil War. A new hotel was built on the site in 1924, and it has been recently renovated into an all-suite hotel with eight luxury suites. A honeymoon suite has an antique four-poster bed, romantic fireplace, and jetted tub built for two. Rates range from $119 to $159; check www.visitlawrence.com for special deals like the Bed-and-Breakfast Package for $89.

The Halcyon House Bed and Breakfast (1000 Ohio Street, 888-441-0314, www .thehalcyonhouse.com) is a charming European style inn built in 1885. Nine rooms are filled with antiques and flourishes and range from the Nooks and Crannies with a shared bath for $55 to the private Carriage House with its own luxurious bath and fireplace for $149. Awaken to the smell of coffee brewing and fresh baked breads. Breakfasts might include scrambled eggs, buttery waffles, fresh fruit, and homemade muffins.

About 15 miles from Lawrence is the Circle S Ranch (3325 Circle S Lane, 785-843-4124, www.circlesranch.com), a country inn that offers plush quarters within a 12,200-acre working ranch. Although the architecture is stylishly rustic (you'll love the hammered copper front door and wraparound porch), the 12 guest rooms with private baths feature antiques and luxurious bed linens. You won't want to miss the hot tub in a silo! The best amenity, however, might be the view of cornflower-blue skies, rolling hills, and meadow flowers. The land has been in owner Mary Stevenson's family since the mid-1880s. Room rates (from $155 to $175 for rooms, $190 to $215 for third-floor suites) include a ranch hand breakfast with all the fixins. Read more about this relaxing destination in the Accommodations chapter. Your hammock is waiting under the giant oak tree.

After breakfast at your hotel or bed-and-breakfast, you can return to downtown to catch all the shops and galleries you missed, or head to one of the area lakes and parks. Anyone who thinks the Kansas prairie is a dull patch of green is in for a pleasant surprise. The Prairie Park Nature Center is a 71-acre park adjacent to

7 acres of virgin prairie with 180 species of wildflowers and native grasses that flow like shimmering satin with the wind. You can explore more than a mile of trails that pass through prairie and wetlands and end at a seven-acre urban lake. Interpretive signs along the path point out habitat elements and identify wildlife.

Located just 3 miles southwest of Lawrence is Clinton Lake, with 7,000 acres for boating, swimming, and fishing. Five developed areas offer bridle, hiking, and mountain biking trails; camper hookups; primitive camping sites; and a complete marina along with a restaurant and convenience store. For more information call (785) 843-7665.

To experience Lawrence, travel west on Interstate 70 from Kansas City, exit at the Lawrence exit (204), and turn left (south) on to Second Street. A visitor center is located in a historic train depot at North Second and Locust Streets. For more information call (785) 865-4499 or (888) LAWKANS (529-5267). Or visit the Web site: www.visitlawrence.com.

WESTON, MISSOURI

Blink twice when you reach Weston and you'll wonder where you left the time machine. Antiques shops, a clothing store like none other, more than its share of historic homes, and two fine dining restaurants should keep you busy for a day or a weekend. Lucky for you Weston has some appealing bed-and-breakfast options and one historic downtown hotel. The hamlet's official tagline might be "the town that time forgot," but you never will.

If it hadn't been for a Missouri River flood in 1881 that shifted the river 2 miles away into Kansas, Weston could have been a major metropolis instead of a side trip. Most of us send a silent thank-you to that watery presence every time we visit this town that's magically stuck in the mid-1880s.

Weston was the first city founded in the six-county Platte Purchase of 1837, and today it remains a hamlet of 1,700 residents—all, it would seem, living or working in a pre–Civil War building or antebellum home. In all, 22 blocks of buildings are listed on the National Register of Historic Places, including the Price-Loyles Home (718 Spring Street, 816–640–2383), an 1857 three-story Federal-style home that was occupied by four generations of Daniel Boone's descendants. The home, filled with original family furnishings and toys, is open for tours. See more of the town's past at the Weston Historical Museum, which features artifacts depicting life here from prehistoric times to World War II.

Main Street has antiques as well, but these are the kind you can buy. In fact, Weston is a magnet for antiques shoppers from surrounding states. With 14 or so Old World emporiums lined up side by side, shoppers look like human rickrack as they go from door to door seeking peeling-paint cabinets and sponged bowls.

Several stores mix old with new, like Currant Cottage, two stories of pinewood tables, handsome museum-quality reproduction cabinets, linens for table and bed, and handpainted pottery from Provence. Weston Grand is just that: a grand collection of furniture and stylish accessories including antique and new tables and beds, pewter, fabulous lamps, and those luscious embellished pillows you covet in the fancy home decor magazines. Look for Evander, the owner's shih tzu, waiting in the window for you.

Attic Window offers primitives and garden antiques in a charming historic building where a cobbler kept the townfolk in shoes in the late 1880s. And Ya Ya (Greek for grandmother) Antiques presents vintage fabrics and quilts, braided and hook rugs, architectural pieces, and well-worn furniture in a pink-and-white house at the top of Main Street.

For a complete 180, head to Old Geezers MANtiques for an interesting array of rare coins, pocketknives, and handsome pocket watches; just look for the long porch where a wheelbarrow is filled with flowers and a 1950s toy pedal car is wait-

Most small towns tend to "roll up the sidewalk" early. That's certainly true in Atchison and Weston, where restaurants tend to close at 9:00 P.M. and there are few nightspots. If you're after relaxation and romance, these towns are fine choices. But if you like variety, from art to music to theater, Lawrence is your kind of getaway.

ing for a tot's grandfather to buy. Maggie's Attic is quite a find on Thomas Street, just around the corner from Main. This old-fashioned emporium has something for every room in your house, including antique and reproduction cabinets, decorative mirrors, candles, and giftware. With its selection of gourmet crackers, chutneys, and mustards and complete wine cellar, you can make a picnic to enjoy on the back deck.

One of the most remarkable shops in the region is a few miles out of town. Locust Grove Antiques (25180 Highway JJ, 816–640–3203) carries a collection of antique and new furniture and accessories arranged in small habitats that make saying, "I'll take the whole room!" easy.

When you're finished sprucing up your home, consider a new outfit at Missouri Bluffs Boutique and Gallery. This is truly the Bermuda Triangle of the Midwest; it's a fact that women who walk in here are never seen again. The store is wall-to-wall with clothing that marries rustic with romance: embroidered and bejeweled vests, sweeping velvet skirts, suede jackets with 6-inch fringe, and hats festooned with fabric roses and netting. You'll also find case after case of jewelry, including artist Kelly Johnson's beaded pins and masks. Red-and-black cowgirl boots to go with your new getup? Size 7, coming up.

By now you're starving, and Weston can oblige. The Vineyards (505 Spring Street, 816–640–5588, www.thevineyards restaurant.com) serves lunch and dinner in an 1845 antebellum home that is delightful during the day and turns intimate with candleglow at night. Cheryl Hartell is a spirited young chef with quite a talent with fresh ingredients and sauces. Start your meal with her baked Brie or house salad with blue cheese crumbles and delightful vinaigrette that fans have been begging her to bottle.

Dinner recommendations include a daily risotto, filet of beef with Merlot sauce and grilled portobello mushrooms, or French-cut pork chops with a caramelized apple, fennel, and red onion sauce. The extensive wine list includes selections from Weston's own award-winning Pirtle Winery. Cheryl hosts wonderful wine-tasting dinners, including one she calls Pinot Envy. Clever girl. The Vineyards is open for lunch Wednesday through Saturday and dinner Wednesday through Sunday. A Sunday brunch menu includes items like a beef tenderloin, mushroom, and smoked Gouda omelet. Reservations are recommended.

Save enough time to visit the winery (502 Spring, 816-386-5200, www.pirtlewine.com) across the street. Housed in a historic church with a wine garden and tasting room, Pirtle's is known for its honey mead, a slightly sweet wine that gives honeymoon its name. The shop is open daily from 10:00 A.M. (it's cocktail hour somewhere in the world!) to 6:00 P.M.

Another favorite dining choice is Avalon Cafe (608 Main Street, 816-640-2835), which we rave about in the Restaurants chapter. This 150-year-old home makes an appealing backdrop for chef David Scott's masterpieces, especially wild game like elk and duck. The Weston Trio takes the guesswork out of ordering; it usually features a wild game dish plus a fish and steak with a selection of marvelous sauces. For lunch, the baked Brie is a gimme. Depending on the season, lunch will include fresh strawberries or grilled eggplant and zucchini, along with buttery baked garlic to slather on French bread. Add a salad and it's plenty to share with a friend for lunch. Avalon is open for lunch and dinner Tuesday through Saturday. Reservations are a must.

If you'd prefer frivolity to fine dining,

take a trip to Ireland at O'Malley's 1842 Pub (Short and Welt Streets, 816-640-5325), carved out of three limestone brewery cellars built 55 feet belowground. Naturally you'll find traditional fare like corned beef and cabbage, bangers and mash, and Irish stew, with plenty of stout and whiskey to wash it all happily down. Sean's pub hosts several big events a year, including a St. Paddy's Day celebration. If you're lucky, local Celtic singer Connie Dover will be home from touring and grace the room with her enchanting voice. If not, balladeer Bob Reeder might turn the same room blue with his repertoire of naughty limericks.

Blues and greens are the colors at Weston Bend State Park, where a scenic overlook offers a view of the Missouri River, Fort Leavenworth in Kansas, and beyond until the line of trees turns into a mist. A hiking trail that meanders through the woods and along the edge of the bluff also has great views of water, prairie, and rugged cliffs. Hikers and bicyclists have the 3-mile paved loop trail all to themselves. Secluded picnic sites, a playground, and open shelter are awaiting your afternoon getaway. For longer park visits, a campground with basic and electric campsites, modern restrooms, hot showers, and laundry facilities is available. For information, or to reserve a campsite, call (816) 640-5443 or go to www.mostateparks.com.

For most of us, however, a getaway means just that: leaving the laundry, cooking, and cleaning to someone else. If that's you, Weston has places for pampering. The Inn at Weston Landing (500 Welt Street, 816-640-5788, 877-249-5788) is a Celtic-style hideaway that is part of the original Weston Brewing Company built in 1842. The inn's four spacious rooms (all with private baths) have distinct personalities. The Andrew O'Malley room reconstructs a delightful cottage on the southern tip of Ireland's Clew Bay with a fireplace, hand-blown windowpanes, and spinning wheel. You might imagine the scent of heather on the highlands in the Rosine Fleming room. New owners Mike and Cyndee Bohaty have added amenities like queen beds and a hot tub in the garden while keeping the authenticity. One of Cyndee's most requested breakfasts is strawberry parfaits, asparagus and mushroom quiche, bacon, and homemade scones.

The Benner House Bed and Breakfast (645 Main Street, 816–640–2616) is a fine example of steamboat gothic architecture. It was built in 1898 for George Shawhan, who owned what is now known as the McCormick Distillery. Strolling from the shops and restaurants, you'll notice the house right away with its wraparound porch, quaint gingerbread details, and large windows overlooking the veranda. Inside, hosts John and Julie Pasley have filled the home with antiques, including a pump organ that dates back to 1911. Julie insists that if one pumps hard enough it will work. You might want to save your energy for breakfast. One morning's repast included baked pears, a sausage-egg casserole, fresh fruit, and blueberry muffins.

Breakfast will be waiting after a night's rest in one of the four upstairs guest rooms, each with private bath. The front bedroom offers a view of downtown and features a yo-yo quilt and oak bedroom set. Across the hall, a brass bed and Main Street view make the room a favorite with guests. Other amenities include a hot tub set in the backyard garden, a parlor for socializing, and a sitting room where you can curl up in a rocking chair with a book. Rates are $90 on weekdays and $120 for holidays and weekends. The Benner House is an ideal place for a wedding for up to 50 guests.

Weston tempts you with festivals and special events throughout the year, including antiques shows in March and April, one of the reasons *Midwest Living* ranked it one of the top-10 antiques destinations in the Midwest. In June a citywide garage sale brings in the bargain hunters, and four summer weekends are devoted to free music in the park featuring regional talent. A July 4 festival includes a parade, street fair, and fireworks, and two ice-cream socials keep you cool in August.

In October the town celebrates the German and Irish families that made Weston home in the 1800s with an Octoberfest and a three-day Irish Festival. The annual Applefest, held in October as well, brings together more than 40 folk artists; a garden market; food vendors selling everything from turkey legs to homemade root beer; live music; a parade; and everything you could possibly make apples into, including apple butter, fritters, cider, and dumplings. You can also celebrate the harvest at the source; two nearby orchards offer such fall treats as pumpkin patches, hayrides, caramel apples, and free cider. Call Vaughn Orchard and Country Store (816–386–2900) and Weston Red Barn Farm (816–386–5437) for details.

Before the first frost, townspeople begin planning the annual Candlelight Homes Tour in December, when five historic homes are dressed for the season. Street activities feature carolers, carriage rides, and a chance to whisper wishes to Father Christmas. Call the Weston Development Company for tickets.

Weston is 30 miles northwest of Kansas City; take exit 20 off Interstate 29 and follow the signs. For information, including an online tour of 23 historic homes, visit www.ci.weston.mo.us; another helpful site is www.westonwares.com. Or call the Weston Development Company at (816) 640–2909 or (888) 635–7457. A visitor center at 502 Main Street has brochures on shops, lodging, and restaurants. Please be aware that many of the shops and restaurants are closed on Monday.

ATCHISON, KANSAS

A trolley ride past grand Victorian mansions on brick-paved streets, sweeping views of the Missouri River valley from a tree-shaded park bench, and a hot fudge sundae at an old-fashioned soda fountain downtown: If this sounds like an idyllic afternoon, then this lovely riverfront town is for you.

When you come to Atchison you'll be following in the footsteps of the Kansa

Sometimes tiny shops and 10-table restaurants keep strange hours, so to keep from driving 40 minutes only to see a display of CLOSED signs on doors, call to check on open days. In Weston, for instance, it seems the whole place shuts down on Monday. Maybe they're all driving to Kansas City

Indians, who gave the state its name, and Lewis and Clark, who passed through on July 4, 1804. Fifty years later Atchison became one of the first settlements in the Kansas Territory. The town was named for David R. Atchison, then president of the Missouri Senate, who became president for a day when Zachary Taylor refused to take office on a Sunday.

Its location at the westernmost bend of the Missouri River turned the town into a leading commercial center, a role that was expanded when the Atchison, Topeka & Santa Fe Railroad was founded in 1860. Soon bankers and railroad magnates were building impressive mansions and minicastles, many of which still line Third, Fourth, and Fifth Streets.

Other settlers were building grand stone structures as well; the Benedictine monks established St. Benedict's Abbey (1020 North Second Street, 913–367–7853) in 1858. It's easy to tell the church didn't come until a century later. A student of Frank Lloyd Wright, Barry Byrne, designed this handsome limestone structure with a 44-foot-high nave ceiling. His wife created many of the interior frescoes. Self-guided tours are available, and if you wish to spend more time in this spiritual setting, weekend retreats can be arranged. Contact Fr. Matthew Habiger (913–367–5340) for details.

In 1863 the Benedictine Sisters established Mount St. Scholastica College for women, and in 1938 their beautiful chapel (801 South Eighth Street) was dedicated. The interior is rich with beautiful marble, including pillars that contain many fossils. A large rose window, stained-glass win-

dows, and magnificent Romanesque vaulted ceiling make this worth a look. Tours can be arranged by calling (913) 367–6110. The chapel overlooks the river, and a park bench under an ancient tree provides a pleasant stop.

Enough reflection, now it's time to shop! Atchison's claim to fame, of course, is as the birthplace of Amelia Earhart. But these days another woman is putting the town on the map. Mary Carol Garrity's famous home interiors store, Nell Hill's (501 Commercial, 913–367–1086), is a phenomenon that's been covered in *Victoria* magazine, *Kansas City Home Design,* and even the *Wall Street Journal.* Customers from Topeka, Omaha, and of course Kansas City make regular road trips to stock up on European antiques, home furnishings, accessories, and gifts at jaw-dropping prices. Don't worry about getting it all home; Mary Carol ships. And be sure to ask about her interior design book while you're there.

Other antiques shops on Commercial Street are worth checking out as well. This outdoor pedestrian plaza is landscaped with brick walls, seasonal plantings, and fountains. Hungry? Pop into Marigold Bakery and Cafe (913–367–3858), a cozy place for crisp salads, sandwiches on focaccia, and homemade pies. Take an extra cookie to go. Or belly up to the lunch counter at one of two vintage soda fountains. Most downtown locations are open every day except Sunday.

And don't miss G. Diebolt's (913–367–2395), Mary Carol's other store in a converted bank at 608 Commercial. You'll want to climb into one of the antique iron beds layered with oodles of pillows, fluffy comforters, and embroidered neck rolls. Silver picture frames, scented candles, and other surprises are artfully displayed as well. Garrity's, 121 North Fifth Street (913–367–1523), is Mary Carol's "new" place for "old" items—as in antiques—as well as her exciting new furniture line. Does this woman *never* sleep?

Now that you've experienced the town's sanctuaries (both religious and 400-

count Egyptian cotton) it's time to discover her history. The visitor center (913–367–2427, 800–234–1854) is historical itself, housed in the restored Santa Fe Depot at 200 South 10th Street. Open every day except major holidays, the center provides maps, a brochure, and a gift shop for souvenirs of your visit. The same address is home to the County Historical Society Museum, which has artifacts from steamboats and wagon trains, and the Atchison Rail Museum, owned by a voluntary group of railroad enthusiasts who operate a miniature railroad during the summer.

The depot is also where you can catch the Atchison Trolley for a 45-minute narrated tour past 18 sites on the National Register of Historic Places. The ride departs each hour on the hour on different days and times from May through October and during special events. Fares are $4.00 for adults, $2.00 for children 4 to 12. As you clack, clack, clack over brick streets you'll see some of the most impressive Victorian homes in the Midwest as well as the Romanesque-style post office that was completed in 1894. You may want to hop off at one of the following stops to explore.

The Evah C. Cray Historical Home Museum (815 North Fifth Street, 913–367–3046) is a 25-room mansion that offers a look at the opulence of the Victorian era. Built in 1882, it is distinguished by a three-story fairy-tale tower, ornate fireplaces, and original chandeliers. The carriage house has a video viewing room, country store, and exhibits. A minimal fee is charged. The museum is open daily May through August, closed November through February, and open Friday through Monday all other months. Got that?

The Muchnic Art Gallery (704 North Fourth Street, 913–367–4278) is in a spectacular Queen Anne mansion that was built in 1885 for lumber merchant George W. Howell. His profession dictated the home's lavish use of carved woods like the intricate parquet floors of walnut, mahogany, and oak and faces carved on the ornate newel posts in the lower hall; the eight faces are said to represent the

Howell family. Cast-bronze hardware and stained glass in the conservatory are other masterful touches. H. E. Muchnic, founder of LFM (now Atchison Casting), purchased the home in 1922 for $9,000. The furnishings and paintings on the main floor are just as when the Muchnic family lived here. Since 1970 the second floor has been dedicated as exhibition space for the Atchison Art Association. The home is open on weekends and Wednesday afternoons from March through December; there is a small fee.

The Amelia Earhart Birthplace Museum (223 North Terrace Street, 913–367–4217, www.ameliaearhartmuseum.org), also on the trolley route, is a pretty Gothic Revival cottage built in 1861 by the famous flyer's grandfather, Judge Alfred G. Otis. The Ninety-Nines, a women's pilot organization Earhart helped found in 1929, now operates the museum, which features period furnishings. Open daily, but hours vary throughout the year. Donations are appreciated.

You'll find more memorials to the aviatrix at the International Forest of Friendship at Warnock Lake. A life-size bronze gazes over the grounds and a forest that was established during the town's bicentennial. Each June, new plaques are set into a walkway to honor people involved in aviation and space exploration. Trees representing all 50 states and more than 35 countries are planted here, including the "Moon Tree," which was grown from a seed taken to the moon aboard Apollo 14. It is encircled by a memorial to the 10 astronauts who have lost their lives.

A deck on a hill within the lake provides a spectacular view of the Amelia Earhart Earthwork. Kansas artist Stan Herd created this one-acre portrait of permanent plantings and stones in 1997. Now it's time to plant yourself in a booth at the River House Restaurant (913–367–1010) at 101 Commercial. Here you'll find elegant dining in a century-old building that has been a railroad hotel, peanut butter factory, and bordello. There's a pun in there somewhere, folks; we'll let you work on it. Lovely views of the river are part of the restaurant's many charms, but the big draw is the menu, which includes salmon prepared a number of ways and a veggie sandwich, a mélange of grilled eggplant, red pepper, red onion, and portobella mushrooms served with sundried tomato puree and garlic mayonnaise on focaccia. The children's menu offers a Little Mo Hamburger with fries. Lunch and dinner are available Monday through Saturday.

If you prefer something a little more casual, Lopez de Mexico (112 South Sixth, 913-367-2422) is a third-generation restaurant that prides itself on incredible fajitas, enchiladas, and a homemade guacamole that's not to be missed. Thursday is "cheap margarita" night; we'll be the ones with the coarse-salt mustaches. It's closed Monday. The Roastery at Neuforth's (913-367-0465) at 901 North Seventh Street is the place to stop for a cappuccino and dessert.

Ready for bed? Part of the allure of tiny towns is that lodging choices always seem to include a bed-and-breakfast. Atchison has two delightful options. St. Martin's Bed and Breakfast is perched on a stone wall and provides a glorious view of the river from the back patio. You may never want to leave the luxury of the spacious Gold Suite, with its grand king-size bed, claw-footed bathtub, and shower for two. Four other rooms are available, including the ultraromantic Anna's Room in shades of taupe and mauve with a dreamy view.

All rooms have a private, adjoining bath and are $95 per night. Owners John and Janet Settich are well known for their continental breakfasts, which include

made-from-scratch baked goods like pumpkin bread, cheddar cheese biscuits, and cinnamon rolls and a delightful platter of fresh fruit and gourmet cheeses. Cereals and yogurt are also available. John is an amateur historian of the town and can tell you fascinating stories and suggest must-see attractions. St. Martin's is at 324 Santa Fe Street. Call (913) 367–4964 or (877) 367–4924. You may view the rooms online at www.stmartinsbandb.com.

Jan and Robert Denny offer heavenly respite at their bed-and-breakfast built by the brothers of St. Benedict's in 1890. The appropriately named Majestic House is an imposing stone structure set in 30 acres of deep woods and cool, shaded gardens. Five bedrooms will tempt you, including the spacious Christmas Memories on the third floor. This suite features elegant iron beds that can be twin or king and a window seat that provides a treetop view. Old-fashioned sleds give the room its name.

The Garden Room on the main floor is so close to the flowers you'll be able to tell which ones are in bloom. Many consider the Music Room the prettiest in the house. Rooms range from $89 to $130. Breakfast is a hearty country affair with hotcakes, eggs, bacon, sausage, fresh fruit, and juice. Take your time; the glassed-in porch is so lovely you'll want to linger over another cup of coffee. You can reach Jan and Robert at (913) 367–3696 or www.thema jestichouse.com. The address is 18936 262nd Road, just a few miles from Atchison's downtown.

But you'll find reasons to visit Atchison other than cinnamon rolls and hotcakes; there seems to be a special event nearly every weekend, especially in summer. Things really start jumping in March for the St. Patrick's Day parade, with floats downtown and corned beef and cabbage at the Elks. Later in the month, get on track for the annual Artrain, when five railcars serve as art galleries and studios for local and regional artists. In May 3 downtown blocks are transformed into the Kiwanis Spring Flea Market, and the following week an Antique Airport Fly-in displays vintage air-

---

i *If you're planning to stay at a bed-and-breakfast, the host can become your new best friend even before you sign the register. Call before your visit, if possible, to request information about upcoming events, what not to miss, and restaurant recommendations. That way you can get the most from your visit.*

---

craft at the airport named for the town's famous daughter. That same month, the Riverbend Art Fair features artists from a six-state area with live music, children's activities, and food vendors.

In July a celebration on the Fourth serves up food, music, and fireworks at the Amelia Earhart Stadium, and two weeks later the Annual Amelia Earhart Festival treats residents and guests to outdoor concerts, arts and crafts, food, a carnival and street dance, and a spectacular fireworks display on the Missouri River. In October the Atchison Homes Tour lets us peak into some of the fabulous old homes. Tickets are $15, and money raised goes to the Mount St. Scholastica Academy. The Oktoberfest Arts and Crafts Festival is a downtown event with more than 100 arts and crafts vendors plus German food and music. And count us in for the Haunted Homes Tour, which extends through Halloween. This narrated trolley tour takes you around "the most haunted town in Kansas." Perhaps Sallie will make an appearance; you can read about the famed "Heartland Ghost" at www.prairieghosts.com. The tour costs $5.00, and children from 4 to 12 get a goodie bag. The rest of us just get goosebumps.

The trolleys are rolled out again for the annual Tour of Lights each December, an hour's round-trip of festive holiday lights and decorations all around Atchison. Fares are $4.00 for adults and $2.00 for children. For more information on all these events, call the Atchison Area Chamber of Commerce at (913) 367-2427 or (800) 234-1854. Details are also available on the Web site, www.atchison.org. To reach Atchison, head north on I-29, take exit 20, and follow Missouri Highway 273 to Missouri Highway 45. Go north on MO 45 to U.S. Highway 59, and then go west 4 miles to the town.

MEDIA

Perhaps Kansas Citians have so many media choices because more than half of us live in the Show Me state. Our need-to-know mentality can be appeased through a breathtaking variety of ways, including five daily newspapers, a handful of weeklies, 10 television stations, 20 FM and 23 AM radio stations, and a growing list of public interest sites on the World Wide Web. And whatever your livelihood or hobby, from golf to computers, fine dining to fitness, chances are there's a special-interest publication to help you do it better, find out where to enjoy it, or at least commune with others who share your passion.

Following are some of our more interesting means of communicating, listed by category. Companies are located in Kansas City, Missouri, unless otherwise noted.

DAILIES

The *Examiner*
P.O. Box 459
Independence, MO 64051-0459
(816) 254-8600
Owned by Morris Communications Corporation, which serves the towns of Independence, Sibley, Buckner, Blue Springs, Grain Valley, and Oak Grove under its two mastheads: the *Independence Examiner* and the *Blue Springs Examiner.* This century-old newspaper is published afternoons Monday through Friday and Saturday morning. Local home delivery costs $100 per year.

The *Kansas City Kansan*
901 North Eighth Street
Kansas City, KS
(913) 371-4300
Strong political leadership (finally!) and exciting new tourism destinations west of the state line have given this daily more to

cheer about in the past few years. The paper has covered Wyandotte and northern Johnson Counties since 1921, so the 14-year-old 4-H'er who once had his prize-winning pig pictured in the paper might now be turning his bifocals to the monthly senior section. In fact community news is the strong suit of the *Kansan* for folks who feel slighted by the big paper across the river. Published Tuesday through Friday plus a weekend edition with a circulation of 10,000. Subscriptions cost $80 per year.

The *Kansas City Star*
1729 Grand
(816) 234-7827
www.kansascity.com and
www.kcstar.com
Although the *Star* is the only daily newspaper that serves the entire metroplex, it has never used its "only game in town" status to deliver less-than-stellar reporting. It mirrors our town's tragedies and triumphs with insight and depth. And despite the nationwide trend of decreasing newspaper readership, the *Star* remains a vibrant and growing communicator. Indeed, a preholiday edition can weigh as much as your Thanksgiving turkey!

The paper's five metropolitan bureaus contribute a neighborhood feel to each zoned issue. Its editorial coverage has evolved with the lifestyle interests of its readers, adding a daily FYI section that deals with fitness, family, pets, home fashion, and just enough celebrity gossip to keep us from turning to supermarket tabloids. The Friday Preview provides a week's worth of entertainment and arts coverage throughout the region. The *Sunday Star* magazine brings us profiles of people, places, and events in our area worth a closer look.

On-staff photographers provide sometimes humorous and often poignant glimpses of the city's inhabitants. When journalists like Eric Adler share stories about hometown heroes we cheer; when his four-part series features a teenager fighting drugs and a tough home life hundreds of us mail checks to pay for her college tuition. Sportswriter Mike Polanski's prose is so remarkable that even nonsports buffs often turn to his section first.

The paper's online version displays news, story archives, and extensive links to other area sites. A classified section lets viewers search for a house, car, or job from their computer screens. Daily delivery costs $198 a year; Saturday and Sunday only delivery is $144. Newsstand cost is 50 cents. See the Close-up in this chapter for a look at the history of the *Star*.

The *Olathe Daily News*
514 South Kansas
Olathe, KS
(913) 764-2211
This community paper is the place to find news about local schools, business, and social events in the booming southwest region of the metroplex. Daily circulation on Tuesday through Saturday is around 8,000 except on Wednesday, when it jumps to 42,000 and includes a Home Living section with new home community profiles, real estate listings, and gardening and home decorating tips. Yearly subscriptions are $111.

WEEKLIES

The *Business Journal*
1101 Walnut, Suite 800
(816) 421-5900
www.bizjournals.com/kansascity
Kansas City's edition of American City Business Journals Inc. is delivered to nearly 11,000 offices each Friday. Its editorial focus—banking, sales and marketing, business owner profiles, growth strategies—is geared to decision makers in companies with fewer than 100 employees. Each issue takes an in-depth look at a business category such as family businesses, health care, or banking. The annual *Book of Lists* is an excellent tool for area salespeople and job seekers; it names top managers and lists revenue for segments such as manufacturing, minority businesses, advertising agencies, property managers, lenders, architects, and travel industries. The online version is easy to navigate and provides links to the publisher's other city journals. An annual subscription gets you 53 issues plus the *Book of Lists* for $86; the newsstand price is $1.75 per copy.

Along with the Kansas City Star, *the Nelson-Atkins Museum of Art, and our city's many boulevards, parks, and gardens, William Rockhill Nelson left another, more furry, legacy. He imported squirrels from neighboring states and let them loose in Kansas City's new green spaces. So some fall, as you're watching the long-tailed creatures leap around in search of acorns, you can say, "Nuts to you, Mr. Nelson."*

The *Call*
1715 East 18 Street
(816) 842-3804
"We call it like it is," was the motto of Chester A. Franklin, an ambitious businessman and community activist who founded one of the nation's most respected African-American papers in 1919. The paper quickly developed a reputation as an advocate for social justice, with articles about lynchings, police brutality, segregation, and discrimination in housing and employment. In 1955 Lucille Bluford took the helm after writing for the paper for more than two decades. Known for her thoughtful and thought-provoking columns Bluford has been called "the conscience of Kansas City." Her own conscience guided her when she sued the University of Missouri for not allowing her to attend its school of journalism in the late 1930s. She lost the case, but in 1984 she received the school's Honor Medal and five years later MU presented her with an hon-

orary doctorate of humanities. But this petite lady's highest honor came not in bronze but in bricks: The Kansas City Missouri Public Library system named a new branch library at 3050 Prospect for her in 1988. The *Call* has a paid circulation of 20,000 and costs $26 a year. Single issues cost 50 cents.

The *Independent*
306 East 12 Street, Suite 630
(816) 471-2800

If you're *anyone* in Kansas City society, your engagement, wedding, and birth announcements will have been covered by the city's oldest magazine; if your last name appears on a street sign, building, or museum anywhere in town chances are your photo accompanied the write-up. Since 1899 the city's crème de la crème have turned these oversized black-and-white pages to see who wore what designer's gown to the latest ball or muse about gentle gossip in "Over My Shoulder." The readership represents Kansas City's most influential, active, and civic-minded citizens. . . and certainly some of its most affluent. The average household income is $277,000, with an average net worth of $1.5 million. The *Independent* arrives in polished brass mailboxes on Saturday morning 45 times a year and is available at a select number of newsstands. The annual subscription price is $45.

The *Leaven*
12615 Parallel Parkway
Kansas City, KS
(913) 721-1570
www.theleaven.com

The weekly newspaper of the Archdiocese of Kansas City in Kansas is distributed free to families who belong to Catholic parishes throughout Wyandotte, Johnson, and Leavenworth Counties. Each issue covers national and local news, book reviews, and a calendar that lists upcoming social and educational events, retreats, and meetings. The commentary pages answer questions regarding religion and provide a deeper look into the current Sunday's scripture.

Pitch Weekly
1701 Main Street
(816) 561-6061
www.pitch.com

This free weekly with a 80,000 circulation is the city's most recognized alternative tabloid. The editor boasts that the paper is dedicated to "hard-hitting journalism, smart criticism, lively features and good old-fashioned muckraking," but the real reason folks pick it up is to see what band is playing at the Hurricane or what food critic Charles Ferruzza thinks of the new restaurant in town. In fact, anyone who whines "There's nothing to do in Kansas City" has somehow missed tripping over stacks of the *Pitch* in doorways of bookstores, coffeehouses, and bistros and in red kiosks all over town. Its calendar offers the area's most complete coverage of live music, dance, and theater (including some in Lawrence, Kansas, a college town about half an hour away). And for a paper with such a Gen-X base it provides a respectable listing of events for kids. Even the ads are pretty entertaining; here's where to find outlets for any vice from martinis to water pipes, sexy lingerie to sex partners (you might need to read the abbreviation code for any designation beyond SWM in the personal ads titled "Romance" and "Wildside").

The annual Best of Kansas City issue—usually in mid-October—has the typical "best brunch" categories along with a few fresh options such as best guilty pleasure. Just thinking about those answers gives us goosebumps. The paper's online incarnation provides a repeat of the printed page with added links to other sites, Web-exclusive features, and essays.

Sun Publications
7373 West 107 Street
Overland Park, KS
(913) 381-1010
www.sunpublications.com

Founded in 1918 by Stan Rose, this company publishes nine weekly newspapers serving communities in Johnson County, Kansas, and Missouri's Northland. On the

Kansas side the papers provide a handy soapbox for the political views of the founder's son, Steve Rose, who retains a title despite having sold the company a few years ago. Don't expect to find much on the main Web site, but the printed versions offer residents a chance to keep up on the social, school, and business scene in their regions.

MAGAZINES

Ingram's
306 East 12 Street, Suite 1014
(816) 842-9994
www.ingramsonline.com
For more than a century this monthly, and its predecessor, *Corporate Report,* has been a staple among area business leaders. The average reader's annual income is close to $172,000, and nearly half are millionaires. Each issue contains editorials about law, sales and marketing, technology and e-commerce, profiles of the city's movers and shakers, coverage of area philanthropic activities, and a short calendar of upcoming events. The magazine does a fine job at promoting Kansas City's strengths by profiling a geographical portion of the city including schools, economic growth, and real estate options. There's stiff competition to make the magazine's annual Corporate Report 100, a list of Kansas City's fastest growing companies, and perhaps even tougher competition for the annual best-of survey published each August. Within days plaques declaring "Best Barbeque" or "Best Golf Course" start going up all over town. *Ingram's* is delivered free of charge to qualified readers; subscriptions are available for $36 per year.

Kansas City
7101 College Boulevard
Overland Park, KS
(913) 894-6923
www.kcmag.com
Every city has one: a glossy magazine that celebrates the region's most interesting people and places. Lucky for us, *Kansas City* is a beaut with great writing and photography. Published monthly, each issue offers late-breaking takes on around-town happenings, profiles of home-town celebrities, tips on making your space more livable, and handy guides to restaurants and events. Once a year the magazine publishes the Best of Kansas City survey in which community readers provide their own favorites along with readers' top picks. *Kansas City* is $3.50 per issue. An annual subscription is $12.98.

Kansas City Home and Garden
5301 West 75 Street
Prairie Village, KS
(913) 648-5757
www.kchomesandgardens.com
The fact that Kansas City can support two home and garden magazines is testament to our appreciation for graceful living, lovely gardens, and gracious entertaining. This magazine also has a lake living section to appease the hundreds of residents who spend summer weekends at the Lake of the Ozarks, four hours south of Kansas City. Published monthly, the magazine costs $26 for an annual subscription, $4.95 for an individual copy.

Kansas City Home Design
7101 College Boulevard
Overland Park, KS
(913) 894-6923
www.kansascityhomedesign.com
Although *Home Design* shares its editorial staff, office space, and a handful of writers with *Kansas City* magazine, it is by far the more elegant, better-dressed sister. In each issue, two or three homes, often belonging to our town's toniest couples, are profiled along with stunning photography to show us how the other half lives and entertains. And after drooling over a four-page photo essay of a dinner party, complete with recipes, you'll feel as if you'd been a guest. Other topics include gardening, home renovations, coverage of

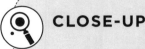

William Rockhill Nelson

Many of us read all about it in the *Kansas City Star,* the venerable newspaper founded by William Rockhill Nelson on September 18, 1880. In Kansas City this newspaperman from Indiana saw a town where he could make both money and a difference—and he eventually did both. His other legacies include our parks and boulevard systems and the art gallery that bears his name.

Nelson quickly showed his business acumen by charging two cents for his paper instead of the nickel that the other three dailies already in print did. The last of his competitors, the *Kansas City Journal,* held on until 1942. As Nelson's fame and legend grew—thanks in great part to his unconventional tastes and famed battles with the establishment—he was often interviewed by national magazines like the *Saturday Evening Post.* Theodore Roosevelt became a personal friend who often came to Kansas City to seek his advice.

Nelson's paper's reach expanded along with his waistline when in 1891 he delivered the *Weekly Kansas City Star* to country towns throughout Kansas, Missouri, Nebraska, Colorado, and Oklahoma. For 25 cents a year subscribers were treated to reprints from the daily Star and the editor's political views.

By 1901 he had purchased the *Kansas City Times,* a morning daily, and began calling his empire "the 24-hour Star." The *Star's* afternoon edition ceased in 1990. In 1911 the paper moved to its current location, a redbrick Italian Renaissance-style building at 18 and Grand where there were no private offices. Nelson said the layout was designed so that everyone could feel equal; employees knew it was so that the boss could keep his eyes on them.

By the time he died on April 13, 1915, Nelson's fortune was estimated at between $5 and $10 million and the *Star's* circulation was more than

A big man with big dreams for Kansas City, William Rockhill Nelson pushed forward the city's beautiful parks and boulevards system among other accomplishments. SPECIAL COLLECTIONS DEPARTMENT, KANSAS CITY PUBLIC LIBRARY, KANSAS CITY, MISSOURI

200,000. His will stipulated that after the death of his heirs the entire fortune would be converted to cash and given to the arts. His majestic home, Oak Hall, is now the site of the Nelson-Atkins Gallery of Art. He had already made our city a work of art; he used his paper to campaign for paved roads and streets, sidewalks and streetlights. And he was instrumental in creating the city's parks system in 1881 when he hired landscaper George E. Kessler to design a boulevard and park system that is still considered one of the finest in the world.

As for the *Star*, Nelson thought it couldn't continue without him. But survive it has, and has thrived under the helm of talented and forward-thinking managers and through pens of award-winning journalists. Its reporters and editors have won eight Pulitzer prizes and four Polk awards. Yet its most famous reporter wasn't around long enough to earn more than a paycheck: Ernest Hemingway joined the staff in October 1917 but left the next April to drive ambulances in the war. Hemingway credited a *Star* editor, C. G. "Pete" Wellington, with teaching him to write clearly and provocatively. The paper's style sheet at the time admonished, "Use short sentences. Use short first paragraphs. Use vigorous English." Okay.

When Nelson's daughter, Laura Nelson Kirkwood, died in 1926, the paper was sold in accordance with his will. With financial help from her husband Irwin, 30 *Star* employees purchased the paper for $11 million. In 1977 it was sold to Capital Cities Communications Inc. for $125 million; today it is part of the Knight-Ridder family.

During the 1980s, under editor James H. Hale, the *Star* greatly expanded its zoned suburban operations and extended its coverage of business and sports, just in time to herald the city's first baseball championship in 1985. Hale's 15-year tenure also saw a continuation of Nelson's philanthropic legacy by establishing Project Warmth, which has raised millions of dollars and tons of clothes and blankets for the city's poor.

Under its current president and publisher, Arthur S. Brisbane, the *Star* has explored innovative methods of delivering news and information through technology. StarTouch, an interactive telephone news and information service, was launched in 1991; within four years the system was logging six million calls a year. And in 1996 the paper decided to embrace the emerging news source that threatened its readership: It introduced a multimedia site in cyberspace just two years after the phrase "World Wide Web" first appeared within its newsprint pages.

And the *Star* continues to find ways to assist the community through programs like Stars in Education, which provides newspapers and training materials to schools; Hooked on Books, a citywide program that delivers books to school libraries; a recycling program; and sponsorship of ongoing health and business seminars.

high-profile society events, and the art scene. The magazine is published monthly; subscriptions are $11.95.

SPECIAL INTEREST PERIODICALS

Dos Mundos
902-A Southwest Boulevard
(816) 221-4747
www.dosmundos.com
Dos Mundos, or *Two Worlds,* has provided a bilingual forum for Kansas City's vibrant and growing Hispanic population since 1981; 80 to 90 percent of the information is translated. The readership is diverse: Of the more than 50,000 Hispanics living in the Kansas City metropolitan area, only about 60 percent are of Mexican origin. The remainder are mostly Puerto Ricans and Cubans. Along with national news, *Dos Mundos* covers local news, sports, and entertainment and provides a much-needed focus on Hispanic heritage. The 70,000 circulation covers the greater Kansas City area with nationwide distribution accounting for 5 percent. Published biweekly, an annual subscription costs $20.

JAM (Jazz Ambassadors Magazine)
P.O. Box 36181
Kansas City, MO 64171
(913) 967-6767
One of the finest regional jazz magazines in the country, *JAM* has covered the Kansas City jazz scene since 1986. It is distributed free to 500-plus Kansas City Jazz Ambassador members (one more great reason to join this organization), and available free at local jazz venues, record stores, bookstores, and libraries. Whether your musical taste runs to jazz, Dixieland, or bebop, *JAM* is the place to find where musicians are jamming at nightclubs and festivals, learn more about our town's musical heritage, and read where to board the bus for the next pub crawl. *JAM* is produced in even-numbered months. Pick up a copy or check out the *Jazz Ambassador*'s Web site at www.jazzkc.org.

Kansas City Small Business Monthly
P.O. Box 754
Shawnee Mission, Kansas 66201
(913) 432-6690
www.kcsmallbiz.com
Small and emerging businesses in the area have a friend in publisher/editor Kelly Scanlon. Her monthly tabloid covers need-to-know topics such as how to keep employees happy, watch out for the latest computer virus, cope with rising health care costs, decide whether to incorporate, measure trade show results, market globally, and write a sales script. And that was just October. Each issue also profiles a successful business, provides strategies for home offices, and includes a comprehensive calendar of seminars and events. There's even a handy guide for the biggest problem facing entrepreneurs today: where to get a decent lunch in 15 minutes. The online version is extremely well designed and offers additional articles about marketing, sales, and cash flow. The annual "Entrepreneur's Guide" is a keeper, covering legal, marketing, e-commerce, taxes, real estate, education, and training subjects. *Small Business Monthly* is distributed free to qualified readers and is also available by subscription for $22 a year.

Liberty Press Kansas City
1509 Westport Road. Suite 203B
(816) 931-3060
www.libertypress.net
Serving Kansas City's gay, lesbian, and bisexual communities, this monthly newspaper provides extensive reporting on relevant events, health issues, and book and movie reviews as well as listing alternative nightclubs. A monthly column addresses legal issues facing gay and lesbian readers, and "Out on Vacation" profiles gay-friendly cities. "Around Kansas City" lists nonprofit support, political, and spiritual organizations in the Kansas City area. The paper also covers general interest news

such as restaurant reviews and tips on throwing the perfect dinner party. *Liberty Press* is distributed free to area bookstores, hair salons, coffee shops, and restaurants throughout the city.

Review
1427 West Ninth Street, Suite 203
(816) 471-2343
Published six times a year, this tabloid covers Kansas City's impressive art scene through previews of upcoming exhibitions and art events, gallery and studio listings, reviews of current works, and artist-on-artist interviews. Here's where to locate art in places outside the galleries: coffeehouses, flower shops, restaurants, and libraries. If you're not familiar with the talent and variety of work to be found within our town, this publication may surprise you. Available free at many bookstores and galleries around town.

TELEVISION

Hundreds of dinners got cold as an estimated 100,000 people crowded around 7,500 television sets throughout the city when our first station, WDAF-TV, went on the air at 6:00 P.M. October 16, 1949. To beam those signals the station built a 724-foot antenna, which was the highest man-made structure in Missouri at that time. It became the 79th TV station in the country. Viewers were treated to three hours of programming every day, starting with a locally produced children's show sponsored by Frito-Lay; during the rest of the day many people tuned in just to watch the test pattern.

The *Kansas City Star* owned WDAF-TV from sign-on until it was indicted by a federal grand jury for monopolistic advertising practices and forced to sell the station in 1958. A year after its first airing, WDAF became an NBC affiliate, a designation it continued until 1994 when it switched to the Fox Network.

Kansas City's pioneer station holds bragging rights to a number of firsts in the market, including the first to offer color,

stereo, Doppler radar, 24-hour programming, and a helicopter for traffic and news reporting.

Today the helicopter from WDAF-TV vies for air space with KMBC-TV's eyes-in-the-skies. But when it comes to on-air time, Kansas City has its favorite personalities. The patriarch is Larry Moore at KMBC-TV, who started as a reporter with the station in 1968 and became primary news hawker in 1972. His warmth has earned him a wall full of awards such as News Anchor of the Year and one of Kansas City's 10 Top Celebrities. But it's his community involvement that has earned him accolades like Man of the Year. Moore helped organize the Dream Factory in 1984, a nonprofit that has helped grant the wishes of nearly 2,500 seriously ill youngsters; the anchor has helped raise $400,000 annually to send kids to Disneyland, get them computers, and travel around the country to meet favorite celebrities. Moore, a cancer survivor, was also lauded by the American Cancer Society for his educational series urging early detection. The entire community watched and sent prayers as he lost his dark, wavy hair to chemotherapy before he bounced back to the robust health he enjoys today.

At KSHB-TV one of the personalities is also known for a luxurious head of hair—or fur, in this case. It's Windy the weather dog, who accompanies meteorologist Gary Lezak on his speaking engagements at retirement communities and schools and often appears on the air. Lezak introduced a new pooch, Stormy, in 2001.

You might be interested to know that the KCTV tower at 125 East 31 Street is taller than the Eiffel Tower in Paris. The KC tower stands at 1,067 feet; the Parisian structure—although admittedly more beautiful—is 1,024 feet tall.

Along with cable programming, Kansas City supports nine local stations, including network affiliates and one independent station. The stations are listed along with their non-cable channels. Kansas City also has two cable companies, Time Warner and Comcast. For these channel settings, check the last page in Star TV found in the *Kansas City Star* Sunday paper.

WDAF Channel 4 (Fox)
KCTV Channel 5 (CBS)
KMBC Channel 9 (ABC)
KCPT Channel 19 (PBS)
KCWE Channel 29 (UPN)
KMCI Channel 38 (Independent)
KSHB Channel 41 (NBC)
KPXE Channel 50 (PAX)
KSMO Channel 62 (WB)

RADIO

Kansas City joined the country's love affair with radio in the spring of 1922 when a furniture dealer and a radio supplier joined forces to put the city's first commercial station, WOQ, on the air. A few weeks later religious programming and poetry readings were being broadcast from the RLDS Church (now Church of Christ) on WPE. WDAF, whose call letters live today, used the airwaves for a more lively purpose as it broadcast the Coon Sanders Nighthawks Orchestra live from the Muehlebach Hotel starting that June. Kansas City radio played an even bigger part in the history of jazz when, in 1935, a record producer heard Count Basie's Barons of Rhythm carried live from the Reno Club at 12th and Cherry Streets on his car radio hundreds of miles away.

Sadly, it's harder to dial in a jazz tune on a local station today as contemporary hits and album rock has taken over the airwaves. A few stations offer jazz programming at various times throughout the week, and KCIY–FM 106.5 provides what it calls "smooth jazz" from a variety of contemporary artists like Diana Krall and David Sanborn. Classical music lovers also go wanting in Kansas City, since its only all-classical station, KXTR, left its FM status in 2000. It now has far less reach on its new home at KXTR, 1660 AM.

Drive-time listeners hoping to get away from the in-your-face ramblings of radio personalities can tune to KCUR–FM 89.3, a noncommercial station that broadcasts National Public Radio and Public Radio International programming. Popular locally produced programs make up the rest of the broadcasting day; at 10:00 A.M. every other Friday foodies listen to restaurant reviews on Walt Bodine's program, while Chuck Haddix (aka Chuck Haddock) shares his passion for blues, soul, and jazz—along with 250,000 recordings housed in the Miller Nichols Library—every Friday and Saturday from 8:00 P.M. to midnight on "Fish Fry." Another music lover got his start on KCUR: Bill Shapiro's "Cyprus Avenue" debuted on the station in 1978 and today his "intelligent rock and roll" can be heard on 50 radio stations across the nation. It's aired from noon to 2:00 P.M on Saturday in Kansas City.

Other stations are listed below.

NEWS/TALK

WIBW 580 AM
KFEQ 680 AM
KCMO 710 AM
KMBZ 980 AM (popular call-in forum for sports fanatics)
KCXL 1140 AM
KCTE 1510 AM

CHRISTIAN/GOSPEL/ FAMILY VALUE

KCCV 760 AM
KGGN 890 AM (Urban gospel)
KCWJ 1030 AM
KEXS 1090 AM
KGNM 1270 AM
KCKN 1340 AM
KCNW 1380 AM(Catholic programming)
KKLO 1410 AM (Sports/Christian)
KPRT 1590 AM
KCCV 92.3 FM

NATIONAL PUBLIC RADIO/CULTURAL/ CLASSICAL/JAZZ

KUPN 1480 AM
KXTR 1660 AM
KCUR 89.3 FM
KKFI 90.1 FM

KCMW 90.9 FM
KANU 91.5 FM
KCIY 106.5 FM

COUNTRY

WDAF 610 AM
KFKF 90.1 FM
KBEQ 104 FM

CONTEMPORARY

KOKO 1450 AM
KMXV 93.3 FM
KRBZ 96.5 FM
KUDL 98.1 FM
KSRC 102.1 FM

KPRS 103.3 FM
KKJO 105.5 FM

ROCK/RHYTHM/SOUL (INCLUDING OLDIES)

KCMO 94.9 FM
KQRC 98.9 FM
KYYS 99.7 FM
KCFX 101.1 FM
KLZR 105.9 FM
KNRX 107.3 FM
KFME 105.1 FM

OTHERS

WHB-810 AM (Sports)
KPHN 1190 AM (Business)
KMEX 1250 AM (Spanish)

WORSHIP

We have, as theologian Martin Marty said when he saw a 1998 *Kansas City Star* poll on religion, "a real believing town here." Indeed. Ninety-six percent of those surveyed said they believed in God or a higher power, 95 percent believed in miracles, 85 percent believed in life after death. And we put our faith to work. Fifty-two percent of Kansas Citians attend worship services weekly, 68 percent pray daily, 23 percent read scripture daily, 16 percent read it several times a week, and 40 percent volunteer for charity.

Through the years, even during our rough-and-tumble early days, we have built monuments to faith in buildings that reach toward the heavens: the dizzying spiral of the Community of Christ Temple, the majestic Unity Tower, the shining golden dome of the Cathedral of the Immaculate Conception, the Steeple of Light piercing the night sky from the Community Christian Church near the Plaza. And a new heaven-sent symbol is being planned for the United Methodist Church of the Resurrection in Leawood, Kansas, home to the fastest-growing Methodist congregation in the country.

There are slightly more than 2,000 congregations here, representing more than a dozen faiths. In addition to the more familiar Protestant, Roman Catholic, Jewish, Eastern Orthodox, and Islamic groups, there are Hindu, Buddhist, Sufi, Baha'i, Native American, Sikh, Jain, pagan, Unitarian Universalist, and New Age groups.

A list of churches, synagogues, and other houses of worship in the area, including links to those with Web sites, can be found at www.kansascityguide .com/church/index.htm.

And to keep pace with the faithful in the suburbs, new houses of worship—huge structures, even some megachurches, defined as those with over 2,000 in attendance—are being built at an amazing pace. Yet even some of these supersize structures are outgrown before the last pew is in place. Our frantic expansion is getting noticed. John Vaughan, director of Church Growth Today, a research center in Bolivar, Missouri, says "to have this kind of growth and this kind of construction is phenomenal. For the size of the city, it makes it even more impressive."

And the fervor of the heartland is evident in the fact that two of the churches mentioned, Community of Christ and Unity School of Christianity, are world headquarters. The third is the Church of the Nazarene.

It certainly was for Joseph Smith III, who in 1852 took the helm of the largest Mormon splinter group to found the Reorganized Church of Jesus Christ of Latter-Day Saints in Independence, Missouri. Why this place? Because Midwest town is where his father, Joseph Smith, had determined Jesus Christ would return to Earth. When the elder Smith was killed in 1844, the son continued his teachings here in the city of Zion. The growing congregation built their massive Auditorium in 1920 and later the Temple with its splendid 300-foot spiral roof that resembles a seashell.

The campus, 1001 West Walnut, Independence, serves as the spiritual center for 250,000 members in more than 50 states. Along with a museum, the campus contains the Children's Peace Pavilion, an interactive museum dedicated to promoting peace through example. The Worshiper's Path, a reflective walkway filled with symbolic artwork, leads to the 1,600-seat Sanctuary. Guests are welcome to visit, and organ recitals are held at various times of the year. You are also invited to take part in a Daily Prayer for Peace beginning at 12:30 P.M. You may contact them at (816) 521-3045 or www.cofchrist.org.

Unity World Headquarters, with its beautiful 165-foot-tall bell tower, is situated among 1,400 acres of beautifully landscaped grounds with meditation chapels, fountains, and reflecting pools. It is home to a magnificent rose garden with more than 800 rose bushes and 50 varieties. Founded in 1889 by American clergyman and educator Charles Fillmore and his wife, Myrtle, the nondenominational religion combines teachings from Christian Science, Hinduism, Theosophy, New Thought, and others.

Unity has been offering ministry, prayer, and education since 1889. Its monthly spiritual publication, *Daily Word,* is translated into nine languages with an annual circulation of 1.3 million, and its Silent Prayer ministry received 2 million requests for prayer assistance in 1999. Free tours start at the visitor center (1901 Northwest Blue Parkway, 816-524-3550, www.unityworldhq.org) Monday through Friday year-round; weekend tours are also available May through October.

The Church of the Nazarene is the third religious organization to be headquartered in Kansas City. The church moved to its present home at 6401 The Paseo shortly after it was organized October 8, 1908, in Pilot Point, Texas.

The International Center provides support services to more than 1.4 million members worshiping in more than 12,600 churches in the United States, Canada, and 143 other world areas. Its publishing house is 5 miles north of the center at 2931 Troost Avenue and is the largest publisher of Holiness (Wesleyan) literature in the world. It prints more than 500,000 books annually.

Although today religious headquarters and even community churches can take over entire blocks or acres of land, Kansas City's first house of worship was a log cabin built in 1834 at what is now 11th and Pennsylvania. It was called "Chouteau's church" because it was funded by the extended family of Francois and Berenice, who came

Roman Catholics wishing to attend mass in Latin may do so at a beautiful Gothic church built in 1924 at 2203 Parallel Avenue in Kansas City, Kansas. Blessed Sacrament Church holds daily Latin mass Monday, Tuesday, Wednesday, and Friday at noon, low mass on Sunday at 7:30 A.M., and high mass at 10:45 A.M. Call (913) 321-1958 for more information.

here in 1820 as the first white settlers. It is the oldest worshipping congregation in Kansas City. Various missionaries built the log cabin and two brick structures, none of which are standing today.

In 1845 Father Bernard Donnelly, a pioneer priest, came to the area. Thanks to his Irish charm as much as his pastoral leadership, he soon became a legend among the settlers and native tribes. In 1880 the area was officially designated a diocese, and Bishop Hogan was named the first bishop.

When the Immaculate Conception Church was relocated to its present site at 416 West 12th Street in 1882, it was the tallest building in Kansas City, Missouri. People bought tickets just to ascend the staircase to see the view. The church became the Cathedral, or the Mother Church, for the newly formed Diocese of Kansas City in 1884. In 1895 one of the most unusual carillons in the city was installed in the tower; the 10 bells are named after saints. The largest of these, St. Thomas, is most often rung.

The church was renamed the Cathedral of the Immaculate Conception in 1893. It is always a lovely site, its graceful lines and stained-glass windows giving visual and spiritual respite among its taller neighbors. But when the sun turns the 23 karat gold dome into a shimmering glow, it's simply beautiful. Call (816) 842-0416.

In 1974 the Cathedral of the Immaculate Conception entered into a covenant with the neighboring Episcopalian Cathedral, Grace and Holy Trinity. This stone structure is quite impressive as well and contains two Tiffany stained-glass windows.

The Kansas City Star *publishes a section each Saturday called "Faith" profiling congregations and individuals, listing upcoming faith events, and providing advertising for area churches, synagogues, and other places of worship. Each week two members of the newspaper's panel of religious leaders answer a reader's question. Once the reincarnation was covered by a Buddhist lama and a Baptist minister.*

One religious landmark, the striking B'nai Jehudah synagogue at 59th and Holmes, has been torn down. Yet even its destruction follows the Jewish values and congregational concepts of shalom—the promotion of harmony in all things. Taking its place will be the University Academy, a charter school that will serve more than 1,000 students in grades 6 through 10. The congregation's new home, at 123rd and Nall in Overland Park, Kansas, will serve a growing faith community that spans more than 130 years.

In 1870, 25 Jewish families gathered, pledged $800, and rented a hall at Sixth and Eight and Main Streets to form the first Jewish congregation in Kansas City, Missouri. Founders included Civil War veterans who had fought on both sides of the conflict, a saloonkeeper, store owners, clerks, and at least one gold prospector.

They called themselves B'nai Jehudah, "children of Judah." It became one of the pioneer congregations of Reform Judaism in America, and its rabbis and hundreds of its people have played prominent roles in the economic, social, and political life of Greater Kansas City from an early day to the present. Today membership numbers about 1,700 families.

The congregation's modest first temple, built in 1875 at Sixth and Wyandotte, was replaced 10 years later by a more substantial structure at the southeast corner of 11th and Oak, opposite the present City Hall. By 1908 the growing congregation needed more space and so built an impos-

ing new structure at Linwood Boulevard and Flora Avenue. Temple membership more than doubled soon after World War II, with the majority of members moving farther south. This led to relocating the facilities to 69th and Homes in 1957 with a new religious school, social hall, and chapel. Ten years later the sanctuary was added. Designed by Kansas City architect Clarence Kivett, the broadly spiraling temple rising nearly 90 feet high was meant to evoke one of the oldest structural forms, the Bedouin tent.

A beautiful learning center, which houses a religious school and 250-seat chapel, has been built at 12320 Nall in Overland Park. Soon a new synagogue and offices will follow and B'nai Jehudah will continue to flourish. Contact the congregation at (816) 363–1050 or www.bnaijehuda.org.

One more area church is of note, both for its architect and for its tower made of light instead of steel. But the heavenly beam almost didn't happen. When Frank Lloyd Wright designed the Community Christian Church (816–561–6531) in the 1930s, technology couldn't produce the shaft of light he envisioned coming from the top of the dome. Sixty years later artist Dale Eldred, who was teaching at the Kansas City Art Institute, created a system to send four xenon lights toward the skies. But not even he lived to see the display. The artist died before the Steeple of Light was finally switched on in December 1994. The lights are on every weekend and nightly during the holiday season. You may visit the church at 47th and Main.

A modern-day church is making history as well. The United Methodist Church of the Resurrection, at 137th Street and Roe Avenue in Leawood, Kansas, is the fastest growing United Methodist church in the country. With its expansion plans it is poised to become the largest as well. Led by the charismatic Reverend Adam Hamilton, the congregation has grown from a handful of families meeting in a funeral home chapel in 1990 to more than 10,000 today.

When complete, the church's 10-year expansion plan will encompass almost one million square feet of worship, educational, fitness, and multipurpose space and a 7,000-seat sancutuary. That's larger than Kemper Arena and Bartle Hall combined.

With its amazing growth, some question the church's ability to serve its congregation's spiritual needs. But those who attend are impressed. The key to the Church of the Resurrection's (or COR, as it's often called) success is its mission to build a faith community for those who don't go to church and have little or no religious background.

There is no doubt that when this many people come together with one goal, things get done. The COR was the Community Blood Center's third largest donor in 2000, behind Sprint and Hallmark. In 2001 alone its congregation provided 5,000 sack lunches to children in Westport, helped build 16 homes for Habitat for Humanity, sponsored 300 children through Compassion International, and donated literally tons of clothing and food to area shelters and food pantries.

We've talked about cathedrals and churches created so that people of one faith can come together to pray, do good work, seek solace, and rejoice in the glory of their God. Kansas City is also home to a church that has no central denomination, the Pilgrim Chapel.

This tiny English Gothic church at 3801 Gillham Road was built in 1941 as a congregation for the deaf and hard of hearing—a rare example of a religious building constructed by and for a special needs membership. The Pilgrim Lutheran Church for the Deaf closed in 1987, and today under the leadership of ordained ministers Roger and Elizabeth Coleman, the facility is open to persons of all faiths. All religions are welcomed: Christian, Jewish, Buddhist, Hindu, Muslim, or New Age.

Behind these massive stone walls and heavy oak doors they come to worship and meditate, hold wedding or funeral cer-

The increasing number of faithful can make it tough to find a seat in church as well as at breakfast. By 11:00 A.M. restaurants serving brunch are packed with churchgoers. Be prepared to wait at First Watch, a breakfast-and-lunch-only restaurant with locations around the city, as well as eateries like the Bristol in Overland Park. Some places take reservations.

emonies, or simply pause in the middle of a hectic day. And what they find is something extraordinary, both spiritually and structurally. Architects incorporated special accommodations for lip-reading and hand signing. For instance, sightlines were important, so the pulpit was built high enough so everyone could see clearly from every position. The rows of windows were positioned to eliminate glare. And its miniature Gothic dimensions created an unplanned benefit for the hearing: perfect acoustics with no echoes and no dead spots.

The church is beautiful in both its simplicity and its special touches. The stained-glass windows of rose and amber provide a pinkish-golden hue, and the oak parquet flooring is laid in lively geometric squares. Even the 24-inch-thick stone walls are special. Instead of the ghostly white of native Missouri limestone, Pilgrim Chapel was built of Wisconsin limestone, a putty-gray color that weathers well. The sacred space has no ornamentation; the lines are clean and pure. And in keeping with the intradenominational theme, there are crosses, a menorah, and portraits of yogis, symbols that can be brought out for a service, then put away.

In 1999 Pilgrim Chapel was placed on the National Register of Historic Places. And across the country there are only a few cities that have anything remotely similar to this tiny space where everyone is welcome. It is a fitting tribute to the City of Faith.

RELOCATION 🏠

All right already, we've convinced you to move here. Congratulations, neighbor. You're going to love living in the Heartland. We've helped you pick your neighborhood, line up some festivals, locate parks and lakes, and find where to get a great meal. Now let's move you in.

To smooth your move we've divided this chapter into topics of major interest to those planning—or just contemplating—a move to Kansas City: Neighborhoods and Real Estate will help you decide where you want to live. Once you've settled on a location, Getting Started will help you get hooked up to utilities. Getting Legal provides basic information about licenses you'll need, and Getting to Know You introduces those little nice-to-know services in town. In Kansas City we take our children's education and well-being seriously. Education and Child Care highlights that commitment, and Higher Education takes the search for knowledge to the next level—for you as well as your kids. As you'll see in Health Care and Wellness, the city's health care infrastructure is second to none, and although we might not be the first place to pop into your mind when you think *retirement*, perhaps we should be. Check out the Retirement section of this chapter and decide for yourself.

Whatever your reasons for making the move, welcome to Kansas City!

The listings are in Kansas City, Missouri, unless otherwise noted.

NEIGHBORHOODS AND REAL ESTATE

Kansas City real estate agents fight over who gets to take the couple from California on a tour of available homes. Once the visitors get a gander at the five-bedroom beauty on two acres for the same price as a two-bedroom bungalow in San Jose, they'll practically wretch the contract out of the agent's hand.

A 2001 survey conducted by the National Association of Homebuilders ranked Kansas City No. 1 in housing affordability among metropolitan areas with populations over one million. In dollars and cents that translates to this: In the first quarter of 2001 the average home in Kansas City cost $111,000. That compares with $550,000 in San Francisco and $230,000 in Boston. And no wonder the transplants from San Jose were eager to buy; the same home there would cost $480,000.

Factor in our low tax burden and the picture gets even better. According to the Tax Foundation, homeowners in Missouri pay 10.49 percent of their income in local and state taxes, and Kansas homeowners pay 10.88 percent. Both numbers are well below the national average of 11.33 percent.

In fact, Kansas City ranks well below the national average in cost of living and costs for housing, utilities, and grocery items. According to the American Chamber of Commerce Researchers, we are one of the nation's best bargains. Our residents average about 28 percent above the national median in real income, which combines "affordable" with "cost-effective." That means we have more disposable money for shopping, dining out, and recreation. No wonder big retailers like Nordstrom can't get here fast enough. Let me at those Johnson County shoppers!

Kansas City also offers solid business opportunities for both corporations and employees. *Fortune* has referred to our town as one of the best places for doing business. Perhaps more important in terms of lifestyle, the same magazine listed

Kansas City as most beloved by its own resident executives.

Perhaps one reason the execs are so happy is that they're not behind the wheel. Kansas City is second only to San Antonio for freeway miles per capita, which means our workforce has a faster and easier commute than other cities our size. On average, most commuters get to the office before the cup of coffee gets cold, in about 20 minutes. One executive who left behind a 90 minute commute each way in Chicago said living 10 minutes from his office has meant a true lifestyle change. He has more time to spend with his family, can easily make a five o'clock tee time, and has far less stress.

Giant corporations are proud to call Kansas City home. Sprint Corporation's 3.9-million-square-foot world headquarters houses 14,500 employees. Hallmark Cards, one of the world's best-known brands with sales of $4.2 billion, is based here.

H&R Block, the nation's largest tax preparation firm, was founded in Kansas City in 1955 and employs 86,500. Its planned move to downtown Kansas City will help to further revitalize that area. American Century Investment Inc., the mutual fund giant, with $50 billion in assets, was begun in Kansas City, and here it stays. And other large corporations are locating here to reap the rewards of our central location and wealth of educated, friendly workers. *Management* magazine rates us among the top 25 "Hottest Real Estate Markets." Once transferred employees gets a chance to experience the Midwest lifestyle and buying power, they're thrilled to call Kansas City home.

Although these corporate giants have helped grow our economy and attract a top-notch work force, Kansas City remains a hotbed of entrepreneurial and small business activities. In fact, 99 percent of local companies employ 250 or fewer workers, accounting for 64 percent of total employment. They find plenty of support through training and specialized programs. *Entrepreneur* magazine rates Kansas City as one of the best three cities for supporting small business, and *Inc.* magazine has called us "an entrepreneur's dream." Our diversity—a healthy mix of big corporations and small companies—is one reason we tend to weather a recession better than most other cities do.

Our job force is consistently ranked among the most educated and productive in the United States, but we realize there's more to life than just work. We are, above all, a city of balance.

We tend to take our city's riches for granted, but newcomers are often surprised at our varied and vibrant arts culture. The Nelson-Atkins Museum of Art features one of the world's finest collections of Asian art and has more Henry Moore sculptures than any place this side of the Atlantic. The museum is undergoing a $133.5 million expansion and renovation that will elevate its standing even more. Down the street, the Kemper Museum of Contemporary Art showcases works by Dale Chihuly and Louise Bourgeois.

Music lovers have the Kansas City Symphony, Lyric Opera, Chamber Music series, and jazz concerts at the Folly Theatre. Art galleries abound here, especially in our revitalized inner city Crossroads Arts District that's home to dozens of small showrooms and artist studios. And just on the horizon is the $300 million Metropolitan Kansas City Performing Arts Center that will make a monumental addition to our city's skyline and way of life. Yet with all our highbrow offerings, one of our most appealing aspects is our mix of cultures. You can enjoy an evening of Beethoven on Saturday night and spend Sunday afternoon at a blues jam.

And we like to exercise our bodies as well as our minds. Long known as a major league sports town, we offer more recreational amenities than most cities our size. With hundreds of parks, lakes, golf courses, recreation centers, and public pools in every community, we offer ample opportunities for family entertainment and a healthy lifestyle. In fact, *Men's Health* magazine ranks Kansas City second in cardiovascular fitness and fourth for running and jogging.

Head out to Lake Jacomo on any given Sunday and it looks like a movie set for Happy Town USA as people fish for bluegill and glide through a sailboat regatta, little kids play soccer, teens take up volleyball, couples bike along trails, dogs catch Frisbees, and Dad catches a snooze under an oak tree. Look up and you'll see kites doing a graceful figure eight in our clean, fresh prairie wind, and hot air balloons dotting the sky with a rainbow of color.

You'll find all four seasons beautifully represented here. Outdoors, in fact, is where Kansas City really shines. Real estate agents tell stories of newcomers who expect to find dusty streets with tumbleweeds scuffing the car door and instead are enchanted by our lush green spaces and acres of forests.

People who have never seen the marvelous seasonal transitions are delighted in spring when our Bradford pear trees turn pink and white and daffodils line every sidewalk. Summers in Kansas City become a paintbox of greens with luxurious lawns and trees in full force, and gardens and flower boxes are ripe with colorful blooms. In autumn we open our jewelry box to decorate trees with purple, deep red, brilliant orange, and gold. And perhaps there's not a more precious sight than a four-year-old at the window with the news that "It's snowing!"

The City of Fountains is also a wellspring of education. We boast a network of highly rated public schools, private and parochial schools, top-notch technical and vocational programs, and private and state-affiliated colleges and universities. Parents are involved in their students' school programs through parent-student-teacher programs and are quick to vote "Yes" when it comes to updating existing schools, building new ones, and improving services.

Many of our public schools and their educators have received state and even national recognition, including Teacher of the Year honorees, Triple A–rated schools, and Blue Ribbon awards from the U.S.

Department of Education. Graduating students find a wide variety of choices, whether they seek the small student-teacher ratio of a private college like William Jewell or the excitement of the University of Missouri–Kansas City with 13,000 students. Graduate degree programs abound, offering working adults a chance to take classes part time while maintaining their careers.

With our great schools, friendly neighborhoods, and abundance of recreational opportunities, Kansas City is a great place to raise a family. In fact, Overland Park, Kansas, is the "kid-friendliest" suburban area in the country (among those with populations over 100,000) according to the Washington-based group Zero Population Growth. The group looked at factors like education, environment, health, public safety, and community life.

On the other side of town, Lee's Summit, Missouri, is one of only 17 cities nationwide, according to Homeadvisor.com, that meet the highest criteria in terms of school ratings, sunny days, and cost of living index below the national average. And on a bigger scale, the Kansas City bistate area of nearly two million was awarded a five-star Quality of Life rating, the highest level possible, from *Expansion Management* magazine in 2001.

Wellness is also an element that puts Kansas City ahead. It's significant that people come here from all over the country to obtain premium health care. More than 60 hospitals and specialized clinics stand ready to meet any medical need from the birth of a baby to the rarest forms of cancer. Greater Kansas City is also home to award-winning medical research based at the University of Kansas Medical Center, the University of Missouri School of Medicine, and the University of Health Sciences.

In 2000 they were joined by the Stowers Institute for Medical Research, a $195 million, 600,000-square-foot facility funded by James Stowers Jr., founder of American Century Investments. With its current endowment of $1 billion, the center is devoted to studying gene-based diseases such as cancer, Alzheimer's disease, and rheumatoid arthritis. Largely due to the Stowers project, eight primary research institutions are collaborating through the Kansas City Area Life Sciences Institute, with a goal of making our city one of the nation's top-10 centers for life sciences and biotechnology research in the years ahead.

Add to the mix our midwestern friendliness and small-town values, and it's easy to see why people who have grown up here wouldn't want to live anywhere else. And people who move here realize they've stumbled upon the nation's best-kept secret.

What newcomers find is more than just a vibrant city. We're an exciting mix of neighborhoods as varied as can be. And naturally, for a metropolis that encompasses more than 9,100 square miles and 18 counties in two states, housing options are diverse. Urban offerings include River Market warehouses converted to sleek lofts, upscale apartments that overlook the Country Club Plaza and Crown Center, and downtown condos not far from where our city began.

If you're willing to put in some sweat equity, you can find century-old homes in historic districts that need your tender loving or expertise with a sledge hammer. For considerably more you can own a restored 1909 Colonial Revival minimansion complete with original stained-glass windows and a fireplace in every room.

Looking for land, lots of land under starry skies above? We can set you up with a suburban lifestyle next to a lush golf course or a country estate with room for horses or overlooking a shimmering lake. More modest means will still land you in a desirable neighborhood of trim ranch houses where strollers and yellow Labs are part of the landscape.

You'll have your pick of neighborhoods and homes here, and chances are for far less money than you'd ever imagine possible. And you'll be amazed at how quickly you'll be welcomed into the neighborhood. No matter what your interests, you'll soon find a garden club or singles' group to join, an invitation to a Chiefs' tailgating party, or another soccer mom who's happy to let you take Tuesday. Let's take a drive around the neighborhoods. Notice all the people waving? Yes, we really are that friendly in Kansas City.

Ready for the grand tour? We divide this section into counties, then by city. Each community, whether it's populated by 334 or 134,000, is governed by a mayor and city council. Granted, this gets a little confusing when a dividing street has a different speed limit depending whether you're heading north or south. But on the plus side, having so many communities with their own histories and sense of pride means more festivals and Fourth of July fireworks displays for the rest of us.

Missouri

CASS COUNTY

If you prefer the quiet, scenic countryside to a metropolitan environment, you may want to explore some of the many advantages Cass County's cities provide. From its rural beginnings, Cass is becoming a hot ticket in terms of new business and residential development thanks to a low cost of living, efficient transportation, and room for expansion. Its diverse economic base includes biotech firms and manufacturers, and new, attractive industrial parks are popping up throughout the region.

Cass County students receive a superb education in 10 school districts that do an excellent job balancing studies with healthy recreational programs. Parents will also like the fact that their dollars go far here in terms of quality housing. Well-kept older homes, bright new subdivisions, or a custom-built estate: You'll find it all in Cass.

And where new homes are built, retail and services are sure to follow. The county has exciting new shopping districts to take care of its residents. Families can also "take it outside" at any number of nearby parks, lakes, and golf courses. Some of the most popular fishing and boating lakes are nearby, including Lake Winnebago, Rain-Tree Lake, and the natural paradise known as Lake Jacomo. Take your pick from the following Cass County cities.

Belton

A sleepy little town that has seen remarkable growth lately as families move south to get nice homes for far less than in town, Belton has its own school district and a population of around 20,000. It's a bit of a drive to the airport (about 45 minutes), but you can be on the Plaza in about 20 minutes. Homes tend to be traditional and cost from $60,000 to more than $1 million for mansions sitting on enormous estates.

Lake Winnebago

Ah, this is the life! Although some people simply maintain a vacation home here, most choose the resort-type amenities every day. Yet even with its Lake of the Ozarks feel, it's just 30 minutes from Downtown.

Housing options are attractive, diverse, and amazingly affordable when compared with resort-caliber cities across the nation. Students attend the highly rated Lee's Summit school district, and health care and shopping options are all within easy reach. About 900 lucky folks live here, and there's always room on the lake for one more boat. Homes range from $90,000 to more than $250,000.

Raymore

Known as a small rural farm community years ago, recently Raymore has had the greatest percentage of population increase of any Kansas City suburb. The population numbers around 8,000 right now, but the growth will continue. Close to Belton, you can expect the same 20-minute drive to the Plaza. Or you can stay home and have a cookout with your neighbors; this is a friendly place. Home prices range from $60,000 to $500,000.

CLAY COUNTY

Surrounded by the natural beauty of rural landscapes, yet with the convenience of urban living, Clay County offers the best of both worlds. In fact, 20 percent of Kansas City, Missouri, extends into Clay. Its residents are proud of the eclectic mix of neighborhoods, its colorful history, and exciting growth.

Clay County is the fourth largest county in the metroplex, ranking third in both total retail sales and total effective buying income. Just 15 minutes from downtown Kansas City, it has attracted giant companies like Citicorp and Union Pacific to its 400-square-mile confines. In fact, the small community of North Kansas City is home to more than 30 of the Fortune 500. Liberty boasts such highly visible names as Ferrellgas and the Hallmark Cards Distribution Center.

Education is a priority as well. Students are served by the respected North Kansas City and Liberty school districts. Also found in Liberty is William Jewell College, a four-year private resident college that is highly regarded nationwide. Newcomers to Clay County enjoy the balance of small town living and metropolitan attractions. Lakes and parks await, and there's excitement to be had as well at two riverboat casinos. And you can bet little ones will love living near Oceans of Fun and Worlds of Fun.

Sound good? When you're ready to move here, you'll have a variety of housing choices, from Tara-like estates on acreage to historic older homes. And if a friendly neighborhood is your style, Clay also offers lots of new subdivisions.

Gladstone

Sometimes referred to as Happy Rock, this community of some 25,800 is about 10 square miles in area and is completely surrounded by Kansas City North. It's a great place for families, thanks to its proximity to Smithville Lake, Worlds of Fun, and Oceans of Fun. The airport is just 20 minutes away. Homes tend to be ranch or traditional and cost $60,000 to $400,000.

Liberty

Historic charm, small-town spirit, and recreational amenities galore appeal to families living in this 27-square-mile city. Its population is on a steady incline (an 18 percent increase each decade since 1940), yet Liberty has a friendly, country town appeal.

As one of Missouri's oldest settlements, Liberty is home to a number of well-preserved original structures like the Jesse James Bank. But families won't need to rob a bank to live here; home prices are favorable. You can choose anything from renovated older homes in quiet neighborhoods for $100,000 to country estates on sprawling acreage for $1 million or more.

North Kansas City

Boasting a large and diverse economic base, North Kansas City is home to more than a thousand businesses that include some of the world's leading corporations. Yet neighborhoods offer the peace and relaxation of well-kept homes set on tree-lined streets.

A highly developed park system offers ball fields, playgrounds, swimming, tennis, and walking trails. And its 4,250 residents can find a full calendar of professional sports events, plus entertainment and shopping at nearby River Market and Country Club Plaza.

Housing options run the gamut from small starter homes to nice-size family homes ranging from $75,000 to well over $150,000.

JACKSON COUNTY

Named for General Andrew Jackson at the height of his popularity, this county is blessed with beautiful rolling hills, wooded sites, and mature greenery. It's the population center of the metroplex, so within its nearly 605-square-mile area are densely populated urban centers as well as growing cities like Lee's Summit and a variety of small towns.

It offers the region's most diversified and exciting cultural avenues, yet affordable and attractive housing options still abound. You'll have your choice of lovingly restored historic homes, sleek renovated lofts, cottages in tree-lined neighborhoods, lakeside estates, and affordable reverse ranch-style homes in new subdivisions.

An excellent network of educational opportunities are here, including two highly rated two-year community colleges, plus the University of Missouri at Kansas City, Kansas City Art Institute, Avila College, Rockhurst College, and DeVry Institute. When it's time to put down the books, Jackson County provides the area's most vibrant entertainment districts. The River Market, Country Club Plaza, and Westport are all here, providing four-star restaurants, charming bistros, and world-class shopping.

Jackson County is also at the heart of our cultural center with its showpiece, the Nelson-Atkins Museum of Art, as well as the stellar collections of the Kemper Museum of Contemporary Art. Art galleries and studios are here as well, too many to count because a new one seems to pop up every week.

For more recreational activities (although a day shopping on the Plaza can get your heart racing), the county has the 1,800-acre Swope Park, home to the Kansas City Zoo, a wonderful nature center with educational facilities and hiking trails, and a golf course. Swope Park also has the exciting Starlight Theatre, one of the most successful professional outdoor theaters in the country.

Yet with all its many delights, Jackson County real estate is surprisingly affordable. Homeowners have a wide array of choices in charming older neighborhoods, downtown high-rises, new subdivisions, and luxurious lakeside locations. Here, too, is where many young professionals and empty-nesters find the city's most exciting apartments and condominiums, including those on the Plaza or Crown Center that provide "city" living at its best.

Blue Springs

The original pioneers found this area to be the ideal stopover due to the abundance of clear, clean water from a nearby spring at the mouth of the Little Blue River. Water is still quite a draw for this community. Lake Jacomo and Longview Lake are nearby, and you'll have your choice of 14 city parks. Three golf courses mean there's no waiting for tee times. About 50,000 lucky people make their homes here and send their children to AAA-rated Blue Springs schools.

Home prices can still be a bargain, beginning at $80,000, but can easily escalate to $1 million for estates on spectacular lands.

Grandview

Situated on the southern edge of Jackson County, Grandview's residents value a stable neighborhood environment yet enjoy the convenience of major interstates a few miles north. A major intersection, the Grandview Triangle, is undergoing a redesign that will make commuting a piece of cake. About 25,000 people live in Grandview, and houses range from $45,000 to around $200,000.

Independence

One of our most vibrant historical areas, this is a great place to visit and an even better place to live. After all, it was good enough for Harry S Truman. About 116,000 people can proudly say the buck stops here, and it can for you, too, for $50,000 to $300,000.

Besides offering a wealth of historical sites, Independence is close to Downtown, the Plaza, and the airport. Travel to each is around 15 to 20 minutes.

Kansas City

Over half a million people live in Kansas City, and who could blame them? You could write an entire book about its lifestyle, fountains, food, and friendliness. . . hey! We did!

The city is made up of three distinct major areas: Midtown, where homes cost $20,000 to $400,000; Country Club, where you would pay between $50,000 and $2 million; and South Kansas City,

where homes range from $80,000 to $750,000. Kansas City is also where to find exciting lofts and condominiums in River Market, Downtown, and the West Bottoms. Prices range from $100,000 to well over $250,000.

Although it takes a bit of a drive to get to the airport (from 30 to 60 minutes), look what's nearby: the Plaza, the zoo, Crown Center, River Market, Nelson-Atkins Museum of Art, and more.

Lake Lotawana

Ideally situated just 20 miles from downtown Kansas City, this lake community offers both summer and year-round homes centered around a sparkling 600-acre lake. It's the perfect backdrop for magnificent waterfront estates. Its 2,200 residents enjoy a vacation-like lifestyle and needn't spend a million dollars to achieve it. Small bungalows and lake cabins are still available for less than $100,000, but there are also showplaces that cost $1 million or more.

Lake Tapawingo

Just west of Blue Springs and close to the urban amenities of Lee's Summit and Kansas City, this small lake community provides a tranquil setting. The lake itself is small, which is how the 890 or so residents like it: no loud motorboats to break the peaceful sound of children playing Red Rover at dusk. Although you'll still see small cottages dotting the rolling wooded landscape, homeowners with real buying power have discovered this beauty and have built magnificent lakeside estates worth well over $1 million.

Lee's Summit

Located in eastern Jackson County, Lee's Summit is the third largest city in Missouri based on geographic size. With more than 90 subdivisions, it's also the fastest growing community in the Kansas City area.

Families love it here thanks to an award-winning school district and plenty of recreational opportunities at nearby Longview Lake and Lake Jacomo. Arrow-

head Stadium is a 15-minute drive. You'll see a wide variety of architectural styles in the neighborhoods, from traditional to contemporary. Expect to pay from $80,000 to $1 million, which would get you a palatial home on a golf course.

Raytown

When Raytown was incorporated in the 1950s, it had a population of 850 in a 2-mile-square land area. Today it has grown to 12 square miles and a population of 31,850. It's close to some of the area's most beautiful lakes, including Blue Springs, Longview, and Lake Jacomo.

Home prices are very reasonable here. You'll see bungalows, ranches, Victorians, and traditionals ranging from $60,000 to more than $250,000.

PLATTE COUNTY

Overlooking the point where the Missouri and Kansas Rivers meet, Platte offers the rolling hills, dramatic limestone overlooks, and lush woods that appeal to so many homeowners. It's home to one of the country's most fetching river towns yet is just minutes away from the vibrancy of downtown Kansas City; in fact, Platte County offers some of the most stunning views of the city's skyline.

Executives who travel on business find this region ideal, with the airport just minutes away. Or you can work close to home at one of dozens of new office and industrial parks that have sprung up here.

The nearly 12,000 students enrolled in four public schools get a quality education thanks to excellent schools and a strong student-teacher-parent system. Undergraduate and graduate programs are also available from Park University and Webster University.

As for lifestyle, many Kansas Citians enjoy visiting towns in Platte for their "day trip" amenities, including antiques shops, galleries, and unique restaurant choices. Lucky for the county's population of nearly 69,000, all that fun is in their own backyards. So are beautiful riverfront parks,

Just moved into town and miss your old friends? You can make new ones through the New Neighbors League Club. Whether you're interested in gardening, travel, antiquing, wine tastings, golf, bowling, or canasta, you'll find a group to join. Contact the area manager, Nadine Crawford, at (913) 681-5103, or check out www.sunflower.org/~nnl .member.htm.

lakes, and acres of wetlands that make fishing a joy.

Parkville

Nestled in the natural beauty of wooded hills and the limestone bluffs of the Missouri River, this is a highly desirable area. It's home to Park University, and its historic downtown area is filled with antiques shops, restaurants, and art galleries. A nature center and riverside park add to its charm.

Parkville affords an extraordinary view of the Kansas City, Missouri, skyline. To get there takes only 15 minutes, and the airport is a pleasant 15-minute drive. About 3,600 people live here, and the architecture varies from traditional to historic, with some cozy cottages around $100,000, to fabulous homes costing more than $1 million.

Riverside

As a Northland suburb of Kansas City, Riverside is known for its pleasing small neighborhoods, large industrial parks, and extensive business district. With a population of less than 5,000, it offers a small town spirit with easy access to the region's finest cultural, educational, and social amenities. Home styles and prices vary greatly, from $75,000 to $250,000.

Weatherby Lake

Only 57 years old, this delightful community is centered around a man-made lake set in panoramic rolling hills and lush woods. Originally developed as an enclave of summer homes, people found it too hard to leave at the end of the season. Now Weatherby supports neighborhoods ranging from lake cabins to gorgeous estates. City leaders were smart enough to put strict zoning laws into place early to maintain the area's rural and rustic feeling that its 1,700 residents find so appealing. Homes range from less than $80,000 to more than $500,000.

Kansas

JOHNSON COUNTY

We've always known Johnson County was in a class all its own in terms of beautiful parks and lakes, lovely neighborhoods, and excellent schools. But the rest of the nation has caught on: *Fortune* magazine calls it one of the premier counties in the nation in terms of business climate and exceptional quality of life. Its many attributes have attracted such corporations as Sprint, Applebee's International, Black and Veatch, Yellow Corporation, Universal Underwriters, Farmers Insurance, Verizon, and Federal Express.

Nationally recognized for its superb public schools, Johnson County offers many choices for private education and parochial schools. The area is also home to excellent opportunities for higher education, including the award-winning Johnson County Community College, and satellite campuses of Baker University, St. Mary College, Mid America Nazarene University, Ottawa University, and the Edwards Campus of the University of Kansas. These programs allow working adults to obtain bachelor's or master's degrees while remaining close to home and work. Excellent health care choices are within the county's boundaries as well.

The living is easy in Johnson County, thanks to its first-rate recreational opportunities at its many lakes, parks, and recreational centers. Golfers can choose from some of the most challenging and luxuri-

ous public and private courses in the metro. And if shopping is your sport, look no further. Overland Park alone offers more than 40 open-air plazas as well as enclosed modern complexes with hundreds of shops, department stores (can you say Nordstrom?), restaurants, and theaters. Historic sites and museums, even ones kids will love, are within JoCo's boundaries.

Its many attributes have made it one of the fastest growing counties in the Kansas City area and state. In fact, Johnson County accounts for 71 percent of the total population growth in Kansas, adding approximately 10,000 new residents each year. And yet with all its natural beauty, tremendous growth, and clean, attractive cities, Johnson County's home prices are among the lowest of any area. From a quaint historic home to a custom masterpiece on a wooded lot, you can afford the lifestyle you deserve. Following are snapshots of Johnson County's various locations.

Countryside

How about holding a block party where the entire city shows up? That's a real possibility in this delightful little community of just 312 citizens and 133 homes. It's bound by Nall and Lamar Streets, 61st Street to the north and Shawnee Mission Parkway to the south, creating a square mile garden. You just have to love a neighborhood whose city tree is the red cedar and city bird is the house wren.

Homes are so choice here that people stand in yards and ask residents, "Are you leaving soon?" as if you're in a prime parking space. The answer is no, usually. Who would want to leave paradise? Houses in Countryside, for the most part, are cute bungalows, some ranch style, and prices can go from $100,000 to $200,000 or so. Good luck.

DeSoto

This has long been a sleepy little town of just over 3,200 residents, but that's all been changing in the past few years. DeSoto's location between Lenexa and

Lawrence on K–10 makes it a prime place for residential, retail, and commercial growth. And with ready access to the desirable lifestyles of both Lawrence and Kansas City, you might say DeSoto is the best of both worlds. Its progressive school system, which also serves residents of Western Shawnee, is another plus. The Plaza is still only 25 minutes away, the airport, 40.

Right now home prices are relatively low, considering that so many of the homes include acreage, but that will start to change. Prices range from $90,000 for a simple ranch to $400,000 plus for an estate set way back on vast acreage. Got horses?

Fairway

This is one of the most desirable addresses thanks to a storybook setting of pretty ranch homes and stone cottages with small but beautifully landscaped yards. The landmass is only about one square mile, but it packs in 4,200 people, and they love the small town in a big city atmosphere. And the location? Let's just say it got its name from the three panoramic golf courses nearby.

Its proximity to the Plaza (just 5 to 10 minutes away) plus parks and the excellent Shawnee Mission School District make this area ideal for singles and for couples with young children. Homes here are snatched up as soon as they hit the market; in fact in the crazy days of the mid-1990s, here's where you might have seen bidding wars on a perfectly manicured lawn. Look for prices from $100,000 to $900,000.

Lake Quivira

Located in both Johnson and Wyandotte Counties, Lake Quivira affords residents a lakeside lifestyle that is still conveniently located in town. Distinctive homes and tranquil neighborhoods are found in this gated community of around 1,900. Swimming, boating, and sailing are all part of the allure, plus a jogging track around the area's 1.3 square miles. Home styles vary greatly from small older bungalows to stunning contemporary showhomes. Prices range from $100,000 to well over $1 million.

Leawood

Answer "Leawood" to a question of where you live and you instantly get more respect. Pure snobbism? Not really. Leawood just happens to be one of the prettiest places around, with lovely homes with nice-size yards and a convenient location (10 minutes to the Plaza, 20 to Downtown) that still feels like it's out in the country. Perhaps that's because it used to be. Leawood dates back to territorial days and was built on farmland acquired by early settlers. Over 25,000 live in this area that primarily sits between State Line and Mission Roads and extends from 83rd Street south to 202nd Street.

The city was named for the original landowner, Oscar G. Lee. The spelling was slightly changed by the developer. Leawood offers a pleasing mix of older, well-kept neighborhoods along tree-lined streets and vibrant new subdivisions. And with its "halfway-mark" between the Country Club Plaza and the new Town Center Plaza, shopping doesn't get much better. Expect handsome traditional homes from $200,000 to more than $2 million.

Lenexa

Ah, suburbia. Lenexa sits in west central Johnson County, south of Shawnee, and is home to more than 40,000 people. You can see the city's roots as a town along the Santa Fe and Oregon Trails in late-19th-century buildings that still stand in Old Town Lenexa.

You can check out hundreds of homes during the Home Builders Association of Greater Kansas City's Parade of Homes. These tours are held for two weeks each spring and fall, and the homes are typically professionally decorated. Contact the association for dates at (816) 942-8800, or check www.kchba.org.

Residents are family oriented; during summer there's a festival or celebration every week including a barbecue contest in June, Spinach Festival in September (perhaps you shouldn't mention that one to your kids), and the Chili Challenge in October. Maybe it's a good thing Lenexa offers so many recreational opportunities to work off all those calories. Shawnee Mission Park, Sar-Ko-Par Trails Park, Ernie Miller Nature Park, and the Overland Park Arboretum are close by.

The Plaza is about a 20-minute drive, and it's 40 minutes to the airport. Look for generally traditional architecture in the price range of $100,000 to more than $500,000.

Merriam

Welcome to Worlds of Fun . . . in Merriam? In 1880 famed architectural designer George Kessler turned 40 acres of wooded hills into a lovely park area, complete with a lake, tennis courts, and boating. And at the turn of the 20th century, Kansas Citians were coming to the Hocker Grove Amusement Park's dancing pavilion, skating rink, and rides. The amusement parks have closed, but Merriam still offers a wonderful lifestyle for its 12,000 residents. With its ready access to the highway system, the Plaza is just 12 minutes away, the airport just 25.

Home prices in Merriam vary dramatically depending on whether the house is a two-bedroom bungalow or a five-bedroom reverse ranch on a landscaped lot. Expect to find homes between $80,000 and more than $300,000.

Mission

A charming burb in the northern section of Johnson County, Mission offers neighborhood shopping centers, excellent schools, and tree-lined streets. And location? You can practically be on the Plaza before you find your charge card. The airport is 30 minutes away. Homes here are typically traditional or ranch style, with a few fairy-tale Tudors tossed in for looks.

The excellent Shawnee Mission School District is a draw for families, but first-time homebuyers often shop here first for homes in the $80,000 range. Larger homes can run higher than $300,000.

Mission Hills

The Beverly Hills of Kansas City, Mission Hills is status plus. Exclusively fine homes, there are no shopping centers to ruin the line of expansive lawn after lawn. And it may be the most impressive art gallery in town: Sculptures and fountains are dotted within its 2.5-mile radius, gifts from developer J. C. Nichols.

The city also contains three of the area's finest golf clubs. This is the only city of its size in the country that can claim this distinction. There are 1,327 homes and villas here in a delightful range of styles that makes rubbernecking fun. You'll see colonial, Tudor, contemporary, Spanish, traditional, and a handful of contemporary homes. Prices range from $250,000 to well over $2.5 million. Pull your Mercedes or Beemer out of the garage and you can be at the Plaza within 5 to 10 minutes, to the airport in 30.

Mission Woods

Exclusive, exquisite, and in demand. Occupying 20 acres of land, yet with only 225 or so residents, Mission Woods has the distinction of having the lowest population of any of the incorporated cities of Johnson County. Homes here quietly go on the market (you'll never see a yard sign) and are quickly sold.

Amenities include a nearby golf country club, tennis club, several parks, and both private and parochial schools. Thanks to its location at the intersection of State Line Road and Shawnee Mission Parkway, the Plaza is at its doorstep.

This is truly one of the most beautiful little cities in the country, and the privilege of living here will cost between $500,000 and $2 million, but we know of a recent $4.5 million sale. All things considered, that may well be a bargain.

Olathe

From the Indian word for beautiful (pronounced *Oh-LAY-thuh*), this city covers 50 square miles. Its size holds many advantages, including two airports, Johnson County Executive and the Industrial Airport, and its own award-winning school district.

It's also home to Hillsdale Lake, a gigantic recreational area, and Olathe Medical Center. Homes here range from $75,000 for a modest starter home (ideal for singles, young couples, and retirees) to more than $1 million for a gorgeous estate overlooking the lake at Cedar Creek. Its diversity means you'll see architecture in a variety of designs, from traditional to Spanish, California contemporary to prairie style.

Overland Park

Overland Park has shaken off its roots as a bedroom community to become a vibrant city with its own personality. Today it's home to 145,000 (no, make that 145,001) with a population growth that's one of the fastest in the metro. Families in particular love it here, and it's been rated among the best places in the country to rear children. Schools are excellent, and it's blessed with nearby parks, lakes, and mile after mile of hiking and biking trails. Other pluses are the Overland Park Arboretum and Deanna Rose Children's Farmstead.

And you'll have just the place to buy all those cute kids' clothes, as well as your own fashions. Overland Park is home to Oak Park Mall, one of the largest malls in the state and the only one with Nordstom as its anchor. The Plaza is just a 20-minute drive, and the airport another 10 minutes or so.

Overland Park is a great place to work as well as live; when we call Corporate Woods an office park, we mean just that. Architecturally stunning buildings are set in 40 acres of wooded, rolling hills with walking paths, streams, and picnic areas that make lunch break a minivacation. And the new multimillion-dollar Sprint world headquarters is here as well. Look for two-story traditional homes for the most part, for mortgages from $100,000 to $1 million.

Prairie Village

Charming is the word that most comes to mind to describe this hamlet of established neighborhoods with an abundance of trees. Located just west of State Line and South of Mission Hills, this is a real draw for affluent singles and families who enjoy a small town atmosphere that's close to everything. Prairie Village is home to two delightful open-air shopping centers, Corinth Square and the Prairie Village Shops, which means a grocery store, a gift shop, and an ice-cream parlor are just a stroll or bike ride away. No wonder people who grew up here tend to stay in the neighborhood.

Big-time shopping and entertainment venues on the Plaza are a short 10 minutes away; although the airport is a 30- to 40-minute drive, you won't want to leave home very often. The typical Prairie Village home is traditional, Cape Cod, or ranch, costing from $120,000 to more than $500,000.

Roeland Park

This is a quaint, older neighborhood in the northeast corner of Johnson County with plenty of pluses. It's 10 minutes away from the Plaza and 10 to 15 minutes from Downtown and is within the desirable Shawnee Mission School District.

The population is around 7,800, and home styles tend toward traditional, ranch, and bungalow. Prices generally run from $100,000 to $250,000.

Shawnee

The Shawnee Mission Park alone is enough reason to want to live in this Johnson County community. It offers the Theatre in the Park, a fabulous lake, and a 450-foot-tall observation tower. Hey! I can see my house from here! Other recreational opportunities, at least for teenagers, can be found at the nearby malls, including Oak Park Mall and The Great Mall of the Great Plains. And the Plaza is a quick 10-minute drive away.

Shawnee has nearly 50,000 residents and is one of the fastest growing cities in the states. Look for traditional-style homes in the $80,000 to $600,000-plus range.

Spring Hill

Located in northeast Kansas, Spring Hill straddles the Johnson and Miami County lines, giving residents amenities of a big city in a rural setting. Incorporated in 1885, Spring Hill has recorded strong residential and commercial growth in the past years and expects that to continue.

It has about 2,500 residents, and an additional 6,000 people live outside its boundaries but within the school district. And like the good neighbors they are, they work together to address community needs. This city is about 20 to 30 minutes from Interstate 435, the main artery. Houses tend to be on large-acreage lots, many with separate garages. The house prices are as varied as the style of homes available, from $50,000 to well over $500,000.

Stanley

Early settlers in this area purchased their home lots for about $10 an acre, and although you can add some zeroes to that now, the lifestyle is worth every penny. Stanley was annexed by Overland Park in 1985 but feels like its own little world with rolling, wooded acres. Many of the homes take advantage of the landmass, with homes set half an acre away from the road down a curving path. Several estates have horse pastures.

Stanley is at the heart of the top-rated Blue Valley School District and is close to Town Center Plaza and fine restaurants. Architectural styles vary greatly, from Colorado lodge to traditional. Prices range from $140,000 to more than $500,000.

Westwood

Looking like a picture postcard of everything you could want in a neighborhood, Westwood offers well-manicured lawns, beautiful older homes, and picturesque neighborhoods. Its tidy size, just one square mile, gives it a small town feeling. Parks and walking trails make Westwood great for families, and a health club with tennis courts and swimming pool are pluses. Ideally situated close to the Plaza and Overland Park, Westwood provides its 1,800 residents with the best of the metroplex.

Home styles range from darling bungalows to handsome Spanish-style structures. Expect to pay from $150,000 to $1 million or more.

Westwood Hills

Although at just three-quarters of a square mile, Westwood Hills is one of the smaller cities, it is one of the loveliest residential choices. It is filled with charming neighborhoods, serene streets lined with mature shade trees, and a showcase of eclectic architectural styles. Many are storybook Tudor-style with stone or brick set amid lush landscaping.

The award-wining Shawnee Mission School District makes this an ideal community for families as well as young professionals. A very desirable address; expect home prices from $200,000 to $2 million.

WYANDOTTE COUNTY

Named for the Wyandot Indians who once made this area their home, Wyandotte County, or WyCo, is steeped in the history of the Old West yet offers a progressive lifestyle. With its central location along river bluffs overlooking the confluence of the Missouri and Kansas Rivers, it offers easy access to the entire region. The airport is just 10 to 15 minutes away, and downtown Kansas City, Missouri, from 5 to 10 minutes.

This county offers something even more appealing to homebuyers: Some of the lowest home prices in the Greater Kansas City area. Triple-A school districts also rank high on the plus side; the New Stanley School, for instance, was singled out for the state's "Next Century" program of excellence. Health care is also tops here thanks to the University of Kansas Medical Center's well-respected programs.

Within the county are exceptional recreational opportunities, including the Agricultural Hall of Fame, an outdoor music theater, and the 1,500-acre natural wonder known as Wyandotte County Lake Park. Among its many amenities are playgrounds, tennis courts, horse paths, and a 400-acre lake for fishing and boating.

If sports are your game, you'll have the Woodlands Race Track for dog racing and simulcast horse racing, and the spectacular Kansas Speedway, a $250 million NASCAR facility with state-of-the-art features. Homebuyers, start your engines!

Bonner Springs

On the western edge of Wyandotte County, Bonner has easy access to many areas of interest such as Verizon Amphitheater, where headline musical acts appear, and the Renaissance Festival in the fall. The Kansas Speedway is nearby as well.

With a population of around 6,750, the city has its own school district. Homes generally go for $60,000 to more than $500,000.

Kansas City

The Wyandot Indians first settled here in 1840, and its oldest home is the Grinter House, whose owner operated a ferry across the Kansas River (which we call the Kaw) in 1857. Today KCK is home to several ethnic groups. Strawberry Hill has a strong Slavic community, and the

Rosedale and Argentine areas have Mexican American settlements. Both groups celebrate their heritage with several festivals during the year.

The city provides excellent access to the other Kansas City's downtown district. It's about 5 minutes across the Lewis and Clark Viaduct, the Plaza is a 10-minute drive, and it's just 20 minutes to the airport. With a strong government in place, KCK is coming into its own. Home prices cover quite a spread, from starter homes in the $40,000 range to grand new estates with large lots for $400,000. The city also has a hidden gem in its historic Westheights Manor neighborhood, where homes average $200,000.

Real Estate Companies

Kansas City is home to hundreds of real estate companies and thousands of agents, most of whom are licensed on both sides of the state line. Although some of these professionals specialize in certain areas of the region or in specific categories such as historic homes or estates with surrounding acreage, most will be happy to locate whatever home you seek.

Some neighborhoods and subdivisions are so desirable they have their own real estate offices, such as Hallbrook in Leawood and Cedar Creek in Olathe. However, any Realtor can take you on a tour of the area.

It's often tricky to find a Realtor in a new city. We suggest you ask friends and family for references; if they've had a good experience with an agent, they'll be thrilled to tell you about it. And if you're being transferred for business, often your company's human resources department can make recommendations.

If in doubt, call the Kansas City Regional Association of Realtors (913–498–1100, www.kcrar.com). Their Web site includes links to related organizations such as the National Association of Homebuilders and area home inspectors. You'll also find a link to a list of available homes in the area that are shown by Realtor members, or go to www.heartlandmls.com. You can find homes by location, price range, or categories such as maintenance provided or acreage. The Better Business Bureau of Greater Kansas City (816–421–7800) is another resource to make sure you're working with a professional firm you can trust.

The following real estate firms were selected based on experience, customer service, and sometimes their expertise for specific areas of homes. This is by no means a complete list; Kansas City has around 7,000 members of the real estate board, and the phone book alone shows 10 pages of offices, individual brokers, and agents. The offices shown here are the top area producers, based on gross sales, according to a recent issue of the Kansas City edition of the *Business Journal.*

The real estate companies here are in Kansas City, Missouri, unless otherwise noted.

To shop for a home in your pajamas, simply click on www.realtor.com/ kansascity and you can scan about 4,000 different homes. You can select your potential abode by region, zip code, price range, or other criteria, like number of bedrooms and whether you want treed acreage or lakefront living.

Prudential Henry & Burrows Realtor
8101 College Boulevard
Overland Park, KS
(913) 491–1550, (800) 444–7206
www.kansascityhomes.com

Although not the largest company in terms of agents, this company packs a punch in sales. According to local Multiple Listing Services statistics, its sales associates had the highest average production and sales transactions completed in a year. And according to *Real Trends,* a national trade publication, Prudential Henry and Burrows is frequently No. 1 in the nation. That's motivation. The com-

pany was founded in 1978 by Richard Henry, who has received Broker of the Year honors, and has more than 100 agents.

Besides the Henry and Burrows team, Prudential has three other franchises in the metropolitan area. You can access their information on www.prudential.com.

Reece & Nichols
11500 Granada
Leawood, KS
(913) 491–1001
www.reeceandnichols.com

When two heavy-hitter real estate firms, J. D. Reece and J. C. Nichols, decided to stop competing and merge in January 2002, the result was a company with incredible marketing strength and depth of services. It now boasts more than 2,100 agents in just over 62 branch offices, reaching all areas of Kansas City and beyond in new homes, resales, and land. And most of us tune into the company's *Home Show* every Sunday morning whether we're in the market for a new home or not; the half-hour program tours current listings that are open for viewing that day.

Other exclusive services include "My Home," a personal tracking system that lets you create custom home searches online. When a home matching your criteria comes on the market you'll be contacted, often before it shows up in the listings. Reece and Nichols also takes the guesswork out of finding home services and products by listing agent-recommended vendors throughout the metropolitan area in categories such as appliance repair, brick and stone contractors, plumbing, and pest control.

The company has a full-time relocation department (913–469–8300, 800–821–6565), staffed by experts who can take you by the hand and lead you through all the details involved in moving.

And before you think Reece and Nichols is too big to care about someone looking for a bungalow for under 100 Gs, remember that the company is made up of lots of individual offices. You'll be a big deal when you call.

One example is the office at 9035 Metcalf in Overland Park, Kansas, where broker and manager Terri McGowen serves as mentor, motivator, and leader to 90 top-notch sales associates. Downturn in the market? Not for Terri's team. They had their best year yet when others were complaining about a lack of listings and sales. You can reach this upbeat professional or one of her associates at (913) 381–4300.

RE/MAX

That red-white-and-blue balloon stops you every time. There are 30 RE/MAX offices in Kansas City that share the attention-getting logo with more than 4,100 other independently owned RE/MAX offices around the world. Having a network with offices in 38 countries and on six continents gives them marketing moxy and ongoing training opportunities—and gives you a leg up when you're ready to buy that second home in Mexico, where they have offices. Following are some of the top-performing RE/MAX offices in town; each is independently owned and operated.

RE/MAX of Eastern Johnson County
14500 East 42nd Street
Independence, MO
(816) 373–8400
www.tdavidrogers.com
T. David Rogers knows how to make the real estate process smooth for buyers and sellers; he's been at it since 1975. The decades of hard work have paid off with dozens of awards, including Realtor/Broker of the Year four times. He and his 135 associates like to provide what they call "one-stop real estate," which starts with the backing of a global network and adds special services like on-site title and escrow, access to in-house mortgage resources, and property management all under one roof.

RE/MAX First Realtors
11251 Nall Avenue
Shawnee Mission, KS
(913) 338–1880, (800) 394–1880
www.firstkc.com
RE/MAX First has been serving clients in both Kansas and Missouri since 1992, but their 60 sales associates were at work long before that. They average more than 15 years of experience, and along the way they have earned enough awards and plaques to nearly require a separate office and full-time duster. Broker of the Year, Relocation Specialist of the Year, Top Sales in the Region: This is a group of professionals who must go around singing the company's jingle, "Above the crowd!"

RE/MAX of Kansas City/Liberty
2850 Kendallwood Parkway
(816) 454–6540
www.remax.com
Talk about fast workers! This three-location franchise skyrocketed to the No. 3 position of all Kansas City real estate offices in just over 10 years. Greg Koons and his team of 150 agents and brokers handled more than $403 million in residential sales in 2001 alone, an increase of $62 million at a time when others were struggling. Although the three offices are on the Missouri side, agents are licensed to move you into a home in Kansas as well.

RE/MAX State Line/Suburban Real Estate
10200 State Line Road
Leawood, KS
(913) 649–3100
www.realtykc.com
With a whopping 98 percent customer satisfaction rating, you can bet this office gets plenty of referrals.

Realty Executives
With more than 675 associates and 30 locations in the Kansas, Missouri, and Nebraska area, this company has connections. It's part of a worldwide network with locations in 44 states, seven countries, and five Canadian provinces. That

kind of power provides clients with some super bonuses, like an international corporate relocation division and major savings in intrastate moving expenses. Following are some of the offices in Kansas City under the Realty Executives banner.

Realty Executives of Kansas City
11115 Ash Street
Leawood, KS
(913) 642-4888
www.realtyx.com
This hardworking team of more than 90 agents and brokers moved into the top spot in overall sales for Realty Executives offices recently. Leaders Steve Shumate, Greg Franklin, and Fred Perry have more than 90 years of real estate experience among them. Steve, buddy, you don't look a day over 32. One of the keys to their success is the quality of the listings. Along with resales, this team is the exclusive marketer for around 20 of Kansas City's most exciting developments, including Riss Lake (risslake.com) in Parkville, Missouri. This community of gorgeous upscale residences is spread out over acres of rolling, treed hills centered by a 134-acre lake.

In 2001 Scottie Broderick, one of Kansas City's top-producing agents, came on board as one of the owners. This franchise also owns the Realty Suburban office and another location, called Premiere, at 75th and Mission Road. When the agents aren't out showing homes they're involved in the Children's' Miracle Network, WDAF-TV4's Love Fund for Children, or building homes for Habitat for Humanity.

Other winning Realty Executives offices are Metro One (816-525-7000) in Lee's Summit and Realty Executives Area Realtors (816-453-9100) in Gladstone.

OTHER REALTORS

Century 21 Heartland Realty
7709 West 151st Street
Overland Park, KS
(913) 681-8215, (800) 581-8215
www.century21heartland.com

If Century 21 is the world's largest residential real estate company, this office is one of the reasons. As the No. 1 Century 21 office in the metropolitan area for four years straight, as well as being rated top office in the state of Kansas twice, this is one motivated team. The company has three locations in Johnson County.

The office makes it easy to buy or sell a home. Buyers can answer a few questions on the Web site and receive automatic updates when their dream home becomes available. Sellers can choose "Market Analysis" on the same site to learn the fair market value of their home. Heartland also has a full-time relocation agent on staff to help you transfer to your new home.

Char MacCallum Real Estate Team
1819 South Ridgeview Road
Olathe, KS
(913) 782-8857, (888) 782-8857
www.char4homes.com
You've got to love a Realtor who will don Easter rabbit ears to get her ads noticed. That, and a big smile, let you in on her secret to success: Buying or selling a house is serious business, but that doesn't mean you can't have fun. You'll still get top professionalism from this award-winning agent. A licensed Realtor and broker since 1978, Char has been named Olathe's No. 1 Realtor, in the top 10 of Johnson County Realtors and Kansas City metropolitan Realtors, and singled out in the Kansas City *Business Journal.*

Coldwell Banker Advantage
7501 College Boulevard
Overland Park, KS
(913) 345-9999
www.coldwellbanker.com
Looking for a real estate company that's secure? Coldwell Banker fits the bill—it's been around since 1906. One of the reasons is the growth in the number of its independently owned and operated offices: 3,000 offices globally with more than 75,000 sales associates. The Advantage office is the top dog in the Kansas

City area, with $180 million in sales in one recent year with just 38 agents. That's a lot of open houses. This team taps into the special services available through a giant like Coldwell Banker, including the international Concierge program that provides deep discounts on everything from car rentals to custom closets. You can even print the coupons using your computer.

Crown Realty
2099 East 151st Street
Olathe, KS
(913) 782-1155
www.crownrealty.com
Since 1973 this family-owned agency has been getting buyers into the saddle, literally. As specialists in horse and rural properties, these 70 professionals in five offices can find you the right home whether your taste runs to Green Acres or Dallas. Dallas, indeed; their biggest transaction to date took place in late 2001 and included 92 farm properties running along two counties and reaching into both Kansas and Missouri. One buyer, one seller, $13.9 million. Must have been a lot of Christmas bonus checks at Crown.

If you're more the city type, a Crown agent can find you a sleek loft or in-town Tudor just as easily. But if you're coming to Kansas City with a horse trailer, this should be your first stop.

Keller Williams Realty
8005 West 110th Street, Suite 100
Overland Park, KS
(913) 906-5400
kw.com
Keller Williams is an innovative firm that has been in the forefront of using the Internet to make buying and selling a home faster, easier, and less stressful. The company has 50 agents in the Kansas City area who are putting technology to good use.

New Home Developments

These are new homes in resortlike areas that are offered exclusively by on-site real estate offices. With one stop you'll be able to view several homes in the development, usually decorated to the nines, along with a look at available land. Expect to be overwhelmed; these areas usually are built around a luxurious golf course or lake (or both) and are affiliated with some of Kansas City's finest builders.

Cedar Creek
K-10 Highway at the
Cedar Creek Parkway exit
Olathe, KS
(913) 829-6500
www.cedarcreek-kc.com
Long, graceful vistas of deep forests, emerald-green freeways, and stone bluffs with waterfalls and stepping-stones: Could life get any more relaxing than this? Not for the 600 families that call this paradise home. Cedar Creek is made up of neighborhoods set among rolling hills in southwest Johnson County, centered by a 65-acre sailing and fishing lake, 1,500 acres of undisturbed natural green space, and the gorgeous Shadow Glen Golf Club. It's all part of a 4,500-acre master-planned community that will offer more neighborhoods to keep up with the demand. It will also expand on the adjacent retail shops and an office park and eventually include a hotel.

It's already a city you may never want to leave; among the amenities are its own fire station, elementary school, indoor gymnasium, lighted tennis complex, miles of hiking and biking trails leading through some of the most stunning landscape in the region, and four private parks, including one of 600 acres. Ready to move in? We thought so. You'll find a wide variety of home styles here, from all-brick traditional to Colorado contemporary with prices ranging from the mid-$200,000s to well over a million. And folks who move to

Cedar Creek find something else: friendly neighbors. The area has several informal special interest clubs to join, such as early-morning walkers, a Bible-study group, and a gourmet dinner club.

Find out why the Greater Kansas City Home Builders Association calls this "Kansas's Best Single Family Community." But hurry. Resales go fast. New lots go even faster.

The National
6701 Birkdale
Parkville, MO
(816) 746-0200
www.thenationalgolfclub.com

Say, isn't that Tom Watson playing one hole ahead of you? It certainly could be at the National Golf Club. The hometown hero built this course and belongs to the club. You can join him by owning one of these breathtaking homes built amid massive oaks and sycamores, perched on lime stone bluffs, or overlooking the lake and incredible course. Homes range in price from the $200,000s for villas in the Links to a French-style knockout with a tile roof and outdoor fireplace for $2 million. The lower-level golf cart storage will come in handy, because the lucky homeowner will have a private cart path to the club.

The National's clubhouse is pretty spectacular as well, with 40,000 square feet of amenities including a dining room that's actually one of the best restaurants in town. It has hosted wine tastings with another famous Watson, Tom's brother Ridge, who owns a vineyard in Carmel. Another impressive guest has been former Missouri State coach Norm Stewart, who showed up for a fireside chat. Check out the homes available online, and then call the office to arrange a private tour. You might just see Tom.

Other New Home and Resale Resources

For Sale by Owner
10635 Roe
Overland Park, KS
(913) 498–FSBO (3726)
www.fsbo-kc.com

This service makes locating a commission-free "fizz-bow" a piece of cake. The Web site lists properties in Kansas and Missouri and provides a photo, description, and price along with the owner's phone number and e-mail address, if available. You'll see everything from houses in midtown for $45,000 to luxurious retreats in the upper ranges for sale by owners and builders.

The Pearson Company has been Kansas City's leader in private home sales since 1996 and provides excellent services for both buyers and sellers, including paperwork assistance and access to attorneys if necessary. Along with the Internet listing, the company distributes 30,000 copies of its free listing magazine every month to shopping centers, grocery stores, airports, and hotels.

Homes for Sale
(913) 621–HOME (4663)
www.kchomes.com

Chuck Boyles, Inc., publishes three big, fat magazines showing resale property, acreage, builders, new construction, and new home communities in the Greater Kansas City area. Areas covered are Kansas, Suburban North, and Jackson/Cass Counties. The free guides are distributed biweekly to grocery stores, bookstores, and some retailers across town, or you can request one sent free of charge by phone or online. The Web site also has links to Realtors and homes for sale.

Homefinder.com
A service of the *Kansas City Star,* this Internet site lets you search listings from the *Star* and real estate brokers from all over the Kansas City area. You can also

locate an agent who meets your needs, get information such as an Affordability Calculator, and get tips on moving.

Kansas City New Homes Guide
(913) 385–2772
www.kcnewhomes.com

This glossy magazine covers new home subdivisions throughout the entire metro area in a well-organized format. Comprehensive maps are included for each area, along with a listing for each community by price range, home size, builder name, and contact information. This magazine is also a boon for new residents, as it lists helpful phone numbers for each area's chamber of commerce, utility contacts, and attractions. The magazine is distributed free each month to area grocery stores, libraries, and other outlets.

Condominiums, Lofts, and Apartments

Our affordable real estate costs make it possible for the vast majority of residents to buy homes (nearly 75 percent in Johnson County alone), but often an apartment is the way to go. We offer a dazzling variety of options, from sleek lofts overlooking Downtown to minicities situated around a lake in the suburbs.

In fact, condo living is one of the fastest growing markets in the area. Since the early 1980s developers have been converting century-old warehouses into loft spaces at an amazing rate, yet they can't keep up with the demand. At this writing thousands of units are being built throughout the River Market, Downtown, and Quality Hill areas. The high-ceilinged, open spaces appeal to young professionals as well as empty nesters who are thrilled to give up yard maintenance in lieu of a balcony with a breathtaking view of Downtown at night. Following are a few of the more notable selections in town.

Conover Place Lofts
5th and Wyandotte, River Market
(816) 421–0572
www.conoverplace.com

This premier loft development in the vibrant River Market district offers such amenities as inside garages, a workout room and pool, 13- to 20-foot ceilings, fabulous stainless-steel kitchens, polished concrete floors, and huge windows overlooking the Downtown skyline. Toss in the exposed-brick walls and heavy-timbered ceilings and it's a glossy-magazine shot of upscale urban living. A two-bedroom complete with a 266-square-foot terrace goes for around $325,000. That is, if you move fast.

Mallin/Gibson Loft Properties
201 Wyandotte
(816) 471–6789
www.kclofts.com

Mel Mallin, a lovable and sharp-as-a-tack octogenarian, is considered the grandfather of loft living in Kansas City. He fell in love with the bohemian lifestyle while courting his wife in New York's SoHo neighborhood after World War II and decades later decided to try to sell the idea to his hometown. He nearly lost his shirt. Live downtown? In a big brick box without walls? But Mel persevered, kept to his "For God's sake, cheer up!" mantra, and today is one of our town's most successful and respected real estate developers.

His company, which includes his son-in-law, Dana Gibson, is beloved by tenants for its old-fashioned service. Need a jump-start or someone to feed your cat and pick up your mail when you're out of town? Mel's even been known to help get careers off the ground or chins off the floor with his positive energy.

Oh, and did we mention he has great lofts available? The locations are in the hot and happening River Market area, with the farmers' market, restaurants, and entertainment at your doorstep. These are true lofts, with all the romance of those days Mel remembers from New York: open floor plans, high ceilings, exposed-brick walls, majestic wood columns and beams, wood floors, and plenty of windows. Options include the Art Space at 201 Wyandotte, which was originally built in 1900 and renovated in 1985. Your neighbors include several artists and the Kansas City Artists Coalition, an organization so dear to Mel's heart that a gallery space has been named in his honor. Then there's Delaware Lofts at 219 Delaware, with 40 apartments ranging from 625 to 3,000 square feet. Landmark Lofts, 425 Washington, are located in a handsome brick structure that was originally built in 1885; renovations were completed in 1998.

San Francisco Tower at Crown Center
2450 Grand Avenue
(913) 649–6100
www.sanfranciscotower.com

Just steps away (and through a covered walkway at that) from Crown Center, this 31-story high-rise offers in-town living at its best. The views from these one- and two-bedroom units range from Liberty Memorial to the Crown Center Square, where there's always a festival or event going on. The overhead Link also connects residents to Union Station and the Hyatt Regency. The largest home here is a 1,592-square-foot marvel with a $350,000 price tag.

OTHER RESOURCES FOR APARTMENTS

The *Kansas City Star* maintains an online listing of apartments (www.apartments.com), where you can search all developments throughout the Kansas City metro area. Options range from studios starting at $350 to major league palaces in the sky for $2,000 or more a month. The site also provides information about renter's insurance, moving, and more. And of course you can always find an apartment the old-fashioned way, through the newspaper. On Saturday the *Star* publishes a separate guide showing apartments available; in Sunday's real estate broadsheet, you'll find houses for rent.

The *Pitch Weekly* includes a few choice apartments around town, usually in the coolest inner-city areas near the Art Institute, the Plaza, and Westport. Here, too, is where you'll find listings for roommates wanted. You can pick up a copy free at hundreds of outlets throughout the city.

Apartments for Rent (913-888-1200) is a slick magazine that showcases more than 300 rental units throughout Kansas City, including lofts, apartments, corporate housing, and even senior communities. Many of the ads include special deals, such as first month's rent free or $100 savings with a year's lease. The publication is available free at grocery stores and convenience stores around town, or go online (www.forrent.com) to see the goods.

GETTING STARTED

Naturally, you'll want to get the lights, water, and gas turned on and the telephone hooked up, so we'll start with the basics. Sounds easy, until you remember that the Kansas City metro area comprises more than 150 cities in an 18-county area (more or less, depending on who's counting). To make it more confusing, some counties use two or more utility companies. This creates a new version of the old joke: How many newcomers does it take to turn on the lights? Two: one to find out who to call and the other to bang his head on the wall. If you can get through this maze of numbers, more power to you.

That task taken care of, we can move on to more interesting things like how to learn more about Kansas City and where to meet new friends. We'll also cover some essentials about living here and provide valuable resources. Most important, we'll clue you in to some of the top services that are often so hard to find when you're new to a city: hair stylists, dog trainers, florists, landscapers, and more. These are names we've culled over the years from hundreds of interviews, lots of referrals, "best-of" surveys in local publications, and personal experience.

Utilities

If you have questions about what service provider serves your area, check with your realtor, landlord, your homeowners association, or the city or county clerk. When you call the utility customer service representative, be prepared to make a security deposit to establish service. Requirements for service deposits vary and are usually based on an amount totaling two months' worth of bills.

Most deposits are refunded after one year or when service is terminated. Water deposits range from about $20 to $75 or more, but rural dwellings can have a much heftier fee—as much as $1,500—if a meter must be installed. Just one more thing to ask your Realtor before you sign on the dotted line. Following are the basics. And honestly, once you make it past the conundrum of our utility providers, you're home safe. With the lights on.

ELECTRICITY

Missouri
Independence
(816) 325–7880

Kansas City Power & Light
(Western Cass and Jackson,
southern Clay and Platte, and
most of Johnson Counties)
(816) 471–5275
www.kcpl.com

Missouri Public Service/Energy One
(Platte City, Lee's Summit, Blue
Springs, Smithville, Raytown, Belton)
(800) 303–0752

Platte-Clay Electric Cooperative
(Northern Platte, northern Clay,
and Ray Counties)
(800) 431–2131

Union Electric Company
(Northeast Clay and northwest
Ray Counties)
(800) 552–7583

Kansas
Board of Public Utilities
(Kansas City, Kansas)
(913) 573–9190

KPL/KGE (Also known as Westar)
(Olathe, Bonner Springs,
Leavenworth, Lawrence, De Soto)
(800) 794–4780
www.kgas.com

GAS

Missouri
Missouri Gas Energy
(Jackson, Platte, Clay, Ray,
and Cass Counties)
(816) 756–5252

Kansas
Greeley Gas Company
(Portions of Johnson, Wyandotte,
Leavenworth, and Douglas Counties)
(913) 441–2123, (888) 442–1313
www.greeleygas.com

Kansas Gas Service
(Parts of Johnson, Wyandotte, Franklin,
Miami, Douglas, Anderson, Osage, and
Leavenworth Counties)
(800) 794–4780

United Cities Gas Company
(Olathe, parts of Lenexa, and
Overland Park in Johnson County)
(888) 824–3434

WATER

Missouri
Missouri Water Department
(Kansas City)
(816) 221–6505

*To get underground utility lines marked
before digging, call (800) 344-7483 in
Missouri and (800) 344-7233 in Kansas.*

Kansas
Board of Public Utilities
(Kansas City, Kansas)
(913) 573-9190

Water District No. 1
(Johnson County)
(913) 895-1800
www.waterone.org

Telephone

Birch Telecom
(888) 772-4724

Southwestern Bell
Residential customers
(800) 464-7928
www.swbell.com

Sprint
(800) 788-3500
www.sprint.com

Cellular Phone Service

Southwestern Bell Mobile
(800) 331-0500

Sprint PCS
(816) 559-1000

Verizon (formerly Cellular One)
(800) 458-3047

Cable

Greater Kansas City
American Cablevision
(816) 358-5360

Direct TV
(816) 421-4004

Time Warner Cable
(816) 358-2292

Johnson County
Time Warner Cable
(913) 451-6464

Trash

Many homeowners associations provide curbside trash pickup as part of their dues. And many cities in the metropolis offer a curbside recycling program or have developed convenient drop-off centers at churches and shopping areas. Check with your Realtor or your homeowners associate contact. For more information on recycling, call the Mid-America Regional Council's recycling hotline at (816) 474-TEAM.

The following companies cover the greater Kansas City area; you may also contact them for information regarding items for recycling.

Defenbaugh Disposal Service
(913) 631-3300

Hickman Disposal Service
(913) 831-2072

REB Trash Service
(913) 779-6592

Post Offices

Kansas City
(816) 374-9173

Kansas City, Kansas
(913) 573-2600

Shawnee Mission/Johnson County,
Kansas
(913) 831-5302

GETTING LEGAL
Motor Vehicle Registration

In both Kansas and Missouri, license plates are issued upon vehicle registration. Yearly renewals are required and indicated by a renewal sticker. New residents are expected to register within 90 days. Contact the following for current requirements, any necessary inspections, and fees.

MISSOURI
**Motor Vehicle & Driver's License Fee Office
(816) 931-5252**

KANSAS
**Johnson County DMV
Mission Office: (913) 826-1800
Olathe Office: (913) 715-2400**

Voter Registration

Generally, registration for voting must be completed at least 20 days prior to primary or general elections. However, in Jackson, Cass, Clay, and Platte Counties, residents must wait 28 days after registration before they're eligible to vote. In Johnson County it's 14 days. You must reregister each time you change your residency or name.

Application information includes your name, birthplace, birth date, mailing address, telephone number, place of previous registration, and usually your Social Security number. An oath or signature is required to verify that all information is true.

To register in both Kansas and Missouri, you must submit information with a current address and meet the following requirements: You must be a U.S. citizen or have a naturalization number if you were born outside of the country, be at least 18

years of age, and meet the residency requirements for your voting precinct.

Registration centers are located throughout the metroplex, and any of the centers below can direct you to the one most convenient to you. Kansas residents have the option of mail-in registration. In Missouri, that option is restricted to those who are unable to travel to a registration center in person.

**Kansas City, Missouri, Board of Election:
(816) 842-4820
Johnson County Board of Election:
(913) 782-3441
Wyandotte County Board of Election:
(913) 334-1414**

Driver's License and Permit

To receive a driver's license with full privileges in either Kansas or Missouri, you must be at least 16 years of age. New Kansas residents must pass only a vision test if your out-of-state license is current.

In Missouri, if your out-of-state license is valid, you are required to take a vision and road sign recognition test. If your current license has been expired for more than 90 days, you will be required to take the driving and written test as well.

Kansas offers a special restricted license for young adults at least 14 years old for the purpose of going to or from school or work; this license requires the written permission of a parent or guardian.

MISSOURI
Licenses are issued on a six-year basis (every three years for those older than 69), and new residents are required to apply immediately. Bring a valid out-of-state license. You'll be required to pass a vision and road sign recognition test. If your license has expired you'll need to take a written test and will be sitting in a car with a Missouri State Highway Patrol

officer. Contact the following office for examination and testing; there may also be an area office closer to you:

Kansas City
(816) 889-2461

KANSAS

Licenses are issued every four years, and new residents are required to apply immediately. Bring your valid out-of-state driver's license with you. New residents must pass only a vision test, unless your current license has been expired for more than 90 days. Then a driving and written test is required. (We were serious when we said to apply immediately.) For examination and testing, contact one of the following offices:

Kansas City, Kansas
(913) 287-2900

Olathe
(913) 829-2501

Shawnee Mission
(913) 432-2266

Hunting and Fishing Licenses

Licenses are required in both states for fishing as well as hunting small and large game. In Kansas the waiting time after registration is 60 days. In Missouri new residents are eligible for a license after 30 days. And just wait till you see the bass in Lake Jacomo!

The cost for licenses varies depending on your age (seniors and youth get reduced rates), residency status, and the duration of the license. Nonresident licenses carry significantly higher price tags. Fishing licenses can be purchased for as long as one year or a mere 24 hours. They're available for purchase at local sporting good stores and most public lake marinas. For current rates or questions on

specific game stamps or licenses, contact the respective state offices:

Missouri Department of Conservation
(816) 356-2280

Kansas Department of Wildlife & Parks
(913) 894-9113

GETTING TO KNOW YOU

Area convention and visitor bureaus are great sources for newcomers to town as well. Keep in mind that nearly every city within the vast metropolis has its own center ready to welcome you with brochures, maps, and information. Check the telephone book for contact information. Following are the organizations that cover the entire metropolitan area.

Convention & Visitor's Bureau
of Greater Kansas City
(816) 221-5242
www.kansascity.com
This should be your first call, even before you move. These fine folks will set you up with information about Kansas City in general as well as contacts for your particular area of town. Plus they'll give you a dandy little coupon book with free or discounted admissions to several attractions around town.

Kansas City Area Chamber of Commerce
(816) 221-7440
www.kcchamber.com

Online Visitor's Guide
www.visitkc.com,
www.experiencekc.com

Gifts, Grooming, and Various Good Things to Know

You're new in town. Where do you find your new best friend, your confidant, the most important person in your life . . . in other words your hair stylist? Pick a name out of the phone book? We think not. There are other fine salons in town, but following are a few where you and your locks will be treated incredibly well. After you're coifed or trimmed, we'll introduce you to other services that are difficult to find.

DAY SPAS AND SALONS

Bangs Hair Salon
1115 West 47th Street
(816) 756–1422

Bijin Salon & Day Spa
6960 Mission Lane
Shawnee Mission, KS
(913) 671–7777

Mario Tricoci Salon & Day Spa
111 Nichols Road
(816) 931–9922

Serenity The Rejuvenating Day Spa
7211 West 95th Street
Overland Park, KS
(913) 341–0025
www.serenitydayspa.net
When Judy Hohn's doctors couldn't diagnose her various aches and pains, she found relief through massage. That was decades ago, and now her spa is providing the same healthful benefits to clients. Along with a variety of massage options they offer manicures, pedicure, and facials. Make a day of it with a beauty package or invite your girlfriends for a spa party.

FLORISTS

Most large grocery stores have floral departments these days, and the quality and variety is good enough for a gift on the way home or to cheer a sick friend. But when you need a floral design guaranteed to impress a boss or delight your sweetheart, the following florists can arrange it.

One of the best ways to get in tune with a new city is through its daily newspaper. In our case it's the Kansas City Star. You can find it at newsstands throughout town, or subscribe by calling (816) 234–STAR (7827). And the newspaper's Web site, www.kansascity.com, is a 24-hour gateway to local news, weather, events, and more.

Beco Flowers
1922 Baltimore
(816) 472–4242
www.becoflowers.com
A serene collection of baby artichokes in a wooden bowl. A fat pineapple in a base of bright gerbera daisies. Collette Keenan and Rebecca Ederer like to play with their food. These talented florists also do amazing things with flowers, from show-off displays for an entryway to sweet floral bouquets. There is no minimum price for orders. The florist is also an art gallery, called the CUBE, which showcases a different artist's work every month.

Dan Meiners Studio
1700 Wyandotte
(816) 842–7244
www.danmeiners.com
If you want to get a "Wow!" from someone, send one of Dan's arrangements. His work can be contemporary or very traditional depending on your needs, and he's known for incorporating unusual vessels and groupings. Dan and his talented staff are also high society's first call for weddings and special events. At his new shop, the giftware and home decor are nearly as spectacular as the flowers.

Matney Floral Design
2708 West 53rd Street
Fairway, KS
(913) 362–5419
If the flowers at a black tie gala get more attention than the ball gowns, Chuck Matney is probably to blame. From a single exquisite orchid to stunning arrangements

Good Phone Numbers to Know

Fire, police, sheriff, and ambulance: 911
Child abuse: (800) 392-3738
Missouri Poison Control Center: (816) 234-3430
Kansas Poison Control Center: (913) 588-6633
Directory assistance (local): 1411
Local from pay phones: 411
Long distance: 1 + area code (if different from yours) + the seven-digit number
Assistance in calling: Dial "0" for Operator
Weather forecast: (913) 831-4141
Road condition information (Kansas Highway Patrol): (913) 782-8100
Legal Aid of Western Missouri: (816) 474-6750
Legal Aid for Wyandotte and Leavenworth Counties: (913) 621-0200

that use Granny Smith apples in tall vases, his designs are fresh, inventive, and in perfect taste.

Making New Friends

Perhaps the toughest thing about moving to a new city is meeting people who share your interests. You should have no trouble in Kansas City; in fact newcomers are often surprised when strangers strike up a conversation at the bookstore, grocer's produce section, and in the elevator. We even have an entire club to welcome you with open arms. And if you're single, check out the many opportunities to meet someone new.

MATCHMAKING SERVICES

If it's time to let a professional handle your love life, the following are a few companies that can take you in hand.

Heart to Heart Introductions, Inc.
(913) 491-9110
www.hearttoheart.com
This company is the compatibility specialist and will screen and match potential clients with a low-key approach. Fees vary.

Supper Club
(913) 851-8400
www.kcsupperclub.com
Three women, three men, one table. What could be intimidating about that? This service provides a way to meet other singles during a casual dinner at one of Kansas City's best restaurants. The clientele tends to be successful, attractive professionals.

SINGLES GROUPS

Singles of the world—unite! Sometimes new cities can seem like couples-ville, but Kansas City has some terrific organizations where like-minded singles can meet, whether they're looking for a date or a way to volunteer their time.

Colonial Presbyterian Church
9500 Wornall
(816) 942-3272
www.colonialkc.org
One of the city's most expansive organizations to meet others through activities, parties, and outings. Groups are generally divided by age from twenties to sixties and beyond. All denominations are welcome.

Friends of Art Solos
(816) 751-1246
www.nelson-atkins.org
This group, which is sponsored by the Nelson-Atkins Museum of Art, has so many varied and interesting activities that happily married couples are jealous. Actually, anyone can attend the events, but it's a boon for singles. You'll be invited to attend parties throughout the metro area, dinners in the glamorous Rozzelle Court, and visits to artists' studios.

Johnson County Unos
(913) 262-7658
This group, which meets at Pius X Church in Mission, Kansas, provides social and spiritual contact for widows and widowers throughout the metropolitan area.

Midwest Singles Dances
(816) 254-6493
www.midwestsinglesdances.com
Gotta dance? You'll find a willing partner at these weekly dances held at hotel ballrooms throughout the area. The age range is from mid-thirties through late sixties, and attendance can be high, as many as 160 to 250.

Singles Available for Service
St. Joseph Hospital,
Interstate 435 and State Line at
Community Service Building D
www.sacskc.com
Volunteer your time to a worthy cause and possibly make a love-match? Sounds like the perfect combination to us. This group gets involved with organizations like the Harvesters, Big Brothers and Big Sisters, and Special Olympics. Show up the first Thursday of every month at 7:00 p.m. and they'll put you to good work.

Village Singles
Village Presbyterian Church
6641 Mission Road
Prairie Village, KS
(913) 262-3195
www.members.aol.com/villagers
One of the best ways to meet singles in town through a variety of club activities, trips, classes, and parties.

SPECIALTY GROUPS

New Neighbors of Kansas City
www.newfriendsofkc.com
Clean your social calendar! Join this fun-loving group of women and you'll be kept busy with shopping trips, tours, gourmet dinners, and luncheons complete with speakers. This lively bunch also gives of time and money to charities.

Pet Projects

Here's where to find a new pet in Kansas City, how to report a lost one, or where to have yours trained, groomed, and housed when you're out of town.

Keep in mind that in Kansas and Missouri, each community develops and maintains rules and regulations for pet registration, leash laws, and other pet-related policies. For details in your community, contact your local city courthouse; numbers are listed in the blue government section of the telephone directory.

If you find a lost dog or cat or lose your beloved family pet, call the numbers below. The *Kansas City Star also* provides a free listing in their daily "Lost or Found" section. Call (816) 234-4000 to place a notice. The shelters are also the best place to find a new buddy. Visit in person or check out the online adoptions and just try to keep from losing your heart to a new little Fido or Fluffy.

Animal Haven
9800 West 67th Street
Merriam, KS
(913) 432-7548
www.animalhavenkc.com

Humane Society of Greater Kansas City
(913) 596-1000
www.hhskc.org

Lakeside Nature Center (To report an injured or abandoned wild animal in Missouri) (816) 513-8960

Pet owners are lucky that one of the world's most respected pet behavior authorities lives and practices in Kansas City. Dr. Wayne Hunthausen has trained hundreds of other veterinarians as well as pet owners around the world on how to keep dogs from biting, barking, or ruining your carpet—and how to keep cats out of the houseplants.

Wayne has also provided expert advice on programs such as *20/20, PBS Health Week,* and *Today.* He's available for consultation and has produced a video for families called *Dogs, Cats and Kids* to teach children how to act around animals. His Westwood Animal Hospital also offers services in animal health and surgery, training, and has excellent boarding and grooming facilities.

Lost Dog Registry (816) 333-0020

Operation Wildlife (Helps with wild animals found injured in Kansas) (913) 631-6566

Wayside Waifs (816) 761-8151 www.waysidewaifs.org

Publications and Books

We cover local magazines and newspapers in Media, but here's a refresher course about Kansas City–based periodicals or books that belong in your mailbox or on your coffee table.

Kansas City: An American Story

This gem of a book by Rick Montgomery and Shirl Kasper, published by the *Kansas City Star,* is a comprehensive, richly illustrated account of a river town that made it big. The book came out in time for our 150th birthday, and we can't imagine a better gift. It's available for around $50 at area bookstores or through the *Star.* Call (816) 234-4636 and ask for "Star Books." Other titles have covered everything from barbecue to a major flood.

Kansas City magazine

Available by subscription and on newsstands, this is the quintessential city magazine that covers celebrities, restaurants, and upcoming events. And—because the editor, Leigh Elmore, is a bit of a history nut—you'll learn fascinating tidbits like where Daniel Boone's great-grandson is buried. Or was it his nephew? Check it out online at www.kcmag.com, or call (816) 421-4111 or (800) 214-8119 to subscribe.

Tours

When you go to Paris, you take a tour. Rome, same thing. In Kansas City you can simply drive around to acquaint yourself with our many charms, or you can hire a tour guide to take you to all the most interesting attractions. It's also a great way to learn about Kansas City's history and see our most impressive attractions while somebody else drives, and at least you'll have no problem with the language. Here are some ways to go sightseeing. We list other options in Getting Here, Getting Around and Attractions.

Historic Kansas City Foundation

Three cheers for this organization for fighting to keep Kansas City's historical buildings and districts alive and well. Volunteers offer guided tours by advance appointment and can provide self-guided tour brochures on areas like the Historic Northeast District, Quality Hill, and the Plaza. They also host walking tours at various times of the year and an annual fund-raiser when they offer tours of homes in wonderful neighborhoods. Call (816) 931-8447.

Kansas City Adventures

Tour guide Ann Malita-Smith wants to introduce you to the city she loves. She can custom design a tour for your group or suggest one of her itineraries, such as Kansas City's Heritage, Historical Churches, or finding all the little art galleries you might miss on your own. She can be reached at (816) 920-5513 and www.kansascityadventures.com.

Passage Unlimited

This group offers customized tours from the African-American perspective. Choices include jazz, the Underground Railroad, historic sites, and more for groups of 10 or more. For more information call (816) 483-4919.

Spunky Senior Tours, LLC

If you love the name, you'll really love the variety and professionalism of these tours designed with seniors in mind. Watching monarchs on their journey south, minivacations to Branson, day trips to Independence: There's no end to the number of adventures you can have. Call (816) 805-0166 or go to www.spunky-senior-tours.com.

Weddings
Kansas City Style

Planning a wedding for yourself or someone else is stressful enough; we can't imagine handling all the details if you're new to

Here's a tour of Kansas City's past that doesn't even require a vehicle. On www.kcstories.com you'll read memoirs from older Kansas Citians who participated in writing teacher Michael Humphrey's Thousand Stories project. These are fascinating essays from people who lived through the Great Depression, went to work on Kansas City's streetcars, and watched stage acts at long-gone palace theaters.

the area. Your first stop should be to the newsstand to pick up the latest copy of *KC Weddings,* a wonderful magazine that covers every element of getting married in town, including catering, musicians, gowns, reception sites, and photographers. It's published by Grand Communications, a subsidiary of the Kansas City Star. Call (816) 234-4234 for back issues, or visit www.kansascity.com/kcweddings/.

Following are two tried-and-true professionals who can help make this important ceremony . . . well, a piece of cake. You'll find romantic honeymoon ideas in the Accommodations chapter.

Final Touch Studios
(wedding coordinator, florist)
(913) 492-5864

Rosemary Dennis is a miracle worker. She can whip up the most incredible floral displays and bouquets, coordinate the reception hall, and hire the band, baker, and limousine so that you won't have to worry about a thing. She brings the most important element to the party: resourcefulness. We've seen her rip up a slip to create lovely pew bows when the bride's mom left them at home. Not really, but we know she could. Rosemary also creates incredible arrangements with silk and dried arrangements for clients and interior designers.

Simple Elegance
(913) 397-9932

Kendra Brown is the wedding coordinator Rosemary Dennis recommends when the bride needs the whole works, from hiring the caterer to fluffing the train before the walk down the aisle. Her company's name says it all; her weddings tend to be elegant and very romantic.

EDUCATION AND CHILD CARE

Our city's commitment to education shows up in one of the first questions parents ask when shopping for a home: "How are the schools around here?" The answer, particularly in our suburban areas, is "excellent." Here in the heartland, Junior isn't the only one bringing home a bright red A on his report card; many of the institutions in our 36 school districts have achieved the highest distinctions awarded by their states.

That's not to say they all make the grade. Our largest district, Kansas City, Missouri, with 32,000 students in 70 different schools, is plagued by the same problems most other urban cities have: poor attendance, below-average test scores, and low graduation rates. And these troubles remain despite spending $2 billion to create impressive magnet schools with themes like science, foreign languages, performing arts, and college preparation.

Yet families with inner-city addresses still have excellent options such as Montessori, private schools (both religious and nonreligious), and 20 charter schools, which are independent public schools designed and operated by educators, parents, community leaders, and others.

These institutions, along with our top-notch suburban public schools, have elevated our overall educational rankings to some of the highest in the nation. Banners boasting A-plus rankings are posted next to glass cases crowded with 3-foot-tall basketball trophies. Elementary schools proudly show off Blue Ribbon certificates at parent-teacher meetings. And quality schools help produce students who are eager to continue their education: Greater Kansas City's 82 percent high school graduation rate beats the national average by at least seven points. In three Johnson County districts, more than 90 percent of the graduates are college bound.

We take a look at some of the elementary and secondary education choices available, both public and private, as well as list resources for day care programs within the metroplex. In the following section we graduate to our many fine colleges and universities as well as other learning options for adults and seniors.

Public Schools

Following is an overview of area public schools that have achieved impressive state and national honors. The accolades are shared by administrators, teachers, and students, as well as the parents who stay involved in school activities and tend to vote "Yes" on school bonds. The schools are listed alphabetically by state.

MISSOURI
Blue Springs
Jackson County's second largest district has two high schools, four middle schools, and 12 elementary schools; yet despite this escalating enrollment, it has garnered state and national recognition. Thanks to a $30 million bond election, which received an 85 percent approval, a districtwide technology program will make computers accessible to each staff member and student. *Expansion Management* magazine consistently bestows its highest Gold

Medal award on the district, and the *Wall Street Journal* named it one of the top 10 in the nation.

Grandview

Students who live in south Kansas City don't have a problem finding their lockers; they go to one school from kindergarten through eighth grade. And the kids aren't the only ones singing this one-school system's praises: The state named it one of the best small schools in language arts and science. The district's high schools also receive high marks from the state in journalism, art, music, and business, and 75 percent of its students participate in extracurricular activities.

Independence

For a district that's more than 135 years old, Independence looks remarkably fit. It has been accredited with distinction by the Missouri Department of Education, making it the largest district in the state to be so honored. Two of its high schools have received A-plus ratings, and three elementary schools are national Blue Ribbon winners. Its 21st-century early childhood education program is a model for the nation.

North Kansas City

Parents, businesses, and community members work together in this district through projects such as YouthFriends, Partners in Education, the Community Committee, and educational foundations. The results are schools that consistently earn A-plus rankings and students who score above state and national averages. The district also features the GED Online series, a pilot program for the state, as well as all-day kindergarten, summer enrichment classes, and before- and after-school child care. High school graduates who meet academic requirements are eligible to receive free books, tuition, and fees for two years at a community or vocational school in Missouri.

Park Hill

In southern Platte County parents, educators, and students work together through programs like Parents as Teachers and Community Education. This commitment has helped earn the district Accredited with Distinction status from Missouri as well as a Gold Medal from *Expansion Management* magazine. In 1999 Park Hill's superintendent was named the state's Superintendent of the Year. Students in the district have earned perfect SAT scores and the state Heisman trophy for athletics.

KANSAS

Blue Valley

Serving more than 17,000 students in 28 schools, this southern Johnson County district has earned a reputation for high academic performance. Eleven schools have received the prestigious Blue Ribbon Award, and in 2000 Blue Valley was awarded the Multicultural Education Award. That same year graduating seniors were offered more than $12.8 million in college scholarships. The district has also implemented successful community outreach programs, including SHARE (Seniors Helping and Refining Education), which places seniors in the schools to share time and talents, and YouthFriends, which pairs adults with children who benefit from individualized attention.

DeSoto

Administrators in the fastest growing school district in Johnson County planned for growth by building eight new facilities in the late 1990s. And not just any square box will do: The elementary school design has won international acclaim as a "Kid Friendly School." Technology plays a big part in learning, with computers in each classroom and additional computer labs for students that include CAD (computer-aided drafting) units.

Mr. K—High on Education

On a spring day in 1988 a man was ushered into Kansas City, Missouri's Westport Middle School auditorium to offer 200 eighth graders an opportunity of a lifetime. "Stay in school and away from drugs," said Ewing Kauffman, the multimillionaire founder of Marion Laboratories and owner of the Royals baseball team, "and I'll pay your college tuition." Thus was the start of Project Choice, a program that later made the same promise to students at Harmon, Schlagle, Sumner, Washington, and Wyandotte High classes in Kansas City, Kansas.

Project Choice would ultimately encourage 767 students to graduate on time and pay for college or vocational school for 709 of them. In all, the Ewing Marion Kauffman Foundation provided degrees to 308 students and spent $22.4 million. But beyond dollars, the foundation's administrators and staff gave time and encouragement to the students through a tutoring program, counseling, and lots of personal attention. Team members often visited students during their high school days and stayed in touch throughout college.

The results were gratifying: Before the program about 20 percent of the Westport graduating class went on to college or vocational school. Just a year later 98 percent of the first Project Choice class went on to higher education. But the administrators feel the program's no-drugs rule was its biggest success. Random drug testing results ranged from 97 percent to 100 percent drug free. Kauffman, the spunky entrepreneur, was first in line to take the tests until one day his sample came back positive, the result of narcotics he was taking for bone cancer. He died in 1993, a year after the first of what came to be known as the Kauffman Kids graduated from Westport.

The last of the group—the classes of 1992 to 1995 at Westport High and 1993 to 1996 from five Kansas City, Kansas, schools—graduated from college in 2001. But Kauffman's legacy lives on: The foundation, one of the 25 largest philanthropic organizations in the country, now distributes grants directly to school districts and community-based groups that serve Kansas City's children.

Read how Ewing Kauffman, affectionately known as "Mr. K," became a hero to kids of all ages when he saved our hometown baseball team in the Sports chapter.

Kansas City

With more than 20,000 students speaking 16 languages, this district is making a concerted effort to expand special programs for students with limited English proficiency. This district also supports Sumner Academy, the only magnet school on the Kansas side of the state line to offer college prep courses. Stanley Elementary is the district's only year-round elementary school. In 2001 voters approved a $120 million bond to upgrade technology, air-condition schools, and make other improvements. And thanks to a $10 million grant from the Ewing Marion Kauffman Foundation, the "First Things First" program will be expanded to the entire district. This program, which has been tested at a few schools since 1998, has achieved remarkable results. At Wyandotte High School suspensions dropped 57 percent, and at Washington High 289 students, one-quarter of the enrollment, increased their reading levels by three or more grades in just one year. The dropout rate has been cut in half. To read more about how the Kauffman Foundation has helped this and other school districts succeed, read the Close-up in this section.

Olathe

An expanding student population makes this southwest Kansas district the fourth largest in Kansas, but it may be the teachers who put it on top. Among their honors are 12 Presidential Awards for Excellence in math and science teaching and 14 National Blue Ribbon Awards from the Department of Education. Voters recently passed a $60 million bond to continue the district's good works.

Shawnee Mission

This school district challenges students to do their best through such initiatives as the International Baccalaureate Program, an advanced system of studies that earns students college credit, and the Center for International Studies, which gives students in grades 9 through 12 an opportunity to develop skills in Arabic, Chinese, Japanese, Russian, and geopolitics. National Merit Scholarships are well represented here; recently 44 district students took home honors.

Private Schools

The Kansas City area offers a variety of choices for private education at the elementary and secondary levels. In Missouri the Missouri Council for American Private Education publishes a directory of private schools for around $10. For more information write to the organization at 334 Nantucket Drive, Ballwin, MO 63011 or call (314) 214-8255.

The Kansas State Board of Education publishes an annual Kansas Educational Directory listing private schools in the state. The directory is available at libraries, online at www.ksbe.state.ks.us/pubs.html, or by calling (785) 296-4961.

Nearly every Catholic Church in Kansas City has an affiliated school where children receive an outstanding education along with lessons in religion. For information about schools call the specific church directly or the area's diocese. In Missouri contact the Roman Catholic Diocese of Kansas City-St. Joseph at (816) 756-1850 or www.diocese-kcsj.org/schools. In Johnson and Wyandotte Counties in Kansas, contact the Archdiocese of Kansas City in Kansas at (913) 721-2082 or www.archkckcs.org.

For information on schools affiliated with the Lutheran Church in Kansas and Missouri, contact the Director of Lutheran Schools in Missouri (314-268-1508) or Kansas (785-357-4441).

Many of our prestigious private schools teach children from tots to teens, so students don school colors from the morning they arrive in a stroller until the afternoon they drive away in their SUV or mom's BMW. Combining as many as five different grade levels is a practice that instills a sense of family and school spirit that extends far beyond the campus gates. A diploma from one of these schools, coupled with a diploma from a top university, can almost guarantee an interview with Kansas City's best companies; alumni tend to look after their own.

The schools listed here are arranged alphabetically by state.

MISSOURI

Barstow
11511 State Line Road
(816) 942-3255
www.barstowschool.org
In 1884 two Wellesley College grads, Mary Barstow and Ada Brann, came to Kansas City to establish a local school comparable to the independent schools in the

East. With the financial backing of several notable city leaders, including William Rockhill Nelson and August Meyer, their "School for Girls" was officially opened. Although lofty in goal—Brann's motto was "to educate a woman is to educate a nation"—the school had humble beginnings. The first class consisted of five girls sitting in a sparsely furnished parlor at 1204 Broadway. The school moved frequently, all within the posh Quality Hill area, and by 1897 began accepting a few boys in its college preparatory program. That same year Miss Brann returned to her home in New England, which left the dynamic redhead, Miss Barstow, to continue the school. It thrived after moving to a four-story schoolhouse in an apple orchard at 15 Westport Road—what is now an Osco Drug Store parking lot at Westport and Main. Parents of 93 students paid $62.50 per term.

In 1909 boys were admitted to the lower school only, and by 1923 Barstow had a new home at 50th and Cherry in the flourishing Rockhill section of town. By 1954 the school's enrollment of 170 was expected to quickly double after the board voted to allow coeducation. This created a need to move to 40 acres "in the country" at 115th and State Line Road. The new school was dedicated on May 5, 1962, where it stands today surrounded by lovely neighborhoods and massive estates. All 560 students, from preschool through 12th grade, share the campus, providing a sense of family in the communal lunchroom and extra cheering power during varsity pep rallies.

Pembroke Hill School
5121 State Line
(816) 936-1200
www.pembrokehill.org
Alumni still call their alma mater Pem-Day from when this private school was known as Pembroke-Country Day, an all-boy school founded in 1910. Some of Kansas City's most prominent families sent their sons to Pem-Day and their daughters to Sunset Hill, which opened in 1913. The two

schools had many similarities: Both were highly regarded and independent; teachers often taught at both institutions; and several activities, especially theatrical programs, involved students from both campuses. When the two schools merged in July 1984, the newly named Pembroke Hill School adopted traditions from both facilities. For example, students voted to keep Pem-Day's colors of red and blue on the school's banner; the motto "Freedom with Responsibility" came from Sunset Hill. Another beloved tradition remains from the girls' school days: May Day, complete with music, poetry, and dancing around the Maypole, is observed each spring.

PHS is located on two campuses less than a mile apart near the Country Club Plaza; it's quite a stirring sight to see a football game in play while driving past the field on your way to dinner on fall evenings. Make sure to lower your car window to get the full effect. The school offers an extended day program until 6:00 P.M. for children through fifth grade, a service that continues during winter and spring breaks. And its students learn the importance of giving back to the town that has provided so much: All upper school students must complete 60 hours of community service before graduation; many easily surpass this requirement. Currently 1,200 students are enrolled from age two through 12th grade.

St. Teresa's Academy
5600 Main Street
(816) 501-0011
www.stteresasacademy.com
The oldest school in Kansas City remains one of its best. This Catholic, independent college-preparatory school for young women was founded in 1866 and is sponsored by the Sisters of St. Joseph of Carondelet. Students are treated to a 20-acre collegelike campus in one of the most elegant residential areas of Kansas City, Missouri, near Loose Park. A newly renovated quadrangle draws students from more than 70 elementary schools and various ethnic, social, and economic

backgrounds. In 2001, 100 percent of St. Teresa's graduates continued their education, with more than 60 percent receiving academic scholarships. Many of these had a head start on their secondary education by earning up to 30 hours of college credit. The school emphasizes a well-rounded experience by encouraging involvement in sports (it has one of the most respected athletic programs in the area) and community service. Volunteering a minimum of 90 hours is a prerequisite to graduation. The academy enrolls just over 500 students.

KANSAS

Christots Country Day School
21403 Midland Drive, Shawnee
(913) 422-5684
With activities that include gardening, music, and visiting the school's rabbit and baby goats, it's enough to make you want to revert to childhood. Students from 18 months to third grade also learn phonics, geography, math, science, and computer skills through a Montessori-based teaching discipline. The school is set in wooded acreage, and the children spend plenty of time outdoors participating in games and watching for the deer that live just beyond the facility's fence. The school has been in operation since 1986; all classes are led by certified teachers.

Hyman Brand Hebrew Academy
5801 West 115 Street, Overland Park
(913) 327-8180
www.hbha.edu
In 1966 parents who wanted to provide a Jewish day school for their children rented space at Ohev Shalom Synagogue and began with 33 students. In 1973 a high school department was added. Over the years the academy has moved several times to adjust to its growing enrollment needs; in fall 1988 it found its permanent home when the architecturally stunning Jewish Community Campus opened in south Overland Park. Since then space has been added to support a biology lab, fine

arts center, Judaic studies rooms, two computer labs, and a foreign language classroom. Speaking of language skills, the admissions form states that new applicants entering grades 4 through 12 must be able to read and write Hebrew. The children come from a variety of racial, national, and economic backgrounds (over 50 percent receive financial assistance), yet all are being raised in the Jewish faith. Currently 340 students are enrolled from kindergarten to grade 12.

Kansas City Christian School
4801 West 79 Street, Prairie Village
(913) 648-5227
www.kcchristianschool.org
The hallmarks of this 50-year-old institution are its Biblical integration, character training, and parental involvement. In fact, parents don't just bake cookies for the booster club, they sign a form promising to be active in their child's academic and spiritual upbringing. Advanced placement classes in English and math provide college credit. The 14:1 student-to-teacher ratio helps turn out quality students, and the Discover Program caters to students with learning disabilities. The emphasis is on academic competence as well as compassion; for example, many teens the class of 2000 spent their senior trip in the sunshine, but instead of frolicking in Ft. Lauderdale they were constructing classrooms in a tiny village in northern Belize. The school enrolls 575 students from preschool to 12th grade, representing more than 100 churches from across the area.

Child Care

Kansas City is a family-oriented community with hundreds of day care options for working parents. Churches offer programs ranging from daily child care to weekly "mom's day out" relief, and the phone book is filled with Montessori and other organizations that accept children from several weeks of age through kindergarten and beyond. National companies such as Kindercare and La Petite Academy are well represented.

Several agencies provide resources and referrals to help you find a competent center, including the Johnson County Child Care Association (913-341-6200), Heart of America Resource and Referral (800-753-9981), and Day Care Connection (913-962-2020).

The two state organizations that oversee day care licensing and registration are the Missouri Department of Health's Bureau of Child Care Safety and Licensure (816-325-5860) and the Kansas Department of Health's Johnson County Branch of Health and Human Services Child Care Programs (913-894-2525).

HIGHER EDUCATION

Kansas City, it should be noted, is a university town. Never mind that the homecoming parade is an hour or so away. In fact, the traffic you hear on crisp fall evenings is alumni driving to Kansas University in Lawrence, the University of Missouri–Columbia, or Kansas State University in Manhattan to cheer at ball games before heading to favorite beer joints from school days. But woe is the couple with mixed allegiances; the ride home from a game between dueling schools can be pretty chilly. After all, one team has to lose.

Yet despite the lure of these Big 12 schools, degree seekers can choose in-town options without sacrificing prestige. Several of our colleges are nationally recognized for excellence yet offer students smaller class sizes for more personal attention. And don't worry that the little darlings will be denied interaction with other cultures by staying close to home; we draw students from around the world.

High school grads can select from an array of universities, community colleges, and trade schools. Several out-of-town entities maintain classrooms within our geographical area, an ideal way for working adults to obtain a four-year or advanced degree.

In addition, to help fuel our reputation as the life sciences center of the country, we have a number of respected schools in the health care field training medical doctors and researchers. Other professional schools offer degrees in chiropractic, dentistry, and osteopathy. See the Health Care and Wellness chapter for these options.

We cover some of Kansas City's classiest institutions and then take a look at other learning choices for adults and seniors, including dance and cooking classes. There could be tap shoes or a sauté pan in your future.

The listings are arranged in alphabetical order by type of institution and are located in Kansas City, Missouri, unless otherwise noted.

Two-Year Institutions

Johnson County Community College
12345 College Boulevard
Overland Park, KS
(913) 469-8500
www.jccc.net
Hear the deep grinding sound of a bulldozer? Must be another building going up at Johnson County Community College. In the sleepy suburb of Overland Park sits a community college with the sheer size and academic power to rival many four-year universities. JCCC's 17 redbrick buildings are linked by walkways and gardens dotted with outdoor sculptures and rimmed by 13 parking lots. Plans call for a gorgeous new art gallery and a research center to open in 2005. No wonder first-timers need a map to get around; each fall campus security staffers help a dozen or so dazed students find their cars.

The campus has to be immense to support its enrollment: With more than 34,000 students each semester, JCCC is the third largest institution of higher education in the state. It offers a full range of undergraduate credit courses that form the first two years of most college curricula as well as more than 50 one- and two-year career certificate programs that prepare students to enter the job market.

Its Center for Professional Education is the largest continuing education program in the region, enrolling more than 12,000 students in more than 600 certification workshops and seminars each year. More than 150 companies take advantage of training courses tailored for them and presented at the college or on-site at the workplace. And more than 11,000 people attend JCCC's public events, including a writers' conference, travelogue series, and youth programs.

But it's the three-year Chef Apprenticeship program that's brought the school national acclaim. Here's where some of the country's best chefs have trained; in fact the school has placed extremely well in international cooking exhibitions, usually bringing home gold and silver prizes.

The 234-acre campus is also home to the Carlsen Center, one of the most sophisticated performing and visual arts complexes in the city. Within its space is the 1,250-seat Yardley Hall. (Read more about Carlsen Center in The Arts chapter.)

Take a virtual tour of JCCC on its Web site or stop by in person. It's easy to find, particularly during warm weather when kite enthusiasts use its windswept hillside to maneuver huge, brightly colored flying contraptions.

Metropolitan Community Colleges
3200 Broadway (Administrative Center)
(816) 795-1000
www.kcmetro.cc.mo.us
Metropolitan Community Colleges is actually a system of four colleges—Blue River, Longview, Maple Woods, and Penn Valley—in nine locations throughout the Kansas City area. More than 40,000 students choose these schools every year for more than just economic reasons (although parents are thrilled with the $55 per credit hour cost). These modern facilities on beautiful campuses offer more than 70 career certificates or transfer

degrees in technology, health care, and business, even auto mechanics and veterinary sciences.

Yet educational quality isn't short-changed. For instance, in 2000 Longview Community College was one of four institutions named "College of the Year" by *Time Magazine*/the *Princeton Review*, putting it right up there with Sarah Lawrence and Cornell University.

Four-Year Colleges and Universities

Avila College
11901 Wornall Road
(816) 501-2400
Avila's history started in the 17th-century when the Sisters of St. Joseph of Carondelet in France crossed the Atlantic and half a continent to begin St. Teresa's Academy, a private school for girls. In 1916 the Sisters founded Saint Teresa College on the same campus and in 1963 moved the college to 50 acres at the edge of Kansas City for a new location and a new name. In 1969 Avila opened its enrollment to men. Today more than 1,400 students from more than a dozen different countries and all parts of the United States are drawn to Avila each year.

The Catholic college has continued the Sisters' pioneering ways. It was the first college in Kansas City to offer programs in nursing, gerontology, and social work. It is also the first (and currently only) four-year college in the city to offer a paralegal program approved by the American Bar Association and one of only 23 colleges in the country to offer a four-year degree in radiological technology.

Park University
8700 N.W. River Park Drive
Parkville, MO
(816) 741-2000
www.park.edu
It's hard enough to keep students focused on lessons, but when the classrooms are

high on a limestone bluff with views of the Missouri River peeking through leaves that change colors with the seasons, it must be downright impossible. Yet the 1,000 or so students attending this four-year coeducational Christian institution continue to excel.

The campus is arguably the most beautiful in the Midwest thanks to its picturesque site overlooking the bend of the river, the quaint town of Parkville, and the skyline of downtown Kansas City, Missouri. Opened in 1875, the buildings were constructed of native limestone; in fact the campus is a geologist's dream, with fossils from the Paleozoic period visible in building blocks and stone stairways. The boulder at the entrance of Copley Hall is a glacial deposit. Poets might find inspiration in walking the 800 acres of woodlands, waterfalls, and wildflowers.

The main campus is home to the School of Arts and Sciences, Nursing Bridge program, accelerated weekend and evening courses, and graduate programs in education and business administration. Its School for Extended Learning, which has served the nontraditional, working adult student since 1972, has 36 resident centers in 20 states across the United States. Of these sites, 34 are on military installations.

A diverse population is treated to Park's charms: The student body represents 30 states and more than 50 foreign countries. And more than 85 percent of undergraduate students receive some form of financial aid in the form of grants, loans, and work-study positions.

It was the students who built the school's most stunning building, Mackay

Hall, to pay for tuition. Construction of the limestone building—topped with a 135-foot-tall clock tower—began in 1886 and took seven years to complete. Another impressive site is Herr House, an upper-class residence hall built in 1927 that sports a handsome lounge and large rooms with—get this—*walk-in closets.*

But perhaps the university's most inspiring site is the Black History Wall located near the Sixth Street entrance. The landmark is inscribed with the names of four African-American employees who contributed to Park's rich history, including Spencer Cave, head groundskeeper from 1875 until his death in 1946 and who, one alumnus said "taught us more than our professors."

Rockhurst University
1100 Rockhurst Road
(816) 501-4000
www.rockhurst.edu

The spirit behind Rockhurst University was born in 1521 when a Spanish soldier took a cannonball in the leg at Pomplona. That soldier, later to be known as St. Ignatius of Loyola, used his recovery time for spiritual growth, which led to the formation of the Society of Jesus. The Jesuit tradition of service to others through a liberal education came to Kansas City in 1910 with the founding of Rockhurst University.

Today the university serves approximately 3,000 students (about 72 percent Catholic) at the main campus in Kansas City's cultural district and the Ignatius Center of Rockhurst University/Saint Louis University, located in suburban Kansas City. Rockhurst alumni are achievers; 1 in 10 is president, chief executive officer, or owner of his or her own company or organization. There's even a presidential appointee: Hector V. Barreto, class of '83, became head of the U.S. Small Business Administration in 2001.

Older students also choose Rockhurst for a superior education. Its Continuing Education Center, through subsidiary National Seminars, is the nation's largest provider of adult continuing education.

i *To get the best view of the prettiest campus in town, request a window or balcony table at Piropos, an Argentine restaurant in Parkville. You'll be treated to Park University's 135-foot-tall clock tower illuminated at night. During a full moon it's the most romantic spot in the city.*

And Rockhurst's Executive Fellows MBA program boasts an alumni list that includes more than 400 top leaders in major organizations throughout the Kansas City area and the nation.

"The Rock" has been ranked consistently as one of the top 15 universities in the Midwest by *U.S. News and World Report,* listed in *Barron's* "Best Buys in College Education," and received accolades in *Money* magazine. And it hosts PeaceJam, an annual event where Nobel Peace Prize winners and students discuss global issues and perform community service projects together, making it perhaps the only forum where you could hear, "So what do you consider the biggest threat to peace in the Middle East . . . and could you hand me that hammer, please?"

In fact, 85 percent of students participate in community work. They're also active in internship and co-op work programs thanks to the university's ties with local companies and its nonprofit leadership program. Yet there's time for sports as well: The Hawks and Lady Hawks routinely participate in national play-offs in soccer, volleyball, and basketball.

University of Missouri–Kansas City
5100 Rockhill Road
(816) 235-1111
www.umkc.edu

In the heart of Kansas City's cultural and entertainment zone stand the red tile-roofed buildings of the University of Missouri–Kansas City. The campus was established in 1933 when local philanthropist William Volker, presented the school with a 40-acre parcel in the Rockhill district. The main campus is named in his honor.

Soon other colleges were merging with the school to form an arts and sciences focus. The Kansas City School of Law joined in 1938, followed by dental, pharmacy, medical, and nursing schools. Today 13 schools and colleges offer more than 125 degree options to more than 13,000 students. In 1963 the University of Kansas City became part of the 160-year-old University of Missouri system, joining three other campuses located in Columbia, Rolla, and St. Louis.

UMKC is also home to the Henry W. Bloch School of Business and Public Administration; the Conservatory of Music; Missouri Repertory Theatre, the premier resident theater company of the Midwest (read more about this in The Arts chapter); National Public Radio's local affiliate, KCUR–FM (see Media); and a Gallery of Art.

The campus also has the area's largest academic library system, with more than 5 million volumes, including the Linda Hall Library of Science and Technology, second only to Harvard University Library in scientific material. Miller Nichols Library houses several fascinating exhibits on Kansas City's history; for example, get a taste of our jazz heritage, complete with recordings, at "Club Kaycee" at www.umkc.edu/orgs/kcjazz.

Although the school's facilities are state of the art, the 70-year-old ivy-covered stone buildings and tree-lined walkways retain an aura of pre–World War II innocence and a slower pace.

William Jewell College
500 College Highway
Liberty, MO
(816) 781-7700
www.jewell.edu

Being named *Time* magazine's "Liberal Arts College of the Year, 2000–2001" is impressive, indeed, for a school that was derided for being on the edge of civilization when chartered in 1849. Named for Dr. William Jewell, a prominent physician from Columbia, Missouri, the college adheres to the principles of a century and a half ago: Provide a superior quality education while retaining its Missouri Baptist heritage. The college became coeducational in 1921.

Jewell pulls from some of the most academically talented students in the region; in a recent entering class of 300, nearly 10 percent had graduated as valedictorian or salutatorian. These top achievers can choose from several advanced programs including the Oxford Honors Program, which combines British tutorial methods of instruction with a year of study in Oxford or Cambridge.

One of the college's strengths is its incoming freshman program that links new students with five mentors, including two faculty members and three students. Newbies get acquainted fast thanks to team-building exercises held at the new Tucker Leadership Lab. This same facility, including rock climbing walls and towers, challenging rope and bridge courses, and the "Sweet Chariot" 250-foot swing ride, is also popular with corporate teams and not-for-profit groups.

A sense of camaraderie can also be found by joining a fraternity or sorority or a Bible-study group or by helping construct houses in the inner city through Habitat for Humanity. And class sizes are kept small, averaging 15 students, so that the nearly 1,200 students enjoy one-on-one attention.

Graduate and Master's Programs

Adults who want to further their careers have plenty of options through universities that offer MBAs, including schools that have primary campuses in Kansas City and off-site universities that have developed a satellite presence in town.

Baker University School of Professional and Graduate Studies
8001 College Boulevard
Overland Park, KS
(913) 491-4432
www.bakerspgs.edu

Working adults can complete a degree almost as fast as they can say the name of this program. Well, almost. Students can obtain an undergraduate degree in just three years of intense work. Baker's SPGS also offers accelerated MBA and MSM degrees as well. It's quite a commitment; students typically attend one three-hour class a week with interim group study assignments. With a main campus in Baldwin City, Kansas, the university maintains satellite locations in Overland Park, Kansas, and Lee's Summit, Missouri.

Henry W. Bloch School of Business and Public Administration
5100 Rockhill Road
(816) 235-1111
www.umkc.edu
This school, located at the University of Missouri–Kansas City campus, offers both an MBA, which can be completed as a part-time student, and an Executive MBA, which is a 21-month, intensive program with classes that meet every other Friday and Saturday. One of the school's strongest points is its connections with and support from area businesses that can lead to job placement.

MidAmerica Nazarene University
2030 East College Way
Olathe, KS
(913) 782-3750
www.mnu.edu
Busy professionals can complete an MBA degree within two years at MidAmerica with the help of other students, caring instructors, and a personal laptop computer that's part of tuition. Here, courses are laid out in a structured manner in which each class builds upon the last to provide a feeling of integrated knowledge. This system is one reason the university has such a successful completion rate for its program.

University of Kansas Edwards Campus
12600 Quivira Road
Overland Park, KS
(913) 897-8400
www.kuec.ukans.edu

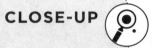

Kansas City Art Institute

If you could point to one reason our town is so flush with art galleries and artist studios, it's the Kansas City Art Institute. Young creative minds come here from 45 states and five foreign countries to study with some of the best instructors in the world. And if at first they mumble about being stuck in a cowtown, they soon fall in love with our exciting, urban city, and many of them stay after graduation.

Yet as a frontier town in the mid-1880s, Kansas City was an unlikely place for the founding of an art school. It began in 1885 when a small group of art enthusiasts organized a Sketch Club to "talk over art matters in general and to judge pictures." The club moved into quarters in the Deardorf Building at Eleventh and Main Streets and held its first public exhibition in the spring of 1887. The Kansas City Art Association and School of Design was incorporated in July of that year.

As the rowdy town's first cultural institution, KCAI has enjoyed support from prominent business and civic leaders, starting with Howard Vanderslice, who in the 1920s purchased a stone mansion and surrounding eight acres at 44th and Warwick for the school. Four years later the Art Institute renamed the residence "Vanderslice Hall." Today the school shares its neighborhood with the Nelson-Atkins Museum of Art and the Kemper Museum of Contemporary Art.

The college recently expanded its campus within the Southmoreland Neighborhood by purchasing two properties at 43rd and Walnut and opening the H&R Block Art Space, a gallery for contempo-

rary work by students and other artists. The new Jannes Library, situated in a stately old mansion known as the Cunningham Estate, recently opened.

The private four-year college awards bachelor of fine arts degrees in ceramics, design/illustration, fiber, painting and printmaking, photo and new media, sculpture, and art history or creative writing with a studio art emphasis. The 600 students join an impressive roster that includes Walt Disney, painters Jackson Pollock and Keith Jacobshagen, ceramicists Richard Notkin and Akio Takamori, sculptor Robert Morris, and photographer Thomas Barrow.

For more than three decades KCAI has hosted a lecture series, open to students and the public, starring some of the world's most respected artists and scholars. In spring 2001 a Visiting Scientists series was added as another dimension to the agenda. The program has partnered with Science City at the Union Station to exhibit artists' interpretations of the themes being explored.

KCAI also offers many outreach programs, including evening and weekend continuing education courses for credit and noncredit, family studio workshops, and a high school summer residency program. Student exhibits are held twice a year on campus, providing an opportunity for the public to experience and buy the work on display.

For more information contact the Kansas City Art Institute at 4415 Warwick Boulevard, Kansas City, MO 64111; (816) 474-5224; www.kcai.edu.

Now adults in Kansas City can chant "rock-chalk Jayhawk" while driving just a few miles to campus. The master's program is designed to meet the needs of a typical student who is 33 years old, works full-time, and has a family; most classes meet one night a week, and computer labs are open days, evenings, and weekends.

Mini-Medical Schools

These sessions may be just what the doctor ordered if you've ever wondered what makes you tick or what progress is being made to diagnose and treat various diseases. Two Kansas City medical schools have opened their doors to the public through classes taught in lively, understandable formats by some of the schools' top physicians and researchers. Although "graduates" won't come away with a medical degree, it's a sure thing they'll be more proactive about their own health care, and without living through a 36-hour intern shift.

KU Medical Center School of Medicine
3901 Rainbow Boulevard
Kansas City, KS
(913) 588-1227
www.kumc.edu/som/minimed
When KU Medical Center decided to offer these sessions a few years ago they hoped for 50 students. They got 250, with 100 on the waiting list. The eight-week sessions cover the same medical and research topics medical students receive. The curriculum changes each year, but past programs have covered cancer research, pain management, trauma center techniques, and diabetes. The result is a public that's informed and more at ease about communicating with their own physicians. Tuition is $95 and includes a detailed notebook covering each topic, a reception with the instructors before each session, and a gift (one year it was scrubs!) presented during the graduation ceremony. Some scholarships are available.

UMKC School of Medicine
2411 Holmes Street
(816) 235-1801
This fascinating seven-week fall session covers topics such as asthma, women's health, stroke, and complementary and alternative medicine. Each one-hour presentation is followed by a question-and-answer session, often the most popular part of the evening. All age groups have attended, from one very sharp teen to an incredibly feisty 89-year-old woman. On graduation night students receive a certificate, T-shirt, and tour of nearby Truman Medical Center. The tuition is $35, and registration is required, as this is always a sellout.

Other Learning Experiences

With so many credit and noncredit classes available around town, adults can expand their minds or their waistlines. You'll find classes for sports enthusiasts (think sailing and ice-skating) in the Parks, Lakes, and Recreation chapter.

Communiversity
5327 Holmes
(816) 235-1448
www.umkc.edu/commu
Called the university without walls, this is a mixed bag of adult education classes taught by volunteer instructors at various homes, gardens, and classrooms throughout the city. Want to learn how to buy a house, and then decorate it the feng shui way? Learn breathing techniques from a "recovering lawyer"? Here's where to find these and dozens of other classes in categories like Arts and Crafts, Inner and Outer Paths (yoga to reading auras), Food (tamales and paella to dim sum), and Business and Legal Issues that tackle reading an investment prospectus or writing a news story. This last one is taught by a Pulitzer Prize–winning news correspondent. Other teachers, called conveners,

include professional chefs, financial planners, and artists.

Classes cost between $9.00 and $16.00 each; materials, if needed, are extra. Communiversity offers two semesters a year starting in August and January. The free printed catalog is available at the office located on the UMKC campus or at bookstores, coffee shops, and other outlets around town a month or so before classes begin. The online version is up and running by then as well. Popular classes fill quickly.

The Culinary Center of Kansas City
7917 Foster
Overland Park, KS
(913) 341-4455
www.kcculinary.com
Follow your nose to Old Overland Park and join fellow culinarians, both skilled and novice, in hands-on cooking classes and demonstrations. The classes are fun and educational, and the best part is you get to taste the results afterward.

Instructors are chefs from some of Kansas City's top restaurants as well as other talented area cooks. CCKC has four to eight classes per week, and many of the favorites sell out as soon as the 20-page newsletter hits the mailboxes. Popular offerings include a Wine Country Dinner, with comice pear and Stilton salad, crispy crusted salmon with thyme-infused zucchini broth, and black bottom coconut cream pie; and a Bistro Dinner Under the Tuscan Sun, with penne *putanesca,* honey-glazed pork tenderloin with fennel, and winter pears in wine served with Gorgonzola and walnuts. Are you drooling on the page yet? Classes are matched to the season, so you'll learn barbecuing techniques in summer and holiday entertaining tips in winter. There are plenty of basic cooking classes as well, covering topics such as choosing a knife or stocking the pantry.

Classes are held in a lovely space, a cross between a Tuscan country house and villa in the south of France, that's also available for private parties, weddings, and corporate team-building events. Join the Frequent Fryers Club and get a discount on your fifth class.

New Writer's Workshop
6000 Lamar
Mission, KS
(816) 630-7063
If you long to unleash your writing potential or want to find out how to get your work published, this is the course for you. New writers will find a relaxed, supportive atmosphere and an instructor (always a published writer) who will help develop creativity, writing skills, and marketing techniques. Classes are held mornings for eight consecutive sessions each fall and cover fiction, nonfiction, and poetry. The fee is $50.

Theatre for Young America Acting Classes
4881 Johnson Drive
Mission, KS
(913) 831-2131
www.tya.org
Some students at this theater and education center are seeking acting careers; others simply want to improve their voices, body movements, creativity, and self-esteem. Classes for ages 3 through 18 are taught by professional actors and experienced theater craftspeople. The center also provides work/study programs to give students a chance to learn scene crafts, lighting, directing, and other behind-the-scenes skills. The classes are affiliated with the not-for-profit Theatre for Young America; for more information on performances see the Kidstuff chapter.

The Writers Place
3607 Pennsylvania
(816) 753-1090
www.writersplace.org
Newcomers to the craft of writing as well as frequently published sages come together in this grand stone mansion in Kansas City's elegant Valentine Neighborhood. Before its rebirth as classroom, library, and literary community center for

readers and writers, the handsome build-ing—complete with turret—spent time as a private home, brothel, and church. It could even serve as inspiration for one genre of fiction: the ghost story: Some say it's haunted.

William Hickok and local writer Gloria Vando founded The Writers Place in 1992 with the goal of providing a venue where writers could come together and discuss their work. They can also improve it, through a series of courses and workshops on everything from fiction writing and poetry to dialogue, usually taught by regional published authors.

The Writers Place also hosts ongoing events, open to the public, that include book discussions, poetry readings, and dramatic presentations. Fund-raising events are always a lively soiree. The organization currently has 1,000 members; dues are $40 per year for individuals, $60 for families, and $20 for students.

HEALTH CARE AND WELLNESS

When moving to a new city, even more important than locating the nearest ice-cream parlor is finding the closest hospi-tal. In Kansas City, chances are you'll have one practically in your backyard.

Even more good news is that many of our hospitals are nationally known for spe-cialties like cardiac care, cancer diagnos-tics and treatment, and even kidney transplants. Chalk it up to the fact that Kansas City is home to three medical schools: the KU Medical Center, known for its outstanding research programs; the University of Missouri–Kansas City, offer-ing a unique six-year program combining B.A. and M.D. degrees; and the University of Health Sciences, with a focus on osteopathy. Practitioners of chiropractic have the highly respected Cleveland Chi-ropractic College. While we're busy train-ing the best physicians and health care workers in the world, they're busy falling in love with this town. After graduation

they tend to plant their comfortable white shoes right here.

We're also making medical break-throughs that can help eliminate disease, speed the recovery process, and improve the patient's quality of life. For instance, our neurosurgeons were the first in the region to operate on tumors and lesions near the brainstem that were once thought to be inoperable. Heart surgeons per-formed the first endoscopic vein removal from the leg in the Midwest; the resulting incision was less than 2 inches long instead of the previous method, which created a scar the length of the leg.

And our KU Med was one of the first hospitals to perform deep-brain stimula-tion surgery to help control tremors asso-ciated with Parkinson's disease. It has performed more of these surgeries than any other hospital in the world.

Kansas City is fast becoming a world leader in the exciting field of life sciences with the opening of the Stowers Institute for Medical Research. This $200 million facility is devoted to finding cures to gene-related diseases like cancer and Alzheimer's. Find out more about this bio-medical research center in this chapter's Close-up.

As for immediate care, we'll start our rounds by covering the area's three largest health care organizations with multiple facilities and then follow up with individual medical centers and other health care providers. And we promise, no "cutting-edge" jokes.

All institutions are located in Kansas City, Missouri, unless otherwise noted.

Saint Luke's–Shawnee Mission Health System

www.saint-lukes.org
This organization consists of nine hospi-tals, a home health and wellness agency, 15 physician practices, and thousands of affiliated physicians in the Kansas City metropolitan and surrounding regions.

Following is a look at each hospital in the immediate area.

Saint Luke's Hospital
4401 Wornall Road
(816) 932-2000

For more than a century, Saint Luke's has been serving the health care needs of a growing city. Founded in 1882 as a 50-bed institution at 10th and Campbell Streets, the hospital moved to its present location near the Country Club Plaza in 1923, when a six-story, 150-bed facility was dedicated. Today the hospital campus covers more than eight square blocks and includes more than a dozen major facilities. The 650-bed tertiary-care hospital offers more than 56 medical specialties through its network of 550 physicians.

One of its primary focuses is on cardiac health. The Mid America Heart Institute, located at the Wornall Road campus, is the number-one preferred heart care facility in the region. The institute performed the world's first coronary angioplasty for an acute heart attack in 1980, revolutionizing heart attack treatment worldwide. This 210-bed specialty heart center is complemented by six different groups of doctors who specialize in cardiac and pulmonary research and care.

St. Luke's Hospital is also highly regarded for its cancer prevention, diagnosis, and treatment centers. Its Centers for Breast Care of the Cancer Institute provides the latest in imaging and diagnostic techniques, including stereotactic core biopsy.

Saint Luke's South
12300 Metcalf Avenue
Overland Park, KS
(913) 317-7000

This 75-bed facility offers a range of health care services including emergency, physical and occupational therapies, happy-mom-happy-baby birthing suites, prenatal services and a Level II nursery, cardiac diagnostic testing and rehabilitation, sleep disorder center, pain management clinic, and radiology services, along with surgery center.

Saint Luke's South was designed to be exceedingly patient friendly, with new technology such as wireless communication, electronic patient records, and bedside registration. Now that's a brilliant idea! It also offers a 90,000-square-foot medical office building on its campus.

Shawnee Mission Medical Center
9100 West 74th Street
Shawnee Mission, KS
(913) 676-2000

Back in the days of $4.00 house calls, residents of northeast Johnson County had few choices when it came to health care. Eight doctors practiced in the county, and the nearest hospital was a four-bed facility in Gardner, Kansas. Thanks to two doctors, Al Armbruster and Donald Smith, Shawnee Mission Hospital opened in 1962. Its 15-acre campus was donated by J. C. Nichols, a gift that was appraised at nearly $6.5 million at the time. Dr. Smith delivered the first two babies born at the 102-bed hospital.

Today the campus has expanded to 54 acres, which includes a 383-bed acute care hospital, a freestanding outpatient surgery facility, a community health education building, five medical office buildings, an employee child care center, and a community fitness course.

A member of the Saint Luke's–Shawnee Mission Health System, it has 640 physicians on staff and employs 2,500 associates. Its primary medical services are cardiovascular, women's care, surgery, and outpatient programs.

Most of the larger hospitals and health care groups provide community outreach programs including nutritional counseling, fitness programs, CPR training, and even babysitting classes. Many of these programs are free or inexpensive. Call around; often the hospitals publish schedules in a newsletter or on their Web sites.

The Stowers Institute—Hope for Life

In 1994 Jim and Virginia Stowers decided they wanted to give back something "more valuable than money" to the millions of investors in American Century mutual funds who made their success possible. As cancer survivors, they decided to put their fortune to work to find the causes of cancer and other gene-based diseases.

Starting with an initial gift of $50 million, they created the Stowers Institute as a nonprofit medical research organization. They purchased the 10-acre site formerly occupied by Menorah Hospital in the heart of the city and began construction of the 600,000-square-foot complex in 1998. Since then the Stowers have followed their initial gift with stock and cash that raised the institute's endowment above $500 million. Their most recent gift was securities valued at $1.14 billion.

The center is well on its way to turning Kansas City into "Biomed Valley," attracting top researchers and scientists from around the world. And although experts tried to convince the Stowers that the best-of-the-best would never transfer to Kansas City, they were soon proved wrong. Bill Neaves, the institute's president, and Robb Krumlauf, its scientific director, are beginning to staff the facility with the world's top minds. They tend to be impressed with the city, but they are overwhelmed by the institute. Its laboratory and research support space is unsurpassed. And the buildings and grounds at 1000 East 50th Street are simply magnificent. The general architect is the Kansas City firm of Peckham Guyton Alvers & Viets, but MBT Architecture of San Francisco, one of the few firms in the country specializing in research facilities, designed the laboratory and research spaces.

The landscaped grounds include waterfalls and walking trails, and the building's entrance is defined by a 31-foot double helix sculpture. The sculpture and the glass panels in the library's fireplace contain the institute's slogan, Hope for Life.

At its opening, the center was staffed with four laboratories headed by independent scientists. Since then it has recruited five additional scientists plus two highly ranked experts in bioinformatics and transgenic technology. When fully operational, the institute will house at least 50 independent research programs focused on understanding the genes and proteins that control how cells in our bodies divide, differentiate, migrate, and die. By studying these fundamental processes in cells, scientists hope to discover how genes cause many diseases, particularly cancer. For more information about the Stowers Institute, log on to www.stowers-institute.org or call (816) 926–4000.

The Stowers center served as a catalyst for the Kansas City Area Life Sciences Institute, a coalition of businesses, hospitals, and universities with a common goal: to improve the quality of life.

Other programs associated with Saint Luke's–Shawnee Mission follow.

ADDITIONAL SERVICES

Ask-A-Nurse
(816) 932–6220, (800) 932–6220
www.saint-lukes.org
Stubbed toe? Chest pain? Is it a cold or the flu . . . or perhaps that potato salad that sat out all day? You can get immediate answers to your medical questions 24 hours a day, seven days a week through this free service. It's also a handy way to find out about upcoming community education classes and register at the same time. And if you're new in town, you can find a physician (within the Saint Luke's–Shawnee Mission family, of course) who meets your specific needs.

The Cancer Institute
(913) 676–8156
This oncology partnership, affiliated with Saint Luke's–Shawnee Mission Health System, provides the community with a wide variety of services from a single source.

The institute collaborates with Kansas City's academic and research communities to provide research, therapies, and ongoing care. Specific services include inpatient oncology treatment, radiation therapy, breast centers at Menorah Medical Center and Saint Luke's Hospital, the Blood and Marrow Transplant program, a gynecologic oncology practice, and Gamma Knife services at Research Medical Center.

Crittenton Behavioral Health
10918 Elm Avenue
(816) 767–4101
Located on a picturesque 156-acre site near Longview Lake in southeast Kansas City, Crittenton is Kansas City's premier provider of psychiatric care for children and their families.

Founded in 1896, the center has evolved into a comprehensive system of care that includes acute inpatient hospitalization, partial hospitalization, community-based services, and prevention services. On any given day, more than 100 children and

young people receive treatment in one of the therapeutic programs. Additional behavioral health programs, for children and adults, are available at several locations through the system. These include addictions services and assessment centers.

Home Care and Hospice
(816) 756–1160
As the largest full-service home care organization in Kansas City, this organization provides home health services to help patients remain independent and decrease the time they need to spend in the hospital; hospice services, which provide caring medical and emotional support to patients and their families during the last days of life; plus home pharmacy infusion, medical equipment, and private-duty services.

Carondelet Health

This national network of hospitals is operated by the Sisters of St. Joseph Health System. In Kansas City they operate the two hospitals described below, as well as other facilities and services, including St. Mary's Manor, Carondelet Manor, and Villa Saint Joseph long-term care facilities; and home care services, a hospice, a pharmacy, and eight physician offices under the Carondelet name.

Saint Joseph Health Center
1000 Carondelet Drive
(816) 942–4400
Established in 1874 as the first private hospital in Kansas City, today this facility has 300 beds and is served by more than 720 staff physicians. With its handsome central atrium and architecture, it looks more like a hotel than a hospital. Patients also like the smaller waiting rooms spread throughout the place rather than having one huge Grand Central Station with screaming kids and four television sets, all tuned to a different station. The attached Medical Mall has a nice food court that beats most cafeteria choices hands down.

Saint Joseph's specialized services include Level II trauma care, a chest pain center, cardiac and pulmonary rehabilitation center, Lifeflight Eagle air medical services, and family-centered maternity care including neonatal intensive care.

Also on-site are an asthma center; the pain management center; a sleep lab; and programs for wellness, sports medicine, and nutrition.

ℹ️ *The Web site of Leawood's American Academy of Family Physicians, www.familydoctor.org, has health information fact sheets in both Spanish and English, self-care flowcharts, drug data, and more. By the way, Kansas City is home to the international headquarters of the American Academy of Family Physicians.*

St. Mary's Hospital of Blue Springs
201 West R.D. Mize Road
Blue Springs, MO
(816) 228-5900

This 111-bed acute care hospital opened the first Birthing Center in Missouri, providing a homelike environment for families. The hospital also has a 24-hour emergency room, Lifeline, hospice care, pain clinic, mobile CT scanner, and physical therapy unit.

Ongoing community wellness programs include coping with diabetes, prenatal and postnatal education, and CPR classes. St. Mary's Manor, a skilled nursing and residential care facility, is located adjacent to the hospital campus.

Independently Operated Hospitals

Baptist-Lutheran Medical Center
6601 Rockhill Road
(816) 276-7000

When Baptist Medical Center and Trinity Lutheran Hospital merged in 2000, it created a new entity to serve the south Kansas City community better. Licensed for 354 beds, the medical center is located on a 37-acre campus that includes outpatient facilities, medial office buildings, and a Pavilion Health Club that's dedicated to the rehabilitation and prevention of illness and disease. Baptist-Lutheran has approximately 1,000 employees and more than 700 physicians on its medical staff.

In addition to the traditional hospital services such as emergency, critical care, surgery, and other offerings, the center maintains the Center for Radiation Therapy; the Goppert Family Care Center, an extended-hour program that treats all aspects of the community's health needs; and the Center for Eye Surgery, which provides glaucoma and cataract surgery and features two suites specifically for laser procedures. The Pain Management department (816-276-7094) provides services relating to acute and chronic inpatient and outpatient situations. Patients can be referred by their physicians or self-admitted.

The medical center is involved with several community activities. It teams with the Yellow Cab Company to provide free rides home to people who can't (or shouldn't) drive from restaurants, parties, or bars during the holidays. Since its inception, Holiday Cab has provided more than 23,000 rides. Baptist-Lutheran is the exclusive local provider of the Lifeline 24-hour emergency response system. Subscribers keep a small pager with them at all times, so help is just a push-button away.

Children's Mercy Hospital
2401 Gillham Road
(816) 234-3000
www.childrens-mercy.org

You and your child will immediately know this is a special place when you see the lobby filled with bright colors, children's artwork on the walls, and physicians who often wear Hawaiian shirts instead of white jackets.

The hospital's history can be traced to 1897 when two sisters, Dr. Alice Berry

Graham, a dentist, and Dr. Katharine Berry Richardson, established the Free Bed Fund Association to treat "sick, crippled, deformed and ruptured" children from families that couldn't afford health care. Today the Children's Mercy health care system includes the state-of-the-art, 194-bed hospital in Kansas City, busy outpatient clinics in midtown, and a hospital in suburban Johnson County (described separately).

The hospital serves children from birth to age 18 and provides outpatient care in 35 pediatric subspecialties. Children's Mercy has the region's only Level I pediatric trauma center and emergency department as well as a Level IV neonatal intensive care nursery.

Along with providing the very best care possible, the hospital caters to young patients' emotional needs. Little ones are encouraged to bring a favorite stuffed animal or doll along with them, which promptly receives a bracelet that matches the child's. Kids can get an online tour of the hospital with Mercy Bear, with helpful tips for parents along the way.

The hospital continues to expand its services, thanks to several generous gifts from Kansas City citizens and annual fundraising efforts. It is involved in a 10-year, $129 million expansion that will increase services at the two locations and continue its ongoing research programs in genetics, cancer, neonatal, immunology, and nursing. The sisters who began this service with one child more than a century ago would be proud to see that their work continues: Children's Mercy provides more than $20 million in charity care per year.

Children's Mercy South
5808 West 110th Street
Overland Park, KS
(913) 696-8000

This facility brings the nationally recognized pediatric expertise closer to families in the south metropolitan area. It offers convenient access to outpatient pediatric surgery, 16 pediatric specialty clinics, a short-term stay inpatient unit, after-hours

clinic, and radiology services. More important, it continues the central hospital's renowned kid-glove treatment for little patients that takes much of the fear out of surgery and medical procedures.

Independence Regional Health Center
1509 West Truman Road
Independence, MO
(816) 836-8100

As the oldest hospital in Eastern Jackson County, this 3,666-bed acute care facility has a rich history of serving its community. It works in tandem with the Medical Center of Independence to provide an array of services through 400 physicians, nearly 250 registered nurses, 300 active volunteers, and more than 1,200 employees.

The health center is the only Level II Trauma Center in eastern Jackson County and offers a team approach to treat patients with severe injuries. Its Cancer Institute provides early detection screenings and services. And Independence Regional's Cardiac Center includes surgery facilities for open-heart surgery, as well as a complete rehabilitation program, the second largest in the Kansas City area.

KU Medical Center
3901 Rainbow
Kansas City, KS
(913) 588-5000
www.kumed.com

For nearly a century the hospital at the University of Kansas Medical Center has been providing leading-edge medicine and care to the people of the region. And since the hospital was separated from the University of Kansas system and placed under its own authority in 1998, we can now legitimately call it what we always have: KU Med.

As the region's only true academic medical center, the physicians at KU Med are dedicated researchers, scientists, and educators. Their achievements are many. Neurosurgeons were the first in the region to operate on tumors and lesions near the brain stem that were once thought inoperable. Heart surgeons performed the first endoscopic vein harvesting in the Midwest, creating an incision a mere inch and a half long rather than one the length of the leg.

KU Med was one of the first hospitals in the world to perform deep-brain stimulation surgery, which significantly controls tremors associated with Parkinson's disease and other brain disorders; it has performed more of these surgeries than any other hospital in the world. The hospital also performed the first kidney transplant in the state and has the first and only liver and pancreas transplant program in the area. A heart transplant program opened in 2002. Its Kidney Institute is one of the top programs in the world in fighting polycystic kidney disease.

The facility also has the region's only burn center certified by the American College of Surgeons and the American Burn Association. And its new heart-lung program features the most advanced diagnostic and treatment technology in the region. A $23 million investment added two state-of-the-art catheterization labs, operating suites, and therapeutic procedures. Its PET (positron emission tomography) scanner is the most accurate imaging technology available for tracking cancer and heart disease, allowing doctors to view a patient's internal organs at the cellular level.

Along with treating more than 200,000 inpatients and outpatients a year, KU Med provides health and wellness programs to another 10,000 people. For instance, about 3,700 people line up in their vehicles for a flu shot every fall. "Like fries with that?" is not an option.

Lee's Summit Hospital
530 Northwest Murray Road
Lee's Summit, MO
(816) 969-6000

Serving one of the fastest growing regions in the Kansas City area, this 102-bed acute care facility offers a wide array of inpatient and outpatient medical and surgical care.

Among its many programs are same day surgery, including suites for laser and microsurgery, and a Phase II and Phase III cardiac rehabilitation center, available on an outpatient basis. Additional rehabilitation services are available for physical, occupational, and speech therapy.

Prevention is also important here, so the center offers a variety of wellness programs, including aerobics classes; CPR training; free and discounted health screenings; and a weight management workshop that includes eight weekly sessions to teach individuals about healthy eating, exercise, and reading food labels. Thank goodness our famous barbecued ribs don't come with a label.

Menorah Medical Center
5721 West 119th Street
Overland Park, KS
(913) 498-6000

Menorah first opened its doors on Rockhill Road in Kansas City in 1931 and moved to its new location in 1996. The new campus includes a 158-bed acute care hospital, doctors building, and outpatient clinics. It may be the most beautiful facility in the city with its handsome architecture, fountains, and gardens that can be viewed from patient rooms and waiting areas. An appendectomy in 15 minutes? Sure, doc, but did you see the daffodils in bloom?

Within the 110,000-square-foot center is a sophisticated cardiology center including open-heart surgery, angioplasty, pacemakers, diagnostics, and a full range of modern cardiac care. The Family Birthing Center has 12 luxurious birthing suites that cater to new parents by providing private baths and showers with a jetted tub, sleeping facilities for Dad or a support person, and in-room private dining. We'd like to make a reservation for Friday, please.

Other patient-care touches include a pre-op pediatric party where younger patients get a firsthand look at the operating room to help ease any fears. They can also try out the kid-size electronic jeep they'll be driving into surgery. A Kosher kitchen takes care of the special needs of Jewish patients, and the arboretum is a tranquil garden with a walking trail that beckons caregivers and patients to relax.

Numbers for Health-Related Questions or Emergencies

Look to these organizations for help. Crisis lines are answered 24 hours a day.

Life-Threatening, Police, and Fire Emergencies: 911
AIDS Counseling & Information Hotline: (800) 590-2437
AIDS Testing Council of Greater Kansas City: (816) 751-5166
Al-Anon, Alateen: (816) 373-8566
Alcoholics Anonymous: (816) 471-7229
Alzheimer's Disease & Related Disorders Help Line: (913) 831-0003
American Cancer Society of Wyandotte & Johnson Counties: (913) 432-3277
American Diabetes Association: (816) 361-3361
American Heart Association: (913) 648-6727
American Lung Association: (816) 842-5242
American Red Cross: (816) 931-8400
ANSWER Network Teen Suicide Hotline: (800) 784-2433, www.teenanswer.org
Arthritis Foundation: (816) 753-2220
Battered Women's Hotline & Shelter: (816) 861-6100
Domestic Violence Network: (816) 995-1000
Kidney Foundation: (913) 262-1551
Mental Health Crisis Hotline: (888) 279-8188; TDD (800) 955-8339
Narcotics Anonymous: (816) 531-2250
Poison Control Center, Kansas: (913) 588-6633, (800) 332-6633
Poison Control Center, Missouri: (800) 366-8888
Rape Crisis Hotline: (816) 531-0223
Safehome Sexual Assault Hotline & Shelter: (913) 262-7273
Substance Abuse Center: (913) 362-0045
Sudden Infant Death Syndrome Resources: (913) 649-6996
Suicide Prevention Hotline: (913) 831-1773

PHYSICIAN REFERRALS

The following are referral centers that are not tied to any particular hospital or health care group.

Cass County Referral: (816) 884-3291
Jackson/Clay/Platte County Referrals: (816) 531-8432
Johnson County Medical Society: (913) 432-9444
West Central Missouri Medical Society: (816) 679-4135
Wyandotte County Referral: (913) 573-6702

North Kansas City Hospital
2800 Clay Edwards Drive
North Kansas City, MO
(816) 691–2000
www.nkch.org

For more than 40 years this hospital has expanded to meet the growing needs of its community north of the river. Today it's a fully equipped 350-bed regional medical center with more than 550 physicians representing 45 medical specialties.

It's perhaps known best for its superb maternity unit, which treats the birthing process as the magical time it is. For example, the private labor, delivery, recovery, and postpartum (LDRP) rooms are designed to pamper Mom and baby with all the comforts of home, including a specially designed birthing bed, private bath with jetted tub, television, and VCR. Dad can rest on a foldout sleeper chair and enjoy meals at the dining table. To celebrate the big moment, parents receive a decorative birth announcement and a diaper bag filled with gifts, including a logo T-shirt. No wonder more than 1,800 births take place here every year. Extraordinary medical care is close by if needed: The Level II neonatal intensive care nursery is on the same floor.

Cardiac care is also a specialty. North Kansas City Hospital was the first health care provider in Kansas City to use minimally invasive techniques for open-heart surgery. This advanced surgery offers less discomfort and a quicker return to home and everyday activities. To diagnose and treat heart problems before surgery is necessary, the hospital offers one of the area's most advanced cardiac catheterization labs.

North Kansas City Hospital has also made strides in its cancer treatment program. It was the area's first medical facility to eliminate the need to remove the prostate when cancer is confined to the area. And new gastrointestinal procedures take advantage of fiber-optic technology to allow the detection of polyps in the colon and remove them without major surgery. The center also offers the Northland's only

hospital-based radiation therapy services.

Its new Health Services Pavilion is just what the patients ordered. This $94.8 million facility consists of six levels and offers expanded outpatient services in one easily accessible location. Along with plenty of covered parking, the center has large, visitor-friendly waiting areas; Tiny Town, a section designed just for kids; and a health and wellness center for fitness and rehabilitation programs.

Olathe Medical Center
20333 West 151st Street
Olathe, KS
(913) 791–4200
www.ohsi.com

Founded in 1953 as the Olathe Health Foundation, the hospital established new facilities at its present location in 1987. When it built the expansive campus it was truly out in the boondocks. Today it's surrounded by homes, shopping centers, and office parks.

The 150-bed center's comprehensive patient services include anesthesiology, dermatology, diabetic, education, cardiac care and rehabilitation, community service, emergency medicine, general surgery, laser surgery, and MRI. Also on-site are facilities for pain management, oncology treatment, speech and audiology, support groups, and wellness programs. Many of Olathe Medical Center's more than 300 active staff physicians have offices located on the center's health campus and at health care facilities of Olathe Medical Services, Inc. The new Miami County Medical Center in Paola, Kansas, is a subsidiary.

Overland Park Regional Medical Center
10500 Quivira Road
Overland Park, KS
(913) 541–5000

This center was among the first health care facilities to bring quality patient care to southern Johnson County. Opened in 1978, today it encompasses a 249-bed acute care hospital, three medical office buildings, three pharmacies, and offices for more than 100 physicians.

Overland Park Regional offers several services that set it apart from other centers in the area. For instance, it has the only nationally verified Level II Trauma Program in Johnson County, including 24-hour emergency services. It also offers a Stroke Prevention and Recovery Program through its emergency department.

The hospital's Diabetes Wellness center is recognized for excellence by the American Diabetes Association. Its Burn and Wound Care Program is known as one of the region's most comprehensive. And the Geropsychiatry Program offers special care for the elderly, including crisis stabilization in the 24-bed unit; comprehensive psychiatric, medical, and neurological evaluations; individualized, ongoing treatment programs; and free follow-up visits.

Overland Park Regional is also home to a Sleep Disorders Center that evaluates, diagnoses, and treats patients with sleep problems. There's no question that new parents have a hard time sleeping, but they'll have a nice time with delivery thanks to the center's Pre-Delivery Program that includes "Birth Day Beepers" for the dad or birthing coach and 20 luxurious suites that pamper the new family. You can even let friends and family across the world see the new little miracle through the "StorkBytes" program that allows you to put your baby's photo, first name, and vital statistics on a Web site. And if problems should arise, the center has Johnson County's only Level III Neonatal Intensive Care Unit (NICU), providing the highest level of care for premature or sick infants.

Providence Medical Center
8929 Parallel Parkway
Kansas City, KS
(913) 596-4000
www.pmc-sjh.org
The Sisters of Charity opened Providence Hospital in 1920, and in 1976 the center relocated to a new building on a spacious campus in western Kansas City, Kansas. In 1994, Saint John Hospital in Leavenworth, Kansas, became an affiliate of Providence to further expand regional health care delivery.

The mission continues to focus on Providence's special identity as a Catholic hospital while expanding its services. Some of these programs include a radiation oncology center, a cardiac center offering open-heart surgery and rehabilitation; geropsych services, and a broad range of general and specialized surgical services including neurosurgery and ophthalmology.

Along with the 400-bed hospital, the campus maintains Providence Place, a 90-bed nursing facility that provides diverse health education and screening programs.

Finding the right doctor in the Yellow Pages is nearly impossible. To save time, and make sure the doc matches your particular needs—including coverage by your insurance—call the referral centers shown in this chapter. Most hospitals and groups also provide referrals, but be aware that the list will come from their own rosters.

Research Belton Hospital
17065 South Missouri Highway 71
Belton, MO
(816) 348-1200
This 70-bed medical center provides optimum care to the citizens of southern Jackson and northern Cass Counties through an array of services. Along with general and specialty surgeries, radiology services, and occupational and physical therapy programs, the hospital is one of only six Health Midwest providers to offer a new stroke treatment program. Services available include use of the Tissue Plasminogen Activator (TPA). Patients who received this treatment within three hours of the onset of stroke symptoms were found to be 30 percent more likely to escape permanent disability. In 1995 Research Belton opened its Skilled Nursing Unit to provide special services to patients who are medically stable but require skilled nursing care before returning home.

 **RELOCATION**

ADDITIONAL SERVICES

Kansas City Hospice
Main Office: 9221 Ward Parkway,
Suite 100
(816) 363-2600
www.kansascityhospice.org
For more than 20 years, Kansas City Hospice has provided medical, emotional, and spiritual support to area residents approaching the last stage of life. More than 130 professional staff in three Kansas City Hospice offices serve more than 2,000 Kansas and Missouri families each year, regardless of their ability to pay.

These families receive individually tailored care from a team that can include nurses, medical social workers, home health aides, art and music therapists, bereavement counselors, chaplains, and specially trained volunteers. Together they manage pain and provide caring, gentle support.

The Carousel Program (913-894-8228), Kansas City's only pediatric hospice in the region, cares for newborns through teenagers.

The organization's new resale shop, Top Drawer, offers great bargains on gently used clothing and estate items. People who donate their goods have excellent taste: Offerings include designer duds, furs, and antiques. Located at 3826 West 95th Street, Leawood, Kansas, in the Ranch Mart Shopping Center. Call (913) 642-2292 for hours.

OpenScan MRI
Baptist Medical Center
(816) 444-3198
Magnetic Resonance Imaging, or MRI, is a powerful innovation in diagnostic imaging. Its special qualities enable a trained radiologist to see the inner workings of the human body in details so clear they approach the appearance of fine line drawings in anatomy books.

The superior clarity enables swift and accurate diagnosis, which can eliminate the need for other prolonged and expensive testing. And because the 45-minute procedure is noninvasive, it is pain free with no side effects. Verbal reports are available the same day; written reports are sent to your doctor within 48 hours. MRI facilities are provided at three locations within the Kansas City area.

The Rehabilitation Institute of Kansas City
3011 Baltimore
(816) 751-7700
The Institute is a not-for-profit Heart of America United Way agency that helps children and adults with disabilities realize their highest physical, social, and vocational potential. Programs include community integration, day treatment, and outpatient medical services. It is also one of the largest vocational rehabilitation centers in the state of Missouri, with extensive work evaluation, counseling, and placement programs. The institute has a team of more than 100 full-time staff who help those disabled by stroke and spinal cord injury along with those affected by birth, childhood, or adult-onset diseases.

More than 1,700 people come to the institute each year to increase their functional capacity through medical rehabilitation; another 1,800 patients receive vocational rehabilitation to enhance their employment opportunities. Programs are available at six locations throughout Kansas City and outlying areas.

Research Psychiatric Center
2323 East 63rd Street
(816) 444-8161
This center offers a full continuum of behavioral health services, including inpatient and partial hospitalization programs, as well as a CareNet Clinic that provides crisis intervention, outpatient counseling, and community support groups. The 40-member medical staff and 100-member allied staff provide services available to the Greater Kansas City area.

The center's Senior Adult Inpatient Treatment is known regionally and nationally for its quality and longevity. Patients are treated based on their needs, either as high-functioning seniors or those who suffer from organic or chronic mental illness. Separate treatment programs are available through the Child and Adolescent Program, which includes a tutorial system that helps patients from ages 13 to 18 keep up with schoolwork.

Visiting Nurse Services of Health Midwest
(816) 751-3751

Established in 1891, this not-for-profit home health care agency offers the area's most comprehensive range of in-home services. As a United Way agency, it cares for adults throughout metropolitan Kansas City and surrounding rural areas regardless of the patient's ability to pay.

Home care can be as simple as providing skilled services that allow an older adult to live independently, such as physical therapy and nutritional counseling, or as complex as administering chemotherapy. Nursing visits, personal care assistance, and antibiotic treatments can all be handled in the comfort of the patient's home.

Mental Health

Johnson County Mental Health Center
Northeast: 6000 Lamar, Suite 130
Mission, KS
(913) 831-2550

Southwest: 1125 West Spruce
Olathe, KS
(913) 782-2100

This community mental health center provides professional assistance to service the emotional and mental health needs of Johnson County residents. Programs include individual, family, and group counseling and treatment.

Fees are based on the client's ability to pay. A 24-hour crisis service is available for situations requiring immediate attention; the after-hours emergency number is (913) 384-3535.

Mental Health Association of the Heartland
739 Minnesota Avenue
Kansas City, KS
(913) 281-2222

This center is dedicated to promoting the mental health of the community and improving the quality of life of persons with mental illness through advocacy, education, and support. A new service for people diagnosed with a mental disorder who just want to talk can be reached at (913) 281-2251. The Teen Help Line is (913) 281-2299.

Two Rivers Psychiatric Hospital
5121 Raytown Road
(816) 356-5688
www.tworivershospital.com

Set in a serene, parklike environment, this 80-bed facility provides short-term treatments for adults, children, and adolescents suffering with mental illness or chemical dependency. Some of the services offered are a Masters and Johnson Trauma and Dissociative Disorders program, eating disorders treatment, on-site accredited school program, and free assessments.

Underlining its treatment is a commitment to safety and confidentiality. The center is CHAMPUS approved and has received accreditation with commendation from JCAHO.

Diagnosis and treatment are available 24 hours a day, seven days a week.

Western Missouri Mental Health Center
600 East 22nd Street
(816) 512-4000

This academic training and research center provides acute care to the seriously mentally ill in its role as the regional inpatient and emergency psychiatric hospital for the state of Missouri and the University of Missouri–Kansas City School of Medicine. The center also operates supervised housing, prevocational services, and outpatient substance abuse treatment.

RETIREMENT

We'll be the first to admit that Kansas City hasn't made its reputation as the retirement center of the universe. Maybe we should. After all, the wonderful attributes that make this town great for families— low cost of living, a wealth of recreational choices, vibrant arts and culture environment, friendly people, and excellent health care options—make it a terrific place to retire. And if you're leaving one career and thinking about starting another, our network of college courses and entrepreneurial programs will help you get started, you young whippersnapper, you.

Best of all, we treat older Americans as the gems they are. Want proof? The Shepherds Centers of America started right here in Kansas City. This seniors-helping-seniors program helps participants maintain independent and productive lifestyles while they enjoy newfound creative outlets. Activities range from meal delivery, to legal counseling, to classes in art, to writing, to travel. Today the concept has been copied at more than a hundred centers nationwide, with new sites opening every year.

Kansas City is also home to one of the country's most respected retirement communities, John Knox Village, which has been instrumental in developing programs and excellent living options for seniors for more than 30 years. In fact, our senior communities are so stellar, Mom and Dad might have to fight off their kids wanting to move in with them. Again.

You'll find the right living arrangement to fit your lifestyle, including luxurious villas with a health club, salon, and garden outside your door; assisted care facilities;

One of the best ways to make friends in Kansas City is through volunteering, and perhaps there's no better place to lend a hand than at your friendly neighborhood hospital. You can serve as an escort for patients or even as a rocker in the nursery!

---

and even services that care for patients with Alzheimer's.

Let's take a look at all the services and programs available for our mature residents. You might find yourself fudging on your birth certificate just to be able to participate.

Opportunities are listed in alphabetical order by category, followed by a Retirement Communities section. Organizations are located in Kansas City, Missouri, unless otherwise noted.

Education

It's never too late to learn. Teachers and professors adore having mature students in the classroom to provide a unique view on a subject and serve as role models for the younger generation. Many of our universities and colleges offer discounts to seniors; check out "Colleges and Universities" in this chapter's Higher Education section. In addition, our parks and recreation departments offer educational programs in everything from art to tap dancing. You'll find individual listings in the Parks, Lakes, and Recreation chapter.

And if you live in Johnson County, you're really in luck; there's a club just for you at JCCC. Read on.

Brown & Gold Club
Johnson County Community College
12345 College Boulevard
Overland Park, KS
(913) 469-8500, ext. 4305
www.jccc.net/academic/brownandgold
If you're a Johnson County resident aged 55 and older, this is your ticket to ride. For a mere $10 a year you can take credit classes free (some restrictions apply), get discounted fees for continuing education courses, and attend parties, special lectures, and events throughout the year. Since the club began in 1972, more than 5,000 members have joined. Programs include travel, from trips as close as Overland Park's New Theatre Restaurant to a

10-day Caribbean cruise; social events such as dance parties for St. Valentine's Day; special lectures; and discounted or free tickets to entertainment at the college's Carlsen Center. It's enough to make you lie about your age.

SeniorNet
Johnson County Community College
(913) 469-2323
www.seniornet.org

Keep in touch with friends around the world, learn more about health issues, or sell your rocking chair on e-Bay. Older Americans are jumping onto the computer with help from programs like SeniorNet. This nonprofit organization provides computer instruction and access to an online network in an easy-to-learn and fun environment.

SeniorNet has more than 22,000 members in the Western Hemisphere and more than 125 sites across the country. In the Kansas City area, classes are taught at several locations, including KCPT, the public television station, and the Johnson County Community College campus in Overland Park. Membership is $35 a year. For information or to join, contact the area coordinator, John Duff, at the number shown above.

Recreation

In Kansas City, seniors can keep active and healthy, thanks to a plentitude of programs through organizations like banks and savings and loans. Check with yours to see if they host travel groups and special events. Several area hospitals also offer programs specifically geared toward older citizens. These include free or reduced-cost health screenings and classes for CPR, fitness, and nutrition. For more information see the Health Care and Wellness chapter.

Our parks and recreation departments provide dozens of programs for seniors. Each county has its own parks and rec department; you'll find them listed in Parks, Lakes, and Recreation.

Classic Senior Games
Jackson County Parks and Recreation
(816) 795-8200, ext. 1278

Each September, this Olympic-style event brings out the competitive nature in men and women who don't feel 50 years old. But that's the *minimum* age for these games; you'll also see plenty of participants pushing 80. Sports include swimming, tennis, track and field, and horseshoes. Medals are awarded for a variety of categories. This four-day event is recognized by the United States National Senior Sports Organization.

50 Plus Program
Johnson County Park and
Recreation District
(913) 831-3355
www.jcprd.com,
www.50plusprogram.com

Arts and crafts classes, group travel, cards and games, gardening . . . do these folks ever slow down? Johnson County's 50 Plus Program offers so many classes and events there's no time to grow old and creaky. A recent list of springtime activities included West Coast Swing, Latin Rhythm Workout, Working with Digital Photography, Hands-On Investing, Basic Spanish, and a rather curious new class, New Spouse Checklist. Travel opportunities have included trips to China and the Yangtze River, Spain and Portugal, and Branson, Missouri.

Other programs include regular health screenings at reduced or no cost, CPR training, yoga, and joining friends for regular nature walks. What are you waiting for?

Senior Arts Council
(913) 897-4165

This group began in 1977 as a way for senior arts and crafters to showcase their talent and continue to learn new creative skills. Each meeting, held the last Monday of each month at 1:00 P.M., includes a guest artist or speaker. The fee is $10.

One of the best ways to stay active is to volunteer. Share your expertise as a SCORE volunteer, serve as an usher, serve at a soup kitchen, or pull weeds at a community garden. You'll find opportunities in this section, or contact the Heart of America United Way (816-235-6675), which can match your interests with an organization that needs you.

Senior Peers Actively Renewing Knowledge (SPARK)
4825 Troost
(816) 235-2870
www.umkc.edu/spark
You've got to love this acronym, eh, Sparky? This program, hosted by the University of Missouri–Kansas City and affiliated with Elderhostel Institute for Learning in Retirement, provides courses each summer at the school's campus. Noncredit courses touch on such topics as computers, the Internet, Spanish, music, and Kansas City history.

Most classes meet once a week for four, six, or eight periods. An annual SPARK membership costs $51 and includes three classes and admission to various social activities throughout the year. There is a fee, usually around $10, for each additional class. Call the number above for more information. Persons with speech or hearing impairment may call Relay Missouri at (800) 735-2966 (TT), or (800) 735-2466 (voice).

Shepherd's Center of Kansas City Central
5200 Oak (and other locations)
(816) 444-1121
www.shepherdcenters.org
The Shepherd's Center movement was started in 1972 by 25 Catholic, Jewish, and Protestant congregations in one area of Kansas City. The goal was to create programs that would enrich the lives of seniors, help them to remain independent, and to celebrate life.

The first center was a smashing success from the start. Each Friday, 400 to 500 men and women took classes on everything from painting and journaling to learning to play bridge. Soon the center was helping 4,000 people stay active and engaged in life. The genius of the program is that it is an interfaith ministry by and with older adults rather than a ministry to them. Many of the programs are taught by senior volunteers.

Shepherd's Center soon became a model for other programs throughout the country, and an ad hoc committee was formed in 1973 to respond to requests from other communities. The Shepherd's Centers of America was incorporated a year later. Today this organization coordinates nearly 100 independent Shepherd's Centers throughout the country. Centers in the Kansas City area provide classes in foreign language, computers, tai chi, and creative writing; there are dozens of classes and groups.

In addition, senior volunteers go into the community to help their neighbors. A few of the 25 services are Meals on Wheels to deliver a hot noontime meal to those who can't leave their home; Wheels That Care, providing free transportation to doctor's visits, pharmacies, and grocery stores; Respite Care to offer short-term relief for caregivers of homebound loved ones; and Care Home Contacts, to visit nursing home residents who don't have family or friends. There are other Shepherd's Centers throughout the city. Contact the number above or go online to learn more.

Services

American Association of Retired Persons
700 West 47th Street, Suite 110
(866) 389-5627
www.aarp.org
It's a rite of passage: Turn 50 and get a big packet of information from AARP. Frankly, we can't imagine anyone who

would say no to this collection of benefits for $12.50 a year. A sampling includes discounts on everything from lodging and car rentals to cruises and information and resources on health, fitness, and insurance, as well as legal and consumer issues. And with more than 30 million members, AARP is the largest advocacy group for older adults in the United States.

Joining the local chapter will net you invitations to social events, provide opportunities to volunteer your time and expertise, and give you access to the organization's home-delivery prescription drug service and much more. Plus, your spouse gets in free whether he or she is 50 or not. Membership also includes subscriptions to the monthly AARP Bulletin and the bimonthly Modern Maturity.

AARP's 55 Alive/Mature Driving Program
700 West 47th Street, Suite 110
(866) 389-5627
www.aarp.org
This program is just what is says: teaching older Americans how to drive defensively. The comprehensive, eight-hour course covers topics such as age-related changes that can affect vision, hearing, and physical strength. Check with your auto insurance carrier; some agencies provide discounts to seniors who have completed the course.

Area Agency on Aging–Johnson County
11875 South Sunset, Suite 200
Olathe, KS
(913) 894-8811
(Press "1" for Aging Information)
www.jocoks.com/humanservices-aging
The goal of the AAA is to help older adults in Johnson County maintain independence and dignity in their own homes and in the community. A few of the programs include in-home services such as minor repairs and preparing for winter; noon meals and fellowship at senior centers and through home-delivered meals for homebound seniors; legal services and insurance counseling; and client assess-

ment referral and evaluation (CARE), which provides preadmission assessments for persons considering nursing facilities or long-term care services.

In addition, the Catch-A-Ride program (913–477–8105) provides older adults and persons with disabilities with a free ride to grocery stores, senior centers, and health care appointments.

Area Agency on Aging–Kansas City
600 Broadway, 300 Rivergate Center
(816) 474-4240
www.marc.org
This initiative of the Mid-America Regional Council serves older residents in Cass, Clay, Jackson, Platte, and Ray Counties in Missouri. Some of the programs and services include providing hot meals and activities at senior centers; delivering meals to residents who are unable to leave their homes; offering adult day care services and homemaker and personal care services such as grocery shopping; providing transportation to medical appointments, and offering advocacy in legal and consumer situations.

Generally, the MARC adult programs are available to those aged 60 and over, regardless of income. There are no predetermined fee scales, but participants are encouraged to make voluntary contributions to offset the cost of the services they receive. In addition, a limited number of programs are available to those between the ages of 18 and 59 with significant disabilities.

Volunteering

That friendly face who shows you to your seat at the ballet? That's a volunteer, and not only does she get to meet new people and contribute to the community, she gets a free seat for the *Nutcracker Suite*. Pretty sweet, indeed. Kansas City provides thousands of opportunities for seniors to donate time, talent, and expertise. You've read about some of them here, such as the seniors-helping-seniors programs through the Shepherd's Centers. In addition mature adults can mentor at-risk youth, read to little kids, teach English to immigrants, and yes, serve as ushers or guides at one of our many cultural centers. Call your favorite venue found in The Arts chapter; chances are they're holding a nifty uniform in just your size.

Following are other worthwhile volunteer opportunities.

Catholic Charities
(913) 621-1504
2220 Central Avenue
Kansas City, KS
www.catholiccharitiesks.org

The volunteer opportunities at this organization are as big as your heart. This nondenominational group is always grateful for people who serve at community kitchens, read to small children, mentor youths in need, set up households for immigrants, and serve as hospice caregivers. Catholic Charities helps more than 75,000 people every year; you can make it 75,001.

Heart of America United Way
(816) 235-6675
www.hauw.org

The umbrella organization services hundreds of not-for-profit groups throughout the greater Kansas City area and serves as a resource center for volunteer opportunities. Give them a call to match your talents with a need, or show up at their annual Day of Caring, held every June. This communitywide service event mobilizes volunteers from over 126 companies, federal agencies, and labor unions.

Retired & Senior Volunteer Program (RSVP)

This program gives seniors a chance to learn new skills and share their expertise with others while making new friends through volunteering. Opportunities include serving as ambassador at the air-

port, becoming a resource guide at Union Station, or mentoring students at area schools. Contact the United Way at Jackson, Clay, and Platt Counties at (816) 474-5111, ext. 245; in Wyandotte County it's (913) 371-3674. Or call the Johnson County Volunteer Center, (913) 341-1792.

The Service Corps of Retired Executives (SCORE)
4747 Troost
(816) 235-6675
www.scorekc.org

If you've ever run a company, managed a department, or written a brochure, someone in the business world needs your talents. This organization pairs retired executives with small business owners in need of advice. Sponsored by the Small Business Administration, the program has experts in virtually every area of free enterprise, including management, finance, marketing, and human resources.

The Kansas City chapter's volunteers join more than 11,500 nationwide who donate their time and talent to help nearly 300,000 entrepreneurs every year. The satisfaction that you helped should be enough, but sometimes there are more immediate bonuses, like the one a businessman in Johnson County who provided advice to a young woman starting a candy company got. He has enough chocolate to last another lifetime.

Retirement Communities

John Knox Village
400 Northwest Murray Road
Lee's Summit, MO
(816) 524-8400, (800) 892-5669
www.johnknoxvillage.org

This 40-acre retirement community is practically its own town. Residents find everything they could need or want for the best years of their lives, including a variety of housing options, a maintenance-free lifestyle, plenty of activities, and a full continuum of health care services.

There are nearly 15,000 homes at John Knox, providing more than 70 different floor plans including apartments, cottages, duplexes, town houses, and single-family homes. All maintenance and utilities (except telephone) are included in a monthly fee. No shoveling snow or cutting the lawn, but many of the residents enjoy tending the garden. And with all those chores done for you, you'll have more time to enjoy the fitness center, two swimming pools, fishing lake, nine-hole golf course, bowling alley, and 2,000-seat pavilion for dances and shows.

The Village also offers plenty of choices when it comes to dining. The Villager Restaurant has sit-down table service and a Sunday Family Brunch once a month. A more casual choice is the cafeteria-style dining room with a spectacular view of the golf course and lake. And for date night, take your sweetie to the Fireside Dining Room, with dishes that range from soup and sandwiches to grilled tuna steak.

Part of the real joy of living here are the ongoing activities like craft lessons, musical groups, a variety of clubs to join, and trips to take as a group. Security is another benefit; the campus has its own security force with officers patrolling the area 24 hours a day, 365 days a year. Residents also have access to health and wellness programs and services, including nutritional and rehabilitation services. And because John Knox Village is a continuing care retirement community, it also offers access to 24-hour nursing care, an assisted living facility, a fully accredited, 430-bed skilled nursing center complete with an Alzheimer's unit, a physician's clinic, and the adjacent 102-bed acute care Lee's Summit Hospital, all on the campus.

Residents may choose to pay an annual rental fee or enter into an entry fee agreement that's available in four different levels of care.

Town Village Leawood
4400 West 115th Street
Leawood, KS
(913) 491-3681
www.townvillage.com
You've got a lot of living to do, and Town Village is just the place to enjoy it. It's close to entertainment, outdoor activities like parks and golf courses, and some of the best shopping and restaurants in the region, so you'll have plenty to keep you busy. But you might find yourself spending most of your time at this campus, especially once you taste the four-star quality food served in the light-filled dining room. No mush here; how about Cornish game hens, trout amandine, chicken stir-fry, or another one of the delicious entrees that rotate on a four-week cycle, so diners are never bored.

Other amenities include arts and crafts, an indoor pool, resident gardening area, fitness center, and a Cultural Guild, which brings in artists, musicians, and actors to entertain the residents. Spacious apartments are available, from studios through two-bedroom, two-bath homes.

Village Shalom
5500 West 123rd Street
Overland Park, KS
(913) 317-2600
www.villageshalom.org
A retirement village with its own award-winning art gallery? This beautiful campus in south Johnson County was designed as a nurturing—even exciting—environment for seniors. Near the Jewish Community Campus, Menorah Medical Center, and a number of activities, it provides fellowship

One of the best things about turning 60 in Johnson County is getting a free subscription to Best Times. *This monthly publication of Aging International Action of Johnson County provides information about services and events for seniors. Call (913) 477-8242 for subscriptions.*

for those who value Jewish traditions. The villas, apartments, and suites are beautifully designed for comfort and luxury, and the grounds are landscaped with lovely gardens and walking paths. Community-oriented services include Rachel's Cafe, a kosher dining room; a day spa; and the ElderSpa Wellness Center. The Epsten Gallery is a two-story, museum-quality art showroom that features exhibits from around the world. In addition, within the community are a full-service bank, children's outdoor playground for visiting family members, and a social hall and synagogue.

Village Shalom offers maintenance-free villas, apartments, and Shalom Suites, which provide assisted living or skilled nursing services. The Weinberg Health Center has additional facilities to meet the special needs of those residents with Alzheimer's and other diseases.

INDEX

A

AARP's 55 Alive/Mature Driving Program, 347

Abdallah Shrine Rodeo, 221

accommodations. *See* bed-and-breakfasts and inns; extended-stay facilities; hotels and motels; RV campsites and resorts

Act II, 128

Adam's Mark, 45–46

Aesthetica, 140

AIDS Walk, 257–58

air travel, 14, 16–17

Aixois, 68, 89

Alexander Majors Historic House and Museum, 155

alfresco dining restaurants, 103

All Fired Up, 186

American Association of Retired Persons, 346–47

Americana Weekend, 209–10

American Cablevision, 310

American/Continental restaurants, 60–77

American Heartland Theatre, 179–80

American Jazz Museum, 159

American Livestock Horse Show & Rodeo, 232, 234–35

American Restaurant, The, 60, 68

American Royal Museum and Visitor Center, 196

Ameristar Casino, 112

Ameristar Casino Hotel, 47, 147

AMF College Lanes, 260

AMF Ice Chateau, 189, 261

Andre's Confiserie Suisse, 78, 136

Angie's Italian Ice and Frozen Custard, 78

Animal Haven, 315

Animania, 138

Annual Bachathon, 210

Annual Easter Egg Hunt, 205–6

annual events, 201–38

Annual Home Show, 206

Annual Jazz Ambassador's Fund-Raiser, 204

Annual Kansas City Boat Show, 204

Annual "Little House" Birthday Celebration, 205

Antioch Park, 241

antiques and collectibles stores, 121–25

Antiques Garden & Home Design Show, 228

Antiques on the Common, 210, 223

Antiquities & Oddities Architectural Salvage, 121

apartments, condominiums, and lofts, 307–8

Arabia Steamboat Museum, 160

Area Agency on Aging–Johnson County, 347

Area Agency on Aging–Kansas City, 347

Argosy Casino, 112, 147

Art at the Center, 207

Art Auction, 202

Arthur Bryant's Barbeque, 79–80

arts
    art galleries and showrooms, 172–73
    art museums, 146–47, 173
    artspaces, 174–75
    child-oriented theater, 198–99
    dance, 174
    literary arts, 175, 178
    music, 178–79
    performing arts venues, 183–85
    theater companies, 179–83

Art Westport, 223

Asian restaurants, 77–78

Asiatica Ltd., 121

Ask-A-Nurse, 335

Athletic Club of Overland Park, The, 262–63

attractions
    art museums, 146–47, 173
    casinos, 147, 150–51
    entertainment districts, 151–53
    historical churches, 153–54
    historical homes, 155–59
    historical museums and sites, 159–64
    landmarks, 164–65
    neighborhood drives, 165–66
    observation points, 166–68
    outdoor attractions, 168–70
    tours, 170–71

auto rental companies, 17

Avalon Cafe, 60–61

Aviation Expo, 221

Avila College, 325

Azteca Fiesta, 211

B

bakeries, 78–79
Baker University School of Professional and Graduate Studies, 328
Ballet in the Park, 221–22
Bally Total Fitness, 263
Bangs Hair Salon, 313
Baptist-Lutheran Medical Center, 336
barbecue restaurants, 79–85
Bar Natasha, 108
Barney Allis Plaza, 241–42
Barn Players, 180
bars, taverns, and cocktail lounges, 105–6
Barstow, 321–22
Barstow Organic Farmer's Market, 132–33
Barumba in Mi Cocina, 107
Basswood Country Inn and RV Resort, 57, 258–59
bath and bed gifts stores, 125–26
BB's Lawnside Bar-B-Q, 80, 109
Beast, The, 231
Beaumont, The, 113
Beco Flowers, 313
bed and bath gifts stores, 125–26
bed-and-breakfasts and inns, 52–57
Belton, Grandview & Kansas City Railroad Company Train Rides, 223–24
Belton Parks & Recreation, 246
Best of Kansas City, The, 145
Better Cheddar, The, 136
Bijin Salon & Day Spa, 313
biking, 255–57
Bingham-Waggoner Estate, 155
Birch Telecom, 310
Black Bamboo, 140
Blayney's, 109
Bloch, Henry, 35
Bloomsday Books, 126–27
Blue Bird Bistro, 68, 102
Blue Gallery, 172–73
Blue Koi, 87–88
Blue Room, The, 115
blues, 12, 108–12
Blues and Bar-Be-Q Benefit, 222
Blue Springs Lake, 240
Bluestem, 61
Blue Valley Parks & Recreation, 246
Blue Valley Recreation Pumpkin Patch, 231
Board of Public Utilities, 309, 310
Boardroom Bar-B-Que, 80

Bob Jones Shoes, 128
Bo Lings, 88
Bonner Springs Park, 242
Bonner Springs Parks & Recreation, 247
Boo at the Zoo, 231
bookstores, 126–28
Booms and Blooms, 219
Boulevard Brewing, 170
bowling, 260
Boy and Frog Fountain, 177
Breakfast with the Easter Bunny, 206
Bristol Bar and Grill, 97
Brookside Antiques, 121–22
Brookside Art Fair, 210–11
Brookside Irish Festival, 224
Brookside St. Pat's Warm-Up Parade, 206–7
Brookside Toy & Science, 197
Browne's Market, 136–37
Brown & Gold Club, 344–45
Build-A-Bear Workshop, 186–87
buses, 15–16
Bushnell Factory Outlet, 128–29
Business Journal, The, 275

C

cable service, 310
Cafe Casbah, 103–4
Cafe des Amis, 68, 89
Cafe Garozzo, 93–94
Cafe Maison, 68, 102–3
Cafe Provence, 89–90
Cafe Sebastienne, 61–62, 68
Cafe Trocadero, 62, 68
Cajun/Creole restaurants, 85
Californo's, 62–63
Call, The, 275–76
camping, 258–59
Cancer Institute, The, 335
CANstruction, 228
Canyon Cafe, 96
Capital Grille, The, 98–99
Cargo Largo, 129
Carlsen Center, 183
Carmen's Cafe, 93
Carondelet Health, 335–36
car rentals, 17
casinos, 112–13, 147, 150–51
Cathedral of the Immaculate Conception, 153

Catholic Charities, 348
Cedar Creek, 305–6
cellular phone service, 310
Century 21 Heartland Realty, 304
Charlie Parker Memorial, 164
Char MacCullum Real Estate Team, 304
Chateau Avalon, 50–51
Cheep Antiques, 122
child care, 323–24
children, activities for. *See* kidstuff
Children's Fountain, The, 177
Children's Mercy Hospital, 336–37
Children's Mercy South, 337
Children's Museum of Kansas City, 194
children's sports, 262
Chinese restaurants, 87–88
Christmas Card Lane, 236
Christmas Carol, A, 232
Christmas in October, 228
Christmas in the Park, 233
Christmas in Weston, 237
Christopher Elbow Artisanal
    Chocolates, 137
Christots Country Day School, 323
churches, 284–87
churches, historical, 153–54
Churchill at Crestwood, 122
Cinco de Mayo Fiesta, 211
Circle S Ranch Guest Ranch & Country
    Inn, 52–53
City Hall Observation Deck, 166–67
City Market, 133
City Tavern, 68
Civil War on the Border, 207
Classic Cup Cafe, 63, 103
Classic Senior Games, 345
Clay County Parks & Recreation, 246
Clay-Platt Baseball League, 246
Cliff Drive, 167
climate, 13
clothing and accessories stores, 128
Club at Plaza III, The, 115
cocktail lounges, bars and taverns, 105–6
Coldwell Banker Advantage, 304–5
collectibles and antiques stores, 121–25
Collector's Choice Trains, 139
colleges and universities
    four-year, 325–28
    graduate programs, 328–30
    two-year, 324–25

Colonial Presbyterian Church, 314
ComedyCity, 107
comedy clubs, 106–7
Community Christian Church, 153
Community of Christ Temple and
    Auditorium, 154
Communiversity, 330–31
Complete Traveler, The, 127
condominiums, lofts, and apartments,
    307–8
Conover Place Lofts, 307
Continental/American restaurants, 60–77
convention and visitor bureaus, 312
Convention & Visitor's Bureau of Greater
    Kansas City, 5, 312
Cool Crest Family Fun Center,
    187–88, 260
Corbin Bronze Ltd., 134
Corporate Woods Jazz Festival, 213
Coterie, The, 180, 198–99
Country Club Plaza, 130–32, 151–52, 236
Country Club Plaza Holiday Lights, 201–2
country music, 113
Crayola Cafe, The, 188
Crayola Store, 197
Creole/Cajun restaurants, 85
Crittenton Behavioral Health, 335
Croatian Day Picnic, 213
Crossroads Arts District, 143–44
Crown Center, 152
Crown Center Fountain on the Square, 176
Crown Center Ice Terrace, 189, 202,
    232, 261
Crown Realty, 305
Culinary Center of Kansas City, The, 331
Curious Sofa, The, 122–23

D

dance (performing art), 174
dancing, 107–8
Dan Meiners Studio, 313
Danny Edwards Famous Kansas City
    Barbecue, 80–81
day care, 323–24
day spas and salons, 313
day trips and weekend getaways
    Atchison, Kansas, 269–73
    Lawrence, Kansas, 264–66
    Weston, Missouri, 266–69
d'Bronx Deli, 78–79

Deanna Rose Children's Farmstead, 168, 190–91, 242
Deer Creek Golf Club, 252–53
Defenbaugh Disposal Service, 310
delis, 78–79
Denim and Diamonds, 113
desserts restaurants, 78–79
Direct TV, 310
discount malls and stores, 128–29
Dog-N-Jog Run-Fur-Fun, 213
Donovan's Grille & Pub, 114
Dos Mundos, 280
Doubletree, The, 48–49
Doubletree Hotel, 44
Downtown Overland Park Days, 213
Downtown Parkville, Missouri, 144
driver's licenses, 311–12
Drive-Through Living Nativity, 237
Drury Inn Stadium, 46

E
Earth Day at the Zoo, 208
EBT Restaurant, 63–64
Eden Alley, 102
Edge of Hell, The, 232
education. See schools
1859 Jail, Marshal's Home, and Museum, 155–56
18th and Vine Historic District, 160–61
El Caribe Cafe & Lounge, 107
electricity service, 309
Elms Resort & Spa, The, 47–48
Elmwood Cemetery, 161
Elvis Parade, 222
Embassy Suites Hotel, 39–40
emergency phone numbers, 314, 339
Empire Room, 105–6
English Landing Park, 242
entertainment districts, 151–53
Ernie Miller Park and Nature Center, 198
Ethnic Enrichment Festival, 222
Ewing and Muriel Kauffman Memorial Garden, 242, 244
Examiner, The, 274
extended-stay facilities, 51–52

F
Fairmont Kansas City at the Plaza, 40–41, 176
Fairy Princess, The, 232

Fall Parade of Homes, 229
Family Golf Park, 188, 260
family history, 37
family style restaurants, 86–87
farmers' markets, 132–34
Federal Reserve Bank of Kansas City, 170–71
fencing, 255
Fervere Bread, 137
Festival of Butterflies, 222
Festival of Creativity, 211–12
Festival of Trees, 236
Festival of Wines, 208
festivals, 201–38
Fiesta Hispanic, 224
Fiesta in the Heartland, 211
50 Plus Program, 345
Figlio, 103
FilmFest Kansas City, 229
Final Touch Studios, 317
fine art stores, 134–36
Fiorella's Jack Stack Barbecue, 81
Fire in the Sky Fourth of July Celebration, 219–20
First Fridays in the Crossroads Arts District, 205
fishing, 259–60, 312
fitness centers/health clubs, 262–63
Fleming Park, 239–40
florists, 313
Folly Theatre, 183
food and gifts stores, 136–39
Foo's Fabulous Frozen Custard, 79
For Sale by Owner, 306
45th and State Line Antique, Art & Design Center, 123
40 Sardines, 64, 68
Frankie's on the Plaza, 68
French restaurants, 88–91
Friends of Art Solos, 315
Friends of Chamber Music, The, 178
Fritz's Railroad Cafe, 188–89
Frondizi's, 68, 103

G
galleries and showrooms, art, 172–73
Gallery of Art, 174–75
Gallup Map Company, 139
garbage pickup, 310
Gardener's Railway, The, 237

Garozzo's Ristorante, 93–94
Garozzo's Ristorante Due, 93–94
gas service, 309
Gates Bar-B-Q, 81, 84
gay and lesbian clubs, 108
Gem Theater, The, 115
genealogy, 37
Genghis Khan Mongolian Grill, 88
Gia's Italian Cucina, 68
gifts and food stores, 136–39
golf, 252–54
Gorilla Theatre, 180–81
Governor's Meeting House Restaurant & Catering, 69
Grand Emporium, 109–10
Grand Street Cafe, 64–65
Grandview Parks & Recreation, 246
Great Lenexa Barbecue Battle, 214
Great Mall of the Great Plains, The, 129
Great Wolf Lodge, 51
Greek Cuisine, 104
Greek Festival, 224
Greeley Gas Company, 309
Grille on Broadway, The, 65
GR Interiors, 123–24
Groundhog Run, 202–3, 258

H
Halfway to Hollywood Film Festival, 214
Hall, Donald and Adele, 35–36
Hallbrook neighborhood drive, 165
Halloween Family Concert Fest, 231
Hampton Inn & Suites, 40–41
Handel's Messiah, 232–33
Hannah Bistro Cafe, 90
Happy Rock Park, 254
Hare, Sid and Herbert, 243
Harlem Globetrotters, 203–4
Harley-Davidson Final Assembly Plant, 171
Harling's Upstairs, 114
Harpo's, 119
Harrah's, 112–13
Harrah's North Kansas City Casino & Hotel, 48, 147, 150
Harry S Truman Home, 156
Harry S Truman Library and Museum, 161–62
Harry S Truman Office and Courtroom, 156
Have a Heart for Hope House, 203

Hayward's Pit Bar-B-Que, 84
health care
    auxiliary services, 335, 342–43
    Carondelet Health, 335–36
    hotlines/helplines, 314, 339
    independent hospitals, 336–38, 340–41
    mental health services, 343
    physician referrals, 339
    Saint Luke's-Shawnee Mission Health System, 332–33, 335
health clubs/fitness centers, 262–63
Heart of America Shakespeare Festival, 214
Heart of America United Way, 348
Heart to Heart Introductions, Inc., 314
Helzberg, Barnett and Shirley, 36
Helzberg Diamonds, 142
Henry W. Bloch School of Business and Public Administration, 328
Hereford House, 69, 99–100
Heritage Fountain, 177
Heritage Hikes, 212
Heritage Park, 244
Heritage Park Golf Course, 253
Hickman Disposal Service, 310
Hidden Glen Arts Festival, 229
higher education. See colleges and universities
historical churches, 153–54
historical homes, 155–59
historical museums and sites, 159–64
Historic Kansas City Foundation, 171, 317
Historic Kansas City Homes Tour, 229
Historic Suites of America, 44
history
    colorful events in, 26–27
    early inhabitants, 20
    1800s, 20–24
    1900 to 1960, 24–29
    1960 to present, 29–34
    timeline, 11–12
Holiday Inn Express-Westport, 41–42
Home Care and Hospice, 335
Homefinder.com, 306–7
Home for the Holidays Tour, 233
home furnishings and accessories stores, 140–42
Home Gallery, The, 140
homes, historical, 155–59

Homes for Sale, 306
hospitals. *See* health care
Hotel Phillips, 45
hotels and motels
    Country Club Plaza and Westport,
       39–43
    Crown Center, 43–44
    downtown, 44–45
    east metro, 45–47
    north of the river, 47–48
    Overland Park, Kansas, 48–50
    Wyandotte County, Kansas, 50–51
    See also bed-and-breakfasts and inns;
       extended-stay facilities; RV camp-
       sites and resorts
Hotel Savoy, 46–47
hotlines/helplines, 314, 339
H&R Block Artspace, 175
Humane Society of Greater Kansas
    City, 315
hunting and fishing licenses, 312
Huron Indian Cemetery, 162
Hurricane, The, 110
Hyatt Regency Crown Center, 43, 238
Hyde Park Historic Homes Tour and
    Festival, 229–30
Hyman Brand Hebrew Academy, 323

I
ice skating, 261
Iliki Cafe, 104
Incred-A-Bowl, 188, 260
Independence Day at Ft. Osage, 220
Independence Day at Missouri Town
    1855, 220
Independence Regional Health
    Center, 337
Independence Square, 156
Independent, The, 276
Indian Creek Recreation Center, 254
Indigo Wild, 125–26
Ingram's, 277
Inn on Crescent Lake, The, 53–54
inns and bed-and-breakfasts, 52–57
international restaurants, 91–93
Irish pubs, 113–15
Ironhorse Golf Club, 253
Isle of Capri Casino, 113, 150
Italian restaurants, 93–96
Ivy's Restaurant & Jazz Club, 65–66, 118

J
J. C. Nichols Memorial Fountain, 176
J. Gilbert's, 100
Jackson County Parks and Recreation
    Campgrounds, 57–58, 259
Jackson County Parks & Recreation, 246
Jacomo, Lake, 240
Jacomo Sailing Club, 255
Jaegers Subsurface Paintball, 188
James Inn, The, 54
JAM (Jazz Ambassadors Magazine), 280
Jardine's Restaurant & Jazz Club, 66,
    69, 118
Jasper's, 94–95, 103
jazz, 12, 115–19
Jazz, Blues & Fine Arts Riverjam, 214–15
Jazz—A Louisiana Kitchen, 85
Jazz Community Carol Fest, 237
Jazz Lover's Pub Crawl, 215
Jazzoo, 215
Jeepers!, 192–93
Jesse James Bank Museum, 156
Jesse James Farm and Museum, 156–57
Jess & Jim's Steak House, 100–101
jewelry stores, 142–43
Jewish Arts Festival, 224
Jilly's on Broadway, 110
JJ's, 66, 69
Joe D's on 39th, 67, 69, 103
Joe D's Wine Bar-Cafe, 67, 69, 103
Joey O'Connor Antiques and Oriental
    Rugs, 124
John Knox Village, 348–49
John's Food and Drink, 110
Johnson, Rhett and Kelly, 135
Johnson County Bicycle Club, 255–56
Johnson County Board of Election, 311
Johnson County Community College, 200,
    324–25
Johnson County DMV, 311
Johnson County Mental Health
    Center, 343
Johnson County Museum of History,
    162–63
Johnson County Parks & Recreation, 246
Johnson County Unos, 315
John Wornall House Museum, 157
Juneteenth Celebration, 215
Junior League of Kansas City Holiday
    Mart, 230

K

Kaleidoscope, 187
Kansas City
    getting more information about, 5
    metropolitan areas, 4–8
    outlying areas, 8–9
    overview of life in, 288–91
    prominent citizens, 35–37
    vital statistics, 10–11
Kansas City, 277, 316
Kansas City: An American Story, 316
Kansas City, Kansas Parks &
    Recreation, 247
Kansas City, Missouri, Board of
    Election, 311
Kansas City Adventures, 317
Kansas City Area Chamber of
    Commerce, 312
Kansas City Art Institute, 329
Kansas City Art Institute Annual Ceramics
    Sale, The, 134–35
Kansas City Artists Coalition, 175
Kansas City Ballet, 174
Kansas City Bicycle Club, The, 256–57
Kansas City Chiefs, 251
Kansas City Christian School, 323
Kansas City Fencing Center, 255
Kansas City Home and Garden, 277
Kansas City Home Design, 277, 280
Kansas City Hospice, 342
Kansas City Indian Market and Southwest
    Show, 208
Kansas City International Airport, 14, 16–17
Kansas City Jaycees Pro Rodeo and Wild
    West Extravaganza, 220
Kansas City Kansan, The, 274
Kansas City Marriott Downtown, 44–45
Kansas City Missouri Parks &
    Recreation, 246
Kansas City Museum of History and Sci-
    ence, 163, 200
Kansas City New Homes Guide, 307
Kansas City Power & Light, 309
Kansas City Power & Light Building,
    The, 164
Kansas City Renaissance Festival, The,
    226–27
Kansas City Repertory Theatre, 181
Kansas City Royals, 250–51
Kansas City Royals Opening Day, 209

Kansas City Ski Club, 261
Kansas City Small Business Monthly, 280
Kansas City Spirit Festival, 217–18
Kansas City Star, The, 274–75
Kansas City Symphony, 178–79, 228
Kansas City Track Club, 258
Kansas City Wizards, 251
Kansas City Zoo, The, 168–69, 191–92
Kansas Department of Wildlife &
    Parks, 312
Kansas Gas Service, 309
Kansas Sampler, 145
Kansas Speedway, 169, 256–57
Kauffman, Ewing and Muriel, 36–37, 320
Kauffman Stadium Fountain, 177
Keller Williams Realty, 305
Kelly's Westport Inn, 106
Kemper, R. Crosby, Jr., 36
Kemper Museum of Contemporary Art,
    The, 146–47, 173
Kessler, George, 243
Kids Fishing Derby, 211
kidstuff
    animal-related activities, 190–92
    creative activities, 186–87
    fun centers, 187–88
    ice and snow activities, 189–90
    museums, 193–96
    observatories, 199–200
    parks, 197–98
    restaurants, 188–89
    shopping, 196–97
    theater, 198–99
    water activities, 192–93
KPL/KGE, 309
KU Medical Center, 337–38
KU Medical Center School of
    Medicine, 330

L

L. C.'s Bar-B-Q, 84
La Bodega, 69, 91–92
La Fonda El Taquito, 96–97
LaFontaine Inn Bed & Breakfast, 55
Lake Fest, 215
lakes, 239–41
Lakeside Nature Center, 316
landmarks, 164–65
Last Chapter Bookshoppe, The, 127
La Strada dell'Arte, 230

Leaven, The, 276
Leedy-Voulkos Art Center, 173
Lee National Denim Day, 230
Lee's Summit Festival of the Arts, 216
Lee's Summit Hospital, 338
Le Fou Frog, 69, 90–91
Lenexa Community Days, 220
Lenexa Parks & Recreation, 247
Lenexa Spinach Festival, 224–25
lesbian and gay clubs, 108
Levee, The, 110–11
Lewis and Clark Point, 167
Liberty Memorial Observation Tower, 167–68
Liberty Parks & Recreation, 246
Liberty Press Kansas City, 280–81
Lidia's, 95, 103
Linda Hall Library, 244
literary arts, 175, 178
Locust Grove Antiques & Interiors, 124
lofts, apartments, and condominiums, 307–8
Longview Lake Golf Course, 253
Loose Park, 244, 246
Loose Park Garden Center, The, 247
Lost Dog Registry, 316
Lyric Opera of Kansas City, 179

M
Macaluso's, 69, 95–96
Madrid, The, 111
Madry's Dash of Flavor, 97–98
magazines, 277, 280–81
Majestic Steakhouse, The, 69, 101, 118–19
Mallin/Gibson Loft Properties, 307–8
Marche du Jour, 133–34
March of Dimes Annual Bikers for Babies, 225
Mardi Gras Blues Pub Crawl, 204–5
Marina Grog and Galley, 69
Mario Tricoci Salon & Day Spa, 313
Markus and Sheryl Pierson, 135
Marriott, The, 49
Martin Luther King Jr. Celebration, 202
Master Gardeners' hotlines, 247
matchmaking services, 314
Matney Floral Design, 313–14
Mayor's Christmas Tree Lighting Ceremony, 233
McCormick & Schmick's, 97

media. *See* news media
medical care. *See* health care
MelBee's Bar & Restaurant, 67, 69, 70
Menorah Medical Center, 338
Mental Health Association of the Heartland, 343
mental health services, 343
Metropolis Lawn & Garden Show, 203
Metropolitan Community Colleges, 325
Metropolitan Kansas City Performing Arts Center, 183–84
Mexican/Southwestern restaurants, 96–97
MidAmerica Nazarene University, 328
Midland Theatre, The, 184
Midwest Singles Dances, 315
Mike's Tavern, 106
miniature golf, 260
Mission Community Center, 247
Mission Hills, Kansas, 236
Mission Hills neighborhood drive, 165
Mission Road Antiques, 124
Missouri Department of Conservation, 312
Missouri Gas Energy, 309
Missouri Public Service/Energy One, 309
Missouri Water Department, 309
Moon Marble Company, 139, 197
Mormon Visitors Center, 154
motels. *See* hotels and motels
Motor Vehicle & Driver's License Fee Office, 311
motor vehicle registration, 311
Municipal Auditorium, The, 184–85
Murray's Ice Creams & Cookies, 79
museums
    art, 146–47, 173
    child-oriented, 193–96
    historical, 159–64
    music, 178–79
Mutual Musician's Foundation, The, 119

N
Nate's Swap Shop, 139
National, The, 306
Negro Leagues Baseball Museum, 163–64
neighborhood drives, 165–66
neighborhoods. *See* real estate
Nell Hill's, 140–41
Nelson, William Rockhill, 278–79
Nelson-Atkins Museum of Art, The, 148–50, 173

New Neighbors of Kansas City, 315
news media
    cable television service, 310
    daily newspapers, 274-75
    magazines, 277, 280-81
    radio stations, 282-83
    television stations, 281-82
    weekly newspapers, 275-77
newspapers, 274-77
New Theatre Restaurant, The, 181
New Writer's Workshop, 331
nightlife
    blues and rock 'n' roll, 108-12
    casino entertainment, 112-13
    cocktail lounges, bars, and taverns, 105-6
    comedy clubs, 106-7
    country music, 113
    dancing, 107-8
    gay and lesbian clubs, 108
    Irish pubs, 113-15
    jazz, 115-19
    sports bars, 119
North Kansas City Hospital, 340
North Kansas City Parks & Recreation, 246
Nutcracker, The, 237

O
observation points, 166-68
observatories, 199-200
Oceans of Fun, 170, 193
O'Dowd's Little Dublin, 114
Oklahoma Joes' BBQ, 84-85
Olathe, Lake, 259
Olathe Daily News, The, 275
Olathe Medical Center, 340
Olathe Parks & Recreation, 247
Old Ballgame Training Academy, 262
Old Settlers Celebration, 225
Old Shawnee Days, 216
O'Malley's Pub, 114
Online Visitor's Guide, 312
OpenScan MRI, 342
Operation Wildlife, 316
Ophelia's, 55, 70, 102
Original Juan Specialty Foods, Inc., 137
Overland Park Arboretum & Botanical Gardens, 246-47
Overland Park Civic Band Concerts, 218
Overland Park Fall Festival, 225

Overland Park Farmers' Market, 134
Overland Park Fireworks Spectacular, 220-21
Overland Park Golf Club, 253-54
Overland Park Mayor's Lighting Ceremony, 236
Overland Park Parks & Recreation, 247
Overland Park Regional Medical Center, 340-41

P
Pachamama's, 70-71
Park Place Hotel, 48
parks and gardens, 197-98, 241-48
parks & recreation departments, 246-47
Park University, 325-26
Parkville Concert and Fireworks Display, 221
Party 'Arty, 225-26
Party at Barney, 212
Passage Unlimited, 317
Paul Mesner Puppets, 199
Pembroke Hill School, 322
Pembroke Hill School Clothesline Sale, 208-9
Pendergast, Thomas J., 30-31
Peppercorn Duck Club, 71
Pepsi Ice Midwest Skating Rink and Fitness Center, 189-90, 261
Perfect Scents, 126
performing arts venues, 183-85
pet services, 315-16
Phillips Chophouse, 71-72
Phoenix Piano Bar & Grill, 119
physician referral services, 339
Pierpont's, 69, 72
Pierson, Markus and Sheryl, 135
Pig-Pickin' Chicken-Lickin' Feast, 226
Pioneer Mother, 164
Piropos, 69, 92, 103
Pitch Weekly, 276
Planters Seed & Spice Company, 137-38
Platte-Clay Electric Cooperative, 309
Platte County Parks & Recreation, 246
Plaza Art Fair, 226
Plaza III The Steakhouse, 101-2
Plaza Live! Courtyard Concerts, 212
Plaza Pzazz, 226
Plaza Tennis Center, 254-55
Polar Bear Plunge, 205

post offices, 310
PotPie, 69
Powell Gardens, 169, 245
Powell Observatory, 200
Powell Pumpkin Patch, 231
Prime Outlets, 129
private schools, 321–23
Project Choice, 320
Prospero's Books, 175
Providence Medical Center, 341
Prudential Henry & Burrows Realtor, 302
Pryde's Old Westport, 141
public schools, 318–21
public transit, 15

Q

Quality Hill Playhouse, 179
Quarterage Hotel-Westport, The, 42

R

Race for the Cure, 223
radio stations, 282–83
Rainforest Cafe, 189
Rainy Day Books, 127–28
Raoul's Velvet Room, 72–73, 111
Raphael Hotel, The, 42–43
Raphael Restaurant, 69, 73
Raytown Parks & Recreation, 246
Reading Reptile, 128, 197
real estate
    Cass County, Missouri communities,
        291–92
    Clay County, Missouri communities,
        292–93
    condominiums, lofts, and apartments,
        307–8
    Jackson County, Missouri communities,
        293–95
    Johnson County, Kansas communities,
        296–300
    new home and resale resources,
        306–7
    new home developments, 305–6
    Platte County, Missouri communities,
        295–96
    real estate companies, 301–5
    Wyandotte County, Kansas
        communities, 300–301
Realty Executives of Kansas City, 304
REB Trash Service, 310

recreation. *See* sports and recreation
Reece & Nichols, 302–3
Rehabilitation Institute of Kansas City,
    The, 342
relocation. *See* convention and visitor
    bureaus; driver's licenses; hunting
    and fishing licenses; motor vehicle
    registration; real estate; utilities;
    voter registration
RE/MAX First Realtors, 303
RE/MAX of Eastern Johnson County, 303
RE/MAX of Kansas City/Liberty, 303
RE/MAX State Line/Suburban Real
    Estate, 303
Remodeling & Decorating Show, 203
Research Belton Hospital, 341
Research Psychiatric Center, 342–43
Residence Inn by Marriott-Union Hill, 51–52
resorts and RV campsites, 57–58
restaurants
    alfresco dining, 103
    American/Continental, 60–77
    Asian, 77–78
    bakeries, delis, and desserts, 78–79
    barbecue, 79–85
    Cajun/Creole, 85
    casual dining family style, 86–87
    child-oriented, 188–89
    Chinese, 87–88
    French, 88–91
    hidden gems, 103–4
    international, 91–93
    Italian, 93–96
    Kansas City Originals, 68–70
    Mexican/Southwestern, 96–97
    seafood, 97
    soul food, 97–98
    steakhouses, 98–102
    Sunday brunch, 102–3
    vegetarian, 102
Retired & Senior Volunteer Program
    (RSVP), 348
retirement and senior services
    education, 344–45
    recreation, 345–46
    retirement communities, 348–50
    services, 346–47
    volunteering, 347–48
Retro Inferno, 141–42
re:Verse, 69, 92

Review, 281
Rhett and Kelly Johnson, 135
Rice-Tremonti Home, 157
Rich & Famous Tour, 165–66
River Market, 152–53
River Market Antique Mall, 125
River Market Brewing Company, 119
River's Bend Gallery, 173
Riverside Riverfest, 227
Roasterie, The, 138
Robyn Nichols, The Pearl Gallery, 135–36
Rockhurst University, 326–27
rock 'n' roll, 108–12
Roller Hockey Rink, 198, 262
Rosedale Barbecue, 85
Rosedale Memorial Arch, 165
Rose Day in the Park, 216
Rotisserie, 102
Rozzelle Court, 73–74
running and walking, 257–58
RV campsites and resorts, 57–58
RV Show, The, 204

S
Saigon 39, 77
sailboat racing, 255
Saint Joseph Health Center, 335–36
Saint Luke's Hospital, 333
Saint Luke's-Shawnee Mission Health System, 332–33, 335
Saint Luke's South, 333
salons and day spas, 313
San Francisco Tower at Crown Center, 308
Santa-Cali-Gon-Days, 227
Savoy Grill, 74
Scandia Down—Kansas City, 126
schools
    adult/other learning, 330–32
    four-year colleges and universities, 325–28
    graduate programs, 328–30
    Kansas private schools, 323
    Kansas public schools, 319–21
    Missouri private schools, 321–23
    Missouri public schools, 318–19
    two-year colleges, 324–25
Science City, 195
Scottish Highlands Games, 216
Scout, The, 165
seafood restaurants, 97

Senior Arts Council, 345
SeniorNet, 345
Senior Peers Actively Renewing Knowledge (SPARK), 346
senior services. *See* retirement and senior services
Serenity The Rejuvenating Day Spa, 313
Service Corps of Retired Executives, The (SCORE), 348
Shawnee Mission Medical Center, 333
Shawnee Mission Park, 248, 259
Sheila Kemper Dietrich Park, 198
Shepherd's Center of Kansas City Central, 346
Sheraton Overland Park Hotel at the Convention Center, 49–50
Shields Manor Bistro, 69
Shiraz, 92–93, 103
shopping
    antiques and collectibles, 121–25
    bed and bath gifts, 125–26
    bookstores, 126–28
    child-oriented, 196–97
    clothing and accessories, 128
    discount malls and stores, 128–29
    farmers' markets, 132–34
    fine art, 134–36
    florists, 313
    food and gifts, 136–39
    home furnishings and accessories, 140–42
    jewelry, 142–43
    shopping districts, 143–45
    souvenirs, 145
Simple Elegance, 317–18
Singles Available for Service, 315
singles groups, 314–15
Skateboard Park, 198, 262
Skies, 74
Sky Stations/Pylon Caps, 165
Smithville Lake, 259–60
Snake Saturday Parade and Festival, 206
Snow Creek Ski Lodge, 190, 202, 261–62
snow skiing, 261–62
soul food restaurants, 97–98
Southmoreland on the Plaza, 55–56
Southwestern Bell, 310
Southwestern Bell Mobile, 310
Southwestern/Mexican restaurants, 96–97
souvenirs stores, 145

Spencer, Kenneth and Helen, 37
Spirit of Christmas Past Progressive
	Gala, 233
Spooktacular at Powell Gardens, 231
sports, spectator, 250–51
sports and recreation
	biking, 255–57
	bowling, 260
	camping, 258–59
	children's sports, 262
	fencing, 255
	fishing, 259–60
	fitness centers/health clubs, 262–63
	golf, 252–54
	hunting and fishing licenses, 312
	ice skating, 261
	miniature golf, 260
	running and walking, 257–58
	sailboat racing, 255
	snow skiing, 261–62
	tennis, 254–55
sports bars, 119
Spring Homes Tour, 209
Sprint, 310
Sprint PCS, 310
Spunky Senior Tours, LLC, 317
St. Dionysios Greek Orthodox Church
	Festival, 217
St. Mary's Hospital of Blue Springs, 336
St. Patrick's Day Parade, 207
St. Teresa's Academy, 322–23
Stanford & Sons Comedy Club, 107
Starker's Reserve, 74–75
Starlight Theatre, 181–82
steakhouses, 98–102
Stephenson's Old Apple Farm, 86
"Still More Things People Collect"
	Exhibit, 221
Stowers, James and Virginia, 36
Stowers Institute, 334
Stroud's, 86–87
Strut with Your Mutt, 227–28
Sugar Creek Slavic Festival, 217
Summerfest, 218
Summer Skies, 223
Sunday brunch restaurants, 102–3
Sun Publications, 276–77
Sunset Safaris, 217
Supper Club, 314
Suzi's, 69

Swirk Jewelry, 142–43
Swope Park, 248
Swope Park Memorial Golf Course, 254
Symphony Designer's Showcase, 209

T
Tatsu's, 69, 91
taverns, cocktail lounges, and bars, 105–6
taxis, 15
telephone service, 310
television, 281–82, 310
tennis, 254–55
Thai Place, 77–78
theater, children's, 198–99
theater companies, 179–83
Theater League, 182
Theatre for Young America, 199, 331
Theatre in the Park, 182, 218
Thomas Hart Benton Home and Studio,
	157–58
Three Dog Bakery, 138
Three Friends' Restaurant & BBQ, 98
Time Warner Cable, 310
Tivol, 143
Tomfooleries Restaurant & Bar, 103
tours, 18–19, 170–71, 316–17
Town of Kansas 1850 Mural, The, 177–78
Town Village Leawood, 349
Toy and Miniature Museum of Kansas City,
	The, 194–95
trails, 248–49
trains, 15–16
transportation
	air travel, 14, 16–17
	buses, 15–16
	car rentals, 17
	car travel, 16–18
	public transit, 15
	taxis, 15
	tours, 18–19
	trains, 15–16
trash pickup, 310
Trolley Run, 258
Truman Days, 212
TV, 281–82, 310
Two Rivers Psychiatric Hospital, 343

U
UMKC School of Medicine, 330
Unicorn Theatre, 182–83

Union Cemetery Walking Tour, 164
Union Electric Company, 309
Union Station, 158–59
Union Station's New Year's
    Celebration, 238
United Cities Gas Company, 309
Unity World Headquarters, 154
universities. *See* colleges and universities
University of Kansas Edwards Campus,
    328, 330
University of Missouri-Kansas City, 327
Uptown, The, 111–12
utilities, 309–10

V

Vaile Victorian Mansion, 159
Vanity Fair Plaza Suites, 52
vegetarian restaurants, 102
Velvet Dog, The, 106, 238
Verizon, 310
Village Shalom, 349–50
Village Singles, 315
Visiting Nurse Services of Health
    Midwest, 343
voter registration, 311
V's, 70

W

W. J. McBride's Irish Pub, 114–15
walking and running, 257–58
Ward Parkway and Romany Road, 236
Ward Parkway neighborhood drive, 166
Warkoczewski Observatory, 200
Water District No. 1, 310
Water Garden Tour, 218–19
water service, 309–10
Wayside Waifs, 316
weather, 13
Webster House Antiques and Restaurant,
    70, 76, 125

weddings, 317–18
weekend getaways. *See* day trips and
    weekend getaways
wellness. *See* health care
Western Missouri Mental Health
    Center, 343
Westin Crown Center, The, 43–44
Weston Irish Festival, 230
Westport, 144–45, 153
Westport Irish Festival, 212–13
Westwood Hills neighborhood drive, 166
White Haven Motor Lodge, 50
Wild Lights at the Kansas City Zoo, 236
Wild West Border Deli and Bar, The, 112
William Jewell College, 327–28
Windsong Corporate Apartments, 52
Winstead's, 87
Winter Skies, 237
Wonderscope Children's Museum, 196
Woodlands, The, 150–51
Woodson Place Antiques & Interiors, 125
Woodstock Inn, 56–57
World of Wheels at Bartle Hall, 204
Worlds of Fun, 170, 193
Writers Place, The, 175, 178, 331–32
Wyandotte County Board of Election, 311
Wyandotte County Fair, 219
Wyandotte County Lake Park, 241

X

XO, 107–8

Y

Yahooz, 75, 103
Yardley Hall, 183
YiaYia's Eurobistro, 75–76, 103
YMCA, 263

Z

Zin, 70, 76–77

ABOUT THE AUTHOR

Katie Van Luchene has written travel articles for *Midwest Living* and *Kansas City* magazine, where she now serves as editor. Her copywriting work has won awards and her graphic design work has appeared in the *Best of Business Card Design*. But her favorite writing honor was when *Insiders' Guide to Kansas City* won the Mark Twain Award for Travel Book of the Year from the Midwest Travel Writers Association.

Katie lives in Overland Park, Kansas, a suburb of Kansas City, with husband Jerry Foulds, an engineer by day and metal sculptor at night. Together they enjoy traveling, especially to a different warm-weather spot each winter, but her home will always be here, in the Heartland.

WALT WHITAKER

HELP US KEEP THIS GUIDE UP TO DATE

Every effort has been made by the author and editors to make this guide as accurate and useful as possible. However, many things can change after a guide is published—phone numbers change, facilities come under new management, etc.

We would love to hear from you concerning your experiences with this guide and how you feel it could be improved and be kept up to date. While we may not be able to respond to all comments and suggestions, we'll take them to heart and we'll also make certain to share them with the author. Please send your comments and suggestions to the following address:

> The Globe Pequot Press
> Reader Response/Editorial Department
> P.O. Box 480
> Guilford, CT 06437

Or you may e-mail us at:

> editorial@GlobePequot.com

Thanks for your input, and happy travels!